Ancient and Medieval Legacies

THE LIVING THEOLOGICAL HERITAGE
OF THE UNITED CHURCH OF CHRIST

Barbara Brown Zikmund
Series Editor

VOLUME ONE

Ancient and Medieval Legacies

Edited by Reinhard Ulrich

The Pilgrim Press
Cleveland, Ohio

The Pilgrim Press, Cleveland, Ohio 44115
© 1995 by The Pilgrim Press
Copyright information accompanies each reprinted document.
We have made every effort to trace copyrights on the materials
included in this publication. If any copyrighted material has
nevertheless been included without permission and due
acknowledgment, proper credit will be inserted in future
printings after receipt of notice.
All rights reserved. Published 1995
Printed in the United States of America on acid-free paper
00 99 98 97 96 95   5 4 3 2 1
Library of Congress Cataloging-in-Publication Data
The living theological heritage of the United Church of Christ /
Barbara Brown Zikmund, series editor.
p. cm.
Includes bibliographical references and index.
Contents: v. 1. Ancient and medieval legacies / edited by Reinhard Ulrich.
ISBN 0-8298-1064-1 (v. 1 : alk. paper)
1. United Church of Christ — Doctrines — History.
2. Theology, Doctrinal — History.
3. United Church of Christ — History.
I. Zikmund, Barbara Brown.
BX9886.L58   1995
230′.5834 — dc20
95-12480
CIP

Contents

The Living Theological Heritage of the United Church of Christ	xi
Ancient and Medieval Legacies	1
Part I. Consolidating the Christian Witness (United)	7

Prophets and Apostles

1. The Didache (c. 100)	15
2. Clement's First Letter (c. 95) CLEMENT	25
3. The Faith in Scripture and Tradition from *Against Heresies* (c. 189) IRENAEUS	32
4. The Rule of Faith and the Uses of Scripture from *Prescription Against Heretics* (c. 189) TERTULLIAN	41
5. On the Right Way of Reading the Scriptures from *On First Principles IV* (c. 230) ORIGEN	48
6. New Testament Canon from *39th Easter Letter* (367) ATHANASIUS	55

Persecution

7. Letter from the Churches of Lyon and Vienne (177) from *The History of the Church* (4th century) EUSEBIUS	58
8. The Martyrdom of Perpetua and Felicitas (203)	69
9. The Problem of the Lapsed from *Letter 33* (c. 250) CYPRIAN	81

Defenders of the Faith

10. Letter to Diognetus (c. 150)	84

11. First Apology (c. 155) JUSTIN MARTYR	94
12. Plea Regarding the Christians (c. 177) ATHENAGORAS	109

Visions of Church Unity

13. Letter to the Philadelphians (c. 113) IGNATIUS OF ANTIOCH	123
14. Outside the Church, There Is No Salvation from *Letter 73* (c. 256) CYPRIAN	129
15. The Church as the Body of Christ from *Commentary on John XI, II (On John 17:20–21)* (c. 430) CYRIL OF ALEXANDRIA	135
16. The Church as the Company of the Elect from *On Baptism V* (c. 400) AUGUSTINE OF HIPPO	140

Part II. Giving Account of the Faith (Christ)   145

Antioch and Alexandria

17. On the Incarnation VII and Commentary on Galatians 4:24 (c. 420) THEODORE OF MOPSUESTIA	157
18. Dialogue of Origen with Heraclides and the Bishops with Him Concerning the Father and the Son and the Soul (c. 235) ORIGEN	166
19. On Sin and Salvation from *Catechetical Oration 5–8* (late 4th century) GREGORY OF NYSSA	175

Augustinian Theology

20. Faith and the Creed (393) AUGUSTINE OF HIPPO	184
21. Sermon on 1 John 4:12–16 from *Eighth Homily* (415) AUGUSTINE OF HIPPO	201
22. Sermon on Holy Communion from *Sermon 272* AUGUSTINE OF HIPPO	210
23. On Nature and Grace (415) AUGUSTINE OF HIPPO	213

Early Creedal Controversies

24. The Confession of the Presbyters at Smyrna (c. 180) PRESBYTERS AT SMYRNA	226
25. The Rule of Faith from *Against Praxeas* (213) TERTULLIAN	228

26. The Letter of Eusebius of Caesarea Describing the Council 230
of Nicaea (325)
EUSEBIUS
27. Constantinople: Creed of the 150 Fathers (381) 235
28. The Nicene Creed (325) from the UCC *Book of Worship* 237
(1986)
29. The Definition of the Council of Chalcedon (451) 240
30. The Athanasian Creed: A Western Creed of the Fifth 242
Century
31. The Apostles' Creed of the Seventh Century 246

Worship and Work

32. O Gladsome Light (early 3rd century) 249
33. The Apostolic Tradition of Hippolytus (c. 200) 250
34. Six Hymns of the Early Church 255
CLEMENT OF ALEXANDRIA, CYPRIAN OF CARTHAGE,
AMBROSE OF MILAN, AMBROSE OF MILAN OR
BISHOP NICETA OF REMESIANA, AURELIUS CLEMENS
PRUDENTIUS, AND ST. PATRICK
35. A Sermon on Faith and Works from *Homilies on Ephesians* 264
1:1–2 (on Eph. 1:4–5) (4th century)
JOHN CHRYSOSTOM
36. On Female Dress (c. 200) 268
TERTULLIAN
37. On Human Sexuality and Christian Marriage from 274
Miscellanies, Book III (c. 200)
CLEMENT OF ALEXANDRIA
38. On Public and Military Service from *Against Celsus VIII,* 279
73–75 (c. 248)
ORIGEN

Eastern Orthodoxy

39. Communion as Participation from *Homilies on 1 Corinthians* 282
24:1–2 (on 1 Cor. 10:16–17) (4th century)
JOHN CHRYSOSTOM
40. Symbols and Images (726–30) 286
JOHN OF DAMASCUS
41. The Image Controversy from the Synod of Constantinople 293
(753) and the Council of Nicaea (787)

Part III. Being God's People in the World (Church) 297

The Rise of the Papacy

42. The Edict of Milan from *The History of the Church* (c. 313) 304
EUSEBIUS

43. Christmas Sermon on the Two Natures of Christ from *Sermon 28*, the Tome (448)   308
   POPE LEO I
44. Dedicatory Letter to His Commentary on Job (587)   314
   POPE GREGORY I
45. Letter to Childebert, King of the Franks (late 6th century)   324
   POPE GREGORY I
46. Popes and Emperors: The Struggle Over Investiture (1076–1122)   327
47. The Fourth Lateran Council, Canon I (1215)   333
   INNOCENT III
48. Unam Sanctam (1302)   337
   BONIFACE VIII

Mission to the Barbarians
49. Mission Work in England (c. 590–604)   340
   POPE GREGORY I
50. The Decrees of the Council of Hertford (673)   344
51. The Council of the Germans: The Decrees of the Frankish Synods (742–43)   347
52. Letter to Cuthbert, Archbishop of Canterbury on the German Synods and Other Matters of Church Discipline (747)   352
   BONIFACE
53. Supported by Spiritual Women (c. 725–50)   362
   BONIFACE, LUL, AND LIOBA

Definitions of Christendom
54. The Lord's Body and Blood (c. 832)   367
   RADBERTUS
55. Christ's Body and Blood (c. 833)   369
   RATRAMNUS
56. Why Did God Become Human? from *Cur Deus Homo?* (1097–99)   376
   ANSELM OF CANTERBURY
57. Five Ways to Prove the Existence of God from the *Summa Theologica* (1266–73)   380
   THOMAS AQUINAS
58. Whether the Trinity of the Divine Persons Can Be Known by Natural Reason? from the *Summa Theologica* (1266–73)   390
   THOMAS AQUINAS
59. Natural and Theological Virtues from the *Summa Theologica* (1266–73)   395
   THOMAS AQUINAS

60. Whether the Substance of Bread and Wine Remain in the Sacrament after Consecration? from the *Summa Theologica* (1266–73) — 405
   THOMAS AQUINAS

Part IV. Keeping and Renewing the Faith (Church) — 411

Moral and Spiritual Renewal

61. The Twelve Degrees of Humility from the *Rule of St. Benedict* (early 6th century) — 417
   BENEDICT

62. The Four Degrees of Love from *On the Love of God* (early 12th century) — 423
   BERNARD OF CLAIRVAUX

63. Exposition of the Lord's Prayer and Pray and Work from the *Rule of St. Francis* (1209–23) — 429
   FRANCIS OF ASSISI

64. On Spiritual and Mystical Ecstasy from *The Soul's Journey into God* (c. 1259) — 434
   BONAVENTURE

65. The Divine Spark in the Soul from *Sermon 48* and Blessed Are the Poor! from *Sermon 28* (early 14th century) — 442
   MEISTER ECKHART

66. The Flowing Light of the Godhead (1250–65) — 452
   MECHTHILD OF MAGDEBURG

67. God in Christ, Our True Mother from *Showings* (c. 1388) — 457
   JULIAN OF NORWICH

68. German Theology (late 14th century) — 474

Reformation Beginnings

69. Tractate on the Unity of the Church (1409) — 478
   JOHN GERSON

70. On the Eucharist (1:1–15, 17) (1380) — 488
   JOHN WYCLIFFE

71. Treatise of Divine Providence (1378) — 496
   CATHERINE OF SIENA

72. The Congregation of the Elect from *De Ecclesia* (1413) — 500
   JOHN HUSS

73. Reformers Against the Reformers (1414–18) — 510
   THE COUNCIL OF CONSTANCE

Praise and Prayer

74. Two Twelfth-Century Hymns — 522
   PETER ABELARD AND BERNARD OF CLAIRVAUX

75. The Song of the Virtues from the *Scivias* (1141–51)   525
    HILDEGARD OF BINGEN
76. The Canticle of the Sun (1225)   536
    FRANCIS OF ASSISI
77. Canon of the Mass or The Great Eucharistic Prayer   539

Sources   549

Index   553

Scriptural Index   574

The Living Theological Heritage of the United Church of Christ

Remember me, O LORD, when you show favor to your people; help me when you deliver them; that I may see the prosperity of your chosen ones, that I may rejoice in the gladness of your nation, that I may glory in your heritage.
Psalm 106:4–5 (NRSV)

The United Church of Christ is a microcosm of the history of Christian theology. Although the UCC was not officially "born" until 1957, it draws upon a long-standing and rich theological legacy. A living theological heritage has shaped, and continues to support, its common life.

Unfortunately, a perception exists that the UCC is without any roots, that it is unsure about its faith. Lutherans quote the works of Martin Luther; Methodists revere the ideas of John Wesley; Episcopalians have the division of the Church of England. But members of the United Church of Christ often seem uncertain about their theological heritage and identity.

The United Church of Christ was created out of a mid-twentieth-century ecumenical passion to heal the divisions of the Christian church. Its focus was on the future, not on the past. Nevertheless it has a remarkable theological and historical legacy. This volume, and others in this series, offers resources from Congregational Christian history and German Evangelical and Reformed traditions, along with many hidden histories, to leaders and members of the United Church of Christ and to the wider society. We hope that these materials will strengthen the denomination and inform those seeking a better understanding of the past and present life of the UCC.

For example, New England Congregationalism leaned on the theological insights of key English separatist thinkers in the late sixteenth and early seventeenth centuries. Participants in American frontier religion developed six theological principles to guide their Christian witness. The theological work of John Nevin and Philip Schaff shaped and reshaped the German Reformed church. German Evangelical immigrants brought with them a theology forged by a European "church union" movement. Few people know their heritage, and when they look for more information, it is difficult to find the sources.

For the past ten years the Office for Church Life and Leadership and the Board for Homeland Ministries of the United Church of Christ have been working on *The Living Theological Heritage of the United Church of Christ.* They designed this series of seven volumes to enable the United Church of Christ to recover its theological past and strengthen contemporary faith and practice. They offer the series to the churches and their members to enable them to move beyond their theological inferiority complex and to claim their heritage.

• • •

The series brings together key materials that undergird UCC faith and practice. A team of thirteen editors, guided by an editorial board of seven, present these volumes as a "quarry" of resources to be mined by the churches for years to come.

The design of each volume does three things:

First, it gathers together important materials that have shaped the theological identity of the United Church of Christ — ancient Christological discourses, sixteenth-century treatises by Reformation theologians, the Heidelberg Catechism, writings and sermons from colonial Congregationalism, the Cambridge Platform, mission statements, popular hymns, prayers, official ecumenical materials, resolutions from wider church meetings, minority reports, and even protest literature. Some of the materials are obvious and known, some are fugitive, and some are new discoveries. The editors chose all of them from the first century to the twentieth century, not simply because they are part of the historical record, but because the editors believe these documents have shaped the theological identity of the UCC.

Second, each volume contains brief introductions to individual documents or groups of source materials, giving the reader background information needed to understand what is printed. Who wrote it? When was it written? Why was it written? What was the result? These document introductions help make the materials understandable "in and of themselves."

Third, each volume has one or more introductory essays to highlight broader insights and theological interpretations of the materials. Obviously any selection of documents can distort by highlighting some things and excluding others, but the editors have attempted to make the selections as inclusive as possible. The introductory essays, written by the editors, weave the materials into meaningful patterns and gather up the collective wisdom of the UCC to make it more assessable in the present.

•••

The Living Theological Heritage of the United Church of Christ has seven volumes:

Volume One, *Ancient and Medieval Legacies*, grounds the theological life of the United Church of Christ in the search for unity and theological clarity within the ancient and medieval church. As a Protestant denomination, why should the UCC concern itself with pre-Reformation theology and history? Because not to begin with the early church betrays its understanding of Christian unity. This volume explores the themes of unity ("united"), ecclesiology ("church"), and Christology ("Christ") from the time of Jesus to the Reformation. It highlights the fact that the United Church of Christ stands in a long line of faithful Christians who have sought to understand and name their faith from the first century to the present.

Volume Two, *Reformation Roots*, explores the theological legacies of the United Church of Christ found in the sixteenth-century Protestant Reformation. From reformers like Erasmus, Zwingli, Luther, Calvin, English separatists, and the irenic leaders of the Palatinate, the UCC has forged its theological core. Volume Two provides a collection of Reformation materials especially meaningful to the United Church of Christ.

Volume Three, *Colonial and National Beginnings*, examines the development of early Congregationalism and German Reformed theology. It lifts up the ideas and concerns that motivated colonial thinking and demonstrates how they evolved with the migration and increasing diversity of the population.

Volume Four, *Consolidation and Expansion*, documents the story of the Christians and the German Evangelicals on the American frontier and tracks later developments in Congregational and German Reformed history. It illustrates how the Christian movement brought together Methodists from North Carolina, Baptists from New England, and Presbyterians from Kentucky. It reveals the contributions of German Evangelicals on the Mississippi frontier. At the same time, it follows the development of German Reformed and Congregational faith and practice as the nation matured, and the people migrated west.

Volume Five, *Outreach and Diversity*, brings together a mix of materials flowing from the mission outreach of all of these groups. It also explores the experiences of minority and immigrant communities. The call to evangelize, educate, and serve stretched the theological mind of those groups that later created the UCC. African American contributions, encounters with indigenous peoples, social witness, and new immigrants raised new theological issues and encouraged a pattern of theological engagement with the world.

Volume Six, *Growing Toward Unity*, celebrates the long-standing commitment of the UCC to an ecumenical vision and the search for Christian unity. It steps back from the complex history of peoples and ideas documented in the earlier volumes to examine the vision of Christian unity that eventually gave birth to the United Church of Christ. It is a theological heritage that takes seriously the prayer of Jesus "that they might all be one."

Volume Seven, *United and Uniting*, documents the evolution of the United Church of Christ's theological identity since 1957. It looks at almost four decades of UCC life and gathers up its theological treasures. It recognizes that the theological journey of the UCC has been wide ranging, one that has produced a distinctive living theological heritage. It also invites the UCC to become more theologically self-conscious.

• • •

We hope that *The Living Theological Heritage of United Church of Christ* will enable those who are members of the UCC to find new courage to speak with pride about their UCC faith and theological inheritance and give those who are not members of the church a clear understanding of this unique community of Christians.

BARBARA BROWN ZIKMUND
Series Editor

Ancient and Medieval Legacies

Why does a collection of documents that traces the "living theological heritage" of the United Church of Christ need a volume on the ancient and the medieval church? What do the quarrels of ancient theologians have to do with the concerns of a late twentieth-century denomination that stresses active Christian commitment and takes pride in its theological diversity? A "living" theological heritage must address the issues of the day and direct us toward the future. A person well might wonder what influence the classic theological literature of the church, especially before the Protestant Reformation of the sixteenth century, has on the contemporary United Church of Christ.

We have precedents for objecting to irrelevant theological discourse. Luther's friend Melanchton, a reasonable theologian in his own right, prayed God to save us from "the ravings of the theologians." Yet a relentless pursuit of modernity causes its own problems of relevance. An irreverent student of Karl Barth rewrote the words to a popular hymn of early social gospel days. The original words were "Rise up, O men of God! His kingdom tarries long, Bring in the day of brotherhood and end the night of wrong." The heady optimism of those words seemed unsuited to the prevailing gloom between the two World Wars. So Barth's student changed what was essentially a strategic plan for the reign of God into a neo-Calvinist description of the human condition — "Sit down, O men of God, His kingdom He shall bring, whenever it shall please His will, you cannot do a thing."

Obviously Christian truth lies somewhere between what our forebears called the theology of glory and the theology of the cross. By current standards of relevance, we might reject both versions of that hymn because they lack inclusive language. Our rejection, however, misses the point. Christianity is a "historical" religion. It has no message to proclaim apart from the mysterious "dogma" or teaching that "Jesus Christ, the man of Nazareth, [is] our crucified and risen Lord" (UCC "Statement of Faith," 1959). At all times in history, the church derives whatever relevance it has from that belief.

The founders of modern theology, German scholars like Friedrich D. E. Schleiermacher and Adolf von Harnack, and American Philip Schaff, have argued consistently that although understandings of the Christian faith change in time, the Christian gospel must always be identifiable. For instance, Schleiermacher (d. 1834) challenged the traditional idea that creeds and confessions are objective statements of "the truth about God." He argued that they are expressions of "religious consciousness," which are subject to historical circumstance and change. The church does not receive the doctrines of the Christian religion from heaven on tablets of stone. Doctrines develop in a cultural context as the Christian community seeks to teach and to explain what it believes to be true. The official pronouncements of churches and synods, says Schleiermacher, are "declarations of what is considered valid by a given church association (*Kirchengesellschaft*) at a given time." Yet Schleiermacher also suggests that the very fact of change implies a constant. Something definable does the changing: "Christianity is a teleological, monotheistic religion which is distinguished from all other religions of its kind in that it is related to redemption accomplished by the person of Jesus of Nazareth."[1]

In a similar fashion, von Harnack (d. 1930) studied the historical development of the church's dogma and defined that constant in *What Is Christianity?* (1901), a book that tries to capture the essence (*Wesen*) or abiding truth of the Christian faith. In United Church of Christ history, Philip Schaff (d. 1893) spoke of the classical creeds of Christendom "not [as] a word of God to men, but [as] a word of men to God, in response to God's revelation."[2]

United Church of Christ

What is relevant? Many mainline liberal Protestants, such as members of the United Church of Christ, reject rigid "tests of faith" as divisive and

---

1. Friedrich Schleiermacher, *The Christian Faith,* ed. and trans. by H. R. Mackintosh and J. S. Stewart (Philadelphia: Fortress Press, 1928), 52.
2. Philip Schaff, *Creeds of Christendom,* vol. 1 (Grand Rapids: Baker Book House, 1977), 16.

inconsistent with Jesus' mandate that Christians ought to love one another. They stress the practical conduct of the Christian life over formal expressions of faith and uniformity in worship. Perhaps that choice is appropriate. But a quip attributed to Oliver Powell carries a sobering truth. The United Church of Christ is "like a latter day Diogenes looking for an honest movement." Mainline liberal Protestants in the late twentieth century have a tendency to act as if their "present consciousness" is all there is and to treat current convictions on contemporary issues as formal confessions of faith. The danger for liberal Christians lies more in losing their identity as a distinctly Christian community than in being trapped in some theological intransigence.

The United Church of Christ often rejects the binding force of confessional norms in the church, seeking in its much vaunted diversity to locate the marks of Christian commitment and identity in the secular culture. Yet, when the culture writes the church's agenda, some people ask if we will hear the voice of Yahweh. Henry Ford's opinion that "history is bunk!" not withstanding, we can learn some interesting lessons from the past.

To benefit from the early theological heritage, however, we need a shift away from any bias for religion-in-general to a greater appreciation of religion-in-particular, which, as Schleiermacher wrote, "distinguishes Christianity from all other religions." This situation is very similar to that of the ancient church, which developed in a Hellenistic culture. The theological and ethical constant in the Christian heritage is the person and work of Jesus Christ. From that Christological center, it is possible to bridge the chasm of time and to discover Christian membership in the holy catholic church of all ages (see Matt. 28:19–20).

"All Christians have the church as their mother," stated Cyprian, the third-century bishop of North African Carthage. He was not talking about the church at Carthage alone. Rather he spoke about a larger household of the faith, the one holy universal Christian church, both hidden and revealed. Across the centuries, Christians have proclaimed "redemption accomplished by Jesus of Nazareth" in the theological language of the scriptures and the early Christian community. Contemporary Christians may appreciate that language, demythologize it, or try to explain it away. Yet, the centrality of Jesus continues to be a living and essential part of any ecumenical Christian consciousness. Nothing in the church can be more relevant.

Revisiting ancient theological controversies is not always helpful because normative expressions of the Christian faith are inherently divisive.

Since the language of dogma presumably threatens the bond of peace, some believe we should avoid it at all cost. Theological controversy can be as acrimonious as any other form of human conflict, including all-out war.

At the Seventh Ecumenical Council (787 C.E.), Greek and Latin monks supposedly engaged in a major brawl on the steps of the Church of St. Sophia in Constantinople. The basis of the brouhaha was the Holy Spirit. To be more precise, their understanding of the Trinity divided along the line of whether the Holy Spirit proceeded from the Father alone (the view of the Greeks) or whether the Holy Spirit proceeded from both Father and Son (the view of the Latins). Theologically, it was a draw. At the Council, where they kept score, Eastern and Western representatives agreed to disagree. But it was a fight of some substance.

The 1986 edition of the United Church of Christ *Book of Worship* still reflects that ancient argument. It contains a version of the Nicene Creed, which affirms that the Holy Spirit "proceeds from the Father [and the Son]." People no longer care much about the inner workings of the Trinity. Yet the church is the loser when no one agitates about theology in the halls of our conferences or on the steps in our synods. "By their fights you shall know them!"

It is important to remember that throughout the history of the church theological controversy is not the enemy of Christian unity — indifference is. In fact, the love of Christ is manifest only where differences exist. Historically, an absence of theological activism often has signaled either official intransigence or rank apathy. Christian theology is an ongoing, reasoned debate about what matters to people of faith in any given epoch in history. When people talk about things that really matter, moments of discord and harmony will arise, as well as opportunities for the Holy Spirit's revitalization of the church.

A Living Heritage

Volume one of the Living Theological Heritage of the United Church of Christ traces the common beginnings of Christian theological debate that inform the life of all Christian groups in all times and places. It explores a succession of documents that dates from the second century to the fifteenth century. Any selection from this vast array of material might seem arbitrary. However, the editors have resisted the temptation to use history as a reinforcement of contemporary causes or to develop any critical history of dogma. Hopefully, the selections strike a compromise between personal involvement and historical detachment.

Christians living in modern times share a common faith with sisters and brothers from the first century to the present. Church members at Immanuel United Church of Christ in Town Herman, Wisconsin, for instance, would have no difficulty recognizing their Christian roots in the celebrations and preaching of the ancient congregations of Carthage or Lyons. Schleiermacher was right: The faith has a "living" content, a perennial theology that "distinguishes the Christian religion from all others." Karl Barth called this core essence "dogma" (*das Dogma*), distinct from "doctrines" (*die Dogmen*), historical and cultural affirmations that are subject to change.

A healthy tension exists between dogma and its expression in the historical doctrines of the church, because they have no fixed boundaries between them. "The wind blows where it chooses" (John 3:8). At first, the Christian community made no attempt to chisel its teachings into tablets of stone. Later, as sectarian dispute and heretical attack threatened the unity of faith and the bond of peace, testimony hardened into test. The lesson is twofold: A "religious association," which uses its own sectarian teachings as an exclusive standard of truth, separates itself from the body of Christ and from the world Christ came to save. On the other hand, a "religious association" that confines its teachings to the limited wisdom of its own brief moment in time, separates itself from the "one holy universal" church and from the truth of Christ.

When Jesus asked his disciples, "Who do you say that I am?" (Matt. 16:15), he was not soliciting opinions or asking for a correct answer. He was inviting his disciples to an affirmation of faith. Peter understood this and confessed, "You are the Christ, the Child of the living God" (Matt. 16:16). Over time the Christological problem has shaped Christian consciousness with remarkable consistency. All Christian theologizing begins and ends with that choice and confession.

A living theological heritage does not consist of a collection of facts about God, nor is it an unfailing barometer of "ortho-doxy" (correct teaching). It does not rest easily with religions-in-general, nor is it an expression of sentiment like Freud's "oceanic feeling." Its claims are embarrassing in their concreteness. The history of theology records how Christians affirmed, and sometimes denied, a specific belief that God was in Christ reconciling the world. Interestingly enough, much of what the ancients debated about Christ in the councils of Nicea (325) and Chalcedon (451) continues to be the mark of sound teaching for most ecumenical Christians twenty centuries later.

Each generation, however, must find its own answer to the question of What does it means to be "a religious association, where everything depends on the redemption accomplished by Jesus of Nazareth"? The question implies that each religious association encounters a constant truth that it may discover and reclaim in each era.

"What does it mean to be the United Church of Christ?" The words *united, church,* and *Christ* suggest an orderly way of looking at the theological testimony of the centuries. Consequently the materials in this collection are grouped according to four major sections: unity, Christology, and ecclesiologies (dominant and dissenting). The first section addresses the problem of unity: What are the forces moving the early Christian communities from theological diversity toward growing uniformity? The second section focuses on understanding the person and work of Christ. It traces the struggles of the pre-Nicene church to comprehend what it already believed; i.e., that Jesus is Christ and that Christ is God. The third and fourth sections contain documents of the post-Nicene church with primary emphasis on the Latin West. They document the expansion of Christendom and the rise of the medieval papacy and explore early voices of dissent that were challenging and changing the Christian community under the guidance of the Spirit.

PART I

Consolidating the Christian Witness (United)

Christianity arrived on the scene in the best of times and in the worst of places. During the first century of the struggling Christian movement, imperial Rome was at the height of its political power and its greatest territorial expansion. Under Roman law, trade and commerce flourished. The arts and ideas of the ancient Greeks found new expression and Roman statecraft blended with Hellenistic culture to sustain a global civilization under the *Pax Romana* (Roman peace).

The Greco-Roman world combined practical professionalism with cultural diversity, leaving considerable space for cultural and religious pluralism. A bewildering variety of political, ethnic, and religious interests pressed for favors and protection under Roman rule. Hated symbols of oppression for some were signs of progress for others. Roman soldiers and officials saw themselves as harbingers of a civilization that was triumphing over barbarism; Stoic philosophers envisioned a global community — neither barbarian, Roman, or Greek — where human beings were citizens of the universe.

Into this world, came Christian missionaries with a confident redeeming "knowledge of the Lord." They traveled the trade routes along the shores of the Mediterranean Sea, spreading west from the frontier of the empire — the province of Palestine, known mainly for its ethnic and religious fanaticism. With incredible zeal, the "prophets and apostles" of this small Christian movement visited the settlements of the Jewish Diaspora, preached the gospel of Jesus, and established "Christian synagogues"[1] in most of the cities in the eastern half of the Mediterranean

---

1. W. H. C. Frend, *The Rise of Christianity* (Philadelphia: Fortress Press, 1984), 119.

basin. By the turn of the second century, Christianity was commonplace in Asia Minor, Syria, Macedonia, and Greece, reaching west as far as the imperial city of Rome.

The earliest Christian communities had close ties to their Palestinian origins, often physically located in or near the Jewish sections of town. Unlike traditional Judaism, however, Christianity did not enjoy the status or protection of an "approved religion" under imperial law. Even after Palestinian influence began to wane and non-Jewish Christians became the majority, Roman officials continued to treat Christians as members of an unauthorized Jewish sect. Their unwillingness to compromise with the authorities and their uncertain legal status made Christians the target of frequent persecutions. Most Roman bureaucrats considered this oppression to be the victims' fault. To practical Roman minds, refusing to pledge allegiance to the "divine genius" of the emperor seemed irrational or worse. It suggested some hidden subversion or danger to the state.

History relates many vivid accounts of the conflict between individual Christians and Roman authorities during the first three centuries of Christian history. Of the three narratives included in this volume, the most moving is the story of two Carthagenian women, Perpetua and Felicitas, who died in the arena of Carthage on March 7, 203 (see vol. 1:69–80). The courage and sacrifice of the martyrs became the seed of the church, inspiring many of the serious to join the Christian community. Not all Christians, of course, courted martyrdom. As their movement spread across the Roman world, Christians enjoyed increasing respectability and long intervals free of persecution.

Unfortunately, the picture changed in the middle of the third century, when severe and universal persecution resumed under emperors Decius and Valerian. Many Christians weakened, denouncing their faith or offering sacrifices to the Roman gods. Later, they regretted their actions and came back to the church. What to do with these penitent "lapsed" Christians became the cause of a major schism in the North African church.

The issue involved a conflict over ultimate allegiance. In 180, for instance, the Scillitan Christian martyr Speratus insisted before a Roman proconsul at Carthage that he could recognize no emperor but God, who was the true and only emperor of all kings and nations. The six Christian men and five Christian women with him agreed, refusing all compromise between their understanding of authority and the proconsul's vision of empire. Their vision was simple and direct, a stubborn insistence on the prime directive of their faith: *Jesus kyrios.* "Jesus is [the only] Lord!" Confident in that confession, they went to their death.

As the apostle Paul had been quick to note, the story of the cross and resurrection of Christ challenged the cherished beliefs of both Jews and Greeks, confounding the wisdom of the wise. To faithful Jews that confession was "blasphemy"; to educated Romans or Greeks, it was plain "foolishness." Then as now, the perennial "scandal" of Christianity does not lie in the rigor of Jesus' moral teachings. It lies in the word of the cross, the story of the crucified and risen Christ (see 1 Cor. 1:20–25). Within the Christian community, ancient disputes between "Judaizers" and "Hellenizers" sound surprisingly like modern polemics over the "Jesus of history" and the "Christ of faith."

Prophets and Apostles

The first task of early "catholic" or ecumenical theology, therefore, was to hold the Christological center against the extremes of either biblical literalism (the "Judaizers") or eclectic syncretism (the "Hellenizers"). Paul himself triggered that discussion by compelling the early Christian community to decide between an ethnic or a global mission for the church at the Council of Jerusalem (see Acts 15). Theologian Bruno Bauer (d. 1882) may not have been wrong altogether, when he claimed that the development of the "catholic" church was the outcome of a synthesis or compromise between Peter and Paul; i.e., between the partisans of Jerusalem and those of Athens in the ancient church.

It is significant that the roots of Christianity were planted firmly in the religion of the Hebrew Scriptures. From the beginning, Christians considered themselves rightful heirs of the covenant given by Yahweh to the people of Israel. They were the "new" Israel. The first Christian writers used the Hebrew Scriptures to support a claim that Christ's new covenant fulfilled and restored the promises of God made to Moses and to the prophets of Israel. When Marcion, a second-century Christian writer, threw out the Hebrew Scriptures, because, he argued, they upheld the goodness of the created world, he triggered a major division in the Christian church that lasted well into the fifth century. Christian gnostics sought holiness by escaping from the sinful world of "matter" to live "spiritual" lives.

The early Christians read the Hebrew Scriptures "backwards." They interpreted the history of Israel from the perspective of their Christian faith. For example, biblical theologian Irenaeus (d.c. 200) used the narrative of Adam's fall to support the Christian doctrine of salvation by grace. Christ, the second Adam, "recapitulates" the first. Thus, by his obedience unto death, Christ, the second Adam, atones for our first parents' disobedience and restores "God's image" to humankind. Tertullian, a younger contemporary (d.c. 225), claimed that only Christians have a right to use the Hebrew Scriptures, for they alone know how to interpret them correctly (see vol. 1:41–47). Tertullian chides the gnostics for using allegorical interpretations of the scripture to support their views on the dualism of matter and spirit. Irenaeus targets the gnostics for rejecting the goodness of God's creation which, he says, the Father has made with his two hands, that is with the Son and the Spirit.

Other Christian writers did not object to allegory if it suited their purpose. Origen of Alexandria (d.c. 254), an early proponent of the allegorical method, became one of the first systematic theologians of the Christian church. For him, a literal reading of the scriptures occurred on a "simple" or preliminary level of understanding "barely touching the flesh of scripture" (see vol. 1:48–54). Those more advanced in the gifts of the Spirit were empowered to move to higher ground, to a "spiritual" (allegorical) comprehension, a "Christian gnosis" beyond the "obvious" meaning of the text.

Irenaeus or Tertullian considered Origen's views heretical. Yet both sides agreed that scripture ought to play a central role in shaping and defining the teachings of the Christian faith. Already Christians were using a common text of the Hebrew Scriptures, the Greek version of the Septuagint that dated from the third century B.C.E. In fact, when discrepancies between the Septuagint and the Hebrew Masoretic texts arose, Christian scholars stayed with the Greek. They even accused their Jewish colleagues of deliberately falsifying the Hebrew text where it differed from their Greek version.

The authority of the emerging New Testament was more precarious. While most of the writings of the New Testament canon were known and read by the end of the first century, no generally accepted list was forthcoming. Some writings, including Hebrews and Revelation, continued to be controversial. A group of "lesser" gospels beyond Matthew, Mark, Luke, and John, and some apocryphal epistles circulated freely in the churches. Ironically, the first "official" list of New Testament writings was made by Marcion (c. 150), who was considered a heretic by many because he wanted to replace the Hebrew Scriptures with a new Christian canon. Marcion's canon included the Gospel of Luke and the letters of Paul. Irenaeus, the bishop of Lyon (d.c. 200), began calling these Christian "scriptures" a "New Testament." Irenaeus's list of books shows that the New Testament canon was almost complete by the end of the second century, including the four Gospels, Acts, Paul's epistles, Peter, Jude, John, Revelation, and several apocryphal books. The first complete listing of all twenty-seven New Testament books finally canonized dates from 367, when Athanasius, the bishop of Alexandria, included the list in his 39th Easter Letter (see vol. 1:55–57). It took at least another century or so before the canon became "official" in the West.

Popular "Christian" literature of dubious origin, such as charming stories of Jesus' childhood, sundry epistles attributed to various apostles, and the gnostic gospels of St. Thomas and St. Peter continued to circulate. The problem was not too little literature but too much. Faced with a variety of conflicting literary sources, it became increasingly important for the church to decide what to accept as genuine and what to reject as inconsistent with the "tradition of the apostles" or as a serious threat to Christian unity.

Toward the end of the second century, a theological consensus began to emerge. Irenaeus of Lyon referred to a normative teaching tradition (c. 189). Though Christians are scattered across the whole world, noted Irenaeus, Christians everywhere "share this preaching and this faith": (1) a widely accepted body of teaching known as the "tradition of prophets and apostles," (2) an open list of written affirmations known as the "Rule of Faith (or Truth)" based on that tradition, (3) the Septuagint version of the Hebrew Scriptures, and (4) a group of canonical books known as the New Testament that were being tested against antiquity and apostolic origin constantly.

The early Christian search for theological consensus was forced in part by (1) the delay of the anticipated, imminent return of Christ (the parousia); (2) the rise of "false prophets," i.e., of schismatic or heretical teachers who caused confusion in Christian ranks; and (3) the rising tide of criticism and outright defamation from religious rivals, intellectual critics, and political enemies who wanted to halt the rapid growth of the new religion.

Along with the emerging biblical canon, another group of writings developed to provide rules for Christian living. Apostolic authors produced the *Didache* (Teaching) and an anonymous letter known as Clement's First Letter (see vol. 1:15–24 and vol. 1:25–31). Written about 100 C.E., they give practical guidance concerning Christian life and worship to diverse and often poorly educated Christian communities. They reflect the "congregational" autonomy of local churches that have an elected resident bishop (or presbyter) assisted by a team of deacons. They also show how the charismatic, itinerant ministry of prophets (evangelists) and apostles (teachers), which characterized most of the first century, began to change. Early apocalyptic hopes gave way to martyrdom and extensive mission outreach as the primary means for Christian witness.

Persecutions

Many Christian "confessors," especially in North Africa, chose martyrdom as their own parousia (end time), welcoming personal reunion with Christ (see vol. 1:69–80). When Ignatius, the bishop of Antioch, traveled to Rome under guard to die a martyr's death (c. 113), Christians gathered along the route to honor him as a conquering hero and future saint. Although Ignatius was troubled over his fitness to wear the martyr's crown, he used his power to speak out against a rising tide of discord in the churches he visited (see vol. 1:123–28). At Smyrna, for instance, he found that Docetists, who wanted to deny that Jesus was human at all, were causing a schism. In Philadelphia radical Judaizers were creating factions in one of the oldest Christian congregations with their extreme legalism. Calling himself "a man utterly devoted to unity," Ignatius called for a hierarchical solution to the problem of unity. The bishop, he said, is the living symbol of Christ's presence in the congregation. Christians must follow their bishop as Christ followed the Father, their presbyters as the apostles, and their deacons as God's commandments. Gradually the terms *bishop* and *presbyter* ceased to be interchangeable. In the cause of unity Christians argued that bishops had more authority (oversight) than local elders.

Within the next century Irenaeus carried that logic to its conclusion, arguing that only leaders in "apostolic succession," the "catholic" bishops who have descended in direct line from Peter and the apostles, ought to have the final word in matters of faith. Irenaeus used this argument to refute Christian gnostics, who claimed their own private revelation. Unfortunately, his "argument from antiquity" tied church authority to the monarchical episcopate. It was a less than happy combination, carrying unpleasant consequences for the subsequent development of Christian doctrine.

Apologetics

The search for orderly church life also encouraged growing expectations of doctrinal uniformity. External and internal challenges created pressures for generally agreed upon, authoritative understandings of

Christian belief. As Christianity spread across the empire, attacks by religious rivals, intellectual critics, and political enemies became commonplace. Christians were accused of an assortment of crimes and misdemeanors: civil disobedience; atheism; and gross immoralities, such as incest and cannibalism.

Under intense pressure, the teachings of prophets and apostles needed to be preserved for future generations. Theological "apologists" wrote furiously to defend the faith, entering into reasoned dialogue with their pagan detractors. Origen (d.c. 254), in his apologetic treatise "Against Celsus," preserved most of the "True Discourses" (c. 180) — an astute critique of early Christianity. Celsus ridiculed Christians for many things, including their reluctance to recognize the truth of other religions and their refusal to participate in public and military service, omitting only the more esoteric moral charges (see vol. 1:118–21 and 279–81). Like another scholarly baiter of Christians, Porphyry, Celsus had done his homework. An eclectic in matters of religion, Celsus took pains to "spiritualize" (understood as allegorize) the popular polytheistic mythologies. He found many central Christian doctrines, such as creation *ex nihilo* (from nothing) and the physical birth, death, and resurrection of Jesus to be crude and unreasonable. He considered the belief that God gave the free gift of eternal life to all Christians a moral disincentive. He found eternal life inconsistent with the classical postulate about an immortal human soul.

Unlike the preposterous charges of immorality or political subversion that fueled persecutions, this type of philosophic and theological criticism highlighted the real dispute between classicism and Christianity. It challenged Christian writers to respond with a reasoned and reasonable defense of the faith. Consequently, "apologetics" remained an important part of the Christian theological repertoire long after the ancient church had won the day.

Three early apologetic works, the anonymous "Letter to Diognetus" (c. 150) (see vol. 1:84–93), the "First Apology" of Justin Martyr (c. 155) (see vol. 1:94–108), and "Plea Regarding the Christians" (c. 177) by Athenagoras, the Athenian, a philosopher and a Christian (see vol. 1: 109–22) are classic examples of this genre. As a group, the apologists fought their battles as much as possible on the grounds of their adversaries. They argued that (1) Christians could hardly be guilty of political subversion, because there was no conflict between them and the empire since the realm of God was not of this world. They argued that (2) it was unworthy of Roman justice to punish Christians "just for bearing the name" of Christ. They argued that (3) accusations of atheism and immorality were based on ignorance, malicious gossip, or both; and that unless these absurd charges could be substantiated, they had to be rejected by every fair-minded person. And finally they argued that (4) the teachings of classical philosophers supported the teachings of the Christian scriptures. If the Hebrew Scriptures were older than any other book, Plato must have been instructed by Moses. Christianity was actually superior philosophy.

Visions of Unity

In the shadow of real persecution, however, ecclesiastical order and unity were even more important than philosophic victories. Ignatius of Antioch (d.c. 113) and Irenaeus of Lyon (d.c. 200) felt the need for a strong, hierarchical episcopate validated by apostolic tradition (see vol. 1: 123–28). Cyprian (d. 258) saw the marks of the true church in the succession of the episcopal office, the unity of the trinitarian faith, and the validity of the sacraments (vol. 1:129–34). Cyril of Alexandria (d. 444) followed Cyprian by thinking of the church as the sacramental, mystical body of Christ, which can be broken but not divided (see vol. 1:135–39). And finally, Augustine (d.c. 430) addressed the question of who belongs to the communion of saints in his treatise on Baptism (see vol. 1:140–44).

The struggle to define and preserve the oneness of the Christian faith is an ongoing challenge for the church. These efforts of early Christians to discover and uphold Christian unity are a continuing resource for contemporary Christians.

Prophets and Apostles

1. The Didache
(c. 100)

*"The teaching (*didache*) of the Lord through the twelve apostles to the gentiles" is a composite work compiled about 150 in Alexandria from two earlier sources: a moral treatise known as "Two Ways" and a first-century manual on church order. Internal evidence suggests Palestinian or Syrian origins in the late first or very early second century. The writer appeals to an emerging tradition of true apostolic teaching to address three practical problems facing the scattered Christian communities at the turn of the century: (1) What does it mean to live as a Christian, to "bear the yoke of the Lord?" (2) What is the correct way of observing the sacraments, that is, baptism and Holy Communion? and (3) What are the marks of a true "apostle," or minister of Christ?*

The first section of the document (1–6) is a series of commandments and rules based on the "Two Ways," which defines the Christian "way of life" as a struggle for moral perfection (6). The second part (7–12) con-

---

SOURCE: Cyril C. Richardson, ed., *Early Christian Fathers*, vol. 1 of *The Library of Christian Classics* (Philadelphia: Westminster Press, 1953). Used by permission of Westminster John Knox Press.

tains liturgical material, an agenda for celebrating baptism and Holy Communion. Here fasting precedes baptism in the triune name. Interestingly, this part reverses the order of serving bread and wine at communion. The final section (11–16) is a manual on church governance and contains some very practical advice on how to distinguish between true and false prophets. In the Didache, church governance clearly is still congregational. The manual vests authority in the local Christian community, which elects its own clerical leadership (bishops and deacons). The Christian community may judge the authenticity of itinerant prophets (charismatic preachers) and apostles (teachers) by their life and message.

The Lord's Teaching to the Heathen by the Twelve Apostles:

There are two ways, one of life and one of death; and between the two ways there is a great difference.

Now, this is the way of life: "First, you must love God who made you, and second, your neighbor as yourself."[1] And whatever you want people to refrain from doing to you, you must not do to them.[2]

What these maxims teach is this: "Bless those who curse you," and "pray for your enemies." Moreover, fast "for those who persecute you." For "what credit is it to you if you love those who love you? Is that not the way the heathen act?" But "you must love those who hate you,"[3] and then you will make no enemies. "Abstain from carnal passions."[4] If someone strikes you "on the right cheek, turn to him the other too, and you will be perfect."[5] If someone "forces you to go one mile with him, go along with him for two"; if someone robs you "of your overcoat, give him your suit as well."[6] If someone deprives you of "your property, do not ask for it back."[7] (You could not get it back anyway!) "Give to everybody who begs from you, and ask for no return."[8] For the Father wants his own gifts to be universally shared. Happy is the man who gives as the command-

---

1. Matt. 22:37–39; Lev. 19:18.
2. Cf. Matt. 7:12.
3. Matt. 5:44, 46, 47; Luke 6:27, 28, 32, 33.
4. 1 Pet. 2:11.
5. Matt. 5:39, 48; Luke 6:29.
6. Matt. 5:40, 41.
7. Luke 6:30.
8. Ibid.

ment bids him, for he is guiltless! But alas for the man who receives! If he receives because he is in need, he will be guiltless. But if he is not in need he will have to stand trial why he received and for what purpose. He will be thrown into prison and have his action investigated; and "he will not get out until he has paid back the last cent."[9] Indeed, there is a further saying that relates to this: "Let your donation sweat in your hands until you know to whom to give it."[10]

The second commandment of the Teaching: "Do not murder; do not commit adultery"; do not corrupt boys; do not fornicate; "do not steal"; do not practice magic; do not go in for sorcery; do not murder a child by abortion or kill a newborn infant. "Do not covet your neighbor's property; do not commit perjury; do not bear false witness";[11] do not slander; do not bear grudges. Do not be double-minded or double-tongued, for a double tongue is "a deadly snare."[12] Your words shall not be dishonest or hollow, but substantiated by action. Do not be greedy or extortionate or hypocritical or malicious or arrogant. Do not plot against your neighbor. Do not hate anybody; but reprove some, pray for others, and still others love more than your own life.

My child, flee from all wickedness and from everything of that sort. Do not be irritable, for anger leads to murder. Do not be jealous or contentious or impetuous, for all this breeds murder.

My child, do not be lustful, for lust leads to fornication. Do not use foul language or leer, for all this breeds adultery.

My child, do not be a diviner, for that leads to idolatry. Do not be an enchanter or an astrologer or a magician. Moreover, have no wish to observe or heed such practices, for all this breeds idolatry.

My child, do not be a liar, for lying leads to theft. Do not be avaricious or vain, for all this breeds thievery.

My child, do not be a grumbler, for grumbling leads to blasphemy. Do not be stubborn or evil-minded, for all this breeds blasphemy.

But be humble since "the humble will inherit the earth."[13] Be patient, merciful, harmless, quiet, and good; and always "have respect for the teaching"[14] you have been given. Do not put on airs or give yourself up to

---

9. Matt. 5:26.
10. Source unknown.
11. Ex. 20:13–17; cf. Matt. 19:18; 5:33.
12. Prov. 21:6.
13. Ps. 37:11; Matt. 5:5.
14. Isa. 66:2.

presumptuousness. Do not associate with the high and mighty; but be with the upright and humble. Accept whatever happens to you as good, in the realization that nothing occurs apart from God.

My child, day and night "you should remember him who preaches God's word to you,"[15] and honor him as you would the Lord. For where the Lord's nature is discussed, there the Lord is. Every day you should seek the company of saints to enjoy their refreshing conversation. You must not start a schism, but reconcile those at strife. "Your judgments must be fair."[16] You must not play favorites when reproving transgressions. You must not be of two minds about your decision.[17]

Do not be one who holds his hand out to take, but shuts it when it comes to giving. If your labor has brought you earnings, pay a ransom for your sins. Do not hesitate to give and do not give with a bad grace; for you will discover who He is that pays you back a reward with a good grace. Do not turn your back on the needy, but share everything with your brother and call nothing your own. For if you have what is eternal in common, how much more should you have what is transient!

Do not neglect your responsibility[18] to your son or your daughter, but from their youth you shall teach them to revere God. Do not be harsh in giving orders to your slaves and slave girls. They hope in the same God as you, and the result may be that they cease to revere the God over you both. For when he comes to call us, he will not respect our station, but will call those whom the Spirit has made ready. You slaves, for your part, must obey your masters with reverence and fear, as if they represented God.

You must hate all hypocrisy and everything which fails to please the Lord. You must not forsake "the Lord's commandments," but "observe" the ones you have been given, "neither adding nor subtracting anything."[19] At the church meeting you must confess your sins, and not approach prayer with a bad conscience. That is the way of life.

But the way of death is this: First of all, it is wicked and thoroughly blasphemous: murders, adulteries, lusts, fornications, thefts, idolatries, magic arts, sorceries, robberies, false witness, hypocrisies, duplicity, deceit, arrogance, malice, stubbornness, greediness, filthy talk, jealousy, audacity, haughtiness, boastfulness.[20]

---

15. Heb. 13:7.
16. Deut. 1:16, 17; Prov. 31:9.
17. Meaning uncertain.
18. Literally, "Do not withhold your hand from . . ."
19. Deut. 4:12; 12:32.
20. Cf. Matt. 15:19; Mark 7:21, 22; Rom. 1:29–31; Gal. 5:19–21.

Those who persecute good people, who hate truth, who love lies, who are ignorant of the reward of uprightness, who do not "abide by goodness"[21] or justice, and are on the alert not for goodness but for evil: gentleness and patience are remote from them. "They love vanity,"[22] "look for profit,"[23] have no pity for the poor, do not exert themselves for the oppressed, ignore their Maker, "murder children,"[24] corrupt God's image, turn their backs on the needy, oppress the afflicted, defend the rich, unjustly condemn the poor, and are thoroughly wicked. My children, may you be saved from all this!

See "that no one leads you astray"[25] from this way of the teaching, since such a one's teaching is godless.

If you can bear the Lord's full yoke, you will be perfect. But if you cannot, then do what you can.

Now about food: undertake what you can. But keep strictly away from what is offered to idols, for that implies worshiping dead gods.

Now about baptism: this is how to baptize. Give public instruction on all these points, and then "baptize" in running water, "in the name of the Father and of the Son and of the Holy Spirit."[26] If you do not have running water, baptize in some other. If you cannot in cold, then in warm. If you have neither, then pour water on the head three times "in the name of the Father, Son, and Holy Spirit."[27] Before the baptism, moreover, the one who baptizes and the one being baptized must fast, and any others who can. And you must tell the one being baptized to fast for one or two days beforehand.

Your fasts must not be identical with those of the hypocrites.[28] They fast on Mondays and Thursdays; but you should fast on Wednesdays and Fridays.

You must not pray like the hypocrites,[29] but "pray as follows"[30] as the Lord bid us in his gospel:

"Our Father in heaven, hallowed be your name; your Kingdom come; your will be done on earth as it is in heaven; give us today our bread for

---

21. Rom. 12:9.
22. Ps. 4:2.
23. Isa. 1:23.
24. Wisd. 12:6.
25. Matt. 24:4.
26. Matt. 28:19.
27. Ibid.
28. I.e., the Jews. Cf. Matt. 6:16.
29. Matt. 6:5.
30. Cf. Matt. 6:9–13.

the morrow; and forgive us our debts as we forgive our debtors. And do not lead us into temptation, but save us from the evil one, for yours is the power and the glory forever.

You should pray in this way three times a day.

Now about the Eucharist:[31] This is how to give thanks: First in connection with the cup:[32]

"We thank you, our Father, for the holy vine[33] of David, your child, which you have revealed through Jesus, your child. To you be glory forever."

Then in connection with the piece[34] [broken off the loaf]:

"We thank you, our Father, for the life and knowledge which you have revealed through Jesus, your child. To you be glory forever.

"As this piece [of bread] was scattered over the hills[35] and then was brought together and made one, so let your Church be brought together from the ends of the earth into your Kingdom. For yours is the glory and the power through Jesus Christ forever."

You must not let anyone eat or drink of your Eucharist except those baptized in the Lord's name. For in reference to this the Lord said, "Do not give what is sacred to dogs."[36]

After you have finished your meal, say grace[37] in this way:

"We thank you, holy Father, for your sacred name which you have lodged[38] in our hearts, and for the knowledge and faith and immortality

---

31. I.e., "the Thanksgiving." The term, however, had become a technical one in Christianity for the special giving of thanks at the Lord's Supper. One might render the verbal form ("give thanks"), which immediately follows, as "say grace," for it was out of the Jewish forms for grace before and after meals (accompanied in the one instance by the breaking of bread and in the other by sharing a common cup of wine) that the Christian thanksgivings of the Lord's Supper developed.

32. It is a curious feature of the Didache that the cup has been displaced from the end of the meal to the very beginning. Equally curious is the absence of any direct reference to the body and blood of Christ.

33. This may be a metaphorical reference to the divine life and knowledge revealed through Jesus. It may also refer to the Messianic promise (cf. Isa. 11:1), or to the Messianic community (cf. Ps. 80:8), i.e., the Church.

34. An odd phrase, but one that refers to the Jewish custom (taken over in the Christian Lord's Supper) of grace before meals. The head of the house would distribute to each of the guests a piece of bread broken off a loaf, after uttering the appropriate thanksgiving to God.

35. The reference is likely to the sowing of wheat on the hillsides of Judea.

36. Matt. 7:6.

37. Or "give thanks." See note 31.

38. For the phrase cf. Neh. 1:9.

which you have revealed through Jesus, your child. To you be glory forever.

"Almighty Master, 'you have created everything'[39] for the sake of your name, and have given men food and drink to enjoy that they may thank you. But to us you have given spiritual food and drink and eternal life through Jesus, your child.

"Above all, we thank you that you are mighty. To you be glory forever.

"Remember, Lord, your Church, to save it from all evil and to make it perfect by your love. Make it holy, 'and gather' it 'together from the four winds'[40] into your Kingdom which you have made ready for it. For yours is the power and the glory forever."

"Let Grace[41] come and let this world pass away."

"Hosanna to the God of David!"[42]

"If anyone is holy, let him come. If not, let him repent."[43]

"Our Lord, come!"[44]

"Amen."[45]

In the case of prophets, however, you should let them give thanks in their own way.[46]

Now, you should welcome anyone who comes your way and teaches you all we have been saying. But if the teacher proves himself a renegade and by teaching otherwise contradicts all this, pay no attention to him. But if his teaching furthers the Lord's righteousness and knowledge, welcome him as the Lord.

Now about the apostles and prophets: Act in line with the gospel precept.[47] Welcome every apostle on arriving, as if he were the Lord. But he must not stay beyond one day. In case of necessity, however, the next day too. If he stays three days, he is a false prophet. On departing, an apostle must not accept anything save sufficient food to carry him till his next lodging. If he asks for money, he is a false prophet.

---

39. Wisd. 1:14; Sir. 18:1; Rev. 4:11.
40. Matt. 24:31.
41. A title for Christ.
42. Cf. Matt. 21:9, 15.
43. Or perhaps "be converted."
44. Cf. 1 Cor. 16:22.
45. These terse exclamations may be versicles and responses. More likely they derive from the Jewish custom of reading verses concerning Israel's future redemption and glory, after the final benediction.
46. I.e, they are not bound by the texts given.
47. Matt. 10:40, 41.

While a prophet is making ecstatic utterances,[48] you must not test or examine him. For "every sin will be forgiven," but this sin "will not be forgiven."[49] However, not everybody making ecstatic utterances is a prophet, but only if he behaves like the Lord. It is by their conduct that the false prophet and the [true] prophet can be distinguished. For instance, if a prophet marks out a table in the Spirit,[50] he must not eat from it. If he does, he is a false prophet. Again, every prophet who teaches the truth but fails to practice what he preaches is a false prophet. But every attested and genuine prophet who acts with a view to symbolizing the mystery of the Church,[51] and does not teach you to do all he does, must not be judged by you. His judgment rests with God. For the ancient prophets too acted in this way. But if someone says in the Spirit, "Give me money, or something else," you must not heed him. However, if he tells you to give for others in need, no one must condemn him.

Everyone "who comes" to you "in the name of the Lord"[52] must be welcomed. Afterward, when you have tested him, you will find out about him, for you have insight into right and wrong. If it is a traveler who arrives, help him all you can. But he must not stay with you more than two days, or, if necessary, three. If he wants to settle with you and is an artisan, he must work for his living. If, however, he has no trade, use your judgment in taking steps for him to live with you as a Christian without being idle. If he refuses to do this, he is trading on Christ. You must be on your guard against such people.

Every genuine prophet who wants to settle with you "has a right to his support." Similarly, a genuine teacher himself, just like a "workman, has a right to his support."[53] Hence take all the first fruits of vintage and

---

48. Literally, "speaking in a spirit," i.e., speaking while possessed by a divine or demonic spirit. This whole passage (ch. 11:7–12) is a sort of parallel to Matt. 12:31 ff. There is an interpretation of the sin against the Holy Ghost, followed by a comment on good and evil conduct (cf. Matt. 12:33–37), and concluded by the prophets' signs which are suggested by the sign of the Son of Man (Matt. 12:38 ff.).

49. Matt. 12:31.

50. The sense is not clear, but suggests a dramatic portrayal of the Messianic banquet. It was characteristic of the biblical prophets to drive home their teaching by dramatic and symbolic actions (cf. Jer., ch. 19; Acts 21:11; etc.).

51. Literally, "acts with a view to a worldly mystery of the Church." The meaning is not certain, but some dramatic action, symbolizing the mystical marriage of the Church to Christ, is probably intended. The reference may, indeed, be to the prophet's being accompanied by a spiritual sister (cf. 1 Cor. 7:36 ff.).

52. Matt. 21:9; Ps. 118:26; cf. John 5:43.

53. Matt. 10:10. The provision for the prophet or teacher to settle and to be supported by the congregation implies the birth of the monarchical episcopate. Note the connection

harvest, and of cattle and sheep, and give these first fruits to the prophets. For they are your high priests. If, however, you have no prophet, give them to the poor. If you make bread, take the first fruits and give in accordance with the precept.[54] Similarly, when you open a jar of wine or oil, take the first fruits and give them to the prophets. Indeed, of money, clothes, and of all your possessions, take such first fruits as you think right, and give in accordance with the precept.

On every Lord's Day—his special day[55]—come together and break bread and give thanks, first confessing your sins so that your sacrifice may be pure. Anyone at variance with his neighbor must not join you, until they are reconciled, lest your sacrifice be defiled. For it was of this sacrifice that the Lord said, "Always and everywhere offer me a pure sacrifice; for I am a great King, says the Lord, and my name is marveled at by the nations."[56]

You must, then, elect for yourselves bishops and deacons who are a credit to the Lord, men who are gentle, generous, faithful, and well tried. For their ministry to you is identical with that of the prophets and teachers. You must not, therefore, despise them, for along with the prophets and teachers they enjoy a place of honor among you.

Furthermore, do not reprove each other angrily, but quietly, as you find it in the gospel. Moreover, if anyone has wronged his neighbor, nobody must speak to him, and he must not hear a word from you, until he repents. Say your prayers, give your charity, and do everything just as you find it in the gospel of our Lord.

"Watch" over your life: do not let "your lamps" go out, and do not keep "your loins ungirded"; but "be ready," for "you do not know the hour when our Lord is coming."[57] Meet together frequently in your search for what is good for your souls, since "a lifetime of faith will be of no advantage"[58] to you unless you prove perfect at the very last. For in the final days multitudes of false prophets and seducers will appear. Sheep will turn into wolves, and love into hatred. For with the increase of iniquity men will hate, persecute, and betray each other. And then the world deceiver will appear in the guise of God's Son. He will work "signs

---

of this with the high priesthood (cf. Hippolytus, Apost. Trad. 3:4) and tithing. No provision is made for the support of the local clergy in ch. 15.

54. Deut. 18:3–5.
55. Literally, "On every Lord's Day of the Lord."
56. Mal. 1:11, 14.
57. Matt. 24:42, 44; Luke 12:35.
58. Barn. 4:9.

and wonders"[59] and the earth will fall into his hands and he will commit outrages such as have never occurred before. Then mankind will come to the fiery trial "and many will fall away"[60] and perish, "but those who persevere" in their faith "will be saved"[61] by the Curse himself.[62] Then "there will appear the signs"[63] of the Truth: first the sign of stretched-out [hands] in heaven,[64] then the sign of "a trumpet's blast,"[65] and thirdly the resurrection of the dead, though not of all the dead, but as it has been said: "The Lord will come and all his saints with him. Then the world will see the Lord coming on the clouds of the sky."[66]

---

59. Matt. 24:24.
60. Matt. 24:10.
61. Matt. 10:22; 24:13.
62. An obscure reference, but possibly meaning the Christ who suffered the death of one accursed (Gal. 3:13; Barn. 7:9). Cf. two other titles for the Christ: Grace and Truth.
63. Matt. 24:30.
64. Another obscure reference, possibly to the belief that the Christ would appear on a glorified cross. Cf. Barn. 12:2–4.
65. Matt. 24:31.
66. Zech. 14:5; 1 Thess. 3:13; Matt. 24:30.

2. Clement's First Letter
(c. 95)

CLEMENT

Clement's First Letter (c. 95) is the oldest Christian writing known outside the New Testament canon. It is also a letter of counsel and rebuke from one Christian congregation to another, from the Romans to the Corinthians. It reflects the fact that these two local churches shared a unique "pastoral" relationship. Although the text does not identify an author, scholars agree that it was probably written on behalf of the Roman church by its presbyter/bishop Clement between 95 and 97. Clement wrote it because of the crisis in the Corinthian church caused by the dismissal of its pastoral leadership.

Apart from the interesting notion that beyond the duty of charity, Christian congregations have a pastoral responsibility for one another, Clement's First Letter tries to reconcile Stoic philosophy with the Hebrew Scriptures and Pauline theology. In the process, some of the power of the Hebrew prophetic witness and Paul's exuberant embrace of the mysteries of Christ is lost.

SOURCE: Cyril C. Richardson, ed., *Early Christian Fathers,* vol. 1 of *The Library of Christian Classics* (Philadelphia: Westminster Press, 1953). Used by permission of Westminster John Knox Press.

The church of God, living in exile[1] in Rome, to the church of God, exiled in Corinth — to you who are called and sanctified by God's will through our Lord Jesus Christ. Abundant grace and peace be yours from God Almighty through Jesus Christ.

Due, dear friends, to the sudden and successive misfortunes and accidents we have encountered,[2] we have, we admit, been rather long in turning our attention to your quarrels. We refer to the abominable and unholy schism, so alien and foreign to those whom God has chosen, which a few impetuous and headstrong fellows have fanned to such a pitch of insanity that your good name, once so famous and dear to us all, has fallen into the gravest ill repute. Has anyone, indeed, stayed with you without attesting the excellence and firmness of your faith? without admiring your sensible and considerate Christian piety? without broadcasting your spirit of unbounded hospitality?[3] without praising your perfect and trustworthy knowledge? For you always acted without partiality and walked in God's laws. You obeyed your rulers and gave your elders the proper respect. You disciplined the minds of your young people in moderation and dignity. You instructed your women to do everything with a blameless and pure conscience, and to give their husbands the affection they should. You taught them, too, to abide by the rule of obedience and to run their homes with dignity and thorough discretion.

You were all humble and without any pretensions, obeying orders rather than issuing them, more gladly giving than receiving.[4] Content with Christ's rations and mindful of them, you stored his words carefully up in your hearts and held his sufferings before your eyes.

• • •

With this hope, then, let us attach ourselves to him who is faithful to his promises and just in his judgments. He who bids us to refrain from lying

---

1. The Greek word implies a colony of aliens without full civic rights. Christians are strangers and pilgrims on earth, their true fatherland being heaven. Cf. 1 Pet. 2:11; Phil. 3:20; Heb. 11:9.

2. The reference is to persecution under Domitian — the same persecution reflected in John's Apocalypse.

3. Hospitality is emphasized several times in the letter. It is a virtue appropriate to churches on the great trade route of the Empire, Corinth being a natural halt between Rome and the East.

4. Cf. Acts 20:35.

is all the less likely to lie himself. For nothing is impossible to God save lying.[5] Let us, then, rekindle our faith in him, and bear in mind that nothing is beyond his reach. By his majestic word he established the universe, and by his word he can bring it to an end. "Who shall say to him, What have you done? Or who shall resist his mighty strength?"[6] He will do everything when he wants to and as he wants to. And not one of the things he has decreed will fail. Everything is open to his sight and nothing escapes his will. For "the heavens declare God's glory and the sky proclaims the work of his hands. Day pours forth words to day; and night imparts knowledge to night. And there are neither words nor speech, and their voices are not heard."[7]

Since, then, he sees and hears everything, we should fear him and rid ourselves of wicked desires that issue in base deeds. By so doing we shall be sheltered by his mercy from the judgments to come. For where can any of us flee to escape his mighty hand? What world is there to receive anyone who deserts him? For Scripture says somewhere: "Where shall I go and where shall I hide from your presence? If I go up to heaven, you are there. If I go off to the ends of the earth, there is your right hand. If I make my bed in the depths, there is your spirit."[8] Where, then, can anyone go or where can he flee to escape from him who embraces everything?

We must, then, approach him with our souls holy, lifting up pure and undefiled hands to him, loving our kind and compassionate Father, who has made us his chosen portion. For thus it is written: "When the Most High divided the nations, when he dispersed the sons of Adam, he fixed the boundaries of the nations to suit the number of God's angels.[9] The Lord's portion became his people, Jacob: Israel was the lot that fell to him."[10] And in another place it says: "Behold, the Lord takes for himself a people from among the nations, just as a man takes the first fruits of his threshing floor; and the Holy of Holies shall come forth from that nation."[11]

Since, then, we are a holy portion, we should do everything that makes

---

5. Cf. Heb. 6:18.
6. Wisd. 12:12.
7. Ps. 19:1–3.
8. Ps. 139:7, 8.
9. The idea is that each nation has its guardian angel.
10. Deut. 32:8, 9.
11. A conflation of a number of O.T. phrases: Deut. 4:34; 14:2; Num. 18:27; 2 Chron. 31:14; Ezek. 48:12.

for holiness. We should flee from slandering, vile and impure embraces, drunkenness, rioting, filthy lusts, detestable adultery, and disgusting arrogance. "For God," says Scripture, "resists the arrogant, but gives grace to the humble."[12]

• • •

"Each of us," brothers, "in his own rank"[13] must win God's approval and have a clear conscience. We must not transgress the rules laid down for our ministry, but must perform it reverently. Not everywhere, brothers, are the different sacrifices — the daily ones, the freewill offerings, and those for sins and trespasses — offered, but only in Jerusalem. And even there sacrifices are not made at any point, but only in front of the sanctuary, at the altar, after the high priest and the ministers mentioned have inspected the offering for blemishes. Those, therefore, who act in any way at variance with his will, suffer the penalty of death. You see, brothers, the more knowledge we are given, the greater risks we run.

The apostles received the gospel for us from the Lord Jesus Christ; Jesus, the Christ, was sent from God. Thus Christ is from God and the apostles from Christ. In both instances the orderly procedure depends on God's will. And so the apostles, after receiving their orders and being fully convinced by the resurrection of our Lord Jesus Christ and assured by God's word, went out in the confidence of the Holy Spirit to preach the good news that God's Kingdom was about to come. They preached in country and city, and appointed their first converts, after testing them by the Spirit, to be the bishops and deacons of future believers. Nor was this any novelty, for Scripture had mentioned bishops and deacons long before. For this is what Scripture says somewhere: "I will appoint their bishops in righteousness and their deacons in faith."[14]

And is it any wonder that those Christians whom God had entrusted with such a duty should have appointed the officers mentioned? For the blessed Moses too, "who was a faithful servant in all God's house,"[15] recorded in the sacred books all the orders given to him, and the rest of the prophets followed in his train by testifying with him to his legislation. Now, when rivalry for the priesthood arose and the tribes started quarrel-

---

12. Prov. 3:34; James 4:6; 1 Peter 5:5.
13. 1 Cor. 15:23.
14. Isa. 60:17.
15. Num. 12:7; Heb. 3:5.

ing as to which of them should be honored with this glorious privilege, Moses bid the twelve tribal chiefs bring him rods, on each of which was written the name of one of the tribes. These he took and bound, sealing them with the rings of the tribal leaders; and he put them in the tent of testimony on God's table. Then he shut the tent and put seals on the keys just as he had on the rods. And he told them: "Brothers, the tribe whose rod puts forth buds is the one God has chosen for the priesthood and for his ministry." Early the next morning he called all Israel together, six hundred thousand strong, and showed the seals to the tribal chiefs and opened the tent of testimony and brought out the rods. And it was discovered that Aaron's rod had not only budded, but was actually bearing fruit. What do you think, dear friends? Did not Moses know in advance that this was going to happen? Why certainly. But he acted the way he did in order to forestall anarchy in Israel, and so that the name of the true and only God might be glorified. To Him be the glory forever and ever. Amen.

Now our apostles, thanks to our Lord Jesus Christ, knew that there was going to be strife over the title of bishop. It was for this reason and because they had been given an accurate knowledge of the future, that they appointed the officers we have mentioned. Furthermore, they later added a codicil to the effect that, should these die, other approved men should succeed to their ministry.[16] In the light of this, we view it as a breach of justice to remove from their ministry those who were appointed either by them [i.e., the apostles] or later on and with the whole church's consent, by others of the proper standing, and who, long enjoying everybody's approval, have ministered to Christ's flock faultlessly, humbly,

---

16. In this sentence and the one following there are a number of ambiguities in the Greek, which have given rise to three possible interpretations. (*a*) The apostles provided that, if they themselves should die, other approved men should succeed to the apostolic prerogatives. These men would take over the right to appoint the local presbyteries, and are the ones referred to by the phrase, "Others of the proper standing." (*b*) The apostles provided that should their first converts (i.e., the first local presbyters) die, others should succeed them. This succession would be in the hands of the apostles and, later on, of "others of the proper standing," i.e., men like Timothy and Titus with apostolic rank. (*c*) The apostles provided that should their first converts (i.e., the first local presbyters) die, others should succeed them. This succession, begun by the apostles, would be continued by self-perpetuating presbyteries. In this view, the phrase, "Others of the proper standing," would refer to the same class of persons as does the phrase, "The officers we have mentioned," in the preceding sentence, i.e., to presbyters. The reader will observe that, while the titles "presbyter" and "bishop" appear to be synonymous in Clement, the first two interpretations favor the "episcopal" view of the early ministry, while the third favors the "presbyterian."

quietly, and unassumingly. For we shall be guilty of no slight sin if we eject from the episcopate men who have offered the sacrifices with innocence and holiness. Happy, indeed, are those presbyters who have already passed on, and who ended a life of fruitfulness with their task complete. For they need not fear that anyone will remove them from their secure positions. But you, we observe, have removed a number of people, despite their good conduct, from a ministry they have fulfilled with honor and integrity. Your contention and rivalry, brothers, thus touches matters that bear on our salvation.

You have studied Holy Scripture, which contains the truth and is inspired by the Holy Spirit. You realize that there is nothing wrong or misleading written in it. You will not find that upright people have ever been disowned by holy men. The righteous, to be sure, have been persecuted, but by wicked men. They have been imprisoned, but by the godless. They have been stoned by transgressors, slain by men prompted by abominable and wicked rivalry. Yet in such sufferings they bore up nobly. What shall we say, brothers? Was Daniel cast into a den of lions by those who revered God? Or was Ananias, Azarias, or Mishael shut up in the fiery furnace by men devoted to the magnificent and glorious worship of the Most High? Not for a moment! Who, then, was it that did such things? Detestable men, thoroughly and completely wicked, whose factiousness drove them to such a pitch of fury that they tormented those who resolutely served God in holiness and innocence. They failed to realize that the Most High is the champion and defender of those who worship his excellent name with a pure conscience. To him be the glory forever and ever. Amen. But those who held out with confidence inherited glory and honor. They were exalted, and God inscribed them on his memory forever and ever. Amen.

Brothers, *we* must follow such examples. For it is written: "Follow the saints, because those who follow them will become saints."[17] Again, it says in another place: "In the company of the innocent, you will be innocent; in the company of the elect, you will be elect; and in a crooked man's company you will go wrong."[18] Let us, then, follow the innocent and the upright. They, it is, who are God's elect. Why is it that you harbor strife, bad temper, dissension, schism, and quarreling? Do we not have one God, one Christ, one Spirit of grace which was poured out on us? And is there not one calling in Christ? Why do we rend and tear asunder

---

17. Source unknown.
18. Ps. 18:26, 27.

Christ's members and raise a revolt against our own body? Why do we reach such a pitch of insanity that we are oblivious of the fact we are members of each other? Recall the words of our Lord Jesus. For he said: "Woe to that man! It were better for him not to have been born than to be the occasion of one of my chosen ones stumbling. It were better for him to have a millstone around his neck and to be drowned in the sea, than to pervert one of my chosen."[19] Your schism has led many astray; it has made many despair; it has made many doubt; and it has distressed us all. Yet it goes on!

Pick up the letter of the blessed apostle Paul. What was the primary thing he wrote to you, "when he started preaching the gospel"?[20] To be sure, under the Spirit's guidance, he wrote to you about himself and Cephas and Apollos, because even then you had formed cliques. Factiousness, however, at that time was a less serious sin, since you were partisans of notable apostles and of a man they endorsed. But think now who they are who have led you astray and degraded your honorable and celebrated love of the brethren. It is disgraceful, exceedingly disgraceful, and unworthy of your Christian upbringing, to have it reported that because of one or two individuals the solid and ancient Corinthian Church is in revolt against its presbyters. This report, moreover, has reached not only us, but those who dissent from us as well.[21] The result is that the Lord's name is being blasphemed because of your stupidity, and you are exposing yourselves to danger.

We must, then, put a speedy end to this. We must prostrate ourselves before the Master, and beseech him with tears to have mercy on us and be reconciled to us and bring us back to our honorable and holy practice of brotherly love. For it is this which is the gate of righteousness, which opens the way to life, as it is written: "Open the gates of righteousness for me, so that I may enter by them and praise the Lord. This is the Lord's gate: the righteous shall enter by it."[22] While there are many gates open, the gate of righteousness is the Christian gate. Blessed are all those who enter by it and direct their way "in holiness and righteousness,"[23] by doing everything without disorder.

---

19. Matt. 26:24; Luke 17:1, 2, and parallels.
20. Phil. 4:15.
21. I.e., Jews and pagans.
22. Ps. 118:19, 20.
23. Luke 1:75.

3. The Faith in Scripture and Tradition
From *Against Heresies*
(c. 189)

IRENAEUS

Among the prominent members of the church at Lyon was Irenaeus (c. 130–c. 200), who with his pupil Tertullian was one of the major "biblical" theologians of the ancient church. Like many other Christians in the Roman province of Gaul (now southern France), he seems to have come from Asia Minor, perhaps from Smyrna. Smyrna was the city of Polycarp, a leader whom he greatly admired. When Emperor Marcus Aurelius ordered the persecution of Christians in the province, Irenaeus was on his way to Rome on a mission for his church. This fact almost certainly caused him to escape martyrdom in 177. On his return to Lyon, the survivors elected him to succeed their martyred bishop Pothinus.

Only two of Irenaeus's works survive: "Demonstration of the Apostolic Faith," a pamphlet of theological instruction; and a major polemical work, "Refutation against the so-called Gnosis," better known as "Against Heresies." In the polemical work, Irenaeus's particular concern is the Marcionite and Gnostic rejection of the natural world, which he finds incompatible with the Christian doctrine of creation. To

SOURCE: Cyril C. Richardson, ed., *Early Christian Fathers*, vol. 1 of *The Library of Christian Classics* (Philadelphia: Westminster Press, 1953). Used by permission of Westminster John Knox Press.

Irenaeus the world is good, because the good Creator/God has made all things with God's two hands, the Son and the Spirit. God made the world because of love, not from necessity or accident. In Christ, the second Adam, God "recapitulates" the first humanity, restoring the image that was lost. Thus, Christ becomes human, so that humans may become like Christ. Irenaeus says that Christ "is the only true and steadfast teacher, the Logos of God, who did through his transcendent love become what we are, that he might bring us to be even what he is himself."

These selections from Against Heresies, *written about 189, make the "protestant" point that the church must base its sound teaching on the authoritative proclamation of the Word. Though scattered across the world, Christians everywhere share "this preaching and this faith." The faith community bases its tradition, or story, on three sources: (1) the "rule of truth" or "faith," a widely held series of statements summarizing the major Christian teachings attributed to the original apostles and their immediate disciples; (2) the historical continuity of the body of Christ symbolized by the succession of bishops as a sign of divinely given authority; and (3) the written evidence of the Hebrew Scriptures and the New Testament. For Irenaeus, there can be no argument about the essential affirmations of the tradition: "Since the faith is one and the same, he who can say much about it does not add to it, nor does he who can say little diminish it."*

Preface

The Lord of all gave to his apostles the power of the gospel, and by them we also have learned the truth, that is, the teaching of the Son of God — as the Lord said to them, "He who hears you hears me, and he who despises you despises me, and him who sent me."[1]

The Traditions of the Gospels

For we learned the plan of our salvation from no others than from those through whom the gospel came to us. They first preached it abroad, and then later by the will of God handed it down to us in Writings,[2] to be the

---

1. Luke 10:16.
2. *In scripturis,* doubtless representing "*En graphais,*" not yet quite as technical as "Scripture."

foundation and pillar of our faith. For it is not right to say that they preached before they had come to perfect knowledge, as some dare to say, boasting that they are the correctors of the apostles. For after our Lord had risen from the dead, and they were clothed with the power from on high when the Holy Spirit came upon them, they were filled with all things and had perfect knowledge. They went out to the ends of the earth, preaching the good things that come to us from God, and proclaiming peace from heaven to men, all and each of them equally being in possession of the gospel of God. So Matthew among the Hebrews issued a Writing of the gospel in their own tongue, while Peter and Paul were preaching the gospel at Rome and founding the Church. After their decease Mark, the disciple and interpreter of Peter, also handed down to us in writing what Peter had preached. Then Luke, the follower of Paul, recorded in a book the gospel as it was preached by him. Finally John, the disciple of the Lord, who had also lain on his breast, himself published the Gospel, while he was residing at Ephesus in Asia. All of these handed down to us that there is one God, maker of heaven and earth, proclaimed by the Law and the Prophets, and one Christ the Son of God. If anyone does not agree with them he despises the companions of the Lord, he despises Christ the Lord himself, he even despises the Father, and he is self-condemned, resisting and refusing his own salvation, as all the heretics do.

The Apostolic Tradition

But when they are refuted from the Writings they turn around and attack the Writings themselves, saying that they are not correct, or authoritative, and that the truth cannot be found from them by those who are not acquainted with the tradition. For this [they say] was not handed down in writing, but orally, which is why Paul said, "We speak wisdom among the perfect, but not the wisdom of this world."[3] Each of them utters a wisdom which he has made up, or rather a fiction, so that according to them the truth was once to be found in Valentinus, then at another time in Marcion, at another time in Cerinthus, then later in Basilides, or was also in that opponent, who has no saving message to utter.[4] Each one of them is wholly perverse, and is not ashamed to preach himself, corrupting the rule of faith.

---

3. 1 Cor. 2:6.

4. Probably the unnamed heretic of I. 11:3, whom Irenaeus or his source may have left nameless as a recent and therefore familiar (or painful) defection; attempts to identify him by conjectural restoration of misunderstood Greek do not seem convincing.

But when we appeal again to that tradition which has come down from the apostles and is guarded by the successions of elders[5] in the churches, they oppose the tradition, saying that they are wiser not only than the elders, but even than the apostles, and have found the genuine truth. For the apostles [they say] mixed matters of the Law with the words of the Saviour, and not only the apostles, but even the Lord himself, spoke sometimes from the Demiurge, sometimes from the middle power, sometimes from the highest, while they know the hidden mystery without doubt or corruption, and in its purity. This is in nothing less than shameless blasphemy against their Maker. What it comes to is that they will not agree with either Scripture or tradition. It is such people, my dear friend, that we have to fight with, who like slippery snakes are always trying to escape us. Therefore we must resist them on all sides, hoping that by cutting off their escape we may be able to bring them to turn to the truth. For although it is not easy for a soul which has been seized by error to turn back, still it is not absolutely impossible to put error to flight by putting the truth beside it.[6]

The tradition of the apostles, made clear in all the world, can be clearly seen in every church by those who wish to behold the truth. We can enumerate those who were established by the apostles as bishops in the churches, and their successors down to our time, none of whom taught or thought of anything like their mad ideas. Even if the apostles had known of hidden mysteries, which they taught to the perfect secretly and apart from others, they would have handed them down especially to those to whom they were entrusting the church themselves. For they certainly wished those whom they were leaving as their successors, handing over to them their own teaching position, to be perfect and irreproachable, since their sound conduct would be a great benefit [to the Church], and failure on their part the greatest calamity. But since it would be very long in such a volume as this to enumerate the successions of all the churches, I can by pointing out the tradition which that very great, oldest, and well-known Church, founded and established at Rome by those two most glorious apostles Peter and Paul, received from the apostles, and its faith known among men, which comes down to us through the successions of bishops, put to shame all of those who in any way, either through wicked self-conceit, or through vainglory, or through blind and evil opinion,

---

5. *Presbuteroi* in Irenaeus are sometimes holders of an office in the Church, but often, as probably here, the grand old men who were links in the chain of tradition.

6. Apparently a citation of Justin, Apol. I, ch. 12, *fin*.

gather as they should not.[7] For every church must be in harmony with this Church because of its outstanding pre-eminence, that is, the faithful from everywhere, since the apostolic tradition is preserved in it by those from everywhere.[8]

When the blessed apostles had founded and built up the Church, they handed over the ministry of the episcopate to Linus. Paul mentions this Linus in his Epistles to Timothy. Anencletus succeeded him. After him Clement received the lot of the episcopate in the third place from the apostles. He had seen the apostles and associated with them, and still had their preaching sounding in his ears and their tradition before his eyes — and not he alone, for there were many still left in his time who had been taught by the apostles. In this Clement's time no small discord arose among the brethren in Corinth, and the Church in Rome sent a very powerful letter to the Corinthians, leading them to peace, renewing their faith, and declaring the tradition which they had recently received from the apostles, which declared one almighty God, maker of heaven and earth and fashioner of man, who brought about the Deluge, and called Abraham; who brought out the people from the land of Egypt; who spoke with Moses; who ordained the Law and sent the Prophets; and who has prepared fire for the devil and his angels. Those who care to can learn from this Writing that he was proclaimed by the churches as the Father to our Lord Jesus Christ, and so understand the apostolic tradition of the

---

7. I.e., assemble apart from the gatherings in communion with the Church (cf. Ignatius, Eph., ch. 5); or perhaps more generally, do not gather the harvest with the Lord, and so scatter (Luke 11:23; Matt. 12:30; cf. Lebreton, *The History of the Primitive Church,* p. 676).

8. *Ad hanc enim ecclesiam propter potentiorem principalitatem necesse est omnem convenire ecclesiam, hoc est, eos qui sunt undique fideles, in qua semper ab his qui sunt undique conservata est ea quae est ab apostolis traditio.* This sentence, preserved only in Latin, deserves to be quoted more because of the many discussions of it than for its own importance. Eusebius tantalizingly begins a quotation immediately afterward with what he considered of real interest in this passage. Irenaeus' solid reasons for selecting the Roman Church as his chief sample of the preservation of tradition in all churches have just been given; he seems here to mix them rather confusingly with the thought that as the city of Rome was a microcosm of the Empire, so was the Roman Church a microcosm of the Christian world, and the confluence of Christians there preserved the faith by representing all local traditions; *convenire* might mean simply "meet," but is probably best translated as above; for recent discussion see W. L. Knox, "Irenaeus *Adv. Haer.* III. 3:2." *Journal of Theological Studies,* Vol. 47, 1946, pp. 180–184, and P. Galtier, " '. . . *Ab his qui sunt undique . . .*' Irénée, *Adv. Haer.* III. 3:2," *Revue d'histoire ecclésiastique,* Vol. 44, 1949, pp. 411–428.

Church, since this Epistle is older than those present false teachers who make up lies about another God above the Demiurge and maker of all these things that are.[9] Evarestus succeeded to this Clement, and Alexander to Evarestus; then Xystus was installed as the sixth from the apostles, and after him Telesphorus, who met a glorious martyrdom;[10] then Hyginus, then Pius, and after him Anicetus. Soter followed Anicetus, and Eleutherus now in the twelfth place from the apostles holds the lot of the episcopate. In this very order and succession the apostolic tradition in the Church and the preaching of the truth has come down even to us. This is a full demonstration that it is one and the same life-giving faith which has been preserved in the Church from the apostles to the present, and is handed on in truth.

Similarly Polycarp, who not only was taught by apostles, and associated with many who had seen Christ, but was installed by apostles for Asia, as bishop in the church in Smyrna—I saw him myself in my early youth—survived for a long time, and departed this life in a ripe old age by a glorious and magnificent martyrdom. He always taught what he learned from the apostles, which the Church continues to hand on, and which are the only truths. The churches in Asia all bear witness to this, as do those who have succeeded Polycarp down to the present time; he is certainly a much more trustworthy and dependable witness than Valentinus and Marcion and the other false thinkers. When he visited Rome under Anicetus, he converted many of the above-mentioned heretics to the Church of God, proclaiming that he had received from the apostles the one and only truth, the same which is handed on by the Church. There are those who have heard him tell how when John the disciple of the Lord went to bathe at Ephesus, and saw Cerinthus inside, he rushed out of the bath without washing, but crying out, "Let us escape, lest the bath should fall while Cerinthus the enemy of the truth is in it." Polycarp himself, when Marcion once met him and said, "Do you know us?" answered, "I know you, the first-born of Satan." The apostles and their disciples took such great care not even to engage in conversations with the corrupters of the truth, as Paul also said, "A heretical man after a first and second warning avoid, knowing that such a man has fallen away and is a sinner, being self-

---

9. Irenaeus properly recognizes the Old Testament emphasis of 1 Clement; evidently, like we, he derived his knowledge about it entirely from the document itself, except for the tradition of some connection with Clement.

10. "Gloriously bore his witness"; the verb is doubtless used technically, as is the noun in the next section.

condemned."[11] There is also a very powerful letter of Polycarp addressed to the Philippians, from which those who care to, and are concerned for their own salvation, can learn the character of his faith and [his] preaching of the truth. The church in Ephesus also, which was founded by Paul, and where John survived until the time of Trajan, is a true witness of the tradition of the apostles.

Since there are so many clear testimonies, we should not seek from others for the truth which can easily be received from the Church. There the apostles, like a rich man making a deposit, fully bestowed upon her all that belongs to the truth, so that whoever wishes may receive from her the water of life. She is the entrance to life; all the others are thieves and robbers.[12] Therefore we ought to avoid them, but to love with the greatest zeal the things of the Church, and so to lay hold of the tradition of the truth. What if there should be a dispute about some matter of moderate importance? Should we not turn to the oldest churches, where the apostles themselves were known, and find out from them the clear and certain answer to the problem now being raised? Even if the apostles had not left their Writings to us, ought we not to follow the rule of the tradition which they handed down to those to whom they committed the churches? Many barbarian peoples who believe in Christ follow this rule, having [the message of their] salvation written in their hearts by the Spirit without paper and ink. Diligently following the old tradition, they believe in one God, maker of heaven and earth and of all that is in them, through Christ Jesus the Son of God, who on account of his abundant love for his creation submitted to be born of a virgin, himself by himself uniting man to God, and having suffered under Pontius Pilate, and risen, and having been received up into splendor, is to come in glory as the Saviour of those who are saved, and the judge of those who are judged, and will send into eternal fire those who alter the truth, and despise his Father and his coming. Those who believe in this faith without written documents are barbarians in our speech, but in their convictions, habits, and behavior they are, because of their faith, most wise, and are pleasing to God, living in all righteousness and purity and wisdom. If anyone should preach to them the inventions of the heretics, speaking in their own language, they would at once stop their ears and run far, far away, not enduring even to listen to such blasphemous speech. So by that old tradition of the apostles

---

11. Titus 3:10, 11.
12. Cf. Rev. 22:17; John 10:7, 8.

they do not even take into their minds whatever their impressive words may mean.

• • •

Refutation of Gnosticism

John, the disciple of the Lord, proclaimed the faith and wished by the proclamation of the gospel to destroy the error which had been planted among men by Cerinthus, and much earlier by those who are called Nicolaitans, who are an offshoot of the knowledge which is falsely so called, [writing] to confound them and show that there is one God who made all things by his Word. It is not true, as they say, that the Fashioner is one and the Father of the Lord another, and the Son of the Fashioner one being, the Christ from on high another, who remained free from suffering, descending on Jesus the Son of the Fashioner and returning again to his Pleroma; [they allege] that the Beginning was the Only-begotten, and Logos the true Son of the Only-begotten,[13] and that this world order in which we live was not made by the supreme God but by some power far inferior to him and cut off from contact with those things which are invisible and ineffable.

The disciple of the Lord wished to cut off all such ideas and to establish the rule of truth in the Church, that there is one God Almighty who made all things by his Word, both visible and invisible, and also to indicate that through the same Word through whom God made this world order he also bestowed salvation on the men who belong to this order. So he starts off with the teaching according to the Gospel, thus: "In the beginning was the Word and the Word was with God and the Word was God; this was in the beginning with God. All things were made through him, and without him nothing was made. What was made was life in him, and the life was the light of men, and the light shines in the darkness and the darkness has not seized hold of it."[14] All things, he says, were made through him; this word "all" therefore includes this world order of ours. It must not be conceded to them that "all" means what is within that Pleroma of theirs. For if this Pleroma of theirs contains everything, then this order is not outside it, as I

---

13. A Gnostic interpretation of the Prologue to the Fourth Gospel, which takes Beginning (Arche) and Only-begotten (Monogenes) as entities in a Gnostic system.
14. John 1:1–5.

have shown in the Book before this. But if these things are outside the Pleroma, which really does not seem possible, then this Pleroma of theirs does not comprise "all things," and so [in any case] this vast created order is not merely "outside." John himself indeed takes away all our disputes on this matter when he says: "He was in this world, and the world was made by him, and the world knew him not. He came to his own [things] and his own [people] did not receive him."[15] Now according to Marcion and those who are like him, neither was the world made by him, nor did he come to his own things, but rather to alien. According to some of the Gnostics, this world was made by angels and not through the Word of God. According to the followers of Valentinus again, it was not made through him, but through the Demiurge. For he, as they say, made certain images in imitation of the things above, but the Demiurge carried out the forming of the creation. For they say that the Lord and Demiurge of this created order of things, by whom they say this world was made, was sent forth by the Mother — when the Gospel clearly states that all things were made through the Word, who was in the beginning with God, which Word, he says, was made flesh and dwelt among us.

Now according to them neither was the Word made flesh, nor Christ, nor the Saviour who was made out of all [the Aeons]. For they allege that the Word and Christ never came into this world, and that the Saviour was neither incarnate nor suffered, but that he descended as a dove upon that Jesus who was made by [higher] dispensation, and when he had proclaimed the unknown Father, ascended again into the Pleroma. Some of them indeed say that this Jesus who was by dispensation was incarnate and suffered, and that he had passed through Mary like water through a tube; others say that it was the son of the Demiurge, on whom the Jesus who was by dispensation descended; others again say that Jesus indeed was born of Joseph and Mary, and that Christ who came from above descended on him, being without flesh and free from suffering. But according to none of the views of the heretics was the Word of God made flesh. If one should read over all their credal statements, he would find that they always bring in the Word of God and the Christ who is from above as without flesh and free from suffering. Some think that he was manifested as a transfigured man, but say that he was neither born nor incarnate. Others say that he did not even take the form of a man, but descended like a dove on that Jesus who was born of Mary. So the disciple of the Lord shows them all to be false witnesses when he says, "And the Word was made flesh, and dwelt among us."

---

15. John 1:11.

4. The Rule of Faith and the Uses of Scripture
From *Prescription Against Heretics*
(c. 189)

TERTULLIAN

In the second century, Christianity attracted a growing number of educated converts, who were given to theological reflection on their new faith. Among them was Tertullian (c. 160–c. 225), a native of Carthage, who became a Christian sometime before writing his Apology *in 197. It was the first of thirty-eight surviving theological treatises written by Tertullian. Known for his ascetic lifestyle, Tertullian became disillusioned over the lack of moral and spiritual rigor in the mainline church. Though many of Tertullian's writings defended the orthodox faith against Monarchian (the position of Praxeas that the Father/Christ became human in the Son) and Gnostic denials of Christ's true humanity, Tertullian found much to admire in the moral zeal and charismatic spirit of the Montanists — a schismatic sect, which he seems to have joined sometime after 207.*

Against the Gnostics and other eclectic groups, who allegorized biblical texts to support heretical views, Tertullian asserted that Christians alone have the right to use scriptures. Scripture belongs to the church, to

SOURCE: S. L. Greenslade, ed., *Early Latin Theology,* vol. 5 of *The Library of Christian Classics* (Philadelphia: Westminster Press, 1956). Used by permission of Westminster John Knox Press.

the spirit-guided, believing community. God judges, God does not complement the wisdom of the wise. "What has Athens to do with Jerusalem, the [Platonic] Academy with Christ?" With his mentor Irenaeus, Tertullian insists that the church must be guided by a literal (rather than allegorical) reading of the scriptures. He upholds the traditional "rule of faith" as the only source of sound Christian faith and practice.

Tertullian is the first major Christian writer who wrote in the Latin language. His writings became the source of much of the trinitarian vocabulary of Christianity. The first of the following selections from Prescription Against Heretics *(c. 189) contains his version of the "rule of faith," seemingly borrowed from Irenaeus. The second selection makes a case for a "literal" reading of scripture. For a sampling of his moral rigor, see vol. 1:268–73.*

My first principle is this. Christ laid down one definite system of truth[1] which the world must believe without qualification, and which we must seek precisely in order to believe it when we find it. Now you cannot search indefinitely for a single definite truth. You must seek until you find, and when you find, you must believe. Then you have simply to keep what you have come to believe, since you also believe that there is nothing else to believe, and therefore nothing else to seek, once you have found and believed what he taught who bids you seek nothing beyond what he taught. If you feel any doubt as to what this truth is, I undertake to establish that Christ's teaching is to be found with us. For the moment, my confidence in my proof allows me to anticipate it, and I warn certain people not to seek for anything beyond what they came to believe, for that was all they needed to seek for. They must not interpret, "Seek, and ye shall find," without regard to reasonable methods of exegesis.

10. The reasonable exegesis of this saying turns on three points: matter, time, and limitation. As to matter, you are to consider what is to be sought; as to time, when; and as to limitation, how far. What you must seek is what Christ taught, and precisely as long as you are not finding it, precisely until you do find it. And you did find it when you came to believe. You would not have believed if you had not found, just as you would not have sought except in order to find. Since finding was the object of your search and belief of your finding, your acceptance of the faith debars any prolongation of seeking and finding. The very success of

---

1. A great deal of Tertullian's argument depends on this.

your seeking has set up this limitation for you. Your boundary has been marked out by him who would not have you believe, and so would not have you seek, outside the limits of his teaching.

But if we are bound to go on seeking as long as there is any possibility of finding, simply because so much has been taught by others as well, we shall be always seeking and never believing. What end will there be to seeking? What point of rest for belief? Where the fruition of finding? With Marcion? But Valentinus also propounds: "Seek, and ye shall find." With Valentinus? But Apelles also will knock at my door with the same pronouncement, and Ebion and Simon[2] and the whole row of them can find no other way to ingratiate themselves with me and bring me over to their side. There will be no end, as long as I meet everywhere with, "Seek and ye shall find," and I shall wish I had never begun to seek, if I never grasp what Christ taught, what should be sought, what must be believed.

11. We may go astray without harm if we do not go wrong — though to go astray is to go wrong; we may wander without harm, I mean, if no desertion is intended. However, if I once believed what I ought to believe and now think I must seek something else afresh, presumably I am hoping that there is something else to be found. But I should never have hoped that, unless I had either never believed, though I seemed to, or else had stopped believing. So in deserting my faith I am shown up as an apostate. Let me say once for all, no one seeks unless there is something he did not possess or something he has lost. The old woman in the parable had lost one of her ten pieces of silver, and so she began to seek it. When she found it, she stopped seeking. The neighbour had no bread, so he began to knock. When the door was opened and he was given the bread, he stopped knocking. The widow kept asking to be heard by the judge because she was not being granted an audience. When she was heard, she insisted no longer.[3] So clear is it that there is an end to seeking and knocking and asking. For to him that asketh, it shall be given, it says, and to him that knocketh, it shall be opened, and by him that seeketh, it shall be found. I have no patience with the man who is always seeking, for he will never find. He is seeking where there will be no finding. I have no patience with the man who is always knocking, for the door will never be opened. He is knocking at an empty house. I have no patience with the man who is always asking, for he will never be heard. He is asking one who does not hear.

---

2. From the Ebionite sect ("the Poor") Tertullian wrongly supposes a personal founder called Ebion. Simon Magus (Acts 8) is the conventional "founder" of Gnosticism.

3. Luke 15:8; 11:5; 18:3.

12. Even if we ought to be seeking now and always, where should we seek? Among the heretics, where everything is strange and hostile to our truth, men we are forbidden to approach? What slave expects his food from a stranger, let alone his master's enemy? What soldier hopes to get bounty or pay from neutral, let alone hostile, kings? Unless of course he is a deserter or a runaway or a rebel! Even the old woman was seeking the piece of silver inside her own house. Even the man who was knocking hammered at his neighbour's door. Even the widow was appealing to a judge who, though hard, was not hostile. Instruction and destruction never reach us from the same quarter. Light and darkness never come from the same source. So let us seek in our own territory, from our own friends and on our own business, and let us seek only what can come into question without disloyalty to the Rule of Faith.

13. The Rule of Faith[4] — to state here and now what we maintain — is of course that by which we believe that there is but one God, who is none other than the Creator of the world, who produced everything from nothing through his Word, sent forth before all things; that this Word is called his Son, and in the Name of God was seen in divers ways by the patriarchs, was ever heard in the prophets and finally was brought down by the Spirit and Power of God the Father into the Virgin Mary, was made flesh in her womb, was born of her and lived as Jesus Christ; who thereafter proclaimed a new law and a new promise of the kingdom of heaven, worked miracles, was crucified, on the third day rose again, was caught up into heaven and sat down at the right hand of the Father; that he sent in his place the power of the Holy Spirit to guide believers; that he will come with glory to take the saints up into the fruition of the life eternal and the heavenly promises and to judge the wicked to everlasting fire, after the resurrection of both good and evil with the restoration of their flesh.

This Rule, taught (as will be proved) by Christ, allows of no questions among us, except those which heresies introduce and which make heretics.

14. Provided the essence of the Rule is not disturbed, you may seek and

---

4. *Regula Fidei,* a summary of the apostolic preaching, preserved — one might almost say, instinctively — in the tradition of the churches and used as a test of all teaching. It is similar to baptismal creeds, but not used liturgically nor fixed verbally. Irenaeus gives it in two forms, *Haer.,* I, ii and *Epideixis,* 6; Tertullian in three, here and in *Virg. Vel.,* 1 and *Prax.,* 2. For Tertullian's forms see E. Evans, *Tertullian's Treatise against Praxeas* (S.P.C.K., 1948), and for the subject in general, D. van den Eynde, *Les normes de l'enseignement chrétien* (Paris, 1933) and J. N. D. Kelly, *Early Christian Creeds* (Longmans, 1950).

discuss as much as you like. You may give full rein to your itching curiosity where any point seems unsettled and ambiguous or dark and obscure. There must surely be some brother endowed with the gift of knowledge who can teach you, someone who moves among the learned who will share your curiosity and your inquiry. In the last resort, however, it is better for you to remain ignorant, for fear that you come to know what you should not know.[5] For you do know what you should know. "Thy faith hath saved thee,"[6] it says; not thy biblical learning. Faith is established in the Rule. There it has its law, and it wins salvation by keeping the law. Learning derives from curiosity and wins glory only from its zealous pursuit of scholarship. Let curiosity give place to faith, and glory to salvation. Let them at least be no hindrance, or let them keep quiet. To know nothing against the Rule is to know everything.

• • •

36. Come now, if you are ready to exercise your curiosity better in the business of your own salvation, run through the apostolic churches, where the very thrones of the apostles preside to this day over their districts, where the authentic letters of the apostles are still recited, bringing the voice and face of each one of them to mind.[7] If Achaea is nearest to you, you have Corinth. If you are not far from Macedonia, you have Philippi and Thessalonica. If you can go to Asia, you have Ephesus. If you are close to Italy, you have Rome, the nearest authority for us also.[8] How fortunate is that church upon which the apostles poured their whole teaching together with their blood, where Peter suffered like his Lord, where Paul was crowned with John's death, where the apostle John, after

---

5. The text is corrupt here.

6. Luke 18:42.

7. Eusebius, *H.E.*, VII, 19, believed that the actual throne of James still existed at Jerusalem. Some think that Tertullian means by *cathedrae* here the physical objects. That is unnecessary, and on the whole unlikely, but not impossible. But "authentic" will scarcely mean autograph; he means unmutilated texts.

8. Cf. *Adv. Marc.*, IV, 5, a very similar passage. "Us" means Carthage and the Latin African church which, whether or not it was founded or received its ministry from Rome, certainly looked to that apostolic see for doctrinal authority. *Auctoritas* may have the double sense of origin and authority. It does not imply jurisdiction and sovereignty. I do not feel convinced that it should be taken here as a technical term of Roman law, meaning "title deed to possession," as by T. G. Jalland, *The Church and the Papacy* (1944), p. 147. It is uncertain whether "and Thessalonica" stood in the original text.

he had been immersed in boiling oil without harm, was banished to an island.[9]

Let us see what she learned, what she taught, what bond of friendship[10] she had with the churches of Africa. She knows one Lord God, Creator of the universe, and Christ Jesus, born of the Virgin Mary, Son of God the Creator, and the resurrection of the flesh; she unites the Law and the Prophets with the writings of the evangelists and the apostles; from that source she drinks[11] her faith, and that faith she seals with water, clothes with the Holy Spirit,[12] feeds with the eucharist, encourages to martyrdom; and against that teaching she receives no one. This is the teaching, I will not say now, which foretold heresies, but from which heresies have sprung. But they are not of it, ever since they came to be against it. Even from the kernel of the smooth, rich, and useful olive comes the rough wild olive. Even from the seed of the most pleasant and sweetest of figs springs the empty and useless wild fig. Just so have heresies come from our stock, but not of our kind; they spring from the seed of truth, but in their falsehood they are wild growths.

37. If therefore truth must be adjudged to us "as many as walk according to this rule"[13] which the Church has handed down from the apostles, the apostles from Christ, and Christ from God, the principle which we propounded is established, the principle which ruled that heretics are not to be allowed to enter an appeal to Scripture, since, without using Scripture, we prove that they have nothing to do with Scripture. If they are heretics, they cannot be Christians, since the names which they accept come not from Christ but from the heretics whom they follow of their

---

9. This is the first mention of Peter's crucifixion, but cf. John 21:18 and Tacitus, *Annals,* XV, 44, which speaks of the victims of Nero as *crucibus adfixi.* Origen adds head downwards (*ap.* Eus., *H.E.,* III, 1). Paul was decapitated, according to tradition, like John the Baptist; this would be his right as a Roman citizen. This is the first appearance of the story of John and the boiling oil.

10. Reading *contesserarit,* cf. *contesseratio hospitalitatis* in c. 20, *ad fin.* Breaking a *tessera* and taking a half each was a pledge of friendship. But in this context there is much to be said for the other reading *contestetur,* "what common witness to the faith is shared by Rome and Africa," as in the next sentence; and *contesserarit,* if correct, implies that the friendship is based on a common faith, with Rome as the giver. In the parallel passage, *Adv. Marc.,* IV, 5, *sonent* perhaps supports *contestetur.*

11. *Potat,* which could be transitive, "gives her children to drink."

12. *Aqua signat, sancto spiritu vestit.* On sealing, and the connection between the parts of baptism, see G. W. H. Lampe, *The Seal of the Spirit* (1951).

13. Gal. 6:16.

own choice. So, not being Christians, they acquire no right to Christian literature, and we have every right to say to them: "Who are you? When did you arrive, and where from? You are not my people; what are you doing on my land? By what right are you cutting down my timber, Marcion? By whose leave are you diverting my waters, Valentinus? By what authority are you moving my boundaries, Apelles?[14] This property belongs to me. And all the rest of you, why are you sowing and grazing here at your will? It is my property. I have been in possession for a long time, I came into possession before you appeared.[15] I have good title-deeds from the original owners of the estate. I am heir to the apostles. As they provided in their will, as they bequeathed it in trust and confirmed it under oath, so, on their terms, I hold it. You they permanently disinherited and disowned as strangers and enemies."

---

14. Marcion and Apelles removed awkward passages from the Bible, Valentinus perverted their interpretation.

15. Here is an allusion to the *praescriptio longae possessionis* or *longi temporis,* but surely as an addition to the main argument, though bound up with it.

5. On the Right Way of Reading the Scriptures
From *On First Principles IV*
(c. 230)

ORIGEN

Origen (c. 185–c. 254) was the foremost "Christian philosopher" of the ancient city of Alexandria, a leading theological center of the ancient church. He taught at the city's famous theological school until about 230, when a dispute with Bishop Demetrius forced him to leave. After more than twenty years of teaching and writing in Caesarea (Palestine), he was imprisoned and tortured during the persecution of Christians by Decius. He died soon after his release (c. 254).

Like his teacher Clement before him, Origen was an academic theologian who tried to demonstrate the "reasonableness of Christianity" by using the scholarly tools of his time. Origen's defense of the church's faith against the Gnostics (who wanted to deny the material world) drew heavily from Neoplatonism. Many of Origen's critics felt that he was casting out the devil with Beelzebub. Yet in the process, Origen's fertile mind produced the first systematic theology (On First Principles), *the first text-critical edition of the scriptures; a polyglot edition of the Old Testament (the* Hexapla); *and a method of interpreting scripture (ex-*

SOURCE: Maurice Wiles and Mark Santer, eds., *Documents in Early Christian Thought* (Cambridge: Cambridge University Press, 1979). © Cambridge University Press 1975. Used by permission of Cambridge University Press.

egesis). It has been said that Origen's most significant gift to the churches is the sola scriptura *principle, the idea that sound Christian teaching must be based "on scripture alone."*

Origen's allegorical method of interpreting scripture, however, bears little resemblance to the "simpler" approach of the sixteenth-century reformers. Origen states in On First Principles *that all scripture is edifying, but "simple people" understand only the "flesh of scripture" or its "obvious interpretation." Those who are "spiritually advanced" comprehend the "soul" of the word or its metaphorical sense, while "the perfect" discern its "spirit" or deepest allegorical meaning. For Origen, then, the ultimate key to the scriptures is not faith but a kind of Christian gnosis, a higher or "spiritual" level of understanding which, though consistent with the church's rule of faith, is accessible only to the diligent few.*

---

4. The right way to read the Scriptures and to grasp their meaning is, in our view, the following. It is drawn from the Bible itself. In Proverbs we find this sort of injunction given by Solomon concerning the divine teachings of Scripture: "You are to register them thrice in counsel and knowledge, that you may answer words of truth to those who attack you" [see Prov. 22:20–21 (LXX)]. Accordingly, one must register the thoughts of the holy Scriptures in one's soul in a triple manner. The simple man will be edified by what we may call the flesh of Scripture, by which we mean its obvious interpretation; he who has made some progress will be edified by its soul; whilst the perfect man who is like those of whom the apostle speaks — "We speak wisdom among the perfect, although it is not a wisdom of this age or of the rulers of this age, who are passing away; but we impart a secret and hidden wisdom of God, which God decreed before the ages for our glory" [1 Cor. 2:6–7] — such a man will be edified by "the spiritual law" [Rom. 7:14] which "contains a shadow of the good things to come" [Heb. 10:1]. For just as man consists of body, soul and spirit, so too does the Scripture which God has provided for the salvation of men.

It is for this reason that we interpret as follows the passage in the Shepherd (a book despised by some)[1] where Hermas is told to "write two

---

1. Origen regularly treats the *Shepherd of Hermas* as an inspired book, while acknowledging that it does not have universal acceptance in the Church. For an example of Origen's readiness to quote a work even further removed from general acceptance in the Church, see his use of the Gospel according to the Hebrews in his commentary on St. John, 2:12.

books" and then to "proclaim to the elders of the Church." The text is: "You shall write two books, and shall give one to Clement and one to Grapte. Grapte shall admonish the widows and orphans, Clement shall send to the cities outside, and you shall proclaim to the elders of the church."[2] Now Grapte, who "admonishes the widows and orphans," is the bare letter; it admonishes the infant souls that are not yet even able to claim God as their father and are therefore called "orphans." It also admonishes those who no longer associate with the unlawful bridegroom but are in widow-hood because they are not yet worthy of "*the* bridegroom." Clement has passed beyond the letter. He is said to send the sayings "to the cities outside," that is to say, to such souls as are outside all bodily and lower thoughts. Finally, there is the disciple of the Spirit himself; it is not through letters at all but in living words that he is instructed to "proclaim to the elders" of the whole Church of God, that is, to those who have grown grey in wisdom.

5. However, there are some passages of Scripture which, as we shall show, have no bodily sense at all. There are therefore places where one need look only for the "soul" and the "spirit" of the passage. This is perhaps the reason why the waterpots which are described, as we read in the gospel according to John, as "standing there for the purification of the Jews," "contains two or three measures each" [John 2:6]. The passage alludes to those the apostle calls "Jews in secret" [Rom. 2:29], that is people who are purified by the words of the Scriptures, and suggests that in some places those Scriptures contain "two measures," that is, what I may call the "soul meaning" and the "spiritual meaning," and in other places "three," since some passages also contain a bodily sense capable of edifying its reader. "Six waterpots" is appropriate to those who are being purified in the world, since the world was made in six days — a perfect number.[3]

6. That profit can be had from the first meaning, which is helpful at its own level, is evident from the multitudes of sincere and simple believers. The kind of interpretation which rises to the level of "soul" is exemplified by a passage from Paul's first letter to the Corinthians. "It is written," he says, "'You shall not muzzle a threshing ox.'" He then explains this precept by continuing, "Is it for oxen that God is concerned? Does he not

---

2. A free citation of *Hermas* 8, 3 (= *Vis.* II. 4.3). Origen plays on the fact that the name Grapte means "written."

3. See Philo, *De Opificio Mundi* 3, where it is explained that six is a perfect number because it is both the product and the sum of its factors (i.e., $6 = 1 \times 2 \times 3$ and $1 + 2 + 3$). It is also the product of the first male number, 3, and the first female number, 2.

speak entirely for our sake? It was written for our sake, because the ploughman should plough in hope and the thresher should thresh in hope of a share in the crop" [1 Cor. 9:9–10]. Most of the interpretations current which are suitable for the multitude and edify those incapable of higher truths are of this character.

Interpretation is spiritual when one is able to show of what heavenly things the Jews after the flesh were serving a copy and shadow [see Heb. 8:5], and of what good things to come the law has a shadow [see Heb. 10:1]. In general, one should always follow the apostolic injunction by looking for the "secret and hidden wisdom which God decreed before the ages for the glory" of the righteous, "which none of the rulers of this age understood" [1 Cor. 2:7–8]. Elsewhere the same apostle, after citing various incidents recounted in Exodus and Numbers, says, "These things happened to them as types, but they were written down on our account, upon whom the end of the ages has come" [1 Cor. 10:11]. He gives us hints about what these events were types of, when he says, "For they drank from the spiritual rock which followed them, and the rock was Christ" [1 Cor. 10:4].

In another epistle, while giving a brief account of the tabernacle, he quotes the words, "Make everything in accordance with the type that was shown you on the mountain" [Heb. 8:5]. Again, in the letter to the Galatians, he reproaches those who suppose that they are reading the law while in fact not understanding it; he condemns them for not understanding it inasmuch as they suppose that the Scriptures contain no allegories. "Tell me," he says, "you who desire to be under law, do you not hear the law? For it is written that Abraham had two sons, one by the slave and the other by the free woman. But the son of the slave was born according to the flesh, the son of the free woman through promise. Now these things are an allegory; for these two women are two covenants . . ." [Gal. 4:21–24]. We must be careful to notice exactly what he says. He says, "You who desire to be under the law" (not "You who *are* under the law"), "do you not hear the law?" "Hearing" he judges to consist in knowing and understanding.

In the letter to the Colossians he briefly sums up the purpose of the whole code of law: "Therefore let no one pass judgement on you in questions of food and drink or with regard to a festival or a new moon or a sabbath. These things are a shadow of the things to come" [Col. 2:16–17]. Again, in Hebrews, when discussing those who belong to the circumcision, he writes that "they serve a copy and shadow of the heavenly things" [Heb. 8:5].

Now those who admit the inspiration of the apostle will probably, after this evidence, have no doubts about the five books ascribed to Moses. They will want to know whether the other narratives also "happened as types" [see 1 Cor. 10:11]. But notice the quotation from the third book of Kings in the letter to the Romans: "I have kept for myself seven thousand men who have not bowed the knee to Baal." Paul takes these to stand for the Israelites "according to election" [Rom. 11:4–5]; for it is not only the Gentiles who have profited from the coming of Christ, but also some members of the holy nation.

7. In view of all this we must give a sketch of what, in our view, are the characteristics of a right understanding of the Scriptures. The first thing to indicate is their aim. The principal aim with which the Spirit, by the providence of God through the Word who was "in the beginning with God" [John 1:2], enlightened the servants of the truth, that is, the prophets and apostles, concerns those ineffable mysteries that have to do with the affairs of men (by "men" I refer to souls employing bodies); it is that anyone capable of learning should, by "searching out" and devoting himself to "the depths" [see 1 Cor. 2:10] of the meaning of the words of Scripture, become a partaker of the complete teachings of the divine counsel.

Souls can only reach perfection through the rich and wise truth about God. The most important part of this is of course teachings about God and his only-begotten Son; about the nature of the latter and the mode in which he is God's Son; about the causes of his descent to human flesh and complete assumption of humanity; about the nature of his activity, towards whom it is directed and in what circumstances it is exercised.

Other topics necessarily included in the scriptural records of divine teaching relate to rational beings, to those akin to the Word as well as to others, that is, to the more divine as well as to those that have fallen from blessedness; and to the reasons for the fall of the latter. Other questions are the differences between souls and the origin of these differences; the nature of the world and the reason for its existence; why there is such great and widespread evil on earth, and whether it is to be found not only on earth but elsewhere too. All these are questions about which we need to be taught.

8. It was with these and similar ends in view that the Spirit enlightened the souls of the holy servants of the truth. But Scripture also has a second aim, related to those unable to endure the toil of searching out such great matters. This is to conceal the teaching on the themes I have just mentioned in words that present a narrative account of the visible creation, the formation of men, and the successive descendants from those first hu-

mans to the point when mankind had multiplied; and in other stories it recounts the deeds of the just and the sins that those same men, in that they were human, sometimes committed, as well as the acts of wickedness, licence and greed performed by the lawless and the impious.

But the most remarkable thing is the way in which narratives about wars and about who conquered whom are used to reveal some of these ineffable mysteries to those capable of examining these stories. Even more wonderful is the way in which a written code of law prophetically discloses the laws of truth. All these things are recorded in orderly series, with a skill that truly befits the wisdom of God. The intention was that even the covering of the spiritual truths, that is, the bodily sense of the Scriptures, should be made quite useful and capable in all sorts of ways of improving the multitude in accordance with their capacities.

9. Now if the written law were in its entirety immediately and clearly useful, or if the narratives were similarly smooth and elegant throughout, we should not have come to believe that there was anything to be understood in the Scriptures beyond their obvious meaning. Consequently the Word of God has arranged the insertion of a number of stumbling-blocks, obstacles and impossibilities in the middle of the law and the narrative. For the sheer attractiveness of the language might otherwise have led us either to abandon their teachings entirely, through supposing that there was nothing worthy of God to be learned from the Scriptures, or else, through not moving beyond the letter, never to discover anything of a more divine character.

There is something else that we must realize. The main aim of Scripture is to reveal the coherent structure that exists at the spiritual level in terms both of events and injunctions. Wherever the Word found that events on the historical plane corresponded with these mystical truths, he used them, concealing the deeper meaning from the multitude. But at those places in the account where the performance of particular actions as already recorded did not correspond with the pattern of things at the intellectual level Scripture wove into the narrative, for the sake of the more mystical truths, things that never occurred — sometimes things that could never have occurred, sometimes things that could have but did not. In some cases it is a matter of only a few words being inserted which in the literal sense are not true, in others more.

A similar method can also be found in the law. There one can often find matter which is useful in itself, being relevant to the period when the law was given. Other sayings appear to have no use. And in some places there are utterly impossible injunctions, inserted in order to get the more skilful and inquiring readers to apply themselves to the work of examining what is written and so become thoroughly assured of the necessity of searching for a meaning worthy of God in such instances.

It was not only in relation to the events before the coming of Christ that the Spirit arranged things in this way. Because he is the same Spirit and comes from the one God, he has acted in the same way with the gospels and the writings of the apostles. Even they contain a narrative that is not at all points straightforward; for woven into it are events which in the literal sense did not occur. Nor is the content of the law and commandments to be found in them entirely reasonable.

6. New Testament Canon

From *39th Easter Letter*
(367)

ATHANASIUS

The first Christian Bible was the Greek Septuagint version of the Old Testament. By the second century, Christian writers began quoting certain gospels and epistles as "sacred scripture," and Irenaeus called these writings the "New" Testament. The honor of preserving the first "official" list of Christian writings belongs to Marcion, a heretical Christian who rejected the Old Testament as the record of a lesser God, the Demiurge. His judgment, which some people considered heretical, prodded the church into action. It became important to decide on an "official" list of books that met the "canon" (standard) of the church's "rule of faith" and truly expressed the tradition of the apostles.

Groups and individuals proposed various formal and informal lists. Although the formation of the New Testament canon was generally complete by the end of the second century, the list remained open until well into the fifth century. In 367, Athanasius, bishop of Alexandria, wrote an Easter Letter to his churches. His letter contained the first complete list of the twenty-seven books of the New Testament. Athanasius was also the

---

SOURCE: Lee Martin McDonald, *The Formation of the Christian Biblical Canon* (Nashville: Abingdon Press, 1988). Used by permission of the author.

first Christian writer to use the term canon *to designate this list of sacred books.*

(1.) Since, however, I have spoken of the heretics as dead but of ourselves as possessors of the divine writings unto salvation, I am actually afraid lest in any way, as Paul said in writing to the Corinthians, a few of the undefiled may be led astray from their simplicity and purity by the craftiness of certain men and thereafter begin to pay attention to other books, the so-called sacred books. Therefore, because of this fear of your being deceived by these books possessing the same names as the genuine books and because of the present stress of the Church, I exhort you to bear with me for your own benefit as I actually make mention of these heretical writings, which you already know about.

(2.) As I am about to mention such matters, I will back up my venturesomeness by following the example of the evangelist Luke. And I will also say that since certain men have attempted to arrange for themselves the so-called secret writings and mingle them with the God-inspired Scripture, concerning which we have been fully informed even as they were handed down to our fathers by those who were eye-witnesses and servants of the word from the beginning, having been encouraged by true brethren and learning all from the beginning, I also resolved to set forth in order the writings that are in the list and handed down and believed to be divine. I have done this so that each person, if he has been deceived, may condemn those who led him astray, and that he who has remained stainless may rejoice, being again reminded of the truth.

(3.) There are then of the Old Testament books . . . [omitted here].

(7.) Those of the New Testament I must not shrink from mentioning in their turn. They are these: four Gospels, according to Matthew, according to Mark, according to Luke, and according to John.

(8.) Then after these are the Acts of the Apostles and the seven letters of the apostles, called the "Catholic" letters, which are as follows: one from James, two from Peter, three from John, and after these one from Jude.

(9.) In addition, there are fourteen letters of Paul the apostle, written in the following order: the first to the Romans, then two to the Corinthians, and thereafter one to the Galatians, one to the Ephesians, one to the Philippians, one to the Colossians, two to the Thessalonians, one to the Hebrews, and, without a break, two letters to Timothy, one to Titus, and one written to Philemon. Last, from John again comes the Revelation.

(10.) These are springs of salvation, so that he who is thirsty may be filled with the divine responses in them; in these alone is the good news of the teaching of true religion proclaimed; *let no one add to them or take anything away from them.* It was in regard to these that the Lord was ashamed of the Sadducees, saying: "You are being led astray, since you do know not the scripture," and he exhorted the Jews, saying, "Search the scriptures, for they are the very writings that witness concerning me."

(11.) But for the sake of being more exact in detail, I also add this admonition, writing out of necessity, that there are also other books apart from these that are not indeed in the above list, but were produced by our ancestors to be read by those who are just coming forward to receive oral instruction in the word of true religion. These include: the Wisdom of Solomon, the Wisdom of Sirach, Esther, Judith, Tobias, the so-called Teaching of the Apostles, and the Shepherd.

(12.) And nevertheless, beloved, though the former writings *be in the list* [or "are listed," χανονιζομένov] and the latter are read, nowhere is there any mention of the secret writings (the apocrypha). They are, rather, a device of heretics, who write them when they will furnishing them with dates and adding them, in order that by bringing them forth as ancient books they may thus have an excuse for deceiving the undefiled.

Persecution

7. *Letter from the Churches of Lyon and Vienne*
From *The History of the Church from Christ to Constantine*
(177)

EUSEBIUS

The fourth-century historian of the ancient church, Eusebius, lived and wrote during the "enlightened" rule of Marcus Aurelius, Stoic philosopher and emperor of Rome. Eusebius introduces his account of the severe persecutions in Gaul during the second century by saying that he is not going to talk about the kinds of wars where victorious military leaders slaughter thousands "for the sake of children, country, and possessions." It is the "peaceful wars," he says, "fought for the very peace of the soul, and the people who in such wars have fought for truth rather than country, for true religion rather than their dear ones, that my account of God's commonwealth will inscribe on imperishable monuments."

Eusebius tells of a battle in such a "peaceful war," which was fought

---

SOURCE: Eusebius, *The History of the Church from Christ to Constantine*, trans. and with an introduction by G. A. Williamson (New York: Penguin Classics, 1984). © 1965 G. A. Williamson. Reproduced by permission of Penguin Books Ltd.

at Lyon, a trading center on the Rhone River in what is now southern France. There, about forty-eight Christians refused to renounce their faith. They died in prison or perished in the local arena on August 1, 177. Eusebius preserves a letter that the survivors of Lyon (also known as Lyons) and neighboring Vienne wrote to the churches in Phrygia and Asia Minor, the original home of many of the Christians in Gaul. According to the letter, the most courageous among the confessors and one of the last to die was Blandina, a slave girl whose mistress was also part of the group. The writers extol the fact that Blandina, a young woman and a slave, was the undisputed leader and inspiration of the martyrs. As Frend states in The Rise of Christianity, *this letter shows the "prevalent equality within the second-century church between the genders and social classes."*

The severity of our trials here, the unbridled fury of the heathen against God's people, the untold sufferings of the blessed martyrs, we are incapable of describing in detail: indeed no pen could do them justice. The adversary swooped on us with all his might, giving us now a foretaste of his advent, which undoubtedly is imminent.[1] He left no stone unturned in his efforts to train his adherents and equip them to attack the servants of God, so that not only were we debarred from houses, baths, and the forum: they actually forbade any of us to be seen in any place whatever. But against them the grace of God put itself at our head, rescuing the weak and deploying against our enemies unshakable pillars,[2] able by their endurance to draw upon themselves the whole onslaught of the evil one. These charged into the fight, standing up to every kind of abuse and punishment, and made light of their heavy load as they hastened to Christ, proving beyond a doubt that the sufferings of the present time are not to be compared with the glory that is in store for us.[3]

To begin with, they heroically endured whatever the surging crowd heaped on them, noisy abuse, blows, dragging along the ground, plundering, stoning, imprisonment, and everything that an infuriated mob normally does to hated enemies. Then they were marched into the forum and interrogated by the tribune and the city authorities before the whole population. When they confessed Christ, they were locked up in gaol to await

---

1. 2 Thess. 2:7–9.
2. Gal. 2:9 and 1 Tim. 3:15.
3. Rom. 8:18.

the governor's arrival. Later, when they were taken before him and he treated them with all the cruelty he reserves for Christians, Vettius Epagathus, one of our number, full of love towards God and towards his neighbour, came forward. His life conformed so closely to the Christian ideal that, young as he was, the same tribute might be paid to him as to old Zacharias: he had scrupulously observed all the commandments and ordinances of the Lord,[4] and was untiring in service to his neighbour, utterly devoted to God,[5] and fervent in spirit.[6] As such he found the judgement so unreasonably given against us more than he could bear: boiling with indignation, he applied for permission to speak in defence of the Christians, and to prove that there was nothing godless or irreligious in our society. The crowd round the tribunal howled him down, as he was a man of influence, and the governor dismissed his perfectly reasonable application with the curt question: "Are *you* a Christian?" In the clearest possible tones Vettius replied: "I am." And he, too, was admitted to the ranks of the martyrs. He was called the Christians' advocate, but he had in himself the Advocate,[7] the Spirit that filled Zacharias,[8] as he showed by the fullness of his love when he gladly laid down his own life in defence of his brother Christians.[9] For he was and is a true disciple of Christ, following the Lamb wherever He goes.[10]

Then the rest fell into two groups. It was clear that some were ready to be the first Gallic martyrs: they made a full confession of their testimony with the greatest eagerness. It was equally clear that others were not ready, that they had not trained and were still flabby, in no fit condition to face the strain of a struggle to the death. Of these some ten proved stillborn,[11] causing us great distress and inexpressible grief, and damping the enthusiasm of those not yet arrested. However, in spite of the agonies they were suffering, these people stayed with the martyrs and did not desert them. But at the time we were all tormented by doubts about their confessing Christ: we were not afraid of the punishments inflicted, but looking to the outcome and dreading lest anyone might fall away. But the arrests went on, and day after day those who were worthy filled up the

---

4. Luke 1:6.
5. Rom. 10:2.
6. Rom. 7:11 and Acts 18:25.
7. Paraclete: John 14:16.
8. Luke 1:67.
9. 1 Thess. 2:8; 1 John 3:16.
10. Rev. 14:4.
11. A reference to the "stillborn children" of faith.

number of the martyrs, so that from the two dioceses were collected all the active members who had done most to build up our church life. Among those arrested were some of our heathen domestics, as the governor had publicly announced that we were all to be hunted out. These were ensnared by Satan, so that fearing the tortures which they saw inflicted on God's people, at the soldiers' instigation they falsely accused us of Thyestean banquets and Oedipean incest,[12] and things we ought never to speak or think about, or even believe that such things ever happened among human beings. When these rumours spread, people all raged like wild beasts against us, so that even those who because of blood-relationship had previously exercised restraint now turned on us, grinding their teeth with fury. So was proved true the saying of our Lord: "The time will come when whoever kills you will think he is doing a service to God."[13] From then on the holy martyrs endured punishments beyond all description, while Satan strove to wring even from them some of the slanders.

The whole fury of crowd, governor, and soldiers fell with crushing force on Sanctus, the deacon from Vienne; on Maturus, very recently baptized but heroic in facing his ordeal; on Attalus, who had always been a pillar and support[14] of the church in his native Pergamum; and on Blandina, through whom Christ proved that things which men regard as mean, unlovely, and contemptible are by God deemed worthy of great glory,[15] because of her love for Him shown in power and not vaunted in appearance. When we were all afraid, and her earthly mistress (who was herself facing the ordeal of martyrdom) was in agony lest she should be unable even to make a bold confession of Christ because of bodily weakness, Blandina was filled with such power that those who took it in turns to subject her to every kind of torture from morning to night were exhausted by their efforts and confessed themselves beaten—they could think of nothing else to do to her. They were amazed that she was still breathing, for her whole body was mangled and her wounds gaped; they declared that torment of any one kind was enough to part soul and body, let alone a succession of torments of such extreme severity. But the blessed woman, wrestling magnificently, grew in strength as she proclaimed her faith, and found refreshment, rest, and insensibility to her

---

12. Thyestes ate his sons; Oedipus had children by his mother.
13. John 16:2.
14. 1 Tim. 3:15.
15. A reminiscence of 1 Cor. 1:28.

sufferings in uttering the words: "I am a Christian: we do nothing to be ashamed of."

Sanctus was another who with magnificent, superhuman courage nobly withstood the entire range of human cruelty. Wicked people hoped that the persistence and severity of his tortures would force him to utter something improper, but with such determination did he stand up to their onslaughts that he would not tell them his own name, race, and birthplace, or whether he was slave or free; to every question he replied in Latin: "I am a Christian." This he proclaimed over and over again, instead of name, birthplace, nationality, and everything else, and not another word did the heathen hear from him. Consequently, the governor and his torturers strained every nerve against him, so that when they could think of nothing else to do to him they ended by pressing red-hot copper plates against the most sensitive parts of his body. These were burning, but Sanctus remained unbending and unyielding, firm in his confession of faith, bedewed and fortified by the heavenly fountain of the water of life that flows from the depths of Christ's being.[16] But his poor body was a witness to what he had suffered — it was all one wound and bruise, bent up and robbed of outward human shape, but, suffering in that body, Christ accomplished most glorious things, utterly defeating the adversary and proving as an example to the rest that where the Father's love is[17] nothing can frighten us, where Christ's glory is[18] nothing can hurt us. A few days later wicked people again put the martyr on the rack, thinking that now that his whole body was swollen and inflamed a further application of the same instruments would defeat him, unable as he was to bear even the touch of a hand; or that by dying under torture he would put fear into the rest. However, nothing of the sort happened: to their amazement his body became erect and straight as a result of these new torments, and recovered its former appearance and the use of the limbs; thus through the grace of Christ his second spell on the rack proved to be not punishment but cure.

Biblis again, one of those who had denied Christ, was handed over to punishment by the devil, who imagined that he had already devoured her[19] and hoped to damn her as a slanderer by forcing her to say wicked things about us, being — so he thought — a feeble creature, easily broken. But on the rack she came to her senses,[20] and, so to speak, awoke out of

---

16. A reminiscence of John 7:38 and 19:34.
17. A reminiscence of 1 John 4:18.
18. 2 Cor. 8:23.
19. 1 Peter 5:8.
20. 2 Tim. 2:26.

deep sleep, reminded by the brief chastisement of the eternal punishment in hell.[21] She flatly contradicted the slanderers: "How could children be eaten by people who are not even allowed to eat the blood of brute beasts?"[22] From then on she insisted that she was a Christian, and so she joined the ranks of the martyrs.

When the tyrant's instruments of torture had been utterly defeated by Christ through the endurance of the blessed saints, the devil resorted to other devices — confinement in the darkness of a filthy prison; clamping the feet in the stocks, stretched apart to the fifth hole; and the other agonies which warders when angry and full of the devil are apt to inflict on helpless prisoners. Thus the majority were suffocated in prison — those whom the Lord wished to depart in this way, so revealing His glory.[23] Some, though tortured so cruelly that even if they received every care it seemed impossible for them to survive, lived on in the prison, deprived of all human attention but strengthened by the Lord and fortified in body and soul, stimulating and encouraging the rest. But the young ones who had been recently arrested and had not previously undergone physical torture could not bear the burden of confinement, and died in prison.

Blessed Pothinus, who had been entrusted with the care of the Lyons diocese, was over ninety years of age and physically very weak. He could scarcely breathe because of his chronic physical weakness, but was strengthened by spiritual enthusiasm because of his pressing desire for martyrdom. Even he was dragged before the tribunal, and though his body was feeble from age and disease, his life was preserved in him, that thereby Christ might triumph. He was conveyed to the tribunal by the soldiers, accompanied by the civil authorities and the whole populace, who shouted and jeered at him as though he were Christ Himself. But he bore the noble witness.[24] When the governor asked him "Who is the Christians' god?," he replied: "If you are a fit person, you shall know." Thereupon he was mercilessly dragged along beneath a rain of blows, those close by assailing him viciously with hands and feet and showing no respect for his age, and those at a distance hurling at him whatever came to hand, and all thinking it a shocking neglect of their duty to be behind-hand in savagery towards him, for they imagined that in this way they would avenge their gods. Scarcely breathing, he was flung into prison, and two days later he passed away.

---

21. Matt. 25:46.
22. Acts 15:29.
23. A reminiscence of John 2:11.
24. An allusion to 1 Tim. 6:13.

Then occurred a great dispensation of God, and the infinite mercy of Jesus was revealed to a degree rarely known in the brotherhood of Christians, but not beyond the skill of Christ. Those who when the first arrests took place had denied Him were gaoled with the others and shared their sufferings: on this occasion they gained nothing by their denial, for whereas those who declared what they were were gaoled as Christians, no other charge being brought against them, the others were further detained as foul murderers and punished twice as much as the rest. For the faithful were relieved of half their burden by the joy of martyrdom and hope of the promises, and by love towards Christ and the Spirit of the Father, but the unfaithful were tormented by their conscience, so that as they passed they could easily be picked out from the rest by the look on their faces. The faithful stepped out with a happy smile, wondrous glory and grace blended on their faces, so that even their fetters hung like beautiful ornaments around them and they resembled a bride adorned with golden lace elaborately wrought;[25] they were perfumed also with the sweet savour of Christ,[26] so that some people thought they had smeared themselves with worldly cosmetics. The unfaithful were dejected, downcast, ill-favoured, and devoid of charm; in addition they were jibed at by the heathen as contemptible cowards; they were accused of homicide, and had lost the honourable, glorious, life-giving name. The sight of this stiffened the resistance of the rest: those who were arrested unhesitatingly declared their faith without one thought for the devil's promptings. . . .

From that time on, their martyrdoms embraced death in all its forms. From flowers of every shape and colour they wove a crown to offer to the Father; and so it was fitting that the valiant champions should endure an everchanging conflict, and having triumphed gloriously should win the mighty crown of immortality. Maturus, Sanctus, Blandina, and Attalus were taken into the amphitheatre to face the wild beasts, and to furnish open proof of the inhumanity of the heathen, the day of fighting wild beasts being purposely arranged for our people. There, before the eyes of all, Maturus and Sanctus were again taken through the whole series of punishments, as if they had suffered nothing at all before, or rather as if they had already defeated their opponent in bout after bout and were now battling for the victor's crown. Again they ran the gauntlet of whips, in accordance with local custom; they were mauled by the beasts, and endured every torment that the frenzied mob on one side or the other de-

---

25. Ps. 45:13.
26. 2 Cor. 2:15.

manded and howled for, culminating in the iron chair which roasted their flesh and suffocated them with the reek. Not even then were their tormentors satisfied: they grew more and more frenzied in their desire to overwhelm the resistance of the martyrs, but do what they might they heard nothing from Sanctus beyond the words he had repeated from the beginning — the declaration of his faith.

In these two, despite their prolonged and terrible ordeal, life still lingered; but in the end they were sacrificed, after being made all day long a spectacle to the world[27] in place of the gladiatorial contest in its many forms. But Blandina was hung on a post and exposed as food for the wild beasts let loose in the arena. She looked as if she was hanging in the form of a cross, and through her ardent prayers she stimulated great enthusiasm in those undergoing their ordeal, who in their agony saw with their outward eyes in the person of their sister the One who was crucified for them, that He might convince those who believe in Him that any man who has suffered for the glory of Christ has fellowship for ever with the living God. As none of the beasts had yet touched her she was taken down from the post and returned to the gaol, to be kept for a second ordeal, that by victory in further contests she might make irrevocable the sentence passed on the crooked serpent,[28] and spur on her brother Christians — a small, weak, despised woman who had put on Christ,[29] the great invincible champion, and in bout after bout had defeated her adversary and through conflict had won the crown of immortality.

Attalus too was loudly demanded by the mob, as he was a man of note. He strode in, ready for the fray, in the strength of a clear conscience, for he had trained hard in the school of Christ and had been one of our constant witnesses to the truth. He was led round the amphitheatre preceded by a placard on which was written in Latin "This is Attalus the Christian," while the people were bursting with fury against him. But when the governor was informed that he was a Roman, he ordered him to be put back in gaol with the others, about whom he had written to Caesar and was awaiting instructions.

Their time of respite was not idle or unfruitful:[30] through their endurance the infinite mercy of Christ was revealed; for through the living the dead were being brought back to life, and martyrs were bestowing

---

27. 1 Cor. 4:9.
28. Is. 27:1.
29. Gal. 3:27.
30. 2 Peter 1:8.

grace on those who had failed to be martyrs, and there was great joy in the heart of the Virgin Mother,[31] who was receiving her stillborn children back alive; for by their means most of those who had denied their Master travelled once more the same road, conceived and quickened a second time, and learnt to confess Christ. Alive now and braced up, their ordeal sweetened by God, who does not desire the death of the sinner but is gracious towards repentance,[32] they advanced to the tribunal to be again interrogated by the governor. For Caesar had issued a command that they should be tortured to death, but any who still denied Christ should be released; so at the inauguration of the local festival, at which all the heathen congregate in vast numbers, the governor summoned them to his tribunal, making a theatrical show of the blessed ones and displaying them to the crowds. After re-examination, all who seemed to possess Roman citizenship were beheaded and the rest sent to the beasts. Christ was greatly glorified in those who had previously denied Him but now confounded heathen expectation by confessing Him. These were individually examined with the intention that they should be released, but they confessed Him and so joined the ranks of the martyrs. Left outside were those who had never had any vestige of faith or notion of the wedding-garment[33] or thought of the fear of God, but by their very conduct brought the Way into disrepute[34] — truly the sons of perdition.[35] But the rest were all added to the Church.[36]

During their examination, Alexander, a Phrygian by birth and a doctor by profession, who had lived for many years in Gaul and was known to nearly everyone for his love of God and his boldness of speech[37] — he had a large measure of the apostolic gift — stood by the tribunal and gestured to them to confess Christ. To those surrounding the tribunal it was plain that he was suffering birth-pangs. But the crowds, furious that those who had hitherto denied Christ were now confessing Him, shouted against Alexander as the person responsible. The governor made him come forward and demanded to know who he was; when he replied "A Christian," he lost his temper and condemned him to the beasts. The next day he entered the arena with Attalus, whom the governor, to gratify the mob,

---

31. The Church.
32. A synthesis of Ez. 38 and 2 Peter 3:9.
33. Matt. 22:11.
34. Acts 19:9 and 2 Peter 2:2.
35. John 17:12.
36. Acts 2:47 and 5:14.
37. Acts 4:29.

was again giving to the beasts. The two men were subjected to all the instruments of torture assembled in the amphitheatre, and underwent a supreme ordeal. In the end they were sacrificed. Alexander uttered no cry, not so much as a groan, but communed with God in his heart, while Attalus, when he was put in the iron chair and was being burnt and the reek was rising from his body, called out to the spectators in Latin: "Look! eating men is what *you* are doing: *we* neither eat men nor indulge in any malpractices." When asked what name God had he answered: "God hasn't a name like a man."

To crown all this, on the last day of the sports Blandina was again brought in, and with her Ponticus, a lad of about fifteen. Day after day they had been taken in to watch the rest being punished, and attempts were made to make them swear by the heathen idols. When they stood firm and treated these efforts with contempt, the mob was infuriated with them, so that the boy's tender age called forth no pity and the woman no respect. They subjected them to every horror and inflicted every punishment in turn, attempting again and again to make them swear, but to no purpose. Ponticus was encouraged by his sister in Christ, so that the heathen saw that she was urging him on and stiffening his resistance, and he bravely endured every punishment till he gave back his spirit to God. Last of all, like a noble mother who had encouraged her children and sent them before her in triumph to the King,[38] blessed Blandina herself passed through all the ordeals of her children and hastened to rejoin them, rejoicing and exulting at her departure as if invited to a wedding supper,[39] not thrown to the beasts. After the whips, after the beasts, after the griddle, she was finally dropped into a basket and thrown to a bull. Time after time the animal tossed her, but she was indifferent now to all that happened to her, because of her hope and sure hold on all that her faith meant, and of her communing with Christ. Then she, too, was sacrificed, while the heathen themselves admitted that never yet had they known a woman suffer so much or so long.

Not even this was enough to satisfy their insane cruelty to God's people. Goaded by a wild beast,[40] wild and barbarous tribes were incapable of stopping, and the dead bodies became the next object of their vindictiveness. Their defeat did not humble them, because they were without human understanding; rather it inflamed their bestial fury, and

---

38. 2 Macc. 7:21–41.
39. Rev. 19:9.
40. The devil.

governor and people vented on us the same inexcusable hatred, so fulfilling the scripture: "Let the wicked man be wicked still, the righteous man righteous still."[41] Those who had been suffocated in gaol they threw to the dogs, watching carefully night and day to see that no one received the last offices at our hands. Then they threw out the remains left by the beasts and the fire, some torn to ribbons, some burnt to cinders, and set a military guard to watch for days on end the trunks and severed heads of the rest, denying burial to them also. Some raged and ground their teeth at them, longing to take some further revenge on them; others laughed and jeered, magnifying their idols and giving them credit for the punishment of their enemies; while those who were more reasonable, and seemed to have a little human feeling, exclaimed with the utmost scorn: "Where is their god?[42] and what did they get for their religion, which they preferred to their own lives?" Such were their varied reactions, while we were greatly distressed by our inability to give the bodies burial. Darkness did not make it possible, and they refused all offers of payment and were deaf to entreaty; but they guarded the remains with the greatest care, regarding it as a triumph if they could prevent burial. . . .

Thus the martyrs' bodies, after six days' exposure to every kind of insult and to the open sky, were finally burnt to ashes and swept by these wicked men into the Rhône which flows near by, that not even a trace of them might be seen on the earth again. And this they did as if they could defeat God and rob the dead of their rebirth,[43] "in order," they said, "that they may have no hope of resurrection — the belief that has led them to bring into this country a new foreign cult and treat torture with contempt, going willingly and cheerfully to their death. Now let's see if they'll rise again, and if their god can help them and save them from our hands."[44]

---

41. Rev. 22:11, reworded.
42. Ps. 42:3.
43. Matt. 19:28.
44. Dan. 3:15.

8. The Martyrdom of Perpetua and Felicitas
(203)

After a period of relative calm, persecution of Christians resumed in earnest under Emperor Septimius Severus (193–211). Among the most moving documents of the time is the story of two young women, Perpetua and Felicitas. Perpetua, a wealthy matron from Carthage, had just delivered her first child. Along with Felicitas, her personal slave, Perpetua was in a group of new Christian converts (catechumens) arrested in 202 and asked to renounce their faith. Defying the desperate pleas of Perpetua's pagan father and ignoring the Roman prosecutor Hilarian's appeals to be reasonable, the women persisted in their confession. After their arrest, they asked to be baptized and died in the arena of Carthage on March 7, 203.[1]

Their story and its reverent use by the early church show how the early Christians could think of no honor rivaling the martyr's crown. Wealth, social standing, gender, even the calling of motherhood, paled when compared to the confessor's glory in the realm of Christ. Perpetua

---

SOURCE: Anne Fremantle, ed. *A Treasury of Early Christianity* (New York: Mentor Books, 1960). Used by permission of the author.

1. W. H. C. Frend, *The Rise of Christianity* (Philadelphia: Fortress Press, 1984).

gives her own account of her trial and imprisonment. An early editor, possibly Tertullian, added an introduction and included an eyewitness account of the death of the two women in the amphitheater.

If the ancient examples of faith, such as both testified to the grace of God, and wrought the edification of man, have for this cause been set out in writing that the reading of them may revive the past and so both God be glorified and man strengthened, why should not new examples be set out equally suitable to both those ends? For these in like manner will some day be old and needful for posterity, though in their own time because of the veneration secured to antiquity they are held in less esteem. But let them see to this who determine the one power of the one Spirit by times and seasons: since the more recent things should rather be deemed the greater, as being "later than the last." This follows from the pre-eminence of grace promised at the last lap of the world's race. For "In the last days, saith the Lord, I will pour forth of My Spirit upon all flesh, and their sons and their daughters shall prophesy: and on My servants and on My handmaidens will I pour forth of My Spirit: and their young men shall see visions, and their old men shall dream dreams." And so we who recognize and hold in honour not new prophecies only but new visions as alike promised, and count all the rest of the powers of the Holy Spirit as intended for the equipment of the Church, to which the same Spirit was sent bestowing all gifts upon all as the Lord dealt to each man, we cannot but set these out and make them famous by recital to the glory of God. So shall no weak or despairing faith suppose that supernatural grace, in excellency of martyrdoms or revelations, was found among the ancients only; for God ever works what He has promised, to unbelievers a witness, to believers a blessing. And so "what we have heard and handled declare we unto you also," brothers and little children, "that ye also" who were their eyewitnesses may be reminded of the glory of the Lord, and you who now learn by the ear "may have fellowship with" the holy martyrs, and through them with the Lord Jesus Christ, to whom belong splendour and honour for ever and ever. Amen.

Certain young catechumens were arrested, Revocatus and his fellow-slave Felicitas, Saturninus, and Secundulus. Among these also Vibia Perpetua, well-born, liberally educated, honourably married, having father and mother, and two brothers, one like herself a catechumen, and an infant son at the breast. She was about twenty-two years of age. The whole story of her martyrdom is from this point onwards told by herself, as she left it written, hand and conception being alike her own.

"When I was still," she says, "with my companions, and my father in his affection for me was endeavouring to upset me by arguments and overthrow my resolution, 'Father,' I said, 'do you see this vessel, for instance, lying here, waterpot or whatever it may be?' 'I see it,' he said. And I said to him, 'Can it be called by any other name than what it is?' And he answered, 'No.' 'So also I cannot call myself anything else than what I am, a Christian.'

"Then my father, furious at the word 'Christian,' threw himself upon me as though to pluck out my eyes; but he was satisfied with annoying me; he was in fact vanquished, he and his Devil's arguments. Then I thanked the Lord for being parted for a few days from my father, and was refreshed by his absence. During those few days we were baptized, and the Holy Spirit bade me make no other petition after the holy water save for bodily endurance. A few days after we were lodged in prison; and I was in great fear, because I had never known such darkness. What a day of horror! Terrible heat, thanks to the crowds! Rough handling by the soldiers! To crown all I was tormented there by anxiety for my baby. Then Tertius and Pomponius, those blessed deacons who were ministering to us, paid for us to be removed for a few hours to a better part of the prison and refresh ourselves. Then all went out of the prison and were left to themselves. My baby was brought to me, and I suckled him, for he was already faint for want of food. I spoke anxiously to my mother on his behalf, and strengthened my brother, and commended my son to their charge. I was pining because I saw them pine on my account. Such anxieties I suffered for many days; and I obtained leave for my baby to remain in the prison with me; and I at once recovered my health, and was relieved of my trouble and anxiety for my baby; and my prison suddenly became a palace to me, and I would rather have been there than anywhere else.

"Then my brother said to me: 'Lady sister, you are now in great honour, so great indeed that you may well pray for a vision and may well be shown whether suffering or release be in store for you.' And I who knew myself to have speech of the Lord, for whose sake I had gone through so much, gave confident promise in return, saying: 'Tomorrow I will bring you word.' And I made request, and this was shown me. I saw a brazen ladder of wondrous length reaching up to heaven, but so narrow that only one could ascend at once; and on the sides of the ladder were fastened all kinds of iron weapons. There were swords, lances, hooks, daggers, so that if anyone went up carelessly or without looking upwards he was mangled and his flesh caught on the weapons. And just beneath the ladder was a dragon crouching of wondrous size who lay in wait for those going up and sought to frighten them from going up. Now Saturus went up first, who had given himself up for our sakes of his own accord, because our faith had been of his own building, and he had not been present when we were seized. And he reached the top of the ladder, and turned, and said to me: 'Perpetua, I await you; but see that the dragon bite you not.' And I said: 'In the name of Jesus Christ he will not hurt me.' And he put out his head gently, as if afraid of me, just at the foot of the ladder; and as though I were treading on the first step, I trod on his head. And I went up, and saw a vast expanse of garden, and in the midst a man sitting with white hair, in the dress of a shepherd, a tall man, milking sheep; and round about were many thousands clad in white. And he raised his head, and looked upon me, and said: 'You have well come, my child.' And he called me, and gave me a morsel of the milk which he was milking and I received it in my joined hands, and ate; and all they that stood around said: 'Amen.' And at the sound of the word I woke, still eating something sweet. And at once I told my brother, and we understood that we must suffer, and henceforward began to have no hope in this world.

"After a few days a rumour ran that we were to be examined. Moreover, my father arrived from the city, worn with trouble, and came up the hill to see me, that he might overthrow my resolution, saying: 'Daughter, pity my white hairs! Pity your father, if I am worthy to be called father by you; if with these hands I have brought you up to this your prime of life, if I have preferred you to all your brothers! Give me not over to the reproach of men! Look upon your brothers, look upon your mother and your mother's sister, look upon your son who cannot live after you are gone! Lay aside your pride, do not ruin all of us, for none of us will ever speak freely again, if anything happen to you!' So spoke my father in his love for me, kissing my hands, and casting himself at my feet; and with tears called me by the name not of daughter but of lady. And I grieved for my father's sake, because he alone of all my kindred would not have joy in my suffering. And I comforted him, saying: 'It shall happen on that platform as God shall choose; for know well that we lie not in our own power but in the power of God.' And, full of sorrow, he left me.

"On another day when we were having our midday meal, we were suddenly hurried off to be examined; and we came to the market-place. Forthwith a rumour ran through the neighbouring parts of the market-place, and a vast crowd gathered. We went up onto the platform. The others, on being questioned, confessed their faith. So it came to my turn. And there was my father with my child, and he drew me down from the step, beseeching me: 'Have pity on your baby.' And the procurator Hilarian, who had then received the power of life and death in the room of the late proconsul Minucius Timinianus, said to me: 'Spare your father's white hairs; spare the tender years of your child. Offer a sacrifice for the safety of the Emperors.' And I answered: 'No.' 'Are you a Christian?' said Hilarian. And I answered: 'I am.' And when my father persisted in trying to overthrow my resolution, he was ordered by Hilarian to be thrown down, and the judge struck him with his rod. And I was grieved for my father's plight, as if I had been struck myself, so did I grieve for the sorrow that had come on his old age. Then he passed sentence on the whole of us, and condemned us to the beasts; and in great joy we went down into the prison. Then because my baby was accustomed to take the breast from me, and stay with me in prison, I sent at once the deacon Pomponius to my father to ask for my baby. But my father refused to give him. And as God willed, neither had he any further wish for my breasts, nor did they become inflamed; that I might not be tortured by anxiety for the baby and pain in my breasts.

"After a few days, while we were all praying, suddenly in the middle of the prayer I spoke, and uttered the name of Dinocrates; and I was astonished that he had never come into mind till then; and I grieved, thinking of what had befallen him. And I saw at once that I was entitled, and ought, to make request for him. And I began to pray much for him, and make lamentation to the Lord. At once on this very night this was shown me. I saw Dinocrates coming forth from a dark place, where there were many other dark places, very hot and thirsty, his countenance pale and squalid; and the wound which he had when he died was in his face still. This Dinocrates had been my brother according to the flesh, seven years old, who had died miserably of a gangrene in the face, so that his death moved all to loathing. For him then I had prayed; and there was a great gulf between me and him, so that neither of us could approach the other. There was besides in the very place where Dinocrates was a font full of water, the rim of which was above the head of the child; and Dinocrates stood on tiptoe to drink. I grieved that the font should have water in it and that nevertheless he could not drink because of the height of the rim. And I woke and recognized that my brother was in trouble. But I trusted that I could relieve his trouble, and I prayed for him every day until we were transferred to the garrison prison, for we were to fight with the beasts at the garrison games on the Caesar Geta's birthday. And I prayed for him day and night with lamentations and tears that he might be given me.

"During the daytime, while we stayed in the stocks, this was shown me. I saw that same place which I had seen before, and Dinocrates clean in body, well clothed and refreshed; and where there had been a wound, I saw a scar; and the font which I had seen before had its rim lowered to the child's waist; and there poured water from it unceasingly; and on the rim a golden bowl full of water. And Dinocrates came forward and began to drink from it, and the bowl failed not. And when he had drunk enough of the water, he came forward, being glad to play as children will. And I awoke. Then I knew that he had been released from punishment.

"Then after a few days Pudens the adjutant, who was in charge of the prison, who began to show us honour, perceiving that there was some great power within us, began to admit many to see us, that both we and they might be refreshed by one another's company. Now when the day of the games approached, my father came in to me, worn with trouble, and began to pluck out his beard and cast it on the ground, and to throw himself on his face, and to curse his years, and to say such words as might have turned the world upside down. I sorrowed for the unhappiness of his old age.

"On the day before we were to fight, I saw in a vision Pomponius the deacon come hither to the door of the prison and knock loudly. And I went out to him, and opened to him. Now he was clad in a white robe without a girdle, wearing shoes curiously wrought. And he said to me: 'Perpetua, we are waiting for you; come.' And he took hold of my hand, and we began to pass through rough and broken country. Painfully and panting did we arrive at last at an amphitheatre, and he led me into the middle of the arena. And he said to me: 'Fear not; I am here with you, and I suffer with you.' And he departed. And I saw a huge crowd watching eagerly. And because I knew that I was condemned to the beasts, I marvelled that there were no beasts let loose on me. And there came out an Egyptian, foul of look, with his attendants to fight against me. And to me also there came goodly young men to be my attendants and supporters. And I was stripped and was changed into a man. And my supporters began to rub me down with oil, as they are wont to do before a combat; and I saw the Egyptian opposite rolling in the sand. And there came forth a man wondrously tall so that he rose above the top of the amphitheatre, clad in a purple robe without a girdle with two stripes, one on either side, running down the middle of the breast, and wearing shoes curiously wrought made of gold and silver; carrying a wand, like a trainer, and a green bough on which were golden apples. And he asked for silence, and said: 'This Egyptian, if he prevail over her, shall kill her with a sword; and, if she prevail over him, she shall receive this bough.' And he retired. And we came near to one another and began to use our fists. My adversary wished to catch hold of my feet, but I kept on striking his face with my heels. And I was lifted up into the air, and began to strike him in such fashion as would one that no longer trod on earth. But when I saw that the fight lagged, I joined my two hands, linking the fingers of the one with the fingers of the other. And I caught hold of his head, and he fell on his face; and I trod upon his head. And the people began to shout, and my supporters to sing psalms. And I came forward to the trainer, and received the bough. And he kissed me, and said to me: 'Peace be with thee, my daughter.' And I began to go in triumph to the Gate of Life. And I awoke. And I perceived that I should not fight with beasts but with the Devil; but I knew the victory to be mine. Such were my doings up to the day before the games. Of what was done in the games themselves let him write who will."

But the blessed Saturus also has made known this vision of his own, which he has written out with his own hand. "Methought we had suffered, and put off the flesh, and began to be borne toward the east by four angels whose hands touched us not. Now we moved not on our backs looking upward, but as though we were climbing a gentle slope. And when we were clear of the world below we saw a great light, and I said to Perpetua, for she was by my side: 'This is what the Lord promised us, we have received His promise.' And while we were carried by those four angels, we came upon a great open space, which was like as it might be a garden, having rose-trees and all kinds of flowers. The height of the trees was like the height of a cypress, whose leaves sang without ceasing. Now there in the garden were certain four angels, more glorious than the others, who when they saw us, gave us honour, and said to the other angels: 'Lo! they are come; lo! they are come,' being full of wonder. And those four angels which bare us trembled and set us down, and we crossed on foot a place strewn with violets, where we found Jucundus and Saturninus and Artaxius, who were burned alive in the same persecution, and Quintus who, being also a martyr, had died in the prison, and we asked of them where they were. The other angels said unto us: 'Come first and enter and greet the Lord.'

"And we came near to a place whose walls were built like as it might be of light, and before the gate of that place were four angels standing, who as we entered clothed us in white robes. And we entered, and heard a sound as of one voice saying: 'Holy, holy, holy,' without ceasing. And we saw sitting in the same place one like unto a man white-haired, having hair as white as snow, and with the face of a youth; whose feet we saw not. And on the right and on the left four elders; and behind them were many other elders standing. And, entering, we stood in wonder before the throne; and the four angels lifted us up, and we kissed Him, and He stroked our faces with His hand. And the other elders said to us: 'Let us stand.' And we stood and gave the Kiss of Peace. And the elders said to us: 'Go and play.' And I said to Perpetua: 'You have your wish.' And she said to me: 'Thanks be to God, that as I was merry in the flesh, so am I now still merrier here.'

"And we went forth and saw before the doors Optatus the bishop on the right, and Aspasius the priest-teacher on the left, severed and sad. And they cast themselves at our feet, and said: 'Make peace between us, for you have gone forth and left us thus.' And we said to them: 'Are not you our father, and you our priest? Why should ye fall before our feet?' And we were moved, and embraced them. And Perpetua began to talk Greek with them, and we drew them aside into the garden under a rose-tree. And while we talked with them, the angels said to them: 'Let them refresh themselves; and if ye have any quarrels among yourselves, forgive one another.' And they put these to shame, and said to Optatus: 'Reform your people, for they come to you like men returning from the circus and contending about its factions.' And it seemed to us as though they wished to shut the gates. And we began to recognize many brethren there, martyrs too amongst them. We were all fed on a fragrance beyond telling, which contented us. Then in my joy I awoke."

Such are the famous visions of the blessed martyrs themselves, Saturus and Perpetua, which they wrote with their own hands. As for Secundulus, God called him to an earlier departure from this world, while still in prison, not without grace, that he might escape the beasts. Nevertheless his body, if not his soul, made acquaintance with the sword.

As for Felicitas indeed, she also was visited by the grace of God in this wise. Being eight months gone with child (for she was pregnant at the time of her arrest), as the day for the spectacle drew near she was in great sorrow for fear lest because of her pregnancy her martyrdom should be delayed, since it is against the law for women with child to be exposed for punishment, and lest she should shed her sacred and innocent blood among others afterwards who were malefactors. Her fellow-martyrs too were deeply grieved at the thought of leaving so good a comrade and fellow-traveller behind alone on the way to the same hope. So in one flood of common lamentation they poured forth a prayer to the Lord two days before the games. Immediately after the prayer her pains came upon her. And since from the natural difficulty of an eight-months' labour she suffered much in child-birth, one of the warders said to her: "You who so suffer now, what will you do when you are flung to the beasts which, when you refused to sacrifice, you despised?" And she answered: "Now I suffer what I suffer: but then Another will be in me who will suffer for me, because I too am to suffer for Him." So she gave birth to a girl, whom one of the sisters brought up as her own daughter.

Since, therefore, the Holy Spirit has permitted, and by permitting willed, the story of the games themselves to be written, we cannot choose but carry out, however unworthy to supplement so glorious a history, the injunction, or rather sacred bequest, of the most holy Perpetua, adding at the same time one example of her steadfastness and loftiness of soul. When they were treated with unusual rigour by the commanding officer because his fears were aroused through the warnings of certain foolish people that they might be carried off from prison by some magic spells, she challenged him to his face: "Why do you not at least suffer us to refresh ourselves, 'the most noble' among the condemned, belonging as we do to Caesar and chosen to fight on his birthday? Or is it not to your credit that we should appear thereon in better trim?" The commanding officer trembled and blushed; and so ordered them to be used more kindly, giving her brothers and other persons leave to visit, that they might refresh themselves in their company. By this time the governor of the prison was himself a believer.

Moreover, on the day before the games when they celebrated that last supper, called "the free festivity," not as a "festivity," but, so far as they could make it so, a "love-feast," with the same steadfastness they flung words here and there among the people, threatening them with the judgment of God, calling to witness the happiness of their own passion, laughing at the inquisitiveness of the crowd. Said Saturus: "Tomorrow does not satisfy you, for what you hate you love to see. Friends today, foes tomorrow. Yet mark our faces well, that when the day comes you may know us again." So all left the place amazed, and many of them became believers.

The day of their victory dawned, and they proceeded from the prison to the amphitheatre, as if they were on their way to heaven, with gay and gracious looks; trembling, if at all, not with fear but joy. Perpetua followed with shining steps, as the true wife of Christ, as the darling of God, abashing with the high spirit in her eyes the gaze of all; Felicitas also, rejoicing that she had brought forth in safety that so she might fight the beasts, from blood to blood, from midwife to gladiator, to find in her

Second Baptism her child-birth washing. And when they were led within the gate, and were on the point of being forced to put on the dress, the men of the priests of Saturn, the women of those dedicated to Ceres, the noble Perpetua resisted steadfastly to the last. For she said: "Therefore we came to this issue of our own free will, that our liberty might not be violated; therefore we pledged our lives, that we might do no such thing: this was our pact with you." Injustice acknowledged justice; the commanding officer gave permission that they should enter the arena in their ordinary dress as they were. Perpetua was singing a psalm of triumph, as already treading on the head of the Egyptian. Revocatus, Saturninus, and Saturus were threatening the onlookers with retribution; when they came within sight of Hilarian, they began to signify to him by nods and gestures: "Thou art judging us, but God shall judge thee." The people, infuriated thereat, demanded that they should be punished with scourging before a line of beast-fighters. And they for this at least gave one another joy, that they had moreover won some share in the sufferings of their Lord.

But He who had said: "Ask and ye shall receive" had granted to those who asked Him that death which each had craved. For, whenever they talked amongst themselves about their hopes of martyrdom, Saturninus declared that he wished to be cast to all the beasts; so indeed would he wear a more glorious crown. Accordingly at the outset of the show he was matched with the leopard and recalled from him; he was also (later) mauled on the platform by the bear. Saturus on the other hand had a peculiar dread of the bear, but counted beforehand on being dispatched by one bite of the leopard. And so when he was offered to the wild boar, the fighter with beasts, who had bound him to the boar, was gored from beneath by the same beast, and died after the days of the games were over, whereas Saturus was only dragged. And when he was tied up on the bridge before the bear, the bear refused to come out of his den. So Saturus for the second time was recalled unhurt.

For the young women the Devil made ready a mad heifer, an unusual animal selected for this reason, that he wished to match their sex with that of the beast. And so after being stripped and enclosed in nets they were brought into the arena. The people were horrified, beholding in the one a tender girl, in the other a woman fresh from childbirth, with milk dripping from her breasts. So they were recalled and dressed in tunics without girdles. Perpetua was tossed first, and fell on her loins. Sitting down, she drew back her torn tunic from her side to cover her thighs, more mindful of her modesty than of her suffering. Then, having asked for a pin, she further fastened her disordered hair. For it was not seemly that a martyr should suffer with her hair dishevelled, lest she should seem to mourn in the hour of her glory. Then she rose, and seeing that Felicitas was bruised, approached, gave a hand to her, and lifted her up. And the two stood side by side, and the cruelty of the people being now appeased, they were recalled to the Gate of Life. There Perpetua was supported by a certain Rusticus, then a catechumen, who kept close to her; and being roused from what seemed like sleep, so completely had she been in the Spirit and in ecstasy, began to look about her, and said to the amazement of all: "When we are to be thrown to that heifer, I cannot tell." When she heard what had already taken place, she refused to believe it till she had observed certain marks of ill-usage on her body and dress. Then she summoned her brother and spoke to him and the catechumen, saying: "Stand ye all fast in the faith, and love one another; and be not offended by our sufferings."

Saturus also at another gate was encouraging the soldier Pudens: "In a word," said he, "what I counted on and foretold has come to pass, not a beast so far has touched me. And now, that you may trust me wholeheartedly, see, I go forth yonder, and with one bite of the leopard all is over." And forthwith, as the show was ending, the leopard was let loose, and with one bite Saturus was so drenched in blood that the people as he came back shouted in attestation of his Second Baptism, "Bless you, well bathed! Bless you, well bathed!" Blessed indeed was he who had bathed after this fashion. Then he said to the soldier Pudens: "Farewell! Keep my faith and me in mind! And let these things not confound, but confirm you." And with that he asked for the ring from Pudens's finger, plunged it in his own wound, and gave it back as a legacy, bequeathing it for a pledge and memorial of his blood. Then, by this time lifeless, he was flung with the rest onto the place allotted to the throat-cutting. And when the people asked for them to be brought into the open, that, when the sword pierced their bodies, these might lend their eyes for partners in the murder, they rose unbidden and made their way whither the people willed, after first kissing one another, that they might perfect their martyrdom with the rite of the Pax. The rest without a movement in silence received the sword, Saturus in deeper silence, who, as he had been the first to climb the ladder, was the first to give up the ghost; for now as then he awaited Perpetua. Perpetua, however, that she might taste something of the pain, was struck on the bone and cried out, and herself guided to her throat the wavering hand of the young untried gladiator. Perhaps so great a woman, who was feared by the unclean spirit, could not otherwise be slain except she willed.

O valiant and blessed martyrs! O truly called and chosen to the glory of Jesus Christ our Lord! He who magnifies, honours, and adores that glory should recite to the edification of the Church these examples also, not less precious at least than those of old; that so new instances of virtue may testify that one and the self-same Spirit is working to this day with the Father, God Almighty, and with His Son Jesus Christ our Lord, to whom belong splendour and power immeasurable for ever and ever. Amen.

9. The Problem of the Lapsed
From *Letter 33*
(c. 250)

CYPRIAN

*After a period of calm and of rapid growth, the church was ill-equipped to deal with renewed persecution that came with the reign of Emperors Decius (249–251) and Valerian (251–260). Faced with imprisonment and death, scores of Christians "lapsed," by offering the required sacrifices or purchasing forged certificates of compliance (*libelli*). The Christian community barred those Christians who succumbed (*lapsi*) from communion and shunned them. As a consequence the lapsed Christians lost their hope of eternal salvation. Not surprisingly, many of the "lapsed" asked to be forgiven and restored to the fellowship of believers.*

How to treat the "lapsed" caused serious divisions in the churches, especially in North Africa, where many laity clung to Tertullian's rigorist view that apostasy after baptism can never be forgiven. In Carthage, the church was brought to the verge of schism when local clergy and some of the surviving confessors were accused of coddling those who had betrayed the Lord.

SOURCE: S. L. Greenslade, ed., *Early Latin Theology*, vol. 5 of *The Library of Christian Classics* (Philadelphia: Westminster Press, 1956). Used by permission of Westminster John Knox Press.

Cyprian (c. 200–258), the bishop of Carthage, had been forced into exile early in the persecutions. He returned around 250 to restore order and to mediate between the warring partisans of God's justice and God's mercy. In Cyprian's treatise, On the Unity of the Catholic Church, *he sidesteps the thorny theological problem of God's justice and mercy by arguing the practical case that unity and discipline are essential marks of the body of Christ. He uses the story of Rahab, the harlot (Josh. 6; Heb. 11:31), to express disdain for zealots who have no love and who tear the seamless robe of Christ (the church) with the fury of their discord. "Good persons cannot leave the church," he wrote, and "you cannot be a martyr if you are not in the church" or "if you do not have charity."*

His Letter 33, *on the other hand, makes it clear that forgiveness and restoration do not come cheap. Salvation requires "fear and trembling before God" and "great and noble works before the churches." Remission of sin cannot be granted by certificates (*libelli pacis*) even of confessors, since the power of the keys rests only with properly appointed bishops. The "power of the keys" is the authority to determine communicant membership in the Christian community. Early Christians believed that full membership in the Church was essential to salvation. Cyprian's letter, written in 250, was read a year later at a North African bishops' council in Carthage, which adopted official rules for the restoration of the truly penitent (see vol. 1:129–34).*

When our Lord, whose commands we ought to revere and keep, was settling the office of bishop and the constitution of his Church, he said to Peter in the Gospel: "I say unto thee, that thou art Peter, and upon this rock I will build my Church; and the gates of hell shall not prevail against it. And I will give unto thee the keys of the kingdom of heaven: and whatsoever thou shalt bind on earth shall be bound also in heaven: and whatsoever thou shalt loose on earth shall be loosed also in heaven."[1] Thence, down the changes of years and successions, the appointment of bishops and the constitution of the Church runs on, so that the Church rests on the bishops and every act of the Church is governed by these same prelates.

This being established by divine law, I am astonished that certain persons have boldly and presumptuously taken on themselves to write to

---

1. Matt. 16:18–19.

me in the name of the Church, though the Church is made up of the bishops and clergy and all who stand firm. May the Lord in his mercy and unconquered power never allow a collection of the lapsed to be called the Church, for it is written: "God is not the God of the dead, but of the living."[2] We want them all indeed to be brought to life, and with supplications and groanings we pray that they may be restored to their former state. But if some of them will have it that they are the Church, and if the Church is with them and in them, what remains but that we should request them to be so kind as to receive us into the Church? They ought to be submissive and quiet and modest. Remembering their offence, they should give satisfaction to God, and not write letters in the name of the Church when they know they should rather be writing to the Church.

2. Some of the lapsed, however, have written to me who are humble and meek, fearing and trembling before God, men who have always done great and noble works in their churches without ever demanding payment from the Lord for them, knowing that he said: "And when ye shall have done all these things, say, We are unprofitable servants: we have done that which it was our duty to do."[3] Keeping this in mind and taking no advantage of the certificate which they had received from the martyrs, they have written to me praying that their satisfaction may be acceptable to the Lord, telling me that they acknowledge their sin and are truly penitent, that they are not hurrying rashly or importunately to be reconciled, but are waiting for my presence. They say that the reconciliation which they receive in my presence will be all the sweeter to them. How warmly I have congratulated them, the Lord is witness, who deigned to show what such servants deserve of his goodness.

Having received their letter, and having now read your very different one, I must ask you to discriminate between your various desires, and whoever you are that have sent this letter, I must ask you to append your names to the certificate[4] and send it to me with all your names. I must first know whom I have to answer. Then I will answer each of your points as best fits my humble station and activity. I hope, brethren, that you are well and are living peacefully and quietly according to the discipline of the Lord. Farewell.

---

2. Matt. 22:32.
3. Luke 17:10.
4. *Libellus,* perhaps just "a paper."

Defenders of the Faith

10. Letter to Diognetus
(c. 150)

The Letter to Diognetus *is an excellent example of early apologetic literature (writings that make the case for Christianity in a pagan world). The date of the letter is uncertain. Internal evidence suggests an early date around 150.*

The anonymous author of the letter argues that the pagan gods are dumb idols conceived by human minds and created by human hands. Although the author does credit the Jews with having minimal good sense because they worship the "one God of the universe," the sacrificial system of Jews and pagans is an "exhibition of stupidity." It should be obvious that God, the "one who made all things," does not need human assistance.

The letter argues that Christians follow the one true creator God of the universe who has sent God's Word (i.e., Christ) to redeem the world, just "as a [gracious] king might send out his son who is also a king . . . as

---

SOURCE: Henry G. Meecham, *The Letter to Diognetus* (Manchester: Manchester University Press, 1949).

one who is loving, and not judging." Christians rejoice in the love of Christ that enables them to live in peace and harmony with all people. The spirit of prophecy, the truth of the Gospels, and the blood of the martyrs are visible signs of the divine presence in the Christian community. The strongest argument for the truth of the Christian faith, however, is the superior morality of the Christians.

I

Since I perceive, most excellent Diognetus, that you are exceedingly zealous to learn the religion of the Christians and are making very clear and careful inquiry about them — both who is the God in whom they trust and how they worship Him, so that all disdain the world and despise death, and neither account those to be gods who are esteemed such by the Greeks, nor observe the superstition of the Jews; and what is the affection which they have for one another; and why it is that this new race of men or mode of living has entered into our world now and not formerly — I welcome this eager desire in you, and I ask of God, who bestows on us *the power* both of speech and of hearing, that it may be given to me so to speak that you may be edified as much as possible by your hearing, and to you so to hear that I by my speaking may suffer no regret.

II

1. Come then, clear yourself of all the bias that occupies your mind, and get rid of the habit that deceives you, and become as it were from the beginning a new man, as one too who is to hear a new story, even as you yourself also acknowledged. See not only with your eyes, but also with your understanding, what substance or form they chance *to have* whom you declare and esteem to be gods. 2. Is not one a stone, like that which we tread on, another bronze, no better than the implements which have been forged for our use, another wood already decayed, another silver, which needs a man to guard[1] it lest it be stolen, another iron eaten through by rust, another earthenware, not a whit more pleasing than that made for the meanest service? 3. Are not all these of perishable matter? Have they not been forged by iron and fire? Did not the sculptor fashion one of them, the brass-worker another, the silversmith another, the potter another?

---

1. Reading φυλάξοντος.

Before they were modelled by these men's arts into the form of these *gods,* was not each of them subjected to transformation — and still *is so* even now — at the hands of each artificer? Might not the vessels now formed out of the same material, if they met with the same workmen, be made similar to such *images* as these? 4. Again, could not these things which are now worshipped by you become at the hands of men vessels like the rest? Are they not all dumb? Are they not blind? Are they not without souls? Are they not destitute of feeling? Are they not without motion? Are they not all rotting away? Are they not all in course of decay? 5. These things you call gods! These are what you serve! These you worship and in the end you become like them! 6. For this reason you hate (the) Christians — because they do not think that these are gods. 7. For is it not you, who, although you consider and think that you are praising *the gods,* are much more despising them? Are you not much rather mocking and insulting them, when you worship those of stone and earthenware, which you leave unguarded, and yet those of silver and gold you lock up at night and in the day-time set guards by them, lest they be stolen? 8. And by the honours that you think to offer them you are punishing them rather, if indeed they are endued with sense; but, if they lack sensibility, you are refuting[2] them by the very fact of worshipping them with blood and steaming fat. 9. Let anyone of you endure this treatment, let him bear with these things being done to him! Nay, there is not a single man who will, if he can help it, suffer this infliction, for he has sense and reason. But the stone suffers *it,* for it has no feeling. You do not then (by your offerings) show up its sensibility! 10. Well, I could say many other things about the fact that Christians are not in bondage to such gods. But if to anyone even these arguments should not seem sufficient, I think it needless to say more.

III

1. In the next place I suppose that you are especially anxious to hear why they (Christians) do not worship in the same manner as the Jews. 2. The Jews indeed, since they abstain from the religion described above, rightly deem that they worship the one God of the universe and think of Him as Master; but in offering this service to Him in like fashion to those already mentioned they go utterly astray. 3. For whereas the Greeks furnish an example of foolishness by making offerings to *images* void of

---

2. Perhaps better "exposing," "showing them up."

sense and hearing, these *Jews* ought rather to consider it folly maybe, not piety, in thinking that they are offering these things to God as though He were in need of them. 4. For "He who made the heaven and the earth and all things that are in them" and provides us all with what we need would not Himself need any of these things which He Himself supplies to those who imagine that they give *to Him*. 5. But those who think that they are rendering due sacrifices to Him by blood and fat and whole burnt offerings, and that they are doing Him reverence by these tributes, seem to me in no way better than those who show the same lavish honour to deaf *images*. For the one class seem to offer *sacrifices* to things unable to partake of the honour, the other to Him who is in need of nothing.

IV

1. But, in truth, I do not think that you need to learn from me that, after all, their qualms concerning food and their superstition about the Sabbath, and the vaunting of circumcision and the cant of fasting and new moon, are utterly absurd and unworthy of any argument. 2. For how can it be other than unlawful to receive some of the things created by God for man's use as created 'good' and to refuse others as useless and superfluous? 3. And is it not impious to slander God as though He forbids the doing of a good deed on the Sabbath day? 4. And to glory in the mutilation of the flesh as evidence of their election, as if they were on this account especially beloved by God — does this not call for derision? 5. And their star-gazing and watching of the moon, so as to observe months and days and to distribute at their own inclinations the orderings of God and the changes of the seasons, *making* some into feasts and others into times of mourning — who would consider this an example of piety and not much more of folly? 6. Well then, I think that you have learned sufficiently that Christians are right in keeping aloof from the general fatuity and deceit and from the meddlesomeness and pride of the Jews; but as for the mystery of the Christians' own religion, do not expect to be able to learn this from man.

V

1. For Christians are distinguished from the rest of men neither by country nor by language nor by customs. 2. For nowhere do they dwell in cities of their own; they do not use any strange form of speech or practise a singular mode of life. 3. This lore of theirs has not been discovered by any design and thought of prying men, nor do they champion a mere

human doctrine, as some men do. 4. But while they dwell in both Greek and barbarian cities, each as his lot was cast, and follow the customs of the land in dress and food and other matters of living, they show forth the remarkable and admittedly strange order of their own citizenship. 5. They live in fatherlands of their own, but as aliens. They share all things as citizens, and suffer all things as strangers. Every foreign land is their fatherland, and every fatherland a foreign land. 6. They marry, like all others; they breed children, but they do not cast out their offspring. 7. Free board they provide, but no carnal bed. 8. They are "in the flesh," but they do not live "after the flesh." 9. They pass their days on earth, but they have their citizenship in heaven. 10. They obey the appointed laws, yet in their own lives they excel the laws. 11. They love all men, and are persecuted by all. 12. They are unknown, yet they are condemned; they are put to death, yet they are made alive. 13. "They are poor, yet they make many rich." They suffer the lack of all things, yet they abound in all things. 14. They are dishonoured, and yet are glorified in their dishonour. They are evil spoken of, yet are vindicated. 15. "They are reviled, and they bless"; insulted, they repay with honour. 16. When doing good they are punished as evil-doers; suffering punishment, they rejoice as if quickened into life. 17. By the Jews they are warred against as foreigners, and are hunted down by the Greeks. Yet those who hate them cannot state the cause of their hostility.

VI

1. Broadly speaking, what the soul is in the body, that Christians are in the world. 2. The soul, is dispersed through all the members of the body, and Christians throughout the cities of the world. 3. The soul dwells in the body, but is not of the body; and Christians dwell in the world, but "are not of the world." 4. The soul, itself invisible, is guarded in the body which is visible; so Christians are known as being in the world, but their religion remains unseen. 5. The flesh hates the soul, and, though it suffers no wrong, wars *against it,* because the flesh is hindered from indulging its pleasures; so too the world, though in no wise wronged, hates Christians, because they set themselves against its pleasures. 6. The soul loves the flesh that hates it, and the limbs; so Christians love them that hate them. 7. The soul is enclosed within the body, but itself curbs the body; and Christians are detained in the world as in a prison, but themselves restrain the world. 8. The soul, though immortal, dwells in a mortal tabernacle; and Christians sojourn among corruptible things awaiting the incorruptibility which is in heaven. 9. When faring ill in food and drink the soul

becomes better; so Christians when buffeted day by day flourish the more. 10. To so high a rank has God appointed them, and it is not right for them to refuse it.

VII

1. For this is not, as I said, an earthly discovery which was committed to them, and no mortal idea which they think it their duty to guard with such care, nor have they been entrusted with the stewardship of mere human mysteries. 2. But in truth God Himself, the all-sovereign and all-creating and invisible God, Himself from heaven established among men the truth and the holy and incomprehensible word and fixed it firmly in their hearts, not, as one might surmise, by sending to men some servant, or an angel, or ruler, or one of those who administer the affairs of earth, or one of those entrusted with the ordering of things in heaven, but the very Artificer and Maker of the universe himself, by whom He created the heavens, by whom He confined the sea in its own bounds; whose mysteries all the elements faithfully guard, from whom the sun has received the measure of its daily rounds to keep, whom the moon obeys as he bids her shine by night, whom the stars obey as they follow the course of the moon, by whom all things have been ordered and determined and placed in subjection, the heavens and the things in the heavens, the earth and the things therein, the sea and what is in the sea, fire, air, abyss, the things in the heights, the things in the depths, the things in the realm between — him He sent unto them. 3. Did He send him, as a man might conclude, to rule in tyranny and terror and awe? 4. Not so, but in gentleness and meekness He sent him, as a king sending a son who is a king, He sent him as God, He sent him as Man unto men. He was as it were saving when He sent him, (as) persuading, not compelling (for force is no attribute of God). 5. When He sent him God was calling, not pursuing; He sent him as in love, not in judgement. 6. For He will send him to be our judge, and who shall stand at his coming? 7. *Do you not see them* thrown to wild beasts that they may deny the Lord, and *yet* unconquered? 8. Do you not see that as more of them are punished, so much do others abound? These things do not seem to be the works of man; they are a mighty deed of God; they are proofs of His presence.

VIII

1. For what man had any knowledge at all of what God is, before he came? 2. Or do you accept the vain and trumpery statements of those

specious philosophers of whom some said that God was fire (what they themselves are destined to go to, that they call God!), and others water, and others some other of the elements created by God? 3. And yet, if any of these arguments is admissible, each one of the other created things could in like manner be declared God. 4. But these things are mere miracle-mongering and deceit of the magicians. 5. No man has either seen or known *Him,* but God manifested Himself. 6. And He manifested Himself through faith, by which alone it is given to see God. 7. For God, Master and Maker of the universe, who made all things and disposed *them* in their *due* order, proved Himself not only a lover of man but also long-suffering. 8. Nay, such He ever was and is and will be, kind and good and free from anger and true, and He alone is good. 9. And having conceived a great and unutterable design He communicated it to His Child alone. 10. And so long as He held it in a mystery and guarded His wise counsel He seemed to have no concern or care for us. 11. But when He revealed it through His beloved Child, and manifested the things prepared from the beginning, He bestowed upon us all things at once, both to share in His blessings and to see and understand. Who of us would ever have expected these things?

IX

1. Having therefore planned everything already in His own mind with His Child, He suffered us up to the former time to be borne along by unruly impulses, as we willed, in the clutches of pleasures and lusts. Not at all because He took pleasure in our sins, but out of His forbearance; not in approval of the season of iniquity which was then, but creating the season of righteousness which is now, so that we who in past time were from our own deeds convicted as unworthy of life might now by the goodness of God be deemed worthy, and when we had shown clearly that of ourselves it was impossible "to enter into the kingdom of God," might be made able by the power of God. 2. But when our iniquity was fulfilled and it had been made fully manifest that its reward of punishment and death was awaited, and the season came which God had appointed to manifest henceforth[3] His own goodness and power (O the exceeding kindness and love of God!), He did not hate us or repel us or remember our misdeeds, but was long-suffering, bore with us, Himself in mercy took on Him our sins, Himself gave up His own Son as a ransom for us,

---

3. Or "at last."

the holy One for the wicked, the innocent for the guilty, "the just for the unjust," the incorruptible for the corruptible, the immortal for mortals. 3. For what else could cover our sins but his righteousness? 4. In whom was it possible for us, wicked and impious as we were, to be justified, except in the Son of God alone? 5. O the sweet exchange, O work of God beyond all searching out, O blessings past our expectation, that the wickedness of many should be hidden in one righteous Man and the righteousness of the One should justify many wicked! 6. Having then convinced us in the former time of the powerlessness of our nature to gain life, and having now shown the Saviour in his power to save even powerless creatures, in both these ways His will was that we should believe His goodness, and regard Him as guardian, father, teacher, counsellor, healer, mind, light, honour, glory, strength, life, and have no anxiety about clothing and food.

X

1. If you also long for this faith and first obtain knowledge of the father . . . 2. For God loved men for whose sake He made the world, to whom He subjected all things which are in the earth, to whom He gave reason, to whom He gave mind, whom alone He permitted to look upward to Him, whom He formed after His own image, to whom "He sent His only-begotten Son," to whom He promised the kingdom which is in heaven — and He will give it to them that have loved Him. 3. And when you have this knowledge, with what joy, think you, will you be filled? Or how will you love Him who so first loved you? 4. Loving Him you will imitate His goodness. And do not wonder that a man can become an imitator of God. By the will of God he can. 5. For happiness lies not in lordship over one's neighbours, nor in the desire to have more than one's weaker *brethren,* nor in being rich and coercing the more needy. Not in these things can any man imitate God. Nay, these things are outside His majesty. 6. But whosoever takes upon himself his neighbour's burden, whosoever wishes to benefit another who is poorer in that in which he himself is better off, whosoever by supplying to those in want the things which he has received and holds from God becomes a god to those who receive them — this man is an imitator of God. 7. Then though your lot is on earth you will see that God lives[4] in heaven, then you will begin to speak the mysteries of God, then you will both love and admire those who are being punished for their refusal to deny God, then you will condemn

---

4. Or "rules."

the deceit and error of the world, when you know what is the true life in heaven, when you despise the apparent death here below, when you fear the real death, which is kept for those that shall be condemned to the eternal fire, which shall punish up to the end those that were delivered to it. 8. Then you will admire those that endure for righteousness' sake the fire which is but for a season, and you will count them blessed when you know that *other* fire. . . .

XI

1. My discourse is not of strange matters, nor is my quest perverse; but having been a disciple of apostles I am become a teacher of the heathen. What has been handed down I minister worthily to those who are becoming disciples of the truth. 2. For who that has been rightly instructed and has become a lover of the Word does not seek to learn clearly the things that were openly shown by the Word to disciples, to whom the Word on his appearance manifested them, speaking plainly, not being perceived by unbelievers, but expounding them to disciples, who, deemed by him to be faithful, gained knowledge of the mysteries of the Father? 3. For which cause He sent the Word that he might appear to the world, who was dishonoured by the chosen people, proclaimed by the apostles, believed on by the heathen. 4. This is he who was from the beginning, who appeared as new and was proved to be old, and being born in the hearts of the saints is ever young. 5. This is he who is the eternal one, who to-day was accounted a Son, through whom the Church is enriched and grace is unfolded and multiplied among the saints, grace which confers understanding, makes mysteries plain, announces seasons, rejoices over the faithful, is given to them that seek, that is, those by whom the pledges of faith are not broken nor the decrees of the Fathers transgressed. 6. Then is the fear of the law sung, and the grace of the prophets is known, and the faith of the gospels is established, and the tradition of the apostles is guarded, and buoyant is the grace of the Church. 7. And if you do not grieve this grace you will understand what the Word speaks through those whom he chooses, when he will. 8. For in all things which we were moved to declare under stress,[5] by the will of the Word who commands us, we become sharers with you, out of love for what has been revealed unto us.

---

5. Lit. "with labour."

XII

1. If you chance upon[6] these truths and listen earnestly to them you will know what things God provides for those who love Him rightly, who are become "a Paradise of delight," raising up in themselves a tree all-fruitful and flourishing, and are adorned with divers fruits. 2. For in this garden has been planted "the tree of knowledge and the tree of life." But the tree of knowledge does not kill; disobedience kills. 3. For that which stands written is not without significance, how that God from the beginning planted "the tree [of knowledge and the tree] of life in the midst of Paradise," showing that life is through knowledge. Because our first parents did not make pure use of this knowledge they were left naked[7] by the deceit of the serpent. 4. For there can be neither life without knowledge nor sound knowledge without true life. Wherefore each (tree) stands planted near the other. 5. And when the Apostle saw the force of this, he blamed the knowledge which is exercised apart from the truth of the commandment which tends unto life, and said, "Knowledge puffeth up, but love edifieth." 6. For he who thinks that he knows anything without knowledge that is true and attested by life has learned nothing, but he is deceived by the serpent, not having loved life. But he who has gained knowledge with fear and seeks after life plants in hope, expecting fruit. 7. Let your heart be knowledge, your life the true teaching received (into the heart). 8. If you bear the tree of this and pluck its fruit, you will ever gather in the things desired with[8] God, which the serpent does not touch and deceit does not taint; and Eve is not corrupted, but is believed on as a virgin. 9. And salvation is set forth, and apostles are given understanding, and the Passover of the Lord advances, and the seasons are gathered together and are arranged in order, and the Word rejoices in teaching the saints, the Word through whom the Father is glorified; to whom be glory for ever. Amen.

---

6. Or "read."
7. Or "were deprived of it."
8. I.e. in the sight of God.

11. First Apology
(c. 155)

Justin Martyr

Justin Martyr, a converted Platonist, is the most important of the second-century apologists. He wrote his two apologies in Rome in 155 and 160 respectively. He was martyred in 160.

Justin's apology (c. 155) anticipates the development of Christian theology by blending the authority of scripture with ancient philosophical arguments. In his writing, Justin links prophetic voices of the Old Testament with Greek Stoic concepts of the "logos" (Word/Reason) to explain God's ongoing revelation in Jesus Christ. The divine "logos" inspires both prophet and philosopher.

Arguing from antiquity, Justin asserts that if the wisdom of the Creator-God is older than the wisdom of the Greeks, then Moses inspired Plato. Therefore, he concludes that it is the same "logos," which has informed all rational beings in history and which now is made fully known in Jesus Christ. Thus, all people who have ever lived by the divine "logos," even though called atheists, must be counted among the Christians.

SOURCE: Cyril C. Richardson, ed., *Early Christian Fathers*, vol. 1 of *The Library of Christian Classics* (Philadelphia: Westminster Press, 1953). Used by permission of Westminster John Knox Press.

Plea for a Fair Hearing

1. To the Emperor Titus Aelius Hadrianus Antoninus Pius Augustus Caesar, and to Verissimus his son, the Philosopher, and to Lucius the Philosopher, son of Caesar by nature and of Augustus[1] by adoption, a lover of culture, and to the Sacred Senate and the whole Roman people — on behalf of men of every nation who are unjustly hated and reviled, I, Justin, son of Priscus and grandson of Bacchius, of Flavia Neapolis in Syria Palestina, being myself one of them, have drawn up this plea and petition.

2. Reason requires that those who are truly pious and philosophers should honor and cherish the truth alone, scorning merely to follow the opinions of the ancients, if they are worthless. Nor does sound reason only require that one should not follow those who do or teach what is unjust; the lover of truth ought to choose in every way, even at the cost of his own life, to speak and do what is right, though death should take him away. So do you, since you are called pious and philosophers and guardians of justice and lovers of culture, at least give us a hearing — and it will appear if you are really such.[2] For in these pages we do not come before you with flattery, or as if making a speech to win your favor, but asking you to give judgment according to strict and exact inquiry — not, moved by prejudice or respect for superstitious men, or by irrational impulse and long-established evil rumor, giving a vote which would really be against yourselves. For we are firmly convinced that we can suffer no evil unless we are proved to be evildoers or shown to be criminals. You can kill us, but cannot do us any real harm.[3]

3. But so that no one may think that this is an unreasonable and presumptuous utterance, we ask that the charges against us be investigated. If they are shown to be true, [let us] be punished as is proper.[4] But if

---

1. Lucius was the son of L. Aelius Verus, Caesar under Hadrian, and after his death was adopted by Antoninus Pius, later emperor.

2. In form at least this is the *captatio benevolentiae,* or appeal to the sympathy of the audience, with which a speech opens; the [selection] plays on the emperor's surname Pius and the appellation of philosopher, loved by his family, not forgetting the etymology of the latter, "lover of wisdom."

3. A popular Stoic thought, that no external evil can harm the virtuous man; cf. also Luke 12:4, 5.

4. Omitting, with many editors, the confusing phrase *mallon de kolazein* ("but rather to punish") as gloss or mistaken correction.

nobody has proofs against us, true reason does not allow [you] to wrong innocent men because of an evil rumor — or rather [to wrong] yourselves when you decide to pass sentence on the basis of passion rather than judgment. Every honorable man will recognize this as a fair challenge, and only just, that subjects should give a straightforward account of their life and thought, and that rulers similarly should give their decision as followers of piety and philosophy, not with tyrannical violence. From this both rulers and subjects would gain. As one of the ancients said somewhere, "Unless both rulers and those they rule become lovers of wisdom cities cannot prosper."[5] It is for us, therefore, to offer to all the opportunity of inspecting our life and teachings, lest we ourselves should bear the blame for what those who do not really know about us do in their ignorance. But it is for you, as reason demands, to give [us] a hearing and show yourselves good judges. For if those who learn [the truth] do not do what is right, they have no defense before God.

4. The mere ascription of a name means nothing, good or bad, except for the actions connected with the name. Indeed as far as the name charged against us goes, we are very gracious people.[6] But we do not think it right to ask for a pardon because of the name if we are proved to be criminals — and on the other hand, if neither the appellation of the name nor our conduct shows us to be wrongdoers, you must face the problem whether in punishing unjustly men against whom nothing is proved you will yourselves owe a penalty to justice. Neither reward nor punishment should follow from a name unless something admirable or evil can actually be shown about it. Among yourselves you do not penalize the accused before conviction; but with us you take the name as proof, although, as far as the name goes, you ought rather to punish our accusers. For we are accused of being Christians; and it is not right to hate graciousness. Again, if one of the accused denies the charge, saying he is not [a Christian], you dismiss him, as having no proof of misconduct against him; but if he confesses that he is one, you punish him because of his confession. You ought rather to investigate the life of the confessor and the renegade, so that it would appear from their actions what sort of person each is. There are those who, learning from Christ their teacher,

---

5. A summary of Plato, *Republic* 473 D–E.

6. The play between *christos* and *chrēstos,* "gentle" or "kind" (cf. Luke 6:35), a more familiar Greek word often confused with it, seems impossible to represent in English; Justin may have been the first to see the apologetic value of the confusion (cf. Tertullian, *Apol.* 3:5).

when they are put to the test encourage others not to deny him — and similarly others whose bad conduct gives some excuse to those who like to accuse all Christians of godlessness and crime. This is entirely improper. There are those who assume the name and costume of philosophers, but do nothing worthy of their profession — as you know, men among the ancients who held and taught opposite views are included under the one name of philosophers. Some of them even taught godlessness, and those who became poets proclaim the impurity of Zeus, with his own children. And you do not restrain those among you who follow such teachings, but even offer prizes and honors to those who thus in beautiful words insult them [the gods].

5. What can all this mean? You do not make judicial inquiries in our case, though we are bound neither to commit crimes nor to hold such godless ideas. Instead, you punish us injudicially without deliberation, driven by unreasoning passion and the whips of evil demons. The truth must be told. In old times evil demons manifested themselves, seducing women, corrupting boys, and showing terrifying sights to men — so that those who did not judge these occurrences rationally were filled with awe. Taken captive by fear and not understanding that these were evil demons, they called them gods and gave each of them the name which each of the demons had chosen for himself. When Socrates tried by true reason and with due inquiry to make these things clear and to draw men away from the demons, they, working through men who delighted in wickedness, managed to have him put to death as godless and impious, saying that he was bringing in new divinities.[7] And now they do the same kind of thing to us. For these errors were not only condemned among the Greeks by reason, through Socrates, but among the barbarians, by Reason himself, who took form and became man and was called Jesus Christ. In obedience to him we say that the demons who do such things are not only not rightly called gods,[8] but are in fact evil and unholy demons, whose actions are in no way like those of men who long after virtue.

6. So, then, we are called godless. We certainly confess that we are godless with reference to beings like these who are commonly thought of as gods, but not with reference to the most true God, the Father of righteousness and temperance and the other virtues, who is untouched by evil. Him, and the Son who came from him, and taught us these things, and the

---

7. Part of the formal charges against Socrates (Plato, *Apol.* 24 B).

8. Or, as in the MS., "upright" (*orthous*); but the reading *theous*, first suggested by Thirlby in 1722, seems probable.

army of the other good angels who follow him and are made like him, and the prophetic Spirit we worship and adore,[9] giving honor in reason and truth, and to everyone who wishes to learn transmitting [the truth] ungrudgingly as we have been taught.

• • •

13. What sound-minded man will not admit that we are not godless, since we worship the Fashioner of the universe, declaring him, as we have been taught, to have no need of blood and libations and incense, but praising him by the word of prayer and thanksgiving for all that he has given us? We have learned that the only honor worthy of him is, not to consume by fire the things he has made for our nourishment, but to devote them to our use and those in need, in thankfulness to him sending up solemn prayers and hymns for our creation and all the means of health, for the variety of creatures and the changes of the seasons, and sending up our petitions that we may live again in incorruption through our faith in him.[10] It is Jesus Christ who has taught us these things, having been born for this purpose and crucified under Pontius Pilate, who was procurator in Judea in the time of Tiberius Caesar. We will show that we honor him in accordance with reason, having learned that he is the Son of the true God himself, and holding him to be in the second place and the prophetic Spirit in the third rank. It is for this that they charge us with madness, saying that we give the second place after the unchanging and ever-existing God and begetter of all things to a crucified man, not knowing the mystery involved in this, to which we ask you to give your attention as we expound it.

14. We warn you in advance to be careful, lest the demons whom we have attacked should deceive you and prevent your completely grasping and understanding what we say. For they struggle to have you as their slaves and servants, and now by manifestations in dreams, now by magic tricks, they get hold of all who do not struggle to their utmost for their own salvation—as we do who, after being persuaded by the Word, re-

---

9. It is barely possible to construe the sentence so that the angels are listed as subjects or recipients of Christ's teaching, along with men, rather than as objects of veneration listed in this surprising position; but this seems unnecessary, especially since Justin is here concerned to contrast the good angels who follow the Son with the evil demons who oppose him.

10. The reference is primarily if not exclusively to the Eucharist and the Eucharistic prayer.

nounced them[11] and now follow the only unbegotten God through his Son. Those who once rejoiced in fornication now delight in continence alone; those who made use of magic arts have dedicated themselves to the good and unbegotten God; we who once took most pleasure in the means of increasing our wealth and property now bring what we have into a common fund and share with everyone in need; we who hated and killed one another and would not associate with men of different tribes because of [their different] customs, now after the manifestation of Christ live together and pray for our enemies and try to persuade those who unjustly hate us, so that they, living according to the fair commands of Christ, may share with us the good hope of receiving the same things [that we will] from God, the master of all. So that this may not seem to be sophistry, I think fit before giving our demonstration to recall a few of the teachings which have come from Christ himself. It is for you then, as mighty emperors, to examine whether we have been taught and do teach these things truly. His sayings were short and concise, for he was no sophist, but his word was the power of God.

15. About continence he said this: "Whoever looks on a woman to lust after her has already committed adultery in his heart before God."[12] And: "If your right eye offends you, cut it out; it is better for you to enter into the Kingdom of Heaven with one eye than with two to be sent into eternal fire."[13] And: "Whoever marries a woman who has been put away from another man commits adultery."[14] And: "There are some who were made eunuchs by men, and some who were born eunuchs, and some who have made themselves eunuchs for the Kingdom of Heaven's sake; only not all [are able to] receive this."[15]

And so those who make second marriages according to human law are sinners in the sight of our Teacher,[16] and those who look on a woman to lust after her. For he condemns not only the man who commits the act of adultery, but the man who desires to commit adultery, since not only our

---

11. Specifically in the baptismal renunciation of the devil and all his works.
12. Matt. 5:28; Justin's quotations from the Gospels are often somewhat free, and he summarizes or combines without hesitation; but nearly all can be referred primarily to a particular passage.
13. Mark 9:47 (Matt. 5:29).
14. Matt. 5:32 (Luke 16:18).
15. Matt. 19:11, 12.
16. The reference is mainly to remarriage after divorce, though the phrase could cover remarriage of any kind, which many early Christians disliked and some actually condemned.

actions but our thoughts are manifest to God. Many men and women now in their sixties and seventies who have been disciples of Christ from childhood have preserved their purity; and I am proud that I could point to such people in every nation. Then what shall we say of the uncounted multitude of those who have turned away from incontinence and learned these things? For Christ did not call the righteous or the temperate to repentance, but the ungodly and incontinent and unrighteous. So he said: "I have not come to call the righteous but sinners to repentance."[17] For the Heavenly Father wishes the repentance of a sinner rather than his punishment.

This is what he taught on affection for all men: "If you love those who love you, what new thing do you do? for even the harlots do this. But I say to you, Pray for your enemies and love those who hate you and bless those who curse you and pray for those who treat you despitefully."[18]

That we should share with those in need and do nothing for [our] glory he said these things: "Give to everyone who asks and turn not away him who wishes to borrow. For if you lend to those from whom you hope to receive, what new thing do you do? Even the publicans do this.[19] But as for you, do not lay up treasures for yourselves on earth, where moth and rust corrupt and thieves break in, but lay up for yourselves treasures in heaven, where neither moth nor rust corrupts.[20] For what will it profit a man, if he should gain the whole world, but lose his own soul? Or what will he give in exchange for it?[21] Lay up treasures therefore in the heavens, where neither moth nor rust corrupts." And: "Be kind and merciful, as your Father is kind and merciful, and makes his sun to rise on sinners and righteous and wicked.[22] Do not worry as to what you will eat or what you will wear. Are you not better than the birds and the beasts? and God feeds them. So do not worry as to what you will eat or what you will wear, for your Heavenly Father knows that you need these things. But seek the Kingdom of Heaven, and all these things will be added to you.[23] For

---

17. Luke 5:32 (Matt. 9:13; Mark 2:17).

18. Matt. 5:46 (Luke 6:32; like many of us, Justin finds it easy to exchange one set of Gospel characters for another—here "harlots" for Matthew's "publicans" and Luke's "sinners"); Luke 6:27, 28.

19. Matt. 5:42 (Luke 6:34).

20. Matt. 6:19, 20.

21. Matt. 16:26 (Luke 9:25).

22. Luke 6:35, 36 (Matt. 5:45).

23. Matt. 6:25, 26, 33 (Luke 12:22, 24, 31).

where his treasure is, there is the mind of man."[24] And: "Do not do these things to be seen of men, for otherwise you have no reward with your Father who is in heaven."[25]

16. About being long-suffering and servants to all and free from anger, this is what he said: "To him that smites you on one cheek turn the other also, and to him that takes away your cloak do not deny your tunic either.[26] Whoever is angry is worthy of the fire. And whoever compels you to go one mile, follow him for two. Let your good works shine before men, that they as they see may wonder at your Father who is in heaven."[27]

For we ought not to quarrel; he has not wished us to imitate the wicked, but rather by our patience and meekness to draw all men from shame and evil desires. This we can show in the case of many who were once on your side but have turned from the ways of violence and tyranny, overcome by observing the consistent lives of their neighbors, or noting the strange patience of their injured acquaintances, or experiencing the way they did business with them.

About not swearing at all, but always speaking the truth, this is what he commanded: "Swear not at all; but let your yea be yea and your nay nay. What is more than these is from the evil one."[28]

That God only should be worshiped he showed us when he said: "The greatest commandment is: Thou shalt worship the Lord thy God and him only shalt thou serve with all thy heart and all thy strength, the Lord who made thee."[29] And: "When one came to him and said, Good Teacher, he answered and said, There is none good, except only God who made all things."[30]

Those who are found not living as he taught should know that they are not really Christians, even if his teachings are on their lips, for he said that not those who merely profess but those who also do the works will be saved. For he said this: "Not everyone who says to me, Lord, Lord, will enter into the Kingdom of Heaven, but he who does the will of my Father who is in heaven. For whoever hears me and does what I say hears him

---

24. Matt. 6:21 (Luke 12:34); Justin properly recognizes that the Greek *nous* is a fair equivalent for the Hebraic "heart."
25. Matt. 6:1.
26. Luke 6:29 (Matt. 5:39, 40).
27. Matt. 5:22, 41, 16.
28. Matt. 5:34, 37.
29. A surprising combination of Matt. 4:10 (Luke 4:8) and Mark 12:30 (Matt. 22:37).
30. Mark 10:17, 18 (Luke 18:18, 19).

who sent me. Many will say to me, Lord, Lord, did we not eat in your name and drink and do mighty works? And then I will say to them, Depart from me, you workers of iniquity.³¹ Then there will be weeping and gnashing of teeth, when the righteous will shine as the sun, but the wicked will be sent into eternal fire. For many will come in my name clothed outwardly in sheep's clothing, but being inwardly ravening wolves; by their works you will know them. Every tree that does not bring forth good fruit is cut down and thrown into the fire."³²

So we ask that you too should punish those who do not live in accordance with his teachings, but merely say that they are Christians.

17. More even than others we try to pay the taxes and assessments to those whom you appoint, as we have been taught by him. For once in his time some came to him and asked whether it were right to pay taxes to Caesar. And he answered, "Tell me, whose image is on the coin." They said, "Caesar's." And he answered them again, "Then give what is Caesar's to Caesar and what is God's to God."³³ So we worship God only, but in other matters we gladly serve you, recognizing you as emperors and rulers of men, and praying that along with your imperial power you may also be found to have a sound mind. If you pay no attention to our prayers and our frank statements about everything, it will not injure us, since we believe, or rather are firmly convinced, that every man will suffer in eternal fire in accordance with the quality of his actions, and similarly will be required to give account for the abilities which he has received from God, as Christ told us when he said, "To whom God has given more, from him more will be required."³⁴

18. Look at the end of each of the former emperors, how they died the common death of all; and if this were merely a departure into unconsciousness, that would be a piece of luck for the wicked. But since consciousness continues for all who have lived, and eternal punishment awaits, do not fail to be convinced and believe that these things are true. For the oracles of the dead and the revelations of innocent children, the invoking of [departed] human souls, the dream senders and guardians of the magi, and what is done by those who know about such things — all this should convince you that souls are still conscious after death. Then there are the men who are seized and torn by the spirits of the dead, whom

---

31. Matt. 7:21–23.
32. Matt. 13:42, 43; 7:15, 16, 19.
33. Matt. 22:20, 21 (Mark 12:14–17; Luke 20:22–25).
34. Luke 12:48.

everyone calls demon-possessed and maniacs, and the oracles so well-known among you, of Amphilochus and Dodona and Pytho, and any others of that kind, and the teaching of writers, Empedocles and Pythagoras, Plato and Socrates, and the ditch in Homer and the descent of Odysseus to visit the dead,[35] and other stories like this. Treat us at least like these; we believe in God not less than they do, but rather more, since we look forward to receiving again our own bodies, though they be dead and buried in the earth, declaring that nothing is impossible to God.

• • •

Superiority of Christianity to Paganism

21. In saying that the Word, who is the first offspring of God, was born for us without sexual union, as Jesus Christ our Teacher, and that he was crucified and died and after rising again ascended into heaven we introduce nothing new beyond [what you say of] those whom you call sons of Zeus. You know how many sons of Zeus the writers whom you honor speak of — Hermes, the hermeneutic Word and teacher of all;[36] Asclepius, who was also a healer and after being struck by lightning ascended into heaven — as did Dionysus who was torn in pieces; Heracles, who to escape his torments threw himself into the fire; the Dioscuri born of Leda and Perseus of Danaë; and Bellerophon who, though of human origin, rode on the [divine] horse Pegasus.[37] Need I mention Ariadne and those who like her are said to have been placed among the stars? and what of your deceased emperors, whom you regularly think worthy of being raised to immortality, introducing a witness who swears that he saw the cremated Caesar ascending into heaven from the funeral pyre?[38] Nor is it necessary to remind you what kind of actions are related of each of those who are called sons of Zeus, except [to point out] that they are recorded

---

35. *Odyssey* 11:25 ff.; this portion is mainly an *argumentum ad hominem* — Justin's opponents ought not to object to the idea of survival after death, since they had much of the same in their own traditions.

36. By allegorical interpretation of his mythological function as messenger of Zeus.

37. Legends cited correctly except that Bellerophon's ride on Pegasus did not take him to heaven.

38. As reported in the cases of Julius Caesar and Augustus (Suetonius, *Augustus* ch. 100); it may have become a form on later occasions.

for the benefit and instruction of students — for all consider it a fine thing to be imitators of the gods.[39] Far be it from every sound mind to entertain such a concept of the deities as that Zeus, whom they call the ruler and begetter of all, should have been a parricide and the son of a parricide, and that moved by desire of evil and shameful pleasures he descended on Ganymede and the many women whom he seduced, and that his sons after him were guilty of similar actions. But, as we said before, it was the wicked demons who did these things. We have been taught that only those who live close to God in holiness and virtue attain to immortality, and we believe that those who live unjustly and do not reform will be punished in eternal fire.

22. Now if God's Son, who is called Jesus, were only an ordinary man, he would be worthy because of his wisdom to be called Son of God, for all authors call God father of men and gods. When we say, as before, that he was begotten by God as the Word of God in a unique manner beyond ordinary birth, this should be no strange thing for you who speak of Hermes as the announcing word from God. If somebody objects that he was crucified, this is in common with the sons of Zeus, as you call them, who suffered, as previously listed. Since their fatal sufferings are narrated as not similar but different, so his unique passion should not seem to be any worse — indeed I will, as I have undertaken, show, as the argument proceeds, that he was better; for he is shown to be better by his actions. If we declare that he was born of a virgin, you should consider this something in common with Perseus. When we say that he healed the lame, the paralytic, and those born blind,[40] and raised the dead, we seem to be talking about things like those said to have been done by Asclepius.

23. In order to make this clear to you I will present the evidence that the things we say, as disciples of Christ and of the prophets who came before him, are the only truths and older than all the writers who have lived, and we ask to be accepted, not because we say the same things as they do, but because we are speaking the truth — [second] that Jesus Christ alone was really begotten as Son of God, being his Word and First-begotten and Power, and becoming man by his will he taught us these things for the reconciliation and restoration of the human race — and [third] that before he came among men as man, there were some who, on account of the already mentioned wicked demons, told through the poets as already

---

39. To be understood ironically, and so not requiring emendation.
40. Following the suggested reading *pērous*, "blind" (or "maimed") for *ponērous*, "wicked."

having occurred the myths they had invented, just as now they are responsible for the slanders and godless deeds alleged against us, of which there is neither witness nor demonstration.[41]

• • •

Christian Worship

61. How we dedicated ourselves to God when we were made new through Christ I will explain, since it might seem to be unfair if I left this out from my exposition. Those who are persuaded and believe that the things we teach and say are true, and promise that they can live accordingly, are instructed to pray and beseech God with fasting for the remission of their past sins, while we pray and fast along with them. Then they are brought by us where there is water, and are reborn by the same manner of rebirth by which we ourselves were reborn; for they are then washed in the water in the name of God the Father and Master of all, and of our Saviour Jesus Christ, and of the Holy Spirit. For Christ said, "Unless you are born again you will not enter into the Kingdom of heaven."[42] Now it is clear to all that those who have once come into being cannot enter the wombs of those who bore them. But as I quoted before, it was said through the prophet Isaiah how those who have sinned and repent shall escape from their sins. He said this: "Wash yourselves, be clean, take away wickednesses from your souls, learn to do good, give judgment for the orphan and defend the cause of the widow, and come and let us reason together, says the Lord. And though your sins be as scarlet, I will make them as white as wool, and though they be as crimson, I will make them as white as snow. If you will not listen to me, the sword will devour you; for the mouth of the Lord has spoken these things."[43] And we learned from the apostles this reason for this [rite]. At our first birth we were born of necessity without our knowledge, from moist seed, by the intercourse of our parents with each other, and grew up in bad habits and wicked

---

41. As this section stands, Justin distinguished between mythmakers and poets, which seems unduly complex, and several emendations have been suggested that would identify them; it may be that after referring to the demons Justin continues as if they were the subject of the sentence, which is in any case clumsily phrased.
42. John 3:3, 4.
43. Isa. 1:16–20.

behavior. So that we should not remain children of necessity and ignorance, but [become sons] of free choice and knowledge, and obtain remission of the sins we have already committed,[44] there is named at the water, over him who has chosen to be born again and has repented of his sinful acts, the name of God the Father and Master of all. Those who lead to the washing the one who is to be washed call on [God by] this term only.[45] For no one may give a proper name to the ineffable God, and if anyone should dare to say that there is one, he is hopelessly insane.[46] This washing is called illumination, since those who learn these things are illumined within. The illuminand is also washed in the name of Jesus Christ, who was crucified under Pontius Pilate, and in the name of the Holy Spirit, who through the prophets foretold everything about Jesus.

• • •

65. We, however, after thus washing the one who has been convinced and signified his assent, lead him to those who are called brethren, where they are assembled. They then earnestly offer common prayers for themselves and the one who has been illuminated and all others everywhere, that we may be made worthy, having learned the truth, to be found in deed good citizens and keepers of what is commanded, so that we may be saved with eternal salvation. On finishing the prayers we greet each other with a kiss. Then bread and a cup of water and mixed wine are brought to the president of the brethren and he, taking them, sends up praise and glory to the Father of the universe through the name of the Son and of the Holy Spirit, and offers thanksgiving at some length that we have been deemed worthy to receive these things from him. When he has finished the prayers and the thanksgiving,[47] the whole congregation present[48] as-

---

44. The second birth is also connected with moisture, but is otherwise contrasted with the first in all respects.

45. Thirlby and later editors emend the plurals in this sentence to the singular, unnecessarily — Justin is writing from the point of view of the individual convert, but slips into the plural here, either because the occasion was one regularly repeated, or (more likely) because he was accustomed to group baptisms with a number of officiants, and not to the medieval and modern custom of baptism of a single candidate by a single minister.

46. Justin was aware that the Old Testament divine name was used for magical purposes (as *Iao* and the like), and hence his vigorous condemnation of a practice he considers not only wrong (as all Jews would) but impossible.

47. Or, one could equally well say "the Eucharistic prayer."

48. Literally, "all the people present," i.e., those present as being a gathering of the people of God (*laos*), the laity in the positive sense; cf. Neh. 8:5, 6.

sents, saying, "Amen." "Amen" in the Hebrew language means, "So be it." When the president has given thanks and the whole congregation has assented, those whom we call deacons give to each of those present a portion of the consecrated[49] bread and wine and water, and they take it to the absent.

66. This food we call Eucharist, of which no one is allowed to partake except one who believes that the things we teach are true, and has received the washing for forgiveness of sins and for rebirth, and who lives as Christ handed down to us. For we do not receive these things as common bread or common drink; but as Jesus Christ our Saviour being incarnate by God's word took flesh and blood for our salvation, so also we have been taught that the food consecrated by the word of prayer which comes from him, from which our flesh and blood are nourished by transformation, is the flesh and blood of that incarnate Jesus.[50] For the apostles in the memoirs composed by them, which are called Gospels, thus handed down what was commanded them: that Jesus, taking bread and having given thanks, said, "Do this for my memorial, this is my body"; and likewise taking the cup and giving thanks he said, "This is my blood"; and gave it to them alone.[51] This also the wicked demons in imitation handed down as something to be done in the mysteries of Mithra; for bread and a cup of water are brought out in their secret rites of initiation, with certain invocations which you either know or can learn.

67. After these [services] we constantly remind each other of these things. Those who have more come to the aid of those who lack, and we are constantly together. Over all that we receive we bless the Maker of all things through his Son Jesus Christ and through the Holy Spirit.[52] And on

---

49. Literally, "eucharistized," i.e., blessed by the solemn prayer of thanksgiving, in accordance with the Jewish form of prayer, in which offering thanks to God for his gifts also blesses them for human use (cf. Mark 14:22, 23 and 1 Tim. 4:4, 5); but *eucharisteo* as a transitive verb in this connection seems to be Christian and Gentile.

50. "Eucharistized food," see note 49; "by the word of prayer which comes from him" (*di' euchēs logou tou par' autou*) refers to the pattern of the Eucharistic prayer as instituted by Christ—*para* for the source of a tradition also—the *logos* of baptism learned from the apostles, which probably means its rationale, but may mean the threefold formula.

51. Mark 14:22–24 and 1 Cor. 11:23–25; quoted as from the Gospels, but perhaps representing in brief what Justin was used to hearing recited at the celebration of the Eucharist.

52. Not merely a general statement, but a reference to the custom, binding on Christians as on Jews, of giving thanks to God before receiving God's gifts, which makes every meal a sacred act.

the day called Sunday there is a meeting in one place of those who live in cities or the country, and the memoirs of the apostles or the writings of the prophets are read as long as time permits. When the reader has finished, the president in a discourse urges and invites [us] to the imitation of these noble things. Then we all stand up together and offer prayers. And, as said before, when we have finished the prayer, bread is brought, and wine and water, and the president similarly sends up prayers and thanksgivings to the best of his ability, and the congregation assents, saying the Amen; the distribution, and reception of the consecrated [elements] by each one, takes place and they are sent to the absent by the deacons. Those who prosper, and who so wish, contribute, each one as much as he chooses to.[53] What is collected is deposited with the president, and he takes care of orphans and widows, and those who are in want on account of sickness or any other cause, and those who are in bonds, and the strangers who are sojourners among [us], and, briefly, he is the protector of all those in need. We all hold this common gathering on Sunday, since it is the first day, on which God transforming darkness and matter made the universe, and Jesus Christ our Saviour rose from the dead on the same day. For they crucified him on the day before Saturday, and on the day after Saturday,[54] he appeared to his apostles and disciples and taught them these things which I have passed on to you also for your serious consideration.

Conclusion

68. If what we say seems to you reasonable and true, treat it with respect — if it seems foolish to you, then despise us as foolish creatures and do not decree the death penalty, as against enemies, for those who do no wrong. I have said before that you will not escape the future judgment of God if you continue unjust, while we will cry out, What God desires, let that be done.[55]

---

53. The emphasis on the purely voluntary character of these contributions may have a legal purpose, to stress that the unlicensed Christian societies did not profess to collect dues (cf. Tertullian, *Apol.* 39:5).

54. Justin may be avoiding using the term "day of Aphrodite" for Friday, or referring to the Sabbath and its preparation-day (*paraskeuē*) without using Jewish technical terms; he certainly wishes to disclaim, without dignifying with formal mention, any idea that the Christians were worshipers of the sun, as Jews were sometimes supposed to be devotees of Saturn (Cronus).

55. A familiar quotation from Plato, *Crito* 43 D — used probably with reference both to the *Deo Gratias* with which Christians accepted martyrdom and to their readiness for the final judgment.

12. *Plea Regarding the Christians*
(c. 177)

ATHENAGORAS

This late second-century apology by the Athenian Athenagoras, who calls himself a philosopher and a Christian, follows the usual style of an open letter or "supplication" to the emperor(s). Much of the document (c. 177) is a lengthy defense against the charge of atheism, including an argument that the Greek gods are nothing more than sublimated humans.[1]

Athenagoras attempts to "explain" the Trinity in Platonic terms. He also responds to two other common charges made against Christians, those of incest and cannibalism. His writing provides valuable insights into the life and values of the early Christian community.

To the Emperors Marcus Aurelius Antoninus and Lucius Aurelius Commodus, conquerors of Armenia and Sarmatia, and — what is more important — philosophers:

SOURCE: Cyril C. Richardson, ed., *Early Christian Fathers*, vol. 1 of *The Library of Christian Classics* (Philadelphia: Westminster Press, 1953). Used by permission of Westminster John Knox Press.

1. The word "plea" in the title is sometimes wrongly translated (as by the Latin) "legation" or "embassy." While this is the original meaning of the Greek word *presbeia*, it is used here in the derived sense of a "plea" or "apology."

Preface

1. In your Empire, Your Most Excellent Majesties, different peoples observe different laws and customs; and no one is hindered by law or fear of punishment from devotion to his ancestral ways, even if they are ridiculous.

• • •

But you have not cared for us who are called Christians in this way. Although we do no wrong, but, as we shall show, are of all men most religiously and rightly disposed toward God and your Empire, you allow us to be harassed, plundered, and persecuted, the mob making war on us only because of our name. We venture, therefore to state our case before you. From what we have to say you will gather that we suffer unjustly and contrary to all law and reason. Hence we ask you to devise some measures to prevent our being the victims of false accusers.

The injury we suffer from our persecutors does not concern our property or our civil rights or anything of less importance. For we hold these things in contempt, although they appear weighty to the crowd. We have learned not only not to return blow for blow, nor to sue those who plunder and rob us, but to those who smite us on one cheek to offer the other also, and to those who take away our coat to give our overcoat as well. But when we have given up our property, they plot against our bodies and souls, pouring upon us a multitude of accusations which have not the slightest foundation, but which are the stock in trade of gossips and the like.

2. If, indeed, anyone can convict us of wrongdoing, be it trifling or more serious, we do not beg off punishment, but are prepared to pay the penalty however cruel and unpitying. But if the accusation goes no farther than a name — and it is clear that up to today the tales about us rest only on popular and uncritical rumor, and not a single Christian has been convicted of wrongdoing — it is your duty, illustrious, kind, and most learned Emperors, to relieve us of these calumnies by law.

• • •

It does not befit your sense of justice that others, accused of wrongdoing, are not punished before they have been convicted, while with us the mere name is of more weight than legal proof. Our judges, moreover, do not inquire if the accused has committed any wrong, but let loose against the name as if *it* were a crime. But no name in and of itself is good or bad. It is by reason of the wicked or good actions associated with names that they are bad or good. You know all that better than anyone, seeing you are versed in philosophy and thoroughly cultured.

That is why those who are tried before you, though arraigned on the most serious charges, take courage. For they know that you will examine their life and not be influenced by names if they mean nothing, or by accusations if they are false. Hence they receive a sentence of condemnation on a par with one of acquittal. We claim for ourselves, therefore, the same treatment as others. We should not be hated and punished because we are called Christians, for what has a name to do with our being criminals? Rather should we be tried on charges brought against us, and either acquitted on our disproving them or punished on our being convicted as wicked men, not because of a name (for no Christian is wicked unless he is a hypocrite), but because of a crime.

It is in this way, we know, that philosophers are judged. None of them before the trial is viewed by the judge as good or bad because of his system or profession, but he is punished if he is found guilty. (No stigma attaches to philosophy on that account, for he is a bad man for not being a philosopher lawfully, and philosophy is not responsible.) On the other hand, he is acquitted if he disproves the charges. Let the same procedure be used in our case. Let the life of those who are accused be examined, and let the name be free from all reproach.

• • •

Statement of the Charges

3. Three charges are brought against us: atheism, Thyestean feasts,[2] and Oedipean intercourse.[3] If these are true, spare no class; proceed against our crimes; destroy us utterly with our wives and children, if anyone lives like a beast. Beasts, indeed, do not attack their own kind.

---

2. I.e., cannibalistic feasts, from the legendary banquet where Atreus, in order to avenge the rape of his wife by his brother Thyestes, slew the latter's children and served them to him.

3. I.e., incest, from the legend of Oedipus Rex, who unwittingly killed his father and married his mother.

Nor for mere wantonness do they have intercourse, but by nature's law and only at the season of procreation. They recognize, too, those who come to their aid. If, then, anyone is more savage than brutes, what punishment shall we not think it fitting for him to suffer for such crimes?

But if these charges are inventions and unfounded slanders, they arise from the fact that it is natural for vice to oppose virtue and it is in accord with God's law for contraries to war against each other. You yourselves, moreover, are witness to the fact that we are guilty of none of these things, since it is only the confession of a name that you forbid. It remains for you, then, to examine our lives and teachings, our loyalty and obedience to you, to your house, and to the Empire. By doing so you will concede to us no more than you grant to our persecutors. And we shall triumph over them, giving up our very lives for the truth without any hesitation.

Reply to the Charge of Atheism

4. We are of course not atheists (I will meet the charges one by one) — and I hope it does not sound too silly to answer such an allegation. Rightly, indeed, did the Athenians accuse Diagoras[4] of atheism, since he not only divulged the Orphic doctrine as well as the mysteries of Eleusis and of the Cabiri and chopped up a statue of Heracles to boil his turnips, but he proclaimed outrightly that God simply did not exist. In our case, however, is it not mad to charge us with atheism, when we distinguish God from matter, and show that matter is one thing and God another, and that there is a vast difference between them? For the divine is uncreated and eternal, grasped only by pure mind and intelligence, while matter is created and perishable.

If we shared the views of Diagoras when we have so many good reasons to adore God — the order, harmony, greatness, color, form, and arrangement of the world — we should rightly be charged with impiety and there would be due cause to persecute us. But since our teaching affirms one God who made the universe, being himself uncreated (for what exists does not come into being, only what does not exist), and who made all things through his Word, on two scores, then, we are treated unreasonably — by being slandered and by being persecuted.

• • •

---

4. Melian poet of the fifth century B.C.

Proof from Scripture

9. Were we satisfied with such reasoning, one would think our doctrine was human. But prophetic voices confirm our arguments. Seeing how learned and well-informed you are, I suppose that you are not unaware of Moses, Isaiah, Jeremiah, and the rest of the prophets. Under the impulse of the divine Spirit and raised above their own thoughts, they proclaimed the things with which they were inspired. For the Spirit used them just as a flute player blows on a flute. What, then, did they say? "The Lord is our God: no other can be compared with him."[5] Or again, "I am God the first and the last; and apart from me there is no god."[6] Similarly: "Before me there was no other god, and after me there shall be none. I am God, and there is none besides me."[7] Then, concerning his greatness: "Heaven is my throne and earth is my footstool. What kind of house will you build for me, or in what place shall I rest?"[8] But I leave it to you, when you come on their books, to examine their prophecies in more detail, so that you will have good reason to dispel the false accusations brought against us.

The Trinity

10. I have sufficiently shown that we are not atheists since we acknowledge one God, who is uncreated, eternal, invisible, impassible, incomprehensible, illimitable. He is grasped only by mind and intelligence, and surrounded by light, beauty, spirit, and indescribable power. By him the universe was created through his Word, was set in order, and is held together. [I say "his Word"], for we also think that God has a Son.

Let no one think it stupid for me to say that God has a Son. For we do not think of God the Father or of the Son in the way of the poets, who weave their myths by showing that gods are no better than men. But the Son of God is his Word in idea and in actuality; for by him and through him all things were made, the Father and the Son being one. And since the Son is in the Father and the Father in the Son by the unity and power of the Spirit, the Son of God is the mind and Word of the Father.

But if, owing to your sharp intelligence, it occurs to you to inquire

---

5. Ex. 20:2, 3.
6. Isa. 44:6.
7. Isa. 43:10, 11.
8. Isa. 66:1.

further what is meant by the Son, I shall briefly explain. He is the first offspring of the Father. I do not mean that he was created, for, since God is eternal mind, he had his Word within himself from the beginning, being eternally wise.[9] Rather did the Son come forth from God to give form and actuality to all material things, which essentially have a sort of formless nature and inert quality, the heavier particles being mixed up with the lighter. The prophetic Spirit agrees with this opinion when he says, "The Lord created me as the first of his ways, for his works."[10]

Indeed we say that the Holy Spirit himself, who inspires those who utter prophecies, is an effluence from God, flowing from him and returning like a ray of the sun. Who, then, would not be astonished to hear those called atheists who admit God the Father, God the Son, and the Holy Spirit, and who teach their unity in power and their distinction in rank? Nor is our theology confined to these points. We affirm, too, a crowd of angels and ministers, whom God, the maker and creator of the world, appointed to their several tasks through his Word. He gave them charge over the good order of the universe, over the elements, the heavens, the world, and all it contains.

Christian Moral Teaching

11. Do not be surprised that I go into detail about our teaching. I give a full report to prevent your being carried away by popular and irrational opinion, and so that you may know the truth. Moreover, by showing that the teachings themselves, to which we are attached, are not human, but were declared and taught by God, we can persuade you not to hold us for atheists. What, then, are these teachings in which we are reared? "I say to you, love your enemies, bless those who curse you, pray for those who persecute you, that you may be sons of your Father in heaven, who makes his sun to shine on the evil and on the good, and sends his rain on the just and on the unjust."[11]

Although what I have said has raised a loud clamor,[12] permit me here to proceed freely, since I am making my defense to emperors who are philosophers. Who of those who analyze syllogisms, resolve ambiguities,

---

9. *Logikos,* corresponding to *Logos,* "Word."
10. Prov. 8:22.
11. Matt. 5:44, 45; Luke 6:27, 28.
12. Following a rhetorical device, Athenagoras imagines that his speech has been met by hostile gibes.

explain etymologies, or [teach] homonyms, synonyms, predicates, axioms, and what the subject is and what the predicate — who of them do not promise to make their disciples happy through these and similar disciplines? And yet who of them have so purified their own hearts as to love their enemies instead of hating them; instead of upbraiding those who first insult them (which is certainly more usual), to bless them; and to pray for those who plot against them? On the contrary, they ever persist in delving into the evil mysteries of their sophistry, ever desirous of working some harm, making skill in oratory rather than proof by deeds their business. With us, on the contrary, you will find unlettered people, tradesmen and old women, who, though unable to express in words the advantages of our teaching, demonstrate by acts the value of their principles. For they do not rehearse speeches, but evidence good deeds. When struck, they do not strike back; when robbed, they do not sue; to those who ask, they give, and they love their neighbors as themselves.

12. If we did not think that a God ruled over the human race, would we live in such purity? The idea is impossible. But since we are persuaded that we must give an account of all our life here to God who made us and the world, we adopt a temperate, generous, and despised way of life. For we think that, even if we lose our lives, we shall suffer here no evil to be compared with the reward we shall receive from the great Judge for a gentle, generous, and modest life.

Plato, indeed, has said that Minos and Rhadamanthus[13] will judge and punish the wicked; but we say that, even if a man were Minos or Rhadamanthus or their father, he could not escape God's judgment.

Then there are those who think that life is this: "Eat and drink, for tomorrow we shall die."[14] They view death as a deep sleep and a forgetting — "sleep and death, twin brothers"[15] [as the saying goes]. And men think them religious! But there are others who reckon this present life of very little value. They are guided by this alone — to know the true God and his Word, to know the unity of the Father with the Son, the fellowship of the Father with the Son, what the Spirit is, what unity exists between these three, the Spirit, the Son, and the Father, and what is their distinction in unity. These it is who know that the life for which we look is far better than can be told, if we arrive at it pure from all wrongdoing. These it is whose charity extends to the point of loving not only their friends, for,

---

13. Sons of Zeus, and just men who judged the dead.
14. Isa. 22:13.
15. *Iliad* 16:672.

the Scripture says, "If you love those who love you, and lend to those who lend to you, what credit is it to you?"[16] Since we are such and live this way to escape condemnation, can anyone doubt that we are religious?

These points, however, are trifles from a great store, a few taken from many, lest we should trouble you further. For those who test honey and whey judge by a taste if the whole is good.

The Problem of Pagan Sacrifices

13. Since many of those who charge us with atheism do not have the vaguest idea of God, being unversed in, and ignorant of, physics and theology, they measure religion by the observance of sacrifices, and charge us with not having the same gods as the cities. Heed what I have to say, Your Majesties, on both these counts. And first about our not sacrificing.

The creator and Father of the universe does not need blood or the smell of burnt offerings or the fragrance of flowers or incense. He himself is perfect fragrance. He lacks nothing and has need of nothing. But the greatest sacrifice in his eyes is for us to realize who stretched out the heavens in a sphere, who set the earth in the center, who gathered the water into seas and separated the light from darkness, who adorned the sky with the stars and made the earth bring forth all kinds of seed, who made the animals and fashioned man. When, therefore, we recognize God the creator of the universe, who preserves it and watches over it with the wisdom and skill he does, and lift up holy hands to him, what need has he then of a hecatomb?

> "It is with sacrifices and humble prayer,
> With libation and burnt offering that men implore [the gods]
> And turn [their wrath], when any has offended or sinned."[17]

What need have I of burnt offerings, when God does not need them? Rather is it needful to present a bloodless sacrifice, to offer a "spiritual worship."[18]

• • •

---

16. Luke 6:32, 34.
17. *Iliad* 9:499–501.
18. Rom. 12:1, or "reasonable service" (KJV).

The Christian Views of Demons

We speak of God, of the Son, his Word, and of the Holy Spirit; and we say that the Father, the Son, and the Spirit are united in power.[19] For the Son is the intelligence, reason, and wisdom of the Father, and the Spirit is an effluence, as light from fire. In the same way we recognize that there are other powers which surround matter and pervade it. Of these there is one in particular which is hostile to God. We do not mean that there is anything which is opposed to God in the way that Empedocles opposes strife to love and night to day in the phenomenal world. For even if anything did manage to set itself up against God, it would cease to exist. It would fall to pieces by the power and might of God. Rather do we mean that the spirit which inhabits matter is opposed to God's goodness, which is an essential quality with him and coexists with him as color is inseparable from a body and cannot exist without it. I do not mean it is a part of him, but it is a necessary accompaniment which is united and fused with him as red is with fire and blue is with the sky. This opposing spirit was created by God, just as the other angels were created by him and entrusted with administering matter and its forms.

For God made these angels to exercise providence over the things he had set in order. Thus, while he reserved for himself the universal and general providence over everything, the angels exercise a particular providence over the parts entrusted to them.

Conclusion on the Charge of Atheism

Thus, if the myths about the gods, which the populace and the poets repeat, are false, to reverence them is superfluous. For these gods do not exist if the tales about them are untrue. If on the other hand, all these stories about the gods are true — their births, loves, murders, thefts, castrations, thunderbolts — then they no longer exist, since they have ceased to be, just as they originally had no being before they were created. And what good reason is there to believe some of the tales and to disbelieve others, since the poets told them in order to idealize their heroes? For surely those who so magnified them by their stories that they were taken for gods would not have invented their sufferings.

---

19. Text and meaning doubtful.

That, therefore, we are not atheists, since we worship God the creator of this universe, and his Word, I have proved as best I can, even if I have not done the subject justice.

Two Further Charges

31. Our accusers have made up the further charges against us of impious feasts and intercourse. They do this to convince themselves that they have grounds for hating us. They imagine, moreover, that by fear they will either draw us away from our present mode of life or else, by the enormity of the accusations, render our princes harsh and implacable. But this is a foolish approach toward those who realize that of old, and not merely in our time, wickedness has a habit of warring against virtue, in obedience to some divine law and principle. Thus, for instance, Pythagoras with three hundred companions was put to the flames. Heraclitus and Democritus were banished, the one from the city of Ephesus, the other, charged with insanity, from Abdera. Finally, the Athenians condemned Socrates to death. And just as the virtue of these men suffered no whit from the opinions of the mob, so our uprightness of life is in no way obscured by the reckless calumnies of some persons. For we are in good standing with God.

Nonetheless, I will meet these charges too, although I am very confident that I have made my case by what I have already said. You, who are more intelligent than others, know that those who faithfully regulate their lives by reference to God, so that each of us stands before him blameless and irreproachable, will not entertain even the thought of the slightest sin. Were we convinced that this life is the only one, then we might be suspected of sinning, by being enslaved to flesh and blood and by becoming subject to gain and lust. But since we realize that God is a witness day and night of our thoughts and our speech, and that by being pure light he can see into our very hearts, we are convinced that when we depart this present life we shall live another. It will be better than this one, heavenly, not earthly. We shall live close to God and with God, our souls steadfast and free from passion. Even if we have flesh, it will not seem so: we shall be heavenly spirits. Or else, if we fall along with the rest, we shall enter on a worse life and one in flames. For God did not make us like sheep and oxen, a bywork to perish and be done away with. In the light of this it is not likely that we would be purposely wicked, and deliver ourselves up to the great Judge to be punished.

The Charge of Incest

32. It is nothing surprising that our accusers should invent the same tales about us that they tell of their gods. They present their sufferings as mysteries; and, had they wanted to judge shameless and indiscriminate intercourse as a frightful thing, they should have hated Zeus. For he had children from his mother, Rhea, and his daughter Kore, and married his own sister. Or else, they should have detested Orpheus, who invented these tales, because he made Zeus even more unholy and wicked than Thyestes. For the latter had intercourse with his daughter in pursuance of an oracle, and because he wanted to gain a throne and avenge himself.

But we, on the contrary, are so far from viewing such crimes with indifference[20] that we are not even allowed to indulge a lustful glance. For, says the Scripture, "He who looks at a woman lustfully, has already committed adultery in his heart."[21] We may look only on those things for which God created the eyes to be our light. For us a lustful glance is adultery, the eyes being made for other purposes. How, then, in the light of this and of the fact that we shall be called to account for even our thoughts, can it be doubted that we exercise self-control?

We do not have to reckon with human laws, which a wicked man may evade. (At the outset I assured you, Your Majesties, that our teaching came from God.) Rather do we have a law which requires us to have right relations with ourselves and with our neighbors.[22] Hence, according to their age, we think of some as sons and daughters. Others we regard as brothers and sisters, while we revere those who are older as we would fathers and mothers. We feel it a matter of great importance that those, whom we thus think of as brothers and sisters and so on, should keep their bodies undefiled and uncorrupted. For the Scripture says again, "If anyone kisses a second time because he found it enjoyable . . ."[23] Thus the kiss, or rather the religious salutation,[24] should be very carefully guarded. For if it is defiled by the slightest evil thought, it excludes us from eternal life.

33. Having, therefore, the hope of eternal life, we despise the enjoy-

---

20. Text and meaning doubtful.
21. Matt. 5:28.
22. The text here is corrupt and obscure.
23. The source is unknown and the conclusion is wanting.
24. The reference is probably to the kiss of peace in the liturgy.

ments of the present, even the pleasures of the soul. According to our laws, each of us thinks of the woman he has married as his wife only for the purpose of bearing children. For as the farmer casts his seed on the soil and awaits the harvest without sowing over it, so we limit the pleasure of intercourse to bearing children.

You would, indeed, find many among us, both men and women, who have grown to old age unmarried, in the hope of being closer to God. If, then, to remain virgins and eunuchs brings us closer to God, while to indulge in wrong thoughts and passions drives us from him, we have all the more reason to avoid those acts, the very thought of which we flee from. For we center our attention not on the skill of making speeches but on the proof and lessons of actions. We hold that a man should either remain as he is born or else marry only once. For a second marriage is a veiled adultery. The Scripture says, "Whoever puts away his wife and marries another, commits adultery."[25] Thus a man is forbidden both to put her away whose virginity he has ended, and to marry again. He who severs himself from his first wife, even if she is dead, is an adulterer in disguise. He resists the hand of God, for in the beginning God created one man and one woman. But the adulterer breaks the fellowship based on the union of flesh with flesh for sexual intercourse.[26]

34. Since we are such (and why should I speak of such degrading things?), our situation resembles that of the proverb, "The harlot reproves the chaste." Our accusers have set up a market for fornication, have established infamous houses of every sort of shameful pleasure for the young, and do not even spare the males, "males committing shocking acts with males."[27] In all sorts of ways they outrage those with the more graceful and handsome bodies. They dishonor God's splendid creation, for beauty on earth is not self-made, but has been created by the hand and mind of God. It is these people who revile us with the very things they are conscious of in themselves and which they attribute to their gods. They boast of them indeed, as noble acts and worthy of the gods. Adulterers and corrupters of boys, they insult eunuchs and those once married. They even live like fish. For they gulp down whatever comes their way. The stronger chase the weaker. That means they outrage human flesh, even while the laws are in force which you and your forefathers carefully enacted in view of all that is right. To these very laws they do such

---

25. Matt. 19:9; Mark 10:11.
26. Text and meaning doubtful.
27. Rom. 1:27.

violence that the governors appointed by you over the provinces are not able to keep order. We, however, cannot refrain from turning the cheek when we are struck, nor from blessing when we are reviled. For it is not enough to be just — justice consisting in returning blows — but we have to be generous and to put up with evil.

The Charge of Cannibalism

35. Since this is our character, what man of sound judgment would say that we are murderers? For you cannot eat human flesh until you have killed someone. If their first charge against us is a fiction, so is the second. For if anyone were to ask them if they had seen what they affirm, none of them would be so shameless as to say he had.

Moreover, we have slaves: some of us more, some fewer. We cannot hide anything from them; yet not one of them has made up such tall stories against us. Since they know that we cannot endure to see a man being put to death even justly, who of them would charge us with murder or cannibalism? Who among our accusers[28] is not eager to witness contests of gladiators and wild beasts, especially those organized by you? But we see little difference between watching a man being put to death and killing him. So we have given up such spectacles. How can we commit murder when we will not look at it, lest we should contract the stain of guilt? What reason would we have to commit murder when we say that women who induce abortions are murderers, and will have to give account of it to God? For the same person would not regard the fetus in the womb as a living thing and therefore an object of God's care, and at the same time slay it, once it had come to life. Nor would he refuse to expose infants, on the ground that those who expose them are murderers of children, and at the same time do away with the child he has reared. But we are altogether consistent in our conduct. We obey reason and do not override it.

Relevance of the Doctrine of the Resurrection

36. What man, moreover, who is convinced of the resurrection would make himself into a tomb for bodies that will rise again? The same persons would surely not believe that our bodies will rise again and then eat them as if there were no resurrection. They would not think that the

---

28. Text and meaning doubtful.

earth will give back its dead and then imagine that it will fail to demand those entombed in them.

On the contrary, those who deny they will have to give account of the present life, be it wicked or good, who reject the resurrection and who count on the soul's perishing along with the body and, so to say, flickering out, are likely to stop at no outrage. But those who are convinced that God will look into everything and that the body which has aided the soul in its unreasonable lusts and passions will be punished along with it, they have no good reason to commit even the slightest sin.

But suppose someone thinks it sheer nonsense that the body which has rotted, decomposed, and been reduced to nothing, should again be put together. Those who do not believe this would be wrong in accusing us of wickedness. They should rather accuse us of folly. For we do not harm anyone by having mistaken opinions.

It would be out of place here to show that we are not alone in believing bodies will rise again. Many of the philosophers have taught this. But we do not want to seem to introduce matters beyond the scope of our present task. We will not discuss the intelligible and the sensible and their natures. Nor the fact that the incorporeal is prior to the corporeal, and the intelligible precedes the sensible. It is true, of course, that we first experience the sensible; but the corporeal owes its origin to the incorporeal by being combined with the intelligible. The sensible similarly owes its origin to the intelligible.[29] Even according to Pythagoras and Plato the dissolution of the body does not prevent it from being reconstructed with the very elements of which it originally consisted.

Conclusion

37. But we must defer our discussion of the resurrection. Now that I have disposed of the charges brought against us and shown that we are religious, kindly, and gentle in spirit, I beg you, grant your royal approval to my request. For in every possible way, by nature as well as education, you are kind, temperate, generous, and worthy of the imperium. And who, indeed, are more justified in getting what they ask than we? For we pray for your authority, asking that you may, as is most just, continue the royal succession, son from father, and receive such increase and extension of your realm that all men will eventually be your subjects. This is to our interest too, "so that we may lead a quiet and peaceable life,"[30] and be ready to do all we are commanded.

---

29. Text and meaning doubtful.
30. 1 Tim. 2:2.

Visions of Church Unity

13. Letter to the Philadelphians
(c. 113)

IGNATIUS OF ANTIOCH

Early in the second century, Roman soldiers arrested Ignatius, the bishop of Antioch, during a brief persecution of Syrian Christians by Rome. They sent Ignatius to Rome under guard to stand trial. Ignatius died in the coliseum sometime before the end of Emperor Trajan's reign in 117.

During his long triumphant journey to martyrdom, delegations from Christian communities visited Ignatius and sought his counsel. Returning home, they carried messages from him to his friend Polycarp, bishop of Smyrna, and to various churches. Seven letters survived, four of them written in Smyrna. Ignatius wrote the Letter to the Philadelphians *(c. 113) during his stay with Christians in Troas.*

Ignatius calls himself a "man utterly devoted to unity." He is appalled when he learns that two opposing schismatic movements are threatening

---

SOURCE: Cyril C. Richardson, ed., *Early Christian Fathers,* vol. 1 of *The Library of Christian Classics* (Philadelphia: Westminster Press, 1953). Used by permission of Westminster John Knox Press.

to split the churches. In Philadelphia, a group of legalists is demanding devotion to the Jewish law, something the apostle Paul has condemned already. At Smyrna, Docetic teachers are dividing the church with their denial of the true humanity of Jesus.

Speaking with the authority of a man on his way to martyrdom, Ignatius implores the churches to heal their divisions by cultivating a common loyalty to the local bishop. For Ignatius, the bishop is primus inter pares *("first among equals") in the leadership of the local church (the* mon-episcopate*). The bishop is an almost mystical, living symbol of Christ's presence in the church and the arbiter of sound Christian faith and practice: "Where the bishop is present, there let the congregation gather, just as where Jesus Christ is, there is the catholic Church."*

Greetings in the blood of Jesus Christ from Ignatius, the "God-inspired," to the church of God the Father and the Lord Jesus Christ, which is at Philadelphia in Asia—an object of the divine mercy and firmly knit in godly unity. Yours is a deep, abiding joy in the Passion of our Lord; and by his overflowing mercy you are thoroughly convinced of his resurrection. You are the very personification of eternal and perpetual joy. This is especially true if you are at one with the bishop, and with the presbyters and deacons, who are on his side[1] and who have been appointed by the will of Jesus Christ. By his Holy Spirit and in accordance with his own will he validated their appointment.

I well realize that this bishop of yours does not owe his ministry to his own efforts or to men. Nor is it to flatter his vanity that he holds this office which serves the common good. Rather does he owe it to the love of God the Father and the Lord Jesus Christ. I have been struck by his charming manner. By being silent he can do more than those who chatter. For he is in tune with the commandments as a harp is with its strings.[2] For this reason I bless his godly mind, recognizing its virtue and perfection, and the way he lives in altogether godly composure, free from fitfulness and anger.

Since you are children of the light of truth, flee from schism and false doctrine. Where the Shepherd is, there follow like sheep.[3] For there are

---

1. The phrase seems to imply a schism, and that there were some presbyters and deacons who resisted the bishop.
2. The meaning is not altogether clear.
3. Cf. John 10:7 ff.

many specious wolves who, by means of wicked pleasures, capture those who run God's race. In the face of your unity, however, they will not have a chance. Keep away from bad pasturage. Jesus Christ does not cultivate it since the Father did not plant it.[4] Not that I found schism among you — rather had you been sifted.[5] As many as are God's and Jesus Christ's, they are on the bishop's side; and as many as repent and enter the unity of the church, they shall be God's, and thus they shall live in Jesus Christ's way. Make no mistake, my brothers, if anyone joins a schismatic he will not inherit God's Kingdom.[6] If anyone walks in the way of heresy, he is out of sympathy with the Passion.

Be careful, then, to observe a single Eucharist.[7] For there is one flesh of our Lord, Jesus Christ, and one cup of his blood that makes *us* one, and one altar,[8] just as there is one bishop along with the presbytery and the deacons, my fellow slaves. In that way whatever you do is in line with God's will.

My brothers, in my abounding love for you I am overjoyed to put you on your guard — though it is not I, but Jesus Christ. Being a prisoner for his cause makes me the more fearful that I am still far from being perfect.[9] Yet your prayers to God will make me perfect so that I may gain that fate which I have mercifully been allotted, by taking refuge in the "Gospel," as in Jesus' flesh, and in the "Apostles," as in the presbytery of the Church.[10] And the "Prophets," let us love them too,[11] because they anticipated the gospel in their preaching and hoped for and awaited Him, and were saved by believing on him. Thus they were in Jesus Christ's unity. Saints they were, and we should love and admire them, seeing that Jesus Christ vouched for them and they form a real part of the gospel of our common hope.

---

4. Cf. Matt. 15:13.

5. Literally, "Rather did I find filtering." The idea is that the church had gone through a purge, the heretical element being filtered or sifted out from the genuine Christians.

6. Cf. 1 Cor. 6:9, 10.

7. The implication is that the group of Judaizers held separate Eucharists, perhaps on Saturday instead of Sunday (cf. Mag. 9:1).

8. The term "altar" implies that the Eucharistic meal had a sacrificial meaning.

9. I.e., proximity to martyrdom makes him afraid that his courage will fail him at the crucial hour.

10. A possible reference to the "Gospel" and the "Apostles" as the two divisions of the Christian writings.

11. This is an answer to the criticism of the Judaizers that Ignatius was disparaging the Old Testament.

Now, if anyone preaches Judaism to you,[12] pay no attention to him. For it is better to hear about Christianity from one of the circumcision than Judaism from a Gentile.[13] If both, moreover, fail to talk about Jesus Christ, they are to me tombstones and graves of the dead,[14] on which only human names are inscribed. Flee, then, the wicked tricks and snares of the prince of this world, lest his suggestions wear you down, and you waver in your love. Rather, meet together, all of you, with a single heart. I thank my God that in my relations with you I have nothing to be ashamed of. No one can brag secretly or openly that I was the slightest burden to anyone. I trust, too, that none of those I talked to will need to take what I say as a criticism of them.

Some there may be who wanted in a human way to mislead me, but the Spirit is not misled, seeing it comes from God. For "it knows whence it comes and whither it goes,"[15] and exposes what is secret.[16] When I was with you I cried out, raising my voice — it was God's voice[17] — "Pay heed to the bishop, the presbytery, and the deacons." Some, it is true, suspected that I spoke thus because I had been told in advance that some of you were schismatics. But I swear by Him for whose cause I am a prisoner, that from no human channels did I learn this. It was the Spirit that kept on preaching in these words: "Do nothing apart from the bishop; keep your bodies as if they were God's temple; value unity; flee schism; imitate Jesus Christ as he imitated his Father."

I, then, was doing all I could, as a man utterly devoted to unity. Where there is schism and bad feeling, God has no place. The Lord forgives all who repent — if, that is, their repentance brings them into God's unity and to the bishop's council. I put my confidence in the grace of Jesus Christ. He will release you from all your chains.[18]

I urge you, do not do things in cliques, but act as Christ's disciples. When I heard some people saying, "If I don't find it in the original documents, I don't believe it in the gospel," I answered them, "But it *is*

---

12. It may be noted that a similar Judaizing movement in Philadelphia is attacked in Rev. 3:9.

13. Circumcision does not seem to have been included in this Judaizing movement as it had been in Galatia (Gal. 6:12).

14. Cf. Matt. 23:27.

15. Cf. John 3:8.

16. Cf. 1 Cor. 2:10, 11.

17. An instance of the "God-inspired's" prophetic utterances.

18. Cf. Isa. 58:6.

written there." They retorted, "That's just the question."[19] To my mind it is Jesus Christ who is the original documents. The inviolable archives are his cross and death and his resurrection and the faith that came by him. It is by these things and through your prayers that I want to be justified.

Priests are a fine thing, but better still is the High Priest[20] who was entrusted with the Holy of Holies. He alone was entrusted with God's secrets. He is the door to the Father.[21] Through it there enter Abraham, Isaac, and Jacob, the prophets and apostles and the Church. All these find their place in God's unity. But there is something special about the gospel—I mean the coming of the Saviour, our Lord Jesus Christ, his Passion and resurrection. The beloved prophets announced his coming; but the gospel is the crowning achievement forever. All these things, taken together, have their value, provided you hold the faith in love.

Thanks to your prayers and to the love that you have for me in Christ Jesus, news has reached me that the church at Antioch in Syria is at peace.[22] Consequently, it would be a nice thing for you, as a church of God, to elect a deacon to go there on a mission, as God's representative, and at a formal service to congratulate them and glorify the Name. He who is privileged to perform such a ministry will enjoy the blessing of Jesus Christ, and you too will win glory. If you really want to do this for God's honor, it is not impossible, just as some of the churches in the vicinity have already sent bishops; others presbyters and deacons.[23]

Now about Philo, the deacon from Cilicia. He is well spoken of and right now he is helping me in God's cause, along with Rheus Agathopus—a choice person—who followed me from Syria and so has said

---

19. The point of the argument is that the Old Testament is the final court of appeal. It constitutes the "original documents" which validate the gospel. The New Testament, as a book of canonical authority, is still in process of formation. The Bible of the primitive Church is the Septuagint. Hence a point of doctrine turns on the interpretation of Old Testament texts which are viewed as prophetically pointing to Christianity. When, however, an impasse is reached in the argument, Ignatius makes the tradition of the gospel the final authority. He thus opens himself to the criticism of disparaging the Old Testament.

20. I.e., Jesus Christ. This reflects the theme elaborated in The Epistle to the Hebrews, but Ignatius is not necessarily dependent on it. It must have been a Christian commonplace.

21. Cf. John 10:7, 9.

22. The first indication that the persecution in Antioch, which led to Ignatius' condemnation, has blown over. The news seems to have reached him at Troas.

23. An indication of the deep sense of solidarity that bound together the widely scattered Christian congregations.

good-by to this present life. They speak well of you, and I thank God on your account that you welcomed them, as the Lord does you. I hope that those who slighted them will be redeemed by Jesus Christ's grace. The brothers in Troas send their love and greetings. It is from there that I am sending this letter to you by Burrhus.[24] The Ephesians and Smyrnaeans have done me the honor of sending him to be with me. They in turn will be honored by Jesus Christ, on whom they have set their hope with body, soul, spirit, faith, love, and a single mind. Farewell in Christ Jesus, our common Hope.

---

24. The Greek is ambiguous. Burrhus might be either postman or secretary.

14. Outside the Church, There Is No Salvation
From *Letter 73*
(c. 256)

CYPRIAN

In the spring of 251, Cyprian convened a council of North African bishops at Carthage. The purpose of the council was to reconcile the pastoral concern of the clergy for the "lapsed," with the demands of church discipline. Cyprian began with his statement "On the problem of the lapsed" (see vol. 1:81–83) and an early version of his tract, On Catholic Unity. *The African churches avoided schism and preserved their unity largely through Cyprian's efforts.*

The church in Rome was not as fortunate. Pope Cornelius precipitated a major schism because many Christian leaders thought he was soft on the "lapsed." As a gesture of reconciliation, his successor, Pope Stephen (254–257) admitted the validity of schismatic baptism if the baptism was performed rightly with water in the triune name.

The North African church leaders objected. In 256 they held a second council in Carthage, claiming the right to dissent. Cyprian had worked

---

SOURCE: S. L. Greenslade, ed., *Early Latin Theology.* vol. 5 of *The Library of Christian Classics* (Philadelphia: Westminster Press, 1956). Used by permission of Westminster John Knox Press.

hard to preserve unity in the church. Only Pope Stephen's death in that year and Cyprian's martyrdom in the arena of Carthage two years later prevented a more serious rift between Carthage and Rome.

Cyprian addresses Letter 73 to Jubaianus, a fellow bishop, who had asked about the validity of schismatic baptism. Referring to the two North African councils of 251 and 256, Cyprian insists that the church must bind baptism inseparably to the true apostolic faith of the universal church. The church must administer baptism in the name of the "full and united trinity." Heresy and schism, by their very nature, separate persons from the faith and the fellowship of the apostles. Cyprian clearly states that "Outside the church, there is no salvation."

Cyprian to his brother, Jubaianus, greeting.

1. You write to me, dearest brother, desiring me to tell you what I feel about the baptism of heretics who, though they are beyond the pale and outside the Church, claim for themselves something which is not within their right or power. I cannot hold this to be valid or legitimate, for we all know that they cannot lawfully possess it. As I have already expressed my views on this matter in my letters, to save time I am sending you a copy of them, showing you both what was decided at a Council which many of us attended, and also what I afterwards wrote to our colleague Quintus in reply to his questions on the subject. And now we have met again, seventy-one bishops of the province of Africa and of Numidia, and we have confirmed our previous decision, laying it down that there is *one* baptism, that of the catholic Church, and that in consequence we do not "rebaptize," but baptize, all those who, coming as they do from adulterous and unhallowed water, have to be washed and sanctified by the true water of salvation.

• • •

20. How absurd and perverse it is if, when the heretics themselves repudiate and abandon their former error or crime and acknowledge the truth of the Church, we ourselves mutilate the laws and sacraments of that very truth, telling those who come to us in penitence that they have already obtained the remission of sins — and that when they confess that they have sinned and come expressly to receive the pardon of the Church! Therefore, my dear brother, it is our duty to hold fast to the faith and truth of the catholic Church and teach it, and by means of every precept of the

Gospels and the apostles, to demonstrate the character of the divine order and unity.

21. Can the power of baptism be greater and stronger than the confession which confesses Christ before men, and the suffering by which a man is baptized in his own blood? Yet not even this baptism can profit the heretic who, though he has confessed Christ, is put to death outside the Church.[1] Unless the patrons and protectors of the heretics proclaim them martyrs when they have been put to death for a false confession of Christ, unless, contrary to the testimony of the apostle (who said that, though they were burned and killed, it profited them nothing) they assign to them the martyr's crown and glory! But if not even the baptism of a public confession and of blood can profit a heretic for salvation, since there is no salvation outside the Church,[2] it can certainly not profit him to be baptized in a lair and den of robbers with the infection of polluted water, where, so far from putting off his old sins, he still loads himself with fresh and graver ones.

Baptism cannot be common to us and the heretics, for we do not have God the Father in common, nor Christ the Son, nor the Holy Ghost, nor the faith, nor the Church itself. Therefore those who come from heresy to the Church ought to be baptized, so that, being made ready for the kingdom of God by divine regeneration in the lawful and true and only baptism of the holy Church, they may be born of both sacraments, as it is written: "Except a man be born of water and the Spirit, he cannot enter into the kingdom of God."[3]

22. Referring to this passage and imagining that they can make void the truth of the Gospel teaching by human arguments, some bring up against us the case of catechumens. If a catechumen is arrested for the confession of the name and put to death before he is baptized in the Church, does he lose the hope of salvation and the reward of confession simply because he was not first born again of water? Such champions and supporters of heresy have to learn, first, that those catechumens hold the faith and truth of the Church complete, and go out from the camp of God to fight against the devil with a full and sincere knowledge of God the Father and Christ and the Holy Ghost, and, secondly, that they are not in fact deprived of the sacrament of baptism, in that they are baptized with

---

1. Cf. *De Unit.*, 14.
2. *Salus extra ecclesiam non est,* the original form of the Cyprianic maxim.
3. John 3:5; *utroque sacramento,* water and the Spirit, the two parts of baptism, not baptism and eucharist.

the most glorious and most precious baptism of blood, of which the Lord himself said: "I have another baptism to be baptized with."[4] That those who are baptized in their own blood and sanctified by suffering are made perfect and obtain the grace which God promised is made plain by the Lord himself in the Gospel, when he speaks to the thief who believed in him and confessed him in the midst of his sufferings, and promises that he will be with him in Paradise. Consequently, we who preside over the faith and truth must not deceive and cheat those who come to the faith and truth and do penance and ask for the remission of their sins. We must correct them and reform them and instruct them with heavenly teachings for the kingdom of heaven.

23. It is objected: "What, then, will happen to those who in times past came from heresy to the Church and were received without baptism?" The Lord in his mercy is able to grant them indulgence and not separate from the privileges of his Church those who were received into the Church in good faith and have fallen asleep in the Church. None the less, we are not to go on making a mistake because it has been made once. It befits wise and God-fearing men rather to obey the truth gladly and instantly when it is laid open and made visible to them, than to struggle persistently and obstinately against brethren and bishops on behalf of heretics.

24. Let no one suppose that if heretics are faced with baptism they stumble at it as though a second baptism is being talked of, and so are held back from coming to the Church. On the contrary, when the truth is pointed out and put convincingly to them, they are the more impressed with the necessity of coming. If they see it decided and settled by our own judgment that the baptism which they receive in heresy is to be counted rightful and legitimate, they will think that they rightfully and legitimately possess the Church as well, and all the privileges of the Church. Then there will be no reason for them to come to us, for, having baptism, they may be supposed to have all the rest. When, however, they come to see that there is no baptism outside, and that no remission of sins can be given outside the Church, they hurry to us all the more eagerly and promptly, and beg for the gifts and privileges of mother Church, being assured that they can by no means attain to the true grace of the divine promises unless they come first to the true Church. The heretics will not refuse to be baptized among us with the true and lawful baptism of the Church, when they learn from us how those who had already been bap-

---

4. Luke 12:50, *aliud,* another, is not in the normal Greek texts.

tized with John's baptism were baptized also by Paul, as we read in the Acts of the Apostles.[5]

25. Now some of our own people are upholding heretical baptism. They shrink from the odium of what seems like rebaptism. They count it a crime to baptize after the enemies of God. Yet we find that those whom John had baptized were baptized, and John was reckoned greater than all the prophets, John was filled with divine grace while he was yet in his mother's womb, John was upheld by the spirit and power of Elijah,[6] John was not the adversary of the Lord but his forerunner and herald, John did not merely announce the Lord in words before his coming, but pointed him out for men to see, John baptized the very Christ through whom all others are baptized.

If it is argued that a heretic can acquire the right to baptize by baptizing first, then baptism will belong not to those who are in lawful possession of it, but to those who seize it. Then, since baptism and Church are absolutely inseparable, the first to seize baptism will have seized the Church as well, and *you* begin to be the heretic to him, you who have been forestalled and find yourself left behind, you who, by yielding and throwing in your hand, have relinquished the right which you had received. How dangerous it is to give up one's right and power in the things of God is plain from holy Scripture. In Genesis, Esau lost his birthright and could not afterwards regain what he had once yielded.[7]

26. I have answered you briefly, my dear brother, and given you my poor best. I do not lay down the law to anyone. I do not condemn any bishop beforehand for doing what he thinks best. He has the right to use his own judgment freely.[8] So far as lies in me, I do not contend with my own colleagues and fellow-bishops for the sake of heretics.[9] I keep the harmony of God and the peace of the Lord with them, remembering the words of the Apostle: "If any man thinketh to be contentious, we have no

---

5. Acts 19:1–7.

6. Luke 1:15, 17.

7. Gen. 27, cf. Heb. 12:16–17, which brings out the spiritual danger. Birthright is *primatus,* illustrating the element of temporal priority in this word, even as applied to Peter.

8. This passage is very important for Cyprian's idea of episcopal rights. Cf. *Sententiae,* Cyprian's opening words: "It remains that we should each of us express his opinion, not judging anyone or excommunicating anyone if he thinks differently. For none of us sets himself up as bishop of bishops (cf. Tert., *Pud.,* I) or compels his colleagues to obey him by tyrannical terrorizing, since every bishop has freedom and power to use his own judgment, and cannot be judged by another."

9. A hit at Stephen?

such custom, neither the Church of God."[10] Charity of heart, the honour of our college, the bond of faith, the harmony of the episcopate, these I maintain in patience and gentleness. Accordingly, I have just written, as well as my modest talent allowed, with the permission and inspiration of the Lord, a small book on *The Benefit of Patience*,[11] which I am sending you in token of our mutual affection. Farewell, dearest brother.

---

10. 1 Cor. 11:16.
11. *De Bono Patientiae,* extant, modeled on Tertullian's *De Patientia.*

15. The Church as the Body of Christ
From *Commentary on John XI, II (On John 17:20–21)*
(c. 430)

CYRIL OF ALEXANDRIA

Cyril (c. 375–444) became bishop, or patriarch of Alexandria, in 412. He succeeded his uncle Theophilus, who had had a hand in some of the intrigues that had led to the banishment of Chrysostom from Constantinople (see vol. 1:282–85). Cyril's episcopate was a curious mix of hardball politics and theological clarity. After a monk named Nestorius became patriarch of Constantinople in 428, these two Christian leaders in rival cities became involved in a nasty theological controversy. In 431, the Council of Ephesus condemned Nestorius.

At issue was the use of the term theotokos *("Godbearer") to describe the virgin Mary. Nestorius condemned the use of the word. He argued that it was impossible for Mary to wrap the divine "logos" (Word/Reason) in swaddling clothes. At best, one might call her "Christ-bearer."*

However, orthodox Christianity insisted that the "logos" became flesh. Although Cyril may have envied the imperial power of the bishop of Constantinople, he also was genuinely concerned about Christian doctrine. He accused Nestorius of denying the true incarnation (the be-

---

SOURCE: Maurice Wiles and Mark Santer, eds., *Documents in Early Christian Thought* (Cambridge: Cambridge University Press, 1979). © Cambridge University Press 1975. Used by permission of Cambridge University Press.

coming flesh) of the divine "logos." He insisted that if the Word did not become like us, then we cannot unite with the Word or with one another.

In Cyril's commentary on John 17:20–21, he writes that the unity of the persons in the Trinity is like the union of believers. *"He [Christ] made a sort of union in himself of two things which are utterly distinct and remote from one another in nature, and thereby made humans to share and participate in divine nature."* Where Christ and his church are one sacramentally, the body Christ may be broken; yet it cannot be divided.

I do not wish to dwell on these things more than the present context warrants. But I cannot refrain from reiterating this much. Christ is taking the substantial unity which he has with the Father and the Father with him as an image or model of that indestructible love, harmony and unity which is recognized where there is real and deep concord. He thus expresses his will that in the strength of the holy and consubstantial Trinity, we too should be as it were commingled with one another; so that the whole body of the Church may be seen as one — as moving in Christ, through the union of two peoples, towards the constitution of a perfect single whole. This is what Paul says: "For he is our peace, who has made the two one, and in his own body of flesh and blood has broken down the dividing wall of hostility, by abolishing in his flesh the law of commandments and ordinances, that he might create in himself one new man in place of the two, so making peace, and might reconcile both to God in one body through the cross, thereby bringing the hostility to an end" [Eph. 2:14–16]. And this purpose is actually accomplished when those who put their trust in Christ are of one soul with one another and receive as it were a single heart; and that comes from the total affinity which true religion gives, from the obedience which is implicit in faith and from the mind that is set on the good life.

I think that what we have said so far is not only appropriate but also requisite. However the meaning of the passage, and in particular the words of the Saviour, "As thou, Father, art in me, and I in thee, so also may they be in us" [John 17:21], compel us to enter the realm of more profound doctrines; we need therefore to weigh our words with particular care. We have already emphasized at an earlier stage that the oneness of mind and soul which constitutes the unity of believers ought to be an imitative expression of the pattern of divine unity, the substantial identity and perfect interweaving of the holy Trinity. Now we are concerned to show further that this unity, by which we are bound to one another and all of us to God, is also a natural unity; and so far as our unity with one another is concerned, we shall not exclude unity even at the bodily level — even though we are distinct in virtue of our bodily separation, and each of us can as it were retreat within the frontier of his own individual existence. For no one would suggest that Peter was Paul or Paul was Peter because he recognized them both to be one with the kind of unity which Christ supplies.

Well then, in the case of the Father and the Son — and of course the Holy Spirit — the unity we acknowledge is a natural unity; in the holy Trinity it is a single godhead in which we believe and which we worship. So let us again think carefully about the way in which we too are one in body and spirit in relation to one another and also to God. The Only-begotten has shined on us from the very substance of God the Father; having in his own nature the fullness of the one who begat him, he became flesh, as Scripture says [John 1:14], and mixed himself as it were with our nature by virtue of an inexpressible conjunction and union with this earthly body. So he who is God by nature was called — indeed actually became — a heavenly man (not a god-bearing man as he is called by some who do not correctly understand the profundity of this mystery).[1] So he was God and man in one. He made a sort of union in himself of two things which are utterly distinct and remote from one another in nature, and thereby made man to share and participate in divine nature.

The participation in the Holy Spirit and his abiding presence which began through and in Christ has also been transmitted to us. When he appeared at our level, that is as man, he was the first to be anointed and sanctified, even though in his nature, as he comes from the Father, he is God. With his own Spirit he sanctified his own temple and the whole creation that was brought into being through him, for which the act of sanctification was appropriate. Thus the divine plan was effected in Christ as a beginning of the road whereby we too might receive a share both in the Holy Spirit and in union with God. For we all are sanctified in him in the way that we have just described.

We too then are to be combined and commingled into a unity with God and with one another, in spite of our observable separation as individuals distinct in soul and body. To this end the Only-begotten has found a means devised by the Father's own will and wisdom. With one body, namely his own, he blesses those who believe in him as they partake of the holy mysteries and makes them members of the same body with himself and

---

1. Cyril is referring to teachers of the Antiochene school.

with one another. Who could detach or exclude from a natural unity with one another those who are bound into unity with Christ by the one holy body? For if we all partake of one loaf, then we are all made one body [see 1 Cor. 10:17]; for Christ cannot be divided. And so the Church is also called body of Christ and we individually are limbs, as Paul teaches [see 1 Cor. 12:27]. For we are all united to the one Christ through the holy body, since we receive him who is one and indivisible in our own bodies. Our obligation then as limbs of his is to him rather than to ourselves. The Saviour's role is that of head and the Church is the remainder of the body, made up of the various limbs. This is shown by the words of Paul: "We are no longer to be children, tossed to and fro and carried about with every wind of doctrine, by the cunning of men, by their craftiness in deceitful wiles. Rather, speaking the truth in love we are to grow up in every way into him who is the head, into Christ, from whom the whole body, joined and knit together by every joint with which it is supplied, when each part is working properly, makes bodily growth and upbuilds itself in love" [Eph. 4:14–16]. Paul again testifies that we who come to share in Christ's holy flesh also enjoy a union of a bodily kind with him when he speaks of the mystery of religion "which was not made known to the sons of men in other generations as it has now been revealed to his holy apostles and prophets by the Spirit; that is, how the gentiles are fellow heirs, members of the same body, and partakers of the promise in Christ Jesus" [Eph. 3:5–6]. So if we are all one body with one another in Christ, not simply with one another but clearly also with him who is in us by virtue of his own flesh, then surely we are all of us already one both in one another and in Christ. For Christ is the bond of unity, being at once both God and man.

As to our unity in the Spirit, we can follow the same line of reasoning and say that as we all receive one and the same Spirit, namely the Holy Spirit, we are all in a manner conjoined to one another and to God. As individuals we are many but Christ makes the Spirit of his Father, which is his own Spirit, dwell in each one of us. That Spirit is one and indivisible, and it brings into unity our spirits which are cut off from unity with one another at the level of being by their individual identities, and through his own agency reveals us all as one in him. Thus as the power of the holy flesh makes one body of those in whom it is present, in just the same way the "indwelling" in us all of the one indivisible Spirit makes of us a spiritual unity. So the divine Paul addresses us again: "Be forbearing to one another in love, and eager to maintain the unity of the Spirit in the bond of peace. There is one body and one Spirit, just as you were called to the one hope that belongs to your call, one Lord, one faith, one baptism, one God and Father of all, who is above all and through all and in all" [Eph. 4:2–6]. If the one Spirit makes his dwelling in us, then the God and Father of all will be in us, drawing those who have a share in the Spirit into unity — a unity with one another and with him. The fact that we are made one with the Holy Spirit though sharing in him is also clear from the following consideration. If once we turn our back on the life of the natural man and let the laws of the Spirit control our lives, then the rest must follow; we have as it were said "no" to our own life and adopted the other-worldly mould of the Spirit who is so intimately linked with us; we are as it were being changed into another nature, no longer mere men but also sons of God with the title of heavenly men, in that we have been made partakers of the divine nature.

So we are all one in Father, Son and Holy Spirit, one in identity of attitude (to recall what we said at the beginning), one in conformity to the ways of piety, in participation in the holy flesh of Christ and in participation in the one Holy Spirit, as we have said.

16. The Church as the Company of the Elect
From *On Baptism V*
(c. 400)

AUGUSTINE OF HIPPO

In 395, when Augustine (354–c. 430) became bishop of Hippo, a small coastal town near Carthage, a major schism involving the Donatists divided the Christian community in North Africa. Named after Donatus, the schismatic bishop of Carthage (d. 355), Donatists held an extremely rigorous view that the church is the gathered community of the pure, who after baptism remain free from mortal sin. Donatists venerated the martyrs and excluded the "lapsed" (those whose loyalty had wavered in times of persecution).

Donatism became a popular movement and a serious threat to the church in North Africa. Donatism included a politically revolutionary group known as the Circumcellions. In dramatic fashion, Circumcellions tried to initiate radical change in the social and political order by challenging irresponsible banking practices. Optatus, a Donatist himself, complained to the imperial authorities that "no creditor was free to press his claim . . . if there was any delay in obeying their

SOURCE: Maurice Wiles and Mark Santer, eds., *Documents in Early Christian Thought* (Cambridge: Cambridge University Press, 1979). © Cambridge University Press 1975. Used by permission of Cambridge University Press.

demands, a sudden host of madmen flew to the place . . . soon everyone lost what was owing to them."

In a bit of symbolic mischief, the Circumcellions waylaid the chariots of the rich and forced the masters to run ahead of their chariots *"in servile fashion, in front of their own slaves, seated in their lord's place. By judgment and command of these outlaws, the condition of masters and slaves was completely reversed."* In this way, although the Circumcellions divided the Donatist ranks, they unintentionally helped keep the church more moderate.

Augustine, bishop of Hippo, wanted to uphold law and order, but he was even more interested in refuting Donatist extremists on theological grounds. The basic differences between the Donatists and Augustine revolved around the doctrines of the church and sacraments.

Against Donatus, Augustine held that the moral rectitude of Christians could not be an essential mark of the church, nor could the unworthiness of a priest invalidate the sacraments. Augustine distinguished between the "validity" and "efficacy" of sacraments: Baptism in the triune name was valid, even if performed by schismatics or heretics of other denominations. Yet, said Augustine, it became efficacious, only when the believer joined the true communion of saints.

In his treatise On Baptism, Augustine defines the true church as the community of the elect. No empirical way to judge who belongs "in or out" of the church exists. "God knows those who are his." The true church is the sacramental community of those whom God has called from eternity, the "ark of salvation." It is possible to be a baptized member of the universal church, yet outside the ark (i.e., not saved). It is not possible to be baptized and in the ark (i.e., saved) while being "in one's heart" outside the church universal.

---

38. The description of the Church in the Song of Songs — "A locked garden is my sister, my bride; a sealed fountain, a well of living water, an orchard with choice fruits" [Song of Songs 4:12–13] — must be interpreted as referring to the holy and the righteous; these words cannot refer to the greedy or to the fraudulent, to robbers or usurers, to drunkards or to the envious. These men admittedly share the same baptism with the righteous, but they do not share the same love with them. All this, as I have often said before, is to be found fully set out in the letters of Cyprian himself; it is from these that we have learned it and from these that we teach it. I should like to be told how these people, whom Cyprian de-

scribes as having renounced the world in word alone and not in deed and yet being within, have got into the locked garden and the sealed fountain. If they too are there, they too must be the bride of Christ. But is this what the one without spot or wrinkle is really like? Is the beautiful dove besmirched in some of her members [see Eph. 5:27; Song of Songs 2:14]? Or are they the thorns in the midst of which she is like a lily, as the same song declares [Song of Songs 2:2]? She is a closed garden and a sealed fountain precisely in so far as she is a lily — namely in the persons of those righteous people who are Jews secretly by circumcision of the heart [see Rom. 2:29] (for "all the beauty of the king's daughter is within" [Ps. 45:12]), who moreover constitute the fixed number of the saints predestined before the foundation of the world. The multitude of the thorns, whether their separation be concealed or open, lies outside, beyond this number. "I have proclaimed and spoken," he says, "they are multiplied beyond number" [Ps. 40:5]. It is this number of the righteous, those called according to his will [Rom. 8:28] (and referred to in the text: "The Lord knows those who are his" [2 Tim. 2:19]) who are the locked garden, the sealed fountain, the well of living water, the orchard of choice fruits.

Of this number some live spiritual lives and follow the supreme path of love; if anyone is overtaken in a fault, they instruct him in a spirit of gentleness and look to themselves lest they also be tempted; and if they themselves happen to be overtaken in a fault, that disposition of love receives a set-back but is not extinguished; it rises up, burns strongly once again and resumes its original course. They have learnt to say: "My soul became drowsy through weariness; strengthen me in your words" [Ps. 119:28]. And if there is anything where their knowledge is amiss, God will reveal it to those who remain in the burning ardour of love and do not break the bond of peace.

Then there are some who are still living their lives at the carnal or natural level. They vigorously pursue their own advancement. So that in time they may become ready for the food suited to spiritual men, they are nourished on the milk of the holy mysteries. Things which are obviously corrupt practices even in the eyes of people at large they avoid by reason of their fear of God. They take great care and trouble to diminish by degrees their love of earthly and temporal things. They give careful study to the rule of faith and hold firmly to it. If they do deviate from it, they are soon put right by the authority of what is catholic; but because of their carnal understanding they are liable to find all sorts of extraordinary ideas in its words.

Then there are yet others in that number who are still living evil lives, and as yet still belong to heretical bodies or even to gentile superstitions. But in their case too, "God knows those who are his." For in that ineffable foreknowledge of God, there are many who seem to be outside who are really inside, and many who seem to be inside who are really outside.

All these people — those, if I may so put it, who are inwardly and secretly within — go to make up the locked garden, the sealed fountain, the well of living water, the orchard of choice fruits. And of the gifts which heaven bestows on them some are theirs exclusively (such as unceasing love in this age and in the age to come life eternal) while others are shared with evil and wicked men (including, among all the other gifts, the holy mysteries).

39. The next point which we must consider — the ark built and captained by Noah — will now be even easier and more straightforward to deal with. Peter says: "In Noah's ark a few, that is eight persons, were saved by water. Baptism now saves you in a similar way, not as a removal of dirt from the body but as the appeal of a good conscience" [1 Pet. 3:20–21]. So then those who have been baptized but whose renunciation of the world is a matter of words only and not of deeds may appear outwardly to men to be within the fold of catholic unity, but how can they belong to the mystery of the ark of which Peter speaks when they lack "the appeal of a good conscience"? How can those who make a false use of holy baptism and continue to the very end of their lives in profligate and dissolute ways be "saved by water," even though they may seem to be within? How, too, can those whom Cyprian himself records as having been simply admitted into the Church with the baptism that they had received among the heretics not be "saved by water"? It is the same unity of the ark that saves them and there no one is saved except by water. For Cyprian himself says: "The Lord in his mercy is able to grant forgiveness to those who were simply received into the Church and then died in the Church and not to hold them back from the gifts that belong to his Church."[1] If they are not "by water," how can they be "in the ark"? If they are not "in the ark," how can they be "in the Church"? So if they are in the Church, they must be in the ark and if they are in the ark, they must be by water.

It must therefore be the case that some of those who are baptized outside are by the foreknowledge of God classed as really having been baptized inside; for it is here that the water has begun to be of saving help to them. (After all one cannot speak of their being saved in the ark without

---

1. Cyprian, *Letter 73*, 23. Augustine establishes as a rule what Cyprian admitted as an exception.

their being saved by water.) And on the other hand some of those who looked as if they had been baptized inside are by that same foreknowledge of God classed as really having been baptized outside. Those who misuse baptism die by water and that can only happen to someone who is outside the ark.

It is then perfectly clear that when we speak of people being "inside" or "outside" the Church, we need to think of it as a matter of the heart and not of the body. Everyone who is "inside" in heart is saved in the unity of the ark by the same water, by which everyone who is "outside" in heart (whether or not he is "outside" in body) perishes as an enemy of that unity. It is not some different water but the same water which saves those who are in the ark and destroys those who are outside it; in the same way it is not some other baptism but the same baptism by which the good catholic is saved and the bad catholic or the heretic perishes.

PART II

Giving Account of the Faith (Christ)

Within the Christian community, as Christianity spread and generations passed, the church had to teach the "tradition of the faith" to new converts and youth who needed to understand what Christians believed and why. This education in the faith became the primary task of exegetical or biblical theology.

Although philosophical theology, namely the encounter of the apologists with classicism, continued, Christianity could not enter the mainstream of Hellenistic culture until it was able to give a coherent account of the biblical faith in the conceptual language of the period. It was important for Christian theologians to maintain their dialogue with the "cultured despisers" of Christianity in order to support the church's massive missionary effort. Making the "case for Christ" to skeptics and unbelievers was the task of apologetics and/or speculative theologians.

Biblical and speculative theology centers on the question of Jesus Christ. From the second to the fifth centuries, many of the early trinitarian and christological controversies among Christians provided a "heady mix" that (1) set the parameters of theological debate for centuries and (2) focused the church's thinking on the person and work of Jesus Christ. The inherent tension between nurture and teaching grounded in the Bible and apologetic concerns for relevance shaped Christian theological debate. Tertullian, one of the first "biblical" theologians, named the tension with his famous quip, "What has Athens to do with Jerusalem?" His understandings of scripture stand in interesting contrast with Origen's views (see vol. 1:41–47 and 48–54).

Antioch and Alexandria

After the Christian victory over classicism, new tensions between Athens and Jerusalem surfaced in a bitter quarrel between the great theological schools of Alexandria in Egypt, the intellectual center of the ancient world; and Antioch in Asia Minor, one of the oldest and most venerable Christian communities.

Questions raised by Celsus about the Christian savior persisted into the third century. Thus, in his treatise "On the Incarnation," the Antiochian monk and bishop, Theodore of Mopsuestia (d. 428), makes a strong plea for the humanity of Christ on scriptural grounds. His commentary on Galatians 4:24 calls for a "literal" reading of the scriptures, rejecting Origen's allegorical method as "nonsense" (see vol. 1:157–65). However, Origen's earlier "Dialogue with Heraclides" illustrates how difficult it is to "explain" scriptural references to the divine/human nature of Christ literally without denying one or the other attribute (see vol. 1:166–74).

In his *Catechetical Orations,* Gregory of Nyssa (d. 394) tried to combine the biblical doctrine of creation with prevailing classical understandings of spirituality (see vol. 1:175–83). A strong supporter of the Nicene faith, he drew the line dividing creature from creator just below the Trinity. Yet at the same time, he endorsed the conflicting classical doctrine of a preexistent human soul. Like Origen before him, Gregory "resolved" any tension between biblical faith and classical spirituality by postulating a prior creation of a "spiritual realm" before God's creation of the physical world.

When read only as the minutes of an arcane colloquy of ancient theologians, these issues sound trivial. In fact, however, for Christians the outcome of this encounter with classicism, particularly in its gnostic or docetic expressions, was a matter of vital significance. The central affirmation of the Christian faith that God was in Jesus Christ reconciling the world (and its people) to the divine was at stake. "Christians" among the gnostic sects challenged central biblical affirmations about creation, the incarnation (literally, the enfleshment), the cross, the resurrection of Christ, and ultimately the promise of personal salvation by grace. Christian gnostics agreed that (1) the process of creation was a decline into particularity; (2) the human soul was immortal, yet held in bondage by the body; (3) the creation and the fall of humankind were simultaneous if not identical; (4) Christ, the divine messenger, came to rescue the human soul from its bondage to bodily existence; (5) salvation required a secret knowledge (*gnosis*) passed on by Christ to the apostles, which in most cases involved ritual purification and rigid asceticism; (6) the goal of salvation was the loss of individuality or the return of the soul into the divine abyss; and (7) Jesus of Nazareth was the facilitator, not the cause of salvation. Jesus was the bodily receptacle of Christ, the divine aeon, but the man Jesus and the aeon Christ could not be a single entity. For instance, Jesus' words "My God, my God, why hast thou forsaken me" (Mark 15:4) were said to be evidence that the Christ ("my God") departed from the dying Jesus at the cross. Much of gnostic teaching was difficult to reconcile with the biblical doctrine of personal salvation.

Augustine of Hippo

By the end of the third century, the threat of gnosticism compelled Christians to reaffirm their faith in basic doctrines grounded in a biblical faith, such as the goodness of God's creation, the fall of humankind, the doctrine of salvation, and above all the "ecumenical" understanding of the person and work of Jesus Christ. Two major developments shaped the later church: (1) the work of Augustine of Hippo (354–430), whose "theology of grace" laid a foundation for a Western theology that could deal with these matters, including that of classical Protestantism; and (2) the development of creedal formulations rooted in the baptismal creed of Hippolytus (c. 200) and leading to the *textus receptus,* the current version of the Apostles' Creed.

Augustine of Hippo was thirty-two years old when he finally decided to become a Christian. He was also a single parent with a son born of a long-term "relationship"; a professor of rhetoric at Carthage, Rome, and Milan; and a former Manichean (a position that considers all physical substance evil), who had embraced Platonic thought. Last but not least, Augustine was a philosopher in the primary sense of the term; a seeker of wisdom whose "heart was restless, until it rested in God."

Augustine's decision for Christianity came about in part because of an encounter with Ambrose of Milan, who convinced him that being a Christian does not necessarily require the sacrifice of one's intellect. Ambrose, the bishop of Milan, was known for his outstanding preaching and his political activism. In a famous instance, he had forced the emperor Theodosius to do public penance for a gross abuse of imperial power. Following his baptism by Ambrose, Augustine returned to his native North Africa, intent on dedicating his life to study and meditation at a monastic retreat he had established at Cassiciacum.

Such a future was not to be. On a visit to Hippo, a sleepy harbor town west of Carthage, the local Christian congregation asked Augustine to serve as presbyter (391) and eventually as their bishop (395). Augustine remained the pastor and bishop of Hippo until his death in 430, in spite of his rapidly growing reputation as the foremost theologian of the Latin church.

A major classical scholar in his own right, Augustine of Hippo brought Athens to Jerusalem by combining the conceptual language of classical Platonic thought with the biblical substance of Paul's theology of the cross. His work moved Western theology beyond its preoccupation with the inner workings of the Trinity to the more concrete concerns of the human condition and Christ's work of salvation. Augustine's realism is key to his enduring influence.

We can link the development of Augustine's thought to a series of controversies: (1) Out of his own struggle against "concupiscence" or sensuality, Augustine insisted that it was impossible for humankind to achieve moral perfection. (2) In his rejection of the dualism of the Manicheans, who considered all physical things evil, denounced human procreation, and mortified the body to gain a spiritual state of being, Augustine observed that if everyone followed the Manicheans' advice, the human race would soon disappear. (3) Speaking out against the Donatists, Christian fundamentalists of the day, whose moral rigor and charismatic zeal attracted many converts in North Africa, Augustine insisted that grace not works led to salvation. (4) Writing to refute Pelagius, an Irish monk, who upheld a theology of good works, Augustine found a perfect foil against which he could test and develop his own theology of grace.

The overwhelming gift of divine grace is the theme that runs through all of Augustine's life and work. In his *Confessions,* it is easy to see how his theology grows out of his personal struggle for moral perfection and the cataclysmic impact of the barbarian invasions on the Empire. For him, limitations on the human will were the stuff of daily experience. The need for divine grace was evident in the lives of individuals and in the terrors of history. As Augustine saw it, the Manicheans made grace impossible by denying the goodness of God's creation. The Pelagians made grace unnecessary by insisting that humans were free to obey God's law. And the Donatists misused the proper means of grace.

Augustine used the biblical story of Adam and Eve in the garden of

Eden to make the case that evil is always present in the world and that it is deeply rooted in the human desire "to be like God." God created human nature and saw that it was good. As a "superadded gift" of grace, God gave to humans the power of "ordinate love," to love God and all beings as each ought to be loved. When, by free choice, our first parents sinned against God, they lost their freedom and God's grace. What remained was nature and a chain of causes that actually led away from God.

Augustine notes that in the third chapter of Genesis, Adam blames Eve, Eve blames the snake, and the angel at the gate of Eden marks broken relationships. However, Augustine does not regard sin as simple sensuality or moral turpitude. The root cause of sin is a disturbance of the order of love. In their "inordinate love" of the world, human beings are alienated from God, the ground of their being. As a pastor and bishop, he knew that the tragic undercurrents of human existence do not bend to human will. He believed that only grace could restore the proper order of love, preaching that the cross of Christ restores God's gracious gift of ordinate love by empowering those who are in Christ to love God as God ought to be loved.

Four writings by Augustine of Hippo are especially useful: An early address given before a North African bishops' council in 393, while Augustine was still a presbyter. It is an exposition of the Apostles' Creed, which anticipates views that he later expanded into his monumental treatise "On the Trinity" (see vol. 1:184–200). It shows his shifting the emphasis from the "nature" of the persons of the Trinity to their "relation." Within the Trinity and toward the world, the way of that relation is love. According to Augustine, God's reconciling love reaches out in Christ to "bring us back to friendship."

A sermon from a series of sermons on First John, written after Augustine had successfully lobbied for an imperial decree against the Donatists (412), shows the ways in which Augustine could stretch his views to serve diverse goals (see vol. 1:201–9). Referring to Jesus' commandment to love one's enemy, Augustine invites Christians "to love [in the enemy], not what he is, but what you would have him be." This premise opens the way to all sorts of possibilities, including the use of imperial power to straighten out the Donatists and a justification of war if (1) the cause of the war is just, (2) a properly constituted government conducts the war, and (3) the motive of military action is love.

In another sermon on Holy Communion, Augustine discusses the sacrament as a "means of grace" (see vol. 1:210–12). If Christians cannot earn grace, how can they have assurance of salvation? According to Augustine, this assurance comes by being indelibly joined to the body of Christ. We can be certain by our faith in Christ, by the sacrament of Baptism, and by participation in the Holy Communion of the body and blood of Christ. Beyond that, we must trust God's irresistible grace! Later Protestants leaned on these words of Augustine, "We are saved by faith through grace." Yet Augustine might have added, only if you are part of Christ's body, the church. While it is possible to be in the church and not be saved; it is not possible to be saved outside of the church.

Finally, Augustine wrote extensively against the Pelagians, those who insisted that human freedom and works were the key to salvation. In his treatise, "On Nature and Grace" (see vol. 1:213–25), Augustine comes right to the point, accusing Pelagius of "rendering the cross of Christ to no effect." Although both Pelagius and Augustine taught and lived simple, monastic lives, they disagreed over how to reconcile justice with grace.

With the logic of Athens, Pelagius argued that "ought" implies "can." A just God does not command anything humans are unable to do. Augustine, on the other hand, brought the more realistic perspective of Jerusalem: "People will not do what is right," he said, "either because they have no idea of what it is, or because it is no fun." Both Pelagius and Augustine wrestled with the scope and limits of human justice.

Augustine was a pivotal thinker who set the agenda for the development of later theology. He recognized the theological achievements of the early church and put together the first great "summa" (theological summary) of early Christian thought. For three centuries, Christians struggled to reach consensus on the church's understanding of Jesus Christ, including the doctrine of the Trinity. Theological work culminated but did not end with the creedal definitions of Nicaea (325), Constantinople (381), and Chalcedon (451).

Testimony and Tests

Christianity has always been a faith seeking understanding. Rooted in the rabbinical tradition of Palestine, Christians took it for granted that their faith must be taught and confessed. In fact, from the perspective of the early church, a Christian community without theology or creeds was a contradiction.

The best known creedal statement in the Hebrew Scriptures was Deut. 6:4–5. The earliest Christian affirmations of faith were simple testimonials to the reign of Christ: "Jesus is Lord!" (Acts 10:36–38; 1 Cor. 12:3; Rom. 10:9; see also Acts 2:36, Rom. 1:3–4). Congregational worship made use of statements of faith (1 Cor. 15:3–7) and baptismal liturgy (Matt. 28:19). Later the Interrogatory Creed of Hippolytus (c. 215), an early version of the Apostles' Creed, became part of a Latin order of Baptism.

Early Christians scratched the symbols of their faith into Roman walls, using the Greek letters Chi Ro, for CHR-istos; or a line drawing of a fish, the word "IXOYS" in Greek, which was an acronym for the confession that Jesus Christ was the Son of God and Savior (I=Jesus, X=Christ, O=of God, Y=the Son, S=Savior.) These random declarations of faith reflect an emerging theological consensus in the Christian community, which aided the rapid expansion of Christianity beyond its Palestinian origins.

By the end of the second century, the Christian community reached a consensus about the declarations of faith, which became known and acknowledged as the "apostolic tradition" or the "Rule of Faith" (see vol. 1:32–40 and 41–47). This "Rule of Faith" was an open list of creedal affirmations developed by the Christian community as it responded to various internal and external challenges. The church at Smyrna used the Rule of Faith against the Monarchian heresy (see vol. 1:226–27). Against Noetus, a local presbyter who had taught that God/Father suffered on the cross, the local clergy issued a "confession" strongly affirming a clear distinction between the Father and the Son. We find another one of three versions of the "Rule of Faith" in Tertullian's treatise, "Against Praxeas" (see vol. 1:228–29).

Although he used it, Tertullian clearly did not consider the text of the "Rule" as normative and freely adapted it to the context in which he was writing. In "Against Praxeas," Tertullian makes it clear that God/Father sent none other than the divine Son (the *logos*) "into the virgin to be Mary's son." For Tertullian, human nature's salvation rested upon supporting the human side of the *logos*. Furthermore, Tertullian calls Monarchian teaching a faddish innovation. He upholds the biblical *logos* Christology of the divine/human Son against speculation, because it was closer to the ancient "Rule of Faith."

Tertullian's position reflects the contextual and the normative functions of any creedal statement. He writes in a historical context and seems to overstate the humanity of the *logos* to the point of "subordinating" the Son to the Father. At the same time, he holds to the "sound teaching" of the community (as reflected by the Rule of Faith) that Jesus must be both Son (of God) and son (of Mary).

The creedal controversies of the early church were more than historical phenomena. Confessions of faith cannot be compelled. The Councils at Nicaea and, to a lesser extent, Chalcedon produced an ecumenical consensus that has sustained the majority of Christians in all times and places.

In 324, the emperor Constantine defeated his last political rival, the eastern emperor Licinius and became the undisputed ruler of the whole Roman Empire. For the first time, Christians had a friend on the imperial throne. However, Christian controversies continued to cause political unrest. Christian divisions interfered with Constantine's plans to unite the empire with the blessings of the Christian God. Therefore, in 325, Constantine summoned a council of the whole church, both East and West, to his palace at Nicaea in Asia Minor and challenged the church leaders to settle the latest version of the ongoing Christological controversy.

The most recent controversy had been touched off by Arius, a presbyter at Alexandria, who, following the speculative tradition of that city, insisted that "there was a time, when Christ was not." In other words, he argued that Christ was a created being. This assertion sounded like an earlier subordination claim that Christ was "subordinate," or a "lesser god." It also revived dualistic ideas about the differences between the Creator and Redeemer, which the gnostics had raised over a hundred years earlier. Persons on both sides of the argument could cite ancient authorities and scripture (Col. 1:15; John 1:1–3).

Opposing Arius was Athanasius, a fellow Alexandrian who was still a deacon at the time. Athanasius was less interested in the metaphysics of the case and more in the implications of Arian teaching for the doctrine of redemption. Athanasius argued that if Christ is not human, he cannot save *us;* and if Christ is not God, he cannot *save* us. Athanasius's objections were biblical rather than speculative.

Constantine attended the gathering, now known as the First Ecumenical Council (325) and suggested the famous term *homo-ousios* ("consubstantial"), meaning that God and Christ are of the same substance. By the close of the gathering, the views of Athanasius prevailed (see vol. 1:235–36). According to the Nicene Creed, Jesus Christ is "true God from true God, begotten not created, of the same essence [*homo-ousios*] as the Father." The Nicene Creed is trinitarian, but barely, building upon a passing reference to the Holy Spirit, followed by a more substantial paragraph condemning the Arian side. "For the sake of peace," Eusebius and most of his fellow bishops signed the creed. Constantine banished only Arius and four others.

Unfortunately, the Council at Nicaea did not settle the dispute. Many

Eastern Christians were sympathetic to Arian views. They had lost at the council, but they were able to regain lost ground by seeking political influence and episcopal appointments. For the next fifty years, theology in the eastern Mediterranean was dominated by disputes among Arians, semi-Arians, Athanasians, and new-Nicenes over the Nicene settlement. Under the leadership of the Cappadocians (see vol. 1:175–83), a consensus developed that moderated the strict Athanasian interpretation of the creed. The consensus opinion interpreted the term *homo-ousios* ("consubstantial," or of the *same* substance) to mean that the Son and the Holy Spirit were of *like* (*homoi-ousion*) substance as the Father.

In 381, a second Council at Constantinople revised the original Nicene settlement. The Constantinople Council's statement, traditionally called the "Creed of the 150 Fathers," is more decidedly trinitarian and omits the "anathemas" (condemnations) of the 325 version (see vol. 1:235 and 232). This Constantinople version is actually what became known as the Nicene Creed (see vol. 1:237–39). The real authority of any creedal statement depends on two things — sound Christian teaching and shared consensus within a believing community.

It was not until the "Definition of Chalcedon" (451) that the early Christological controversies drew to a close (see vol. 1:240–41). Although Nicaea/Constantinople eliminated the threat of dualism by upholding a "high" trinitarian doctrine of one God in three persons (*hypostases*), arguments continued about the inner workings of the Trinity and the two natures of Christ.

The Council of Chalcedon (451) produced a compromise among three major approaches to these issues: Antiochian Christians upheld the two natures: one divine and one human; Alexandrian thinkers insisted on only one divine nature; and the Latin theologians argued for two natures in one person, or hypostasis. Chalcedon "settled" the issue by applying the term *homo-ousios* to the two natures of Christ. It stated that Christ is consubstantial (*homo-ousios*) with us according to his humanity and consubstantial with God according to his divinity. The last paragraph of the Chalcedonian settlement anticipates a host of objections. Yet the settlement stood unchallenged in the Western, or Roman, church for many centuries, postulating a "theology of salvation" grounded in both the full humanity and the full divinity of Christ.

Two additional important creedal documents developed later: the Athanasian Creed and the Apostles' Creed. In its present form, the Athanasian Creed is a ninth-century Latin document (see vol. 1:242–45). It is a heavy-handed condemnation of anyone who dares to deviate, ever so slightly, from the canons of Nicene/Chalcedonian orthodoxy. It shows how creeds and confessions can become instruments of ecclesiastical power and authority that stifle dissent rather than support a faith community. The Athanasian Creed echoes the "anathemas" (condemnations) of Nicaea (325), demonstrating how the church could use creeds negatively to enforce doctrinal uniformity.

By way of contrast, although the so-called Apostles' Creed came out of the same theological soil, it conveys a very different feeling (see vol. 1:246–48). This creed is the most popular of all Western creeds. It also affirms the Nicene/Chalcedonian position. But rather than defining what Christians must believe, it celebrates what Christians do believe. Worshiping congregations have formed and nurtured The Apostles' Creed over the centuries. Its origins are in the baptismal confessions of the first and second centuries, such as the Interrogatory Creed of Hippolytus (c. 200) (see vol. 1:246), even though its standard or "received" text was not fixed until well into the seventh century. The version from Philip Schaff's *Creeds of Christendom* and the ecumenical text found in the 1986 *Book of Worship* of the United Church of Christ witness to its timeless strength.

Worship and Work

An ancient axiom states that "The rule of prayer is the rule of faith." Later the Protestant reformers stated that faith without worship and works is dead; and worship and works without faith is blind. So it is that worship and work in the early church provide important insights into its theological character. Ancient hymns and prayers show how early theologians addressed practical questions of Christian conduct (see vol. 1:255–63).

Even more revealing of early Christian values are the efforts of Christian thinkers to deal with practical issues (see vol. 1:268). Faith seeking understanding finds its expression in the writings of church leaders about dress, sex, and military service (see vol. 1:268–81).

The trinitarian definitions of Nicaea and Chalcedon were able to capture many of the common faith affirmations for Christians in the West and in the East. As the years went by, the Nicene understanding of "God in three persons" (Greek: *hypostases,* or what Karl Barth calls divine "ways of being" in the twentieth century) and the Chalcedonian definitions of the two natures of Christ as "one with us in our humanity and one with God in God's divinity" became a generally accepted common confession.

Eastern Orthodoxy

However, these affirmations did not end diversity nor did they end Christological controversies — especially in the Eastern church. As is the case with most "bases of union," varying interpretations existed. The most controversial variation was the Western addition of the phrase *filioque* ("and the Son") to the 381 version of the "Nicene" creed known as the "Creed of the 150 Fathers." This issue became a major one between the Eastern and Western churches at the Council of Toledo (589) and was resolved many years later through a compromise at Florence (1439).

The underlying concern related to *filioque*, revolves around the ways in which Christians choose to affirm the relational life of God *within* the Trinity. Augustine greatly influenced Western Christians. He argued that the Holy Spirit is the essence of God's love, which flows (proceeds) among the persons within the Trinity and reaches out as grace to the created world. Stressing God's unity, Augustine held that all of God's works — creation, redemption, and sanctification — are the work of the Trinity. It is appropriate, therefore, to affirm that the Spirit proceeds from the Father *and the Son.*

The "filioque" debate indicates how theology in the Western church moved away from a central focus upon the incarnation to an increasing interest in the theology of the cross. As a result, Western theology increasingly turned to the question of God's grace and human salvation; while Eastern theologians, upheld the doctrine of salvation in its relationship to the incarnation, i.e., God becomes human, so that humans may become like God.

Eastern theologians, like John Chrysostom (c. 345–407), continued to probe the meaning of the incarnation. This eloquent preacher took Eastern theology to new heights in his sermon on Holy Communion, where he defined the sacrament as "participation" in Christ; i.e., as the mystical union by which the mortal believer becomes one with the immortal body of Christ (see vol. 1:282–85).

John of Damascus (d.c. 749) strengthened Eastern preoccupation with the incarnation in the so-called image controversy (see vol. 1:286–92). Touched off by an imperial decree in 726 against the time-honored Eastern church custom of venerating images, John of Damascus defended the use of "icons" on the grounds that God became visible, i.e., an image, through the incarnation of Christ. The crisis necessitated two major councils (see vol. 1:293–95). In 753, Constantine V called a council to Constantinople (753) that ratified measures against the use of images and condemned John of Damascus, posthumously. In 787 at Nicaea, the Second Ecumenical Council rehabilitated John and vindicated his views by ruling that images may be honored as long as they are not worshiped. Worship (*latreia*) belongs to God alone. "Idolatry" is idol-latreia.

How Christians understood Jesus Christ was central to the theological life of the early church. Its early struggles and controversies continue to inform contemporary Christian life and practice.

Antioch and Alexandria

17. On the Incarnation VII and Commentary on Galatians 4:24
(c. 420)

THEODORE OF MOPSUESTIA

Theodore, a monk and bishop of Mopsuestia (392–428), is one of the major exponents of Antiochene Christology. Antiochian theology acknowledges the complete harmony of the divine and the human will in the one personality (prosopon) *of Jesus but also argues on scriptural grounds that to save humans, Christ himself must be fully human. In his treatise, "On the Incarnation," Theodore places "Christ" on the human side of the "creation line" and the "logos" on the other. (The "creation line" distinguishes between the created order and the creator.) The "logos," he says, is "indwelling" the human Christ from the moment of conception in perfect unity of will but as a distinct nature.*

In "On the Incarnation," Theodore states that the word/flesh

SOURCE: Maurice Wiles and Mark Santer, eds., *Documents in Early Christian Thought* (Cambridge: Cambridge University Press, 1979). © Cambridge University Press 1975. Used by permission of Cambridge University Press.

Christology of his Alexandrian opponents wipes out the distinction between God and God's creation and leads to pantheism. "If we say that in his essence God is everywhere present, then he must give a share of his indwelling also to everything — not only to all people but also to the irrational and to inanimate creation." Hence, if everything is God, can anything be God?

In his "Commentary on Galatians 4:24," Theodore attacks the Alexandrian method of biblical interpretation (exegesis). He calls Origen's allegorical method "nonsense" (see vol. 1:48–54) and makes a strong argument for a "literal" reading of the scriptures. His discussion of the conflict between "historical" and "spiritual" understandings of scripture is very contemporary.

On the Incarnation VII

If we can discover how the indwelling is effected, then we shall know both the mode in which it is effected and also what makes for differentiation within that mode. Some people have asserted that the indwelling was a matter of essence (*ousia*), others that it was a matter of activity (*energeia*). Let us consider whether either of these is correct. First we must ask whether the indwelling is universal or not. Obviously the answer is "No." It is promised by God as something special for the saints or, in general terms, for those whom he wills to devote themselves to him. What would be the point of his promise, "I will dwell among them and will walk among them and will be their God and they shall be my people" [2 Cor. 6:16; see Lev. 26:12], which implies some kind of special favour to them, if that is something enjoyed by all men[1] in the ordinary run of things? If indwelling then is not universal (and clearly it is not) even for men let alone for all existents, then we need to be able to define some special meaning of "indwelling" according to which he is present only to those whom he is said to indwell. This makes it quite out of the question to say that indwelling is a matter of essence. For then either we would have to find God's essence only in those whom he is said to indwell and he would be outside everything else, which is absurd since he is of a boundless nature that is everywhere present and not spatially circumscribed at all; or else, if we say that in his essence God is everywhere present, then he must

---

1. Reading πάντες for παρέντες.

give a share also of his indwelling to everything — not only to all men but also to the irrational and even to the inanimate creation; this would be a necessary corollary of claiming that God's indwelling was a matter of essence. But both these are obviously out of the question. For to say that God indwells everything has been agreed to be the height of absurdity, and to circumscribe his essence is out of the question. So it would be naive in the extreme to say that the indwelling was a matter of essence.

Precisely the same reasoning applies in the case of activity. Either one has to confine it to these particular cases only — and then how could we go on talking about God's foreknowledge of everything, his governing everything, and his acting appropriately in everything? Or else if one allows that his activity is universal in its scope — and that is clearly appropriate and logical since it is by him that everything is empowered with its individual existence and with its own way of functioning — then one will have to say that his indwelling is universal.

So God's indwelling cannot be a matter of essence or of activity. What remains? What other concept can we use which will not destroy its particular character as applying to certain particular people? It is obviously appropriate to speak of indwelling being a matter of good pleasure (*eudokia*). "Good pleasure" is the name for that very good and excellent will of God which he exercises because pleased with those who are earnestly devoted to him; the word is derived from his "good" and excellent "pleasure" in them. Scripture frequently speaks of God being thus disposed. So the blessed David says, "He will not base his will on the strength of a horse nor will he find his good pleasure in the legs of a man. The Lord has good pleasure in those who fear him and in those who hope in his mercy" [Ps. 147:10–11]. This implies that he does not plan to work with or choose to cooperate with anyone other than those who fear him; they are the ones he values, they are the ones he chooses to cooperate with and to assist. This therefore is the appropriate way to define indwelling. For being of an infinite and uncircumscribed nature he is present to everyone; but in his good pleasure he is far from some and near to others. That is the meaning of these two texts: "The Lord is near to the broken in heart and will save the humble in spirit" [Ps. 34:18] and "Do not cast me away from thy presence and do not take thy Spirit from me" [Ps. 51:11]. He comes near in disposition to those who are worthy of such nearness and he goes far away from sinners. It is not a matter of being separated or coming nearer in actual nature; in both cases what happens is a question of attitude of mind.

The argument as we have developed it so far shows why we use the phrase "good pleasure," and we have discussed the meaning of the term in full detail in order to establish this. We are now in a position to say that just as it is in his good pleasure that God can be both near and far, so too it is in his good pleasure that his indwelling operates. He does not circumscribe his essence or his activity by being present in certain people only and being separated from everyone else; he is present universally in his essence, but he is separated from the unworthy in his attitude and disposition. In this way the uncircumscribed character of his being is fully preserved; it can be seen that he is not in this respect subject to any external necessity. If on the other hand he were universally present in his good pleasure, this again would make him in a different way subject to external necessity. In that case he would not be determining his presence by choice of will; it would be a matter of his uncircumscribed nature and his will would be simply consequent on that. But as it is he is universally present in nature and separated from those he chooses in will; the unworthy are not benefited by the presence of God which they do have, while the truth is preserved intact of the uncircumscribed character of his nature.

So then in his good pleasure he is present to some and separated from others, just as if he were actually in his essence with the one group and separate from the rest. Moreover, just as the indwelling is a matter of good pleasure, so also in precisely the same way the good pleasure varies the mode of indwelling. That which effects God's indwelling and explains how the one who is universally present in his essence can indwell only some — indeed only a very small proportion — of the whole of mankind is, as I have said, good pleasure; and this good pleasure also qualifies the particular mode of indwelling in every case. Just as God is described as present to all in his essence yet not indwelling all but only those to whom he is present in his good pleasure, so similarly when he is spoken of as indwelling it is not always an identical indwelling but the particular mode of indwelling will depend on the good pleasure. Thus when he is said to indwell the apostles, or more generally the righteous, then it is an indwelling as being well pleased with the righteous, according to the mode of the pleasure he has in the virtuous. But we would never describe the indwelling in his [i.e. Christ's] case as of that kind — that would be sheer madness; in his case it is as in a son; that is the form of good pleasure by which the indwelling took place. What is the significance of this "as in a son"? It is an indwelling in which he united the one who was being assumed wholly to himself and prepared him to share all the honour which he, the indweller, who is a son by nature, shares. Thereby he has constituted a single person (*prosopon*) by union with him and has made him a partner in all his authority. So everything he does he does in him, effecting even the ultimate testing and judgement through him and through his coming. The difference of course [i.e. between the Word and the man] is one that we can recognise by the distinguishing characteristics of each nature.

Although it is in the future that we shall be perfectly controlled in body and soul by the Spirit, yet even now we have a partial foretaste of this in that we are so assisted by the Spirit that we are not forced to succumb to the reasonings of the soul. In the same way although it was in the end that the Lord had God the Word working in him so perfectly and completely that they were inseparably joined in every action, yet even before that he had the Word bringing to perfection in him to the highest possible degree all that he must do; in that period before the cross he was being given free room because of the necessity to achieve virtue on our behalf by his own will, though even then he was being stirred on by the Word and was being strengthened for the perfect fulfilment of what needed to be done. He had received union with him right from the start at the moment of his formation in the womb. Then at the age when men normally begin to be able to distinguish between good and bad, indeed even before that age, he demonstrated far more rapidly and quickly than other people this power of discrimination. This ability to discriminate does not arise in the same way and at the same moment for each person. Some with greater insight achieve the goal more quickly; others acquire it with the help of training over a longer period. He was exceptional in comparison with all others and it came to him at an earlier age than is normal; this is not surprising since even at the human level he was bound to have something extra by virtue of the fact that even his birth was not by the normal method of intercourse between a man and a woman but he was formed by the divine working of the Spirit. Thanks to his union with God the Word, which by foreknowledge he was deemed worthy to receive when God the Word from above united him to himself, he had an outstanding inclination to the good. For all these reasons, as soon as he was in a position to discriminate, he had a great antipathy to evil and attached himself to the good with unqualified affection. In this he received the cooperative help of God the Word proportionate to his own native will and so remained thereafter unaffected by any change to the worse. On the one hand this was the set of his own mind, but it was also a matter of this purpose of his being preserved by the cooperative help of God the Word. So he proceeded with the utmost ease to the highest peak of virtue, whether it were a matter of keeping the law before his baptism or of living the life of grace after it; in doing so he provided a type of that life for us also, becoming a path to that goal for us. Then in the end after his resurrection and assumption into heaven, he showed himself worthy of the union even on the basis of his own will, though he had received the union even before this by the good pleasure of his Maker at the time of his very creation. Thus finally he provides a perfect demonstration of the union; he has no activity separate or cut off from God the Word, but he has God the Word as the effective agent of all his actions by virtue of the Word's union with him.

Commentary on Galatians 4:24

These things are said allegorically.

There are some people who make it their business to pervert the meaning of the divine Scriptures and to thwart whatever is to be found there. They invent foolish tales of their own and give to their nonsense the name of "allegory." By using the apostle's word, they imagine that they have found a way to undermine the meaning of everything in Scripture — they keep on using the apostle's expression "allegorical." They do not realize what a difference there is between their use of the term and the apostle's use of it here. For the apostle does not destroy history; he does not get rid of what has already happened. He sets things out as they happened in the past and uses the history of what happened in support of his own purpose — as when he says, "it corresponds to the Jerusalem that now is" and "as then the one who was born according to the flesh persecuted the one who was born according to the spirit." This shows that he acknowledged the history to be primary. Otherwise he would not have described the things that happened in relation to Hagar as corresponding to "the Jerusalem that now is" — something, that is to say, which he acknowledges to be a present reality. And he would not have said "as" except with reference to something he believed to exist; for the use of the word "as" clearly implies a comparison, and one cannot draw a comparison where the terms of the comparison do not really exist. And by the addition of the word "then" he declares himself uncertain of the length of time involved; but the whole question of time would be irrelevant, if it never happened.

That is how the apostle speaks. But they act in a totally opposite way; their wish is to deny any difference between the whole of the history recorded in divine Scripture and dreams that occur at night. Adam, they say, is not Adam — this being a place where they are especially prone to interpret divine Scripture in a spiritual way (spiritual interpretation is what they like to have their nonsense called) — paradise is not paradise and the serpent is not a serpent. What I would like to say in reply to them is that once they start removing bits of history they will be left without any history at all. In that case, they must tell us how they will be in a position to say who was the first man to be created or how man became disobedient or how the sentence of death was introduced. If it is from the Scriptures that they have learnt their answers to these questions, it follows that their talk of "allegory" is obvious nonsense, because it is clearly irrelevant at all these points. If on the other hand they are right and what is written is not a record of things that happened but is a pointer to some other profound truth in need of interpretation — some spiritual truth it may be, to use the phrase they like, which they have grasped through being such spiritual people themselves — then they must tell us by what means they have acquired these notions. How can they assert these notions, as if they were things they had learnt from the teaching of divine Scripture?

I pass over in silence for the moment the fact that if this were the case, one would be unable to see any reason for the events concerning Christ. The apostle says that he revoked the disobedience of Adam and did away with the sentence of death. What are these things that are said to have happened in the past and where did they happen, if (as they say) the historical account of them does not mean that but means something else? What is to be made of the apostolic saying, "I am afraid that as the serpent seduced Eve" [2 Cor. 11:3], if there was no serpent, no Eve, and no seduction by him at all? Many other passages too show clearly that the apostle always treated the history of the ancients as something real.

So in this passage he is at pains to prove his point on the basis of things that had happened and which were acknowledged by the Jews. That was his intention all along. And the substance of that intention was to show the superiority of the things of Christ to those of the law and the far greater dignity of the righteousness we have compared to that of the law. So he says there are two testaments, one given through Moses and the other through Christ. What he calls the testament in Christ is the resurrection Christ promised to us all when he was the first to rise from the dead. We have dealt with this point more explicitly in our commentary on the Epistle to the Hebrews.[1] The things that were given by Moses had the intention of enabling those who received the law to live under it and to

---

1. The surviving fragments of this commentary have been edited by K. Staab, *Pauluskommentare aus der griechischen Kirche* (Münster, 1933), pp. 200–12.

receive the righteousness that comes from it. (That was why they came out of Egypt and were established in a distant place where they could be free from all intermingling with other nations and could keep the law given to them with appropriate care.) In a similar way the things concerning Christ have the intention and goal of doing away with death, of bringing about the resurrection of all men who have lived at any time, of enabling them to live the life of an immortal and, greatest of all, making it impossible for them to sin any more by virtue of that grace of the Spirit which is in them and by which we will be kept safe from every kind of sin. This is true and complete justification. He appropriately gave them both the same name "testament"; for the things taught by the law were the very things put into practice by grace, namely love of God and neighbour. These are the commands that the law told us to keep, clearly teaching that we ought not to sin in any way. Grace brings it to practical fulfilment by means of the resurrection and of that immortality which will then be ours through the Spirit by whom we will then be controlled and so enabled not to sin at all.

So there is justification both in the law and also with Christ. With the law it is achieved by anyone who is able with much effort and sweat to achieve it. It is very hard, or to speak more accurately, impossible — if one chooses to judge the matter with full legal exactitude. For it is impossible for any living man to be wholly free of sin. That can be acquired only by grace; for we shall be enabled not to sin any more at that future time when all effort having been laid aside we will receive the justification that comes from Christ.

He mentions Hagar and Sarah. One of them had a child in the ordinary course of nature while the other was unable to bear a child but had Isaac by grace; and of the two the child born by way of grace turned out to be much the more highly esteemed. He compares them in order to show that now too the justification by Christ is far better than the other, because it is acquired by grace. He relates the one who had a child in the course of nature to the justification which is according to the law and makes the one who had a child against all hope correspond to that justification which is according to grace. This is because a life according to law is appropriate to the present, whereas for those who have once risen again and been made free of corruption, circumcision and the offering of sacrifices, not to mention the observation of special days, are all irrelevant.

There are things that happen in the course of nature — for example the entry into this life by birth — where life according to the law does seem still to have a place. But there is also a birth of grace, by which everyone rises again and is born into a future life in which the justification of Christ is fully implemented. So to represent the justification according to the law he has taken the one who bore a child in the order of nature, since the law has a role in controlling those who are born in this life, born according to the order of nature. To represent the justification according to Christ, he has taken the one who bore a child by grace, since this is fulfilled in those who are seen to have risen again at some time and who by grace look forward to that second birth beyond all hope.

This then is why he said: "These things are said allegorically." By allegory he means the comparison which can be made between things which have happened in the past and things which are the case now.

18. Dialogue of Origen with Heraclides and the Bishops with Him Concerning the Father and the Son and the Soul
(c. 235)

ORIGEN

In 1941, British soldiers discovered a library of sixth-century papyri in a cave south of Cairo, which included a previously unknown manuscript called the "Dialogue of Origen with Heraclides and the bishops with him concerning the Father and the Son and the soul."[1] Scholars generally agree that the document is the work of Origen (c. 185–c. 254) and records a bishops' council called to examine the views of Heraclides, an unknown cleric of questionable orthodoxy. Though only a presbyter, Origen, the foremost theologian of his time, participated in the council as a theological consultant.

In the "dialogue," Origen sounds like an overly zealous attorney cross-examining a hostile witness. He asks Heraclides the barbed ques-

---

SOURCE: Henry Chadwick and J. E. L. Oulton, eds., *Alexandrian Christianity*, vol. 2 of *The Library of Christian Classics* (Philadelphia: Westminster Press, 1954). Used by permission of Westminster John Knox Press.

1. The original scribe only wrote the title in the final colophon at the end of the work: "Dialogues of Origen: with Heraclides and the bishops with him." A later reviser added to this final colophon "Concerning the Father and the Son and the Soul" and also inserted this full title at the head of the work.

tion, "Do we confess two Gods?" Heraclides responds cautiously, "Yes. The power is one."

*Although it is not clear what happened to Heraclides, Origen shocks the council by overstating the duality of God and then deftly recovering with an argument for the unity of the "two-in-one" based on neo-Platonic "chain of being" thinking (the idea that creation is arranged in a descending chain from God to the Son to the angels to humans to animals to plants to rocks). However, at the same time for the common people, Origen invokes the liturgical principle that the rule of prayer is the rule of faith (*lex orandi, lex credendi*). In worship, he suggests we must preserve the duality for humanity's sake and the unity for God's sake. Any prayerful consideration of God's solidarity with creation affirms that we must worship Christ as both our risen sovereign and as our brother Jesus of Nazareth.*

After the bishops present had raised questions concerning the faith of the bishop Heraclides, that he might confess before all the faith which he held, and after each one had said what he thought and asked questions, Heraclides said:

I also believe what the sacred Scriptures say: "In the beginning was the Word, and the Word was with God, and the Word was God. He was in the beginning with God. All things were made by him, and without him nothing was made."[2] Accordingly, we hold the same faith that is taught in these words, and we believe that Christ took flesh, that he was born, that he went up to heaven in the flesh in which he rose again, that he is sitting at the right hand of the Father, and that thence he shall come and judge the living and the dead, being God and man.

Origen said: Since once an inquiry has begun it is proper to say something upon the subject of the inquiry, I will speak. The whole church is present and listening. It is not right that there should be any difference in knowledge between one church and another, for you are not the false church.

I charge you, father Heraclides: God is the almighty, the uncreated, the supreme God who made all things. Do you hold this doctrine?

Heracl.: I do. That is what I also believe.

Orig.: Christ Jesus who was in the form of God,[3] being other than the

---

2. John 1:1–3.
3. Phil. 2:6.

God in whose form he existed, was he God before he came into the body or not?

Heracl.: He was God before.

Orig.: Was he God before he came into the body or not?

Heracl.: Yes, he was.

Orig.: Was he God distinct from this God in whose form he existed?

Heracl.: Obviously he was distinct from another being and, since he was in the form of him who created all things, he was distinct from him.

Orig.: Is it true then that there was a God, the Son of God, the only begotten of God, the firstborn of all creation,[4] and that we need have no fear of saying that in one sense there are two Gods, while in another there is one God?

Heracl.: What you say is evident. But we affirm that God is the almighty, God without beginning, without end, containing all things and not contained by anything;[5] and that his Word is the Son of the living God, God and man, through whom all things were made,[6] God according to the spirit, man inasmuch as he was born of Mary.[7]

Orig.: You do not appear to have answered my question. Explain what you mean. For perhaps I failed to follow you. Is the Father God?

Heracl.: Assuredly.

Orig.: Is the Son distinct from the Father?

Heracl.: Of course. How can he be Son if he is also Father?

Orig.: While being distinct from the Father is the Son himself also God?

Heracl.: He himself is also God.

Orig.: And do two Gods become a unity?

Heracl.: Yes.

Orig.: Do we confess two Gods?

Heracl.: Yes. The power is one.

Orig.: But as our brethren take offence at the statement that there are two Gods, we must formulate the doctrine carefully, and show in what sense they are two and in what sense the two are one God. Also the holy Scriptures have taught that several things which are two are one. And not only things which are two, for they have also taught that in some instances more than two, or even a very much larger number of things, are

---

4. Col. 1:15.
5. A theological commonplace; cf. Origen, *de Princ.,* I, 3:3, etc.
6. John 1:3.
7. Cf. Rom. 1:3.

one. Our present task is not to broach a problematic subject only to pass it by and deal cursorily with the matter, but for the sake of the simple folk to chew up, so to speak, the meat, and little by little to instil the doctrine in the ears of our hearers. . . . Accordingly, there are many things which are two that are said in the Scriptures to be one. What passages of Scripture? Adam is one person, his wife another. Adam is distinct from his wife, and his wife is distinct from her husband. Yet it is said in the story of the creation of the world that they two are one: "For the two shall be one flesh."[8] Therefore, sometimes two beings can become one flesh. Notice, however, that in the case of Adam and Eve it is not said that the two shall become one spirit, nor that the two shall become one soul, but that they shall become one flesh. Again, the righteous man is distinct from Christ; but he is said by the apostle to be one with Christ: "For he that is joined to the Lord is one spirit."[9] Is it not true that the one is of a subordinate nature or of a low and inferior nature, while Christ's nature is divine and glorious and blessed? Are they therefore no longer two? Yes, for the man and the woman are "no longer two but one flesh," and the righteous man and Christ are "one spirit." So in relation to the Father and God of the universe, our Saviour and Lord is not one flesh, nor one spirit, but something higher than flesh and spirit, namely, one God. The appropriate word when human beings are joined to one another is flesh. The appropriate word when a righteous man is joined to Christ is spirit. But the word when Christ is united to the Father is not flesh, nor spirit, but more honourable than these — God. That is why we understand in this sense "I and the Father are one."[10] When we pray, because of the one party let us preserve the duality, because of the other party let us hold to the unity. In this way we avoid falling into the opinion of those who have been separated from the Church and turned to the illusory notion of monarchy, who abolish the Son as distinct from the Father and virtually abolish the Father also. Nor do we fall into the other blasphemous doctrine which denies the deity of Christ. What then do the divine Scriptures mean when they say: "Beside me there is no other God, and there shall be none after me," and "I am and there is no God but me"?[11] In these utterances we are not to think that the unity applies to the God of the universe . . . in separation from Christ, and certainly not to Christ in separation from God. Let us rather say that the sense is the same as that of Jesus' saying, "I and my Father are one."

---

8. Gen. 2:24; Matt. 19:5.
9. 1 Cor. 6:17. Cf. *contra Celsum*, II, 9; VI, 47; *Comm. in Matt.*, XIV, 16.
10. John 10:30.
11. Isa. 43:10; Deut. 32:39.

It is necessary to study these doctrines because there has been much disturbance in this church. Often people write and demand a signature of the bishop and of those they suspect, asking that they should give their signatures in the presence of all the people, that there may be no further disturbance or dispute about this question. Accordingly, with the permission of God and secondly of the bishops, thirdly of the presbyters, and also of the people, I will again say what I think on this subject. Offering is universally made to Almighty God through Jesus Christ inasmuch as, in respect of his deity, he is akin to the Father. Let there be no double offering, but an offering to God through God. I shall seem to be speaking in a daring manner. When we pray let us abide by the agreements.[12] If the word: "Thou shalt not respect the person of man, nor allow thyself to be impressed by the person of the mighty"[13] is not realized . . . If this is not realized . . . these agreements, it will give rise to fresh disputes. . . . If a man is a bishop or a presbyter, he is not a bishop, he is not a presbyter. If he is a deacon, he is not a deacon, nor even a layman. If he is a layman, he is not a layman, nor is there a meeting of the congregation. If you assent, let these agreed usages prevail.

Some people raise the objection that, with reference to the problem of deity, while I have thus attributed deity to Jesus Christ substantially, I have professed before the church my faith that at the resurrection the body which rose had been a corpse.[14] But since our Saviour and Lord took a body, let us examine what the body was. The church alone in distinction from all the heresies that deny the resurrection confesses the resurrection of the dead body. For from the fact that the firstfruits were raised from the dead, it follows that the dead are raised. "Christ the firstfruits";[15] on that account his body became a corpse. For if his body had not become a

---

12. Origen uses *sunthekai* of the promises and credal confession made in baptism (e.g., *Exh. Mart.,* 12, 17). Cf. Clem. *Strom.* VII, 90. "The terms of the baptismal confession" would perhaps be a possible translation here. But the general idea of this corrupt passage is an appeal to the universal sense of the church. It is likely that Origen means the agreed formulas of liturgical prayer: *lex orandi lex credendi.* Scherer, however, thinks it means the agreements which are to constitute the practical conclusion of the debate.

13. Lev. 19:15. The quotation is odd. Scherer is probably right in taking this to refer to interference in the affairs of the church by powerful people without authority; but the precise sense of the allusion is lost, and the passage, the text of which is more corrupt than any other in the Dialogue, was not understood by the original scribe. The general sense is that if unauthorized people interfere, there will be chaos and the authorized ministry deprived of all meaning.

14. See H. Chadwick and J. E. L. Oulton, eds., *Alexandrian Christianity* (Philadelphia: Westminster Press, 1954), 434.

15. 1 Cor. 15:12 ff.

corpse, capable of being wrapped in a grave-cloth, of receiving the ointment and all the other things applied to dead bodies, and of being laid in a tomb[16] — these are things that cannot be done to a spiritual body. For it is entirely impossible for that which is spiritual to become a corpse, neither can that which is spiritual become insensible. For if it were possible for that which is spiritual to become a corpse, we would have reason to fear lest after the resurrection of the dead, when our body is raised, according to the apostle's saying, "It is sown animate, it is raised spiritual,"[17] we shall all die. . . . In fact "Christ being raised from the dead dies no more."[18] And not only Christ, but those who are Christ's,[19] when they are raised from the dead, die no more. If you agree to these statements, they also with the solemn testimony of the people shall be made legally binding and established.[20]

What else is there to be said concerning the faith? Do you agree to this, Maximus? Say.

Maximus: May everyone hold the same doctrines as I do. Before God and the Church I both give my signature and make my oath. But the reason why I raised a certain question was in order that I might be in no doubt or uncertainty at all. For the brethren know that this is what I said: "I need the help of my brother and instruction on this point." If the spirit was truly given back to the Father, in accordance with the saying, "Father, into thy hands I commend my spirit,"[21] and if without the spirit the flesh died and lay in the tomb, how was the tomb opened and how are the dead to rise again?

Orig.: That man is a composite being we have learnt from the sacred Scriptures. For the apostle says, "May God sanctify your spirit and your soul and your body," and "May he sanctify you wholly, and may your entire spirit and soul and body be preserved unblameable at the coming of our Lord Jesus Christ."[22] This spirit is not the Holy Spirit, but part of the constitution of man, as the same apostle teaches when he says: "The spirit

---

16. Cf. Matt. 27:59; Mark 15:46; Luke 23:53.
17. 1 Cor. 15:44.
18. Rom. 6:9.
19. 1 Cor. 15:23.
20. The procedure appears to have been that at the end of the synod the doctrinal decisions would have been formally set forth, and the congregation would have declared their adherence thereto.
21. Luke 23:46.
22. 1 Thess. 5:23. Cf. Origen, *de Princ.*, II, 8:4, where he suggests that Christ's soul was "a kind of medium between the weak flesh and the willing spirit."

bears witness with our spirit."²³ For if it were the Holy Spirit he would not have said: "The spirit bears witness with our spirit." So then our Saviour and Lord, wishing to save man in the way in which he wished to save him, for this reason desired in this way to save the body, just as it was likewise his will to save also the soul; he also wished to save the remaining part of man, the spirit. The whole man would not have been saved unless he had taken upon him the whole man. They do away with the salvation of the human body when they say that the body of the Saviour is spiritual. They do away with the salvation of the human spirit, concerning which the apostle says: "No man knows the things of man except the spirit of man that is in him."²⁴ . . . Because it was his will to save the spirit of man, about which the apostle said this, he also assumed the spirit of man. At the time of the passion these three were separated. At the time of the resurrection these three were united. At the time of the passion they were separated — how? The body in the tomb, the soul in Hades, the spirit was put in the hands of the Father.²⁵ The soul in Hades: "Thou shalt not leave my soul in Hades."²⁶ If the spirit was put into the hands of the Father, he gave the spirit as a deposit. It is one thing to make a gift, another thing to hand over, and another to leave in deposit. He who makes a deposit does so with the intention of receiving back that which he has deposited. Why then had he to give the spirit to the Father as a deposit? The question is beyond me and my powers and my understanding. For I am not endowed with knowledge to enable me to say that, just as the body was not able to go down to Hades, even if this is alleged by those who affirm that the body of Jesus was spiritual,²⁷ so also neither could the spirit go down to Hades, and therefore he gave the spirit to the Father as a deposit until he should have risen from the dead. . . . After he had entrusted this deposit to the Father, he took it back again. When? Not at the actual moment of the resurrection, but immediately after the resurrection. My witness is the text of the gospel. The Lord Jesus Christ rose again from the dead. Mary met

---

23. Rom. 8:16.

24. 1 Cor. 2:11.

25. J. Crehan, "The Dialektos of Origen and John 20:17," in *Theological Studies,* XI (1950), 368–372, compares the Paschal homily ascribed both to John Chrysostom and Hippolytus, edited by P. Nautin, *Homélies Pascales,* I (1950), 185: "The heavens have thy spirit, paradise thy soul . . . the earth thy body. The indivisible is divided."

26. Ps. 16 (15):10; Acts 2:27. Cf. *contra Celsum,* II, 16.

27. The Marcionites believed that their docetic Christ had descended to Hades to save all who had resisted the God of the Jews such as the Sodomites. Cf. *contra Celsum,* VI, 53, with my note thereon.

him and he said to her: "Touch me not."[28] For he wished anyone that touched him to touch him in his entirety, that having touched him in his entirety he might be benefited in body from his body, in soul from his soul, in spirit from his spirit. "For I am not yet ascended to the Father." He ascends to the Father and comes to the disciples. Accordingly, he ascends to the Father. Why? To receive back the deposit.

All the questions about the faith which disturbed us have been examined. But we must realize that at the divine tribunal we are not judged for faith alone,[29] as if our life were left unexamined, nor for our life alone, as if our faith were not subject to scrutiny. We are justified on the ground that both are correct. We are punished for both if both are incorrect. There are some, however, who will not be punished for both, but for one of the two: some for their faith because it is defective, but not because their life is lacking in right conduct; others, again, will not be punished for their faith, but will be for their life, on the ground that they have lived a life contrary to right reason. My opinion is that in the Proverbs of Solomon these two kinds (I mean that which concerns our belief and knowledge and that which concerns our manner of life) are mentioned by Solomon in the following words: "Who shall boast that he has a pure heart? Or who shall present himself saying that he is free from sins?"[30] The difference between these we take to be this: the "heart" means the thought, the "sins" refer to actions. "Who shall boast that he has a pure heart" which is undefiled by the knowledge falsely so-called,[31] undefiled by falsehood? Or "who shall present himself saying that he is free from sins," having done nothing amiss in his practical conduct? If then we wish to be saved, let us not be concerned about faith to the neglect of practical conduct of life, nor again let us place our confidence in our life. Let us realize, let us comprehend, let us believe that it is on the ground of both that we either receive our acquittal or blessedness, or receive the opposite of these. The things that are liable to punishment, therefore, are not merely the terrible and fearful sins which should not even be named,[32] whether sins of life or of thought, but also sins commonly thought to be of less importance. That is why, it seems, the apostle puts side by side with acts which are abominable, infamous, and revolting (if I may so say) things which are regarded by most people as of little significance. What does he say? "Be not

---

28. John 20:17.
29. Cf. James 2:24.
30. Prov. 20:9.
31. 1 Tim. 6:20.
32. Eph. 5:3.

deceived; neither fornicators, nor adulterers, nor effeminate men, nor homosexuals, nor thieves, nor drunkards, nor revilers, shall inherit the kingdom of God."[33] You see that together with such gross sinners as the homosexual person, the effeminate man, the adulterer, the fornicator, he enumerates the drunkard, the reviler — sins thought by all of us to be of small account, so that we may be taught that it is not for the great sins alone that we are excluded from the kingdom of God, but also for these which are commonly supposed to be of minor significance. Therefore, let us not revile, nor be drunkards, nor extort, nor steal, nor do anything wrong, even if we are "deceived."[34]

---

33. 1 Cor. 6:9–10. Cf. Origen, *in 1 Cor.*, XXVI (Jenkins, *J.T.S.*, IX (1908), 367): "Most of us can know in our consciences that we are not guilty of these vices; but with regard to those that follow, even I myself fear lest I may be guilty of the other sins...."

34. This strange phrase is explained by *Hom. in Jerem.*, XX, 3, where Origen says that 1 Cor. 6:9–10 might cause those who do not understand that God's punishments are purifying to lose heart. "For which of us is not aware in his conscience of having drunk not wisely and too well? Which of us is pure from theft . . . ?" The truth that minor sins are punished by God no less than serious vices is a mystery which providentially is not understood by the ignorant multitude of believers who, if they were not deceived, would abandon hope, not realizing that God's punishments and harsh words are remedial and not retributive.

19. On Sin and Salvation
From *Catechetical Oration 5–8*
(late 4th century)

GREGORY OF NYSSA

The so-called "Cappadocian Fathers," Gregory of Nyssa (d.c. 394–95); his older brother Basil, "the Great" (d. 379); and Gregory of Nazianzus (d. 390) were prominent members of the "new Nicene" party, which after the death of Athanasius played a major role in keeping Eastern Mediterranean Christians loyal to the Nicene creed. All three men were well-educated. They advocated the monastic life and reluctantly accepted the office of bishop. Their work helped to unite the church against the Arians (those who denied that Jesus was of the same substance as God and considered Jesus to be the highest of created beings).

Although Basil's leadership may justify the title "great," his brother Gregory was the group's principal theologian. Together, they laid the foundation for a "Byzantine," or Eastern Christian, theology by blending classical Greek learning with mystical intuition and Nicene orthodoxy.

Gregory's Catechetical Oration *shows the lingering influence of Platonism and Alexandrian Origenist (chain of being) teaching. He borrows*

SOURCE: Maurice Wiles and Mark Santer, eds., *Documents in Early Christian Thought* (Cambridge: Cambridge University Press, 1979). © Cambridge University Press. Used by permission of Cambridge University Press.

Origen's concept of two distinct levels of creation: the "intelligible" creation of a spiritual realm and the "sensible" one of the physical world. Human beings belong to both; and in their original state, humans are free. However, the soul has an "immortal element" that recognizes and longs for the transcendent and eternal. Evil is a deprivation of the good, just as death is a deprivation of being. Sin is a willful turning away from God who is the source of all good and all being. Finally, Gregory brings up the Nicene point that the Word (Jesus Christ) is "substance-ial and distinct," yet embraces the whole creative "power" in himself. For Gregory the line dividing the creator from the creature is just below the Trinity.

---

5. The existence of God's Word[1] and Spirit is unlikely to be contested either by the Greek whose notions are those common to mankind or by the Jew with his notions derived from Scripture. But the dispensation by which the divine Word became man will be rejected by both alike as an incredible and improper thing to affirm about God. So on this issue we will have to take a different starting-point in order to convince our opponents.

They believe that all things were created by the reason and wisdom of him who constructed the whole universe — unless they have difficulty in believing even that! But if they will not grant that reason and wisdom govern the structure of things, that would amount to setting up unreason and unskilfulness as ruling principle of the universe. And that surely is both absurd and impious; so there can be absolutely no question about their admitting that reason and wisdom govern existing things.

Now it has been shown in what has been said already that the Word of God is no mere utterance nor a state of possessing some knowledge or wisdom. He is a power with an existence of his own, freely choosing all that is good and with the power to do whatever he chooses. And since the world is good this power which both possesses in advance and effects the good is its cause. Now if the existence of the world in its totality depends on the power of the Word, as our argument has shown, it follows logically that we cannot ascribe the combination of the various parts of the world to

---

1. Gregory's argument depends on the two meanings of the Greek word, Logos — reason and word. In translation a choice between them has to be made. Also where the personal sense of "the divine Word" seems to be uppermost we have used a capital *W* and the masculine rather than the neuter pronoun — distinctions not present in the Greek.

any other cause; it too must be due to the Word himself, through whom everything received its entry into being. Whether people choose to call him Word or Wisdom or Power or God or any other sublime and honorific title is a matter of indifference to us. Whatever term or name is produced to indicate this reality, the meaning of the various phrases used is identical — namely, that eternal power of God which creates what exists, contrives what does not yet exist, sustains what has been brought into being and foresees what is to come. The logic of the argument shows that this reality — the divine Word, Wisdom, Power — is the creator of human nature. He was not compelled to make man by any kind of necessity; it was the overflowing of love which led him to fashion the existence of a living creature of this particular kind. It was not right that his light should remain without anyone to see it, his glory without anyone to witness it, his goodness without anyone to enjoy it and all the other attributes of deity that we apprehend lie useless with no one to share in them or to enjoy them.

Now if man came into existence for this purpose — namely to be made a partaker of the divine goodness, he must have been created with a propensity for sharing in that goodness. In the case of physical sight the eye partakes of light by virtue of a beam of light with which the eye itself is endowed by nature; this innate power enables it to attract to itself that which is akin to its own nature.[2] In the same way something akin to the divine had to be included in human nature, so that by virtue of that relationship man would have a desire for that which corresponds to his own nature. In the case of creatures without reason, animals whose natural habitat is the water or the air are formed with natures corresponding to their pattern of life; the particular way their bodies are constructed in each case makes air or water, as the case may be, natural and congenial to them. So, since man was created for the purpose of enjoying the divine goodness, he had to have something in his nature akin to that of which he was designed to partake. He was therefore endowed with life and reason and wisdom and all the other good things which are characteristic of God so that each of these might provide him with a desire for something which is related to his own nature. Now since one of the good things that belongs to divine nature is eternity, it would not have been right for the constitution of our nature to have had no share in that whatever; there is therefore within man's nature an immortal element so that by virtue of this inherent

---

2. For the idea that the eye has a light of its own by which it is enabled to attract light from outside, see Plato, *Timaeus* 45B.

capacity he might recognize the transcendent and come to long for the divine eternity.

The account of the creation sums this up in a single phrase when it says that man was created in the image of God [Gen. 1:27]. For the likeness which consists in being in the image of God is a summation of all the characteristically divine attributes. And everything that Moses goes on to relate in his narrative account (for that is the form in which he presents us with his doctrine) has the same teaching in view. The garden of which he speaks and the peculiarity of the fruit which does not satisfy the belly when eaten but which gives knowledge and eternal life — all these are in full accord with what we have already seen about man: namely that in its origins our nature was good and was surrounded by goodness.

But someone looking at the situation as it is now may oppose what has been said and think he can prove it false in view of the fact that we do not see man in that condition now but in an almost exactly opposite condition. Where is the soul's likeness to God? Where is the body's freedom from passion? Where is eternal life? Fleeting, subject to passion, mortal, liable to every kind of suffering in body and soul — with these and similar descriptions he will run down our nature and expect thereby to refute the account of man that we have given. We will deal with these points briefly so as not to interrupt the sequence of our argument.

The fact that human life is now in so evil a state is not sufficient proof that man was never in a state of goodness. Since man was the work of God and since it was God's goodness that brought such a creature into existence at all, one cannot reasonably suppose that man's being in an evil state derives from his maker; for goodness was the very reason for his creation. There must be some other cause of our present condition and of our having lost our more desirable state.

Our basic premise on this issue is once again not one to which our opponents will object. God made man for the purpose of sharing in his own goodness. To that end he endowed his nature with potentialities for attaining excellence in all its forms, so that his aspirations might be conveyed by those varied potentialities in the direction of their corresponding forms of excellence. He would not therefore have deprived him of the most excellent and precious form of goodness, namely the gift of liberty and free-will. For if human life were ruled by necessity of any kind, that would make it wholly unlike its archetype and the image would be falsified at that point. For how could a nature that was enslaved and subject to necessity be called an image of the sovereign nature? That which has been endowed with a likeness to the divine at every point must include in its nature self-determination and liberty; so that participation in all that is good may be the reward of virtue.

How then, you will ask, did it come about that he who was honourably endowed with excellence in all these ways exchanged these blessings for something worse? The answer to this too is clear. The existence of evil did not have its origin in the divine will. Evil would not be blameworthy if it could claim God for its creator and father. Evil comes in some way or another from within. It is the product of free choice, whenever the soul withdraws in any way from the good. Just as sight is an activity of nature and blindness a privation of this natural activity, so virtue stands in the same kind of antithesis to evil. The origin of evil can only be understood as the absence of virtue. If light is removed darkness ensues; if light is present darkness does not exist. In the same way, as long as good is present in a nature, evil as such is non-existent; but the withdrawal of the good is the beginning of the existence of its opposite. And since the distinctive character of free-will is freely to choose what pleases it, God is not the cause of your present evil state. He provided you with a free and independent nature; it is your folly that has chosen the worse instead of the better.

6. You may ask the further question: what is the cause of this total misdirection of the will? That is the issue raised by the argument so far. Once again we can find a very reasonable starting-point for the clarification of this further question. We have inherited from the fathers a kind of explanation, which is not just a legendary tale but one which gains credence from our nature itself. Our experience and observation of existing things is two-fold; it is divided between the intelligible and the sensible. Nothing can be apprehended as having real existence which does not fall within this two-fold classification. It is a vast gulf that separates them from one another. The sensible has none of the characteristics of the intelligible, nor the intelligible of the sensible; rather they have opposing characteristics. Intelligible nature is incorporeal, intangible and without form; while sensible nature, as its very name indicates, is apprehended through the senses. Within the sensible world itself, different elements are directly opposed to one another; yet a harmony in which these opposing elements have their place has been devised by the wisdom which governs the universe; thereby the whole creation is in self-consistent harmony and the opposing nature of the different elements does not destroy the bond of union. In the same way divine wisdom provides a mixture and a blending of the sensible with the intelligible, so that all things partake equally in the good and no existing thing is deprived of a share in the better nature. The

sphere appropriate to intelligible nature is a subtle and mobile essence, which with its transcendent location has in its distinctive nature a close affinity to the intelligible; yet a higher wisdom has brought about a commingling of the intelligible with the sensible creation so that, as the apostle says, "no part of the creation may be rejected" [1 Tim. 4:4] or be deprived of participation in the divine.

Therefore it is in the form of a mixture made up of the intelligible and the sensible that man has been produced by the divine nature, as the creation story teaches. God, it says, made man by taking the dust of the earth and by his own breath implanted life in what he had made [Gen. 2:7]. Thereby the earthly has been raised into union with the divine; this blending of the lower nature with the transcendent means that the same grace is present to the same extent throughout the whole of creation.

The intelligible creation was in existence first. Each of the angelic powers was allocated by the authority which governs all things with a particular activity in connection with the framing of the universe. One such power was appointed to maintain and take charge of the region of the earth. He had been empowered for this specific purpose by the power which governs the universe. Then there was formed that earthly creation which is an image of the power above (namely the creature, man); in this creation was present the godlike beauty of the intelligible nature, blended in by a power that surpasses all description. The angelic power who had been allocated the governance of the earth regarded it as intolerable that out of that nature which was subject to him there should be produced an essence akin to the supreme dignity of all.

• • •

Empowered by God's blessing man held a lofty position. He was appointed to rule over the earth and everything on it. His form was beautiful, for he was created as an image of the archetypal beauty. In nature he was free from passion, for he was a copy of him who is without passion. He was wholly free and open, revelling in the direct vision of God. But all this was fuel to the flames of the adversary's passionate envy. He could not fulfil his purpose by violence or brute force, for the power of God's blessing was stronger than such force. So he contrived to detach man from the power which strengthened him and thus to render him an easy prey to his intrigue. To give an illustration: if the flame of a lamp catches the wick and it is impossible to blow it out, the device of mixing water with the oil will dim the flame. By a similar trick the adversary mixed evil with man's free-will and thereby affected a sort of quenching or dimming of the blessing. And as the blessing failed, its opposite inevitably came in in its place. Now the opposite of life is death, of power weakness, of blessing a curse, of openness shame, and so on with whatever is thought of as the contrary of each form of goodness. This is why humanity is now in its present evil plight. In that beginning lay the starting-point which has led to such a conclusion.

7. Now we ought not to ask whether God embarked on the creation of man with foreknowledge of the disaster that would overtake him as a result of his folly, implying that it might have been better for him not to have been made at all rather than to be in such a plight. It is people who have been misled by Manichaean teaching who put forward that argument in support of their error; their aim in doing so is to prove that the creator of man's nature is evil.

• • •

I would . . . like to call on the apostle to support our charge against them on this issue. In writing to the Corinthians he distinguishes between fleshly and spiritual conditions of the soul [see 1 Cor. 2:14–15]. I think that in what he says he is indicating that one ought not to make judgements about good and evil on the basis of sensation, but that one needs rather to detach the mind from bodily phenomena altogether and to discriminate between good and its opposite in their own intrinsic character. "The spiritual man," he declares, "judges all things."

The reason why such fabulous doctrines have arisen among people who advance these views is, I believe, the following. They define good with reference to the enjoyment of bodily pleasure. And since the nature of the body (being composite and liable to dissolution) is necessarily subject to suffering and weakness, and such sufferings give rise in some way to painful sensations, they imagine that the creation of man is the work of an evil god. But if they had set the sights of their mind higher, detached their thoughts from concern with pleasure and considered the nature of reality in freedom from the influence of the passions, they would have concluded that nothing is evil except wickedness. All wickedness is characterized by the privation of good; it does not exist in its own right, nor is it observed to have any subsistence of its own. For evil has no existence of its own outside the will; it is a name given to the non-existence of good. Non-being has no subsistence; and the creator of subsistent things is not the creator of that which has no subsistence. God, therefore, has no responsibility for evil for he is the author of being and not of non-being, the creator of sight and not of blindness, the source of virtue and not of its privation. The reward of the will which he holds out to those who live virtuously is the enjoyment of all that is good. He has not subjected human nature to any kind of forcible compulsion to do what he wills; he does not drag man unwillingly, like a lifeless object, in the direction of the good. If a man of his own choice closes his eyes in broad daylight, the sun is not responsible for his inability to see.

• • •

Therefore anyone who bears in mind the goal which in his wisdom the ruler of the universe has in view could not be so unreasonable and small-minded as to attribute the cause of evil to the creator of man, alleging either that he was ignorant of what would happen or that if he did know and still created man he played a part in the first steps in the direction of evil. He did know what would happen and he did not prevent the first steps which led to its happening. He was not ignorant that humanity would deviate from the good, seeing that in knowledge he is the complete master over all things and has as clear a vision of the future as he does of the past. So he did see man's turning away; but in the same way he also perceived man's restoration once more to the good. Which then would have been better? Not to have brought our nature into being at all since he foresaw that the one to be created would stray from the good? Or to bring him into being and then (when he had become sick) to restore him again by repentance to his original grace?

Calling God the creator of evil because of bodily sufferings, which are an inevitable consequence of our nature being in flux, or actually denying that he is the creator of man at all so as to avoid attributing the cause of our sufferings to him — that is the height of small-mindedness. It is the view of people who distinguish good and evil on the basis of sensation and do not realize that nothing is good by nature except what is unaffected by sensation, and nothing is evil except alienation from the truly good. Judging good and evil on the basis of pain and suffering is characteristic of irrational nature, because not sharing in intelligence or understanding they are in no position to grasp what is truly good. But that man is a work of God, created good and for the noblest ends, is evident not only from what we have already said but for thousands of other reasons, most of which we must leave on one side because there are such an infinite number of them.

In calling God the creator of man, we have not forgotten the careful distinction we made in that part of our introduction directed to the Greeks. We showed there that God's Word is a substantial and distinct being and is in himself both God and Word. He embraces in himself all creative power—or, better, he *is* power. His inclinations are wholly in the direction of good. And since he has power that keeps pace with his will, whatever he desires he brings to pass. His will and his work is the life of all that is. It is by him that man was brought to life and endowed in godlike fashion with every noble attribute.

Changelessness of nature belongs only to what did not come into being by way of creation. Everything that stems from the uncreated nature has its subsistence from non-being; so having begun its existence by change at the very start, it progresses all the time by way of change. If it acts according to its nature, this continual change is for the better; but if it is diverted from the straight path, movement in the opposite direction ensues. This was man's condition. His mutable nature had slipped off course and was going in the opposite direction. Having once departed from the good, every kind of evil came in as a result. Turning from life brought in death instead. Loss of light produced darkness. Absence of virtue brought in vice. In place of every form of good was listed the set of opposing evils. That was the condition into which man fell through his folly. Once he had turned from prudence, it was impossible for him to be prudent; once he had abandoned wisdom it was impossible for him to decide wisely. By whom was he to be restored once more to his original grace? Whose part was it to raise him up when he had fallen, to restore him when he was lost, to lead him back when he had gone astray? Who conceivably but the Lord of his nature? Only the one who had originally given him life was able and fitted to restore it when it was lost. This is what we learn from the revelation of the truth when it teaches us that God made man in the beginning and saved him when he had fallen.

Augustinian Theology

20. Faith and the Creed
(393)

AUGUSTINE OF HIPPO

In August of 392, Augustine (354–430), former professor of rhetoric and newly ordained catholic presbyter at Hippo, engaged in a formal public debate against Fortunatus, a fellow presbyter of the heretical Manichean sect. Not unlike contemporary sports, formal theological debates were a favorite spectator sport in the fourth century. They drew large crowds of excited fans, who cheered on their favorites.

This public debate was a two-day marathon, and it was a good match. Augustine trounced Fortunatus, a former friend from his own Manichean days (373–382). After the first day, Augustine took the lead. A large crowd roared its disapproval of Fortunatus's doctrine of Christ. By the end of the second day, he left town.

A year later, Aurelius, newly elected bishop of Carthage, asked Augustine, who was still a presbyter, to address a plenary council of Afri-

---

SOURCE: Saint Augustine, *Augustine: Earlier Writings*, ed. J. H. S. Burleigh, vol. 6 of *The Library of Christian Classics* (Philadelphia: Westminster Press, 1957). Used by permission of Westminster John Knox Press.

can bishops at Hippo. Aurelius called the council to initiate reforms that would heal the schism caused by Donatists. Donatists held an extremely rigorous view that the church is the gathered community of the pure. Their moral rigor and charismatic zeal made them attractive as the fundamentalists of their day.

The council met at Hippo in October. Augustine's address, "Faith and Creed," is an exposition of the Apostles' Creed. As he put it, the Apostles' Creed "is [to be] handed over to young Christians . . . that with a pure heart they may know what to believe." The speech includes a sketch of Augustine's trinitarian views (16,–.20), which later grew into the fifteen volumes of a monumental treatise, On the Trinity. In this early work, Augustine demonstrates a genius for using the theological heritage of the church to move in new directions.

Traditionally, Eastern theologians tried to safeguard Christian monotheism by stressing the divine unity of the creator/father. Western theologians, less given to philosophical subtlety, insisted on the humanity of the "logos," thereby compromising divine unity with the idea of two, or even three, gods. Eastern Christians continued to have a nagging uneasiness about the Nicene Creed. When talking about the Trinity, they preferred the idea that Jesus was "of like being" (homoi-ousios), rather than the harsher Nicene formula, "of the same being" (homo-ousios).

Even the Cappadocians (see vol. 1:175–83) intended the divine unity when they talked about three distinct hypostases (modes of being) within the one creator/God. Such language, however, tended to call attention to the differences within the Trinity. When Western Christians translated the Greek hypostasis into the Latin persona, it magnified the differences even further. "Person" implies separation and individuality.

Augustine moves beyond these alternatives by shifting the emphasis from the "nature" of the Trinity to a new appreciation of the loving "relation" among the three persons. He talks about the Trinity in conjunction with the Holy Spirit. We dare not neglect the doctrine of the Spirit, because the Spirit teaches that "nature" or "being" is manifest in the proper relation or order of love. The nature of the Holy Spirit is love. Spirit/love is twofold: the inward love embracing Father and Son and that of God in Christ reaching outward to reconcile the world and to "bring us back to friendship." Furthermore, those reconciled by love must love their neighbor also. Unless the Christian faith joins people in loving community, it does not bear fruit. Augustine insists that this is why Christians need the church. The church is that loving and beloved community.

Finally, Augustine adds the noteworthy caveat that, while God is love, love is not God. However, in the depth of the divine, in the Trinity, love is not just an attribute of the divine being, love is *the Holy Spirit,* homoousios *("of the same being") with the Father and the Son.*

---

i, 1. It is written and confirmed by the strong authority of apostolic teaching that the just shall live by faith. And faith imposes on us a duty to be fulfilled both by the heart and by the tongue. "With the heart man believeth unto righteousness; and with the mouth confession is made unto salvation" (Rom. 10:10). We must therefore be mindful both of righteousness and of salvation. Though we are to reign hereafter in eternal righteousness, we cannot be saved from the present evil age unless, earnestly seeking the salvation of our neighbours, we profess with the mouth the faith which we hold in our heart. We must see to it with careful and pious vigilance that that faith shall not be violated in any way for us by the fraudulent craft of the heretics. But the Catholic Faith is made known to the faithful in the Creed, and is committed to memory, in as short a form as so great a matter permits. In this way for beginners and sucklings, who have been reborn in Christ but have not yet been strengthened by diligent and spiritual study and understanding of the divine Scriptures, there has been drawn up in few words a formula they must accept in faith, setting forth what would have to be expounded in many words to those who are making progress and are raising themselves up to attain the divine doctrine in the assured strength of humility and charity. Under colour of the few words drawn up in the Creed many heretics have endeavoured to conceal their poison. But the divine mercy withstands and resists them by the instrumentality of spiritual men, whose merit has permitted them not only to receive and believe the Catholic Faith as expressed in these words, but also to know and understand it by revelation from God. It is written "Except ye believe ye shall not understand" (Isa. 7:9, LXX). But the exposition of the Faith serves to fortify the Creed, not that it is given to be committed to memory or repeated instead of the Creed by those who obtain the grace of God. But it guards the things contained in the Creed against the wiles of heretics with full Catholic authority and with a stronger defence.

ii, 2. Some have endeavoured to argue that God the Father is not omnipotent. Not indeed that they have ventured to put it in that way, but their teaching proves that this is their opinion and belief. When they say that there is something which God omnipotent did not create, but of which he made the world, beautifully ordered as they admit, they so far deny that God is omnipotent in that they believe he could not have made the world unless, in making it, he had used a material which already existed and which he had not made. They base their argument on the ordinary carnal observation that smiths and builders and other workmen cannot put their art into effect without the aid of material already to hand. So they understand that the maker of the world is not omnipotent, if he could not have made the world without the aid of some kind of material which he had not himself made. If they admit that the world was made by an omnipotent God they must admit that he made what he has made out of nothing. If he were omnipotent there could be nothing of which he was not the Creator. Even if he did make something out of something else, as he made man out of clay, he did not make it out of something which he had not himself made. For he made the earth out of nothing, and clay comes from the earth. If he made the heaven and the earth, i.e., the world and all it contains, out of some matter — as it is written: Thou didst create the world out of invisible, or even, as some copies read, formless matter (Wisdom 11:17) — we must by no means believe that the matter out of which the world was made, however formless or invisible, could have existed as it was by itself, as if it were co-eternal and coeval with God. Only from God omnipotent did it receive whatever mode of being it had, and whatever potentiality it had to receive other different forms. For it is by his gift that any formed thing not only has its being but even is capable of receiving form. There is this difference between what is formed and what is capable of receiving form. That which is formed has already received form. That which is "formable" is capable of receiving form. He who gives form to things also gives capacity for form, for from him and in him is the unchangeable form which is the highest form of all. He is one, who has given to everything not only its beauty but also its power to be beautiful. Most correctly, therefore, do we believe that God has made all things of nothing; for if the world was made out of matter, matter itself was made of nothing, to be, by God's gift and appointment, the primal "formable" substance from which all that has form should be formed. We have said this in order that no one should suppose that Scripture contradicts itself when it says, in one place, that God made all things of nothing, and in another, that the world was made of formless matter.

3. Accordingly, believing *in God the Father Almighty* we ought to believe that there is no creature which has not been created by his omnipotence. Moreover, because he created all things through his Word which is also called the Power and Wisdom of God, and is hinted at by

many other titles which commend the Lord Jesus Christ to our faith as the Son of God, our Saviour and ruler; and because none could generate the Word by whom all things are made save he who made all things through him; iii. we also believe *in Jesus Christ our Lord, the Only Son of God, Only-begotten of the Father.* We must not think that the Word is like our words which proceed from our mouths and are passed on by vibrations in the air and abide no longer than the sound of them remains. That Word abides unchangeable. For of him Scripture says, speaking of wisdom: "Remaining in herself she reneweth all things" (Wisdom 7:27). He is called the Word also because through him the Father is made known. For as by our words, when we speak truly, our mind lets him who hears them know something, and by signs of that kind brings to the knowledge of another what we hold secretly in our heart, so wisdom whom God the Father begat is most appropriately called his Word, because through him the Father who dwells in utmost secrecy becomes known to worthy minds.

4. But there is a vast difference between our minds and the words with which we try to show what is in our minds. We do not beget verbal sounds but make them; and in making them we make use of the body as material. Now there is a great difference between mind and body. When God begat the Word, the Begetter was "he who is." He did not make the Word out of nothing nor out of any ready-made material but from his eternal nature. This is what we, too, try to do when we speak the truth, though not when we lie, if we closely consider the purpose we have in mind in speaking. What else are we trying to do but to bring our mind, as far as it can be done, into contact with the mind of him who listens to us, so that he may know and understand it? We remain in ourselves and take no step outside ourselves, but we produce a token whereby there may be knowledge of us in another; so that, if opportunity is afforded, one mind, as it were, produces another mind to indicate its meaning. We do this with words and sounds and looks and bodily gestures — so many devices that serve our purpose to make known what is within our minds. But we cannot produce anything exactly like our minds, and so the mind of the speaker cannot make itself known with complete inwardness. Hence also there is room for lying. But God the Father had the will and the power to make himself most truly known to those who were destined to know him, and to make himself known he begat one who is like himself, and who is called the Power and Wisdom of God because God operated through him and arranged all things. Wherefore it is written of wisdom that she "reacheth from one end of the world to the other with full strength, and ordereth all things graciously" (Wisdom 8:1).

iv, 5. Wherefore the only-begotten Son of God was not made by the Father, because, as the Evangelist says, "All things were made through him" (John 1:3). Nor was he born of time for the eternally wise God has his Wisdom with him eternally. Nor is he unlike the Father, i.e., less in any way, for the apostle says: "Who being in the form of God thought it not robbery to be equal with God" (Phil. 2:6). Hence the Catholic Faith excludes those who say that the Son is the same as the Father [i.e., Sabellians], because the Word could not be with God unless it were with God the Father, and he who is alone is equal to none. Likewise those are excluded who say that the Son is a creature, though not as the other creatures [i.e., the Arians]. Any creature however great, if it be a creature, is fashioned and made. To fashion is the same as to create, although in the usage of the Latin language "to create" is sometimes used as a synonym for "to beget." The Greeks, however, observe the distinction. What we call a "creature" they call a κτίσμα or a κτίσις. If we wish to speak without ambiguity we must say not *creare* but *condere*. Therefore if the Son is a creature, however great he may be, he is made. We believe in him by whom all things were made, not in him by whom other things were made; and we cannot accept any other sense of the word "all" except as including whatever has been made.

6. "The Word became flesh and dwelt among us" (John 1:14). The Wisdom who was begotten of God deigned to be created among men [*creari*]. Here it is pertinent to quote Proverbs 8:22 (after LXX) "The Lord created me in the beginning of his ways." The beginning of his ways is the Head of the Church, which is Christ incarnate, through whom there was to be given us an example of living, i.e., a certain way by which we might reach God. We had fallen through pride; for it was said to the first creature of our race: "Taste and ye shall be as Gods" (Gen. 3:5). We cannot return except through humility. Now our restorer deigned to show in his own person an example of this humility, i.e., of the way by which we must return. "For he thought it not robbery to be equal with God, but emptied himself, taking the form of a servant" (Phil. 2:6). So the Word by which all things were made was created man in the beginning of his ways. According to his nature as the only-begotten, he has no brothers. But according to his nature as first-born, he has deigned to call brethren all who, after him and by means of his headship, are born again into the grace of God by adoption as sons, as the apostolic teaching proclaims. Being Son by nature he was born uniquely of the substance of the Father, being what the Father is, God of God, Light of Light. We are not light by nature, but we are illumined by that light, according as we are able to shine in

wisdom. "He was the true light that lighteth every man coming into this world" (John 1:9). To the Faith we profess with regard to eternal things we add the temporal dispensation of our Lord, which he deigned to carry through for us and to overrule for our salvation. According to his nature as only-begotten Son of God, it cannot be said of him that he was, or that he will be, but only that he is. What was is not now, and what will be is not yet. But he is unchangeable without variation or temporal condition. I think there is no other reason for the name by which he proclaimed himself to his servant Moses. For when he asked by whom he should say he had been sent if the people to whom he was sent should scorn him, he received the answer: "I Am who I Am"; and it was added: "Say to the children of Israel, He who is hath sent me unto you" (Ex. 3:14).

7. From this I am sure it is manifest to spiritual minds that there can be no thing which is the opposite of God. For if God is and this Word [*sc.* I AM] can properly be said of God alone, God has nothing opposite to him. What is true abides unchangeably. What changes, once was and is not now, or will be and is not yet. If we were asked what is the opposite of white, we should answer, black. If we were asked what is the opposite of hot, we should reply, cold. If we were asked what is the opposite of swift, we should reply, slow; and so on. But if the question is asked what is the opposite of that which is, the correct answer is: that which is not.

8. But since, by what I have called a temporal dispensation, our mutable nature was assumed by the unchangeable Wisdom of God, for our salvation and restoration, by the act of God's loving-kindness, we also put faith in temporal things done on our behalf for our salvation. For we believe *in the Son of God who was born by the Holy Spirit of the Virgin Mary.* By the gift of God, that is, by the Holy Spirit, there was shown towards us such humility on the part of God most high that he deigned to take upon him the whole of human nature in the womb of a Virgin, inhabiting the body of his Mother and being born of it, while leaving it pure and entire. The heretics have many insidious ways of attacking this temporal dispensation. But anyone who holds the Church Faith and believes that the Word assumed the whole of human nature, body, soul and spirit, is sufficiently armed against them. The incarnation took place for our salvation, so we must take care not to suppose that any part of our nature was unassumed. Otherwise it will have no part in salvation. Apart from the shape of the limbs, which differs in the different classes of living creatures, man is not different from the cattle except in having a rational spirit, which is also called a mind. How could it be sane to believe that the divine Wisdom assumed that part of our nature which we have in com-

mon with the cattle, but did not assume the part which is illumined by the light of wisdom, and is man's characteristic part?[1]

9. Those likewise are to be detested who deny that our Lord Jesus Christ had Mary as his mother on earth. That dispensation did honour to both sexes male and female, and showed that both had a part in God's care; not only that which he assumed, but that also through which he assumed it, being a man born of a woman. We are not obliged to deny the Mother of Christ because he said: "Woman, what have I to do with thee? Mine hour is not yet come?" (John 2:4). Rather he lets us know that he had no mother so far as his divine nature is concerned, and he was preparing to manifest his majestic character by turning water into wine. When he was crucified, he was crucified in his human character. That was the hour which had not yet come when he spoke as he did, meaning the hour when he would recognize her. For in the hour when he was crucified he recognized his mother's human nature and commended her most considerately to his beloved disciple. Nor should we be moved by the other passage where, when it was announced to him that his mother and brethren were present, he replied: "Who is my mother? and who are my brethren?" (Matt. 12:48). Rather he would teach us that if our parents hinder the ministry which is ours to minister the Word of God to the brethren, we ought not to recognize them. Anyone who thinks that he had no mother on earth because he said, "Who is my mother?" must also necessarily think that the apostles had no fathers on earth, because he bade them "call no man your father upon the earth; for one is your Father, which is in heaven" (Matt. 23:9).

10. Nor should our faith be lessened by any reference to "a woman's internal organs," as if it might appear that we must reject any such generation of our Lord, because sordid people think that sordid. "The foolishness of God is wiser than men" (1 Cor. 1:25); and "to the pure all things are pure" (Tit. 1:15), as the apostle truly says. Those who think in this way ought to observe that the rays of the sun, which indeed they do not praise as a creature of God but adore as actually God, are poured over evil-smelling drains and other horrible things and do their natural work there without being made foul by any contamination, though visible light is by nature more closely related to visible filth. How much less could the Word of God, who is neither visible nor corporeal, have been polluted by the body of a woman when he assumed human flesh along with a human soul and spirit, within which the majesty of the Word was hidden away

---

1. This refers to the heresy of Apollinarius.

from the weakness of the human body? It is manifest that the Word of God could never have been contaminated by the human body, which does not even contaminate the human soul. The soul is not soiled by contact with the body when it rules and animates the body, but only when it lusts after the perishable goods of the body. If these [Manichees] would only avoid stains upon their souls, they would rather fear such lies and sacrilegious doctrines.

v, 11. But our Lord's humility in being born on our behalf was only a small part. In addition, he deigned to die for mortals. "He humbled himself, and became obedient unto death, even the death of the Cross" (Phil. 2:8); lest any of us, even if he could shake off the fear of death, should dread a kind of death which men think most shameful. Accordingly, we believe in him who *was crucified under Pontius Pilate, and buried.* The name of the judge had to be added to mark the date. And when we confess faith in his burial we remember the new tomb which bears testimony to his resurrection to newness of life, as the womb of the Virgin did to his real birth. For just as no other dead body was buried in that tomb before or after, so no other mortal was conceived in that womb before or after.

12. Also we believe that *he rose again from the dead on the third day*, the first-born of his brethren who were to follow him, whom he called into the adoption of the sons of God and deigned to make his co-heirs and co-partners.

vi, 13. We believe that *he ascended into heaven*, the place of beatitude which he promised even to us, saying: "They will be as the angels in heaven" (Matt. 22:30); in that city which is the mother of us all, Jerusalem, eternal in the heavens. It is wont to offend certain impious gentiles or heretics that we believe an earthly body was taken up into heaven. The gentiles mostly ply us eagerly with the arguments of the philosophers who say that an earthly object cannot exist in heaven. They do not know our Scriptures, or how it is written: "It is sown an animal body; it is raised a spiritual body." This does not mean that body is changed into spirit and becomes spirit. The spiritual body is understood as a body so subject to spirit that it may be suited to its celestial habitation, all earthly weakness and corruption being changed and converted into celestial purity and stability. This is the change of which the apostle speaks when he says: "We shall not all sleep, but we shall all be changed" (1 Cor. 15:51). That the change is not for the worse but for the better he teaches, saying in the next verse: We shall be changed. It is the merest vain curiosity to ask where and in what manner the Lord's body is in heaven. It does not become our weakness to discuss the secrets of heaven, but it is befitting our faith to think highly and honourably of the dignity of the Lord's body.

vii, 14. We likewise believe that *he sitteth at the right hand of the Father*. Of course we are not to think that God the Father is limited as it were by a human form in such a way that in thinking about him we should imagine a right side and a left side. When it is said that "the Father sits" we are not to think of him as doing so by bending his legs, lest we fall into the sacrilege which the apostle execrates in those who have changed the glory of the incorruptible God into the likeness of corruptible man. It is sinful to set up an image of God in a Christian temple. Much more nefarious is it to do so in the heart which is truly the temple of God if it be cleansed from earthly cupidity and error. We are to understand "At the right hand of God" to mean in supreme blessedness where righteousness is, and peace and joy; just as the goats are placed on the left hand (Matt. 25:35), i.e., in misery, on account of their iniquities, toils and torments. To say that "God sits" signifies not the position of his members, but his judicial power, which his divine majesty never lacks, but which ever metes out to men their deserts. But at the last judgment the brightness of the only-begotten Son of God, Judge of the living and of the dead, will be much more manifest among men so that none shall doubt it for ever.

viii, 15. We also believe that at the right time, *Thence he will come to judge the quick and the dead.* Possibly these names signify the righteous and the sinners. Or it may be that those are called quick whom he will then find alive upon the earth, while the dead are those who will be raised at his coming. In any case the temporal dispensation is not like his divine generation; for it has both a past and a future. Our Lord was on the earth, is now in heaven and will come in shining raiment to judge the quick and the dead. He will come as he ascended according to the authority of Scripture in the Acts of the Apostles. And of this temporal dispensation it is written in the Apocalypse: "Thus saith he who is and who was and who is to come" (Rev. 1:8).

ix, 16. Having considered and commended to faith the divine generation of our Lord and the dispensation with regard to his manhood, in order to complete what we believe about God, we add: *And in the Holy Spirit.* The Holy Spirit is not by nature less than the Father or the Son, but is, if I may say so, consubstantial and co-eternal with them. That Trinity is one God. Not that Father, Son and Holy Spirit are identically the same. But the Father is Father, the Son is Son and the Holy Spirit is Holy Spirit, and this Trinity is one God, as it is written: "Hear O Israel, the Lord thy God is one God" (Deut. 6:4). And yet if we are asked about the several Persons, e.g., is the Father God, we shall reply, he is God. If the same question is asked about the Son, we shall give the same answer. Nor if the same question were asked about the Holy Spirit ought we to say anything else than that he is God. But we have to be very careful to avoid the sense in which it is said of men: "Ye are gods" (Ps. 82:6). These are not gods by nature who are made and fashioned by the Father through the Son by the gift of the Holy Spirit. The Trinity is signified when the apostle says: "For of him and through him and to him are all things" (Rom. 11:36). Therefore, although when we are asked about the several Persons and answer that each is God, whether it be the Father or the Son or the Holy Spirit, no one is to think that we worship three Gods.

17. It is not surprising that we speak like this about an ineffable nature, for something similar is met with even in things which we see with our bodily eyes and judge with our bodily senses. When we are asked about a fountain we cannot call it a river, and when we are asked about a river we cannot call it a fountain; and if we take a drink from a fountain or a river we cannot call it either a fountain or a river. But we describe all these three things, together or severally, as water. If I ask whether what is in the fountain or in the river or in the tumbler is water, in each case the reply must be that it is; and yet we do not say that there are three waters but only one. Certainly we must take care that no one imagines that the ineffable substance of the Divine Majesty is like a visible corporeal fountain or river or tumbler of water. For the water which is now in the fountain does not remain there but flows out into the river; and when a drink is taken from a fountain or a river it does not remain in the place from which it is taken. Accordingly it can happen that the same water can belong successively to the fountain, the river and the drinking vessel. But in the Divine Trinity the Father cannot be now the Son and again the Holy Spirit. In a tree the root is simply the root, the trunk the trunk and the branches are nothing but branches. We do not use the word "root" of the trunk or the branches. Nor does the wood which belongs to the root pass in any way into the trunk or the branches, but remains only in the root. And yet the rule remains that the root is wood and the trunk and the branches are wood, but we cannot say there are three woods but one only. Possibly because of a difference in strength these portions of a tree may be so unlike that it would not be absurd to speak of three kinds of wood. At least all admit that if three goblets are filled from one fountain, we may speak of three goblets but not of three waters, but of water in the singular only. If you were asked about the goblets severally you would reply that there is water in each of them, although there is no passage from one to the other as we observed there was from the fountain into the river. These corporeal examples have been given not because they bear any real resemblance to the divine nature, but because they show the unity of visible

things, and to let you understand that it is possible for three things not only severally but also together to be designated by a singular noun; so that no one may be surprised and think it absurd that we call the Father and the Son and the Holy Spirit God, but hold that in that Trinity there are not three Gods but One only, one substance.

18. Many learned and spiritual men have discoursed in many books about the Father and the Son, trying to explain, as far as men can explain to men, how the Father and the Son are not one Person but one substance, and what the Father is in himself and what the Son is in himself: how the Father begets, and the Son is begotten; how the Father is not of the Son, but the Son is of the Father; how the Father is the principle of the Son, whence he is called the Head of Christ (1 Cor. 11:3), though Christ also is principle but not of the Father. He is the image of the Father, though in no way dissimilar but altogether and indistinguishably equal. These things are dealt with at greater length by those whose purpose it is to expound more fully than we are doing the profession of the whole Christian faith. The Son as Son has received existence from the Father, while the Father has not received existence from the Son. So far as, according to the temporal dispensation, the Son in ineffable compassion assumed human nature, a mutable creature, in order to change it for the better, many things are found written in Scripture which mislead the impious minds of heretics who wish to teach rather than to learn, and give them an excuse for thinking that the Son is not equal to the Father, nor of the same substance. Such are: "The Father is greater than I" (John 14:28). "The head of the woman is the man; and the head of the man is Christ, and the head of Christ is God" (1 Cor. 11:3). "Then shall the Son also himself be subject unto him that put all things under him" (1 Cor. 15:28). "I go to my Father and your Father, to my God and your God" (John 20:17). And some other similar passages. These things are not written to signify any inequality of nature or substance. Otherwise these other passages would be false: — "I and the Father are one" (John 10:30); "He who hath seen me hath seen the Father" (John 14:9); "The Word was God" (John 1:1) — for he was not made, since all things were made through him; "He thought it not robbery to be equal with God" (Phil. 2:6). And there are other such passages. The former passages are written partly on account of the economy of the incarnation, for it is said that he emptied himself — not that Wisdom was changed, for he is completely unchangeable, but that he wished to make himself known to men in this humble manner. Partly, then, on account of this economy these passages were written which the heretics falsely interpret; but partly also for this reason that the Son owes

the Father his existence, but owes him also his equality with the Father. The Father on the other hand owes his existence to none.

19. But great and learned commentators of the divine Scriptures have not as yet discussed the doctrine of the Holy Spirit with the same fullness and care, so that we may easily understand his peculiar character as Holy Spirit, by which he is to be distinguished from the Father and the Son. But they declare that he is the gift of God, so that we may believe that God gives no gift inferior to himself. They take care, however, to declare that the Holy Spirit is not begotten of the Father like the Son, for Christ is unique. Nor was he begotten of the Son as if he were the grandson of the Father, most high. Moreover, he owes his existence to the Father from whom are all things. He does not exist in himself; that would be to set up two independent principles instead of one, which is utterly false and absurd, and is the mark not of the Catholic Faith but of the error of some heretics. Some have even dared to believe that the Holy Spirit is the communion or deity, so to speak, of the Father and the Son, their θεότης as the Greeks call it. So, as the Father is God and the Son is God, the very deity which embraces both—the Father who begets the Son and the Son who cleaves to the Father—is equated with God by whom the Son is begotten. This "deity," by which they would have understood the mutual love and charity of both Father and Son, they say is called the Holy Spirit, and they adduce many proofs from Scripture for their opinion. For example: "The love of God is shed abroad in our hearts by the Holy Spirit which is given unto us" (Rom. 5:5). There are many other similar testimonies. And because we are reconciled to God through the Holy Spirit, whence also he is called the gift of God, they would have it clearly indicated that the Holy Spirit is the Love of God. For we are not reconciled to him save through Love, whereby we are also called sons. For we are not under fear as slaves, but perfect love casteth out fear, and we have received the Spirit of liberty "whereby we cry Abba, Father" (Rom. 8:15). Because by love we are reconciled and brought back to friendship, and can know all the secret things of God, it is of the Holy Spirit that it is written: "He will bring you into all truth" (John 16:13). Hence the confidence in preaching the truth which filled the apostles when the Spirit came is rightly attributed to Love. For diffidence comes from fear which is excluded by perfect Love. Likewise he is called the gift of God, because no one enjoys what he knows unless he loves it. To enjoy the Wisdom of God is nothing else but to cleave to him in love; and no one has an abiding grasp of anything unless he loves it. Moreover he is called *Holy* Spirit, since whatever is made holy is made holy in order to abide for

ever. And there is no doubt that the word sanctity is derived from *sancire*, to make holy. Above all the asserters of this opinion make use of this testimony from Scripture: "That which is born of the flesh is flesh and that which is born of the Spirit is Spirit. For God is a Spirit" (John 3:6; John 4:24). Here he speaks of our regeneration which is not after the flesh according to Adam, but after the Holy Spirit according to Christ. If, they say, it is the Holy Spirit that is spoken of in the words, God is a Spirit, it ought to be observed that what is said is that God is a Spirit, not that the Spirit is God. Hence the deity of the Father and the Son is here called God, that is the Holy Spirit. Besides, there is this other testimony where the apostle John says that God is love. He does not say love is God but God is love, so that deity may be understood to be love. There is of course no mention of the Holy Spirit in that passage where many things are linked together: "All things are yours, and ye are Christ's and Christ is God's" (1 Cor. 3:21, 23); and in the other passage: "The head of the woman is the man, and the head of the man is Christ and the head of Christ is God" (1 Cor. 11:3). But they say that this is due to the fact that where things are linked together the link that holds them together is not usually included among them. Hence those who read with close attention seem to recognize the Trinity in the passage where it is written: "Of him and through him and in him are all things." "Of him" points to him who owes existence to none; "through him" points to the Mediator; and "in him" points to him who contains all things and binds them together.

20. This view is contradicted by those who think that that communion, whether we call it Deity or Love or Charity, is not a substance. They want to have the Holy Spirit explained according to his substance, and do not understand that God could not be said to be love unless love were a substance. They are influenced by ordinary corporeal experience. If two bodies are joined together so as to be set side by side, the junction is not a body. For if the two things which had been joined together are separated, nothing else remains. The "junction" cannot be understood to have moved away, as the bodies parted company. Let such people make for themselves a clean heart so that they may be able to see that there cannot be in the substance of God both substance and accidents. All that can be understood to be there is substance. It is easy to speak about such things and even to believe them, but they cannot be seen as they are save by the pure heart. Whatever the true view may be in this matter, we must hold with unshaken faith that the Father is God and the Son is God and the Holy Spirit is God; that there are not three Gods, but that the Trinity is One God; that the persons are not diverse in nature but are of the same

substance; that the Father is not now the Son and now the Holy Spirit; but that the Father is always the Father and the Son always the Son and the Holy Spirit always the Holy Spirit. We must not rashly affirm anything about invisible things as if we knew, but only as those who believe. These things can only be seen by the pure heart. He who, in this life, sees them in part and in an enigma, as it is written, cannot by speaking about them let another see them, who is hindered by uncleanness of heart. "Blessed are the pure in heart for they shall see God" (Matt. 5:8). This is our faith concerning God our maker and renewer.

x, 21. We are commanded to love not only God but also our neighbour; as it is written: "Thou shalt love the Lord thy God with all thy heart and with all thy soul and with all thy mind and thy neighbour as thyself." Unless the Christian faith gather men together into a society in which brotherly love can operate, it remains less fruitful. Hence we believe [in] *the Holy Church,* that is to say, *the Catholic Church.* Heretics and schismatics also call their congregations churches. But heretics do violence to the faith by holding false opinions about God; and schismatics, although they believe as we believe, have broken away from brotherly love by wicked separations. Wherefore heretics do not belong to the Catholic Church which loves God; nor do schismatics, for the Church loves its neighbour, and easily forgives his sins because it prays to be forgiven by him who has reconciled us to himself, blotting out all past transgressions and calling us to new life. Until we attain perfect life we cannot be without sins, but it makes all the difference what kind of sins we commit.

22. There is no need now to deal with the differences between sins, but we must by all means believe that our sins will not be forgiven if we are inexorable in refusing to forgive. We accordingly believe in *the forgiveness of sins.*

23. Man consists of three parts, spirit, soul and body. Sometimes there are said to be only two, for soul and spirit are spoken of often as one thing, whereof the rational part, which beasts lack, is called spirit. Then the life-force by which we are united to our bodies is called the soul. Finally there is the body which, because it is visible, is called our lowest part. This whole creature "groaneth and travaileth until now" (Rom. 8:22), but has put forth the first-fruits of the spirit because it has believed God and has already a good will. The spirit is also called mind, of which the apostle says: "I serve the law of God with my mind" (Rom. 7:25). In another place he says: "God is my witness, whom I serve in my spirit" (Rom. 1:9). But the soul is called "flesh" so long as it desires carnal goods. For part of it resists the spirit, not by nature but by sinful custom and habit.

Hence it is written: "With my mind I serve the law of God, but with the flesh the law of sin." This custom has been changed into a veritable natural state in his mortal descendants by the sin of the first man. Therefore it is written: "We too were at one time by nature the children of wrath," that is, of the punishment by which we were made to serve the law of sin (Eph. 2:3). The soul is by nature perfect when it is subject to its own spirit, and follows the spirit as the spirit follows God. The natural [*animalis,* soulish] man receiveth not the things of the Spirit of God. The soul is not so speedily subjected to the spirit in order to perform good works, as the spirit is subjected to God to produce true faith and a good will. Sometimes its impulse to seek carnal and temporal things is with difficulty restrained. But sometimes it is cleansed and recovers the stability of its nature under the mastery of the spirit—for the spirit is the head of the soul as Christ is the head of the spirit. Hence there is no need to despair of the body, too, being restored to its proper nature, but not so speedily as the soul, still less speedily than the spirit, but at the opportune time, at the last trump, when the dead shall arise incorruptible and we shall be changed (1 Cor. 15:52). Therefore we believe in *the resurrection of the flesh.* That is to say; not merely is the soul restored which is now called "flesh" (in Scripture) on account of its carnal affections, but also this visible flesh, which is naturally flesh and which gives its name to the soul on account of the latter's carnal affections in spite of its higher nature—this visible flesh, properly so-called, we must believe without hesitation, rises again from the dead. The apostle Paul seems to have directly pointed his finger at the flesh when he wrote: "*This* corruptible must put on incorruption." When he says *This* he as good as points with his finger. That which is visible can be pointed at in this way. The soul cannot be pointed at, though it can be called corruptible because it is corrupted by moral vices. [Therefore Paul is here speaking of flesh in its natural acceptation.] When we read: "This mortal must put on immortality," again the visible flesh is signified, for again we have the same demonstrative pronoun. For the soul can be said to be mortal as well as corruptible on account of its moral vices. The death of the soul is to depart from God (cp. Ecclesiasticus 10:12). This first sin committed in paradise is related in the sacred books.

24. The body will rise again according to the Christian faith which is infallible. He who finds this incredible is fixing his attention on what the flesh is like now, and is not considering what it will be like hereafter. When it has been changed into an angelic thing, there will be no longer flesh and blood, but simply body. Speaking of flesh the apostle says:

"There is one flesh of beasts, another of birds, another of fishes and serpents. There are also bodies celestial and bodies terrestrial." Notice he does not say celestial flesh, but celestial and terrestrial bodies (1 Cor. 15:40). All flesh is corporeal, but every body is not flesh. Among terrestrial things wood is a corporeal thing but is not flesh, while the body of man and beast is also flesh. Among celestial things there is no flesh, but simple and shining bodies, which the apostle calls spiritual; but some call them ethereal. So he does not deny the resurrection of the flesh when he says: "Flesh and blood shall not possess the kingdom of God," but declares what flesh and blood are to become. If any man does not believe that common flesh can be changed into a nature of this sort, he is to be led on to faith by gradual steps. If you ask him whether earth can be changed into water, that will not seem to him incredible because there is no great distance between these two elements. Again if you ask whether water can be changed into air, he will agree that that is not absurd because these two elements are close neighbours. Let him next be asked about air, whether it can be transformed into an ethereal body, and again the close relation of the two elements will make it plausible. Now when he has admitted the possibility that earth can be transmuted by these stages into ethereal body, why should it not be possible directly when God so wills it, who once made it possible for a human body to walk upon the waters? Why should he not believe that it can happen without these intermediate steps, "in the twinkling of an eye," as it is written (1 Cor. 15:52); just as smoke is often turned into flame with marvellous speed? Our flesh is no doubt derived from the earth. Philosophical arguments in proof of the assertion that no earthly object can be in heaven are often urged against faith in the resurrection of the flesh; and yet the philosophers admit that any body can be changed and transformed into any other. When the resurrection of the body has taken place we shall be freed from our temporal condition, and shall enjoy eternal life in ineffable charity and with a constancy that knows no corruption. Then shall it be as it is written: "Death is swallowed up in victory. O Death, where is thy sting? O Death, where is thy contention?" (1 Cor. 15:54).

25. This is the faith which is handed over to young Christians, expressed in a few words, which they are to hold faithfully. These few words are made known to believers, that, believing, they may subject themselves to God, being so subject may live righteous lives, living righteously they may cleanse their hearts, and with a pure heart may know what they believe.

21. Sermon on 1 John 4:12–16
From *Eighth Homily*
(415)

AUGUSTINE OF HIPPO

During the Easter season of 415, Augustine (354–430) preached a series of ten sermons on the First Epistle of John. Scholars believe that his treatment of the epistles reflect, at least in part, the final stage of his protracted battle against Donatism, a schismatic movement that had its roots in the great persecution of Diocletian and whose popularity at one time seriously threatened the existence of the church in North Africa.

The outcome of Augustine's campaign, begun in 399, was an imperial decree in 412, which recognized that the true church did not depend upon the purity of its members. It condemned Donatism, imposed heavy fines on violators (not prison or death), and ordered the seizure of Donatist churches and property.

In 404, Augustine wrote the Donatist bishop of Cartenna: "Originally my opinion was that no one should be coerced into the unity of Christ, that we fight only by arguments, and prevail by force of reason, lest we should have those whom we knew to be avowed heretics feigning to be Catholics. But this opinion of mine was overcome. . . . In the first place,

---

SOURCE: Saint Augustine, *Augustine: Later Works,* ed. John Burnaby, vol. 8 of *Library of Christian Classics* (Philadelphia: Westminster Press, 1955). Used by permission of Westminster John Knox Press.

there was set over against my opinion my own town, which although it was once almost totally on the side of Donatus was brought over to the catholic unity by fear of the Imperial Edicts. . . . There were so many others which were mentioned to me by name, that from the facts themselves, I was persuaded that in this matter the word of Scripture may apply, 'Give opportunity to a wise man and he will become wiser.'" In the same letter, Augustine uses Luke 14:23 (*"compel people to come in"*) to justify religious coercion.

Augustine, however, is ever wary of religious pride. In his "Sermon on 1 John 4:12–16," he warns against the sin of pride and argues that persons can do any good work for wrong reasons. Motivation, "the heart," is what ultimately matters — not the outward appearance of an act. We are to judge all actions by the norm of love.

Augustine wonders why Jesus' command to love our enemies does not appear in First John, which commands only that we love our brothers and sisters. Augustine's answer is persuasive: To love an enemy is to love a potential brother or sister; it is to change enemies into friends. "You love in [your enemy], not what he is, but what you would have him be." If one extends this line of reasoning to the schismatic or heretic, however, coercion can become an instrument of salvation. Augustine believes that while it is possible to be in the universal church "only seemingly" (i.e., not saved), everyone outside the church is not saved "in reality."

---

4. It may have occurred to some of you, since we have been expounding this Epistle of John, to ask why the charity which he so strongly commends is only brotherly love. He speaks of "him that loveth his brother," and of the "commandment given to us that we love one another." Brotherly charity is continually spoken of; but of the charity of God, the charity (that is) whereby we love God, there is not such constant mention — though it is not altogether passed over in silence. On the other hand, there is scarcely a word in the whole Epistle about the love of enemies. In all his urgent preaching and commendation of charity, he does not tell us to love our enemies, only to love our brethren. Yet just now, in our reading of the Gospel, we heard the text: "If ye love them that love you, what reward have you? Do not the publicans the same?"[1] How is it then that John the apostle enjoins brotherly love upon us as the great means towards our

---

1. Matt. 5:46.

perfecting, while our Lord says that it is not enough for us to love our brothers, but that love itself must stretch so far as to reach our enemies? The reaching to enemies does not mean the passing over of brothers. Our love, like a fire, must first take hold of what is nearest, and so spread to what is further off. A brother is nearer to you than a casual stranger: and again you are closer to the man whom you do not know but who is not opposed to you, than to the enemy who is. Your love should extend to your neighbours; but that is not to be called extension. Love for those who are linked to you is much the same as love for yourself. Extend it to such as you do not know, who yet have done no harm to you; and now go further than them, and reach to the love of enemies. That, certainly, is our Lord's command. Why then has John said nothing of loving an enemy?

5. All love, even the love we call carnal — for which the more usual Latin word is not *dilectio* but *amor, dilectio* being commonly used and understood in a higher sense — all love, my dear brothers, implies necessarily an element of goodwill towards those who are loved. Whether we use the word *diligere* or *amare* — as the Lord did when he said to Peter, Lovest (*amas*) thou me? — we should not, indeed we cannot love men in the sense in which a glutton will say, I love partridges: the object of his love being the killing and eating them. He says he loves, but the effect for the partridges is to put an end to their existence: he loves their destruction. The love of food can only purport its consumption and our own refreshment. Men are not to be loved as things to be consumed, but in the manner of friendship and goodwill, leading us to do things for the benefit of those we love. And if there is nothing we can do, goodwill alone is enough for the lover. We should not want there to be unfortunates, so that we may exercise works of mercy. You give bread to the hungry; but it would be better that no one should hunger, and that you should not have to give. You clothe the naked; would that all were so clothed that there were no need for it! You bury the dead: but we long for that life in which there is no dying. You reconcile men at law with one another: but we long for the everlasting peace of Jerusalem where all quarrels are at an end. All these are the services called out by man's needs. Remove distress, and there will be no place for works of mercy. Works of mercy will cease, but there will be no quenching of the fire of charity. You may have the truest love for a happy man, on whom you have nothing to bestow: such love will have a greater sincerity and a far more unspoilt purity. Once you have bestowed gifts on the unfortunate, you may easily yield to the temptation to exalt yourself over him, to assume superiority over the object of your benefaction. He fell into need, and you supplied him: you feel yourself as

the giver to be a bigger man than the receiver of the gift. You should want him to be your equal, that both may be subject to the one on whom no favour can be bestowed.

8. The true Christian will never set himself up over other men. God gave you a place above the beasts, in which you are of more value than they. That is your natural privilege, always to be better than a beast. If you would be better than another man, you will grudge to see him as your equal. You ought to wish all men equal to yourself; and if you have gone beyond another man in wisdom, you should want him too to show himself wise. While he is still backward, he may learn of you: while he is ignorant, he has need of you; and you appear as teacher, he as learner. As teacher, you are the superior; as learner, he is the inferior. Unless you want him to be your equal, you will be for having him always as the learner, and that will make you a grudging teacher. But what sort of teaching will a grudging teacher give? I can only beg you not to teach him your grudgingness. Listen to the apostle's words, which come from the true heart of charity: "I would that all men were such as I myself."[2] See how he wanted all to be his equals; and just because charity made him so desire, he was raised above all. Man has transgressed his proper limit: created higher than the beasts, he has let covetousness carry him away, so that he might be higher than other men. And that is pride.

9. Consider now the works that pride may do: notice how they may resemble or even equal those of charity. Charity feeds the hungry, so does pride: charity, to the praise of God, pride, to the praise of itself. Charity clothes the naked, so does pride; charity fasts, so does pride; charity buries the dead, so does pride. All the good works that are willed and done by charity, may be set in motion by its contrary pride, like horses harnessed to a car. But when charity is the inward driver, pride must give place — place which is not so much misgoverning as misgoverned. It goes ill with the man who has pride for his charioteer, for he is sure to be overturned. How can we know or see that it be not pride which governs the good deed? Where is the proof? We see the works: hunger is fed by compassion, but also by pride; strangers are entertained by compassion, but also by pride; poverty is protected by compassion, but also by pride. In the works themselves we can see no difference. I would go further — though it is not I, but Paul who says it: charity goes to death, a man (that is) who has charity confesses the name of Christ and becomes a martyr; and pride also may do both. The one has charity, the other has not; but let

---

2. 1 Cor. 7:7.

this other mark the apostle's words: "If I give all my goods to the poor, and if I give my body to burn, and have not charity, it profiteth me nothing."[3] So Holy Scripture recalls us from all this outward showing, recalls us from the surface appearance displayed before men, to the inward truth. Come back to your own conscience, and question it: pay heed, not to the visible flowering but to the root beneath the ground. Is covetousness at the root? Then you may have a show of good deeds, but of works truly good there can be none. Is charity at the root? Be easy, for no evil can be the issue. The proud may speak fair words, love may show anger: the one may clothe, the other may smite: the one clothes for the pleasing of men, the other smites for the correction of discipline. The stroke of charity is more to be welcomed than the alms of pride. Come back, then, my brothers, into the place within, and in whatsoever you do, look for the witness of God. See, as he sees, the intention of your acts. If your heart does not accuse you of acting for the sake of display, it is well, you may be easy. And when you do well, have no fear of another's seeing. Fear only to act so that you may have praise for yourself; let the other see, so that God may have the praise. If you hide what you do from man's eyes, you are hiding it against man's imitation, and robbing God of his praise. There are two parties for whose benefit you give alms, two are hungry, the one for bread, the other for righteousness; for it is written, "Blessed are they that hunger and thirst after righteousness, for they shall be filled."[4] Between these two hungering ones, you are set for the working of good: if charity is the worker, it has compassion for both, it seeks to give help to both. For while the one looks for food, the other looks for an example to follow. As you feed the first, offer yourself to the second, and you have given alms to both. You have enabled the one to give thanks for the ending of his hunger, the other to imitate the example shown him.

10. Let your works of mercy, then, proceed from a merciful heart; for then even in your love of enemies you will be showing love of brothers. Do not think that John has given no charge concerning love of one's enemy; for he has said much of brotherly charity, and it is always the brother that you love. How so? you ask. I ask in turn, Why do you love your enemy? Because you wish him to have good health in this life? but suppose that is not in his interest? Because you wish him to be rich? but if riches themselves should rob him of his sight? To marry a wife? but if that should bring him a life of bitterness? To have children? but suppose they

---

3. 1 Cor. 13:3.
4. Matt. 5:6.

turn out badly? Thus there is uncertainty in all the things you seem to desire for your enemy, because you love him: uncertainty everywhere. Let your desire for him be that together with you he may have eternal life: let your desire for him be that he may be your brother. And if that is what you desire in loving your enemy — that he may be your brother — when you love him, you love a brother. You love in him, not what he is, but what you would have him be. Once before, if I remember right, my dear people, I put to you this parable: Imagine the trunk of a tree lying before you: a good carpenter may see such a piece of timber, unhewn, as it was cut in the forest. He loves it at sight, but because he means to make something out of it. The reason for his love is not that it may always remain as it is: as craftsman, he has looked at what it shall be, not as lover at what it is; and his love is set upon what he will make of it, not upon its present state. Even so has God loved us sinners. God, we say, has loved sinners; for we have his word, "They that are whole need not a physician, but they that are sick."[5] But surely his love for us sinners is not to the end that we remain in our sin. Like trees from the wood, we have been looked on by the Carpenter, and his thought turns to the building he will make of us, not to the timber that we were. So may you look upon your enemy, standing against you with his angry passion, his biting words, his provoking insults, his unrelenting hate. But in all this you need think only that he is a *man*. You see all the hostility to yourself as of the man's making; and you say in your heart? "Lord, have mercy on him: forgive him his sins: of God: his hatred of you, his malice against you, is his own. And what do your say in your heart? "Lord, have mercy on him: forgive him his sins: put fear in him, and change him." You love in him, not what he is but what you would have him be; and thus when you love your enemy, you love a brother. Therefore the perfection of love is the love of an enemy, and this perfect love consists in brotherly love. It is not to be held that the apostle John enjoins upon us a lesser degree of charity, and the Lord Jesus a greater. John, indeed, instructs us to love our brothers, Christ to love even our enemies. But you must consider why Christ has bidden you love your enemies. It cannot be with the intent that they should always remain such: that would be an instruction to hate, not to love. Consider the manner of his own love for them, which was a will that they should not continue his persecutors: "Father," he says, "forgive them, for they know not what they do."[6] The will for their pardoning was a will for their transformation: in willing that they should be transformed, he deigned to make brothers

---

5. Matt. 9:12.
6. Luke 23:34.

out of enemies; and so in very truth he did. He was killed, and buried. He rose again and ascended into heaven, he sent the Holy Spirit upon his disciples. They began with confidence to preach his name, they worked miracles in the name of the crucified and slain; and those who had done the Lord to death saw what was done: that blood which they had shed in fury, they drank in faith.

11. I have spoken of all this, my brethren, somewhat lengthily; but if charity was to be urged upon you, my people, with the force demanded, there was no other way. If there is in you nothing of charity, all I have said comes to nothing. But if it exists at all in you, my words should be as oil upon the flames; and perhaps they may have kindled it even where it was not. In one, what was already there will have grown: in another, what was not may have begun to be. I have spoken in order to stir up your backwardness in the love of enemies. If a man is passionate against you, meet his passion with prayer: if he hates you, meet his hatred with pity. It is the fever in his soul that hates you: when he is cured, he will show his gratitude. Think of the physician's love for the sick: he does not love them *as* sick men. If he did, he would want them always to be sick. He loves the sick, not so that they may remain sick men but so that they may become healthy instead of sick. And how much he may have to suffer from them in their delirium — abuse, not seldom blows! The physician attacks the fever and excuses the man: is this loving his enemy? Truer to say that he is hating his real enemy, disease: that is what he hates, while he loves the man that strikes at him. His hatred, then, is for the fever; for the blows are struck at him by the disease, the sickness, the fever. The physician takes away the thing that shows hostility to him, in order that the man may live to give him thanks. So with you. If your enemy hates you, and hates you unjustly, you know that it is because the lusts of this world have the mastery in him. If you meet his hate with hate, you are returning evil for evil; and what comes of that? I had to lament for one sick man, who hated you: now, if you are hating also, I must mourn for two. But, you say, he has attacked your property, he is robbing you of some earthly possession or other: you hate him, because he is making this life strait for you. You need not suffer such straitening: for you can take your journey into the heaven above, lifting up your heart to the wide realm of freedom where in the hope of life eternal there is no straitness to be borne. Think what it really is of which he would rob you, and remember that he could not even do that, were he not permitted by the Father who "chasteneth every son that he receiveth."[7] Your enemy himself is as it were God's operating

---

7. Heb. 12:6.

instrument to work your own healing: if God knows it to be for your good that he should despoil you, he allows it; if God knows it to be for your good to be beaten, he allows your enemy to strike you. God is using him to make you whole; pray that he too may be given healing.

12. "No man hath ever seen God." See, my beloved! "If we love one another, God shall abide in us, and his love shall be perfected in us." Make a beginning of love, and you shall be made perfect. For if you have begun to love, God has begun to dwell in you: love him who has begun to dwell in you, so that by a more perfect indwelling he may make you perfect. "Hereby we know that we abide in him, and he in us, because he has given us of his Spirit." It is well: thanks be to God! We know that he dwells in us; and how do we know that we know it? Because John himself tells us, that "he has given us of his Spirit." How do we know that? How do you know that he has given you of his Spirit? Ask your heart: if it is full of charity, you have the Spirit of God. How do we know that this is evidence for you of God's Spirit dwelling in you? Ask Paul the apostle: "Because the charity of God is shed abroad in our hearts through the Holy Spirit that is given us."[8]

13. "And we have seen, and are witnesses, that the Father sent his Son to be the Saviour of the world." Sick men, be at your ease: if such a physician has come to you, there can be no despairing. Grave were your diseases, incurable your wounds, desperate your sickness. But if you think of the gravity of your trouble, think also of the omnipotence of the Physician. You are desperate, but he is omnipotent; and his witnesses are they who first were healed, and who now proclaim the Physician — although their own healing were in hope rather than in fulfilment, as the apostle says: "In hope we are saved."[9] So we have begun to be healed in faith, and our salvation will be perfected, when this corruptible shall have put on incorruption, and this mortal shall have put on immortality. That is hope, not fulfilment; but he that rejoices in hope shall lay hold of the fulfilment, to which he that has not hope can never attain.

14. "Whosoever confesses that Jesus is the Son of God, God abideth in him, and he in God." We need not now insist at length, that this confessing must be not in word but in deed, not of the tongue but of the life; for there are many that confess in words what their deeds deny. "And we have known, and have believed, what love God hath in us." Again, how have you known this? "God is love." He has said it before, and now says it again. You could not have a fuller commendation of love than the naming

---

8. Rom. 5:5.
9. Rom. 8:24.

of it with God's name. You might possibly have thought little of God's gift, but can you think little of God? "God is love, and he that abideth in love, abideth in God and God abideth in him." There is a mutual indwelling of the holder and the held: your dwelling in God means that you are held by him, God's dwelling in you means that he holds you, lest you fall. Think of yourself as being made a house of God, but not like the house of bricks and mortar that carries you in the body. If that house should go from under you, you fall; but God does not fall, if you go from under him. He is whole and entire, when you desert him, whole and entire when you return to him. Your healing brings no gift to him: it is you that are cleansed, you that are amended and re-created. He is medicine to the unhealthy, rule to the crooked, light to the darkened, dwelling to the homeless. The imparting is all to you, and you may not suppose that when you come to God there is aught imparted to him — even the possession of a slave. God will not lack servants, though you refuse, though all refuse his service. God has no need of servants, but servants have need of God. Hence the words of the Psalm: "I have said unto the Lord, thou art my God" — yes, God is the true Lord — "because thou needest not my goods."[10] You need the good your servant provides. He needs the good you provide for him in feeding him, and you need the good he provides for you by his service. For yourself you cannot do all the drawing of water, the cooking, the running before your carriage, the grooming of your beast. You are in want of the good your servant furnishes, you are in want of his attendance; and inasmuch as you want an inferior, you are no true lord. The true lord is he who seeks nothing from us; and it goes ill with us, if we seek not him. He seeks nothing from us, yet he sought us when we were not seeking him. One sheep had gone astray: he found it and brought it home upon his shoulders rejoicing.[11] Was the sheep a necessity for the shepherd, or not rather the shepherd a necessity for the sheep?

    I am loth, you see, to reach the end of this Epistle, just because there is no theme on which I would fainer speak than charity; and no other Scripture extols charity with greater warmth. For you there can be no sweeter matter of discourse, no food more healthful for your souls — but only if by good living you confirm in yourselves the gift of God. Be not unthankful for this wondrous grace of God — God, who, possessing one only-begotten Son, willed not that Son to be alone, but adopted us to be his brothers and share with him eternal life.

---

10. Ps. 16:2.
11. Luke 15:4 f.

22. Sermon on Holy Communion
From *Sermon 272*

AUGUSTINE OF HIPPO

In this brief Easter sermon, Augustine (354–430) addresses newly baptized catechumens (converts) who are about to take their first communion. After a long period of preparation, they had renounced evil ("been exorcised") and were baptized at a solemn service the night before. They had confessed their faith before the congregation and now they were finally ready to participate fully in the life of the church.

Augustine seeks to help these new believers understand what they believe. He asserts that faith must precede understanding. In effect he says, don't argue about it, just listen to the creed and the scriptures. Know that you really are *the body of Christ. Yet faith does not want to be blind; "faith craves understanding."*

To enhance understanding, Augustine uses the process of baking bread and of making wine to illustrate the sacramental union between Christ and the church. Just as kernels of grain are ground and baked into bread, so the believer is indelibly joined to the body of Christ by God's irresistible grace given to us in the sacraments. This understand-

---

SOURCE: Maurice Wiles and Mark Santer, eds., *Documents in Early Christian Thought* (Cambridge: Cambridge University Press, 1979). © Cambridge University Press 1975. Used by permission of Cambridge University Press.

ing of sacramental grace is liberating. Many years later Martin Luther was able to survive deep spiritual anguish (Anfechtung) by telling himself, "I have been baptized!"

What you now see on God's altar, you also saw last night.[1] But you have not yet learnt what it is, what it signifies, or how great is the reality of which it comprises the sacrament. What you see is bread and a cup; that is what your eyes tell you. But what your faith (as yet uninstructed) insists is that the bread is the body of Christ and the cup the blood of Christ. That can briefly be stated and it may be all that faith needs. Yet faith does crave instruction. The prophet says: "Unless you believe, you will not understand" [Isa. 7:9]. So[2] you can now say to me: "You have told us so that we can believe; now explain to us so that we can understand."

Perhaps the following argument has arisen in someone's mind: "Our Lord Jesus Christ, we know, took flesh from the virgin Mary; he was suckled as a baby, was reared, grew up, reached manhood, underwent persecution by the Jews, was hung upon a cross, put to death on the cross, taken down from the cross; was buried, rose again on the third day, and on the day of his own choosing ascended into heaven. Thither he raised his body; thence he will come to judge the living and the dead; there he now is seated at the right hand of the Father. How then can the bread be his body and the cup (or rather the contents of the cup) be his blood?"

These things, my brothers, are called sacraments because there is a difference between their appearance and their true meaning. In appearance they have a physical form; in their true meaning they have a spiritual effect. If you want to understand what is meant by "the body of Christ," you must attend to the words of the apostle: "You are the body of Christ and his members" [1 Cor. 12:27]. So then if you are the body of Christ and his members it is the mystery of yourselves that is placed on the Lord's table; it is the mystery of yourselves that you receive. It is to what you are that you make the response "Amen," and in making that response you give your personal assent. You hear "the body of Christ" and you answer "Amen." Be a member of Christ's body and make your "Amen" true.

---

1. Augustine is preaching to the newly baptized at the second mass of Easter, on Easter morning. He is speaking after the dismissal of all but the baptized, when the bread and wine already stand ready on the altar for the Eucharist. See F. van der Meer, *Augustine the Bishop* (London, 1961), pp. 371–73.

2. Reading *ergo* (with Fulgentius) rather than *enim*.

But why the bread? Here too, let us not use any arguments of our own but continue to listen to the apostle himself and to what he has said about the sacrament: "One bread, one body are we, many that we are" [1 Cor. 10:17]. Understand and rejoice: unity, truth, virtue, love. "One bread." Who is this one bread? The "one body many that we are." Remember that bread is not made from a single grain, but from many. When you were exorcized, that was a kind of grinding; when you were baptized, that was a kind of moistening; and when you received the fire of the Holy Spirit, that was a kind of baking. Be what you see and receive what you are. That is what the apostle said about the bread.

What about the meaning of the cup? He makes this clear enough even though he does not spell it out in so many words. To produce the bread that we see many grains are moistened into unity (the result is like what holy Scripture says of the faithful: "they were of one soul and one heart towards God" [Acts 4:32]). It is the same with the wine. Remember, my brothers, how wine is made. There are many grapes hanging on the vine, but the juice of the grapes is mixed up together in unity. In this the Lord Christ was giving us a picture of ourselves. He wanted us to belong to him; at his table he consecrated the mystery of our peace and of our unity. He who receives the mystery of unity but does not keep the bond of peace, receives not a mystery that will profit him but a testimony that will witness against him.

Let us turn to the Lord, to God the Father almighty, and with pure hearts let us offer true thanks to him as fully as our weakness will allow. With all our powers let us implore him that in his matchless kindness he will graciously deign to hear our prayers; that by his power he will drive the enemy far away from our actions and our thoughts, that he will increase our faith, direct our minds, grant us spiritual thoughts and bring us in the end to his own blessedness through Jesus Christ his Son. Amen.

23. On Nature and Grace
(415)

AUGUSTINE OF HIPPO

In 411, at the Conference of Carthage, Augustine (354–430) played a major role in the defeat of Donatism. A year later, Marcellinus, the imperial arbitrator at the Carthage conference, asked Augustine's advice on the teachings of Pelagius, a lay theologian. Pelagius had come to Carthage with his disciple Caelestius in 410, following the Visigoths' conquest of Rome. Pelagius and Caelestius caused quite a stir by denying the widely held doctrine of original sin according to which "propagation" transmitted Adam's transgression to the whole human race.

Augustine responded to Pelagius with On the Rewards and the Remissions of Sins, *the first in a long series of anti-Pelagian writings. Pelagius argued that a just God cannot possibly demand the impossible, making moral perfection attainable to people of good will. Augustine insisted that people do not do what is right, either because the right is hidden from them or because they find no delight in it. He believed that the strength of our will to do anything is proportionate to our knowledge of its goodness and to the warmth of our delight in it. Thus ignorance and*

SOURCE: Whitney Oates, ed., *The Basic Writings of Saint Augustine,* vol. 1 (New York: Random House Publishers, 1948). Copyright © 1948 by Random House, Inc. Used by permission of Random House, Inc.

infirmity are failings that hinder the will from being moved to perform a good action or to abstain from a bad one.

However, what is hidden may become clear and what fails to delight may become sweet due to the grace of God, which aids the human will. If people lack that aid, however, the cause lies in themselves and not in God, whether they are predestined for damnation because of the wickedness of pride; or whether they are predestined for judgment and instruction against their pride as children of mercy.[1]

It is difficult to understand Augustine's rigid predestinarianism. Both he and Pelagius agreed on the merits of the ascetic life. They agreed that psychologically, the will is free. (We "feel free" to make choices.) Pelagius preached the ethics of the Sermon on the Mount to worldly Christians in Rome for almost thirty years. Known for his ascetic life, many people thought he was a monk. "A Christian," according to Pelagius, "is not known just 'by the name' but by good works; Christians are people who imitate and follow Christ in everything they do."[2]

Augustine's quarrel with Pelagius was not about ethics but about grace. If humans can heal themselves by their own will, they do not need a physician. In On Nature and Grace, Augustine charges Pelagius with "rendering the cross of Christ to no effect . . . if he contends that righteousness and everlasting life may be attained by any other means than through Christ's own sacrament."

If human perfection is just an extra effort away, the cross is unnecessary. Jesus is not merely our teacher; the gospel is not a program for moral reform; and the vision of God's realm is not a blueprint for the perfect society. Against the Pelagian theology of glory, Augustine advances a theology of the cross. Sin is not merely a misstep; it is a flaw in the human condition. Its remedy is healing, not mere instruction. And healing comes only through God's sacramental act in the cross of Christ. Following Paul, Augustine argues that justification is the process of growing towards righteousness by faith active in love. Grace therefore does not oppose nature; it liberates and controls nature.

In Christian history, Augustine's view of the human condition proved to be more enduring than Pelagius's ethical positivism. Christians know the power of "Adam's sin" and discover the difficulty in addressing in-

---

1. From *On the Rewards and Remissions of Sins*, II, 26, xvii, cited by John Burnaby in *Library of Christian Classics*, vol. 8, 187, revised.
2. From *On the Christian Life*, 6, cited by Lhose, 114.

justice without facing "concupiscence," Augustine's term for the human preoccupation with things and self that separate men and women from the love of Christ and the neighbor.

Chapter 1

The Occasion of Publishing This Work; What God's Righteousness Is

The book which you sent to me, my beloved sons, Timasius and Jacobus, I have read through hastily, but not indifferently, omitting only the few points which are plain enough to everybody; and I saw in it a man inflamed with most ardent zeal against those, who, when in their sins they ought to censure human will, are more forward in accusing the nature of men, and thereby endeavor to excuse themselves. He shows too great a fire against this evil, which even authors of secular literature have severely censured with the exclamation: "The human race falsely complains of its own nature!"[1] This same sentiment your author also has strongly insisted upon, with all the powers of his talent. I fear, however, that he will chiefly help those "who have a zeal for God, but not according to knowledge," who, "being ignorant of God's righteousness, and going about to establish their own righteousness, have not submitted themselves to the righteousness of God."[2] Now, what the righteousness of God is, which is spoken of here, he immediately afterwards explains by adding: "For Christ is the end of the law for righteousness to every one that believeth."[3] This righteousness of God, therefore, lies not in the commandment of the law, which excites fear, but in the aid afforded by the grace of Christ, to which alone the fear of the law, as of a schoolmaster,[4] usefully conducts. Now, the man who understands this understands why he is a Christian. For "If righteousness came by the law, then Christ is dead in vain."[5] If, however, He did not die in vain, in Him only is the ungodly man justified, and to him, on believing in Him who justifies the ungodly, faith is reckoned for righteousness.[6] For all men have sinned and

---

1. See Sallust's Prologue to his *Jugurtha*.
2. Rom. 10:2, 3.
3. Rom. 10:4.
4. Gal. 3:24.
5. Gal. 2:21.
6. Rom. 4:5.

come short of the glory of God, being justified freely by His blood.[7] But all those who do not think themselves to belong to the "all who have sinned and fall short of the glory of God," have of course no need to become Christians, because "they that be whole need not a physician, but they that are sick";[8] whence it is, that He came not to call the righteous, but sinners to repentance.[9]

Chapter II

Faith in Christ Not Necessary to Salvation, If a Man Without It Can Lead a Righteous Life

Therefore the nature of the human race, generated from the flesh of the one transgressor, if it is self-sufficient for fulfilling the law and for perfecting righteousness, ought to be sure of its reward, that is, of everlasting life, even if in any nation or at any former time faith in the blood of Christ was unknown to it. For God is not so unjust as to defraud righteous persons of the reward of righteousness, because there has not been announced to them the mystery of Christ's divinity and humanity, which was manifested in the flesh.[10] For how could they believe what they had not heard of; or how could they hear without a preacher?[11] For "faith cometh by hearing, and hearing by the word of Christ." But I say (adds he): Have they not heard? "Yea, verily; their sound went out into all the earth, and their words unto the ends of the world."[12] Before, however, all this had been accomplished, before the actual preaching of the gospel reaches the ends of all the earth — because there are some remote nations still (although it is said they are very few) to whom the preached gospel has not found its way — what must human nature do, or what has it done — for it had either not heard that all this was to take place, or has not yet learnt that it was accomplished — but believe in God who made heaven and earth, by whom also it perceived by nature that it had been itself created, and lead a right life, and thus accomplish His will, uninstructed with any faith in the death and resurrection of Christ? Well, if this

---

7. Rom. 3:23, 24.
8. Matt. 9:12.
9. Matt. 9:13.
10. 1 Tim. 3:16.
11. Rom. 10.
12. Rom. 10:17, 18.

could have been done, or can still be done, then for my part I have to say what the apostle said in regard to the law: "Then Christ died in vain."[5] For if he said this about the law, which only the nation of the Jews received, how much more justly may it be said of the law of nature, which the whole human race has received, "If righteousness come by nature, then Christ died in vain." If, however, Christ did not die in vain, then human nature cannot by any means be justified and redeemed from God's most righteous wrath—in a word, from punishment—except by faith and the sacrament of the blood of Christ.

Chapter III

*Nature Was Created Sound and Whole;
It Was Afterwards Corrupted by Sin*

Man's nature, indeed, was created at first faultless and without any sin; but that nature of man in which every one is born from Adam, now wants the Physician, because it is not sound. All good qualities, no doubt, which it still possesses in its make, life, senses, intellect, it has of the Most High God, its Creator and Maker. But the flaw, which darkens and weakens all those natural goods, so that it has need of illumination and healing, it has not contracted from its blameless Creator—but from that original sin, which it committed by free will. Accordingly, criminal nature has its part in most righteous punishment. For, if we are now newly created in Christ,[13] we were, for all that, children of wrath, even as others,[14] "but God, who is rich in mercy, for His great love wherewith He loved us, even when we were dead in sins, hath quickened us together with Christ, by whose grace we were saved."[15]

Chapter IV

Free Grace

This grace, however, of Christ, without which neither infants nor adults can be saved, is not rendered for any merits, but is given *gratis,* on

---

13. 2 Cor. 5:17.
14. Eph. 2:3.
15. Eph. 2:4, 5.

account of which it is also called *grace*. "Being justified," says the apostle, "freely through His blood."[16] Whence they, who are not liberated through grace, either because they are not yet able to hear, or because they are unwilling to obey; or again because they did not receive, at the time when they were unable on account of youth to hear, that bath of regeneration, which they might have received and through which they might have been saved, are indeed justly condemned; because they are not without sin, either that which they have derived from their birth, or that which they have added from their own misconduct. "For all have sinned" — whether in Adam or in themselves — "and come short of the glory of God."[17]

Chapter V

It Was a Matter of Justice That All Should Be Condemned

The entire mass, therefore, incurs penalty; and if the deserved punishment of condemnation were rendered to all, it would without doubt be righteously rendered. They, therefore, who are delivered therefrom by grace are called, not vessels of their own merits, but "vessels of mercy."[18] But of whose mercy, if not His who sent Christ Jesus into the world to save sinners, whom He foreknew, and foreordained, and called, and justified, and glorified?[19] Now, who could be so madly insane as to fail to give ineffable thanks to the Mercy which liberates whom it would? The man who correctly appreciated the whole subject could not possibly blame the justice of God in wholly condemning all men whatsoever.

Chapter VI

The Pelagians Have Very Strong and Active Minds

If we are simply wise according to the Scriptures, we are not compelled to dispute against the grace of Christ, and to make statements attempting to show that human nature both requires no Physician — in infants, because it is whole and sound; and in adults, because it is able to

---

16. Rom. 3:24.
17. Rom. 3:23.
18. Rom. 9:23.
19. Rom. 8:29, 30.

suffice for itself in attaining righteousness, if it will. Men no doubt seem to urge acute opinions on these points, but it is only word-wisdom,[20] by which the cross of Christ is made of none effect. This, however, "is not the wisdom which descendeth from above."[21] The words which follow in the apostle's statement I am unwilling to quote; for we would rather not be thought to do an injustice to our friends, whose very strong and active minds we should be sorry to see running in a perverse, instead of an upright, course.

Chapter VII

He Proceeds to Confute the Work of Pelagius; He Refrains As Yet from Mentioning Pelagius' Name

However ardent, then, is the zeal which the author of the book you have forwarded to me entertains against those who find a defence for their sins in the infirmity of human nature; not less, nay even much greater, should be our eagerness in preventing all attempts to render the cross of Christ of none effect. Of none effect, however, it is rendered, if it be contended that by any other means than by Christ's own sacrament it is possible to attain to righteousness and everlasting life. This is actually done in the book to which I refer—I will not say by its author wittingly, lest I should express the judgment that he ought not to be accounted even a Christian, but, as I rather believe, unconsciously. He has done it, no doubt, with much power; I only wish that the ability he has displayed were sound and less like that which insane persons are accustomed to exhibit.

Chapter VIII

A Distinction Drawn by Pelagius Between the Possible and Actual

For he first of all makes a distinction: "It is one thing," says he, "to inquire whether a thing can be, which has respect to its possibility only; and another thing, whether or not it is." This distinction, nobody doubts, is true enough; for it follows that whatever is, was able to be; but it does not therefore follow that what is able to be, also is. Our Lord, for instance,

---

20. 1 Cor. 1:17.
21. Jas. 3:15.

raised Lazarus; He unquestionably was able to do so. But inasmuch as He did not raise up Judas, must we therefore contend that He was unable to do so? He certainly was able, but He would not. For if He had been willing, He could have effected this too. *For the Son quickeneth whomsoever He will.*[22] Observe, however, what he means by this distinction, true and manifest enough in itself, and what he endeavors to make out of it. "We are treating," says he, "of possibility only; and to pass from this to something else, except in the case of some certain fact, we deem to be a very serious and extraordinary process." This idea he turns over again and again, in many ways and at great length, so that no one would suppose that he was inquiring about any other point than the possibility of not committing sin. Among the many passages in which he treats of this subject, occurs the following: "I once more repeat my position: I say that it is possible for a man to be without sin. What do you say? That it is impossible for a man to be without sin? But I do not say," he adds, "that there is a man without sin; nor do you say, that there is not a man without sin. Our contention is about what is possible, and not possible; not about what is, and is not." He then enumerates certain passages of Scripture,[23] which are usually alleged in opposition to them, and insists that they have nothing to do with the question, which is really in dispute, as to the possibility or impossibility of a man's being without sin. This is what he says: "*No man indeed is clean from pollution;* and, *There is no man that sinneth not;* and, *There is not a just man upon the earth;* and, *There is none that doeth good.* There are these and similar passages in Scripture," says he, "but they testify to the point of not being, not of not being able; for by testimonies of this sort it is shown what kind of persons certain men were at such and such a time, not that they were unable to be something else. Whence they are justly found to be blameworthy. If, however, they had been of such a character, simply because they were unable to be anything else, they are free from blame."

Chapter IX

Even They Who Were Not Able to Be Justified Are Condemned

See what he has said. I, however, affirm that an infant born in a place where it was not possible for him to be admitted to the baptism of Christ, and being overtaken by death, was placed in such circumstances, that is to

---

22. John 5:21.
23. Job. 14:2; 1 Kings 8:46; Eccles. 8:21; Ps. 14:1.

say, died without the bath of regeneration, because it was not possible for him to be otherwise. He would therefore absolve him, and, in spite of the Lord's sentence, open to him the kingdom of heaven. The apostle, however, does not absolve him, when he says: "By one man sin entered into the world, and death by sin; by which death passed upon all men, for that all have sinned."[24] Rightly, therefore, by virtue of that condemnation which runs throughout the mass, is he not admitted into the kingdom of heaven, although he was not only not a Christian, but was unable to become one.

Chapter X

He Could Not Be Justified, Who Had Not Heard of the Name of Christ; Rendering the Cross of Christ of None Effect

But they say: "He is not condemned; because the statement that all sinned in Adam, was not made because of the sin which is derived from one's birth, but because of imitation of him." If, therefore, Adam is said to be the author of all the sins which followed his own, because he was the first sinner of the human race, then how is it that Abel, rather than Christ, is not placed at the head of all the righteous, because he was the first righteous man? But I am not speaking of the case of an infant. I take the instance of a young man, or an old man, who has died in a region where he could not hear of the name of Christ. Well, could such a man have become righteous by nature and free will; or could he not? If they contend that he could, then see what it is to render the cross of Christ of none effect,[25] to contend that any man without it, can be justified by the law of nature and the power of his will. We may here also say, then is Christ dead in vain,[26] forasmuch as all might accomplish so much as this, even if He had never died; and if they should be unrighteous, they would be so because they wished to be, not because they were unable to be righteous. But even though a man could not be justified at all without the grace of Christ, he would absolve him, if he dared, in accordance with his words, to the effect that, "if a man were of such a character, because he could not possibly have been of any other, he would be free from all blame."

• • •

---

24. Rom. 5:12.
25. 1 Cor. 1:1.
26. Gal. 2:21.

Chapter L

God Commands No Impossibilities

What he says, however, is true enough, "that God is as good as just, and made man such that he was quite able to live without the evil of sin, if only he had been willing." For who does not know that man was made whole and faultless, and endowed with a free will and a free ability to lead a holy life? Our present inquiry, however, is about the man whom "the thieves"[27] left half dead on the road, and who, being disabled and pierced through with heavy wounds, is not so able to mount up to the heights of righteousness as he was able to descend therefrom; who, moreover, if he is now in "the inn,"[28] is in process of cure. God therefore does not command impossibilities; but in His command He counsels you both to do what you can for yourself, and to ask His aid in what you cannot do. Now, we should see whence comes the possibility, and whence the impossibility. This man says: "That proceeds not from a man's will which he can do by nature." I say: A man is not righteous by his will if he can be by nature. He will, however, be able to accomplish by remedial aid what he is rendered incapable of doing by his flaw.

Chapter LI

State of the Question Between the Pelagians and the Catholics. Holy Men of Old Saved by the Self-Same Faith in Christ Which We Exercise

By why need we tarry longer on general statements? Let us go into the core of the question, which we have to discuss with our opponents solely, or almost entirely, on one particular point. For inasmuch as he says that "as far as the present question is concerned, it is not pertinent to inquire whether there have been or now are any men in this life without sin, but whether they had or have the ability to be such persons"; so, were I even to allow that there have been or are any such, I should not by any means therefore affirm that they had or have the ability, unless justified by the grace of God through our Lord "Jesus Christ and Him crucified."[29] For the same faith which healed the saints of old now heals us — that is to

---

27. Luke 10:30.
28. Luke 10:34.
29. 1 Cor. 2:2.

say, faith "in the one Mediator between God and men, the man Christ Jesus"[30] — faith in His blood, faith in His cross, faith in His death and resurrection. As we therefore have the same spirit of faith, we also believe, and on that account also speak.

Chapter LII

The Whole Discussion Is About Grace

Let us, however, observe what our author answers, after laying before himself the question wherein he seems indeed so intolerable to Christian hearts. He says: "But you will tell me this is what disturbs a great many — that you do not maintain that it is by the grace of God that a man is able to be without sin." Certainly this is what causes us disturbance; this is what we object to him. He touches the very point of the case. This is what causes us such utter pain to endure it; this is why we cannot bear to have such points debated by Christians, owing to the love which we feel towards others and towards themselves. Well, let us hear how he clears himself from the objectionable character of the question he has raised. "What blindness of ignorance," he exclaims, "what sluggishness of an uninstructed mind, which supposes that that is maintained and held to be without God's grace which it only hears ought to be attributed to God!" Now, if we knew nothing of what follows this outburst of his, and formed our opinion on simply hearing these words, we might suppose that we had been led to a wrong view of our opponents by the spread of report and by the asseveration of some suitable witnesses among the brethren. For how could it have been more pointedly and truly stated that the possibility of not sinning, to whatever extent it exists or shall exist in man, ought only to be attributed to God? This too is our own affirmation. We may shake hands.

• • •

---

30. 1 Tim. 2:5.

Chapter LXXXIII

God Enjoins No Impossibility, Because All Things Are Possible and Easy to Love

But "the precepts of the law are very good," if we use them lawfully.[31] Indeed, by the very fact (of which we have the firmest conviction) "that the just and good God could not possibly have enjoined impossibilities," we are admonished both what to do in easy paths and what to ask for when they are difficult. Now all things are easy for love to effect, to which (and which alone) "Christ's burden is light"[32] — or rather, it is itself alone the burden which is light. Accordingly it is said, "And His commandments are not grievous";[33] so that whoever finds them grievous must regard the inspired statement about their "not being grievous" as having been capable of only this meaning, that there may be a state of heart to which they are not burdensome, and he must pray for that disposition which he at present wants, so as to be able to fulfil all that is commanded him. And this is the purport of what is said to Israel in Deuteronomy; if understood in a godly, sacred, and spiritual sense, since the apostle, after quoting the passage, "The word is nigh thee, even in thy mouth and in thy heart"[34] (*and,* as the verse also has it, *in thine hands,* for in man's heart are his spiritual hands), adds in explanation, "This is the word of faith which we preach."[35] No man, therefore, who "returns to the Lord his God," as he is there commanded, "with all his heart and with all his soul,"[36] will find God's commandment "grievous." How, indeed, can it be grievous, when it is the precept of love? Either, therefore, a man has not love, and then it is grievous; or he has love, and then it is not grievous. But he possesses love if he does what is there enjoined on Israel, by returning to the Lord his God with all his heart and with all his soul. "A new commandment," says He, "do I give unto you, that ye love one another";[37] and "He that loveth his neighbor hath fulfilled the law";[38] and again, "Love is the fulfilling of the law."[39] In accordance with these sayings is

---

31. See 1 Tim 1:8.
32. Matt. 11:30.
33. 1 John 5:3.
34. Deut. 30:14, quoted Rom. 10:8.
35. Rom. 10:8.
36. Deut. 30:2.
37. John 13:34.
38. Rom. 13:8.
39. Rom. 13:10.

that passage, "Had they trodden good paths, they would have found, indeed, the ways of righteousness easy."[40] How then is it written, "Because of the words of Thy lips, I have kept the paths of difficulty,"[41] except it be that both statements are true: These paths are paths of difficulty to fear; but to love they are easy?

Chapter LXXXIV

The Degrees of Love Are Also Degrees of Holiness

Inchoate love, therefore, is inchoate holiness; advanced love is advanced holiness; great love is great holiness; "perfect love is perfect holiness" — but this "love is out of a pure heart, and of a good conscience, and of faith unfeigned,"[42] "which in this life is then the greatest, when life itself is contemned in comparison with it." I wonder, however, whether it has not a soil in which to grow after it has quitted this mortal life! But in what place and at what time soever it shall reach that state of absolute perfection, which shall admit of no increase, it is certainly not "shed abroad in our hearts" by any energies either of the nature or the volition that are within us, but "by the Holy Ghost which is given unto us,"[43] and which both helps our infirmity and co-operates with our strength. For it is itself indeed the grace of God, through our Lord Jesus Christ, to whom, with the Father and the Holy Spirit, appertaineth eternity, and all goodness, for ever and ever. Amen.

---

40. Prov. 2:20.
41. Ps. 17:4.
42. 1 Tim 1:5.
43. Rom 5:5.

Early Creedal Controversies

24. The Confession of the Presbyters at Smyrna
(c. 180)

PRESBYTERS AT SMYRNA

The earliest creedal statements of the church were simple affirmations of faith for use in worship and instruction. Although there were no formal, normative texts, there was an emerging consensus on what could be accepted as sound "apostolic" teaching. For example, Ignatius asks the Trallians to "be deaf to any talk that ignores Jesus Christ, of David's lineage, of Mary; who was really born, ate, and drank; was really persecuted under Pontius Pilate, was really crucified and died in the sight of heaven, and earth and the underworld. He was really raised from the dead, for his Father raised him, just as his Father will raise us, who be-

---

SOURCE: John H. Leith, ed., *Creeds of the Churches: A Reader in Christian Doctrine from the Bible to the Present* (Atlanta: John Knox Press, 1978). © 1963, 1978, 1982 John H. Leith. Used by permission of Westminster John Knox Press.

lieve in him, through Christ Jesus, apart from whom we have no genuine life."[1]

The confession of the church at Smyrna (c. 180) was written as an affirmation of faith of a local Christian community against the Monarchian heresy of Noetus who was expelled by the presbyters of Smyrna for teaching that God/father himself suffered and died on the cross. Noetus's teachings conflicted with the church's rule of faith or with "what has been handed down to us." It is an early instance of the "declarative use" of a confession as a norm for church discipline.

We also know in truth one God,
we know Christ, we know the Son,
suffering as he suffered,
dying as he died,
and risen on the third day,
and abiding at the right hand of the Father,
and coming to judge the living and the dead.
And in saying this we say what has been handed down to us.

---

1. From Trall. 9:1–2, Cyril C. Richardson, ed., *Early Christian Fathers,* vol. 1 of *Library of Christian Classics* (Philadelphia: Westminster Press, 1953), 100.

25. The Rule of Faith
From *Against Praxeas*
(213)

TERTULLIAN

Three times in his writings, Tertullian cites the "rule of faith" (an informal summary of the church's teaching tradition) to support what he considers to be sound Christian teaching. Each time (in Prescription Against Heretics, *in* On the Virgin's Veil, *and in* Against Praxeas*), Tertullian expresses the commonly held affirmations of the tradition's "rule" but modifies the "rule" to suit his purpose.*

Against Praxeas is a product of Tertullian's Montanist years. Flirting with schism, Tertullian defends the traditional "logos" doctrine of Western Christianity against Monarchian "novelties." Monarchians Praxeas and Noetus upheld that the incarnation was not of the "logos" but of the first person of the Trinity. Understood this way, the God/father himself suffered on the cross (see vol. 1:226–27), which was an unacceptable position.

Tertullian had little sympathy for speculative theology. Appealing to the "rule of faith," he objected: (1) The Son (logos) has been with the Father from the creation; nothing was made without him. This same divine Son was sent by the Father "into the virgin" to be Mary's son. (2)

SOURCE: Anne Fremantle, ed., *A Treasury of Early Christianity* (New York: Mentor Books, 1960). Used by permission of the author.

According to God's promise, God has sent the Paraclete (the Holy Ghost) to those who believe (a mild acknowledgment of Montanism). (3) The views of Praxeas and all other heretics are nothing more than faddish innovations. Only the "rule of faith" meets the test of time.

We believe one God; but under this dispensation which we call the economy there is the Son of the only God, his Word who proceeded from Him, through whom all things were made, and without whom nothing was made. This One was sent by the Father into the Virgin, and was born of her, Man and God, the Son of Man and the Son of God, and called Jesus Christ; He suffered, He died and was buried according to the Scriptures; and raised again by the Father, and taken up into the heavens, and He sits at the right hand of the Father; He shall come again to judge the quick and the dead: and He thence did send, according to His promise, from the Father, the Holy Ghost, the Paraclete, the Sanctifier of the faith of those who believe in the Father and the Son and the Holy Ghost. That this rule has come down from the beginning, even before any of the earlier heresies, much more before Praxeas, who is of yesterday, the lateness of date of all heresies proves, as also the novelties of Praxeas, a pretender of yesterday. . . .

26. The Letter of Eusebius of Caesarea Describing the Council of Nicaea
(325)

EUSEBIUS

In 325, the emperor Constantine convened a general council of bishops at his residence in Nicaea. Constantine wanted to settle, once and for all, the persistent theological squabbles over the nature of Christ that threatened the unity of the church and *eroded Constantine's objective to make Christianity the new religion of his empire. Eusebius, bishop of Caesarea and ancient church historian, attended. The earliest record of the Nicene Creed appears in a letter from Eusebius to his home church in Caesarea.*

In the letter, Eusebius writes that he was able to present the Caesarean views at the opening of the conference. He makes it sound as if the Nicene compromise, which upheld the full humanity and full divinity of Jesus, was merely an extension of the Caesarean Creed. He writes that the council and "our most pious emperor . . . declared [it] to be sound and approved . . . with [only] some additions to our phrases."

Arriving at the Nicene Creed was certainly not that simple. Eusebius himself credits the emperor with adding the word "consubstantial"

SOURCE: Edward Rochie Hardy, ed., *Christology of the Later Fathers*, vol. 3 of *Library of Christian Classics* (Philadelphia: Westminster Press, 1954). Used by permission of Westminster John Knox Press.

(homo-ousios) *to the final document. Like many Eastern Christians whose sympathies were Origenist or semi-Arian (emphasizing the human more than the divine nature of Christ), Eusebius says that he "agreed to this idea" to serve "the aim of peace."*

For the sake of peace, the Nicene Creed tried to capture the mystery of Christ by affirming that he was "of the same being" as God the father and by confessing that he was "begotten, not made." This fourth-century "basis of union with interpretations" actually led to a fifty-year family feud between Eastern and Western Christians.

You have very likely, beloved, already learned from some other source of the action taken at the great synod convened at Nicaea with reference to the faith of the Church, since rumor commonly outruns the true account of what has been done. But lest you should receive an inaccurate impression from such reports, I[1] have found it necessary to send you, first the statement of faith which I presented, and then the second which [the bishops] issued, making some additions to our phrases. My document, then, which was read in the presence of our most pious emperor and declared to be sound and approved, read as follows:

"As I received my tradition from the bishops before me, both in my first instruction and when I was baptized, and as I have learned from the divine Scriptures, and as I believed and taught both in the [office of] the presbyterate and in the episcopate itself — so still believing I present to you my Creed,[2] which is this:

"We believe in one God, Father, Almighty, the maker of all things visible and invisible,

"And in one Lord Jesus Christ, the Word of God, God of God, Light of Light, Life of Life, unique[3] Son, first-born of all creation, begotten of the Father before all the ages, through whom also all things came to be, who for our salvation was incarnate and dwelt among men and suffered and rose on the third day and ascended to the Father and will come again with glory to judge living and dead.

---

1. Eusebius, as a bishop, uses the plural of dignity throughout; except in the Caesarean Creed I have translated it by the singular, since he is obviously referring to himself — though when he speaks of his reservations in accepting the conciliar Creed he may wish to include others who agreed with him.

2. *Pistis,* here in the sense of "confession of faith."

3. *Monogenēs.*

"We also believe in one Holy Spirit.

"Believing that each of these is and exists, the Father truly [as] Father, the Son truly Son, and the Holy Spirit truly Holy Spirit, as also our Lord said when sending forth his disciples for the preaching, 'Go and make disciples of all nations, baptizing them in the Name of the Father and of the Son and of the Holy Spirit' — of which I firmly assert that this is what I hold, and so I am convinced,[4] and so I have held, and will stand for this faith till death, anathematizing every godless heresy.

"That I have always been convinced of these things, heart and soul, since I was first conscious of myself, and so I am now convinced and profess — [this] I witness in truth before God Almighty and our Lord Jesus Christ, and am prepared to demonstrate and prove to you that so I believed and preached in times gone by."

When I had presented this statement of faith there was no room for opposition — indeed our most pious emperor himself, first of all, testified that its contents were very sound. He further confessed that he himself was so convinced, and urged all to agree to it and to subscribe and assent to these very teachings, with the addition of the one word "consubstantial," which he himself interpreted as follows: "The Son is not to be called 'consubstantial' according to what happens to bodies, nor is he constituted by a division or some kind of cutting up of the Father, nor can the immaterial and intellectual and bodiless nature undergo what happens to bodies, but these things must be conceived of in divine and ineffable terms." Such were the theological observations of our most learned and pious emperor. But [the bishops], on the ground[5] of adding the *homoousios,* produced the following statement:

(The Creed drawn up at the Council)[6]

"We believe in one God, Father, Almighty, maker of all things, visible and invisible,

"And in one Lord Jesus Christ, begotten of the Father uniquely,[3] that is, of the substance of the Father, God of God, Light of Light, true God of true God, begotten, not made, consubstantial with the Father, through whom all things were made, both things in heaven and those in earth, who

---

4. Or "think," though the Greek *phroneō* does not suggest the tentativeness that "think" implies in English.

5. Or "pretext," the Greek *prophasis* being ambiguous as to whether the reason alleged is the real one or not.

6. An explanatory heading found in Athanasius and Theodoret, and obviously not part of the original letter.

for us men and for our salvation came down and was incarnate, [and] became man; he suffered and rose on the third day, ascended into heaven, and is coming to judge living and dead,

"And in the Holy Spirit.

"But those who say, there was once when he was not, and before he was begotten he was not and he came into being out of things that are not, or allege that the Son of God is of a different subsistence or essence, or created or alterable or changeable, the catholic and apostolic Church anathematizes."

When they formulated this statement, I did not let it pass without examination in what sense they said "of the substance of the Father" and "consubstantial with the Father." So questions were raised and answered and the meaning of the phrases was tested by reason. Thus it was declared that they used the phrase "of the substance" to indicate his being of the Father, but not as if he were a part of the Father. So I agreed to subscribe to this in the sense of the pious teaching which declares that the Son is of the Father, but not as being a part of his essence. So I agreed to this idea, not rejecting the word *homoousios,* having before me the aim of peace, and that of not falling away from the sound doctrine.

In the same way I also accepted the phrase "begotten and not made," since they alleged that "made" is a term shared with the other creatures of God which came into being through the Son, which the Son is in no way like, since he is not a work of God comparable to those things that came into being through him, but is of a nature superior to everything made, which the divine oracles teach was begotten of the Father, the manner of his generation being ineffable[7] and indescribable for every nature that came into being.

So also the phrase "the Son is consubstantial with the Father" stands up if properly examined — not in the manner of bodies or similarly to mortal animals, nor by division or cutting up of the essence — nor by any suffering or alteration or change of the essence and power of the Father; for the unbegotten nature of the Father is free from all these things. But the phrase "consubstantial with the Father" indicates that the Son of God bears no similarity with the creatures of God that came into being, but is in every way made like only to the Father who begot him, and is not of any other *hypostasis* or essence, but of the Father. It seemed proper to

---

7. Isa. 53:8 (LXX) reads, "Who shall declare his generation?" a favorite patristic text in this connection, though even in Greek the reference is to the contemporaries of the Suffering Servant rather than to his mysterious birth.

assent to the term itself, expounded in this manner, since I knew of some learned and distinguished bishops and writers among the ancients who made use of the term *homoousios* in the doctrinal discussion about the Father and the Son.

This will be sufficient with reference to the Creed that was set forth, to which we all assented—not without examination, but according to the senses indicated, which were inquired into in the presence of our most devout emperor himself, and supported by the arguments given above. And I did not find the anathematism set forth by them after the Creed distressing, since it forbids the use of non-Scriptural terms, from which has come almost all the disorder and confusion of the Church. For as none of the inspired Scriptures uses the phrases "Out of things that are not" and "There was once when he was not," and the others that follow, it did not seem proper to use or teach them. I agreed to this too as a sound decision, since I had not been accustomed to use these terms previously.

Nor did I think it improper to anathematize the term, "Before he was begotten he was not," since all confess that the Son of God was before [his] generation according to the flesh. Our most pious emperor similarly supported the principle that He existed before all ages according to his divine generation, since before he was actually begotten he existed potentially in the Father, unbegottenly. For the Father is always Father as he is always King and Saviour, being all potentially, and always standing in the same relations and [being in himself] the same.[8]

I have thought it necessary to report to you these things, beloved, showing you the process of our examination and assent. I properly resisted up to the last moment, as long as what was written in unaccustomed language was offensive, but then I accepted without disputing what was unobjectionable, when it became clear to me, on examining fairly the meaning of the terms, that they harmonized with what I myself had professed in the Creed that I previously issued.

---

8. This paragraph, one sentence in the original, is omitted by Socrates; doubtless he (or his source) found it incredible in a writer who was considered generally orthodox. As shown before, Eusebius did believe in the pre-existence of the Son, though not clearly in his eternity; but tries to argue that this anathema committed him to nothing in particular.

27. Constantinople: Creed of the 150 Fathers
(381)

The Council of Nicaea (325) did not settle the Arian controversy. For the next fifty years the arguments continued among (1) the "pure" Arians who insisted that a time existed when the logos *("Word") was not; (2) the traditional Origenists or semi-Arians who supported the idea of a preexistent* logos *but wanted a clearer distinction between the Father and the Son; and (3) those who strongly advocated the Nicene settlement (the Athanasians).*

For a time, it seemed as if the Arians would win. After the death of Emperor Constantius (361), Athanasius struck an alliance with the Cappadocians (see vol. 1:175–83). Finally the Nicene settlement served the needs of Eastern and Western Christians, and they pushed the remnants of Arianism beyond the borders of the empire.

In 381, the Council of Constantinople reaffirmed the original Nicene Creed. It made some minor changes in the first and second articles, but it greatly expanded the third article on the Holy Spirit. Persons refer to the Council of Constantinople's statement as the "Creed of the 150 Fathers" or the Nicene-Constantinopolitan Creed.

SOURCE: John H. Leith, ed., *Creeds of the Churches: A Reader in Christian Doctrine from the Bible to the Present* (Atlanta: John Knox Press, 1978). © 1963, 1978, 1982 John H. Leith. Used by permission of Westminster John Knox Press.

This creed assumes that the Spirit is of the same being as the Father and the logos. *The Eastern bishops interpreted its meaning a year later in an official letter to Western Christians. In the letter, they state explicitly that the three persons, or* hypostases *of the Trinity are of one being.*

The Council of Chalcedon (451) further refined the Nicene Creed, and the creed has established itself in the worship of the church as the most widely acknowledged ecumenical confession of faith.

We believe in one God, the Father All Governing [*pantokratora*], creator [*poiētēn*] of heaven and earth, of all things visible and invisible;

And in one Lord Jesus Christ, the only-begotten Son of God, begotten from the Father before all time [*pro pantōn tōn aiōnōn*], Light from Light, true God from true God, begotten not created [*poiēthenta*], of the same essence [reality] as the Father [*homoousion tō patri*], through Whom all things came into being, Who for us men and because of our salvation came down from heaven, and was incarnate by the Holy Spirit and the Virgin Mary and became human [*enanthrōpēsanta*]. He was crucified for us under Pontius Pilate, and suffered and was buried, and rose on the third day, according to the Scriptures, and ascended to heaven, and sits on the right hand of the Father, and will come again with glory to judge the living and dead. His Kingdom shall have no end [*telos*].

And in the Holy Spirit, the Lord and life-giver, Who proceeds from the Father, Who is worshiped and glorified together with the Father and Son, Who spoke through the prophets; and in one, holy, catholic, and apostolic Church. We confess one baptism for the remission of sins. We look forward to the resurrection of the dead and the life of the world to come. Amen.

28. The Nicene Creed

From the UCC *Book of Worship*
1986

The definitions of the Christian faith worked out at Nicaea (325) and Constantinople (381) proved to be amazingly durable. In fact, the Nicene Creed has been the most widely acknowledged Christian statement of faith. Centuries later, most churches still share it.

In the twentieth century, the Nicene Creed provides the doctrinal basis for the ecumenical rapprochement between Eastern orthodoxy and churches of the West. As a truly ecumenical confession of faith, it is not divisive but provides a common ground where disparate believers from the broken household of the church can meet.

In the early 1970s the International Consultation on English Texts (ICET) developed a modern translation for the English-speaking world, which became part of the 1986 United Church of Christ Book of Worship.

The bracketed phrase in the third article of the creed — "and the Son"

SOURCE: United Church of Christ Office for Church Life and Leadership, *Book of Worship, United Church of Christ* (United Church of Christ Office for Church Life and Leadership: New York, 1986). English translation prepared by the English Language Liturgical Consultation (ELLC). Used by permission of the English Language Liturgical Consultation.

(the filioque *phrase) — was a last addition of the Western church. It stresses the equality of the Father and the Son and reflects the widely accepted Augustinian (Western/Latin) doctrine of the Trinity. It also points out that while a creed or confession may be a place to meet, even the most ecumenical of statements rarely removes all theological differences.*

We believe in one God,
    the Father, the Almighty,
    maker of heaven and earth,
    of all that is, seen and unseen.
We believe in one Lord, Jesus Christ,
    the only Son of God,
    eternally begotten of the Father,
    God from God, Light from Light,
    true God from true God,
    begotten, not made,
    of one Being with the Father.
    Through him all things were made.
    For us and for our salvation
    he came down from heaven:
    by the power of the Holy Spirit
    he became incarnate from the Virgin Mary,
    and was made man.
    For our sake he was crucified under Pontius Pilate;
    he suffered death and was buried.
    On the third day he rose again
    in accordance with the scriptures;
    he ascended into heaven
    and is seated at the right hand of the Father.
    He will come again in glory
    to judge the living and the dead,
    and his kingdom will have no end.
We believe in the Holy Spirit, the Lord, the giver of life,
    who proceeds from the Father [and the Son].
    With the Father and the Son
    he is worshiped and glorified.
    He has spoken through the prophets.

We believe in one holy catholic and apostolic church.
We acknowledge one baptism for the forgiveness of sins.
We look for the resurrection of the dead,
and the life of the world to come. Amen.

29. The Definition of the Council of Chalcedon
(451)

For all practical purposes, the Nicene Creed and Augustine's monumental treatise on the Trinity finally settled the protracted controversy over the Trinity. Theological concern began to shift away from the problem of God (the relationship among the three persons of the Godhead) to the problem of the divine/human nature of Christ. The Apollinarians resolved the issue by downplaying the human nature of Christ, since "the life given to us by God cannot be found in a mere human being." The Nestorians, on the other hand, made a clear separation between the Jesus of history and the logos *of faith.*

In 451, an ecumenical council gathered in Chalcedon to discuss the matter. The council reaffirmed the Nicene Creed and, at the request of the emperor, drafted a creedal definition about Jesus Christ. Jesus Christ is one person, wholly human and wholly divine; hence of one being (homo-ousios) *with God and also with us. In spirit and language, the Chalcedonian Creed complements Nicaea, focusing on Christ's work of salvation. If Christ has to be divine to* give us life, *he must be human to give* us *life.*

SOURCE: Philip Schaff, *The Greek and Latin Creeds,* vol. 2 of *The Creeds of Christendom* (Grand Rapids: Baker House, 1977).

The Chalcedonian definition brought together the theological wisdom of the ancient church by integrating major elements of Alexandrian, Antiochian, and Western thought while avoiding the excesses of each. "After endless disputes over the nature of Christ, Chalcedon said simply yet with utmost clarity what it is that Christians believe, namely that Jesus Christ is one person, and that he is at once both truly human and divine."

We, then, following the holy Fathers, all with one consent, teach men to confess one and the same Son, our Lord Jesus Christ, the same perfect in Godhead and also perfect in manhood; truly God and truly man, of a reasonable [rational] soul and body; consubstantial [coessential] with the Father according to the Godhead, and consubstantial with us according to the Manhood; in all things like unto us, without sin; begotten before all ages of the Father according to the Godhead, and in these latter days, for us and for our salvation, born of the Virgin Mary, the Mother of God, according to the Manhood; one and the same Christ, Son, Lord, Only-begotten, to be acknowledged in two natures, *inconfusedly, unchangeably, indivisibly, inseparably;* the distinction of natures being by no means taken away by the union, but rather the property of each nature being preserved, and concurring in one Person and one Subsistence, not parted or divided into two persons, but one and the same Son, and only begotten, God, the Word, the Lord Jesus Christ, as the prophets from the beginning [have declared] concerning him, and the Lord Jesus Christ himself has taught us, and the Creed of the holy Fathers has handed down to us.

30. The Athanasian Creed: A Western Creed of the Fifth Century

Debates about the Trinity and the nature of Christ continued long after Nicaea and Chalcedon. The Athanasian Creed appears in a ninth-century prayerbook of Charles the Bald (843–877) of France, one of the sons of Charlemagne. Internal evidence suggests that the document is a composite, containing segments of North African theology that go back to the fifth or sixth century. It restates the definitions of Nicaea and Chalcedon from a Western, and strictly Augustinian, point of view.

The Athanasian Creed is interesting, not so much for its content, but because of its pounding didactic tone. "Anathemas" (condemnations of heretics or unbelievers) frame its creedal statements, which serve as a kind of "reverse exorcism" that bars unbelievers from access to the realm of heaven. Its intention may have been a test of faith as much as it was a testimony.

Eastern Christians have never accepted the Athanasian Creed because of its filioque clause (see vol. 1:237–39). It has been a favorite among Western Christians. Luther considered it to be one of the greatest things written since the days of the apostles. In spite of the fact that he

---

SOURCE: Philip Schaff, *The Greek and Latin Creeds*, vol. 2 of *The Creeds of Christendom* (Grand Rapids: Baker Book House, 1977).

did not like the anathemas, Puritan Richard Baxter deemed it the best thing ever written on the Trinity.

---

1. Whosoever will be saved: before all things it is necessary that he hold the Catholic Faith:

2. Which Faith except every one do keep whole and undefiled: without doubt he shall perish everlastingly.

3. And the Catholic Faith is this: That we worship one God in Trinity, and Trinity in Unity;

4. Neither confounding the Persons: nor dividing the Substance [Essence].

5. For there is one Person of the Father: another of the Son: and another of the Holy Ghost.

6. But the Godhead of the Father, of the Son, and of the Holy Ghost, is all one: the Glory equal, the Majesty coeternal.

7. Such as the Father is: such is the Son: and such is the Holy Ghost.

8. The Father uncreate [uncreated]: the Son uncreate [uncreated]: and the Holy Ghost uncreate [uncreated].

9. The Father incomprehensible [unlimited]: the Son incomprehensible [unlimited]: and the Holy Ghost incomprehensible [unlimited, or infinite].

10. The Father eternal: the Son eternal: and the Holy Ghost eternal.

11. And yet they are not three eternals: but one eternal.

12. As also there are not three uncreated: nor three incomprehensibles [infinites], but one uncreated: and one incomprehensible [infinite].

13. So likewise the Father is Almighty: the Son Almighty: and the Holy Ghost Almighty.

14. And yet they are not three Almighties: but one Almighty.

15. So the Father is God: the Son is God: and the Holy Ghost is God.

16. And yet they are not three Gods: but one God.

17. So likewise the Father is Lord: the Son Lord: and the Holy Ghost Lord.

18. And yet not three Lords: but one Lord.

19. For like as we are compelled by the Christian verity: to acknowledge every Person by himself to be God and Lord:

20. So are we forbidden by the Catholic Religion: to say, There be [are] three Gods, or three Lords.

21. The Father is made of none: neither created, nor begotten.

22. The Son is of the Father alone: not made, nor created: but begotten.

23. The Holy Ghost is of the Father and of the Son: neither made, nor created, nor begotten: but proceeding.

24. So there is one Father, not three Fathers: one Son, not three Sons: one Holy Ghost, not three Holy Ghosts.

25. And in this Trinity none is afore, or after another: none is greater, or less than another [there is nothing before, or after: nothing greater or less].

26. But the whole three Persons are coeternal, and coequal.

27. So that in all things, as aforesaid: the Unity in Trinity, and the Trinity in Unity, is to be worshiped.

28. He therefore that will be saved, must [let him] thus think of the Trinity.

29. Furthermore it is necessary to everlasting salvation: that he also believe rightly [faithfully] the Incarnation of our Lord Jesus Christ.

30. For the right Faith is, that we believe and confess: that our Lord Jesus Christ, the Son of God, is God and Man;

31. God, of the Substance [Essence] of the Father; begotten before the worlds: and Man, of the Substance [Essence] of his Mother, born in the world.

32. Perfect God: and perfect Man, of a reasonable soul and human flesh subsisting.

33. Equal to the Father, as touching his Godhead: and inferior to the Father as touching his Manhood.

34. Who although he be [is] God and Man; yet he is not two, but one Christ.

35. One; not by conversion of the Godhead into flesh: but by taking [assumption] of the Manhood into God.

36. One altogether; not by confusion of Substance [Essence]: but by unity of Person.

37. For as the reasonable soul and flesh is one man: so God and Man is one Christ;

38. Who suffered for our salvation: descended into hell [Hades, spirit-world]: rose again the third day from the dead.

39. He ascended into heaven, he sitteth on the right hand of the Father God [God the Father] Almighty.

40. From whence [thence] he shall come to judge the quick and the dead.

41. At whose coming all men shall rise again with their bodies;

42. And shall give account for their own works.

43. And they that have done good shall go into life everlasting: and they that have done evil, into everlasting fire.

44. This is the Catholic Faith: which except a man believe faithfully [truly and firmly], he can not be saved.

31. The Apostles' Creed of the Seventh Century

Lorenzo Valla, the fifteenth-century Italian humanist and critic of sacred texts, was first to debunk the pious myth that Christ's disciples wrote the Apostles' Creed ten days after the Ascension. Even Calvin doubted its apostolic authorship. Now scholars generally agree that this most popular creed of the Western church had its origins in the worship of the Christian community, in the language of scripture, in the "tradition" of prophets and apostles, and in the more formal expressions of the "rule of faith" that were the basis for catechetical instruction and baptism in the early church.

The Apostles' Creed builds upon the Interrogatory Creed of Hippolytus (c. 215), which was part of the baptismal liturgy. As the catechumens presented themselves for baptism, leaders asked them to affirm their faith by answering three questions:

- *Do you believe in God the Father all Governing?*
- *Do you believe in Christ Jesus, the Son of God, Who was begotten by the Holy Spirit from the Virgin Mary, Who was crucified under Pontius Pilate, and died (and was buried) and rose the third day living*

SOURCE: Philip Schaff, *The Greek and Latin Creeds*, vol. 2 of *The Creeds of Christendom* (Grand Rapids: Baker Book House, 1977).

from the dead, and ascended into the heavens, and sat down on the right hand of the Father, and will come to judge the living and the dead?
- *Do you believe in the Holy Spirit, in the holy church, and (in the resurrection of the body)?*

Similar statements of faith, collectively known as the "Roman" symbol because of their popularity in the Latin (or "Roman") part of the church, came into general use in the Western church just as the Nicene Creed emerged as the most popular confession of the Eastern church. Our present, or "received," text did not appear until the sixth or seventh century. It took yet another century before the Western church recognized it as an official confession.

Two different English translations of the "received" Latin text show the creed's evolution. We find the earlier of the two in the work of Philip Schaff (d. 1893), a leading American theologian in the nineteenth century, who began his career at the Mercersburg Seminary of the German Reformed Church. In the second volume of his Creeds of Christendom, originally published in 1877, Schaff calls the Apostles' Creed a "liturgical poem and an act of worship . . . which is intelligible and edifying to a child, and fresh and rich to the profoundest Christian scholar, who, as he advances in age, delights to go back to primitive foundations and first principles. . . . It is a bond of union between all ages and sections of Christendom."

The 1986 Book of Worship *of the United Church of Christ contains a contemporary version of the Apostles' Creed.*

Received Form

I believe in the HOLY GHOST; the holy catholic Church; the communion of saints; the forgiveness of sins; the resurrection of the body [flesh]; conceived by the Holy Ghost, born of the Virgin Mary; suffered under Pontius Pilate, was crucified, dead, and buried; he descended into hell [Hades, spirit-world]; the third day he rose from the dead; he ascended into heaven; and sitteth at the right hand of God the Father Almighty; from thence he shall come to judge the quick and the dead.

I believe in the HOLY GHOST; the holy catholic Church; the communion of saints; the forgiveness of sins; the resurrection of the body [flesh]; and the life everlasting. Amen.

UCC Book of Worship, *1986*

I believe in God,
    the Father almighty,
    Creator of heaven and earth.
I believe in Jesus Christ, his only Son, our Lord.
    He was conceived by the power of the Holy Spirit
    and born of the Virgin Mary.
    He suffered under Pontius Pilate,
    was crucified, died, and was buried.
    He descended to the dead.
    On the third day he rose again.
    He ascended into heaven,
    and is seated at the right hand of the Father.
    He will come again to judge the living and the dead.
I believe in the Holy Spirit,
    the holy catholic church,
    the communion of saints,
    the forgiveness of sins,
    the resurrection of the body,
    and the life everlasting.
  Amen.

SOURCE: United Church of Christ Office for Church Life and Leadership, *Book of Worship, United Church of Christ* (United Church of Christ Office for Church Life and Leadership: New York, 1986). English translation prepared by the English Language Liturgical Consultation (ELLC). Used by permission of the English Language Liturgical Consultation.

Worship and Work

32. O Gladsome Light (Phōs hilaron)
(early 3rd century)

This early third-century hymn is one of the oldest Christian hymns preserved outside the biblical literature. It is still used in worship, especially in the Greek Orthodox church. This version appears in the Pilgrim Hymnal *(1958).*

O gladsome light, O grace of God the Father's face,
Th'eternal splendor wearing; Celestial, holy, blest,
Our Savior Jesus Christ, Joyful in thine appearing.

Now, ere day fadeth quite, We see the evening light,
Our wonted hymn outpouring; Father of might unknown,
Thee, his incarnate Son, And Holy Spirit Adoring.

To thee of right belongs All praise of holy songs,
O Son of God, Lifegiver; Thee, therefore, O Most High,
The world doth glorify, And shall exalt forever.

SOURCE: *Pilgrim Hymnal* (Boston: The Pilgrim Press, 1958).

33. The Apostolic Tradition of Hippolytus
(c. 200)

Around 200, Tertullian wrote that Praxeas had done "a two-fold service for the devil in Rome: he drove out prophecy and brought in heresy; he put to flight the Paraclete and crucified the Father" ("Against Praxeas," see vol. 1:228–29). Tertullian was referring to the dispute between the Montanists and the Monarchians. He considered Praxeas, a Monarchian, to be a heretic because the Monarchians blurred the distinction among the "persons" of the Trinity.

Hippolytus, a presbyter and teacher in Rome, supported Tertullian. As the leader of a theological school that defended the traditional logos *Christology, Hippolytus accused the Roman bishops of being soft on heresy. After Callistus became pope in 217, Hippolytus declared himself to be the true bishop of Rome and caused schism. In 235 he suffered martyrdom in Sardinia.*

Nevertheless, the concern of Hippolytus was to preserve the true faith. He wrote a treatise "on what is proper for the churches," prompted by "that apostasy or error which was recently invented out of ignorance and because of certain ignorant men." "The Apostolic Tradition of Hip-

---

SOURCE: Bard Thompson, ed., *Liturgies of the Western Church* (Philadelphia: Fortress Press, 1980). Used by permission of the Estate of Bard Thompson.

polytus" provides the earliest record of the liturgical practices of the ancient church.

The consecration service for a bishop opens with a kiss of peace after the consecration and then leads directly into the celebration of Holy Communion. Although it contains some of the familiar elements of the Latin mass, at this stage of liturgical development, the eucharistic prayer is still informal and encourages the use of "free" intercessory prayers.

iv. (*The Liturgy*)

Kiss of Peace

1 And when he has been made bishop let every one offer him the kiss of peace saluting him, for he has been made worthy (*of this*).

Offertory

2 To him then let the deacons bring the oblation and he with all the presbyters[1] laying his hand on the oblation shall say giving thanks:
3 The Lord be with you. And the people shall say: And with thy spirit. [*And the bishop shall say:*] Lift up your hearts. [*And the people shall say:*] We have them with the Lord. [*And the bishop shall say:*] Let us give thanks unto the Lord. [*And the people shall say:*] (*It is*) meet and right. And forthwith he shall continue thus:

Canon

4 We render thanks unto thee, O God, through Thy Beloved Child Jesus Christ, Whom in the last times Thou didst send to us (*to be*) a Saviour and Redeemer and the Messenger of Thy counsel;
5 Who is Thy Word inseparable (*from Thee*), through Whom Thou madest all things and in Whom Thou wast well-pleased;
6 (*Whom*) Thou didst send from heaven into (*the*) Virgin's womb and

---

1. On the practice of "concelebration," in which the presbyters were associated with the bishop in the celebration of the Eucharist, see Gregory Dix, *The Shape of the Liturgy* (Westminster, 1947), 126.

Who conceived within her was made flesh and demonstrated to be Thy Son being born of Holy Spirit and a Virgin;
7 Who fulfilling Thy will and preparing for Thee a holy people stretched forth His hands for suffering that He might release from sufferings them who have believed in Thee;
8 Who when He was betrayed to voluntary suffering that He might abolish death and rend the bonds of the devil and tread down hell and enlighten the righteous and establish the ordinance and demonstrate the resurrection:
9 Taking bread (*and*) making eucharist [i.e., giving thanks] to Thee said: Take eat: this is My Body which is broken for you [*for the remission of sins*]. Likewise also the cup, saying: This is My Blood which is shed for you.
10 When ye do this [ye] do My "anamnesis."
11 Doing therefore the "anamnesis" of His death and resurrection we offer to Thee the bread and the cup making eucharist to Thee because Thou hast bidden us [or, *found us worthy*] to stand before Thee and minister as priests to Thee.
12 And we pray Thee that [*Thou wouldest send Thy Holy Spirit upon the oblation of Thy holy Church*] Thou wouldest grant to all [*Thy Saints*] who partake to be united [*to Thee*] that they may be fulfilled with the Holy Spirit for the confirmation of (*their*) faith in truth,
13 that [we] may praise and glorify Thee through Thy [*Beloved*] Child Jesus Christ through whom glory and honour (*be*) unto Thee with (*the*) Holy Spirit in Thy holy Church now [and for ever] and world without end. Amen.

v. (*Blessing of Oil*)

1 If any one offers oil, he [*i.e., the bishop*] shall make eucharist [or, *render thanks*] as at the oblation of bread and wine. But he shall not say word for word (*the same prayer*) but with similar effect, saying:
2 [O God] who sanctifiest [this] oil, as Thou dost grant unto all who are [anointed] and receive of it [the hallowing] wherewith Thou didst anoint kings (*and*) priests and prophets, so (*grant that*) it may give strength to all that taste of it and health to all that use it.

vi. (*Blessing of Cheese and Olives*)

1 Likewise if any one offers cheese and olives he shall say thus:
2 Sanctify this solidified milk, solidifying us also unto Thy charity.

3 Grant also that this fruit of the olive depart not from Thy sweetness, (*this fruit*) which is the type of thy fatness which Thou hast caused to flow from the Tree[2] for the life of them that hope in Thee.

4 But in every blessing shall be said: To Thee be glory, to the Father and to the Son with (*the*) Holy Spirit in the holy Church now and for ever and world without end. Amen.

xxiii. (*The Paschal Mass*)

Offertory and Consecration

1 And then let the oblation [at once] be brought by the deacons to the bishop, and he shall eucharistize [first] the bread into the representation [*which the Greek calls the antitype*] of the Flesh of Christ; [and] the cup mixed with wine for the antitype, [*which the Greek calls the likeness*] of the Blood which was shed for all who have believed in Him;

Milk and Honey

2 and milk and honey mingled together in fulfillment of the promise which was (*made*) to the Fathers, wherein He said I will give you a land flowing with milk and honey; which Christ indeed gave, (*even*) His Flesh, whereby they who believe are nourished like little children, making the bitterness of the (*human*) heart sweet by the sweetness of His word;

Water

3 water also for an oblation for a sign of the laver, that the inner man also, which is psychic, may receive the same (*rites*) as the body.

4 And the bishop shall give an explanation concerning all these things to them who receive.

Communion

5 And when he breaks the Bread in distributing to each a fragment he shall say:

The Bread of Heaven in Christ Jesus

6 And he who receives shall answer: Amen.

---

2. "Tree" here seems to mean the Cross, not the olive tree.

7 And the presbyters — but if there are not enough (*of them*) the deacons also — shall hold the cups and stand by in good order and with reverence: first he that holdeth the water, second he who holds the milk, third he who holds the wine.

8 And they who partake shall taste of each (*cup*) thrice, he who gives (*it*) saying:

In God the Father Almighty

and he who receives shall say: Amen.

9 And in the Lord Jesus Christ;

(*and he shall say: Amen.*)

10 And in (*the*) Holy Spirit [*and*] in the Holy Church; and he shall say: Amen.

11 So shall it be done to each one.

12 And when these things have been accomplished, let each one be zealous to perform good works and to please God, living righteously, devoting himself to the Church, performing the things which he has learnt, advancing in the service of God.

13 And we have delivered to you briefly these things concerning Baptism and the Oblation because [*you have already been instructed*] concerning the resurrection of the flesh and the rest according to the Scriptures.

14 But if there is any other matter which ought to be told, let the bishop impart it secretly to those who are communicated. He shall not tell this to any but the faithful and only after they have first been communicated. This is the white stone of which John said that there is a new name written upon it which no man knows except him who receives [*the stone*].

34. Six Hymns of the Early Church

CLEMENT OF ALEXANDRIA, CYPRIAN OF CARTHAGE, AMBROSE OF MILAN,
AMBROSE OF MILAN OR BISHOP NICETA OF REMESIANA, AURELIUS CLEMENS
PRUDENTIUS, AND ST. PATRICK

Most liturgical scholars believe that the Christian practice of chanting or singing hymns originated with the use of Hebrew psalms in early Christian worship. Clearly parts of the New Testament epistles contain fragments of ancient Christian hymns (see Eph. 5:14; Phil. 2:5–11; 1 Tim. 3:16; 2 Tim. 2:11–13). Eventually, however, hymnody became regularized. Probably the oldest complete Christian hymn is the third-century Greek hymn, "O gladsome light" (see vol. 1:249).

Six additional hymn texts (four of which the United Church of Christ still use in worship) capture the flavor of early Christian worship.

*(1) Clement of Alexandria is credited with "Curb for wild horses" (c. 200). As a great teacher, Clement believed that the Christian life was a process of growth (*paideia *or education) whereby the whole person's moral and spiritual life is transformed toward God. Nineteenth-century British poet Elizabeth Barrett Browning translates Clement's hymn beautifully.*

(2) Cyprian of Carthage (c. 200–258) writes "The Church of Christ Is One." In this hymn, Cyprian uses the sun and its rays, a tree and its branches, and a river with its source as metaphors of the organic unity of Christ's church. It is a unity that allows no parting or division.

Scholars often remember Cyprian for his axiom that "outside the church, there is no salvation" (see vol. 1:129–34). A 1971 translation of De Unitate Eccleasiae *by F. L. Battles (1971) appears in the 1974* Hymnal of the United Church of Christ.

(3) Ambrose, gifted preacher and bishop of Milan (c. 340–97), is known also as the father of Latin hymnody. During the fourth century, responsive singing of hymns by soloists and congregations, a pattern familiar to Eastern Christians, became commonplace in Latin worship. According to Augustine, Ambrose encouraged the use of hymns in public and private worship. He was one of the earliest writers of strophic and metric hymns. Ambrose's hymn, "O splendor of God's glory bright," translated by John Chandler (1837) and Louis F. Benson (1910) appears in the 1941 Hymnal *of the Evangelical and Reformed Church.*

(4) The Te Deum Laudamus *("We praise you, O God") is a fourth-century Latin hymn that, according to legend, burst from the lips of Ambrose of Milan as he baptized Augustine. Probably the highly stylized original Latin text is a composite of earlier Greek sources or, as most scholars believe, the work of Bishop Niceta of Remesiana (d. 414).*

(5) Aurelius Clemens Prudentius (348–c. 410) was a native of Saragossa, Spain. He became a high ranking official at the court of Emperor Theodosius (379–95), a fellow Spaniard known as the "the Great" in recognition of his support for the Nicene faith. After Theodosius's death, Prudentius resigned and devoted himself to a life of religious contemplation. He is noted for his Latin hymns and religious poetry. The Hymnal of the United Church of Christ *(1974) includes a nineteenth-century translation of Prudentius's hymn "Of the Father's love begotten" (translated by John M. Neale and Henry W. Baker).*

(6) The "Lorica of St. Patrick" is a devotional hymn attributed to St. Patrick (c. 389–c. 461), the apostle of Ireland. A native Briton, Irish raiders kidnapped Patrick as a child and sold him into slavery in Ireland. After six years, he escaped to Gaul, where he was ordained to the priesthood. In 431 he was consecrated bishop in Auxerre, France, and commissioned by Pope Celestine (d. 432) to return to Ireland as a missionary. He laid the foundations for a Christian Ireland and for the great missionary expeditions of Irish monks more than a century later.

According to an ancient Irish introduction, "Patrick made this hymn [the Lorica] . . . for the protection of himself and his monks against the deadly enemies that lay in ambush for the clerics. And it is a lorica *[breastplate] of faith for the protection of body and soul against demons and men and vices."*

Curb for Wild Horses
(c. 200)
CLEMENT

Curb for wild horses,
Wing for bird-courses
Never yet flown!
Helm, safe for weak ones,
Shepherd, bespeak once,
The young lambs Thine own.
Rouse up the youth,
Shepherd and Feeder,
So let them bless Thee,
Praise and confess Thee —
Pure words on pure mouth —
Christ, the child-leader!
Oh, the saints' Lord,
All-dominant Word!
Holding, by Christdom,
God's highest wisdom!
Column in place
When sorrows seize us —
Endless in grace
Unto man's race,
Saving one, Jesus!
Pastor and ploughman,
Helm, curb, together —
Pinion that now can
(Heavenly of feather)
Raise and release us!

SOURCE: Anne Fremantle, ed., *A Treasury of Early Christianity* (New York: Mentor Books, 1960). Used by permission of the author.

The Church of Christ Is One
(3rd century)
CYPRIAN OF CARTHAGE

1. The church of Christ is one: Many are the rays of the sun,
but only one parent light.
Take a ray from the sun, Uncleft the sun remains;
The church of Christ is bathed — suffused in the Lord's undying light;
Although on all the earth diffused, Ever its light is one.

2. The church of Christ is one: Many are the branches of a tree,
but rooted in the earth one trunk.
Break a branch from a tree, The branch will cease to grow;
The branches of the church are spread through the earth, and still
The body of the church remains, Whole, unbroken, one.

3. The church of Christ is one: Many are the streams of a spring:
the source undivided stands.
Choke a stream at the source, The stream will fail — go dry;
The Well-spring of the church outflows in many streams, and still
The Head thereof is always one, One alone the source.

SOURCE: John Ferguson and William Nelson, eds., *Hymnal of the United Church of Christ* (Philadelphia: United Church Press, 1974).

O Splendor of God's Glory Bright

AMBROSE OF MILAN

1. O splendor of God's glory bright, From light eternal bringing light;
Thou Light of life, light's living Spring, True Day, all days illumining.

2. Confirm our will to do the right, And keep our hearts from envy's blight; Let faith her eager fires renew, And hate the false, and love the true.

3. O joyful be the passing day With thoughts as clear as morning's ray. With faith like noontide shining bright, Our souls unshadowed by the night.

4. Dawn's glory gilds the earth and skies; Do thou, our perfect Morn, arise; The Father's help His children claim, And sing the Father's glorious name. AMEN.

SOURCE: General Synod of the Evangelical and Reformed Church, *The Hymnal* (St. Louis: Eden Publishing House, 1941).

Te Deum Laudamus
(4th century)
AMBROSE OF MILAN OR NICETA OF REMESIANA

1 We praise you, O God,
2 we acclaim you as Lord;
3 all creation worships you,
4 the Father everlasting.
5 To you all angels, all the powers of heaven,
6 the cherubim and seraphim, sing in endless praise:
7   Holy, holy, holy Lord, God of power and might,
8   heaven and earth are full of your glory.
9 The glorious company of apostles praise you.
10 The noble fellowship of prophets praise you.
11 The white-robed army of martyrs praise you.
12 Throughout the world the holy Church acclaims you:
13   Father, of majesty unbounded,
14   your true and only Son, worthy of all praise,
15   the Holy Spirit, advocate and guide.

16 You, Christ, are the king of glory,

17 the eternal Son of the Father.
18 When you took our flesh to set us free
19 you humbly chose the Virgin's womb.
20 You overcame the sting of death
21 and opened the kingdom of heaven to all believers.
22 You are seated at God's right hand in glory.
23 We believe that you will come to be our judge.
24   Come then, Lord, and help your people,
25   bought with the price of your own blood,
26   and bring us with your saints
27   to glory everlasting.

SOURCE: English Language Liturgical Consultation, *Praying Together* (Nashville: Abingdon Press, 1988). Copyright © 1988 by English Language Liturgical Consultation. Used by permission of Abingdon Press.

Of the Father's Love Begotten
(4th century)
AURELIUS CLEMENS PRUDENTIUS

1. Of the Father's love begotten Ere the worlds began to be,
He is Alpha and Omega, He the Source, the Ending He
Of the things that are, that have . . . been, And that future
years shall see, Evermore and evermore!

2. O ye heights of heaven adore Him, Angel hosts, His praises sing;
Powers, dominions, bow before Him, And extol our God and King;
Let no tongue on earth be silent, Every voice in
concert ring, Evermore and evermore!

3. Christ, to Thee with God the Father, And, O Holy Ghost, to Thee,
Hymn and chant and high thanksgiving And unwearied praises be:
Honor, glory, and dominion, And eternal
victory, Evermore and evermore! AMEN.

SOURCE: General Synod of the Evangelical and Reformed Church, *The Hymnal* (St. Louis: Eden Publishing House, 1941).

Lorica of St. Patrick
(5th century)
SAINT PATRICK

I

I arise today:
    in vast might, invocation of the Trinity;
    belief in a Threeness;
    confession of Oneness;
    towards the Creator.

II

I arise today:
    in the might of Christ's Birth and His Baptism;
    in the might of His Crucifixion and Burial;
    in the might of His Resurrection and Ascension;
    in the might of His Descent to the Judgment of Doom.

III

I arise today:
    in the might of the order of Cherubim;
    in obedience of Angels;
    in ministration of Archangels;
    in hope of resurrection for the sake of reward;
    in prayers of Patriarchs;
    in predictions of Prophets;
    in preachings of Apostles;
    in faiths of Confessors;
    in innocence of holy Virgins;
    in deeds of righteous men.

IV

I arise today:
   in the might of Heaven;
   brightness of Sun;
   whiteness of Snow;
   splendour of Fire;
   speed of Lightning;
   swiftness of Wind;
   depth of Sea;
   stability of Earth;
   firmness of Rock.

V

I arise today:
   in the might of God   for my piloting;
      Power of God   for my upholding
      Wisdom of God   for my guidance;
      Eye of God   for my foresight;
      Ear of God   for my hearing;
      Word of God   for my utterance;
      Hand of God   for my guardianship;
      Path of God   for my precedence;
      Shield of God   for my protection;
      Host of God   for my salvation;
   against snares of demons;
   against allurements of vices;
   against solicitations of nature;
   against every person that wishes me ill, far and near;
   alone and in a crowd.

VI

I invoke therefore all these forces:
   against every fierce merciless force that may come upon my body and my soul;
   against incantations of false prophets;
   against black laws of paganism;
   against false laws of heresy;

against encompassment of idolatry;
against spells of women and smiths and druids;
against all knowledge that is forbidden the human soul.

VII

Christ for my guardianship today:
    against poison, against burning,
    against drowning, against wounding,
    that there may come to me a multitude of rewards;
Christ with me, Christ before me,
Christ behind me, Christ in me,
Christ under me, Christ over me,
Christ to right of me, Christ to left of me,
Christ in lying down, Christ in sitting, Christ in rising up,
Christ in the heart of every person who may think of me!
Christ in the mouth of everyone who may speak to me!
Christ in every eye which may look on me!
Christ in every ear which may hear me!

I arise today:
    in vast might, invocation of the Trinity
    belief in a Threeness;
    confession of Oneness;
    meeting in the Creator;
Domini est salus, Domini est salus, Christi est salus;
Salus tua, Domine, sit semper nobiscum.

SOURCE: Anne Fremantle, ed., *A Treasury of Early Christianity* (New York: Mentor Books, 1960). Used by permission of the author.

35. A Sermon on Faith and Works
From *Homilies on Ephesians 1:1–2 (on Eph. 1:4–5)*
(4th century)

JOHN CHRYSOSTOM

John "Chrysostom, the golden mouthed" (c. 347–407), was one of the great preachers of the Eastern church. The son of a high ranking imperial military officer and a Christian mother, he studied rhetoric and theology in Antioch. He was baptized in 370 and, as was common in Syria, he lived in a monastic retreat following his baptism until poor health forced him to return to Antioch.

In 398 John "Chrysostom" became the bishop of Constantinople. He made himself unpopular by his indiscriminate candor, denouncing Jews, Goths, and the rich. His repeated diatribes against the vices of the imperial court (calling Empress Eudoxia a Jezebel) led to his banishment in 404.

John Chrysostom's preaching finds roots in the interpretive tradition of his native Antioch. It combines a close reading of scripture with a prophetic emphasis on the moral life. In his sermon on Ephesians 1:4–5, he proclaims many themes that dominate later Protestant theology. "The Father predestined us, Christ brought us over," he preaches. Good works are the outcome of God's grace, not its prerequisite. Yet God's

---

SOURCE: Maurice Wiles and Mark Santer, eds., *Documents in Early Christian Thought* (Cambridge: Cambridge University Press, 1979). © Cambridge University Press 1975. Used by permission of Cambridge University Press.

"primary will" is that sinners should not perish. John Chrysostom's sermon on the Eucharist also witnesses to his timeless eloquence (see vol. 1:282–85).

Even as he chose us in him before the foundation of the world, that we should be holy and blameless before him.

His meaning is something like this. The one through whom God has blessed us is also the one through whom he chose us. He is also the one who will give us our heavenly rewards. He is the judge who will say, "Come, you blessed of my Father, inherit the Kingdom prepared for you from the foundation of the world" [Matt. 25:34], and also "Where I am I desire that these also may be" [John 17:24].

In almost all his epistles Paul is keen to show that our faith is no new fangled thing but was designed to be as it is from the very beginning; it was not a matter of divine afterthought but was planned and foreordained as it now is. It is the fruit of long providential care.

What then is the meaning of "chose us in him"? That Christ established this way of faith in himself before ever we came into existence, or rather before the foundation of the world. (The word "foundation" is well chosen because it indicates something being laid down from a great height. And the height of God is great and ineffable, not in terms of spatial distance but in the remoteness of his nature, for there is a great gulf between creation and creator. Let the heretics take note and blush!)

And why did he choose us? "That we should be holy and blameless before him." So that you may not suppose, when you hear that he chose us, that faith alone is sufficient, he goes on to refer to manner of life. This, he says, is the reason and the purpose of his choice — that we should be holy and blameless. Once too he chose the Jews. How so? "He chose this nation," it says, "out of all the nations" [Deut. 14:2]. When men choose, they choose the best; that is even more true of God. Indeed the fact of their being chosen is evidence both of God's loving-kindness and of their virtue. For in choosing them he must certainly have been choosing those who were approved. In our case he has himself made us holy, but we have to stay holy. Being holy is a matter of sharing in faith; being blameless is a matter of living an irreproachable life. But it is not what is holy and irreproachable without any further qualification that he is looking for but people who will appear so "before him." Some are holy and blameless but only in men's eyes; they are like whited sepulchres, like those who wear sheep's clothing. These are not the people he is looking for, but those described by the prophet: "and according to the cleanness of my hands" [Ps. 18:24]. What cleanness? That which is so "in his sight." He is looking for that holiness which God's eye sees.

After speaking of the good works of men, he goes back to the grace of God. For all this does not come about by toil and good works, but by love: yet not by love alone, nor by our virtue alone. For if it were by love alone, then everyone would be saved; and if it were by our virtue alone, then the incarnation and all that it accomplished would be superfluous. So it is not by love alone, nor by our virtue alone, but comes from both. "He chose us," says the text; and the chooser knows what he is choosing. "He predestined us in love." For virtue without love would never have saved anybody. Where would Paul have got to, how would he have achieved what he did, if God had not first of all called him and in his love drawn him to himself? In any case the fact that he bestows such great benefits on us is the outcome of his love and not of our virtue. Our becoming virtuous, our believing and our coming to him — these are all the work of him who called us, though admittedly they are our works also. But to bestow such great honours on those who come to him, translating them immediately from enmity to adopted sonship, is most emphatically the outcome of a love that knows no bounds.

He predestined us, he says, *in love to be adopted as sons to him through Jesus Christ.*

You see how nothing happens apart from Christ and nothing happens apart from the Father. The Father predestined us; Christ brought us over. In saying this he is adding something more to his praise of all that has been done — as he says elsewhere: "Not only so, but we also rejoice through our Lord Jesus Christ" [Rom. 5:11]. God's gifts are great but they are made much greater by the fact that they are given through Christ. It was not one of his servants that he sent to his servants, but the only-begotten Son himself.

According to the good pleasure of his will.

In other words, because he willed it so strongly. His desire, we might call this. "Good pleasure" always indicates antecedent will. There is a further will as well. For example it is God's primary will that sinners should not perish; it is his secondary will that those who do become evil should perish. For their punishment is not a matter of inevitable necessity but of God's will. One can take an example from Paul's case too. First: "I will that all men were even as I am myself" [1 Cor. 7:7]. Secondly: "I will that the younger women marry and bear children" [1 Tim. 5:14]. So here when he speaks of "good pleasure," he means the primary will, the strong will, the will accompanied by inner desire, or what in our own case — for I am not afraid of using quite ordinary terms to make the point clear to the simplest person — we call our firm intention; as when we say: "It is our firm intention." What Paul is saying is this. God earnestly longs for, earnestly desires our salvation. Why does he love us like this? What is the source of such affection? It comes solely from his goodness. For grace itself is a product of goodness. The reason, says Paul, why he predestined us to be adopted as sons was his will and strong intent that the glory of his grace should be displayed. "According to the good pleasure of his will," he says, "to the praise of the glory of his grace, with which he has been gracious to us in the beloved."

36. On Female Dress
(c. 200)

TERTULLIAN

At the turn of the third century, North African Carthage was one of the foremost Christian centers of the Western empire. Tertullian (c. 160–c. 225), its leading theologian, made a major contribution to Western Christian thought by introducing the terms person *and* substance *to denote the distinctness and unity of the tri-une God.*

Like many North African Christians of his time, Tertullian viewed the church as a community set apart from the world. He believed that church members, saved by baptismal grace, should live simple and righteous lives while awaiting the coming of Christ. Not surprisingly, the lack of moral discipline in the church disillusioned him. After the persecutions of Emperor Septimius Severus (d. 211), Tertullian joined the charismatic sect of the Montanists whose views of an ascetic life in anticipation of Christ's second coming were more congenial to his own (see vol. 1:228–29).

Although Tertullian is not without appreciation for sensual beauty, he has a deep commitment to the realm of Christ, which he knows may lead to martyrdom. He writes, "Let us stand ready to face any violence, having nothing that we are afraid to leave behind. These things are but fetters that retard our hope."

SOURCE: Anne Fremantle, ed., *A Treasury of Early Christianity* (New York: Mentor Books, 1960). Used by permission of the author.

His injunctions against "female dress" are a bit overstated, but they raise some of the perennial questions about how Christians should relate to popular culture. It is also important to note that Tertullian is aware of the gender imbalance in his treatment of vanity, and he makes a deliberate effort to give males a fair share of the blame. "My own sex recognizes some tricks of beauty which are peculiarly ours."

My sisters and fellow-servants, handmaids of the living God, the right that ranks me with you in fellow-servantship and brotherhood emboldens me, meanest as I am in that fellowship, to address to you a discourse, not one of affection certainly, but in the service of your salvation taking affection's place. That salvation, in the case of men as well as of women, depends chiefly on the observance of chastity. We are all of us the temple of God as soon as the Holy Spirit has entered into us; but the sacristan and priestess of that temple is Chastity, who must allow nothing unclean or profane to enter, lest God, who dwells within, should be offended and leave the polluted abode. But for the moment we are not speaking of Chastity itself, for the enjoining and exacting of which the urgency of divine precepts is sufficient, but rather of some matters pertaining to it, that is, the fashion in which it behoves you to appear abroad. Very many women — in passing this censure on myself may God allow me to pass it on all — either from simple ignorance or from hypocritical motives have the boldness so to walk in public as though chastity consisted only in the bare integrity of the flesh and in the avoidance of fornication. They seem to think that there is no need of anything further, as regards the manner of their dress, the fashion of their toilet, and the studied graces of form and elegance. In their gait they display the same outward appearance as Gentile women, in whom the sense of true chastity is lacking, inasmuch as in those who know not God, the Guardian and Teacher of truth, there can be nothing that is true. . . .

You, my sisters, in your gait, as in all things, must take a different path from theirs. It is your duty to be perfect, even as your Father is perfect who is in the heavens.

• • •

Someone may say: "Why should we shut out wantonness and only admit chastity? Would it not be permissible then for us to enjoy the praise due to beauty and to glory in our bodily advantages?" Those whose pleasure it is to glory in the flesh must see to that. We have no desire for such "glory," inasmuch as glory is the essence of exaltation, and exaltation suits not those who according to God's precepts are professors of humility. Moreover, if all glorying is vain and foolish, how much more so, especially to us, is glorying in the flesh. Even if glorying is allowable, we ought to wish to give pleasure, not in the flesh, but in the good things of the spirit; for it is of spiritual things that we are suitors. Where our work is, there let our joy be. Let us cull glory where we hope to win salvation. Obviously a Christian may glory sometimes, yea, and glory even in the flesh. But that will be when the flesh has endured laceration for Christ's sake, in order that the spirit thereby may win the crown, not in order that it may draw after it the eyes and sighs of youths. A thing that with you in any case is superfluous you may justly disdain if you have it not and neglect if you have. A holy woman may be beautiful by the gift of nature, but she must not give occasion to lust. If beauty be hers, so far from setting it off she ought rather to obscure it.

• • •

Of course, you must not infer from these suggestions that we should approve of an uncouth roughness in dress. We do not urge that squalor and slovenliness are good things. We merely set forth the limit and bounds and just measure of bodily adornment. You must not overstep the line to which simple and sufficient elegance limits its desires, the line which is pleasing to God. Against Him those women sin who torment their skin with potions, stain their cheeks with rouge, and extend the line of their eyes with black colouring. Doubtless they are dissatisfied with God's plastic skill. In their own persons they convict and censure the Artificer of all things....

I see that some women change the colour of their hair with saffron dye. They are ashamed even of their own nation, ashamed that they were not born in Germany or Gaul; and so by changing their hair they change their country! Evil, most evil, is the omen of those flame-coloured heads, a defilement imagined to be a charm. Moreover, the force of the cosmetics burns the hair and ruins it; the constant application of any sort of moisture, even though it were undrugged, is harmful to the brain; and there is even danger in the warmth of the sun, so desirable for imparting to the hair vigour and dryness. What has grace to do with injury? What has beauty to do with filth? Shall a Christian woman put saffron upon her head, as the Gentiles lay it upon their altars? A substance which is usually burned in honour of the unclean spirit may be considered part of heathen sacrifice, unless it is used for honest and necessary and salutary purposes, to serve the end for which God's creation was provided.

But God says: "Who of you can make a white hair black or a black white?" And so women prove the Lord wrong! "Behold," they say, "instead of white or black, we make it yellow, a more pleasing and graceful colour." Not but what those who repent of having lived to old age do attempt to change from white to black again! Shame on such temerity! The age which we fervently pray to attain blushes for itself; a theft is accomplished; youth, the period of sin, is sighed after; the opportunity for grave seriousness is wasted. Far from wisdom's daughters be such folly! The more old age strives to conceal itself, the more it will be detected. This, then, is your idea of true eternity, hair that is ever young! This is the incorruptibility which we have to put on for the new house of the Lord, one guaranteed by cosmetics! Well do you hasten to greet the Lord, well do you speed to depart from this iniquitous age, you to whom the near approach of your own end seems unsightly!

Of what service to your salvation, moreover, is all the anxious care you spend in arraying your hair? You will not let it have a moment's rest: one day it is tied back, another day it falls loose; now it is lifted high, now it is pressed flat. Some women set their heart on forcing it into curls; others let it float waving in the air with a simplicity that has nothing of virtue in it. Moreover, you affix huge bundles of false tresses to your heads, making of them, now a bonnet to enclose and cover over the top, now a platform jutting out at the back of your neck. All this striving, be assured, is contrary to our Lord's precepts. . . .

You will say, I suppose, that I am a man and that from sex jealousy I am driving women from their own domain. Are there, then, some things that to men also are not permissible, if we are God-fearing, and have a due regard for gravity? There are, indeed; since in men for the sake of women, just as in women for the sake of men, there is implanted by a defect of nature the wish to please. My own sex recognizes some tricks of beauty which are peculiarly ours—for example, to cut the beard too sharply; to pluck it out in places; to shave round the lips; to arrange the hair and conceal grayness by dyes; to remove the first traces of down from every part of the body; to fix the hair with womanly pigments; to smooth the skin by means of rough powder; to consult the mirror at every opportunity and to gaze anxiously into it. But all these tricks are rejected as being frivolous and hostile to chastity, as soon as the knowledge of God has destroyed the wish to please by opportunities for wantonness. Where God is, there is chastity; there, too, is gravity, her helper and ally. How, then, shall we practise chastity without her effective instrument, that is gravity? Moreover, how shall we make gravity useful in the winning of chastity, unless we made strictness manifest in our face, and in our dress, and in the general aspect of the whole man? . . .

Therefore, blessed sisters, take not to yourself such roles and garments as play the part of pimp and pander; and if there be any of you whom reasons of birth or riches or past dignities compel to appear in public so gorgeously arrayed as not to appear to have attained wisdom, take heed to temper this mischief, lest under the pretext of necessity you should seem to give full rein to licence. . . .

Was it God, forsooth, who showed men how to dye wool with the juices of herbs and the saliva of shellfish? He forgot, perchance, when He was bidding the universe to come to birth, to order purple and scarlet sheep! It was God, too, I suppose, who invented the manufacture of garments, which, light in themselves, are still heavy in price; God who devised the gold settings that encircle and enhance the brightness of jewels; God who introduced the tiny wounds that ear-rings require, regarding it of such importance that His own work should be spoiled and innocent children tortured and made to suffer at once, that from the scars on their body — born, forsooth, for the steel — should hang some or other of those grains which the Parthians, as we see, use for studs upon their very shoes! Why, even the gold itself, whose glory so enthrals you, serves a certain tribe, as Gentile literature tells us, for chains! . . .

Perhaps some women will say: "We fear lest the Holy Name be blasphemed in our case, if we make any changes in our old style and dress." Let us not, then, forsooth, abolish our old vices! Let us cling to the same character, if we must cling to the same outward appearance as of yore! Then truly there will be no fear of the heathen blaspheming! It is a splendid blasphemy that says: "From the day she became a Christian she appears abroad in poorer dress." Will you be afraid to seem poorer, now that you have become more rich; fouler now that you have become more clean? Is it according to the Gentiles' pleasure or according to the pleasure of God that Christians ought to walk? . . .

For Christian chastity it is not enough to be; it wishes also to be seen. So great ought to be its plenitude that it overflows from the mind to the dress and bursts out from the conscience to the outward appearance, from the outside gazing, as it were, upon its furniture designed to hold the faith safe for ever. Such delicacies, then, which can by their softness and effeminacy unman the manliness of faith, must be discarded. The arm that has been wont to wear a bracelet will scarce endure to be benumbed to the rigour of a prisoner's chains. The leg that has rejoiced in a jewelled garter will hardly suffer itself to be squeezed in the stocks. I fear that the neck on which coils of pearls and emeralds have rested will never give a place to the executioner's sword. Therefore, blessed sisters, let us practise hardships now, and we shall not feel them; let us abandon luxuries, and we shall not regret them. Let us stand ready to face any violence, having nothing that we fear to leave behind. These things are but fetters that retard our hopes. Let us cast away earthly ornaments, if we desire heavenly. Love not gold; for it is gold that brands all the sins of the people of Israel. You ought to hate that which brought your fathers to ruin and was adored by them who were forsaking God. Even then gold was food for fire.

It is in iron, not in gold, that Christians always, and now more than ever, pass their days. The stole of martyrdom is today prepared for us. We are waiting for the angels to carry us to heaven. Go forth to meet them arrayed in the cosmetics and adornments of the prophets and apostles. Draw your whiteness from simplicity, your rosy hues from chastity. Paint your eyes with modesty and your lips with silence. Fix in your ears the words of God and fasten on your necks the yoke of Christ. Bow your head before your husbands, and you will be sufficiently adorned. Busy your hands with wool; keep your feet at home; and then you will please more than if you were arrayed in gold. Clothe yourselves with the silk of honesty, the fine linen of righteousness, and the purple of chastity. Thus painted you will have God for your lover.

37. On Human Sexuality and Christian Marriage
From *Miscellanies, Book III*
(c. 200)

CLEMENT OF ALEXANDRIA

Clement was the first great Christian scholar of Alexandria, the renowned intellectual center of the Greek world not far from what is today Cairo, Egypt. Unlike Tertullian, who wanted no part of an alliance between Athens and Jerusalem, Clement tried to demonstrate the reasonableness of the Christian faith with the help of Platonic philosophy. In Christian teaching, he said, faith and reason combine to give us a true knowledge (gnosis) of the divine. Clement and his brilliant student Origen made Alexandrian theology a major force in Christian doctrinal controversies for many centuries.

Early Christianity struggled with issues of body and spirit. On the one hand, Clement rejects all teaching that human sexuality is evil. He takes the position, generally accepted by the ancient church, that such teaching is "blasphemy against the creator . . . for [God] does not hate creation or reckon married people of no account." On the other hand, he argues that the Christian life—married or not—should be a life of continence, of the absence of desire, not only in sexual matters but in all other things as well.

SOURCE: Henry Chadwick and J. E. L. Oulton, eds., *Alexandrian Christianity*, vol. 2 of *Library of Christian Classics* (Philadelphia: Westminster Press, 1954). Used by permission of Westminster John Knox Press.

Given the temper of the times, Greek Stoics and most Gnostics would have agreed with his Christian view of marriage. Clement's curious ambivalence shows how Christian affirmations of God's creation and the ethical teachings of Jesus sometimes conflicted with popular versions of neo-Platonic asceticism.

Chapter XVII

102. If birth is something evil, let the blasphemers say that the Lord who shared in birth was born in evil, and that the virgin gave birth to him in evil. Woe to these wicked fellows! They blaspheme against the will of God and the mystery of creation in speaking evil of birth. This is the ground upon which Docetism is held by Cassian and by Marcion also, and on which even Valentine indeed teaches that Christ's body was "psychic."[1] They say: Man became like the beasts when he came to practise sexual intercourse. But it is when a man in his passion really wants to go to bed with a strange woman that in truth such a man has become a wild beast. "Wild horses were they become, each man whinnied after his neighbour's wife."[2] And if the serpent took the use of intercourse from the irrational animals and persuaded Adam to agree to have sexual union with Eve, as though the couple first created did not have such union by nature, as some think, this again is blasphemy against the creation. For it makes human nature weaker than that of the brute beasts if in this matter those who were first created by God copied them.

103. But if nature led them, like the irrational animals, to procreation, yet they were impelled to do it more quickly than was proper because they were still young and had been led away by deceit. Thus God's judgment against them was just, because they did not wait for his will. But birth is holy. By it were made the world, the existences, the natures, the angels, powers, souls, the commandments, the law, the gospel, the knowledge of God. And "all flesh is grass, and all the glory of man as the flower of grass. The grass withers, the flower falls; but the word of the Lord abides"[3] which anoints the soul and unites it with the spirit. Without the body how could the divine plan for us in the Church achieve its end?

---

1. Chadwick and Oulton, *Alexandrian Christianity,* Introduction, p. 32.
2. Jer. 5:8.
3. Isa. 40:6–8.

Surely the Lord himself, the head of the Church,[4] came in the flesh, though without form and beauty,[5] to teach us to look upon the formless and incorporeal nature of the divine Cause. "For a tree of life" says the prophet, "grows by a good desire,"[6] teaching that desires which are in the living Lord are good and pure.

104. Furthermore they wish to maintain that the intercourse of man and wife in marriage, which is called knowledge,[7] is a sin; this sin is referred to as eating of the tree of good and evil, and the phrase "he knew"[8] signifies transgression of the commandment. But if this is so, even knowledge of the truth is eating of the tree of life.[9] It is possible for a sober-minded marriage to partake of that tree. We have already observed that marriage may be used rightly or wrongly;[10] and this is the tree of knowledge, if we do not transgress in marriage. What then? Does not the Saviour who heals the soul also heal the body of its passions? But if the flesh were hostile to the soul, he would not have raised an obstacle to the soul by strengthening with good health the hostile flesh. "This I say, brethren, that flesh and blood cannot inherit the kingdom of God nor corruption incorruption."[11] For sin being corruption cannot have fellowship with incorruption which is righteousness. "Are you so foolish?" he says, "having begun in the Spirit are you now to be made perfect by the flesh."[12]

Chapter XVIII

105. Some, then, as we have shown,[13] have tried to go beyond what is right and the concord that marks salvation which is holy and established. They have blasphemously accepted the ideal of continence for reasons entirely godless. Celibacy may lawfully be chosen according to the sound rule with godly reasons, provided that the person gives thanks for the grace God has granted,[14] and does not hate the creation or reckon married

---

4. Eph. 1:22; 5:23.
5. Isa. 53:2.
6. Prov. 13:12.
7. Cf. *Strom.*, III, 81.
8. Gen. 2:9.
9. Gen. 2:9; 3:22.
10. *Strom.*, III, 96.
11. 1 Cor. 15:50.
12. Gal. 3:3.
13. *Strom.*, III, 40.
14. Cf. 1 Cor. 7:7.

people to be of no account. For the world is created: celibacy is also created. Let both give thanks for their appointed state, if they know to what state they are appointed. But others have kicked over the traces and waxed wanton, having become indeed "wild horses who whinny after their neighbour's wives." They have abandoned themselves to lust without restraint and persuade their neighbours to live licentiously.

• • •

Therefore the apostle nobly says, "I wrote to you in my letter to have no company with fornicators," as far as the words "but the body is not for fornication but for the Lord, and the Lord for the body." And to show that he does not regard marriage as fornication he goes on: "Do you not know that he who is joined to a harlot is one body with her?"[15] Or who will assert that before she is married a virgin is a harlot? "And do not deprive one another," he says, "except by agreement for a time," indicating by the word "deprive" the obligation of marriage, procreation, which he has set forth in the preceding passage where he says: "Let the husband give the wife her due and likewise also the wife to the husband."[16]

108. In fulfilling this obligation she is a helpmeet in the house and in Christian faith. And the apostle expresses the same point even more clearly as follows: "To the married I direct, yet not I but the Lord, that the wife be not separated from her husband (and if she is separated, let her remain unmarried or be reconciled to her husband) and that the husband should not leave his wife. But to the rest I say, not the Lord: If any brother . . . ," down to the words "but now are they holy."[17] What have they to say to these words, these people who disparage the law and speak as if marriage were only conceded by the law and is not also in accord with the New Testament? What reply to these directions have those who recoil from intercourse and birth? For he also lays down that the bishop who is to rule the Church must be a man who governs his own household well. A household pleasing to the Lord consists of a marriage with one wife.[18]

109. "To the pure," he says, "all things are pure: but to the defiled and unbelieving nothing is pure, but their mind and conscience are pol-

---

15. 1 Cor. 5:9; 6:13, 16. Cf. *Strom.*, III, 49.
16. 1 Cor. 7:5, 3.
17. 1 Cor. 7:10–12, 14.
18. Cf. 1. Tim. 3:2–4; Titus 1:16; *Strom.*, III, 79, 90.

luted."[19] With reference to illicit indulgence he says: "Make no mistake: neither fornicators nor idolaters nor adulterers nor effeminate men nor homosexuals nor covetous men nor robbers nor drunkards nor revilers nor thieves shall inherit the kingdom of God. And we," who used to indulge in such practices, "have washed ourselves."[20] But they have a purification, with a view to committing this immorality; their baptism means passing from self-control to fornication. They maintain that one should gratify the lusts and passions, teaching that one must turn from sobriety to be incontinent. They set their hope on their private parts.[21] Thus they shut themselves out of God's kingdom and deprive themselves of enrollment as disciples,[22] and under the name of knowledge, falsely so called, they have taken the road to outer darkness.[23] "For the rest, brethren, whatever is true, whatever is holy, whatever is righteous, whatever is pure, whatever is attractive, whatever is well spoken of, whatever is virtuous, and whatever is praiseworthy, think on these things. And whatever you have learnt and received and heard and seen in me, this do. And the God of peace shall be with you."[24]

110. And Peter in his epistle says the same: "So that your faith and hope may be in God, because you have purified your souls in obedience to the truth,"[25] "as obedient children, not behaving after the fashion of the lusts in which in your ignorance you formerly indulged; but as he who has called you is holy, so also must you be holy in all your conduct; as it is written, Be ye holy for I am holy."[26]

But our polemic, though necessary against those who masquerade under the false name of knowledge, has carried us beyond the limit and made our discussion lengthy. Accordingly this is the end of our third miscellany of gnostic notes in accordance with the true philosophy.

---

19. Titus 1:15.
20. 1 Cor. 6:9–11.
21. Phil. 3:19.
22. Cf. Rev. 20:12, 15; 21:27.
23. Cf. Matt. 8:12.
24. Phil. 4:8 f.
25. 1 Peter 1:21 f.
26. 1 Peter 1:14–16 (Lev. 11:44; 19:2; 20:7).

38. On Public and Military Service
From *Against Celsus VIII, 73–75*
(c. 248)

ORIGEN

Two things shaped the attitudes of most early Christians toward the Roman state: the conviction that earthly authority, even the authority of an unjust ruler, comes from God, and *the experience of persecution. Christians agreed that governments should have the power to curb evildoers. People must fear God's authority so that, in Irenaeus's words, they do "not consume one another as fish do." However, acknowledging that reality, Christians rejected Roman religions as demonic and the Roman lifestyle as immoral. Christians live, as Origen put it, "in another country created by God."*

The Christian veneration of those who died for their faith (the martyrs) was also the ultimate rejection of "eternal Rome" and its values. During a persecution of Alexandrian Christians in 202, Origen's father, Leonidas, a recent convert, was arrested and died a confessor. The ancient historian Eusebius claims that Origen (c. 185–c. 254) survived only because his mother, a woman of Christian virtues and practical sense, hid the boy's clothing to keep him from actively seeking martyrdom.

SOURCE: Maurice Wiles and Mark Santer, eds., *Documents in Early Christian Thought* (Cambridge: Cambridge University Press, 1979). © Cambridge University Press 1975. Used by permission of Cambridge University Press.

Later when Celsus, a second-century pagan philosopher, stirs up the populace against Christians by accusing them of being unpatriotic (1) because they would not serve in the armed forces and (2) because they refused to accept public office, Origen insists that Christians do not shirk the "public services of life." Christians "keep themselves for a more divine and necessary service in the Church of God for the sake of the salvation of [all]."

73. Then Celsus next exhorts us to *help the emperor with all our power, and cooperate with him in what is right, and fight for him, and be fellow-soldiers if he presses for this, and fellow-generals with him.* We may reply to this that at appropriate times we render to the emperors divine help, if I may so say, by taking up even the whole armour of God [see Eph. 6:11]. And this we do in obedience to the apostolic utterance which says: "I exhort you, therefore, first to make prayers, supplications, intercessions, and thanksgivings for all men, for emperors, and all that are in authority" [1 Tim. 2:1–2]. Indeed, the more pious a man is, the more effective he is in helping the emperors — more so than the soldiers who go out into the lines and kill all the enemy troops that they can.

We would also say this to those who are alien to our faith and ask us to fight for the community and to kill men: that it is also your opinion that the priests of certain images and wardens of the temples of the gods, as you think them to be, should keep their right hand undefiled for the sake of the sacrifices, that they may offer the customary sacrifices to those who you say are gods with hands unstained by blood and pure from murders. And in fact when war comes you do not enlist the priests. If, then, this is reasonable, how much more reasonable is it that, while others fight, Christians also should be fighting as priests and worshippers of God, keeping their right hands pure and by their prayers to God striving for those who fight in a righteous cause and for the emperor who reigns righteously, in order that everything which is opposed and hostile to those who act rightly may be destroyed? Moreover, we who by our prayers destroy all demons which stir up wars, violate oaths, and disturb the peace, are of more help to the emperors than those who seem to be doing the fighting. We who offer prayers with righteousness, together with ascetic practices and exercises which teach us to despise pleasures and not to be led by them, are cooperating in the tasks of the community. Even more do we fight on behalf of the emperor. And though we do not become fellow-soldiers with him, even if he presses for this, yet we are fighting for him and composing a special army of piety through our intercessions to God.

74. If Celsus wishes us to be generals for our country, let him realize that we do this too; but we do not do so with a view to being seen by men and to being proud about it. Our prayers are made in secret in the mind itself, and are sent up as from priests on behalf of the people in our country. Christians do more good to their countries than the rest of mankind, since they educate the citizens and teach them to be devoted to God, the guardian of their city; and they take those who have lived good lives in the most insignificant cities up to a divine and heavenly city. To them it could be said: You were faithful in a very insignificant city [see Luke 16:10; 19:17]; come also to the great city where "God stands in the congregation of the gods and judges between gods in the midst," and numbers you even with them, if you no longer "die like a man" and do not "fall like one of the princes" [Ps. 82:1, 7].

75. Celsus exhorts us also to *accept public office in our country if it is necessary to do this for the sake of the preservation of the laws and of piety.* But we know of the existence in each city of another sort of country, created by the Word of God. And we call upon those who are competent to take office, who are sound in doctrine and life, to rule over the churches. We do not accept those who love power. But we put pressure on those who on account of their great humility are reluctant hastily to take upon themselves the common responsibility of the Church of God. And those who rule us well are those who have had to be forced to take office, being constrained by the great King who, we are convinced, is the Son of God, the divine Word. And if those who are chosen as rulers in the Church rule well over God's country (I mean the Church), or if they rule in accordance with the commands of God, they do not on this account defile any of the appointed civic laws.

If Christians do avoid these responsibilities, it is not with the motive of shirking the public services of life. But they keep themselves for a more divine and necessary service in the Church of God for the sake of the salvation of men. Here it is both necessary and right for them to be leaders and to be concerned about all men, both those who are within the Church, that they may live better every day, and those who appear to be outside it, that they may become familiar with the sacred words and acts of worship; and that, offering a true worship to God in this way and instructing as many as possible, they may become absorbed in the word of God and the divine law, and so be united to the supreme God through the Son of God, the Word, Wisdom, Truth, and Righteousness, who unites to Him every one who has been persuaded to live according to God's will in all things.

Eastern Orthodoxy

39. Communion as Participation
From *Homilies on 1 Corinthians 24:1–2 (on 1 Cor. 10:16–17)*
(4th century)

JOHN CHRYSOSTOM

John Chrysostom (c. 345–407), the bishop of Constantinople from 398–404, was known as "chrysostom" or "golden mouthed" because of his oratorical skills. He studied rhetoric and theology in his native city of Antioch and was a staunch defender of Antiochian Christology, holding that in Christ the divine logos *truly unites with human nature so that the human might become part of the divine (see vol. 1:264–67). To save us, Christ had to be human; to save us, Christ had to be divine.*

Preaching on 1 Cor. 10:16–17, John Chrysostom declares that "participation" in communion organically unites believers with Christ and with all other believers. The mortal bodies of the believers are trans-

---

SOURCE: Maurice Wiles and Mark Santer, eds., *Documents in Early Christian Thought* (Cambridge: Cambridge University Press, 1979). © Cambridge University Press 1975. Used by permission of Cambridge University Press.

formed into the one immortal body of Christ. This "participation" in the body of Christ means that all Christians are one.

In history, however, such unity has not been the case. John Chrysostom asks one of the most simple and central questions confronting Christians gathered around the table of the Christ in all centuries: "If then we are all fed from the same loaf and actually become the same body, why do we not all show the same love as well and become one in that respect too?"

The cup of blessing which we bless, is it not a participation in the blood of Christ?

1. How is it, Paul, that you can speak like this? You are seeking to stir your hearers to reverence; you are reminding them of the awesome mysteries. Do you at that point speak of the fearful and most awesome cup as a "cup of blessing"? "Yes," comes Paul's reply, "and it is a term of deep significance. When I say blessing, I mean thanksgiving, and when I say thanksgiving I am unfolding the whole treasure of God's goodness and calling to mind his marvellous gifts." We too recite over the cup the unspeakable mercies of God and all the benefits we enjoy from him, as we approach and partake of it; we give thanks that he has delivered from error the whole race of men, that those who were far off he has made near, and that those who were without hope and without God in the world he has made his own brothers and fellow-heirs. It is for these things and all his other similar gifts that we give thanks, as we approach. So Paul is saying to the Corinthians: "Are you not contradicting yourselves when you bless God for delivering you from idols and then go running back to their tables?"

"The cup of blessing which we bless, is it not a participation in the blood of Christ?" Paul's words are thoroughly persuasive and awe-inspiring. What he is saying is this: "What is in the cup is what flowed from Christ's side; that is what we share in." He has called it a cup of blessing, because when we have it in our hands we praise Christ in wonder and astonishment at his unspeakable gift, by blessing him for pouring out this very cup to free us from error; and not only for pouring it out but also for allowing us all to share in it. So Christ is saying to us: "If you want blood, do not make the altar of idols red with the blood of irrational beasts; let it be my altar with my blood." What could be more awesome, what more profoundly loving than that?

2. This is the way lovers behave. When they find those whom they love

getting tired of their own things and longing for what others have to offer, they make gifts from their own possessions to draw them away from those of others. Lovers express this kind of generosity by means of money or clothes or possessions; no one ever does it with blood. But that is how Christ showed his care and the warmth of his love for us. In the days of the old covenant, since men were at a much more imperfect stage, he was prepared to accept the blood which they offered to idols — with the aim of drawing them away from such things; and that is yet another example of his unspeakable love. But now he has provided in its place a far more awesome and glorious way of worship. He has changed the very sacrifice itself, and in place of the slaughter of irrational beasts, he has commanded us to offer up himself.

The bread which we break, is it not a participation in the body of Christ?

Why did he not use the word "sharing"? He wanted to convey something more than that word implies and to stress the closeness of the union. Our participation is not a matter simply of having or getting a share; it is a matter of participation by union. For as that body is united to Christ, so we are also united to him by means of this bread.

Why did he add: "which we break"? This is something which we actually see happening at the Eucharist, though it did not happen at the cross. Indeed there just the opposite was true. I quote: "Not a bone of him shall be broken" [John 19:36]. But what he did not undergo on the cross, that he does undergo in the oblation for the sake of each one of you. He allows himself to be broken up, so that he may fill all men.

The phrase which he uses, "participation in the body," might suggest a distinction between that which participates and that in which it participates. But even this small distinction is not allowed to stand. Having said "participation in the body," he then looks for another phrase to express an even greater closeness and so adds: *Because there is one bread, we who are many are one body.* In effect he is saying, "Why do I speak of participation? We actually are that body." What is the bread? The body of Christ. And what do those who receive a share of it become? The body of Christ — not many bodies, but one body. For as the loaf is composed of many grains united in such a way that the separate grains cannot be seen at all (they do exist, but the distinction between them cannot be observed when they are united); so are we joined to one another and to Christ. There is no question of your being fed from one body and your neighbour from another; everyone is fed from the same body. So Paul goes on: *For we all share in the one loaf.*

If then we are all fed from the same loaf and actually become the same body, why do we not all show the same love as well and become one in that respect too? For that was true of our forefathers in the old days. I quote: "For the company of those who believed were of one heart and one soul" [Acts 4:32]. But now the exact opposite is true. There are battles of every kind between Christians everywhere and our behaviour to one another is more ferocious than that of wild beasts. Christ united you to himself when you were removed from him. Yet you do not deign to be united with appropriate closeness to your brother; you, who have enjoyed the great benefits of love and life from your master, separate yourself from your brother. Indeed Christ's gift was not simply the giving of his body. Our original fleshly nature, which had been fashioned from the dust, had been killed by sin and had no life left. So he brought in, so to speak, the new dough or leaven of his own flesh. His flesh was of the same nature as ours but free of sin and full of life. This he has given to us all to share, in order that we may feed on it. We are to be rid of the old flesh, which is dead, and, by means of this table, are to be united with the living and immortal flesh.

40. Symbols and Images
(726–30)

JOHN OF DAMASCUS

Although little is certain about his early life, John of Damascus (c. 675–c. 749) probably belonged to a family of Christian civil servants who continued to work for the Islamic rulers of Damascus after the Arab conquest. John himself may have been a treasury official until the anti-Christian policies of Caliph Al-Walid (705–715) forced him out of office. We do know that he entered the famed abbey of St. Sabbas in the Cedron Valley around 715 and that the Patriarch of Jerusalem made him a presbyter before 726. He died at St. Sabbas around 749.

John of Damascus played a major role in the final Christological controversies of the Eastern church. In 726, the Byzantine emperor issued the first of a series of decrees prohibiting the use of images in prayer and worship. Venerating images of saints and martyrs had been common since the days of the catacombs.

Against the "iconoclasts" (those who sought to forbid images) John of Damascus argues (1) that the emperor has no business legislating theology, (2) that God himself became visible by becoming human in Jesus Christ, and (3) that the Fathers saw fit to permit the use of images as a

---

SOURCE: John of Damascus, *Writings*, vol. 37 of *The Fathers of the Church: A New Translation* (New York: Fathers of the Church, Inc., 1958). Used by permission of Catholic University of America Press.

"terse reminder" of the teachings of the gospel. Images, he states, are especially helpful to those who cannot read or have no leisure to do so. John of Damascus reminds the church that symbols or images are not just signs. They enable us to participate in the reality of what they represent.

Unfortunately John's views were not always welcome. He was condemned posthumously by the Council of Constantinople (Hieria) in 753 and vindicated again by the decisions of the Council of Nicaea (787).

Chapter 13

Because of the exceedingly great wealth of His goodness, the good, all-good, and exceedingly good God, who is all goodness, did not rest content that the Good, or His nature, should just be and not be shared by anything.[1] For this reason, He first made the spiritual and heavenly powers, and then the visible and sensible world, and then, finally, man of the spiritual and the sensible. Hence, all things He has made participate in His goodness by the fact that they have being. For He is being to them all, since "in him are all things,"[2] not only because He has brought them from nothing into being, but because it is by His operation that all things He made are kept in existence and held together. Living things, however, participate more abundantly, because they participate in the good both by their being and by their living. But rational beings, while they participate in the good in the aforementioned ways, do so still more by their very rationality. For they are in a way more akin to Him, even though He is, of course, immeasurably superior.

Since man was made both rational and free, he received the power to be unceasingly united to God by his own choice, provided, of course, that he persevere in the good, that is to say, in obedience to his Creator. Then, when man became disobedient to the commandment of Him who had made him and thus became subject to death and corruption, the Maker and Creator of our kind, through the bowels of His mercy, likened Himself to us and became man in all things except sin and was united to our nature. Thus, because we did not keep what He had imparted to us, His own image and His own spirit, He now participates in our poor weak

---

1. Cf. Gregory Nazianzen, *Sermon* 45.5.
2. Rom. 11:36.

nature so that He may render us pure and incorrupt and make us once more participators in His divinity.

It was moreover, necessary not only for the first fruits of our nature, but also for every man who so wished. And it was necessary that every such man should be born with a second birth and nourished with a new food fit for the new birth, and thus attain to the measure of perfection. Hence, by His own birth, or incarnation, and by His baptism and passion and resurrection, He freed our nature from the sin of our first parent, from death and corruption. And He became the first-fruit of the resurrection and set Himself to be a way, a model, and an example, so that we, too, might follow in His footsteps and become by adoption, as He is by nature, sons and heirs of God and joint heirs together with Him.[3] Thus, He gave us, as I have said, a second birth, so that, as we had been born of Adam and had been likened to him, and had become heir to his curse and corruption, we might by being born anew of Him be likened to Him and become heir to His incorruption and blessing and glory.

Now, since this Adam is spiritual, it was necessary that there be a spiritual birth and also a spiritual food. But, since we are individuals of a twofold nature and compounded, it is necessary that the birth also be of a twofold nature and that the food likewise be compounded. Hence, the birth was given us by water and the Spirit, by holy baptism, I mean, while the food was the Bread of Life itself, our Lord Jesus Christ who had come down from heaven.[4] For, when He was about to suffer death freely for our sake, on the night in which He delivered Himself up, He made a new testament for His holy disciples and Apostles and, through them, for all that believe in Him. So, when He had eaten the old Pasch with His disciples in the upper chamber on holy and glorious Mount Sion and had fulfilled the old testament, He washed the feet of His disciples and thus showed a symbol of holy baptism.[5] Then, after He had broken bread, He gave it to them saying "Take ye and eat. This is my body, which is broken for you unto remission of sins."[6] And in like manner He took also the chalice of wine and water and gave it to them, saying: "Drink ye all of this. This is my blood of the new testament, which is shed for you unto remission of sins. This do in commemoration of me. For as often as you

---

3. Cf. Rom. 8:17.
4. Cf. John 6:48.
5. Cf. John 13:1–15.
6. Cf. 1 Cor. 11:24. The "which is broken for you" is not strictly scriptural but belongs to the most ancient liturgical tradition and still survives in most eastern liturgies.

shall eat this bread and drink this chalice, you shall show the death of the Son of man and confess his resurrection, until he come."[7]

• • •

Now, bread and wine are used[8] because God knows human weakness and how most things that are not constantly and habitually used cannot be put up with and are shunned. With His usual condescension, therefore, He does through the ordinary things of nature those which surpass the natural order. And just as in the case of baptism, because it is the custom of men to wash themselves with water and anoint themselves with oil He joined the grace of the Spirit to oil and water and made it a laver of regeneration, so, because it is men's custom to eat bread and drink water and wine He joined His divinity to these and made them His body and blood, so that by the ordinary natural things we might be raised to those which surpass the order of nature.

• • •

The bread and wine are not a figure of the body and blood of Christ — God forbid! — but the actual deified body of the Lord, because the Lord Himself said: "This is my body"; not "a figure of my body" but "my body," and not "a figure of my blood" but "my blood." Even before this He had said to the Jews: "except you eat of the flesh of the Son of man and drink his blood, you shall not have life in you. For my flesh is meat indeed: and my blood is drink indeed." And again: "He that eateth me, shall live."[9]

• • •

It is called *participation* because through it we participate in the divinity of Jesus. It is also called *communion,* and truly is so, because of our having communion through it with Christ and partaking both of His flesh and His divinity, and because through it we have communion with and are

---

7. Cf. 1 Cor. 11:25–26. This form, as well as that of the consecration of the bread just mentioned, is the form of the Liturgy of St. James which was commonly used in Syria and Palestine.

8. Cf. Gregory of Nyssa, *Catechesi* 37.

9. John 6:54–58.

united to one another. For, since we partake of one bread, we all become one body of Christ and one blood and members of one another and are accounted of the same body with Christ.

• • •

They are called antitypes of the things to come, not because they are not really the body and blood of Christ, but because it is through them that we participate in the divinity of Christ now, while then it will be through the intellect and by vision alone.

• • •

Chapter 16

Since there are certain people who find great fault with us for adoring and honoring both the image of the Saviour and that of our Lady, as well as those of the rest of the saints and servants of Christ, let them hear how from the beginning God made man to His own image.[10] For what reason, then, do we adore one another, except because we have been made to the image of God? As the inspired Basil, who is deeply learned in theology, says: "the honor paid to the image redounds to the original,"[11] and the original is the thing imaged from which the copy is made. For what reason did the people of Moses adore from round about the tabernacle which bore an image and pattern of heavenly things, or rather, of all creation?[12] Indeed, God had said to Moses: "See that thou make all things according to the pattern which was shewn thee on the mount." And the Cherubim, too, that overshadowed the propitiatory, were they not the handiwork of men?[13] And what was the celebrated temple in Jerusalem? Was it not built and furnished by human hands and skill?[14]

Now, sacred Scripture condemns those who adore graven things, and also those who sacrifice to the demons. The Greeks used to sacrifice and the Jews also used to sacrifice; but the Greeks sacrifice to the demons, whereas the Jews sacrificed to God. And the sacrifice of the Greeks was

---

10. Cf. Gen. 1:26.
11. Basil, *On the Holy Ghost* 18.45.
12. Cf. Exod. 33:10.
13. Cf. Heb. 8:5; Exod. 25:40, 20.
14. Cf. 1 Kings 6.

rejected and condemned, while the sacrifice of the just was acceptable to God. Thus, Noe sacrificed "and the Lord smelled a sweet savor"[15] of the good intention and accepted the fragrance of the gift offered to Him. And thus the statues of the Greeks happen to be rejected and condemned, because they were representations of demons.

But, furthermore, who can make a copy of the invisible, incorporeal, uncircumscribed, and unportrayable God? It is, then, highly insane and impious to give a form to the Godhead. For this reason it was not the practice in the Old Testament to use images. However, through the bowels of His mercy God for our salvation was made man in truth, not in the appearance of man, as He was seen by Abraham or the Prophets, but really made man in substance. Then He abode on earth, conversed with men,[16] worked miracles, suffered, was crucified, rose again, and was taken up; and all these things really happened and were seen by men and, indeed, written down to remind and instruct us, who were not present then, so that, although we have not seen, yet hearing and believing we may attain to the blessedness of the Lord. Since, however, not all know letters nor do all have leisure to read, the Fathers deemed it fit that these events should be depicted as a sort of memorial and terse reminder. It certainly happens frequently that at times when we do not have the Lord's Passion in mind we may see the image of His crucifixion and, being thus reminded of His saving Passion, fall down and adore. But it is not the material which we adore, but that which is represented; just as we do not adore the material of the Gospel or that of the cross, but that which they typify. For what is the difference between a cross which does not typify the Lord and one which does? It is the same way with the Mother of God, too, for the honor paid her is referred to Him who was incarnate of her. And similarly, also, we are stirred up by the exploits of the holy men to manliness, zeal, imitation of their virtues, and the glory of God. For, as we have said, the honor shown the more sensible of one's fellow servants gives proof of one's love for the common Master, and the honor paid to the image redounds to the original. This is the written tradition, just as is worshiping toward the east, adoring the cross, and so many other similar things.[17]

Furthermore, there is a story[18] told about how, when Abgar was lord of

---

15. Gen. 8:21.
16. Cf. Bar. 3:38.
17. Cf. Basil, *op. cit.* 27.66.
18. The earliest form of the Syriac legend of Abgar, the first Christian king of Edessa, is to be found in Eusebius (*Eccles. Hist.* 1.13). The later and more amplified version

the city of Edessenes, he sent an artist to make a portrait of the Lord, and how, when the artist was unable to do this because of the radiance of His face, the Lord Himself pressed a bit of cloth to His own sacred and life-giving face and left His own image on the cloth and so sent this to Abgar who had so earnestly desired it.

And Paul, the Apostle of the Gentiles, writes that the Apostles handed down a great many things unwritten: "Therefore, brethren, stand fast: and hold the traditions which you have learned, whether by word or by our epistle"; and to the Corinthians: "Now I praise you, brethren, that in all things you are mindful of me and keep my ordinances as I have delivered them to you."[19]

---

containing the incident of the portrait here referred to is to be found in the Syriac document known as the *Doctrine of Addai* (translated and published by G. Phillips, London 1876).

19. 2 Thess. 2:14; 1 Cor. 11:2.

41. The Image Controversy
From the Synod of Constantinople and
the Council of Nicaea
(753 and 787)

The Byzantine Emperor Leo III (reigned 717–740) touched off the last phase of the Christological controversy in 726, when he prohibited the veneration of icons. His motives were unclear; images of Christ, the virgin, and the saints had dominated popular piety since the second century. Most likely Leo wanted to gain better control of the church, which had become the most powerful political force in the empire. First he removed a statue of Christ above the gate of the imperial palace. His actions led to riots in Constantinople and elsewhere. In 730, he called a synod to remove the recalcitrant Germanus, bishop of Constantinople, from office.

After Leo's death, his son and successor, Constantine V (741–775), carried on the iconoclastic (anti-icons) campaign. He criminalized all painting, possession, and adoration of images. In 753 he called a council at Constantinople, which among other things condemned image defender John of Damascus (see vol. 1:286–92). Constantine's harsh measures against nonconformists, particularly the monks, caused growing concern and contributed to the widening rift between the Byzantine empire and the Western church. After his death, the seventh ecumenical council at Nicaea (787) reversed the decisions of 753.

SOURCE: John H. Leith, ed., *Creeds of the Churches: A Reader in Christian Doctrine from the Bible to the Present* (Atlanta: John Knox Press, 1978). © 1963, 1978, 1982 John H. Leith. Used by permission of Westminster John Knox Press.

*The proceedings of the iconoclast council at Constantinople (753) rejected John of Damascus's popular argument that if the incarnate Christ is the "figure" or image of God, images must be permissible. The records of the council of Nicaea (787) vindicate John of Damascus's view that sacred images may be given "honorable reverence," as long as they are not worshiped. Worship (*latreia*) belongs to God alone, and Christians must not be guilty of idolatry (*idol-latreia*).*

The Synod of Constantinople (753)

When, however, they are blamed for undertaking to depict the divine nature of Christ, which should not be depicted, they take refuge in the excuse: We represent only the flesh of Christ which we have seen and handled. But that is a Nestorian error. For it should be considered that that flesh was also the flesh of God the Word, without any separation, perfectly assumed by the divine nature and made wholly divine. How could it now be separated and represented apart? So is it with the human soul of Christ which mediates between the Godhead of the Son and the dullness of the flesh. As the human flesh is at the same time flesh of God the Word, so is the human soul also soul of God the Word, and both at the same time, the soul being deified as well as the body, and the Godhead remained undivided even in the separation of the soul from the body in his voluntary passion. For where the soul of Christ is, there is also his Godhead; and where the body of Christ is, there too is his Godhead. If then in his passion the divinity remained inseparable from these, how do the fools venture to separate the flesh from the Godhead, and represent it by itself as the image of a mere man? They fall into the abyss of impiety, since they separate the flesh from the Godhead, ascribe to it a subsistence of its own, a personality of its own, which they depict, and thus introduce a fourth person into the Trinity. Moreover, they represent as not being made divine, that which has been made divine by being assumed by the Godhead. Whoever, then, makes an image of Christ, either depicts the Godhead which cannot be depicted, and mingles it with the manhood (like the Monophysites), or he represents the body of Christ as not made divine and separate and as a person apart, like the Nestorians.

The only admissible figure of the humanity of Christ, however, is bread and wine in the holy Supper. This and no other form, this and no other type, has he chosen to represent his incarnation. . . .

The Council of Nicaea (787)

Seventh Ecumenical

To make our confession short, we keep unchanged all the ecclesiastical traditions handed down to us, whether in writing or verbally, one of which is the making of pictorial representations, agreeable to the history of the preaching of the Gospel, a tradition useful in many respects, but especially in this, that so the incarnation of the Word of God is shewn forth as real and not merely phantastic, for these have mutual indications and without doubt have also mutual significations.

We, therefore, following the royal pathway and the divinely inspired authority of our Holy Fathers and the traditions of the Catholic Church (for, as we all know, the Holy Spirit indwells her), define with all certitude and accuracy that just as the figure of the precious and life-giving Cross, so also the venerable and holy images, as well in painting and mosaic as of other fit materials, should be set forth in the holy churches of God, and on the sacred vessels and on the vestments and on hangings and in pictures both in houses and by the wayside, to wit, the figure of our Lord God and Saviour Jesus Christ, of our spotless Lady, the Mother of God, of the honourable Angels, of all Saints and of all pious people. For by so much more frequently as they are seen in artistic representation, by so much more readily are men lifted up to the memory of their prototypes, and to a longing after them; and to these should be given due salutation and honourable reverence [ἀσπασμὸν καὶ τιμητικὴν προσκύνησιν], not indeed that true worship of faith [λατρείαν] which pertains alone to the divine nature; but to these, as to the figure of the precious and life-giving Cross and to the Book of the Gospels and to the other holy objects, incense and lights may be offered according to ancient pious custom. For the honour which is paid to the image passes on to that which the image represents, and he who reveres the image reveres in it the subject represented. . . .

PART III

Being God's People in the World (Church)

Christian doctrine has a logic of its own that needs consideration on its own merits. It is equally true that Christian theology responds to the changing context of church and society. Consequently, the radical changes in the life of the Christian community brought about by the end of persecution in the fourth century and by the rise of a "Holy Roman Empire" in the Western half of the ancient Roman empire, supported a unique social experiment and nurtured the vision of a global Christian civilization. The Middle Ages were not the "dark ages"; a new vision of Christendom replaced the political culture of ancient Rome.

Ten years after the Roman emperor Diocletian unleashed the most vicious persecution the church had ever seen, the eastern emperor, Constantine conquered Italy and asked the Roman Senate to make him "senior augustus" of the western half of the empire. Constantine was a friend of Christianity. He and Licinius, his major rival in the east, issued a joint edict of religious toleration as part of a political settlement. This Edict of Milan (313) was an unbelievable turn of events for the Christian community (see vol. 1:304–7), touching the life of individual Christians with new hope and tangible evidence of the grace of God. Overnight, Christians ceased being a hated and persecuted minority.

After Constantine conquered the eastern half of the empire, Christianity became an established religion. Constantine and his Byzantine successors took an active interest in the affairs of the Christian church, setting a precedent for Christian rulers to oversee church and state. For this reason, the life and teachings of Eastern Christianity increasingly became enmeshed in Byzantine imperial politics.

In the western half of the empire, the influence of Constantinople weakened and eventually disappeared completely in the wake of barbarian invasions from northern Europe. In its place, church leadership — especially the bishop of Rome (the pope) — became the most stable political force from North Africa to Ireland. After the Goths and Lombards invaded Italy, the missionary outreach of the bishops of Rome to their barbarian conquerors succeeded where the Roman legions had failed. Even the most humble among the bishops of Rome became princes of the church.

The rise of the papacy from Leo I, "the Great" (reigned 440–461), to Boniface VIII (reigned 1294–1303) shaped the theological heritage of all Western Christians. Leo I, "the first of the modern popes," became wildly popular in Italy among Christians and non-Christians alike, when in 452 he singlehandedly talked Attila the Hun out of attacking the city of Rome and negotiated the withdrawal of Attila's army from Italy.

Leo also tried, albeit not as successfully, to intervene in the Christological controversies of the Eastern church by writing a "Tome" — a letter of instruction in support of Flavian, the archbishop of Constantinople who was on the losing side of an argument about the human nature of Christ, against Eutyches, a local abbot. Leo's definition of Christ as "one person, two substances" (fully human, fully divine) later made a difference at Chalcedon (481). Leo's "Christmas sermon on the two natures of Christ" contains the essence of his argument and his summary of Western Christological position as stated in his Tome (see vol. 1:308–13).

Pope Gregory I (c. 540–604) was the next of the Roman pontiffs to be called "the Great." His "dedicatory letter" preceding his commentary on Job provides important insights into his method of interpreting scripture (see vol. 1:314–23). It also contains one of the first references to the Vulgate, the translation of the Bible into the common or "vulgar" Latin tongue. The Vulgate, translated by Jerome, was the official version of holy scriptures in the Roman church long after Latin ceased to be commonly used.

Gregory I was a person of considerable pastoral and diplomatic skill, and he used his position as a spiritual and political leader to extend papal authority to Spain and into the barbarian kingdoms in Gaul. He sent a monk named Augustine as a reluctant missionary to the Angles and Saxons in England. The pope's extensive correspondence provides important insights into how northern Europeans adopted, or accepted under pressure, the Christian faith. Gregory's letter addressed to Childebert II, King of the Franks and a Christian ruler who retained a fondness for his barbarian ways, is a masterpiece of political tact and spiritual clout (see vol. 1:324–26). Gregory's correspondence also anticipates some of the tensions over investiture, the process by which bishops are chosen and authorized, which later divided popes and emperors.

Popes play important symbolic and political roles during the Middle Ages. On Christmas Day in 800, Pope Leo III (reigned 795–816) placed a crown on the head of Charles, king of the Franks. Charlemagne, as historians remember him, was not pleased. He did not want to receive the crown of Constantine from a pontiff whom earlier he had forced to confess to an assortment of vices in a public apology to the people of Rome. Yet popes and emperors needed one another, even as tensions between church and state in western Europe increased.

By the eleventh century, Pope Gregory VII (reigned 1073–1085) and Emperor Henry IV (1050–1106) squared off over the investiture of German bishops. This contest is a fascinating one, which ended inconclusively with the death of the antagonists and the Concordat of Worms (1122) (see vol. 1:331–32).

Popes and emperors eventually did irreparable harm to the fabric of medieval society and eroded a noble vision of Christendom. The most powerful of the medieval popes, Innocent III (reigned 1198–1216) glorified the principle of papal supremacy by proclaiming that "as the moon gets her light from the sun, so the royal power gets its authority from papal authority." He presided over the Fourth Lateran Council whose pronouncements on transubstantiation, the duties of clergy and laity, and the power of the keys (i.e., the power to lock or unlock the gates of salvation), reflect an image of the medieval church as a universal institution of salvation (see vol. 1:333–37).

One hundred years later, Pope Boniface VIII (reigned 1294–1303) went even further, claiming that papal authority comes directly from God and insisting that mere kings and emperors could not judge the Roman pontiffs (see vol. 1:337–39). Spiritual power is not subject to secular justice. Rather, he argued, all power is delegated from God and exercised by the state on behalf of the church. However, unlike Innocent, Boniface no longer had the political clout to wield the spiritual sword. Philip IV, the French king, was singularly unimpressed and had the pope seized and imprisoned to prevent him from denying sacramental services to his realm (an interdict).

During these centuries of political controversy, the church continued to spread north into Europe. Pope Gregory I (d. 604) launched a great missionary effort among the "barbarian" tribes of England and Germany. He wrote letters of pastoral support to Augustine, a fellow monk of St. Andrew's in Rome, whom Gregory convinced to lead a group of "brothers going to England" (see vol. 1:340–43). After initial disappointments, Augustine visited the Christian Queen of Kent (597) and converted her husband Ethelbert (d. 616). Later, he established a residence at Canterbury and became the first "archbishop of Canterbury."

Pope Gregory suggested a careful missionary strategy that built a network of support among Christian queens and princes along the way by instructing missionaries to concentrate on the nobility. This procedure was efficient but sometimes shallow. It often produced sudden and spectacular reversals. After Augustine's death, monks of St. Andrew's continued to work among the Anglo-Saxons with considerable success. However, when they confronted Scotch-Irish missionaries who had crossed into England from the north, their encounter was less than friendly. Traditional enmity between Celts and Anglo-Saxons led to fights over the liturgy, the Easter date, and even such silly things as the correct tonsure of the monks. Finally, in 673 under the leadership of Theodore, archbishop of Canterbury, the two sides met at the Synod of Hertford and united English Christianity (see vol. 1:344–46). The church's unification took place long before the political unification.

Out of the union of Irish (Celtic) and Anglo-Saxon Christianity came a new missionary impulse in the seventh century. Missionaries from England and Ireland were successful in converting the remaining Germanic tribes on the continent to Christianity. Boniface (680–754), a Saxon monk from England, was a famous apostle to Germany. During his long career as a missionary bishop, he established numerous monasteries and churches east of the Rhine. Like Augustine before him, yet with more enthusiasm and a flair for the dramatic, Boniface cultivated an indigenous German church by converting the nobility and by training a native clergy.

Boniface effectively used regional councils to strengthen church leadership. Among them was the first "Council of the Germans" in 742 (see vol. 1:347–51). Boniface wrote a letter to the archbishop of Canterbury telling him about these councils and about the perils of working among the Germans. His English correspondence, like that of Pope Gregory I before him, shows an unwavering dedication to missionary work and widespread, enthusiastic support by the sisters and brothers of the established religious orders (see vol. 1:352–61).

Medieval Latin theology inherited a great deal of its agenda from

Augustine of Hippo (see vol. 1:184–225). Augustine's concerns for the doctrine of Holy Communion, the question of justification by merit or grace, and the related problem of faith and reason continued to engage medieval writers.

Radbertus (d.c. 860) and Ratramnus (d. after 868), monks and scholars at Corbie in Burgundy, both wrote treatises called "On the Lord's body and blood." Radbertus took the literal or "realist" position that the consecrated bread and wine of the Eucharist are the actual corporeal body and blood of Christ. This understanding came to be known as the doctrine of transubstantiation and was adopted by the Fourth Lateran Council of 1215 (see vol. 1:333–36 and 367–68).

Pushing Augustine's concept of the "sacramental symbol" to the other extreme, Ratramnus opposed the "magical" view of the Mass, which is only a "representation" of Christ's sacrifice on the cross (see vol. 1:367–75). He argued that in the elements of bread and wine "faith receives what the eye does not see."

Together, Radbertus and Ratramnus defined two very different understandings of the "real presence" of Christ in the sacrament. If the church views the Eucharist as a *repetition* of Christ's sacrifice on the cross, offered by the celebrant for the salvation of God's people, the church becomes primarily an institution of salvation. If on the other hand the church views the sacrament as a *representation* of Christ's sacrifice to celebrate God's saving grace in the believing community, the church has its being in Christ by hearing and heeding Christ's story. Within the boundaries of Augustinian teaching, both positions are extreme but possible.

In the eleventh century, Anselm of Canterbury (1033–1109) shifted theological concerns from the person and presence of Christ, to focus upon Christ's work (see vol. 1:376–79). In the title of his famous treatise on the atonement, he asked, "Cur Deus Homo?" ("Why did God become human?") Anselm is important for three reasons: (1) Anselm borrowed imagery for his understanding of the atonement from the feudal society in which he lived. God, he said, is the eternal Lord whose honor has been outraged by the sins of his human subjects. Restoring the broken relationship between them requires satisfaction. Only a person of exceeding nobility can offer satisfaction; a person equal to God yet also fully human, that is Christ. (2) Anselm also concentrated on Christ's work of salvation, becoming one of the first theologians in Christian history to draw attention to Jesus' ministry as an object of theological inquiry. This type of thinking greatly influenced later theology. And finally, (3) Anselm, who is often called the founder of medieval scholasticism, was a master practitioner of the dialectical method used by late medieval thinkers. The method argues opposing sides of a question in order to find a logical middle ground. The method's basis is the assumption that there is but one truth, absolute and indivisible; that faith and reason cannot contradict each other; and that reason illuminated by grace can find God. In his *Proslogion,* Anselm demonstrates how reason can find God with his famous "ontological proof." Later philosophers, like Descartes in the seventeenth century, borrowed his "proof" to bolster arguments for the reliability of human reason.

The greatest of the late medieval scholars was Thomas Aquinas (1224–1274). His *Summa Theologica* produced a "new philosophy" quite different from classic Augustinian theology. As Augustine became an important theological resource for the emerging reformation movements in northern Europe, Thomas became the official theologian of the Roman Catholic church.

Thomas Aquinas focuses on natural theology; i.e., the theory that God can be known by God's "effects." Whereas Augustine and Anselm maintained the primacy of faith over natural reason and denied the ability of natural reason (i.e., reason unaided by grace) to lead humanity to God, Aquinas disagreed. Aquinas was careful not to contradict Augustine directly. Following Aristotle, whom he always referred to simply as "the philosopher," he argued that we can know the creator "analogically" by the "effects" of God in creation. Later deists captured the same idea when they argued that the "watch is to watchmaker as cosmos is to God."

Aquinas bases his "Five Ways," or proofs of God, on the assumptions that (a) humans can perceive cause and effect in the world, (b) humans cannot logically conceive of an infinite chain of causes, hence (c) we must postulate a first, uncaused cause, and (d) that cause is God (see vol. 1:386–89).

In spite of his carefully reasoned method, Aquinas acknowledges that mere rational knowledge of God is limited. Rational knowledge cannot give "saving knowledge," which requires revelation and grace. The limitations of human reason are obvious when one contemplates the central teachings of the church, such as the doctrine of the Trinity or the mystery of the Mass. Theology can only show that what the church teaches is not impossible (see vol. 1:392–93).

Aquinas insists that natural and revealed truth are still only aspects of the one eternal truth of God. According to Aquinas, reason and faith complement each other. Unlike Augustine, Aquinas was optimistic about our ability to obtain both merit and grace. Like truth, we may divide virtue into "natural" and "theological" categories. From Aristotle comes the classical Greek list of "natural" virtues based on reason, prudence, justice, self-control, and courage.

From the biblical writings of Paul, we learn about the three theological virtues: faith, hope, and love (1 Cor. 13). Theological virtues are not demonstrable by natural reason. They are not necessarily prudent, because each involves an element of risk. Theological virtues, says Aquinas, are based on revelation and direct us towards a supernatural end. For Thomas Aquinas, reason and revelation collaborate to provide an authoritative theological system of normative moral truth. Furthermore, depending on one's point of view, they also provide a classical semi-Pelagian or semi-Augustinian treatment of the ancient debate over the justice and grace of God (see vol. 1:395–404).

Finally, using Aristotelian logic, Aquinas offers the most impressive exposition of the doctrine of transubstantiation, the doctrine that states that Christ is physically present in the bread and wine at the Mass. Here Aquinas carefully explores the scope and the limits of natural reason, ending his argument with an appeal to the power of God (see vol. 1:405–9).

The Christian church became the triumphant community in the Middle Ages. Emerging from the decaying Roman Empire, church leadership developed important and lasting arguments to widen ecclesiastical power and spread Christianity throughout western Europe. We are heirs of this legacy. Contemporary Christians can benefit from these theological traditions, even as they seek to move beyond them.

The Rise of the Papacy

42. The Edict of Milan
From *The History of the Church from Christ to Constantine*
(c. 313)

EUSEBIUS

Early in 312, Constantine, one of the four regents of the empire, attacked his closest rival Maxentius in the famous battle of the Milvian bridge. Maxentius drowned in the Tiber River. After the melee, Constantine entered Rome in triumph, and the Senate voted him "senior augustus." Christians everywhere celebrated his victory; Constantine, a monotheist and devotee of the "unconquered sun," despised religious persecution.

The Christian historians of the time, Eusebius and Lactentius, both tell the familiar story that on the eve of battle Constantine saw the Greek

---

SOURCE: Eusebius, *The History of the Church from Christ to Constantine,* trans. and introduced by G. A. Williamson (New York: Penguin Classics, 1965). © 1965 G. A. Williamson. Reproduced by permission of Penguin Books Ltd.

letters chi/rho (CHRist) and read the legend "by this sign you shall conquer" in a vision or dream sent by God.

Whatever his vision, Constantine lived up to the expectations of the Christians. A year later at Milan, he negotiated an agreement with Licinius, the imperial regent of Byzantium. They designed the agreement to eliminate their common rival, Maximinus, "caesar" of the northeastern part of the empire. Constantine insisted that the treaty include a decree of religious toleration signed by both emperors, the so-called "Edict of Milan." While the edict commands tolerance for all religions, it specifically provides that Christians are to be granted freedom of worship and that their properties must be restored.

Eusebius's version of the edict captures the sense of relief that the Christians must have felt after years of persecution. He writes, "At the end of all this, when God, the great and heavenly defender of Christians, had by such means displayed his wrath as a warning to all people in return for the cruel wrongs they had done us, he again restored to us the kindly, cheering radiance of his providence towards us. As if in black darkness, God most wonderfully illumined us with the light of peace from himself making it plain that God himself had been watching over us throughout."

For a long time past we have made it our aim that freedom of worship should not be denied, but that every man, according to his own inclination and wish, should be given permission to practise his religion as he chose. We had therefore given command that Christians and non-Christians alike should be allowed to keep the faith of their own religious beliefs and worship. But in view of the fact that numerous conditions of different kinds had evidently been attached to that rescript, in which such a right was granted to those very persons, it is possible that some of them were soon afterwards deterred from such observance.

When with happy auspices I, Constantinus Augustus, and I, Licinius Augustus, had arrived at Milan, and were enquiring into all matters that concerned the advantage and benefit of the public, among the other measures directed to the general good, or rather as questions of highest priority, we decided to establish rules by which respect and reverence for the Deity would be secured, i.e. to give the Christians and all others liberty to follow whatever form of worship they chose, so that whatsoever divine and heavenly powers exist might be enabled to show favour to us and to all who live under our authority. This therefore is the decision that we reached by sound and careful reasoning: no one whatever was to be denied the right to follow and choose the Christian observance or form of worship; and everyone was to have permission to give his mind to that form of worship which he feels to be adapted to his needs, so that the Deity might be enabled to show us in all things His customary care and generosity. It was desirable to send a rescript stating that this was our pleasure, in order that after the complete cancellation of the conditions contained in the earlier letter[1] which we sent to Your Dedicatedness about the Christians, the procedure that seemed quite unjustified and alien to our clemency should also be cancelled, and that now every individual still desirous of observing the Christian form of worship should without any interference be allowed to do so. All this we have decided to explain very fully to Your Diligence, that you may know that we have given the said Christians free and absolute permission to practise their own form of worship. When you observe that this permission has been granted by us absolutely, Your Dedicatedness will understand that permission has been given to any others who may wish to follow their own observance or form of worship — a privilege obviously consonant with the tranquillity of our times — so that every man may have permission to choose and practise whatever religion he wishes. This we have done to make it plain that we are not belittling any rite or form of worship.

With regard to the Christians, we also give this further ruling. In the letter sent earlier to Your Dedicatedness precise instructions were laid down at an earlier date with reference to their places where earlier on it was their habit to meet. We now decree that if it should appear that any persons have bought these places either from our treasury or from some other source, they must restore them to these same Christians without payment and without any demand for compensation, and there must be no negligence or hesitation. If any persons happen to have received them as a gift, they must restore the said places to the said Christians without loss of time; provided that if either those who have bought these same places or those who have received them as a gift wish to appeal to our generosity, they may apply to the prefect and judge of the region, in order that they also may benefit by our liberality. All this property is to be handed over to the Christian body immediately, by energetic action on your part, without any delay.

And since the aforesaid Christians not only possessed those places where it was their habit to meet, but are known to have possessed other

---

1. The Edict of Galerius.

places also, belonging not to individuals but to the legal estate of the whole body, i.e. of the Christians, all this property, in accordance with the law set forth above, you will order to be restored without any argument whatever to the aforesaid Christians, i.e. to their body and local associations, the provision mentioned above being of course observed, namely, that those persons who restore the same without seeking compensation, as we mentioned above, may expect to recoup their personal losses from our generosity.

In all these matters you must put all the energy you possess at the service of the aforesaid Christian body, in order that our command may be carried out with all possible speed, so that in this also our liberality may further the common and public tranquillity. For by this provision, as was mentioned above, the divine care for us of which we have been aware on many earlier occasions will remain with us unalterably for ever. And in order that the pattern of this our enactment and of our generosity may be brought to the notice of all, it is desirable that what we have written should be set forth by an edict of your own and everywhere published and brought to the notice of all, so that the enactment giving effect to this our generosity may be known to every citizen.

43. Christmas Sermon on the Two Natures of Christ

From *Sermon 28*, the Tome
(448)

POPE LEO I

The ancient church used the title "pope" (father) for all bishops of major Christian centers, such as Carthage or Alexandria. After the invasion of tribes from the north (barbarians), the bishops of Rome became the leaders of the church throughout the whole of western Europe, and the title "pope" referred exclusively to the bishop of Rome. In this sense, Leo I, "the Great" (reigned 440–461), was the first of the modern popes.

When the army of Attila the Hun approached Rome in 452, Leo left the city and went out to meet "the scourge of God." Attila "was so pleased at the presence of the chief Christian priest" that he turned aside and left the city unscathed. Three years later, Pope Leo convinced the Vandal king Geneseric, whose victorious army was plundering Rome, not to burn the city. To Rome's grateful citizens, the successor of Peter had become the successor of Caesar.

Leo was not quite as spectacular when he tried to settle some of the theological quarrels in the eastern European church. The immediate oc-

---

SOURCE: Maurice Wiles and Mark Santer, eds., *Documents in Early Christian Thought* (Cambridge: Cambridge University Press, 1979). © Cambridge University Press 1975. Used by permission of Cambridge University Press.

casion was a dispute between Flavian, the patriarch of Constantinople, and Eutyches, a local abbot. Eutyches argued that Jesus Christ, the Son of God was not of one substance (homo-ousios) with humanity.

In 448 after a local synod chaired by Flavian condemned his views, Eutyches appealed to Leo, who responded with a formal "Tome" (letter of instruction). Pope Leo supported Flavian for his orthodox assertion that Christ was fully human and fully divine (following the biblical tradition of Antioch), but his Tome was not well received in the eastern parts of the empire where friends of Eutyches had garnered the support of the court.

An imperial council held at Ephesus in 449 vindicated Eutyches, condemned Flavian, and told Leo to mind his own business. Leo denounced it as a "robber synod." However in 451, Leo's views did prevail at the Council of Chalcedon. There, Leo's Christology became the basis of the council's affirmation that Christ is one person, complete in his deity and also in his humanity; of one substance with God in his divinity and of one substance (homo-ousios) with humankind in his humanity (see vol. 1:240–41). Chalcedon also clearly indicated that no distinction of rank between Rome and Constantinople existed.

Leo's Christmas sermon contains an outline of his argument against Nestorius and Eutyches. It is a concise summary of the emerging theological consensus in the western European church about the nature of Jesus Christ.

---

1. We are bidden, my beloved, throughout the divine Scriptures always to be rejoicing in the Lord, but we are without doubt more particularly stirred to spiritual joy on this day, when the mystery of the Lord's nativity shines so brightly upon us. We turn once again to that ineffable condescension of the divine love, whereby the creator of man deigned to be made man; our aim is to be found in his nature as we adore him in ours. God, the Son of God, the only-begotten from the eternal and unbegotten Father, continuing eternally in the form of God and possessing beyond all change and time an essence identical with the Father's, took upon him the form of a servant — yet without impairing his own majesty: he did it to promote us to his own state, not to degrade himself to ours. Each nature continued with its own characteristics,[1] but so close a unity was estab-

---

1. This insistence that each nature keeps its own distinctive characteristics goes back to Tertullian. It is also an important point of agreement between Leo and Cyril.

lished between them that the divine was inseparable from the humanity and the human indivisible from the divinity.

2. In celebrating our Lord and Saviour's birthday, my beloved, we must have a complete and true conception of the childbearing of the blessed Virgin. We must believe that there was no moment of time at which the power of the Word was absent from the flesh and soul that were conceived. There was no previously formed and ensouled temple of Christ's body, which the Word was to enter later and claim as a habitation. Rather it was through and in the Word himself that the new man was given his beginning. So there was one Son of God and of man, in whom the divinity was without mother and the humanity without father. By the Holy Spirit a virgin was made fruitful, and without trace of corruption gave birth at one and the same moment to the offspring and founder of her race. It was for this reason too that this same Lord, as the evangelist records, could enquire of the Jews whose son they understood Christ to be on the authority of the Scriptures, and, when they replied that it was taught that he would come from the seed of David, could ask, "How then is it that David in the Spirit calls him 'Lord'? For he says, The Lord said to my Lord, 'Sit at my right hand until I put your enemies under your feet'" [Matt. 22:43-4]. The Jews were unable to answer the question, because they did not realize that the prophecy was speaking both of the offspring of David and of the divine nature within the one Christ.

3. The majesty of the Son of God, who is equal to the Father, clothes itself in the humility of a servant — without fear of diminution and without need of augmentation. By the power of his divinity alone he was able to achieve that operation of the divine love, which was devoted to the restoration of mankind — namely the rescue of the creature made in the image of God from the yoke of a harsh oppressor. But when the devil acted against the first man, he did not use force; he got man on to his own side with the consent of his free will. So, man's sin being voluntary and his hostility to God a matter of deliberate choice, these things had to be overcome in a manner which would not make of the requirements of justice an obstacle to the gift of grace. With the whole human race ruined in its entirety, there was in the secret depths of the divine purpose only one remedy which could help the fallen; that was for one of the sons of Adam to be born free from and innocent of the original transgression so that he could benefit all the rest both by his example and by his merit. But this could not happen by natural birth; no offspring of our tainted root could come except from that seed of which Scripture says: "Who can make clean that which has been conceived of unclean seed? Art not thou the

only one?" [Job 14:4]. So David's Lord became David's son and from the fruit of the promised branch there did arise an offspring without taint. Two natures came together into one person, so that there was a single conception and a single birth of our Lord Jesus Christ, in whom was both true divinity for the working of miracles and true humanity for the endurance of suffering.

4. So then, my beloved, the catholic faith should turn her back on the errors of those heretics who rail against her. Deceived by the vanity of the wisdom of the world, they have deserted the truth of the gospel. They have made the source of true enlightenment into the occasion of their own blindness. We have examined the views of almost every form of false belief, even those which go so far as to deny the Holy Spirit, and we are confident that almost every deviation involves a failure to believe the truth of the two natures in Christ within an acknowledgement of the one person. Some have ascribed humanity only to the Lord, others divinity only. Others have said that he had true divinity but that his flesh was unreal. Others have acknowledged that he took real flesh, but have denied that he had the nature of God the Father; they have ascribed to his divinity what are really marks of his human nature, and so have invented the notion of a greater and a lesser God—although in true divinity there can be no differences of rank, since whatever is less than God is not God. Others have recognized that there is no such separation between Father and Son, but because they could not conceive the unity of the godhead except as a unity of person have affirmed that the Father is the same as the Son; on that understanding birth and growth, suffering and death, burial and resurrection are all acts of that one God, who fulfils the role of the man and of the Word at every point. Others have thought that our Lord Jesus Christ had a body which was not of the same substance as ours but composed of elements of a higher and more refined nature. Others have claimed that there was no human soul in the flesh of Christ but that the divinity of the Word itself filled the role of the soul. This rash opinion easily passes over into the view that there was a soul in Christ but it did not have a rational mind as part of it since the divinity by itself was sufficient to fulfil all the functions of reason for the man. Finally these same people have actually dared to affirm that some part of the Word was changed into flesh. Thus the various forms of this one doctrine do away not only with the nature of the flesh and of the soul but even with the essence of the Word itself.

5. There are many other strange forms of error but we must not weary your patience by listing them all. These varied forms of impiety are linked

together by the family resemblance which exists between one kind of blasphemy and another. But there are two errors in particular which we call on you to avoid with devout and special care. One of these was started some time ago by Nestorius; its attempt to gain ground was checked. The other, which is new, and which merits the same vigorous condemnation, has been propounded by Eutyches. Nestorius dared to proclaim that the blessed Virgin Mary was bearer of Christ's humanity only. This excludes the belief that in her conception and child-bearing a union was affected of flesh and the Word; the Son of God will not himself have become son of man, but will only have joined himself by an act of special favour to a created man. Catholic ears were utterly unable to accept this idea, being well enough trained in the true gospel to be absolutely sure that there is no hope of salvation for the human race unless the one who is the Virgin's son is the very one who is his mother's creator. Eutyches, the irreligious author of the more recent blasphemy, did acknowledge a union of the two natures in Christ; but he said that the outcome of that union was that only one of the two remained and that the substance of the other in no sense continued to exist — but this annihilation could only have happened by a process either of absorption or of separation. But both these notions are so directly opposed to a sound faith that one cannot accept them without losing the name of Christian. Consider what follows if the incarnation is a union of divine and human natures of such a kind that by their coming together what was double becomes single; it is divinity alone that was born of the womb of the Virgin, divinity alone that went through the deceptive appearance of submitting to bodily nourishment and growth; and, if I may omit all the other occasions of mutability that are inherent in being human, it is divinity alone that was crucified, divinity alone that died, divinity alone that was buried. Indeed for those who think thus there can be no ground for hope of resurrection, and Christ cannot be "first-begotten from the dead" [Col. 1:18]; for only someone capable of being put to death could have a right to resurrection.

6. Keep your hearts free, my beloved, from poisonous lies inspired by the devil. You know that the eternal divinity of the Son has not grown or increased in any way in the Father's presence; be careful then to observe that the saying "Sit at my right hand" [Ps. 110:1] is directed to the same nature in Christ as that to which the saying "Earth thou art and to earth thou shalt return" [Gen. 3:19] was directed in the case of Adam. In that nature in which Christ is equal to the Father, the Only-begotten has never been inferior to the greatness of his begetter. The glory which he has with the Father is not a temporal thing. He is on that very right hand of the

Father, of which Exodus and Isaiah speak: "Thy right hand, O Lord, is glorified in power" [Exod. 15:6] and "Lord, who has believed our report? and to whom was the arm of the Lord revealed?" [Isa. 53:1]. So then the man was taken up into the Son of God; he was received at the very outset of his physical existence into the unity of the person of Christ in such a way that he could not be conceived in separation from the divinity, could not be born in separation from the divinity, could not be reared in separation from the divinity. The same person was present in the miracles and in the endurance of insults. In his human weakness he was crucified, dead and buried; in his divine power he was raised on the third day, ascended into heaven and sat down at the right hand of God the Father. In his nature as man he received from the Father what in his nature as God he himself also bestowed.

7. Ponder these things, my beloved, with a dutiful heart; always remember the injunction of the apostle, who gives this general warning: "See that no one deceives you by philosophy or empty deceit, according to human tradition and not according to Christ: for in him the whole fullness of deity dwells bodily, and you are filled in him" [Col. 2:8–10]. He says "bodily," not "spiritually," so that we will realize that it is real fleshly substance in which there is a bodily indwelling of the fullness of deity. Thereby, indeed, the whole Church also is filled; cleaving to its head, it is the body of Christ, who lives and reigns, with the Father and the Holy Spirit, God for ever and ever. Amen.

44. Dedicatory Letter to His Commentary on Job
(587)

POPE GREGORY I

Pope Gregory I, "the Great" (c. 540–604), like Leo a century before him, found himself the guardian of the church and of the people of Rome at a time of political turmoil and tribal invasions. Born to a patrician family in Rome, he grew up as the Eastern (Byzantine) empire was losing its last battles against the Germanic tribal incursions into northern Italy. A brief restoration of imperial authority after the collapse of Theoderic's Ostrogoths kingdom (536) was followed by a Lombard invasion of northern and central Italy (568). After a short but spectacular civil service career, Gregory resigned as imperial governor of Rome sometime before 573, disposed of his wealth and joined a monastic community. Rome was one of seven monastic centers he endowed with his own funds across Italy.

When Gregory became pope in 590, Rome was a disaster — ruined by war, devastated by floods, and ravaged by plague. Imperial authority had broken down, and Lombard raiders were at the gates of the city. Convinced of the need for peace, Gregory negotiated a truce between the Lombard kingdom and the Byzantine empire. As pope, Gregory's ad-

---

SOURCE: George E. McCracken, ed., *Early Medieval Theology*, vol. 9 of *Library of Christian Classics* (Philadelphia: Westminster Press, 1957). Used by permission of Westminster John Knox Press.

ministration restored essential services, including grain shipments from the southern provinces. He gave shelter and food to the city's poor in his official residence, the Lateran palace. A year later, he initiated major reforms to curb corruption and incompetence in the handling of the church's extensive properties.

For the clergy, Gregory was a disciplinarian and a pastor. To the people of Rome, he was the symbol of spiritual and civil authority. He developed the Western church into a strong and unified institution that survived the collapse of its ancient home (Rome). Under his leadership, the Western church's aggressive missionary activity among the invading tribes converted the new landlords to Christianity.

Though scholars consider Pope Gregory to be one of the four "doctors" of the Roman (catholic) church, he was actually more a pastor and leader than an original thinker. His best-known work, the Pastoral Rule, *is a treatise on the spiritual and moral demands of the pastoral office. According to Gregory, pastors should lead a simple, monastic life, "lest those who desire to intercede for the sins of others are disgraced by their own."*

Gregory addresses his dedicatory letter of his Commentary on Job *to his friend Leander, the bishop of Seville, who had been instrumental in converting the Arian Visigoths to the catholic faith in 587. Gregory describes his method of interpreting scripture which, like that of his intellectual mentor Augustine, relies heavily on allegory. He asserts that a scriptural narrative cannot be understood literally because this would "engender in the readers, not instruction, but error." He has a clear preference for what he calls moral instruction by the allegorical method.*

In his Commentary on Job *Gregory tells Leander that he is using the "new translation"—that is, Jerome's Vulgate (Latin) translation, which was two hundred years old at the time. He comments, however, that occasionally he still prefers its predecessor, the "old Latin" version of the scriptures.*

Gregory, servant of the servants of God, to the most reverend and most holy Leander,[1] his brother and fellow bishop.

---

1. Leander, born at Cartagena c. 550 or earlier, was brother to Fulgentius, bishop of Cartagena and Ecija; to Florentina, a celebrated nun; and to Isidore of Seville, his successor, all four of them canonized. He was active in the conversion of Visigothic Spain from Arianism, presided at the third Council of Toledo in 589, and delivered the closing

1. Having first made your acquaintance, most blessed brother, long ago at the city of Constantinople, when I was kept there by business of the Apostolic See and you had been sent there on a Visigothic embassy with a mission connected with the faith,[2] I explained to you everything which displeased me about myself: how I postponed for a long period the grace of conversion, and, even after I was inspired by heavenly desire, thought it better still to wear the garments of secular life. For what I should seek from the love of eternity was already revealed to me but ingrown habit had so enshackled me that I did not change my outward habiliments. And since my spirit up to that point compelled me to serve this world, so far as outward appearance goes, many forces out of the care of this same world began to overwhelm me, so that I was held to it now, not only in appearance, but, what is more serious, in my mind also. At last, in flight from all these burdens, I sought the haven of the monastery and, having left everything of the world behind, as I then believed in vain, I escaped, poor man, from the shipwreck of this life. For as often a ship, carelessly moored, is, when the storm grows strong, drawn out by the billow even from the safest harbor, so suddenly I found myself again, under the cloak of the church's order,[3] on the deep sea of secular affairs, and how tightly I should have held to the quiet of the monastery which, when I had it, I did not hold strongly, this I learned only when I lost it.

For when, as I was on the point of receiving the duty of ministry at the holy altar, my own inclination to decline was opposed by the virtue of obedience, this was undertaken because the church demanded it,[4] a duty which I might, if permitted, with impunity turn aside by fleeing from it again. After this, against my will and though I struggled against it, since the ministry of the altar is heavy, there was also added the weight of pastoral care.[5]

Now I bear this with the greater difficulty since, feeling myself unequal to it, I draw my breath with no consolation of confidence. This because, now that evils are increasing,[6] the end approaching, the temporal affairs

---

sermon *De triumpho ecclesiae ob conversionem Gothorum.* Three of Gregory's letters are addressed to Leander. See J. Bolland *et al., Acta Sanctorum,* March, 2.275–280; J. Mabillon, *Acta Sanctorum ord. S. Benedicti* 1.378–385.

2. The story is in John the Deacon, *S. Gregorii Magni vita* 1:27.
3. The mission to Constantinople.
4. *Sub ecclesiae colore.*
5. Gregory speaks of his unworthiness of the pontificate in Epist. 1:6.
6. On Gregory's actual experience with natural disaster, see Gregory of Tours, *Hist. of the Franks* 10.1 (Dalton's ed., 2.425), and his whole pontificate, even his whole life, was

of the world are in a state of confusion. We ourselves, who believe we serve the inner mysteries, are involved in cares without.[7] As in that moment when I approached the ministry of the altar, action was taken also about me without my knowledge, that I might receive the weight of the sacred order, so that I might more freely serve in the earthly palace, to which, of course, many of my brethren from the monastery, bound to me by kindred affection, followed me. I see that this was done by divine agency so that following their example, at the calm shore of prayer, I might be safely moored by the anchor's hawser when billowed about by the ceaseless forces of secular affairs. To their fellowship I fled, as to the harbor of the safest port, from the rolling waves of earthly stress, though that duty, when I was drawn out of the monastery from a life of former quiet, had almost slain me with the dagger of its activity. Among them, however, through the encouragement of serious reading, the stimulation of daily devotion roused my spirits. Then these same brethren were pleased, and you yourself, as you remember,[8] brought pressure upon them, that they should force me by their urgent pleas to expound the book of blessed Job, and in proportion as the Truth[9] should infuse me with power, to open to them the mysteries of such great depth. Besides the burden of their own plea they placed this upon me also, that I should make known not only the words of the story in their allegorical senses but should apply the allegorical senses to the practice of moral virtues. To this they added something still more difficult: that I should bolster each truth taught with proof texts, and when the proof texts were presented, if they should appear perhaps involved, I should unravel them by further exegesis.

2. Presently, however, when I learned the character and the magnitude of the task to which I was being dragged in this obscure work not hitherto treated, I was beaten down, I admit, solely by the weight of listening to their exhortations, and through weariness I gave in. But at once suspended between the alternatives of fear and duty, when I lifted up my eyes to the Bestower of the gifts of the soul, every hesitation was laid aside and then I realized with certainty that what the love of my brethren's hearts ordered me to do could not be impossible. I had, of course, no hope that I

---

an object lesson in perils caused by failure of the Byzantine emperor to give peace to Italy through appointment of able exarchs.

7. Political activity made necessary by the same disturbing conditions.
8. See *Epist. ad Leandrum* 1.43.
9. Christ.

should be adequate to the task, but strengthened by my very lack of confidence in myself, I forthwith raised my hope to Him by whom "the tongue of the dumb was loosened, who gave eloquence to the tongues of babes";[10] who converted the meaningless and unintelligible brayings of an ass into the perceptibility of human conversation.[11] What would be remarkable if he who expresses his truth, when he wishes, even through the mouths of beasts of burden, should furnish understanding to a stupid human being? Girt up, then, with the strength of this thought, I roused my own parched soul to search for the fountain of such great depth, and though the life of those to whom I was forced to provide this exegesis far surpassed my own, I nevertheless did not believe it wrong if a leaden pipe should be used to provide flowing water for men's use.

Thus, soon afterward, when these same brothers had taken their places before me, I delivered the first parts of the book, and because I found a little free time, I dictated the later parts. And when I had greater hours of leisure, adding much, cutting out a little, leaving a few things as they were found, I put together into books, while I revised, the parts which had been orally delivered by me, and I took care to compose the later parts in the same style as I had spoken the first. Thus, while running through and carefully correcting the parts spoken orally, I succeeded in making them assume the appearance of a written work, and the parts I had first written did not seem far different from spoken language, so that while the one was extended, the other contracted, that which came into being by different method might become something homogeneous. Although I increased by a third the spoken part, I omitted almost as much, because although my brothers drew me on to other subjects, they did not want this to be revised too carefully.

Inasmuch as they kept prescribing numerous items, and I desired to obey them, at times providing expositions, at others lofty contemplation, at still others a tool for teaching morality, the bulk of this work came to thirty-five books, with which I filled six manuscripts. This is why in it I often seem almost to be neglecting the order of exposition and to be devoting myself a bit more to broad reflection and moral instruction. Yet whoever speaks about God must take care to try to instruct the character of his hearers. He must consider it the proper procedure in speaking if, when a chance to edify occurs, he turn aside for personal benefit from the topic on which he began to speak. The expounder of Holy Scripture ought

---

10. Wisd. 10:21.
11. Num. 22:21–30.

to be like a river, for if the stream flowing along in its bed should on its flanks come into contact with curving valleys, it at once turns into them its powerful current, and when it has filled them full, it suddenly pours back again into its channel. That is how, certainly, the expounder of the divine Word should be, so that when he discusses any topic, if perchance he finds an opportunity presented to him suitable for edification, he may turn the streams of his eloquence into it as if it were a nearby valley, and when he has poured over this adjacent field of instruction, he may fall back into the channel of speech he had originally set before him.

3. You must know, however, that we run over some topics in historical exposition, and in some we search for allegorical meaning in our examination of types; in still others we discuss morality but through the allegorical method; and in several instances we carefully make an attempt to apply all three methods. In the first instance we lay the historical foundation; in the second, through the typological sense we erect a structure of the mind to be a citadel of faith; finally, through the grace of moral instruction, we clothe the edifice, as it were, with a coat of color. What must one really believe the words of truth to be but food taken for the refreshment[12] of the mind? When we discuss these topics in various methods, changing them often, we set a feast before the mouth, in such a way as to eliminate distaste from our reader who, dining like a banqueter, scrutinizes what is offered him and takes what he sees is more palatable.

But at times we neglect to expound the obvious words of the narrative so as not to reach too late the obscure meanings. At times they cannot be understood literally because, when the obvious meaning is taken, they engender in the readers, not instruction, but error. For see what is said: "Under whom those who carry the world are bowed down."[13] Who would not know that so great a man as Job is not following the empty tales of the poets so as to view the great bulk of the world as borne aloft on the sweat of a giant?[14] Again, struck by calamities, he says: "My soul has chosen hanging and my bones death."[15] Who in his right mind would believe that a man of such great fame, who, of course, as all agree, received from the eternal Judge rewards in proportion to the virtue of his patience, had determined in the midst of his afflictions to end his life by hanging? In

---

12. Cf. John Chrysostom, *Hom. in Ioh.* 4:1.
13. Job 9:13 (Vulgate; R.S.V. different).
14. The allusion is to the pagan concept of the Titan Atlas as in Hesiod, *Theog.* 517; Aeschylus, *Prom.* 347 ff.
15. Job 7:15.

some instances, also, the words themselves militate against the possibility of their literal interpretation. For he says, "Let the day perish on which I was born and the night on which it was said, 'A man has been conceived.'"[16] And a little later he adds, "Let the darkness seize it and let it be covered over with bitterness."[17] And as a curse for the same night he adds, "Let that night be unique."[18] Surely this day of his birth, rolling round in the onrush of time itself, could not stand still. How, then, could it have become veiled in darkness? Having passed away, of course, it no longer existed, nor yet if, in the nature of creation, it still were to exist, could it feel bitterness. It is clear, then, that he is not speaking at all of an insensate day when he wishes it to be struck by a sense of bitterness. And if the night of his conception had passed away like other nights, how could he wish that it be unique? As from the lapse of time, it could not now be fixed, so also it could not be separated from contact with the other nights. Again he says, "How long wilt thou not spare me nor let me go until I swallow my spittle?"[19] And yet a little while before he had said, "My soul was hitherto unwilling to touch them, and now from necessity they are my food."[20] Who does not know that spittle is more easily swallowed than food? Since he says he is taking food, it is absolutely unbelievable that he cannot swallow spittle. Another time he says, "I have sinned; what shall I do to thee, thou guardian of men?"[21] And surely, "Thou wantest me to consume the iniquities of my youth."[22] And in another reply he adds, "My heart shall not reproach me throughout my whole life."[23] How, then, is he not reproached by his heart throughout his whole life when he openly testifies that he has sinned? For never do guilt of deed and irreproachability of heart coincide in the same man. But surely the literal sense of the words, when they are compared, cannot be made to agree, and it shows that something different should be sought in them, as if the words were explicitly to say, "Though you see that we, in so far as our obvious meaning is concerned, are destroyed, nevertheless seek in us something logical and consistent that may be found to reside in us."

---

16. Job 3:2.
17. Job 3:5.
18. Job 3:7.
19. Job 7:19.
20. Job 6:7.
21. Job 7:20.
22. Job 13:26.
23. Job 27:6.

4. At times, however, he who fails to take the words of the story in a literal sense hides the light of truth that has been offered to him, and when he labors to find in them some other inner meaning, he loses what he could easily have arrived at on the surface. For the holy man says, "If I have denied to the poor what they desired, or have made the eyes of the widow to wait; if I have eaten my morsel alone, and the orphan has not eaten of it; . . . if I have seen anyone perishing because he had no clothing, or a poor man without covering; if his loins have not blessed me, and if he was not warmed with the fleece of my sheep . . ."[24] If we forcibly twist such a passage into an allegorical sense, we make all these deeds of mercy to be as naught. For as the divine Word stimulates the wise with mysteries, so it often kindles the simple with an obvious statement. It holds in the open the means of feeding children, but keeps in secret the means of causing souls to hang upon the adoration of the sublime. Indeed, it is, as I said, like a river, shallow and deep, in which a lamb may walk and an elephant may swim. As therefore the opportunity of each and every passage demands, so the course of exposition is studiously changed. In order that it may the more truly discover the sense of the divine Word, as each topic demands, it varies according to the case.

5. This exposition, then, I have transmitted to your beatitude for revision, not because I owed it to you as something worthy of you, but because I remember that when you asked for it, I promised it. Whatever in it your holiness may find mediocre or unpolished, may you as quickly grant me your pardon as you do not overlook the fact that I speak poorly. For when the body is worn with trouble, so when the mind is afflicted, eagerness for speaking grows dull. Now many years have rolled round in their courses since I began to be tortured by frequent pains of the flesh, and each hour and each moment I grow faint with lack of good digestion,[25] and I breathe with difficulty under mild yet constant fevers.

Meanwhile, I give serious attention to the saying in the Scripture, "Everyone who is received by God is beaten,"[26] and the harder I am pressed by these present evils, so the more certainly do I breathe with anticipation of the eternal. And perhaps it was the design of divine providence that, afflicted thus, I should expound Job who was also thus afflicted, and that I should, under the lash, the better understand the mind of

---

24. Job 31:16–20.
25. Gregory, as well as Leander, suffered much from gout, on which see Epist. 9.121 and 11.32 (ibid. 13.58).
26. Heb. 12:6.

the one who was also lashed. Nevertheless, it is clear to those who rightly think about it that weariness of the flesh is no small obstacle to my enthusiasm for my work, in that when the power of the flesh scarcely is sufficient for the function of speaking, the mind cannot express its feelings in proper fashion. For what is the duty of the body except to serve as the instrument of the heart? And no matter how skilled a man may be in the art of singing, he cannot realize the fulfillment of this art unless for this purpose his external functions are in harmony, because the instruments, when shaken, do not give forth the song in proper tones, nor does the breath produce an artistic sound if the reed rattles when it is split. How much more seriously impaired is the quality of my exposition in which the broken instrument diminishes the grace of rhetoric so that it contains no artistic skill? When you run through the pages of this work, please do not look for literary nosegays, because in expounders of Holy Writ the lightness of fruitless verbosity is carefully repressed, since the planting of a grove in God's temple is forbidden.[27] And we are all clearly aware that as often as the tops of the grain stalks luxuriate into undesirable leafage, the heads of the grain do not fill out so well. This is why I have foreborne to employ the very art of rhetoric which the examples of superficial learning teach. For as the sense of this letter proclaims, I do not flee from the collision of metacism,[28] I do not avoid the confusion of a barbarism, and I disdain to preserve the rules of position and order[29] and the cases of prepositions, because I consider it very unbecoming that I should tie down the words of the heavenly oracles to the rules of Donatus.[30] No precedent of the translators of sacred Scripture requires these rules to be observed by any exegetes. Because our exposition takes its origin surely from this authority, it is surely proper for that which issues forth like a shoot to model itself on the appearance of its mother. I am using here,

---

27. Deut. 16:21.

28. Metacism is the juxtaposition of one *m* before another or of final *m* before a word beginning with a vowel, which in the classical poets is called elision; its avoidance, hiatus.

29. Doubtless he means the *clausulae,* patterns of prose rhythm much used by certain stylists, on which see W. H. Shewring, *Oxford Classical Dictionary* (Oxford, 1949) 738–740.

30. On Aelius Donatus, fourth century grammarian, of whom Jerome had been a pupil, and who was influential in late antiquity and the Middle Ages, see H. Keil, *Grammatici latini* 4.355–402. Gregory's disdain for the rules of grammar is in sharp contrast with what his contemporary Gregory of Tours says of him (*Hist. of the Franks* 10.1), that so "accomplished was he in grammar, dialectic, rhetoric, that he was held second to none in all the city." He doubtless supposes that the pope possessed these qualities without having genuine knowledge that he did.

however, the new translation,[31] but as the necessity of proof demands, I take now the new, now the old, so that, because the Apostolic See, over which, with God's design, I preside, uses both, the labor of my study may be supported by both.

---

31. That is, Jerome's translation, now called the Vulgate, nearly two centuries old, but the *Vetus Latinum* which preceded was not yet superseded.

45. Letter to Childebert, King of the Franks
(late 6th century)

POPE GREGORY I

The greatest achievement of the papacy of Gregory, "the Great" (c. 540–604), was his ability to conquer the conquerors. Pope Gregory I consolidated papal authority over the three tribal realms in what was once the Roman province of Gaul. He firmly established Western catholicism in Spain, whose King Recared had converted to the Nicene (Eastern or Byzantine) understanding of Christianity in 589. Even more important, Gregory promoted a major missionary effort in England.

Under Gregory's commission and encouragement, Augustine, a monk of Gregory's own monastery in Rome, successfully converted the Angles and Saxons to Christianity, becoming the first archbishop of Canterbury. As the old imperial culture and the tribal ways of the new rulers clashed, the church was the only institution linking both worlds. Attila the Hun, at any rate, expressed his delight at meeting "the chief Christian priest," (the pope) on the outskirts of Rome in 452.

Gregory I's letter to Childebert II, King of the Franks, displays the pope's considerable diplomatic skill in dealing with a fairly unruly ruler. Childebert wanted to put a trusted but unordained friend into a bishop's

SOURCE: Anne Fremantle, ed., *A Treasury of Early Christianity* (New York: Mentor Books, 1960). Used by permission of the author.

chair. In his letter, Gregory's tone is pastoral and persuasive and somewhat threatening. He uses arguments taken from his Pastoral Rule. *His voluminous correspondence with local and regional rulers foreshadows the growing tensions between church and state that become so characteristic of the Middle Ages.*

The letter of your Excellency has made us exceedingly glad, testifying as it does that you are careful, with pious affection, of the honour and reverence due to priests. For you thus show to all that you are faithful worshippers of God, while you love His priests with the acceptable veneration that is due to them, and hasten with Christian devotion to do whatever may advance their position. Whence also we have received with pleasure what you have written, and grant what you desire with willing mind; and accordingly we have committed, with the favour of God, our vicariate jurisdiction to our brother Virgilius, bishop of the city of Arelate, according to ancient custom and your Excellency's desire; and have also granted him the use of the pallium, as has been the custom of old.

But, inasmuch as some things have been reported to us which greatly offend Almighty God, and confound the honour and reverence due to the priesthood, we beg that they may be in every way amended with the support of the censure of your power, lest, while headstrong and perverse doings run counter to your devotion, your kingdom, or your soul (which God forbid) be burdened by the guilt of others.

Further, it has come to our knowledge that on the death of bishops some persons from being laymen are tonsured, and mount to the episcopate by a sudden leap. And thus one who has not been a disciple is in his inconsiderate ambition made a master. And, since he has not learned what to teach, he bears the office of priesthood only in name; for he continues to be a layman in speech and action as before. How, then, is he to intercede for the sins of others, not having in the first place bewailed his own? For such a shepherd does not defend, but deceives, the flock; since, while he cannot for very shame try to persuade others to do what he does not do himself, what else is it but that the Lord's people remains a prey to robbers, and catches destruction from the source whence it ought to have had a great support of wholesome protection? How bad and how perverse a proceeding this is let your Excellency's Highness consider even from you own administration of things. For it is certain that you do not put a leader over an army unless his work and his fidelity have first been apparent; unless the virtue and industry of his previous life have shown him to be a fit person. But, if the command of an army is not committed to any but men of this kind, it is easily gathered from this comparison of what sort a leader of souls ought to be. But it is a reproach to us, and we are ashamed to say it, that priests snatch at leadership who have not seen the very beginning of religious warfare.

But this also, a thing most execrable, has been reported to us as well: that sacred orders are conferred through simoniacal heresy, that is for bribes received. And, seeing that it is exceedingly pestiferous, and contrary to the Universal Church, that one be promoted to any sacred order not for merit but for a price, we exhort your Excellency to order so detestable a wickedness to be banished from your kingdom. For that man shows himself to be thoroughly unworthy of this office, who fears not to buy the gift of God with money, and presumes to try to get by payment what he deserves not to have through grace.

These things, then, most excellent son, I admonish you about for this reason, that I desire your soul to be saved. And I should have written about them before now, had not innumerable occupations stood in the way of my will. But now that a suitable time for answering your letter has offered itself, I have not omitted what it was my duty to do. Wherefore, greeting your Excellency with the affection of paternal charity, we beg that all things which we have enjoined on our above-named brother and fellow-bishop to be done and observed, may be carried out under the protection of your favour, and that you allow them not to be in any way upset by the elation or pride of anyone. But, as they were observed by his predecessor under the reign of your glorious father, so let them be observed now also, by your aid, with zealous devotion. It is right, then, that we should thus have a return made to us; and that, as we have not deferred fulfilling your will, so you too, for the sake of God and the blessed Peter, Prince of the Apostles, should cause our ordinances to be observed in all respects; that so your Excellency's reputation, praiseworthy and well-pleasing to God, may extend itself all around.

46. Popes and Emperors: The Struggle over Investiture
(1076–1122)

In 1073, a Burgundian monk named Hildebrand (c. 1025–1085) was elected pope. Hildebrand had been a reformer of the church and advisor to popes since the brief papacy of Gregory VI (1045–1046). He had followed Gregory VI into exile after Gregory resigned under imperial pressure to end a schism that had three rival popes competing for the allegiance of the faithful. On his election, which the people of Rome enthusiastically approved, Hildebrand took the name Gregory VII and set out to reform the church.

Called a "holy Satan" by one of his enemies, because of his campaigns against simony (the sale of clerical offices) and lay investiture (the appointment to clerical office by secular rulers), Gregory VII promoted the primacy of the bishop of Rome. He claimed that the bishop of Rome drew special authority from Saint Peter. He argued that since the church represented the claims of God, the church ultimately had primacy over the temporal claims of the state. All secular rulers, including the emperor, should show fealty to the heir of the "Prince of the Apostles," the bishop of Rome.

Gregory VII tested his power and this principle when Emperor Henry IV (1050–1106), also standing on principle, tried to appoint a new bishop for the city of Milan. The attempt was an obvious challenge to the pope's recent edict against any form of lay investiture.

Gregory VII met the challenge, responding with a prayer that released Henry's subjects from feudal allegiance and excommunicated the emperor. In effect, Gregory VII deposed the emperor.

Henry IV countered by becoming a penitent pilgrim, crossing the Alps in the dead of winter and meeting Gregory VII at Canossa. It was a standoff. For three days, the emperor stood barefoot at the gate of the papal castle, begging forgiveness. With public opinion turning against him, Gregory had no choice but to yield and grant Henry absolution.

Once forgiven, the emperor returned home to deal with his rebellious nobles, who with the pope's encouragement, had prematurely elected a new emperor. In the spring of 1081, Henry crossed the Alps again; this time he brought an army. He captured Rome and forced Pope Gregory VII into exile at the abbey of Monte Casino, where he died in 1085. The struggle between Henry IV and the papacy continued under Gregory's successors until the emperor's death in 1106.

In 1122 Pope Calixtus II (1119–1124) and Emperor Henry V (1081–1125) reached a settlement at the "Concordat of Worms." According to the agreement, bishops were to be elected freely under the rules of the church. The emperor could grant the symbols of worldly authority to clerical princes but investiture into the episcopal office (ring and staff) was the sole prerogative of the church. Gregory VII and the monastic reformers prevailed.

Excommunication of Henry IV
(1076)

GREGORY VII

O blessed Peter, prince of the Apostles, mercifully incline thine ear, we [sic] pray, and hear me, thy servant, whom thou hast cherished from infancy and hast delivered until now from the hand of the wicked who have hated and still hate me for my loyalty to thee. Thou art my witness, as are also my Lady, the Mother of God, and the blessed Paul, thy brother among all the saints, that thy Holy Roman Church forced me against my will to be its ruler. I had no thought of ascending thy throne as a robber, nay, rather would I have chosen to end my life as a pilgrim than to seize upon thy place for earthly glory and by devices of this world. Therefore, by thy favor, not by any works of mine, I believe that it is and has been thy will, that the Christian people especially committed to thee should render obedience to me, thy especially constituted representative. To me is given by thy grace the power of binding and loosing in Heaven and upon earth.

Wherefore, relying upon this commission, and for the honor and defense of thy Church, in the name of Almighty God, Father, Son and Holy Spirit, through thy power and authority, I deprive King Henry, son of the emperor Henry, who has rebelled against thy Church with unheard-of audacity, of the government over the whole kingdom of Germany and Italy, and I release all Christian men from the allegiance which they have sworn or may swear to him, and I forbid anyone to serve him as king. For it is fitting that he who seeks to diminish the glory of thy Church should lose the glory which he seems to have.

And, since he has refused to obey as a Christian should or to return to the God whom he has abandoned by taking part with excommunicated persons, has spurned my warnings which I gave him for his soul's welfare, as thou knowest, and has separated himself from thy Church and tried to rend it asunder, I bind him in the bonds of anathema in thy stead and I bind him thus as commissioned by thee, that the nations may know and be convinced that thou art Peter and that upon thy rock the son of the living God has built his Church and the gates of hell shall not prevail against it.

Gregory's Account of Canossa
(1077)

GREGORY VII

Book IV, 12, p. 311. End of Jan., 1077.

Whereas, for love of justice you have made common cause with us and taken the same risks in the warfare of Christian service, we have taken

---

SOURCE: Gregory VII, *The Correspondence of Pope Gregory VII: Selected Letters from the Registrum*, trans. and introduced by Ephraim Emerton, Records of Civilization Series (New York: W. W. Norton, 1969). Copyright © 1932 by Columbia University Press. Used by permission of Columbia University Press.

special care to send you this accurate account of the king's penitential humiliation, his absolution and the course of the whole affair from his entrance into Italy to the present time.

According to the arrangement made with the legates sent to us by you we came to Lombardy about twenty days before the date at which some of your leaders were to meet us at the pass and waited for their arrival to enable us to cross over into that region. But when the time had elapsed and we were told that on account of the troublous times — as indeed we well believe — no escort could be sent to us, having no other way of coming to you we were in no little anxiety as to what was our best course to take.

Meanwhile we received certain information that the king was on the way to us. Before he entered Italy he sent us word that he would make satisfaction to God and St. Peter and offered to amend his way of life and to continue obedient to us, provided only that he should obtain from us absolution and the apostolic blessing. For a long time we delayed our reply and held long consultations, reproaching him bitterly through messengers back and forth for his outrageous conduct, until finally, of his own accord and without any show of hostility or defiance, he came with a few followers to the fortress of Canossa where we were staying. There, on three successive days, standing before the castle gate, laying aside all royal insignia, barefooted and in coarse attire, he ceased not with many tears to beseech the apostolic help and comfort until all who were present or who had heard the story were so moved by pity and compassion that they pleaded his cause with prayers and tears. All marveled at our unwonted severity, and some even cried out that we were showing, not the seriousness of apostolic authority, but rather the cruelty of a savage tyrant.

At last, overcome by his persistent show of penitence and the urgency of all present, we released him from the bonds of anathema and received him into the grace of Holy Mother Church, accepting from him the guarantees described below, confirmed by the signatures of the abbot of Cluny, of our daughters, the Countess Matilda and the Countess Adelaide, and other princes, bishops and laymen who seemed to be of service to us.

And now that these matters have been arranged, we desire to come over into your country at the first opportunity, that with God's help we may more fully establish all matters pertaining to the peace of the Church and the good order of the land. For we wish you clearly to understand that, as you may see in the written guarantees, the whole negotiation is held in suspense, so that our coming and your unanimous consent are in the highest degree necessary. Strive, therefore, all of you, as you love justice, to hold in good faith the obligations into which you have entered. Remember that we have not bound ourselves to the king in any way except by frank statement — as our custom is — that he may expect our aid for his safety and his honor, whether through justice or through mercy, and without peril to his soul or to our own.

The Concordat of Worms, September 1122

1. Agreement of Pope Calixtus II

I, Calixtus, Bishop, servant of the servants of God, do grant to thee, beloved son, Henry — by the grace of God Emperor of the Romans, Augustus — that the elections of bishops and abbots of the German kingdom, who belong to that kingdom, shall take place in thy presence, without simony or any violence; so that if any dispute shall arise between the parties concerned, thou, with the counsel or judgement of the metropolitan and the co-provincial bishops, shalt give consent and aid to the party which has the more right. The one elected shall receive the regalia from thee by the sceptre and shall perform his lawful duties to thee on that account. But he who is consecrated in the other parts of thy empire [i.e. Burgundy and Italy] shall, within six months, and without any exaction, receive the regalia from thee by the sceptre, and shall perform his lawful duties to thee on that account (saving all rights which are known to belong to the Roman church). Concerning matters in which thou shalt make complaint to me, and ask aid — I, according to the duty of my office, will furnish aid to thee. I give unto thee true peace, and to all who are or have been of thy party in this conflict.

2. Edict of the Emperor Henry V

In the name of the holy and indivisible Trinity I, Henry, by the grace of God Emperor of the Romans, Augustus, for the love of God and of the holy Roman church and of our lord Pope Calixtus, and for the salvation of

---

SOURCE: Henry Bettenson, *Documents of the Christian Church* (New York: Oxford University Press, 1963). Used by permission of Oxford University Press.

my soul do surrender to God, and to the holy apostles of God, Peter and Paul, and to the Holy Catholic Church, all investiture through ring and staff; and do grant that in all the churches that are in my kingdom or empire there may be canonical election and free consecration. All the possessions and regalia of St. Peter which, from the beginning of this discord unto this day, whether in the time of my father or in mine have been seized, and which I hold, I restore to that same Holy Roman Church. And I will faithfully aid in the restoration of those things which I do not hold. The possessions also of all other churches and princes, and of all other persons lay and clerical which have been lost in that war: according to the counsel of the princes, or according to justice, I will restore, as far as I hold them; and I will faithfully aid in the restoration of those things which I do not hold. And I grant true peace to our lord Pope Calixtus, and to the Holy Roman Church, and to all those who are or have been on its side. And in matters where the Holy Roman Church shall ask aid I will grant it; and in matters concerning which it shall make complaint to me I will duly grant to it justice. All these things have been done by the consent and counsel of the princes. Whose names are here adjoined: Adalbert archbishop of Mainz; F. archbishop of Cologne; H. bishop of Ratisbon; O. bishop of Bamberg; B. bishop of Spires; H. of Augsburg; G. of Utrecht; Ou. of Constance; E. abbot of Fulda; Henry, duke; Frederick, duke; S. duke; Pertolf, duke; Margrave Teipold; Margrave Engelbert; Godfrey, count Palatine; Otto, count Palatine; Berengar, count.

I, Frederick, archbishop of Cologne and archchancellor, have ratified this.

47. *The Fourth Lateran Council, Canon I*
(1215)

Innocent III

Innocent the III (1198–1216), the greatest of the medieval popes, was also the first pope to call himself "vicar of Christ." In his inaugural sermon, he argued that the "vicar of Christ" is set over the household of the church, "less than God, more than man, who has to judge all, but is himself judged by no man." In essence, the victories of the church over the state had turned the office of the first among bishops (the pope) into a global theocrat.

Writing to the clergy in Tuscany, Innocent III was very clear about papal supremacy. "As God, the creator of the universe, set two great lights in the firmament of heaven, the greater light to rule the day, and the lesser to rule the night, so he set two great dignities on the firmament of the universal church. . . . These dignities are the papal authority and the royal power. But just as the moon gets her light from the sun, so the royal power gets the splendor of its dignity from papal authority."

Innocent III was as good as his word. Through the interdict (the excommunication of an entire principality or nation), he withheld the sacraments from the subjects of uncooperative monarchs. He humbled the rulers of Europe, including the kings of England, France, and Spain. By

---

source: John H. Leith, ed., *Creeds of the Churches: A Reader in Christian Doctrine from the Bible to the Present* (Atlanta: John Knox Press, 1978). © 1963, 1978, 1982 John H. Leith. Used by permission of Westminster John Knox Press.

fomenting civil war in Germany, he assured the imperial succession he desired, first of Otto IV, then of Frederick II. He called for an armed campaign against the ascetic Albigensian sect in southern France and organized a crusade against Saladin, the able Sultan of Egypt.

Unfortunately when the crusade failed, the crusaders conquered and sacked Christian Constantinople, establishing a short-lived Latin Empire there (1204–1261). Innocent did not approve, but he used the opportunity to appoint a Western (Roman catholic) patriarch for Constantinople, hoping to reunite Western and Eastern (orthodox) Christianity.

In 1215, Innocent III convened the Fourth Lateran Council in his official residence, the Lateran palace. More than a thousand bishops and abbots attended. The council reflected Innocent's exalted views of the papacy and marked a high point in the history of the medieval (Roman catholic) church. The council is best known for making "transubstantiation" an official doctrine of the Roman Catholic church.

Transubstantiation is the belief that when the priests dedicate the wine and bread in the Eucharist, they change "substantially" into the actual body and blood of Christ. Other canons of this important council require annual confession, communion, and attendance at Easter services.

The Fourth Lateran Council sanctions the centralized power of the papacy and passes numerous administrative rules governing the lives of clergy and laity. For example, the council provides a canonical basis for the so-called mendicant orders (Dominicans and Franciscans). These new religious orders supported men who moved out of the monasteries to combine monastic poverty with social action, becoming the conscience of medieval society.

The first canon of the council is a statement of faith in the Nicene and Augustinian tradition with some interesting elaborations, including a "high" view of the priestly function and of the sacraments (using the term transubstantiated*). The canon provides an excellent summary of the faith of the medieval church.*

We firmly believe and openly confess that there is only one true God, eternal, beyond measure and unchangeable, incomprehensible, omnipotent and ineffable, the Father, the Son, and the Holy Spirit: Three persons but a single essence, substance, or nature that is wholly one; the Father proceeding from none, the Son proceeding from the Father alone, and the

Holy Spirit from both in like manner; without beginning and having no end for ever: the Father begetting, the Son being begotten, and the Holy Spirit proceeding; having the same substance, the same equality, the same omnipotence, and the same eternity; the one principle of the universe; the Creator of all things visible and invisible, spiritual and corporeal; who from the very beginning of time by His omnipotent power created out of nothing both the spiritual beings and the corporeal, that is to say the angelic beings and those of the earth, and thereafter human beings, who, as it were, partake of both, being composed of spirit and body. The Devil and other wicked spirits were created by God good by nature, but they became evil of their own accord. Man, however, sinned at the prompting of the Devil. This Holy Trinity, undivided in regard to its essence which is common to all, but distinct in regard to the attributes of the persons, gave the doctrine of salvation to the human race in due process of time, first through Moses and the holy prophets and their other servants.

And finally the only-begotten Son of God, Jesus Christ, made flesh by the Trinity in all its persons together, conceived of Mary, ever Virgin, with the cooperation of the Holy Spirit, made true man, composed of a rational soul and human flesh, one person in two natures, showed the way to life with greater clarity. Though immortal and impassible in His divinity He yet became subject to suffering and death in His humanity; nay more, He suffered and died for the salvation of the human race on the wood of the cross, descended into hell, rose from the dead, and ascended into heaven. But He descended in the soul, and rose in the flesh, and ascended alike in both. He will come at the end of time, and will judge the living and the dead, and will reward every man according to his works, both the reprobate and the elect. These will all arise in their own bodies which they now have, that they may receive their reward according to whether their works were good or evil, in the latter case unending punishment with the Devil, in the former eternal glory with Christ.

There is one universal church of believers outside which there is no salvation at all for any. In this church the priest and sacrifice is the same Jesus Christ Himself, whose body and blood are truly contained in the sacrament of the altar under the figures of bread and wine, the bread having been transubstantiated into His body and the wine into His blood by divine power, so that, to accomplish the mystery of our union, we may receive of Him what He has received of us. And none can effect this sacrament except the priest who has been rightly ordained in accordance with the keys of the church which Jesus Christ Himself granted to the Apostles and their successors. The sacrament of baptism is celebrated in water by prayer to God and each person of the Trinity separately, that is to say, the Father, the Son, and the Holy Spirit. Duly conferred on both infants and adults by any one at all in the form appointed by the church, it promotes our salvation. And if after receiving baptism, anyone should fall into sin, he can always be restored through true repentance. Not only virgins and those practicing continence merit the attainment of eternal blessedness, but married persons also, who are acceptable to God through true faith and good works.

48. *Unam Sanctam*
(1302)

Boniface VIII

The most extravagant claim of pontifical authority in the history of the Western church also marked the decline of papal power. The heavy economic burdens imposed by Rome to finance the political ambitions of the papacy increasingly annoyed the princes of Europe, and they found ways to fight back. In 1279, gifts of land to the church became illegal in England. About the same time, Philip IV, "the Fair" of France, imposed a tax on the clergy.

In 1296, Pope Boniface VIII (reigned 1294–1303) issued his bull Clericis laicos *(clergy and laity) in which he threatened to excommunicate anyone, clergy or layperson, who either levied or paid the clergy tax. Philip, who had the support of the French parliament, retaliated by prohibiting all money payments to Rome, forcing Boniface to compromise. This, of course, did not end the battle between pope and king. In 1302, Boniface issued his famous bull* Unam Sanctam *("one holy church"). This document contains the most extravagant claims ever made on behalf of the pontifical office.*

Unam Sanctam *claims that the power and authority of the church*

SOURCE: Henry Bettenson, *Documents of the Christian Church* (New York: Oxford University Press, 1963). Used by permission of Oxford University Press.

vested in Christ's vicar, the pope, takes precedence over the power of kings and of all other secular authority. Moreover, since the pope's authority comes from God, the papal office cannot be subject to secular governance. On the contrary, any person who resists the Roman pontiff, whether pauper, priest, or king, resists the ordinances of God.

"Unam Sanctam" includes a fascinating interpretation of Luke 22, which Boniface uses to revise the earlier medieval "two swords theory." Instead of holding with the approach of two distinct powers: the spiritual power of the pope (the power of the keys to salvation) and the secular power of the emperor (the power of the sword to punish evildoers), Boniface VIII insists that both powers (or swords) rightfully belong to the church. The spiritual sword is used by *the church; the temporal (or material) sword is used* for, *or on behalf of, the church. Therefore, the state is merely an instrument of the church.*

Not surprisingly, Philip IV did not agree. In 1302, before Boniface VIII could issue an edict of excommunication against him, Philip had the pope seized, roughed up, and imprisoned. This time, the pope refused to compromise, dying shortly after he was released in 1303.

We are obliged by the faith to believe and hold — and we do firmly believe and sincerely confess — that there is one Holy Catholic and Apostolic Church, and that outside this Church there is neither salvation nor remission of sins. . . . In which Church there is "one Lord, one faith, one baptism?"[1] At the time of the flood there was one ark of Noah, symbolizing the one Church; this was completed in one cubit[2] and had one, namely Noah, as helmsman and captain; outside which all things on earth, we read, were destroyed. . . . Of this one and only Church there is one body and one head — not two heads, like a monster — namely Christ, and Christ's vicar is Peter, and Peter's successor, for the Lord said to Peter himself, "Feed My sheep."[3] "My sheep" He said in general, not these or those sheep; wherefore He is understood to have committed them all to him. Therefore, if the Greeks or others say that they were not committed to Peter and his successors, they necessarily confess that they are not of

---

1. Eph. 4:5.
2. Gen. 6:16.
3. John 21:17.

Christ's sheep, for the Lord says in John, "There is one fold and one shepherd."[4]

And we learn from the words of the Gospel that in this Church and in her power are two swords, the spiritual and the temporal. For when the apostles said, "Behold, here" (that is, in the Church, since it was the apostles who spoke) "are two swords" — the Lord did not reply, "It is too much," but "It is enough."[5] Truly he who denies that the temporal sword is in the power of Peter, misunderstands the words of the Lord, "Put up thy sword into the sheath."[6] Both are in the power of the Church, the spiritual sword and the material. But the latter is to be used for the Church, the former by her; the former by the priest, the latter by kings and captains but at the will and by the permission of the priest. The one sword, then, should be under the other, and temporal authority subject to spiritual. For when the apostle says "there is no power but of God, and the powers that be are ordained of God"[7] they would not be so ordained were not one sword made subject to the other. . . .

Thus, concerning the Church and her power, is the prophecy of Jeremiah fulfilled, "See, I have this day set thee over the nations and over the kingdoms," etc.[8] If, therefore, the earthly power err, it shall be judged by the spiritual power; and if a lesser power err, it shall be judged by a greater. But if the supreme power err, it can only be judged by God, not by man; for the testimony of the apostle is "The spiritual man judgeth all things, yet he himself is judged of no man."[9] For this authority, although given to a man and exercised by a man, is not human, but rather divine, given at God's mouth to Peter and established on a rock for him and his successors in Him whom he confessed, the Lord saying to Peter himself, "Whatsoever thou shalt bind," etc.[10] Whoever therefore resists this power thus ordained of God, resists the ordinance of God. . . . Furthermore we declare, state, define and pronounce that it is altogether necessary to salvation for every human creature to be subject to the Roman pontiff.

---

4. John 10:16. "Fold" translates the Vulgate "ovile"; the Greek is ποίμνη, "flock."
5. Luke 22:38.
6. John 18:11.
7. Romans 10:1.
8. Jer. 1:10.
9. 1 Cor. 2:15.
10. Matt. 16:19.

Mission to the Barbarians

49. Mission Work in England
(c. 590–604)

POPE GREGORY I

One of the major achievements of Pope Gregory I, "the Great" (c. 540–604), was his missionary effort among the Germanic invaders who threatened and eventually replaced Byzantine rule in Rome and the western half of the empire. Thanks to Gregory's vision, the medieval church conquered the conquerors.

The significant success story of the day was the conversion of England. Gregory sent Augustine, a monk from his own monastery of St. Andrew's, on a mission to the "Angles." Although Augustine becomes discouraged, Gregory does not let him abandon the mission, writing words of encouragement and support to Augustine and his companions.

Pope Gregory I also addresses practical matters. His correspondence includes a letter to Brunichild, the Christian queen of the Franks, asking her to assist the missionaries to England. In his correspondence with her, Gregory praises Brunichild's "God-pleasing goodness manifested in the governance of her kingdom and by the education of her son." He solicits her active support for Augustine's missionary journey to England.

On a more delicate note, Gregory asks the queen's protection for Candidus, a presbyter and an accountant, whom the pope has sent to restore church property (patrimony) to Roman control.

Another letter, written in 601, chronicles Augustine's success. Despite initial disappointments, the Christian queen of Kent received Augustine in 597, and he succeeds in converting her husband, Ethelbert. Other Saxon rulers soon turn to Christianity, and Augustine becomes the first Archbishop of Canterbury, the capital of Kent. By 601 Gregory advises Augustine to be eclectic in developing a liturgy for the English church, for "things are not to be loved for the sake of places, but places for the sake of good things."

To the Brethren Going to England

Since it had been better not to have begun what is good than to return back from it when begun, you must, most beloved sons, fulfil the good work which with the help of the Lord you have begun. Let, then, neither the toil of the journey nor the tongues of evil-speaking men deter you; but with all instancy and all fervour go on with what under God's guidance you have commenced, knowing that great toil is followed by the glory of an eternal reward. Obey in all things humbly Augustine your provost (*præposito*), who is returning to you, whom we also appoint your abbot, knowing that whatever may be fulfilled in you through his admonition will in all ways profit your souls. May Almighty God protect you with His grace, and grant to me to see the fruit of your labour in the eternal country; that so, even though I cannot labour with you, I may be found together with you in the joy of the reward; for in truth I desire to labour. God keep you safe, most beloved sons.

SOURCE: Anne Fremantle, ed., *A Treasury of Early Christianity* (New York: Mentor Books, 1960). Used by permission of the author.

The Christian Ideal

To Brunichild, Queen to the Franks

... The Christianity of your Excellence has been so truly known to us of old that we do not in the least doubt of your goodness, but rather hold it to be in all ways certain that you will devoutly and zealously concur with us in the cause of faith, and supply most abundantly the succour of your religious sincerity. Being for this reason well assured, and greeting you with paternal charity, we inform you that it has come to our knowledge how that the nation of the Angli, by God's permission, is desirous of becoming Christian, but that the priests who are in their neighbourhood have no pastoral solicitude with regard to them. And lest their souls should haply perish in eternal damnation, it has been our care to send to them the bearer of these presents, Augustine the servant of God, whose zeal and earnestness are well known to us, with other servants of God; that through them we might be able to learn their wishes, and, as far as is possible, you also striving with us, to take thought for their conversion. We have also charged them that for carrying out this design they should take with them presbyters from the neighbouring regions. Let, then, your Excellency, habitually prone to good works, on account as well of our requests as of regard to the fear of God, deign to hold him as in all ways commended to you, and earnestly bestow on him the favour of your protection, and lend the aid of your patronage to his labour; and, that he may have the fullest fruit thereof, provide for his going secure under your protection to the above-written nation of the Angli, to the end that our God, who has adorned you in this world with good qualities well-pleasing to Him, may cause you to give thanks here and in eternal rest with His saints.

Furthermore, commending to your Christianity our beloved son Candidus, presbyter and rector of the patrimony of our Church which is situated in your parts, we beg that he may in all things obtain the favour of your protection....

SOURCE: Anne Fremantle, ed., *A Treasury of Early Christianity* (New York: Mentor Books, 1960). Used by permission of the author.

Liturgical Provision for England

To Augustine

[In 598 Augustine sent to Gregory for direction on certain points of organization and discipline.]

Augustine's Second Question: Whereas the faith is one and the same, are there different customs in different Churches? and is one custom of masses observed in the Holy Roman Church, and another in that of the Gauls?

Pope Gregory answers: You know, my brother, the custom of the Roman Church, in which you remember you were brought up. But my advice is that you should make a careful selection of anything that you have found either in the Roman [Church] or [that] of the Gauls, or any other Church, which may be more acceptable to Almighty God, and diligently teach the Church of the English, which as yet is new in the faith, whatsoever you can gather from the several Churches. For things are not to be loved for the sake of places, but places for the sake of good things. Choose, therefore, from each Church those things that are pious, religious, and seemly, and when you have, as it were, incorporated them, let the minds of the English be accustomed thereto.

SOURCE: Henry Bettenson, *Documents of the Christian Church* (New York: Oxford University Press, 1963). Used by permission of Oxford University Press.

50. The Decrees of the Council of Hertford
(673)

While Augustine and his successors worked in Kent and Wales, Irish monks established Christianity among the Picts in Scotland. Moving south across the English border, Scotch-Irish missionaries came upon churches founded by Augustine's order.

Initially, the significant differences between themselves and the Anglo-Saxon Christians troubled the Scotch-Irish missionaries. They had been traditional enemies, so it was not surprising that tempers flared over the proper tonsure of monks and the correct Easter date (which the north had based on a faulty Roman calendar).

Theodore (602–690) came to England from Tarsus in Asia Minor. In 668, the pope made Theodore archbishop of Canterbury. Soon Theodore managed to pacify the warring factions of the Celts and Saxons and to channel their energy into a highly successful joint missionary effort. In 673, well before any political unity, Theodore convened a landmark synod at Hertford. The synod developed a "basis of union" consisting of ten points recognized by both factions, including an affirmation of the

---

SOURCE: Henry Bettenson, *Documents of the Christian Church* (New York: Oxford University Press, 1963). Used by permission of Oxford University Press.

THE DECREES OF THE COUNCIL OF HERTFORD • 345

Roman Easter date by Celtic Christians in the north. The strong leadership from Canterbury soon unified the English churches.

In the name of our Lord God and Saviour Jesus Christ, in the perpetual reign and government of our Lord Jesus Christ. It seemed good that we should come together according to the prescription of the venerable canons, to treat of the necessary affairs of the Church. We are met together on this 24th day of September, the first indiction, in a place called Hertford, I, Theodore, bishop of the Church of Canterbury, appointed thereto, unworthy as I am, by the Apostolic See, and our most reverend brother Bisi, bishop of the East Angles, together with our brother and fellow-bishop Wilfrid, bishop of the nation of the Northumbrians, who was present by his proper legates, as also our brethren and fellow-bishops, Putta, bishop of the Castle of the Kentishmen, called Rochester, Leutherius, bishop of the West Saxons, and Winfrid, bishop of the province of the Mercians, were present; and when we were assembled and had taken our proper places, I said: I beseech you, beloved brethren, for the fear and love of our Redeemer, that we may faithfully enter into a common treaty for the sincere observance of whatsoever has been decreed and determined by the holy and approved fathers. I enlarged upon these and many other things tending unto charity, and the preservation of the unity of the Church. And when I had finished my speech I asked them singly and in order whether they consented to observe all things which had been of old canonically decreed by the fathers? To which all our fellow-priests answered: we are all well agreed readily and cheerfully to keep whatever the canons of the holy fathers have prescribed. Whereupon I presently produced the book of canons, and pointed out ten particulars, which I had marked as being in a more special manner known by me to be necessary for us, and proposed that all would undertake diligently to observe them, namely:

1. That we shall jointly keep Easter Day on the Lord's Day after the fourteenth day of the moon in the first month.

2. That no bishop invade the diocese [*parochia*] of another, but be content with the government of the people committed to him.

3. That no bishop be allowed to offer any molestation to monasteries consecrated to God, nor to take away by violence anything that belongs to them.

4. That the monks themselves go not from place to place, that is from one monastery to another, without the leave of their own abbot, but

continue in that obedience which they promised at the time of their conversion.

5. That no clerk, leaving his own bishop, go up and down at his own pleasure, nor be received wherever he comes without the commendatory letters of his bishop; but if he be once received and refuse to return when he is desired so to do, both the receiver and the received shall be laid under an excommunication.

6. That strange bishops and clerks be content with the hospitality that is freely offered them, and let not any of them exercise any priestly function without permission of the bishop in whose diocese he is known to be.

7. That a synod be assembled twice in the year. But because many occasions may hinder this, it was jointly agreed by all that once in the year it be assembled on the first of August at the place called Cloveshoo.

8. That no bishop put himself before another out of an affectation of precedence, but that every one observe the time and order of his consecration.

9. We had a conference together concerning increasing the number of bishops in proportion to the number of the faithful, but we determine nothing as to this point at present.

10. As to matrimony: that none be allowed to any but what is lawful. Let none commit incest. Let no one relinquish his own wife, but for fornication, as the Gospel teaches. But if any shall have dismissed a wife to whom he has been lawfully married, let him not be coupled to another if he wish to be a true Christian, but remain as he is, or be reconciled to his wife. . . .

51. The Council of the Germans:
The Decrees of the Frankish Synods
(742–43)

The union of Celtic and Saxon Christianity in England produced a dynamic missionary church in the seventh century. After the conversion of England, English missionaries moved out to share the gospel with Germanic tribes on the European continent. The greatest of these English missionaries was a Saxon monk named Wynfrith, better known as Boniface, apostle to the Germans (680–754).

Boniface began his missionary career among the Frisians in northern Germany under Willibrord, a fellow Saxon and the first archbishop of Utrecht (d. 739). While in Frisia, Boniface visited Rome. As he traveled south, he converted tribal leaders in Bavaria, Thuringia, and Hesse. He baptized them and their subjects and established monasteries on the way. Recognizing Boniface's talents, Pope Gregory III called him back to Rome, asked that he swear fealty to the papacy, and consecrated him bishop of Germany in 722. Ten years later, Boniface became the metropolitan of Germany east of the Rhine with administrative power to establish bishoprics. Gregory's successor made him the apostolic legate to all the Franks and Germans.

SOURCE: *The Letters of Saint Boniface*, trans. and introduced by Ephraim Emerton, Records of Civilization Series (New York: Columbia University, 1940). Copyright © 1940 by Columbia University Press. Used by permission of the publisher.

Boniface was a missionary and church organizer on a grand scale, perfecting methods that Augustine had used in the conversion of England. As the pope's representative, he gained the support and political backing of the Christian rulers of the Franks, Charles Martel and his sons Carloman and Pepin. However, in German-speaking areas, the social organization of the Germanic tribes invited a test of what later became the cuius regio, eius religio *principle — the idea that the religion of the ruler should determine the religion of the people.*

As the years passed, Boniface targeted local rulers for conversion, thereby Christianizing their lands. He consolidated his gains by establishing monasteries and bishoprics as Christian beachheads on pagan soil. Although Boniface was politically successful, he always remained a monk and a missionary. Legend marks a place near the village of Geismar in Hesse where, after one of his trips to Rome, he preached the gospel under a sacred oak dedicated to the Norse god Odin. When his pagan audience threatened his life, he took a battle ax from one of them and, cutting down the tree, defied Odin to punish him. When nothing happened, the chieftain and his tribe, impressed by his courage, were baptized. After his sixty-seventh birthday, Boniface left the relative comfort of his favorite abbey at Fulda, resigned as archbishop of Mainz, and returned to his beginnings. He died a martyr preaching the gospel to the Frisians.

The "Decrees of the Frankish Synods" document the task of building the church in the eighth century. Instruction of clergy and laity often had to wait until after baptism. Local, indigenous clergy generally were untrained and undisciplined. With the support of Carloman, the ruler of the Eastern Franks, Boniface initiated a series of synods for the clergy beginning in 742. Concilium Germanicum *was the first national synod of the Germans. The secular ruler of the realm, Carloman (or Karlmann) published the decrees for the church, creating a troublesome symbiosis between lay and clerical authority in the medieval church.*

In the name of our Lord Jesus Christ, I, Karlmann, duke and prince of the Franks, in the seven hundred and forty-second year of the Incarnation of Christ and the twenty-first day of April, by the advice of the servants of God and my chief men, have brought together in the fear of Christ the bishops of my realm with their priests into a council or synod; namely, Archbishop Boniface, Burchard [Würzburg], Reginfried [Cologne], Wintan [Buraburg], Willibald [Erfurt?], Dadanus [Utrecht or Erfurt], and

Eddanus [Strasburg], together with their priests, that they might give me their advice how the law of God and the service of religion, fallen into decay under former princes, might be reëstablished, and how the Christian people might attain salvation for their souls and not perish through the deceit of false priests.

And, by the advice of my priests and nobles we have appointed bishops for the several cities and have set over them as archbishop Boniface, the delegate of St. Peter.

We have ordered that a synod shall be held every year, so that in our presence the canonical decrees and the laws of the Church may be reëstablished and the Christian religion purified.

Revenues, of which churches were defrauded, we have restored and given back to them. We have deprived false priests and adulterous or lustful deacons of their church incomes, have degraded them, and forced them to do penance.

We have absolutely forbidden the servants of God to carry arms or fight, to enter the army or march against an enemy, except only so many as are especially selected for divine service such as celebrating Mass or carrying relics — that is to say: the prince may have one or two bishops with the chaplains, and each prefect one priest to hear confessions and prescribe penance. We have also forbidden the servants of God to hunt or wander about the woods with dogs or to keep hawks and falcons.

We have also ordered, according to the sacred canons, that every priest living within a diocese shall be subject to the bishop of that diocese. Annually during Lent he shall render to the bishop an account of his ministry, in regard to baptism in the catholic faith, to prayers, and the order of the Mass. Whenever, according to the canon law, the bishop shall make the rounds of his diocese for the purpose of confirmation, the priest is to be ready to receive him with those who are going to be confirmed already assembled and coöperating. On Holy Thursday let him ask the bishop for fresh consecrated oil and bear witness before the bishop of his chastity, his way of life, and his belief.

We have ordered, according to canonical warning, that unknown bishops and priests, wherever they may come from, shall not be admitted into the service of the Church until they shall be approved by the synod.

We have decreed, according to the canons, that every bishop within his own diocese and with the help of the count, who is the defender of the Church, shall see to it that the people of God perform no pagan rites but reject and cast out all the foulness of the heathen, such as sacrifices to the dead, casting of lots, divinations, amulets and auguries, incantations, or offerings of animals, which foolish folk perform in the churches, according to pagan custom, in the name of holy martyrs or confessors, thereby calling down the wrath of God and his saints, and also those sacrilegious fires which they call "Niedfeor," and whatever other pagan practices there may be.

We have further ordered that after this synod held on April the twenty-first, any of the servants of God or the maids of Christ falling into carnal sin shall do penance in prison on bread and water. If it be an ordained priest he shall be imprisoned for two years, first flogged to bleeding and afterward further disciplined at the bishop's discretion. But if a clerk or monk fall into this sin, after a third flogging he shall be imprisoned for a year and there do penance. Likewise a veiled nun shall be bound to do the same penance, and all her hair shall be shaved.

We have decreed also that priests and deacons shall not wear cloaks after the fashion of laymen, but cassocks according to the usage of the servants of God. Let no priest or deacon permit a woman to live in the same house with him. Let cloistered monks and maids of God live after the Rule of St. Benedict and govern their lives accordingly.

The Second Synod

And now, in this synodal assembly, called for the first day of March in the place called Leptines, all the venerable priests of God, the counts and prefects have accepted and confirmed the decrees of the former synod and have promised to carry them out and observe them.

The whole body of the clergy — bishops, priests, deacons, and clerks — accepting the canons of the ancient fathers, have promised to restore the laws of the Church as to morals and doctrine and form of service. Abbots and monks have accepted the Rule of the holy father, Benedict, for the reformation of the regular life.

We order that corrupt and adulterous clerics who have defiled the holy places and monasteries by occupying them until now shall be expelled and made to do penance, and if, after this declaration, they fall into the crime of fornication or adultery they shall suffer the penalties prescribed at the former synod. The same with monks and nuns.

We order also, by the advice of the servants of God and of the Christian people and in view of imminent wars and attacks by the foreign populations which surround us, that a portion of the properties of the Church shall be used for some time longer, with God's indulgence, for the benefit of our army, as a *precarium* and paying a *census,* on condition, however, that annually from each *casata* [of these ecclesiastical estates] one *solidus,* that is twelve *denarii,* shall be paid to the church or monastery which owns it. In case of the death of the persons to whom the property was entrusted as a *precarium,* it shall revert to the Church. Also, if conditions are such that the prince deems it necessary, let the *precarium* be renewed for another term and a new contract be written. But let extreme care be taken that churches and monasteries whose property is granted in *precarium* shall not be reduced to poverty and suffer want; and, if they should thus be distressed, let the whole property be given back to the church and the house of God.

We likewise ordain that, in accordance with the canonical decrees, adultery and incestuous marriages contrary to law shall be forbidden and shall be punished at the discretion of the bishop. And let not Christian slaves be transferred to pagans.

We have also decreed, as my father [Charles Martel] did before me, that whosoever engages in heathen practices of any sort shall be condemned to pay a fine of fifteen *solidi.*

52. Letter to Cuthbert, Archbishop of Canterbury on the German Synods and Other Matters of Church Discipline
(747)

BONIFACE

Throughout his life, Boniface kept in close touch with his home church in England. He carried on an extensive English correspondence with monks and nuns, bishops and priests, and even an occasional slave or king who were close friends. The eighth-century church provided a helpful network of support for Boniface, when, as he wrote, "he was worn out by the storms of the German sea which buffeted him on all sides."

In his letter of 747 to Cuthbert, the Archbishop of Canterbury, Boniface gives an account of the Concilium Germanicum *(742) and the subsequent synods of the German churches. He also hints that he considers his own position as papal legate in Germany equal to the archbishop of Canterbury.*

The most interesting part of the letter is the second half. In the spirit

---

SOURCE: Edward Kylie, ed., *The English Correspondence of St. Boniface* (New York: Cooper Square Publishers, Inc., 1966).

of Gregory I (d. 604), whose Pastoral Rule *he follows, Boniface addresses the problem of clerical discipline. Boniface insists that clergy are "under a great and terrible necessity ... to be an example to the faithful."*

Bishops and priests must not only live just lives in accordance with their words but "may not by their silence be condemned for another's sin." Their prophetic office compels them to speak out against the sins of the rich and powerful. Too many shepherds, he says, say nothing in the presence of sin and power. They feed themselves and not their flock. They "take the fat and the wool of the sheep of Christ with daily offerings and tithes from the faithful; and the care of flock of Christ they put to one side."

Boniface thanks Cuthbert, Archbishop of Canterbury, for gifts and a letter. He indicates some matters which have been determined by him in a synod. He urges zeal. He adds a proposal about checking the pilgrimage of women to Rome. He suggests that monasteries should not be ruled through laymen, and condemns extravagance in dress. 747.

To his brother and fellow-bishop Cuthbert, bound by the tie of spiritual affinity, exalted to the archiepiscopal dignity, Boniface, legate in Germany of the Catholic and Apostolic Roman Church, greetings of truest love in Christ.

It is written in the book of Solomon, "Blessed be he that findeth a true friend, with whom he can speak as with himself." With great thanks to God and to you, we have received from your son, deacon Cyneberht, your munificent gifts and your most welcome letter underlined with fraternal love. You also lovingly communicated with us, through him, your honeysweet words of fraternal counsel. It is our wish that, as long as God grants us to live in this mortal life, such spiritual colloquies and advice may always be imparted with the aid of Him, from whom alone are holy desires, just counsels, and good wishes. Let us seek to instruct one another, you taking the larger and better part, whom God enriched with many powers and with great wisdom and ability, we in a few things, as a faithful and devoted brother, both united by the golden bond of heavenly love which cannot be broken.

For our labour is in the same ministry and for the same cause; and an equal obligation is imposed upon us to care for the Church and for the people, whether this take the form of teaching and restricting and advising, or of protecting canonical or popular ranks. I most humbly beseech you, therefore, not to fail to tell me, when God inspires you with wise counsels and informs your synodal deliberations with His spirit. And we must do the same if God inspires our weakness with anything necessary or agreeable to you. For a greater solicitude for his churches and a greater care for the people are incumbent upon us, through our having received the pall, than upon other bishops, because they care merely for their own parishes. Wherefore, beloved, not that your prudence needs to hear or to read the decrees of our ignorance, but because we think that from your good and humble and holy disposition you would prefer to know rather than not to know, we send you for correction and amendment the rules which the clergy here with us have drawn up.

We decreed and acknowledged in our synod that we wished to preserve to the end of our lives the Catholic faith and unity, and submission to the Roman Church; that we bowed to Saint Peter and to his vicar; that we should call a synod together every year; that the metropolitans would seek their palls from the Holy See; that we desired to follow in everything the precepts of Saint Peter, so as to be numbered among the sheep entrusted to him. To this profession we all agreed, and set our hands; we forwarded it to the body of Saint Peter, Prince of the Apostles, where the Roman clergy and the Pope received it with rejoicing.

We determined that each year the canonical decrees and the laws of the Church and the rule of the monastic life should be read and re-enacted in the synod. We decreed that the metropolitan who has received the dignity of the pall should exhort and admonish the rest and examine who among them is concerned about the welfare of the people, and who is careless. The servants of God we forbade to hunt and wander in the woods with dogs and to keep hawks and falcons. We decreed, that each year, each priest should give to his bishop at Easter an account of his ministry, reporting on the Catholic faith and baptism and on the whole order of his ministry. We decreed that each year each bishop should go carefully through his diocese, to confirm the people and to teach them, examine into and prohibit pagan practices, divinations or drawing of lots, auguries, phylacteries, incantations, and all unclean usages of the Gentiles. We forbade the servants of God to wear showy dress and military cloaks or to use arms.

We decreed that it is binding upon the metropolitan in accordance with the canon law to examine the character of the bishops subordinate to him and their solicitude for their people, of what sort it is; and that he should admonish the bishops, after coming from the synod, to meet the priests and abbots in their own parishes, and to enjoin them to keep the decrees of the synod. And each bishop, if there is anything in his diocese which he has not been able to correct or change, should mention this for correction, in the synod before the archbishop and all, as after our ordination the Roman Church bound us with an oath that if we saw the clergy or people wandering from the laws of God and could not correct them, we should always faithfully point this out to the Apostolic See and the vicar of Saint Peter for correction. Thus, unless I am mistaken, all the bishops ought to make known to the metropolitan, anything which they find it impossible to correct among their people, and he should make it known to the Roman pontiff; and so they will be guiltless of the blood of lost souls.

For the rest, dear brother, equal toil but greater danger hangs over us than over other priests, because as all know the ancient canons enjoin the metropolitan to undertake the care of a whole province, and, to express my fears in a figure, we have undertaken to steer the ship among the waves of a savage sea, though we can neither guide it carefully nor lose it without a sin — because, as some one of the wise says:[1] "If it is dangerous not to guide a ship skilfully amid the waves, how much more dangerous is it to abandon it in the storm, as it struggles with the swelling waves." Therefore, the Church, which like a great ship, sails over the sea of the world, and is buffeted by the many waves of temptation in this life, must not be abandoned, but steered. For examples in this connection we have the early Fathers Clement and Cornelius and several others in the city of Rome, Cyprian in Carthage, Athanasius in Alexandria, who under pagan emperors steered the ship of Christ, nay His beloved spouse, that is the Church, by teaching, and by struggling, and toiling and suffering even to the shedding of their blood. Truly I can speak of myself in the words of the Song of Songs: "My mother's children were angry with me, They made me the keeper of the vineyards: But mine own vineyard have I not kept."[2] The vineyard according to Nahum, the prophet of the Lord of Sabaoth, is the house of Israel; now it must be understood to be the Catholic Church. In it, at the command of the Roman pontiff and the request of the rulers of the Franks and Gauls, I undertook to gather and exhort a synod in the hope of restoring the law of Christ. I dug about it, I brought to it a basket of dung, but I did not guard it. When I looked that it should bring forth grapes, it brought forth but wild grapes. According to

---

1. From the *De vita contemplativa* of Julianus Pomerius, 1. xvi. Migne, Patrologia latina, LIX, 431.
2. Cant. 1:5.

another prophet: "The labour of the olive shall fail, and the fields shall yield no meat."[3] But alas! my duty seems to be like that of a dog on the watch, who sees thieves and robbers breaking into and bursting through and pillaging his master's house, but because he has none to help him in the defence, only complains and grieves. But now, when, as seems just and wise for one placed in such danger, I seek and wish to know your helpful advice, I recommend liberty of speaking; I speak, as in the Acts of the Apostles Paul the apostle advised the priests, saying: "Wherefore I take you to record this day, that I am pure from the blood of all men. For I have not shunned to declare unto you all the counsel of God. Take heed, therefore, unto yourselves, and to all the flock over the which the Holy Ghost hath made you overseers to feed the Church of God, which he hath purchased with his own blood. I preached the Kingdom of God," said he, "as I went about among you: that I might keep myself guiltless of the ruin of all men."[4] For the apostle calls a priest of the Church overseer, the prophet calls him watchman, and the Saviour of the world calls him shepherd, and all agree that a teacher who is silent about the sins of the people is guilty through his silence of the blood of the lost souls. Wherefore, a great and terrible necessity forces us to show, in accordance with the words of the apostle, an example to the faithful: that is, unless my judgment errs, the priest must live so justly that from the contrast with his deeds his words may not be idle, and that, while he lives prudently for himself from his own, he may not by his silence be condemned for another's sin; because for this purpose is one set over the church of Christ, that not only by living well he may instruct others through his example, but also that, by faithful preaching, he may set out before each man's eyes his sins, and show what punishment awaits the obstinate, what glory the obedient. Because according to the word of God to Ezekiel he, to whom the dispensation of the word is entrusted, may live justly, but yet, if he is ashamed or fears to rebuke those who live abandoned lives, together with all who perish through his silence, he likewise perishes. And what will it avail him not to be punished for his own sins, who is to be punished for another's? The silence of the priest, the Lord speaking to Ezekiel condemns terribly and calls the priest a watchman: and just as the watchman must from a loftier place see farther than all, so the priest ought to be raised higher on the elevation of his merits and to have the grace of greater wisdom, whereby he can instruct the rest of men. "Therefore hear

---

3. Hab. 3:17.
4. Acts 20:26–28.

the word of my mouth," said the divine voice, "and thou wilt give them warning from me."[5] He means that the priest is to declare what he has learned from divine reading, what God has given him by inspiration, not what human senses have discovered. "Thou wilt give them warning from me," said He, "from me, not from thyself; thou wilt speak my words, and wilt not boast of them as thine own. "From me," said He, "thou wilt give them warning. When I say unto the wicked, Thou shalt surely die; and thou givest him not warning, nor speakest to warn the wicked from his wicked way, to save his life; the same wicked man shall die in his iniquity, but his blood will be required at thine hand."[6] It is as though He said openly: If thou hast not warned him of his sins, and if thou hast not rebuked him, that he turn from his sins and live, both thee who didst not warn and him who through thy silence sinned, I will hand over to eternal flames. Let us not, therefore, be so stony or iron of heart, that these words of the Lord do not alarm us. Let us not be so barren of faith, that we should not believe these words of the Lord; but let us rouse up and exhort our brethren with the revered words of Saint Peter the apostle: "Be sober, be vigilant; because your adversary the devil, as a roaring lion, walketh about, seeking whom he may devour; whom resist, stedfast in the faith, knowing that the same afflictions are accomplished in your brethren that are in the world."[7] And let us admonish the bishops who are under our synod with the exhortation of Saint Paul the apostle, when he says to Timothy: "I charge thee, therefore, before God, and the Lord Jesus Christ, who shall judge the quick and the dead, at his appearing and his Kingdom: preach the word: be instant in season, out of season, reprove, rebuke, exhort, with all long suffering and doctrine."[8] For now is the time foretold by the apostle "when they will not endure sound doctrine, but after their own lusts shall they heap to themselves teachers"[9] and the rest. Let us, according to the word of the prophet, cry aloud with all our strength, we who announce peace on earth to men of good will. For he cries aloud with all his strength, whom neither fear nor shame hinders from preaching the word of life. Let us strive, with the aid of the Lord, that we may not be among those false shepherds of the sheep, whom the prophet accuses, saying: "Thus saith the Lord God: Woe be to the shep-

---

5. Ezek. 3:17.
6. Ezek. 3:18.
7. 1 Pet. 5:8, 9.
8. 2 Tim. 4:1, 2.
9. 2 Tim. 4:3.

herds of Israel, that do feed themselves! Should not the shepherd feed the flock? Ye eat the fat, and ye clothe you with the wool, ye kill them that are led, but ye feed not the flock. The diseased have ye not strengthened, neither have ye healed that which was sick, neither have ye bound up that which was broken, neither have ye brought again that which was driven away, neither have ye sought that which was lost; but with force and with cruelty have ye ruled them, and they were scattered because there is no shepherd, and they became meat to all the beasts of the field."[10] The woe of which the prophet speaks he has fixed for a curse: by the shepherds he signifies the bishops, by the flocks of the Lord, the faithful to be fed. But they feed themselves, because they strive not for the safety of the people, but for their own pleasure. The fat and the wool of the sheep of Christ they take with daily offerings and tithes from the faithful; and care for the flock of Christ they put to one side. They do not heal with spiritual counsel the man sick in sin; they do not strengthen with priestly aid the man broken by many sufferings; they do not recall the erring one to the way of salvation; they do not seek out with pastoral solicitude the man lost through despair of forgiveness; nor do they defend the afflicted against the violence of the powerful, who rage against them like wild beasts; and so far from rebuking rich and powerful sinners, they do them honour. So with threats the divine word smites the pride of such, saying: "Woe to the prophets of Israel!"[11] And again: "Therefore, O ye shepherds, hear the word of the Lord. Thus saith the Lord God; Behold, I am against the shepherds; and I will require my flock at their hands, and cause them to cease from feeding the flock; neither shall the shepherds feed themselves any more." What is this but to say: The shepherds who feed themselves and not the flock, I will thrust down from their high dignity, among the outcast and the accursed! At all this who will not tremble, unless it be one who believes not in the future? Everything which God wished to have observed He has so clearly fixed and established with the authority of His name, that it would be easier to despise His words—and to say this is itself a sin—than to lie and declare that we did not understand things so clear and divine. When we hear: "Thus saith the Lord," who can believe that what God says will not be, unless it be one who believes not in God? With the thought of these things and things like unto them I am terrified, and "fearfulness and trembling are come upon me, and horror of my sins hath all but overwhelmed me";[12] and gladly should I have abandoned the

---

10. Ezek. 34:2–5.
11. Ezek. 34:2, 9, 10.
12. Ps. 4:6.

helm of the Church once taken up, had I been able to do so or could I have found examples, either from the Fathers or the Holy Scriptures to approve such a course.

Wherefore, my beloved brother, since all these things are so, and truth can be sorely tried but neither conquered nor deceived, let our wearied minds take refuge in Him, who says, through the mouth of Solomon: "Trust in the Lord with all thine heart, and lean not unto thine own understanding. In all thy ways acknowledge Him, and He shall direct thy paths."[13] And elsewhere: "The name of the Lord is a strong tower; the righteous runneth into it, and is safe."[14] Let us stand fast in justice, and prepare our souls against temptation, that we may have the support of God and may say to him: "Lord, Thou hast been our dwelling place in all generations."[15] Let us put our trust in Him, who hath put the burden upon us. What we cannot carry ourselves, let us carry through Him who is Omnipotent, and says: "For my yoke is easy, and my burden is light."[16] Let us stand fast in battle in the day of the Lord because the "days of tribulation and hardship" have come upon us. Let us die, if God wills it, for the sacred laws of our fathers, that with them we may deserve to win an eternal heritage. Let us not be dumb dogs nor silent watchmen, nor hirelings who flee before the wolf, but zealous shepherds, watching over the flock of Christ, preaching the whole counsel of Christ, to high and low, to rich and poor, and to all ranks or ages, so far as God gives us strength, in season, out of season, as Saint Gregory has described it in his *Pastoral Care*.

Wherefore, I do not conceal from your love that all the servants of God, who, either in the study of the Scriptures or in the fear of God are here most approved, feel that it would be for the welfare and the fair name and pure character of your Church, and would serve to conceal the disgrace, if your synod and rulers were to forbid to matrons and veiled women the journey to Rome, and the frequent halts which they make on the way thither and on the return. For the most part they perish, few remaining pure. There are few cities in Lombardy or in France or in Gaul, in which there is not an adulteress or a harlot of English race: which is a scandal and disgrace to your whole Church.

And this too, that a layman, be he emperor or king, or one of the prefects or counts, relying on the secular power, should seize for himself

---

13. Prov. 3:5, 6.
14. Prov. 18:10.
15. Ps. 90:1.
16. Matt. 11:30.

a monastery from the power of the bishop or the abbot or the abbess, and begin to rule in the abbot's stead, and have under him monks and take into his possession the money, which was gathered by the blood of Christ, such a man the Fathers of old called a plunderer, a man of sacrilege, a murderer of the poor, and a wolf of the devil entering into the fold of Christ, to be punished before the tribunal of Christ with the heaviest fetters of anathema. Concerning such remember the words of Saint Paul the apostle to Timothy: "Charge them that are rich in this world that they be not high-minded, nor trust in uncertain riches, but in the living God, who giveth us richly all things to enjoy."[17] With such men, living or dead, if they do not receive the warning of the Church, for they are heathen men and publicans, the Church of God can have naught to do. In their ears let us both — for they are found here and there alike — sound the trumpet of the Lord, that by our silence we may not be condemned.

Seek by every means to check the luxury of dress which is excessive and hateful to God. Because these ornaments upon clothing — such their wearers think them to be though they are a disgrace in the eyes of others — the wide stripes and scarlet borders, are sent by Anti-christ and prepare for his coming: through his ministers he craftily introduces within the gates of the monasteries the licence of youths clad in purple garments, lust, unholy intercourse, indifference to reading and prayer, and the ruin of souls. These garments, betraying a nakedness of soul, display in themselves signs of arrogance and pride and wantonness and vanity, concerning which the wise man says: "Pride and arrogancy, and the evil way and the double tongue and froward mouth do I hate."[18]

In your parishes, it is said, the evil of drunkenness has greatly increased so that some bishops, so far from checking it, themselves become intoxicated through excess of drink, and, by offering cups unduly large, force others to drunkenness. This beyond doubt, is a crime for any servant of God to commit, or to have committed; and the canons of our Fathers bid us remove or degrade a drunken bishop or priest, and the Truth itself says: "And take heed to yourselves, lest your hearts be over charged with surfeiting and drunkenness."[19] And Paul the apostle: "And be not drunk with wine, wherein is excess."[20] And Isaiah, the prophet: "Woe unto them that are powerful to drink wine, and men of strength to mingle strong

---

17. 1 Tim. 6:17.
18. Prov. 8:13.
19. Luke 21:34.
20. Eph. 5:18.

drink."[21] This evil indeed is peculiar to the heathen and to our race. For neither the Franks, nor the Gauls, nor the Lombards, nor the Romans, nor the Greeks have it. Let us crush out this sin, if we can, by decrees of our synods and by the ban of the Scriptures; if we cannot, let us by shunning and forbidding it wash our souls clean of the blood of the damned.

Concerning the violent enslavement of monks for royal works and buildings, which in the whole Christian world has never been heard of, save only among the race of the English, the priests of God must not be silent nor give consent thereto. Such an abuse was unheard of in past ages.

May the hand of God guard you, beloved and honoured brother, unharmed against all adversities, while you intercede for us.

---

21. Isa. 5:22.

53. Supported by Spiritual Women
(c. 725–50)

BONIFACE, LUL, AND LIOBA

Whenever Boniface, English monk and apostle to the Germans, felt "battered by the storms of the German sea," he seems to have renewed contact with his spiritual brothers and sisters in England. A great deal of spiritual and material support for his missionary efforts came from devout women in English convents.

Three letters to and from English women illustrate his reliance on their patronage: A letter to Eadburga, abbess of Thanet, requests a manuscript copy of the Epistle of Peter written in gold. Apparently he wanted to use it as a visual aid in his missionary work (Letter XIV, see vol. 1:363). A letter to "an abbess and a nun," perhaps the same Eadburga, from a young deacon named Lul, Boniface's closest assistant, gives an ardent and poetic description of Boniface's recent illness and the rigors of his life (Letter XVIII, see vol. 1:363–65). And Lioba, a young woman who later joined Boniface's mission in Germany and became the abbess of Bischofsheim, writes to Boniface asking for prayers for her family. She reminds him of her mother's kinship to him and hopes that he will protect her like a brother (Letter XXIII, see vol. 1:365–66).

These letters illustrate the importance of women's support to Christian missionaries laboring among the teutonic tribes of northern Europe in the eighth century.

Source: Edward Kylie, ed., *The English Correspondence of St. Boniface* (New York: Cooper Square Publishers, Inc., 1966).

XIV

Boniface asks Eadburga, Abbess of Thanet, to copy for him the Epistles of Saint Peter in letters of gold. 735.

To his revered and beloved sister, Abbess Eadburga, Boniface, poor servant of the servants of God, kind greetings of love in Christ.

I pray Almighty God, who rewards all good works, that He may grant thee in the heavenly mansions and the everlasting tabernacles, and in the court of the holy angels, an eternal recompense for all the kindnesses which thou has shown me, because, by helpful and consoling gifts of books and vestments, thou hast of thy goodness often relieved my distress. So now I beg thee to carry still further what thou hast begun, and to copy in gold the Epistles of my lord, Saint Peter, that the Holy Scriptures may be honoured and reverenced when the preacher holds them before the eyes of the heathen; and I long, above all else, to have with me, the words of him who guided me into this path. I have chosen the priest Eoba to write this request.

Deal then, my dear sister, with this request of mine, as in thy kindness thou hast always been wont to deal with my petitions, so that here also thy works may shine in letters of gold for the glory of the Heavenly Father.

It is my wish that thou mayst fare well in Christ and advance in holy virtues to still higher things.

XVIII

Some one [Lul] writes to an abbess and a nun, and tells of his pilgrimage to Rome, of his loneliness and sickness. He recalls that formerly he was carefully attended by them. Instructed in the art of poetry by Boniface, he sends them some verses of his own composition. 723–754.

To * * *, endowed with virgin chastity and refreshed from on high by the honey-sweet flood of heavenly dew, ennobled not merely by high birth, but also, as is better, by the dignity of her spiritual office, governess of the daughters of Christ who bear the light yoke of God, tireless guardian of the flock entrusted to her care, and of a rule of monastic life determined in accordance with the authentic opinions of the ancient Fathers; and to the young and distinguished * * *, adorned with the white garment of uncorrupted purity, steeped in the living and ever abundant waters of the broad-flowing heavenly stream, illumined not only by the outer brilliance of learning, but by the inner light of divine wisdom, * * *, who, without the prior claim of merit, discharges the duties of a spiritual office, kindly greetings on the stone of the corner, which is Christ.

I confess to your love: when, touched as I think by the beneficent warning of the divine goodness, I departed from the famous kingdoms of Britain, leaving the fruitful soil of my native island whose craggy coasts the dark green waves of the foaming sea hem in on every side, and conscious of my weakness and mindful in some measure of my sins, together with a band of almost all my kindred, crossed, by the favour of Christ, the threatening hills of the raging sea, and happy in the fulfilment of my wish rejoiced in having reached the shores of this land; then I longed to present myself at the shrine of the blessed apostles, that I might pray to have put off from me the weight of innumerable sins, but there, after almost all my kindred had fallen into the long sleep of peace, I was left alone and widowed in this sad exile. None the less must I tell you in what distress and grief I remained. I did not escape the onslaught of the plague with my former health and robust strength of limb; but, praise and thanks to the Scourger, all the joints of my limbs were shaken and twisted, and I am still weak and outworn . . . from my experience, both new and old, I declare, not to flatter you, but relying on the strength of truth, that I have found, among all those of your sex who dwell here, none more faithful: while for five times five long months the heat and cold of panting fever in turn tortured my sick body, I remember with what loving kindness I was cared for. This mercy, as I am aware, you showed me in my infirmity and sickness, obeying the precepts of the Lord, and hoping for the eternal reward; and to this day you have displayed towards me as towards a brother this same unwearying affection in consideration of the divine love.

Wherefore, when I have found fitting material for writing to you, I shall celebrate, in verse, the spiritual bond of your loving kinship with us. Since Christ, the giver of all good things, in His wonderful clemency, let me share in this gift through the heavenly dew of His grace, I long held it fixed in my mind, and dear to my heart, to send you some poor verses, composed in metrical sequence, because I knew none among those who read, to whom I should more gladly send them: for with you I am certain that the tooth of suspicion will not bite, nor the claw of harsh judgment rend the writer, though the contents be faulty and the composition rough. This poetic art I have but lately learned under the instruction of our common and my special master, our revered leader Boniface, to whom, —

after the Heavenly Lightbearer, before whom the secrets of the heart are revealed, and from whom the dark and the hidden things do not lie concealed — the eye of my mind is open, and by whom my dry heart is watered daily with the heavenly shower of nectar from on high.

The verses you will find designed after a droll fashion, if you will with care scan the capital letters, that is, those which every fourth line enclose with their embrace, the others placed in the centre. Those, with which I designated your name, as that of my spiritual mother, begin at the beginning and run on regularly to the end. My pupils begin from the end of those letters devoted to you, not improperly, because the pupil should follow her mistress as does the maid her lady;

Esto Susanna memor Domini regnantis in ede:

And so they begin at the end:

Ernklind esto memor Domini celorum in arce.

But if you find anything unsuited to the work, anything involved or contrary to the rules of grammatical art, this remember to polish, taking a file from the shop of the grammarians. And I beg of you with earnest prayers by that imperishable bond of spiritual love, not to show this work to any one without my consent, or to betray the author of it without my permission; that a dangerous crop of envy may not grow, where the concord of true peace should flourish. But rather be ever mindful of the plighted troth and the intimacy formed between us by the firm link of our hands. And I do humbly beseech you, deign to lighten the burden of my toil with your pure and holy prayers.

XXIII

Lioba asks Boniface to pray to God for her relatives and herself. She sends a gift. After 732.

To Boniface, revered master, endowed with the highest of dignities, dearly beloved in Christ, bound to me by ties of kinship, Lioba, lowliest servant among those who bear the easy yoke of Christ, wishes for eternal welfare.

I beseech thy clemency to be mindful of the friendship which thou didst form long ago, in the regions of the West, with my father Dynne, who was taken from this light more than eight years since, and not to fail in offering prayers to God for his soul. I commend to thee the memory of my mother, Aebbe, who is joined to thee as thou knowest well, by ties of kinship; she still lives a toilsome life and has been long oppressed by infirmities. I am the only daughter of these my parents, and would, that, unworthy as I am, I could deserve to have thee in place of a brother, for in no one among men do I place such great trust as in thee. This small gift I am sending, not that it may appear worthy in thy sight, but in order that thou mayst retain some recollection of my weakness and not let me fall into oblivion because of the long distance which separates us, but rather that the bond of our love may hold firm for ever. And this I beg of thee fervently, beloved brother, to guard me with the shield of thy prayers, against the poisoned shafts of the hidden enemy. I ask thee too, deign to correct the homely style of this letter, and to send me for a model some words of thine, which I crave eagerly to hear.

These little verses below I tried to compose according to the rules of poetic art, in no spirit of confidence, but wishing to practise the rudiments of a graceful accomplishment and to have thy aid. The art I have learned from the teaching of Eadburga, who continues without ceasing to search into the divine law.

Farewell, pray for me and enjoy a long life here, and the happier life to come.

> May the Omnipotent Judge, sole Creator of all,
> Ever resplendent with light in the Father's heavenly kingdom,
> Where reigns the glory of Christ, amid splendour unfailing,
> Keep thee unharmed in His justice eternal.

Definitions of Christendom

54. The Lord's Body and Blood
(c. 832)

RADBERTUS

St. Augustine of Hippo greatly influenced Western European theology in the early Middle Ages. In the Augustinian tradition, at least three theological problems demanded further attention: (1) What happens in the Eucharist when Christians share bread and wine? (2) If we received God's unmerited grace, why do we need to work to please God? (the Pelagian controversy) (3) How do faith and understanding relate?

In the ninth century, controversy arose over how Christ was present in the bread and wine of communion. Augustine of Hippo had upheld the symbolic, yet real, presence of the Lord in the believing, worshiping

SOURCE: George E. McCracken, ed., *Early Medieval Theology,* vol. 9 of *Library of Christian Classics* (Philadelphia: Westminster Press, 1957). Used by permission of Westminster John Knox Press.

church — Christ's body. Symbol meant more than sign, yet Augustine insisted on staying close to scripture and explicitly warned against unwarranted speculation (see vol. 1:210–12).

At the same time, a renewed interest in the popular tradition of "realism" developed, which went back to Cyprian of Carthage and Ambrose of Milan. Cyprian (d. 258) introduced the concept of communion as a sacrifice. Ambrose (d. 379) taught that the words of dedication transform bread and wine into the flesh and blood of Christ.

About 832, a monk and later Abbot of Corbie, Paschasius Radbertus (c. 790–c. 860), wrote a learned treatise on "The Lord's Body and Blood." The treatise was his attempt to reconcile the conflicting traditions. Without repudiating Augustine's "symbolism," he argued that the "substance" of bread and wine is transformed miraculously into the actual flesh and blood of Christ, even though they seem unchanged to the senses. Radbertus's important point is that, for the believer, the consecrated elements are the physical body and blood of Christ.

---

3. As it is the true flesh of Christ which was crucified and buried, truly is it the sacrament of his flesh, which is divinely consecrated through the Holy Spirit on the altar by the agency of the priest in Christ's word. The Lord himself proclaims, "This is my body."[1] Do not be surprised, O man, and do not ask about the order of nature here; but if you truly believe that that flesh was without seed created from the Virgin Mary in her womb by the power of the Holy Spirit, so that the Word might be made flesh, truly believe also that what is constructed in Christ's word through the Holy Spirit is his body from the Virgin. If you ask the method, who can explain or express it in words? Be assured, please, that the method resides in Christ's virtue, the knowledge in faith, the cause in power, but the effect in will, because the power of divinity over nature effectively works beyond the capacity of our reason. Therefore, let knowledge be held in the teaching of salvation, let faith be preserved in the mystery of truth, since in all these "we walk by faith and not by sight."

---

1. Luke 22:19.

55. Christ's Body and Blood
(c. 833)

RATRAMNUS

Although the doctrine of transubstantiation carried the day at the Fourth Lateran Council in 1215 (see vol. 1:333–36), not everyone in the ninth century was ready for Radbertus's extreme literalism. Among the dissenters were Rabanus Maurus, the archbishop of Mainz (d. 856) and Ratramnus, also a monk of Corbie (d. after 868). Both were prolific writers and staunch defenders of the Augustinian tradition. Both strongly objected to the idea that the "transformed" communion bread becomes the flesh born of Mary.

Ratramnus published a treatise entitled, "Christ's Body and Blood," to refute the one with a similar title written by Radbertus. He dedicated his work to the Carolingian emperor Charles "the Bald" who had taken an interest in the matter.

Quoting Augustine of Hippo, Ratramnus argues against transubstantiation, "for he [Augustine] says that to take [Christ's] flesh and his blood in a fleshly sense involves, not religion, but crime." The sacrifice of the Mass is a representation of Christ's sacrifice on the cross. Bread and wine are "figures" of Christ's body and blood and his real pres-

---

SOURCE: George E. McCracken, Ed., *Early Medieval Theology,* vol. 9 of *Library of Christian Classics* (Philadelphia: Westminster Press, 1957). Used by permission of Westminster John Knox Press.

ence a "mystery," by which we become "partakers of the divine boon, through which we have been freed from death."

Ratramnus objected to the "miracle," not to the mystery of the Mass. Transforming the elements into the corporeal body and blood of Christ obliterates the mystery, "where faith receives what the eye does not see."

---

5. Your majesty inquires whether that which in the church is received into the mouth of the faithful becomes the body and blood of Christ in a mystery or in truth. That is, whether it contains some hidden element which becomes patent only to the eyes of faith, or whether without concealment of any mystery the appearance of the body is seen outwardly in what the mind's eyes see inwardly, so that everything which takes place becomes clearly visible; and whether it is that body which was born of Mary, suffered, died, and was buried, and which, rising again and ascending into heaven, sits on the right hand of the Father.

• • •

32. Here arises that question which many express when they say that these things do not happen in a figure but in truth. When they say this, they are shown to be out of harmony with writings of the holy fathers.

33. Saint Augustine, the great doctor of the church, writes in Book III of his work *On Christian Doctrine*[1] as follows:

> "'Except you shall eat,' says the Saviour, 'the flesh of the Son of Man, and shall drink his blood, you shall not have life in you.' This seems to order a shameful crime. Therefore it is a figure, enjoining that we should have a share in the Lord's suffering, and that we should faithfully[2] remember that for us his flesh was crucified and wounded."

34. We see that doctor says that the mysteries of Christ's body and blood are celebrated in a figurative sense by the faithful. For he says that to take his flesh and his blood in a fleshly sense involves, not religion, but crime. This was the view held by those who, understanding the Lord's

---

1. Augustine, *De doctr. Chr.* 3.16.24.
2. Here Augustine: "sweetly and profitably."

statement in the Gospel not in a spiritual but in a fleshly sense, departed from him, and were already not going with him.[3]

35. The same man, writing in his letter[4] to Bishop Boniface, says among other things:

> "Of course, we often say, as the Pascha is approaching, that tomorrow or the day after is the Lord's Passion, although he suffered many years ago, and his Passion did not occur except once. Likewise, on that Lord's Day we say, 'Today the Lord is risen,' although since the day on which he rose so many years have passed. Why is no one so foolish as to accuse us of lying when we speak in this way because we give these names to such days on account of some resemblance with the events that occurred on them, with the result that the day is called that day although it is not the very day on which the event took place but in the revolution of time it is like it, and the event is said to have occurred on that day on account of its sacramental celebration, although the event took place, not on that day but one long since passed? Was not Christ once for all sacrificed in his person? And yet is he not sacrificed in the sacrament, not only in all the celebrations of the solemnities of the Pascha, but before the congregation daily, so that the man does not lie who says, when asked, that he is sacrificed? For if sacraments did not have some resemblance to the things of which they are sacraments, they would not be sacraments at all. By virtue of this resemblance, however, in most cases they derive their names from those things of which they are the sacraments. So, therefore, as in some manner the sacrament of Christ's body is Christ's body, the sacrament of Christ's blood is Christ's blood, so the sacrament of faith is faith."

36. We see that Saint Augustine says that the sacraments are one thing and that the things of which they are sacraments are another. Moreover, the body in which Christ suffered, and the blood which flowed from his side, are things, but he says that the mysteries of these things are the sacraments of Christ's body and blood which are celebrated for the memory of the Lord's Passion, not only each year in all the solemnities of the Pascha, but even every day in the year.

37. And although the Lord's body, in which he once suffered is one thing, and the blood, which was shed for the salvation of the world, is one

---

3. John 6:66.
4. Augustine, *Epist.* 98.9 (formerly 23.9) *ad Bonifatium episcopum*. Date is 408.

thing, yet the sacraments of these two things have assumed their names, being called Christ's body and blood, since they are so called on account of a resemblance with the things they represent. So also the annual celebrations are called the Pascha and the Lord's resurrection, although he suffered in his own person and rose again once and for all, and those days cannot now be called back since they are past. Yet the days on which the remembrance of the Lord's Passion or of his resurrection is celebrated are called by their name, and for the reason that they have some resemblance to those days on which the Saviour suffered once and for all and rose again once and for all.

• • •

40. Nor is it falsely said that in those mysteries the Lord is both sacrificed and suffers since they bear appearance of his death and Passion, of which they are representations. For this reason they are called the Lord's body and the Lord's blood because they take His name whose sacrament they are. On this account the blessed Isidore in the books of *Etymologies*[5] says:

> "Sacrifice is so called from *sacra* and *fieri,* 'that which is made holy,' because it is consecrated by mystical prayer to commemorate the Lord's suffering in our behalf. For this reason, we, at his bidding, say that the body and blood of Christ is what, though made[6] of the earth's fruits, is consecrated and becomes a sacrament through the invisible action of God's spirit. This sacrament of bread and cup the Greeks call the *Eucharistia*,[7] which in Latin may be rendered *bona gratia*.[8] And what is better than the blood and body of Christ?"

But the bread and wine are likened to the body and blood because, just as the substance of this visible bread and wine nourishes and stimulates the outer man, so the Word of God, who is living bread, refreshes faithful souls that share in it.[9]

---

5. Isidore of Seville, *Etymologiae sive origines* 6.19.48.
6. Isidore has, "It is."
7. See Matt. 26:27; Mark 14:23; Luke 22:17, 19.
8. "Good grace."
9. Both Boileau and Bakhuizen attribute this sentence to Isidore, but it is not in the text. Cf. his *De eccl. off.* 1.18.3 for a somewhat similar passage.

41. That catholic doctor also prescribes that this holy mystery of the Lord's Passion should be practiced in memory of the Lord's suffering in our behalf. When he says this, he shows that the Lord's Passion has taken place once and for all, but that His memorial is represented in the sacred rites.

42. This is why the bread which is offered, although from the fruits of the earth, is transferred into the body of Christ while it is being consecrated. So also the wine, though it flowed out of the vine, is made the blood of Christ through the consecration of the divine mystery — not visibly, of course, but as this doctor says, working invisibly through the Spirit of God.

43. This is why they are called Christ's blood and body, because they are received, not as what they outwardly seem, but as what inwardly, through the agency of the divine Spirit, they have been made.

• • •

73. It must be considered that in that bread not only Christ's body but the body also of the people believing on him should be symbolized by the many grains of flour of which it is made because the body of the people who believe is increased by many faithful ones through Christ's word.

74. Wherefore, as in the mystery that bread is taken as Christ's body, so also in the mystery the members of the people who believe in Christ are suggested, and as that bread is called the body of the believers, not in a corporeal sense but in a spiritual, so of necessity Christ's body must also be understood not corporeally but spiritually.

75. As also in the wine which is called Christ's blood mixing with water is prescribed,[10] the one element is not allowed to be offered without the other, because the people cannot exist without Christ, nor Christ without the people, so also can the head not exist without the body, nor the body without the head. So then, in that sacrament, the water represents the people. Therefore, if that wine which is consecrated by the liturgy of the ministers is changed into Christ's blood in a corporeal sense, the water, likewise, which is mixed with it, must of necessity be converted corporeally into the blood of the people who believe. For where there is one consecration, of a consequence there is one action, and where there is

---

10. On mixing of water with the wine see F. J. Dölger, *Der heilige Tisch in den antiken Religionen und im Christentum* (Münster i. W., 2d ed., 1928), 2.491–496; Ambrose, *De virg.* 3.5.22.

a like transaction, there is a like mystery. But we see that in the water nothing is changed with respect to the body, so also for this reason in the wine there is nothing corporeally exhibited. Whatever is meant in the water concerning the body of the people is accepted spiritually. Therefore it is necessary that whatever in the wine is suggested concerning Christ's blood should be accepted spiritually.

• • •

96. Saint Augustine sufficiently instructs us that as the body of Christ, placed on the altar in the form of bread, is symbolized, so also the body of the people as they receive it, in order that he might clearly show that Christ's own body is that in which he was born of the Virgin, in which he was nursed, in which he suffered, in which he died, in which he was buried, in which he rose again, in which he ascended into the heavens, in which he sits on the right hand of the Father, in which he shall come to the judgment. This, however, which has been placed on the Lord's Table contains his mystery, just as it also contains in the same manner the mystery of the body of the people who believe; in the words of the apostle's witness, "We who are many, one bread, one body" in Christ.

97. May your wisdom take notice, most famous prince, that since the testimonies of the Holy Scriptures and the words of the holy fathers have been cited, it has been most clearly shown that the bread which is called Christ's body, and the cup which is called Christ's blood, is a figure, because it is a mystery, and that there is no small difference between the body which exists through the mystery and that which suffered, was buried, and rose again. Since this body, the Saviour's own, exists, and in it there is neither any figure nor any symbol, but it is recognized as the very manifestation of the thing itself, and those who believe long for sight of it, since it is our Head, and when it is seen our longing will be satisfied; since he himself and the Father are one substance, not with respect to the fact that the Saviour has body but with respect to the fullness of divinity which dwells in Christ and man.

98. But in that which is enacted through the mystery there is a figure not only of Christ's own body, but also of the people who believe in Christ, for it bears the figure of both bodies, that is, the one which suffered and rose again, and the body of the people reborn in Christ through Baptism and quickened from the dead.

99. Let us add also that that bread and cup, which are named and are Christ's body and blood, present a memorial of the Lord's Passion or

death, in the manner in which he himself said in the Gospel: "Do this in remembrance of me." The apostle Paul explains this and says: "As often as you eat this bread and drink this cup, you will proclaim the Lord's death until he comes."[11]

100. We are taught by the Saviour, as well as by Saint Paul the apostle, that that bread and that wine which are placed on the altar are placed there as a figure or memorial of the Lord's death, so that what was done in the past may be recalled to memory in the present; that, made mindful of his Passion, we may through it be made partakers of the divine boon, through which we have been freed from death; recognizing that when we have arrived at the point of seeing Christ we shall have no need of such aids by which we are reminded what that measureless goodness bore for us, since, seeing him face to face, we shall not be moved by any outward remembrances of things temporal, but through contemplation of the truth itself we shall see the manner in which we ought to give thanks to the Author of our salvation.

101. Let it not therefore be thought that, since we say this, in the mystery of the sacrament either the Lord's body or his blood is not taken by the faithful when faith receives what the eye does not see but what it believes; for it is spiritual food, spiritually feeding the soul, and bestowing a life of eternal satisfaction. So also the Saviour himself speaks when he commends this mystery: "It is the spirit which quickens, for the flesh is of no avail."[12]

---

11. 1 Cor. 11:26.
12. John 6:63.

56. Why Did God Become Human?
From *Cur Deus Homo?*
(1097–99)

ANSELM OF CANTERBURY

Scholars often refer to Anselm of Canterbury (1033–1109) as the father of medieval scholasticism, a theological method popular in the Middle Ages that combined a dialectical approach to problem solving (question/alternative answers) with a logical demonstration of the "correct" answer. Anselm was one of its skilled practitioners, accepting the underlying assumption that there is but one universal truth of faith and reason. Faith, he wrote, leads to understanding: "I believe that I may understand" (Credo ut intelligam).

Anselm's life was a curious mixture of scholarship, monastic discipline, and ecclesiastical politics. In 1060 he entered the monastery of Bec in Normandy to study under its distinguished abbot Lanfranc. He succeeded his mentor as abbot in 1078, further enhancing the abbey's fame as a center of scholarship. In 1093 he followed Lanfranc as archbishop of Canterbury, becoming deeply involved in a lengthy dispute with the crown. He died at Canterbury in 1109.

SOURCE: Eugene R. Fairweather, ed., *A Scholastic Miscellany: Anselm to Ockham*, vol. 10 of *Library of Christian Classics* (Philadelphia: Westminster Press, 1956). Used by permission of Westminster John Knox Press.

Anselm's most important theological achievement was a new definition of Christ's work of salvation. He shifted the Christological question from its classical preoccupation with the "person" of Christ, to asking about the "work" of Christ. "Why," asked Anselm, "did God become human?" Borrowing imagery from the feudal system, he developed a surprisingly durable answer — what we call the theory of the atonement.

Anselm's argument noted that human sin has outraged God's honor, and God's honor must receive satisfaction. However, since God is infinite, "no one save God can make [satisfaction] and no one save man ought to make it"; therefore, "it is necessary for a God-man to make it."

In his treatise, "Why did God become human?," Anselm develops his answer with questions and answers (the dialectical method). Like Socrates in the writings of Plato, the teacher "A" (Anselm) says a lot more than "B" (his disciple).

Chapter XIII

Nothing Is Less Tolerable in the Order of Things than for the Creature to Take Away the Honor Due to the Creator and Not Repay What He Takes Away

A. Nothing is less tolerable in the order of things, than for the creature to take away the honor due to the Creator and not repay what he takes away.

B. Nothing is clearer than this.

A. But nothing is more unjustly tolerated than that which is most intolerable.

B. This is not obscure, either.

A. I think, then, that you will not say that God ought to tolerate that than which nothing is more unjustly tolerated — namely, that the creature should not restore to God what he takes away.

B. Quite the opposite; I realize that it must be denied.

A. Again, if nothing is greater or better than God, then the highest justice, which is none other than God himself, maintains nothing more justly than his honor, in the ordering of things.

B. Nothing can be plainer than this.

A. Then God maintains nothing more justly than the honor of his dignity.

B. I must grant this.

A. Does it seem to you that he preserves it wholly if he permits it to be taken away from him, and neither receives recompense nor punishes him who took it away?

B. I dare not say so.

A. Therefore, either the honor that was taken away must be repaid or punishment must follow. Otherwise, God will be either unjust to himself or powerless to accomplish either; but it is impious even to imagine this.

• • •

A. [If a person] is to give something of his own to God, which surpasses everything that is beneath God, it is also necessary for him to be greater than everything that is not God.

B. I cannot deny it.

A. But there is nothing above everything that is not God, save God himself.

B. That is true.

A. Then no one but God can make this satisfaction.

B. That follows.

A. But no one ought to make it except man; otherwise man does not make satisfaction.[1]

B. Nothing seems more just.

A. If then, as is certain,[2] that celestial city must be completed from among men, and this cannot happen unless the aforesaid satisfaction is made, while no man save God can make it and no one save man ought to make it, it is necessary for a God-Man to make it.

B. "Blessed be God!"[3] We have already found out one great truth about the object of our inquiry. Go on, then, as you have begun, for I hope that God will help us.[4]

Chapter VII

It Is Necessary for the Same Person to Be Perfect God and Perfect Man

A. Now we must inquire how there can be a God-Man. For the divine and human natures cannot be changed into each other, so that the divine

---

1. Cf. Augustine, *Enarr. in Ps.* 63:13.
2. Cf. Book I, Chapters XVI and XIX.
3. Ps. 67:36 (P.B.V., 68:35).
4. On this chapter, cf. Leo, *Sermo* 56, I.

becomes human or the human divine. Nor can they be so mingled that a third nature, neither fully divine nor fully human, is produced from the two.[5] In short, if one could really be changed into the other, the person would be God only and not man, or man alone and not God. Or if they were mingled in such a way that a third nature was made out of two corrupted natures—just as from two individual animals, a male and a female, of different species, a third is born, which does not preserve the entire nature either of father or of mother, but possesses a third composed of both—the result would be neither man nor God. Therefore, the Man-God we are seeking cannot be produced from divine and human nature, either by the conversion of one into the other or by the destructive commingling of both into a third, because these things cannot be done, and if they could they would be of no avail for the end we seek.

Moreover, even if these two complete natures are said to be united in some way, but still man is one person and God another, so that the same person is not both God and man, the two natures cannot do what needs to be done. For God will not do it, because he does not owe it, and man will not do it, because he cannot. Therefore, for the God-Man to do this, the person who is to make this satisfaction must be both perfect God and perfect man, because none but true God can make it, and none but true man owes it. Thus, while it is necessary to find a God-Man in whom the integrity of both natures is preserved, it is no less necessary for these two complete natures to meet in one person—just as body and rational soul meet in one man—for otherwise the same person could not be perfect God and perfect man.

B. I am pleased with everything you say.

---

5. Cf. "The Chalcedonian Definition of the Faith," in T. H. Bindley, *The Oecumenical Documents of the Faith,* revised ed. (ed. F. W. Green, Methuen, London, 1950), 183–199, 232–235.

57. Five Ways to Prove the Existence of God
From the *Summa Theologica*
(1266–73)

THOMAS AQUINAS

Thomas Aquinas (c. 1224–1274), the greatest theologian of the high Middle Ages, was born in 1224 or 1225 near Naples, Italy. Like many younger sons of the nobility, his parents educated him for service in the church. At the age of five, they sent Thomas to the Benedictine monastery at Monte Cassino. In 1244, while a student at the University of Naples, he joined the Dominican order.

His family considered the Dominicans a bad career choice and forcibly kept him at the family castle, hoping Thomas would change his mind. Their tactics did not work, and after a year Aquinas made his way to Paris to finish his novitiate and to study under Albertus Magnus (d. 1280), a fellow Dominican and advocate of the "new [Aristotelian] philosophy." Aquinas followed his teacher to Cologne, where for his sheer bulk and taciturn ways, he acquired the nickname "dumb [mutus] ox." His nickname was no reflection on his intellect. Aquinas was a highly educated man and spent the remainder of his life as a Dominican professor of theology, teaching in Cologne, Paris, and Naples.

Aquinas wrote extensively. His two most important works are the

---

SOURCE: Anton C. Pegis, ed., *The Basic Writings of St. Thomas Aquinas*, vol. 1 (New York: Random House, 1945). Used by permission of the Anton C. Pegis Estate.

Summa Contra Gentiles, *a handbook for erudite missionaries; and the* Summa Theologica, *a systematic theology. Long after Aquinas's death, Pope Leo XIII in 1879 named Thomas Aquinas the official teacher (*doctor communis*) of the Roman church.*

Aquinas's Summa Theologica *is the most important theological work of the late Middle Ages. It is a clear, systematic exposition of the Christian faith based on the "new philosophy" of Aristotle, whose writings had been rediscovered by Christian monks in Muslim libraries during the Crusades.*

By the thirteenth century, classic Christian theology grounded in the writings of Augustine of Hippo and Platonic philosophy no longer gave an adequate account of the experienced world. If all human knowledge is contingent and corrupted by sin, as Augustine said, then natural reason cannot demonstrate God's existence. Anselm of Canterbury expressed that theological tradition when he wrote that natural reason cannot demonstrate God's existence ("I believe that I may understand"), though the idea of God's existence ("that than which nothing greater can be conceived") is self-evident.

Thomas Aquinas "gently" repudiates Anselm and his fellow Augustinians. Aquinas says we base human knowledge on our experience of cause and effect in the external world. While reason cannot fathom the mysteries of God, those effects in the world can demonstrate the existence and some of the attributes of God. The created order has its being from the one who "is" (Yahweh). It is possible, according to Aquinas, to have a rational knowledge of God. And rational knowledge can provide a basis for natural theology.

Aquinas offers five ways to demonstrate the existence of God. He uses a thoroughly modern argument against Anselm's metaphysical proof of God by saying that the sentence "God exists" is a tautology (or a statement that cannot be false, such as "A equals A"). He continues his arguments following the scholastic method: first, state the problem under investigation as a question; second, list possible answers arranged by authorities (the "philosopher," i.e. Aristotle; or tradition or scriptures); third, reflecting on the references, provide the correct answer; and fourth, refute all incorrect answers.

BECAUSE the chief aim of sacred doctrine is to teach the knowledge of God not only as He is in Himself, but also as He is the beginning of things and their last end, and especially of rational creatures, as is clear from what has been already said,[1] therefore, in our endeavor to expound this science, we shall treat: (1) of God; (2) of the rational creature's movement towards God;[2] (3) of Christ Who as man is our way to God.[3]

In treating of God there will be a threefold division: —

For we shall consider (1) whatever concerns the divine essence. (2) Whatever concerns the distinctions of Persons.[4] (3) Whatever concerns the procession of creatures from Him.[5]

Concerning the divine essence, we must consider: —

(1) Whether God exists? (2) The manner of His existence, or, rather, what is *not* the manner of His existence.[6] (3) Whatever concerns His operations — namely, His knowledge,[7] will,[8] power.[9]

Concerning the first, there are three points of inquiry: —

(1) Whether the proposition *God exists* is self-evident? (2) Whether it is demonstrable? (3) Whether God exists?

First Article

Whether the Existence of God Is Self-Evident?

We proceed thus to the First Article: —

Objection 1. It seems that the existence of God is self-evident. For those things are said to be self-evident to us the knowledge of which exists naturally in us, as we can see in regard to first principles. But as Damascene says, *the knowledge of God is naturally implanted in all.*[10] Therefore the existence of God is self-evident.

Obj. 2. Further, those things are said to be self-evident which are known as soon as the terms are known, which the Philosopher says is true of the first principles of demonstration.[11] Thus, when the nature of a whole and of a part is known, it is at once recognized that every whole is

---

1. Q. 1, a. 7.
2. *S. T.,* II.
3. *S. T.,* III.
4. Q. 27.
5. Q. 44.
6. Q. 3.
7. Q. 14.
8. Q. 19.
9. Q. 25.
10. *De Fide Orth.,* I, 1; 3.
11. *Post. Anal.,* I, 3.

greater than its part. But as soon as the signification of the name *God* is understood, it is at once seen that God exists. For by this name is signified that thing than which nothing greater can be conceived. But that which exists actually and mentally is greater than that which exists only mentally. Therefore, since as soon as the name *God* is understood it exists mentally, it also follows that it exists actually. Therefore the proposition *God exists* is self-evident.

Obj. 3. Further, the existence of truth is self-evident. For whoever denies the existence of truth grants that truth does not exist: and, if truth does not exist, then the proposition *Truth does not exist* is true: and if there is anything true, there must be truth. But God is truth itself: *I am the way, the truth, and the life* (*Jo.* xiv. 6). Therefore *God exists* is self-evident.

On the contrary, No one can mentally admit the opposite of what is self-evident, as the Philosopher states concerning the first principles of demonstration.[12] But the opposite of the proposition *God is* can be mentally admitted: *The fool said in his heart, There is no God* (*Ps.* liii. 1). Therefore, that God exists is not self-evident.

I answer that, A thing can be self-evident in either of two ways: on the one hand, self-evident in itself, though not to us; on the other, self-evident in itself, and to us. A proposition is self-evident because the predicate is included in the essence of the subject: *e.g., Man is an animal,* for animal is contained in the essence of man. If, therefore, the essence of the predicate and subject be known to all, the proposition will be self-evident to all; as is clear with regard to the first principles of demonstration, the terms of which are certain common notions that no one is ignorant of, such as being and non-being, whole and part, and the like. If, however, there are some to whom the essence of the predicate and subject is unknown, the proposition will be self-evident in itself, but not to those who do not know the meaning of the predicate and subject of the proposition. Therefore, it happens, as Boethius says, that there are some notions of the mind which are common and self-evident only to the learned, as that incorporeal substances are not in space.[13] Therefore I say that this proposition, *God exists,* of itself is self-evident, for the predicate is the same as the subject, because God is His own existence as will be hereafter shown.[14] Now because we do not know the essence of God, the proposi-

---

12. *Metaph.,* III, 3; *Post. Anal.,* I, 10.
13. *De Hebdom.*
14. Q. 3, a. 4.

tion is not self-evident to us, but needs to be demonstrated by things that are more known to us, though less known in their nature — namely, by His effects.

Reply Obj. 1. To know that God exists in a general and confused way is implanted in us by nature, inasmuch as God is man's beatitude. For man naturally desires happiness, and what is naturally desired by man is naturally known by him. This, however, is not to know absolutely that God exists; just as to know that someone is approaching is not the same as to know that Peter is approaching, even though it is Peter who is approaching; for there are many who imagine that man's perfect good, which is happiness, consists in riches, and others in pleasures, and others in something else.

Reply Obj. 2. Perhaps not everyone who hears this name *God* understands it to signify something than which nothing greater can be thought, seeing that some have believed God to be a body.[15] Yet, granted that everyone understands that by this name *God* is signified something than which nothing greater can be thought, nevertheless, it does not therefore follow that he understands that what the name signifies exists actually, but only that it exists mentally. Nor can it be argued that it actually exists, unless it be admitted that there actually exists something than which nothing greater can be thought; and this precisely is not admitted by those who hold that God does not exist.

Reply Obj. 3. The existence of truth in general is self-evident, but the existence of a Primal Truth is not self-evident to us.

Second Article

Whether It Can Be Demonstrated That God Exists?

We proceed thus to the Second Article: —

Objection 1. It seems that the existence of God cannot be demonstrated. For it is an article of faith that God exists. But what is of faith cannot be demonstrated, because a demonstration produces scientific knowledge, whereas faith is of the unseen, as is clear from the Apostle (*Heb.* xi. 1). Therefore it cannot be demonstrated that God exists.

Obj. 2. Further, essence is the middle term of demonstration. But we

---

15. Cf. *C. G.*, I, 20 — Cf. also Aristotle, *Phys.*, I, 4 (187a 12); St. Augustine, *De Civit. Dei*, VIII, 2; *De Haeres.* 46, 50, 86; *De Genesi ad Litt.*, X, 25; Maimonides, *Guide*, I, 53.

cannot know in what God's essence consists, but solely in what it does not consist, as Damascene says.[16] Therefore we cannot demonstrate that God exists.

Obj. 3. Further, if the existence of God were demonstrated, this could only be from His effects. But His effects are not proportioned to Him, since He is infinite and His effects are finite, and between the finite and infinite there is no proportion. Therefore, since a cause cannot be demonstrated by an effect not proportioned to it, it seems that the existence of God cannot be demonstrated.

On the contrary, The Apostle says: *The invisible things of Him are clearly seen, being understood by the things that are made (Rom.* i. 20). But this would not be unless the existence of God could be demonstrated through the things that are made; for the first thing we must know of anything is, whether it exists.

I answer that, Demonstration can be made in two ways: One is through the cause, and is called *propter quid,* and this is to argue from what is prior absolutely. The other is through the effect, and is called a demonstration *quia*; this is to argue from what is prior relatively only to us. When an effect is better known to us than its cause, from the effect we proceed to the knowledge of the cause. And from every effect the existence of its proper cause can be demonstrated, so long as its effects are better known to us; because, since every effect depends upon its cause, if the effect exists, the cause must pre–exist. Hence the existence of God, in so far as it is not self-evident to us, can be demonstrated from those of His effects which are known to us.

Reply Obj. 1. The existence of God and other like truths about God, which can be known by natural reason, are not articles of faith, but are preambles to the articles; for faith presupposes natural knowledge, even as grace presupposes nature and perfection the perfectible. Nevertheless, there is nothing to prevent a man, who cannot grasp a proof, from accepting, as a matter of faith, something which in itself is capable of being scientifically known and demonstrated.

Reply Obj. 2. When the existence of a cause is demonstrated from an effect, this effect takes the place of the definition of the cause in proving the cause's existence. This is especially the case in regard to God, because, in order to prove the existence of anything, it is necessary to accept as a middle term the meaning of the name, and not its essence, for the

---

16. *De Fide Orth.,* I, 4.

question of its essence follows on the question of its existence. Now the names given to God are derived from His effects, as will be later shown.[17] Consequently, in demonstrating the existence of God from His effects, we may take for the middle term the meaning of the name *God*.

Reply Obj. 3. From effects not proportioned to the cause no perfect knowledge of that cause can be obtained. Yet from every effect the existence of the cause can be clearly demonstrated, and so we can demonstrate the existence of God from His effects; though from them we cannot know God perfectly as He is in His essence.

Third Article

Whether God Exists?

We proceed thus to the Third Article: —

Objection 1. It seems that God does not exist; because if one of two contraries be infinite, the other would be altogether destroyed. But the name *God* means that He is infinite goodness. If, therefore, God existed, there would be no evil discoverable; but there is evil in the world. Therefore God does not exist.

Obj. 2. Further, it is superfluous to suppose that what can be accounted for by a few principles has been produced by many. But it seems that everything we see in the world can be accounted for by other principles, supposing God did not exist. For all natural things can be reduced to one principle, which is nature; and all voluntary things can be reduced to one principle, which is human reason, or will. Therefore there is no need to suppose God's existence.

On the contrary, It is said in the person of God: *I am Who am* (*Exod.* iii. 14).

I answer that, The existence of God can be proved in five ways.

The first and more manifest way is the argument from motion. It is certain, and evident to our senses, that in the world some things are in motion. Now whatever is moved is moved by another, for nothing can be moved except it is in potentiality to that towards which it is moved; whereas a thing moves inasmuch as it is in act. For motion is nothing else than the reduction of something from potentiality to actuality. But nothing can be reduced from potentiality to actuality, except by some-

---

17. Q. 13, a. 1.

thing in a state of actuality. Thus that which is actually hot, as fire, makes wood, which is potentially hot, to be actually hot, and thereby moves and changes it. Now it is not possible that the same thing should be at once in actuality and potentiality in the same respect, but only in different respects. For what is actually hot cannot simultaneously be potentially hot; but it is simultaneously potentially cold. It is therefore impossible that in the same respect and in the same way a thing should be both mover and moved, *i.e.*, that it should move itself. Therefore, whatever is moved must be moved by another. If that by which it is moved be itself moved, then this also must needs be moved by another, and that by another again. But this cannot go on to infinity, because then there would be no first mover, and, consequently, no other mover, seeing that subsequent movers move only inasmuch as they are moved by the first mover; as the staff moves only because it is moved by the hand. Therefore it is necessary to arrive at a first mover, moved by no other; and this everyone understands to be God.

The second way is from the nature of efficient cause. In the world of sensible things we find there is an order of efficient causes. There is no case known (neither is it, indeed, possible) in which a thing is found to be the efficient cause of itself; for so it would be prior to itself, which is impossible. Now in efficient causes it is not possible to go on to infinity, because in all efficient causes following in order, the first is the cause of the intermediate cause, and the intermediate is the cause of the ultimate cause, whether the intermediate cause be several, or one only. Now to take away the cause is to take away the effect. Therefore, if there be no first cause among efficient causes, there will be no ultimate, nor any intermediate, cause. But if in efficient causes it is possible to go on to infinity, there will be no first efficient cause, neither will there be an ultimate effect, nor any intermediate efficient causes; all of which is plainly false. Therefore it is necessary to admit a first efficient cause, to which everyone gives the name of God.

The third way is taken from possibility and necessity, and runs thus. We find in nature things that are possible to be and not to be, since they are found to be generated, and to be corrupted, and consequently, it is possible for them to be and not to be. But it is impossible for these always to exist, for that which can not-be at some time is not. Therefore, if everything can not-be, then at one time there was nothing in existence. Now if this were true, even now there would be nothing in existence, because that which does not exist begins to exist only through something already existing. Therefore, if at one time nothing was in existence, it would have been impossible for anything to have begun to exist; and thus even now nothing would be in existence — which is absurd. Therefore, not all beings are merely possible, but there must exist something the existence of which is necessary. But every necessary thing either has its necessity caused by another, or not. Now it is impossible to go on to infinity in necessary things which have their necessity caused by another, as has been already proved in regard to efficient causes. Therefore we cannot but admit the existence of some being having of itself its own necessity, and not receiving it from another, but rather causing in others their necessity. This all men speak of as God.

The fourth way is taken from the gradation to be found in things. Among beings there are some more and some less good, true, noble, and the like. But *more* and *less* are predicated of different things according as they resemble in their different ways something which is the maximum, as a thing is said to be hotter according as it more nearly resembles that which is hottest; so that there is something which is truest, something best, something noblest, and, consequently, something which is most being, for those things that are greatest in truth are greatest in being, as it is written in *Metaph.* ii.[18] Now the maximum in any genus is the cause of all in that genus, as fire, which is the maximum of heat, is the cause of all hot things, as is said in the same book.[19] Therefore there must also be something which is to all beings the cause of their being, goodness, and every other perfection; and this we call God.

The fifth way is taken from the governance of the world. We see that things which lack knowledge, such as natural bodies, act for an end, and this is evident from their acting always, or nearly always, in the same way, so as to obtain the best result. Hence it is plain that they achieve their end not fortuitously, but designedly. Now whatever lacks knowledge cannot move towards an end, unless it be directed by some being endowed with knowledge and intelligence; as the arrow is directed by the archer. Therefore some intelligent being exists by whom all natural things are directed to their end; and this being we call God.

Reply Obj. 1. As Augustine says: *Since God is the highest good, He would not allow any evil to exist in His works, unless His omnipotence and goodness were such as to bring good even out of evil.*[20] This is part of the infinite goodness of God, that He should allow evil to exist, and out of it produce good.

---

18. *Metaph.* Ia, 1.
19. Ibid.
20. *Enchir.*, XI.

Reply Obj. 2. Since nature works for a determinate end under the direction of a higher agent, whatever is done by nature must be traced back to God as to its first cause. So likewise whatever is done voluntarily must be traced back to some higher cause other than human reason and will, since these can change and fail; for all things that are changeable and capable of defect must be traced back to an immovable and self-necessary first principle, as has been shown.

58. Whether the Trinity of the Divine Persons Can Be Known by Natural Reason?

From the *Summa Theologica*
(1266–73)

THOMAS AQUINAS

If, as Thomas Aquinas (c. 1224–74) suggests, natural reason allows for a limited knowledge of God, then the question arises: Where is one to draw the limits? Obviously God's own way of being is beyond human understanding. Therefore, Aquinas devotes a good part of the Summa Theologica *to exploring the limits of reason and the grounds for belief.*

The Trinity is a good case. In the long history of the church, understandings of the Trinity have endured the uses and abuses of natural reason, always retaining a logical dissonance. Aquinas flatly denies that one can attain knowledge of the Trinity by natural reason. It is precisely the particularity of God (the three, not the one) that has been and continues to be the "scandal" (1 Cor. 1:23) of the Christian faith.

Aquinas asserts that resolving the problem of the Trinity by reason, positively or negatively, diminishes faith. He concludes that we must ac-

---

SOURCE: Anton C. Pegis, ed., *The Basic Writings of St. Thomas Aquinas*, vol. 1 (New York: Random House, 1945). Used by permission of the Anton C. Pegis Estate.

cept the Trinity on faith or, failing that, on authority. All theology can do is show that "what faith teaches, is not impossible."

We proceed thus to the First Article: —
Objection 1. It would seem that the trinity of the divine persons can be known by natural reason. For philosophers came to the knowledge of God not otherwise than by natural reason.[1] Now we find that they have said many things about the trinity of persons. For Aristotle says: *Through this number* — namely, three — *we bring ourselves to acknowledge the greatness of one God, surpassing all things created.*[2] And Augustine says: *I have read in their works,* that is, in the books of the Platonists, *not in so many words, but enforced by many and various reasons, that in the beginning was the Word, and the Word was with God, and the Word was God,*[3] and so on; in which passage the distinction of persons is laid down. We read, moreover, in the *Gloss* on *Rom.* 1. and *Exod.* 8 that the magicians of Pharaoh failed in the third sign[4] — that is, as regards knowledge of a third person — *i.e.,* of the Holy Ghost, and thus it is clear that they knew at least two persons. Likewise Trismegistus says: *The monad begot a monad, and reflected upon itself its own desire.*[5] By which words the generation of the Son and the procession of the Holy Ghost seem to be indicated. Therefore knowledge of the divine persons can be obtained by natural reason.

Obj. 2. Further, Richard of St. Victor says: *I believe without doubt that not only probable but even necessary arguments can be found for any explanation of the truth.*[6] So even to prove the Trinity some have brought forward an argument based on the infinite goodness of God, which communicates itself infinitely in the procession of the divine persons;[7] while some are moved by the consideration that *no good thing can be joyfully*

---

1. Cf. R. Arnou, "Platonisme des Pères" (*Dict. de théol. cath.,* XII, 2, 1935, coll. 2322–2327).
2. *De Caelo,* I, 1.
3. *Confess.,* VII, 9.
4. *Glossa ordin.,* super *Exod.* VIII, 19. — Cf. St. Isidore, *Quaest. in Vet. Test., In Exod.,* XIV, super VIII, 19. — Cf. also St. Augustine, *Epist.* LV., ch. 16.
5. Pseudo-Hermes Trismegistus, *Lib. 24 Philosoph.,* prop. 1.
6. *De Trin.*
7. Alexander of Hales, *Summa Theol.,* I, no. 295; St. Bonaventure, *Itin. Mentis in Deum,* VI.

possessed without partnership.[8] Augustine, on the other hand, proceeds to prove the trinity of persons by the procession of the word and of love in our own mind;[9] and we have followed him in this.[10] Therefore the trinity of persons can be known by natural reason.

Obj. 3. Further, it seems to be superfluous to teach what cannot be known by natural reason. But it may not be said that the divine teaching on the Trinity is superfluous. Therefore the trinity of persons can be known by natural reason.

On the contrary, Hilary says, *Let man not think to reach the sacred mystery of generation by his own mind.*[11] And Ambrose says, *It is impossible to know the secret of generation. The mind fails, the voice is silent.*[12] But the trinity of the divine persons is distinguished by origin of generation and procession.[13] Since, therefore, man cannot know, and with his understanding attain to, that for which no necessary argument can be given, it follows that the trinity of persons cannot be known by reason.

I answer that, It is impossible to attain to the knowledge of the Trinity by natural reason. For, as was above explained,[14] man cannot obtain a knowledge of God by natural reason except from creatures. Now creatures lead us to the knowledge of God, as effects do to their cause. Accordingly, by natural reason we can know of God only that which of necessity belongs to Him as the cause [*principium*] of all things, and we have used this as a fundamental principle in treating of God.[15] Now, the creative power of God is common to the whole Trinity; and hence it belongs to the unity of the essence, and not to the distinction of the persons. Therefore, by natural reason we can know what belongs to the unity of the essence, but not what belongs to the distinction of the persons.

Whoever, then, tries to prove the trinity of persons by natural reason, detracts from faith in two ways. First, as regards the dignity of faith itself, which consists in its being concerned with invisible things that exceed human reason; wherefore the Apostle says that *faith is of things that appear not* (*Heb.* 11:1), and the same Apostle says also, *We speak wisdom*

---

8. Richard of St. Victor, *De Trin.*, III, 3.
9. *De Trin.*, IX, 4.
10. Q. 27, a. 1 and 3.
11. *De Trin.*, II.
12. *De Fide*, I, 10.
13. Q. 30, a. 2.
14. Q. 12, a. 4, 11 and 12.
15. Q. 12, a. 12.

among the perfect, but not the wisdom of this world, nor of the princes of this world; but we speak the wisdom of God in a mystery which is hidden (*1 Cor.* 2:6, 7). Secondly, as regards the utility of drawing others to the faith. For when anyone in the endeavor to prove what belongs to faith brings forward arguments which are not cogent, he falls under the ridicule of the unbelievers: since they suppose that we base ourselves upon such arguments, and that we believe on their account.

Therefore, we must not attempt to prove what is of faith, except by authority alone, to those who receive the authority; while as regards others, it suffices to prove that what faith teaches is not impossible. Hence it is said by Dionysius: *Whoever wholly resists Scripture, is far off from our philosophy; whereas if he regards the truth of the sacred writings we are agreed in following the same rule.*[16]

Reply Obj. 1. The philosophers did not know the mystery of the trinity of the divine persons by its proper attributes, namely, paternity, filiation, and procession; according to the Apostle's words, *We speak the wisdom of God which none of the princes of the world* — i.e., "the philosophers," according to the *Gloss*[17] — *knew* (*1 Cor.* 2:6). Nevertheless, they knew some of the essential attributes appropriated to the persons, as power to the Father, wisdom to the Son, goodness to the Holy Ghost; as will later on appear.[18] So, when Aristotle said, *By this number,* etc.,[19] we must not take it as if he affirmed a threefold number in God, but that he wished to say that the ancients used the threefold number in their sacrifices and prayers because of some perfection residing in the number three. In the Platonic books also we find, *In the beginning was the word,*[20] not as meaning the Person begotten in God, but as meaning the ideal model whereby God made all things, and which is appropriated to the Son. And even though it be said that they knew these were appropriated to the three persons, yet they are said to have failed in the third sign — that is, in the knowledge of the third person, because they deviated from the goodness appropriated to the Holy Ghost, in that, knowing God, *they did not glorify Him as God* (*Rom.* 1:21); or because the Platonists, asserting the existence of one Primal Being whom they also declared to be the father of the universe,[21] then maintained the existence of another substance beneath

---

16. *De Div. Nom.,* II 2.
17. *Glossa interl.* (VI, 36r); Peter Lombard, *In 1 Cor.*
18. Q. 39, a. 7.
19. *De Caelo,* I, 1.
20. Cf. St. Augustine, *Confess.,* VII, 9.
21. Macrobius, *In Somn. Scipion.,* I, 14.

him, which they called *mind*[22] or the *paternal intellect*,[23] containing the models of all things, as Macrobius relates.[24] They did not, however, assert the existence of a third separate substance which might correspond to the Holy Ghost. Now we do not thus assert that the Father and the Son differ in substance, which was the error of Origen and Arius, who in this followed the Platonists.[25] When Trismegistus says, *Monad begot monad,* etc.,[26] this does not refer to the generation of the Son, or to the procession of the Holy Ghost, but to the production of the world. For one God produced one world by reason of His love for Himself.

---

22. Op. cit., I, 2.
23. St. Albert, *Metaph.*, I, tr. 4, ch. 12; *De 15 Problem.*, problem. I.
24. *In Somn. Scipion.*, I, 2.
25. Cf. St. Jerome, *Epist.* LXXXIV, 1.
26. Pseudo-Hermes Trismegistus, *Lib. 24 Philosoph.*, prop. 1.

59. Natural and Theological Virtues
From the *Summa Theologica*
(1266—73)

THOMAS AQUINAS

One can clearly see the line dividing rational and revealed truth in Thomas Aquinas's treatment of natural and theological virtues. Based on Aristotle's principle of the "Golden Mean," Aquinas (c. 1224–1274) lists four primary natural or intellectual virtues: prudence, justice, self-control (temperance), and courage (fortitude). These virtues are rationally discernible principles of action whose purpose is beneficial to the agent and the community. (For instance, the practice of dietary self-control is preferable to the extremes of either gluttony or starvation.)

Aquinas also notes that "faith, hope, and love" are the three theological virtues revealed in scripture (1 Cor. 13). These theological virtues transcend rational principles of action, ultimately directing us toward God. (In human experience, these virtues are objectively uncertain. For instance, we may suspend belief and wait for evidence.)

Therefore, Aquinas argues, we must distinguish theological virtues

---

SOURCE: Anton C. Pegis, ed., *The Basic Writings of St. Thomas Aquinas*, vol. 2 (New York: Random House, 1945). Used by permission of the Anton C. Pegis Estate.

from natural virtues. The human "intellect" and the human "will" need "to receive in addition something supernatural to direct humans to a supernatural end." In other words, to be complete, reason needs revelation; merit needs grace. Thus, Aquinas shows how reason and revelation collaborate to guide us toward ultimate truth, just as merit and grace assure us of ultimate happiness.

The Natural Virtues

Third Article

We proceed thus to the Third Article: —

Objection 1. It would seem that the other virtues should be called principal rather than these. For the greatest is clearly the principal in any genus. Now *magnanimity has a great influence on all the virtues.*[1] Therefore, magnanimity should, more than any, be called a principal virtue.

Obj. 2. Further, that which strengthens the other virtues should above all be called a principal virtue. But such is humility, for Gregory says that *he who gathers the other virtues without humility is as one who carries straw against the wind.*[2] Therefore humility seems above all to be a principal virtue.

Obj. 3. Further, that which is most perfect seems to be principal. But this applies to patience, according to *Jas.* 1:4: *Patience hath a perfect work.* Therefore, patience should be reckoned a principal virtue.

On the contrary, Cicero reduces all other virtues to these four.[3]

I answer that, As was stated above, these four are reckoned as cardinal virtues according to the four formal principles of virtue as we understand it here. These principles are found chiefly in certain acts and passions. Thus the good which exists in the act of reason is found chiefly in reason's command, but not in its counsel or its judgment, as was stated above.[4] Again, good as defined by reason, and put into our operations as something right and due, is found chiefly in commutations and distributions in relation to another person, and on a basis of equality. The good of curbing the passions is found chiefly in those passions which are most difficult to

---

1. Aristotle, *Eth.*, IV, 3.
2. *In Evang.*, I, hom. 7.
3. *De Invent.*, II, 53.
4. Q. 57, a. 6.

curb, viz., in the pleasures of touch. The good of being firm in holding to the good defined by reason, against the impulse of passion, is found chiefly in perils exposing us to death, which are most difficult to withstand.

Accordingly, the above four virtues may be considered in two ways. First, according to their common formal principles. In this way, they are called principal, being general, as it were, in comparison with all the virtues; so that, for instance, any virtue that causes good in reason's act of consideration may be called prudence; every virtue that causes the good of rectitude and the due in operations, be called justice; every virtue that curbs and represses the passions, be called temperance; and every virtue that strengthens the soul against any passions whatever, be called fortitude. Many, both holy doctors,[5] as also philosophers,[6] speak about these virtues in this sense. It is in this way that the other virtues are contained under them. — Therefore all the objections fail.

Secondly, they may be considered according as each one of them is named from that which is foremost in its respective matter, and thus they are specific virtues, co-divided with the others. Yet they are called principal in comparison with the other virtues because of the importance of their matter. Thus, prudence is the virtue which commands; justice, the virtue which is about due actions between equals; temperance, the virtue which suppresses desires for the pleasures of touch; and fortitude, the virtue which strengthens against dangers of death. — Thus again do the objections fail; because the other virtues may be principal in some other way, but these are called principal by reason of their matter, as was stated above.

The Theological Virtues

(In Four Articles)

We must now consider the Theological Virtues. Under this head there are four points of inquiry: (1) Whether there are theological virtues? (2)

---

5. St. Ambrose, *De Off. Ministr.*, 1, 36; St. Augustine, *De Mor. Eccl.*, I, 15; St. Gregory, *Moral.*, XXII, 1.
6. Seneca, *Ad Lucilium Epistulae Morales,* Epist. LXVII, ed. R. M. Gummere (New York: G. P. Putnam's Sons), vol. II (1920), pp. 36, 38.

Whether the theological virtues are distinguished from the intellectual and moral virtues? (3) How many, and which are they? (4) Of their order.

First Article

Whether There Are Theological Virtues?

We proceed thus to the First Article:—

Objection 1. It would seem that there are not any theological virtues. For according to *Physics* vii., *virtue is the disposition of a perfect thing to that which is best; and by perfect I mean that which is disposed according to nature.*[1] But that which is divine is above man's nature. Therefore the theological virtues are not the virtues of a man.

Obj. 2. Further, theological virtues are quasi-divine virtues. But the divine virtues are exemplars, as was stated above,[2] which are not in us but in God. Therefore the theological virtues are not the virtues of man.

Obj. 3. Further, the theological virtues are so called because they direct us to God, Who is the first cause and last end of all things. But by the very nature of his reason and will, man is directed to his first cause and last end. Therefore there is no need for any habits of theological virtue to direct the reason and the will to God.

On the contrary, The precepts of law are about acts of virtue. But the divine law contains precepts about the acts of faith, hope and charity: for it is written (*Ecclus.* 2:8, *seqq.*): *Ye that fear the Lord believe Him,* and again, *hope in Him,* and again, *love Him.* Therefore faith, hope and charity are virtues directing us to God. Therefore they are theological virtues.

I answer that, Man is perfected by virtue for those actions by which he is directed to happiness, as was explained above.[3] Now man's happiness or felicity is twofold, as was also stated above.[4] One is proportioned to human nature, a happiness, namely, which man can obtain by means of the principles of his nature. The other is a happiness surpassing man's nature, and which man can obtain by the power of God alone, by a kind of participation of the Godhead; and thus it is written (*2 Pet.* 1:4) that by Christ we are made *partakers of the divine nature.* And because such

---

1. Aristotle, *Phys.,* VII, 3.
2. Q. 61, a. 5.
3. Q. 5, a. 7.
4. Q. 5, a. 5.

happiness surpasses the power of human nature, man's natural principles, which enable him to act well according to his power, do not suffice to direct man to this same happiness. Hence it is necessary for man to receive from God some additional principles, by which he may be directed to supernatural happiness, even as he is directed to his connatural end by means of his natural principles, albeit not without the divine assistance. Such principles are called *theological virtues*.[5] They are so called, first, because their object is God, inasmuch as they direct us rightly to God; secondly, because they are infused in us by God alone; thirdly, because these virtues are not made known to us, save by divine revelation, contained in Holy Scripture.

Reply Obj. 1. A certain nature may be ascribed to a certain thing in two ways. First, essentially, and thus these theological virtues surpass the nature of man. Secondly, by participation, as kindled wood partakes of the nature of fire, and thus, after a fashion, man becomes a partaker of the divine nature, as was stated above. Hence these virtues befit man according to the nature of which he is made a partaker.

Reply Obj. 2. These virtues are called divine, not as though God were virtuous by reason of them, but because by them God makes us virtuous, and directs us to Himself. Hence they are not exemplar virtues but copies.

Reply Obj. 3. The reason and the will are naturally directed to God, inasmuch as He is the cause and the end of nature, but according to the ability of nature. But the reason and the will, according to their nature, are not sufficiently directed to Him in so far as He is the object of supernatural happiness.

Second Article

Whether the Theological Virtues Are Distinguished from the Intellectual and Moral Virtues?

We proceed thus to the Second Article: —

Objection 1. It would seem that the theological virtues are not distinguished from moral and intellectual virtues. For the theological virtues, if they be in a human soul, must needs perfect it either as to the intellectual part or as to the appetitive part. Now the virtues which perfect the intellectual part are called intellectual, and the virtues which perfect the ap-

---

5. Cf. William of Auxerre, *Summa Aurea*, III, tr. 2, ch. 2.

petitive part are called moral. Therefore the theological virtues are not distinguished from the moral and intellectual virtues.

Obj. 2. Further, the theological virtues are those which direct us to God. Now among the intellectual virtues there is one which directs us to God, namely, wisdom, which is about divine things, since it considers the highest cause. Therefore the theological virtues are not distinguished from the intellectual virtues.

Obj. 3. Further, Augustine shows how the four cardinal virtues are the *order of love*.[6] Now love is charity, which is a theological virtue. Therefore the moral virtues are not distinct from the theological.

On the contrary, That which is above man's nature is distinguished from that which is according to his nature. But the theological virtues are above man's nature, while the intellectual and moral virtues are proportioned to his nature, as was shown above.[7] Therefore they are distinguished from one another.

I answer that, As was stated above, habits are distinguished specifically from one another according to the formal difference of their objects.[8] Now the object of the theological virtues is God Himself, Who is the last end of all, as surpassing the knowledge of our reason. On the other hand, the object of the intellectual and moral virtues is something comprehensible to human reason. Therefore the theological virtues are distinguished specifically from the moral and intellectual virtues.

Reply Obj. 1. The intellectual and moral virtues perfect man's intellect and appetite according to the power of human nature; the theological virtues, supernaturally.

Reply Obj. 2. The wisdom which the Philosopher reckons as an intellectual virtue considers divine things so far as they are open to the investigation of human reason.[9] Theological virtue, on the other hand, is about these same things so far as they surpass human reason.

Reply Obj. 3. Though charity is love, yet love is not always charity. When, then, it is stated that every virtue is the *order of love,* this can be understood either of love in the general sense, or of the love of charity. If it be understood of love commonly so called, then each virtue is stated to be the order of love in so far as each cardinal virtue requires an ordered affection. Now love is the root and cause of every affection, as was stated

---

6. *De Mor. Eccl.,* I, 15.
7. Q. 58, a. 3.
8. Q. 54, a. 2, ad 1.
9. *Eth.,* VI, 3.

above.[10] If, however, it be understood of the love of charity, it does not mean that every other virtue is charity essentially, but that all other virtues depend on charity in some way, as we shall show further on.[11]

Third Article

Whether Faith, Hope and Charity Are Fittingly Reckoned as Theological Virtues?

We proceed thus to the Third Article: —

Objection 1. It would seem that faith, hope and charity are not fittingly reckoned as three theological virtues. For the theological virtues are in relation to divine happiness just as the inclination of nature is in relation to the connatural end. Now among the virtues directed to the connatural end there is but one natural virtue, viz., the understanding of principles. Therefore there should be but one theological virtue.

Obj. 2. Further, the theological virtues are more perfect than the intellectual and moral virtues. Now faith is not reckoned among the intellectual virtues, but is something less than a virtue, since it is imperfect knowledge. Likewise, hope is not reckoned among the moral virtues, but is something less than a virtue, since it is a passion. Much less therefore should they be reckoned as theological virtues.

Obj. 3. Further, the theological virtues direct man's soul to God. Now man's soul cannot be directed to God save through the intellectual part, in which are intellect and will. Therefore there should be only two theological virtues, one perfecting the intellect, the other, the will.

On the contrary, The Apostle says (*1 Cor.* 13:13): *Now there remain faith, hope, charity, these three.*

I answer that, As was stated above, the theological virtues direct man to supernatural happiness in the same way as by the natural inclination man is directed to his connatural end. Now the latter direction happens in two respects. First, according to the reason or intellect, in so far as it contains the first universal principles which are known to us through the natural light of the intellect, and which are reason's starting-point, both in speculative and in practical matters. Secondly, through the rectitude of the will tending naturally to the good as defined by reason.

But these two fall short of the order of supernatural happiness, accord-

---

10. Q. 27, a. 4; q. 28, a. 6, ad 2; q. 41, a. 2, ad 1.
11. Q. 65, a. 2 and 4; II–II, q. 23, a. 7.

ing to *1 Cor.* 2:9: *The eye hath not seen, nor ear heard, neither hath it entered into the heart of man, what things God hath prepared for them that love Him.* Consequently, in relation to both intellect and will, man needed to receive in addition something supernatural to direct him to a supernatural end. First, as regards the intellect, man receives certain supernatural principles, which are held by means of a divine light; and these are the things which are to be believed, about which is *faith.* — Secondly, the will is directed to this end, both as to the movement of intention, which tends to that end as something attainable, — this pertains to *hope* — and as to a certain spiritual union, whereby the will is, in a way, transformed into that end — and this belongs to *charity.* For the appetite of a thing is naturally moved and tends towards its connatural end and this movement is due to a certain conformity of the thing with its end.

Reply Obj. 1. The intellect requires intelligible species whereby to understand, and consequently there is need of a natural habit in addition to the power. But the very nature of the will suffices for it to be directed naturally to the end, both as to the intention of the end and as to its conformity with the end. But in relation to the things which are above nature, the nature itself of the power is insufficient. Consequently there was need for an additional supernatural habit in both respects.

Reply Obj. 2. Faith and hope imply a certain imperfection, since faith is of things unseen, and hope of things not possessed. Hence to have faith and hope in things that are subject to human power falls short of the nature of virtue. But to have faith and hope in things which are above the ability of human nature surpasses every virtue that is proportioned to man, according to *1 Cor.* 1:25: *The weakness of God is stronger than men.*

Reply Obj. 3. Two things pertain to the appetite, viz., movement to the end, and conformity with the end by means of love. Hence there must needs be two theological virtues in the human appetite, namely, hope and charity.

Fourth Article

Whether Faith Precedes Hope, and Hope Charity?

We proceed thus to the Fourth Article: —

Objection 1. It would seem that the order of the theological virtues is not that faith precedes hope, and hope charity. For the root precedes that which grows from it. Now charity is the root of all virtues, according to

Ephes. 3:17: *Being rooted and founded in charity.* Therefore charity precedes the others.

Obj. 2. Further, Augustine says: *A man cannot love what he does not believe to exist. But if he believes and loves, by doing good works he ends in hoping.*[12] Therefore it seems that faith precedes charity, and charity hope.

Obj. 3. Further, love is the principle of all our affections, as was stated above. Now hope is a kind of affection, since it is a passion, as was stated above.[13] Therefore charity, which is love, precedes hope.

On the contrary, The Apostle enumerates them thus (*1 Cor.* 13:13): *Now there remain faith, hope, charity.*

I answer that, There is a twofold order, namely, that of generation, and that of perfection. According to the order of generation, in which matter precedes form, and the imperfect precedes the perfect, in one and the same subject faith precedes hope, and hope charity, as to their acts; for the habits are infused together. For the movement of the appetite cannot tend to anything, either by hoping or loving, unless that thing be apprehended by the sense or by the intellect. Now it is by faith that the intellect apprehends what it hopes for and loves. Hence, in the order of generation, faith must precede hope and charity. In like manner, a man loves a thing because he apprehends it as his good. Now from the very fact that a man hopes to be able to obtain some good from someone, he looks on the man in whom he hopes as a good of his own. Hence, for the very reason that a man bases his hopes in someone, he proceeds to love him; so that in the order of generation, hope precedes charity as regards their respective acts.

But in the order of perfection, charity precedes faith and hope, because both faith and hope are quickened by charity, and receive from charity their full complement as virtues. For thus charity is the mother and the root of all the virtues, inasmuch as it is the form of them all, as we shall state further on.[14]

This suffices for the Reply to the First Objection.

Reply Obj. 2. Augustine is speaking of that hope by which a man hopes to obtain beatitude through the merits which he has already; and this belongs to hope quickened by, and following, charity. But it is possible for a man, before having charity, to hope through merits not already possessed, but which he hopes to possess.

---

12. *De Doct. Christ.,* I, 37.
13. Q. 23, a. 4.
14. *S. T.,* II–II, q. 23, a. 8.

Reply Obj. 3. As was stated above in treating of the passions, hope has reference to two things.[15] One is its principal object, viz., the good hoped for. With regard to this, love always precedes hope, for a good is never hoped for unless it be desired and loved. — Hope also regards the person from whom a man hopes to be able to obtain some good. With regard to this, hope precedes love at first, though afterwards hope is increased by love. Because, from the fact that a man thinks that he can obtain a good through someone, he begins to love him; and from the fact that he loves him, he then hopes all the more in him.

---

15. Q. 40, a. 7.

60. Whether the Substance of Bread and Wine Remain in the Sacrament after Consecration?
From the *Summa Theologica*
(1266–73)

THOMAS AQUINAS

The third book of Thomas Aquinas's Summa Theologica *contains his treatment of the sacraments. Aquinas (c. 1224–74) never completed it. Some scholars think that his efforts to explain the sacraments strained the "new philosophy" to the breaking point, since its bias for factual detail clashed with the biblical language of worship.*

In this selection from volume III, Aquinas unequivocally affirms the doctrine of transubstantiation, which he defines as replacing the substance (essential being) of bread and wine with the substance of Christ's body and blood. With Aristotle, he argues that the "accidents" of bread and wine remain. (An "accident" is an Aristotelian term denoting the variable attributes of something, which do not affect its substance. For instance, the essential quality of "being human" does not depend on such "accidental traits" as race, creed, gender, etc.) In the celebration

SOURCE: Henry Bettenson, *Documents of the Christian Church* (New York: Oxford University Press, 1963). Used by permission of Oxford University Press.

of the Eucharist, the substance (or essential quality) of the bread and wine are changed into the substance of Christ's body and blood under the "accidents" of bread and wine.

Aquinas tries to explain this change further by asking the logical question, Whose accidents are the visible bread and wine? In his efforts to respond to this question, he suggests the existence of accidents without a substance; the bread and wine are gone, changed into the body and blood of Christ "by the power of God." Although this statement may work as one of faith, it defies every canon of Aristotelian logic. It also demonstrates an enduring theological problem: the requirements of intellectual "systems" sometimes distort the meaning of biblical language. In Aquinas's earlier treatment of the Trinity (see vol. 1:390–94), he is more cautious.

Summa Theologica, iii. Q. lxxv.

Article II. *Whether the substance of bread and wine remain in this sacrament after consecration.*

... *I reply* that it has been held that the substance of bread and wine remain in this sacrament after consecration. But this is an untenable position, for in the first place it destroys the reality of this sacrament, which demands that in the sacrament there should be the true body of Christ, which was not there before consecration. Now a thing cannot be in a place where it was not before except either by change of position, or by the conversion of some other thing into it; as a fire begins to be in a house either because it is carried there or because it is kindled. But it is clear that the body of Christ does not begin to be in the sacrament through change of position.... Therefore it remains that the body of Christ can only come to be in the sacrament by means of the conversion of the substance of bread into his body; and that which is converted into anything does not remain after the conversion.... This position is therefore to be avoided as heretical.

Article III. *Whether the substance of bread or wine is annihilated after the consecration of this sacrament.*

... *I reply* that, since the substance of bread or wine does not remain in the sacrament, some have thought it impossible that their substance should be converted into that of the body or blood of Christ, and therefore have maintained that through the consecration the substance of bread or wine is either resolved into underlying matter [*sc.* the four elements] or annihilated.... But this is impossible, because it is impossible to suppose the manner in which the true body of Christ begins to be in the sacrament, unless by conversion of the substance of bread; and this conversion is ruled out by the supposition of the annihilation of the substance of bread, or its resolution into underlying matter....

Article IV. *Whether bread can be converted into the body of Christ.*

... *I reply* that this conversion is not like natural conversions but is wholly supernatural, effected solely by the power of God.... All conversion which takes place according to the laws of nature is formal.... But God ... can produce not only a formal conversion, that is, the supersession of one form by another in the same subject, but the conversion of the whole being, that is, the conversion of the whole substance of *A* into the whole substance of *B*. And this is done in this sacrament by the power of God, for the whole substance of bread is converted into the whole substance of Christ's body.... Hence this conversion is properly called transubstantiation.

Article V. *Whether in this sacrament the accidents of bread and wine remain after the conversion.*

... *I reply* that it is apparent to sense that after consecration all the accidents of bread and wine remain. And this indeed happens with reason, by divine providence. First, because it is not customary but abhorrent for men to eat man's flesh and to drink man's blood. Therefore Christ's flesh and blood are set before us to be taken under the appearances of those things which are of frequent use, namely bread and wine. Secondly, lest this sacrament should be mocked at by the infidels, if we ate our Lord under his proper appearance. Thirdly, in order that, while we take the Lord's body and blood invisibly, this fact may avail towards the merit of faith....

Ibid. Q. lxxvi.

Article VI. *Whether the body of Christ is in this sacrament as in a place.*

... *I reply* that ... the body of Christ is not in this sacrament according to the proper mode of spatial dimension [*quantitas dimensiva*], but rather according to the mode of substance. Now any body has a position in space according to the mode of spatial dimension, inasmuch as its extension is measured thereby. Hence Christ's body is not in this sacrament as in a place, but in the mode of substance, i.e. in the way in which a substance is contained by dimensions; for the substance of Christ's body takes the place of the substance of bread. Hence, as the substance of bread was not subject to its own dimensions locally, but in the mode of substance, neither is Christ's body. But the substance of Christ's body is not the subject of these dimensions, as was the substance of bread, and therefore the substance of bread as locally there by reason of its dimensions, because its position was fixed by means of its proper dimensions; whereas the substance of Christ's body has its position fixed by means of dimensions not its own, in such a way that, conversely, the proper dimensions of Christ's body have their position fixed by means of substance, and this is contrary to the principle of a body having position. Wherefore Christ's body is in no way locally in this sacrament. . . .

Ibid. Q. lxxvii.

Article I. *Whether the accidents remain without a subject in this sacrament.*

. . . *I reply* that the accidents which are observed by sense to remain after consecration are not in the substance of bread and wine as in a subject, for that does not remain . . . , nor in the substantial form, for that does not remain, and if it did remain, could not be a subject. . . . It is also clear that accidents of this kind are not in the substance of Christ's body and blood as in a subject, for the substance of the human body can in no way be qualified by these accidents; nor is it possible that the body of Christ, being glorious and impassible, should be changed so as to take on itself qualities of this kind. . . . Therefore it remains that the accidents in this sacrament remain without a subject, and this can indeed be brought about by the power of God. For since the effect depends more on the first cause than on the second, God, who is the first cause of substance and accident, is able, through his infinite power, to keep the accident in being, even after the removal of the substance through which it was kept in being, as through its proper cause. . . .

Article II. *Whether in this sacrament the spatial dimension [quantitas dimensiva] of bread or wine is the subject of other accidents.*

We thus proceed to the second article:
1. It might seem that it is not. . . . For the subject of an accident is not an

accident. . . . But spatial dimension is a kind of accident. Therefore it cannot be the subject of other accidents.

• • •

Therefore, *in reply to the first point,* an accident cannot in itself (*per se*) be the subject of another accident, for it has no existence in itself. But, as having existence in another thing, one accident is said to be the subject of another, inasmuch as one accident is received in the subject through the mediation of another; as surface is said to be the subject of colour. Hence, when an accident is divinely given the power to exist in itself, it is also able to be in itself the subject of another accident. . . .

PART IV

Keeping and Renewing the Faith (Church)

The institutional history of the medieval church confirms the political adage that absolute power corrupts. As the medieval hierarchy gained in strength and political influence, Christian piety and spirituality retreated to the monastery. Increasingly, the actions of popes and bishops dismayed committed nuns and monks, scholars and reformers. Many of them were highly critical of the medieval church and its vision of hierarchical unity.

A story is told that Pope Innocent III (reigned 1198–1216), the mightiest of the medieval popes, had a dream in which he saw the figure of a man holding the whole world in his outstretched hands. However, the figure was not the pope; it was Francis of Assisi, a monk who shunned all worldly power to live like Jesus, preaching to the poor and ministering to the oppressed (see vol. 1:429–33).

Medieval monastic communities played important roles in the missionary spread of Christianity into Britain and Germany. Dedicated monks and nuns also retreated from the world and the church when they found it corrupt or lacking moral rigor or spiritual zeal. "Religious orders" protected the faith and fostered spiritual and theological diversity.

In the second century, for instance, Tertullian left the dominant church to join the Montanists, an apocalyptic sect known for its moral rigor. Led by Montanus and two women prophets, Priscilla and Maximilla, the Montanists were deeply committed to gender equality. Later medieval monastic communities became important centers where women could exercise spiritual leadership both within and outside the walls of their cloister.

Western monasticism was initially a male-dominated enterprise. Its founder, Benedict of Nursia (c. 480–550) began monastic life as a hermit by withdrawing from the world, similar to the anchorites in northern Africa. Because he attracted a large following, Benedict established a cloistered community at Monte Cassino in central Italy and wrote a "rule" to govern their common life (see vol. 1:417–22). Benedict's Rule balanced the contemplative life with the practical needs of a self-sustaining community.

Throughout the Middle Ages, many impulses for the renewal of church and society and for the reform of monasticism itself, came from Christian men (and later women) committed to the monastic ideal. In the tenth century, a low point in the life of the church, the Abbey of Cluny, founded in 906 and located in Burgundy, France, launched a monastic reform movement based on the strict observance of Benedict's Rule. Among the best known of the Cluniac reformers were two popes, Leo IX and Gregory VII (see vol. 1:327–32).

Success and power caused the decline of the Cluniac movement by the end of the eleventh century. Its replacement was new efforts to combine Western monasticism with older Eastern practices of individual asceticism. Bruno of Cologne (d. 1101) founded the Carthusian order, and "Christ's Poor," an itinerant group of male and female ascetics, emerged under the leadership of Robert of Arbrissel. Robert eventually established a "double monastery" at Fontevrault (1100), which became the leading convent in northern France.

The most influential order of the twelfth century was the Cistercians of Citeaux (Cistercium), also in Burgundy. Known for their extreme asceticism and rigorous observance of the Benedictine Rule, the Cistercians established almost 700 houses by the end of the thirteenth century. Cistercian communities for women expanded at about the same rate, in spite of official efforts by the order to prohibit or limit their growth.

The best known among the early Cistercian leaders was Bernard of Clairvaux (1090–1153), mystic, preacher, and "hammer of heretics," who was a great religious leader (see vol. 1:423–28). Bernard of Clairvaux was an advisor to popes and bishops, ranging far beyond the walls of the cloister. His life and ministry resembled the Augustinian canons, an order of ordained clergy who were much less concerned with strict observance of monastic contemplation than with an active ministry of preaching, teaching, and service to the sick and poor.

The Cistercians paved the way for what were known as the mendicant, or begging, orders (Franciscans and Dominicans); and for their "heretical opponents" (Cathars and Waldensians). Although many of these reforming orders were divided in their loyalties to Rome, they shared an ideal of apostolic poverty and stressed a practical ministry of preaching and social service. The piety and ethos of the mendicants is evident in the "Exposition of the Lord's Prayer" and the "Rule of St. Francis of Assisi" (1210). Francis (1182—1226) established his order of friars or brothers in 1210. Two years later, his friend and disciple, Clare of Assisi (1194–1253) added a women's branch, now known as the Second Order of St. Francis.

The Franciscans did not always agree on their calling, developing an internal schism between the "spirituals," who strictly observed the simple life of Francis; and the "conventuals" who practiced a more traditional form of Benedictine monasticism. Bonaventure (c. 1217–1274), a speculative theologian in the Augustinian tradition, is often considered the second founder of the Franciscans, because he was able to reconcile these differences (see vol. 1:434–41). His "The Soul's Journey into God" is a classical statement of medieval spirituality.

By the late Middle Ages, a tradition of classical Christian mysticism grew up. A large number of clergy, nuns, monks, and simple lay people led the tradition to move beyond formal observances to more personal, inward-directed experiences of God. Their vision contrasted sharply with the moral and spiritual poverty of the official church.

Meister Eckhart (1260–1328), a Dominican scholar and the foremost preacher of Germany in his day, sought a vision even "beyond the Trinity" (see vol. 1:442–51). Language and imagery reminiscent of the early writings of Augustine fill his sermons. The sermons also explain why medieval mystics in general, and Meister Eckhart in particular, invariably invited charges of heresy. If God can be born within a divine spark of the human soul, if it is possible to comprehend God "without a medium," then we have no need for the sacraments as means of grace and no need for the church as a universal institution of salvation.

To a large extent, the spiritual revival of the late Middle Ages took on the nature of a "women's movement." Many of its leaders came from convents of the great monastic orders or from their "secular" auxiliaries, the so-called tertiary orders. Their leaders gained popular acclaim and considerable influence in the church. Mechthild of Magdeburg (1210–1297) is an early example of medieval spirituality on the continent which has become known as the *Frauenbewegung* (women's movement).

Julian of Norwich, a female English hermit (1342–c. 1416), is another important example of the ways in which women participated in the movement for spiritual renewal in England, Holland, and Germany in the late fourteenth century (see vol. 1:457–73). Julian's "Showings," or revelations, do not stray from medieval orthodoxy except perhaps in her frequent use of the term *mother* to designate both the first and second persons of the Trinity.

In Italy, the leading woman mystic was Catherine of Siena (1347–1380), one of only two women in history to be named a "Doctor of the Church." Catherine played an active role in ending the so-called "Babylonian captivity" of the papacy, whereby the secular rulers kept the popes powerless in a small city in southern France (Avignon, see vol. 1:496).

Finally, an anonymous fourteenth-century mystical treatise entitled "German Theology," was probably written by the "Friends of God." A group of clergy, lay men and lay women, who in the spiritual tradition of the Rhineland sought the mystical union of the believer with Christ, made up the "friends of God" (see vol. 1:474–77). Martin Luther greatly appreciated the "German Theology." He introduced and published the work again in the early sixteenth century.

As the Middle Ages faded, serious Christians sought shelter from the turbulent state of church and society behind the walls of convents and monasteries; others turned inward to seek the life of the spirit; and still others embarked on a more active role to reform the church "in head and members." The need for reform was great, especially to correct the overriding scandal of papal corruption, which created incredible ecclesiastical legislation through the Canon Law.

Small problems were growing out of the feudal system, such as simony, nepotism, unworthy clergy, and monastic greed. But the grand vision of medieval Christendom collapsed with the Great Schism of the papacy (1309–1377). In its final stages three warring popes, each claiming to be the true head of the church, were flinging decrees of excommunication at one another as they placed whole countries under the interdict (denying sacraments) for the sin of supporting one of their rivals.

Searching for a workable solution, many thoughtful Christian leaders remembered how the councils of the early church had established collective authority to guide patriarchs, matriarchs, and popes. A group of theologians at the University of Paris, including Marsiglio of Padua, William of Ockham, Pierre d'Ailly, and John Gerson, took the lead in a movement for church reform. The objective of this new conciliarism was to restore the balance between papal authority and other power centers in medieval society, such as bishops and secular authorities. John Gerson's

(1363–1429) "Tractate on the Unity of the Church" (see vol. 1:478–87) summarizes the conciliar position.

While Gerson and other conciliarists focused on the immediate problem of healing the papal schism, an English reformer named John Wycliffe (also known are Wyclif) (c. 1325–1384), master at Oxford and rector of Lutterworth parish, looked at the papal schism against the broader context of the doctrine of the church (see vol. 1:488–95). Wycliffe asserted that the pope is only the head of the visible church, which contains both saints and sinners. The true church, drawing upon Augustine's theology, consists of those saved by grace who are known only to God. Unworthy clergy—whether priest or pope—place themselves outside the true church and cannot rightly administer the sacraments. Wycliffe's treatise "On the Eucharist," was controversial, but unlike earlier writers who challenged the papacy, Wycliffe died in bed.

The urgent need for reform created its own tension, pitting "ecclesiastical" reformers against "biblical" reformers. The early efforts of the conciliarists to end the papal schism by holding the Council of Pisa (1409) had actually made things worse. The council had deposed two rival popes and elected another, in effect creating three contenders, none of whom showed any inclination to quit. The conciliarists tried again at the Council of Constance (1414–1418), this time with support from the emperor.

The council's focus on unity was so strong that it would not tolerate a whisper of dissent, not even from the dead. With uncommon zeal, this Council of Constance condemned the teachings of John Wycliffe (d. 1384), whose followers (the Lollards) were being persecuted in England under a 1401 royal decree entitled "De haeretico comburendo" (On the need to burn heretics). To make its point, the council ordered Wycliffe's remains exhumed from the Lutterworth cemetery and burned at the stake. It elected Martin V (d. 1331) to the papacy, a strong and morally upright leader, who was able to restore the lost power and prestige of the papacy. Unfortunately the council literally sacrificed legitimate reformers on the altar of doctrinal and political uniformity.

John Huss (also known as Hus) (c. 1372–1415), a Bohemian reformer who was initially guaranteed safe passage to the council, was tried and executed for heresy (see vol. 1:500–509). His "Treatise on the Church" (*De Ecclesia*) shows the influence of Wycliffe's "biblical" theology on the Bohemian reformers. One official statement of the council, the decree "Sacrosancta," is the statement by which the council declared its own authority (see vol. 1:512).

Another decree condemned forty-three articles of Wycliffe's teachings. Contemporary eyewitness accounts of the trial and execution of Huss and his friend Jerome of Prague (c. 1370–1416) tell of growing intolerance even among the reformers.

In spite of these political and theological controversies, life in the church continued. People still turned to the church to bless their lives from birth to death, to celebrate the cycle of seasons and to keep hope alive — and the language of worship provided a "tie that binds our hearts in Christian love."

Monasteries kept the faith, providing scholars and artists to enrich liturgical practice through hymns and prayers. Peter Abelard (d. 1142), scholar and poet, wrote a "Hymn for Saturday Vespers" as one of a group of hymns for use during the daily prayers in his monastery. One of the best loved hymns, "Jesus the Very Thought of Thee," dates from the twelfth century and is attributed to Bernard of Clairvaux (see vol. 1:522–24). Hildegard of Bingen (1098–1179), a Rhenish abbess and mystic, wrote a "Song of the Virtues" (*Ordo virtutum*, a "morality play" within her larger work, the *Scivias* ("Know the Way of the Lord") (see vol. 1:525–35). Another familiar hymn, "All creatures of our God and King," is an adaptation of Francis of Assisi's "Canticle of the Sun" (1225) (see vol. 1:536–38).

Medieval influences are rooted in the stone and glass of the most humble Romanesque village church to the Gothic splendors of great cathedrals. Contemporary worship continues to draw upon this medieval musical heritage. For example, the familiar Advent carol, "O come, O come, Emmanuel" (*Veni Emmanuel*), is an adaptation of a Latin plainsong dating from the twelfth century.

The Latin Mass has influenced all Protestant worship greatly. Even the most ardent advocates of "free prayer" find that the patterns of praise, confession, supplication, and commitment draw on a common heritage. Doctrine and celebration are one. So it is that sharing bread and cup are a celebration of unity. That sharing calls Christians to the center and away from diversity. The great prayer of the Eucharist (or the "Canon of the Mass") is a theological and liturgical act, which celebrates unity (see vol. 1:539–47). It teaches, confesses, and celebrates the gift of God in Christ.

The struggle to sustain the church has encompassed seasons of grace and times of utter failure. Yet contemporary Christians dare not deny this legacy. Out of the struggles of monks and mystics and through the cycles of worship, we garner insights to renew and sustain the church of the twenty-first century.

Moral and Spiritual Renewal

61. The Twelve Degrees of Humility
From the *Rule of St. Benedict*
(early 6th century)

BENEDICT

The Christian church always depicts its martyrs and ascetics — men and women who turn away from the world and try to imitate Christ with saintly lives — "waiting for the end in cheerfulness and hope." The earliest Christian ascetics were hermits living in the Syrian or Egyptian desert. They regarded time in prison (or in the desert) as a chance to retire from the world. It was the place where all doors were open to the spirit. The first monastic communities were probably "households" of virgins (female ascetics) who lived apart, serving local congregations.

SOURCE: Owen Chadwick, ed., *Western Asceticism*, vol. 12 of *Library of Christian Classics* (Philadelphia: Westminster Press, 1958). Used by permission of Westminster John Knox Press.

By the fourth century, when Christianity entered the cultural mainstream, many "puritan" Christians became disenchanted with the laxity of the growing established and urban church that had "jettisoned its puritans." They formed conventicles, "little primitive churches," at the periphery of the institutional church. In the sixth century, a monk named Benedict established a monastery on Monte Cassino in a remote part of Italy. His written discipline, now the "Rule of St. Benedict," shaped Western monasticism for centuries to come.

The first article of the "Rule" states that monks ought to "dwell in convents under the direction of a rule and an abbot." Although the "Rule of St. Benedict" is rigorous, it is not like Egyptian monasticism, which required mortification of the flesh. The "Rule" regulates a self-contained community whose primary purpose is contemplative; that is, to praise God and to practice evangelical counsels of poverty, chastity, and obedience.

Many of the rubrics deal with the practical life of the monks, regulating their hours of prayer, sleep and work, the duties of office, the care of the sick, etc. Some deal with loftier things like the practice of silence or of obedience. The "Rule" is quite specific about the "twelve degrees of humility," required of all monks.

Brethren, the Scripture asserts that "everyone that exalteth himself shall be humbled, and he that humbleth himself shall be exalted." It shows us thereby that all exaltation is in some measure the pride which the prophet tells us he took care to shun: "O Lord, my heart is not exalted, nor mine eyes lifted up: I have not aspired to great things, nor wonders above myself." And his reason for it is: because (says he): "If I had not thought humbly of myself but had exalted my soul, thou wouldst have driven away my soul like an infant weaned from the breast of its mother."[1]

Therefore, brethren, if we want to attain true humility, and come quickly to the top of that heavenly ascent to which we can only mount by lowliness in this present life, we must ascend by good works, and erect the mystical ladder of Jacob, where angels ascending and descending appeared to him. That ascent and descent means that we go downward when we exalt ourselves, and rise when we are humbled. The ladder

---

1. Luke 14:11; Ps. 131:1–2.

represents our life in this world, which our Lord erects to heaven when our heart is humbled. And the sides of the ladder represent our soul and body, sides between which God has placed several rungs of humility and discipline, whereby we are to ascend if we would answer his call.

The first degree, then, of humility is, to have the fear of God ever before our eyes: never to forget what is his due, and always to remember his commands: to revolve in the mind how hell burns those who have contemned God, and how God has prepared eternal life for them that fear him: to preserve ourselves from the sins and vices of thought, of the tongue, the eyes, hands, feet, self-will and fleshly desires. Man ought to think that God always looks down from heaven upon him, and that all he does lies open to his sight, is daily told him by the angels. The prophet shows this truth, when he describes God as present in our thoughts, "searching the heart and reins"; and, "Our Lord knows the thoughts of men"; and again, "Thou hast understood my thoughts a great way off": and, "The thought of man shall confess to thee." That he may ever watch the perverseness of his thoughts, let the right-minded brother continually repeat in the language of his heart: "Then I shall be without blemish before him, if I keep myself from mine iniquity."[2]

As for our own will, we are forbidden to pursue it by these words of the Scripture: "Turn away from thine own will": and we are required to ask of God in prayer, that his will may be done in us. We have reason to be convinced that we ought not to be guided by our own will, when we take account of what the Scripture tells us: "There are ways which to men appear to be right, whose endings nevertheless plunge us into the very depth of hell." And again, when we reflect fearfully upon the character given to the negligent: "They are corrupt and become abominable in their own pleasures."

As regards our sensual desires, we must remember that God is ever present; as the prophet says to the Lord: "All my desire lies open before thee."[3] So unlawful desires are to be carefully avoided, because death lurks behind the door at the very entrance to pleasure: whence the Scripture forbids us to "pursue our lusts."[4]

If then the eyes of the Lord observe both the good and the wicked, and God looks down from heaven upon the sons of men, to see if there be any

---

2. Ps. 7:9; 94:11 (*Regula Magistri* and a few MSS. add the second half of the versicle); 139:1; 76:10; 18:23.

3. Ecclesiasticus 18:30; Prov. 16:25; Ps. 14:1; 38:9.

4. Ecclesiasticus 18:30.

that understand or seek after God; and again, if night and day our guardian angels give an account of what we do to the Lord; we must, every moment, be on our guard, lest God, at any time, should surprise us, as the Psalmist terms it, "leaning towards evil and rendered unprofitable"; and sparing us in this life (because he is good and waits for our becoming better) should reproach us in the next: "These things didst thou do, and I kept silence."[5]

The second degree of humility is, if anyone, not wedded to his own will, finds no pleasure in the compassing of his desires; but fulfils with his practice the word of our Lord: "I came not to do mine own will, but the will of him that sent me." The Scripture also says: "Pleasure hath its penalty, but need winneth a crown."[6]

The third degree of humility is, when anyone submits himself with obedience to his superior for the sake of the love of God, after the example of the Lord, of whom the apostle says: "He was made obedient even unto death."

The fourth degree of humility is, when anyone, in the practice of obedience, meets with hardships, contradictions, or affronts, and yet bears them all with a quiet conscience and with patience, and continues to persevere. The Scripture says: "He who perseveres to the end, the same shall be saved," and again: "Let your heart be strengthened, and wait for our Lord." And to show that the faithful servant ought to suffer every trial for God, the Scripture speaks in the person of those that suffer: "For thy sake we are killed all the day long: we are accounted as sheep for the slaughter." And afterwards, in full assurance of their reward, they say with happiness, "But in all these things we are conquerors through him that loved us." In another place the Scripture tells us: "Thou, O God, hast proved us: thou has tried us with fire, as silver is tried. Thou hast led us into the snare, and loaded us with afflictions." And to show that we ought to live under a superior, it goes on, "Thou hast set men over our heads."[7]

So these sufferers live up to the command of God, bearing injuries and adversity with patience. But more: Struck on one cheek they offer the other. They give away their coat to him that takes away their cloak. Forced to walk one mile, they go two. They bear with false brethren, like Paul the apostle. They bless them that curse them.

The fifth degree of humility is, humbly to confess to the abbot every

---

5. Prov. 15:3; Ps. 14:3; 53:2–3; 50:21.
6. John 6:38. The second text is not from the Bible but from (e.g.) *Acta Martyrum*.
7. Matt. 10:22; Ps. 27:14; Rom. 8:36–7; Ps. 66:10–12.

unlawful thought as it arises in the heart, and the hidden sins we have committed. The Scripture advises this, saying: "Reveal your way to God and hope in him": and again: "Confess to God because he is good: for his mercy endureth for ever."[8] And in the prophet: "I have made known my sin to thee, and have not covered my iniquities. I have said, I will declare to God my own iniquities against myself: and thou hast forgiven the wickedness of my heart."[9]

The sixth degree of humility is, if a monk be content with anything though never so vile and contemptible; and to think himself inadequate, and unworthy to succeed in whatever he is commanded to do; saying with the prophet: "I was brought to nothing and I knew nothing. I am become like a brute beast before thee, yet I am always with thee."[10]

The seventh degree of humility is, when one does not merely call oneself the least and most abject of all mankind, but believes it, with sincerity of heart: humbling oneself and saying with the prophet: "I am a worm and no man: a scorn of men, and the outcast of the people." "I have been exalted, humbled, and confounded." And again: "It is good for me that thou hast humbled me, that I may learn to keep thy commandments."[11]

The eighth degree of humility is, when a monk does nothing but what is countenanced by the constitutions of the monastery, or the example of the elders.

The ninth degree of humility is, when a monk controls his tongue and keeps silence till a question be asked. For the Scripture teaches that "in much talk you will not avoid sinning"; and "the talkative man shall live out his life haphazardly."[12]

The tenth degree of humility is, not easily to lay hold on occasions of laughing. For it is written: "He who laughs loud is a fool."[13]

The eleventh degree of humility is, when a monk discourses with moderation and composure, mixing humility with gravity; speaking few words, but home, and to the purpose; not raising the voice. "The wise man is known because he speaks little."[14]

---

8. Ps. 37:5; 106:1.
9. Ps. 32:5.
10. Ps. 73:21–2.
11. Ps. 22:6; 88:15; 119:71.
12. Prov. 10:19; Ps. 140:11.
13. Ecclesiasticus 21:20.
14. From the *Sentences of Sixtus,* a book of proverbs and moral sayings.

The twelfth degree of humility is, when the monk's inward humility appears outwardly in his comportment. And wherever he be, in the divine office, in the oratory, in the monastery, in the garden, on a journey, in the fields — wherever he is sitting, walking or standing, he is to look down with bowed head conscious of his guilt, imagining himself ready to be called to give account at the dread judgement: repeating in his heart what the publican in the Gospel said with eyes downcast: "Lord, I am not worthy, sinner that I am, to lift up my eyes to heaven"; and with the prophet "I am bowed down and humbled on every side."[15]

After he has climbed all these degrees of humility, the monk will quickly arrive at the top, the charity that is perfect and casts out all fear. And then, the virtues which first he practised with anxiety, shall begin to be easy for him, almost natural, being grown habitual. He will no more be afraid of hell, but will advance by the love of Christ, by good habits, and by taking pleasure in goodness. Our Lord, by the Holy Spirit, will deign to show this in the servant who has been cleansed from sin.

---

15. Luke 18:13; Ps. 119:107.

62. The Four Degrees of Love
From *On the Love of God*
(early 12th century)

BERNARD OF CLAIRVAUX

Bernard of Clairvaux (1090–1153), who was more powerful than any pope in the twelfth century, has been called the greatest religious figure of his age. His support assured the election of popes Innocent II and Eugenius III. His fiery sermons calling Christians to go on the ill-fated second crusade were so effective that the male population of whole villages left home to do battle with the infidels. He secured papal approval for the Templars, the crusading order of Christian knights, whom he encouraged to wage holy war for the glory of Christ.

Bernard was a traditionalist, the scourge of heretics, and one of the greatest preachers of his time. Yet for all his public visibility, the secret of Bernard of Clairvaux' authority was the simplicity of his life. He was a spiritual reformer and a Cistercian monk.

Bernard entered the monastery of Citeaux in Burgundy, France, in 1113 with four of his brothers and a group of friends. The new order of Cistercians (Latin for "Citeauxian") had established a reputation for

SOURCE: Ray C. Petry, ed., *Late Medieval Mysticism*, vol. 13 of *Library of Christian Classics* (Philadelphia: Westminster Press, 1957). Used by permission of Westminster John Knox Press.

spiritual zeal and strict observance of the Benedictine Rule. Two years later, Bernard was sent to Clairvaux, also in Burgundy, to establish one of the first branches of the order. By 1153, the year of his death, there were 339 Cistercian monasteries.

Under Bernard's leadership, Clairvaux became a center of moral reform and spiritual renewal for the whole church. In his own life, Bernard blended rigorous monastic discipline with mystical spirituality. His writings include eighty-six sermons on the Song of Solomon and a treatise On Loving God. *His spiritual quest seeks more than knowledge; it seeks to experience the love of Christ.*

Chapter Eight

The First Degree of Love, Which Is the Love of Self for Self

Love is a natural affection. . . . And, because love is natural, it would indeed be just for nature to give her service first to Him from whom she takes her being; whence comes, of course, the first and great commandment, "Thou shalt love the Lord thy God."[1] For, though our nature's law directs us thus to love God first of all, our weakness and infirmity require the binding force of the commandment too; because what really takes the first place in our lives is love for self. We have indeed no feeling that is not for self. "First that which is natural and afterward that which is spiritual" — so says Paul.[2] Who ever hated his own flesh? But if this love, according to its wont, run to excess and like a flooded river burst its banks and overflow the plain, it finds its way blocked then by *this* commandment, "Thou shalt love thy neighbor as thyself."[3] Justly should he who shares our nature share our love, and all the more since love is part of the endowment our nature has from God. A man who finds it burdensome to serve his brother's interests and pleasures should discipline his own, if he would keep from sin. Let him show all consideration to himself, indeed, provided only he does not forget to show the same to others! This is the curb imposed on thee, O man, by thine own nature's law and discipline, lest thou go after thine own lusts to ruin and put the gifts, that God has

---

1. Matt. 22:37.
2. 1 Cor. 15:46.
3. Matt. 22:39.

given thee, at the disposal of thine enemy — that is, of wanton, unrestrained desire. It is but just and honest to give of what thou hast to thine own fellow, rather than to a foe. And if you follow the wise man's advice and curb your appetites, and if, content with food and raiment as the apostle bids, you shrink not for a while to keep your love detached, abstaining from those "fleshly lusts that war against the soul," you will, I think, have little trouble in bestowing on your fellow men what you have taken away from your soul's enemy. A love both just and balanced will be yours, if you deny not to your brother's need what you refuse to your own base desires. The love of God extended thus becomes benevolence.

But what if, by giving to our neighbor, we find ourselves in want? What should we do save go with confidence to God, "who giveth to all men liberally and upbraideth not," and openeth his hand and all things living are filled with plenteousness? Without a doubt he who gives most men more than what they need will not deny us bare necessities. Has he not told us, "Seek ye first the Kingdom of God and his righteousness, and all these things shall be added unto you"?[4] He has bound himself to give all things needful to him who disciplines himself and loves his neighbor; and you do seek his Kingdom and strive against the tyrant of sin, if you refuse to let sin reign in your mortal body and take the yoke of purity and self-control upon yourself instead. It is moreover (as I said before) but justice that we should share the blessings of this life with other men.

But for our love of others to be wholly right, God must be at its root. No one can love his neighbor perfectly, unless it is *in God* he holds him dear. And nobody can love his fellow men in God who loves not God Himself. We must begin by loving God; and then we shall be able, *in* him, to love our neighbor too. God, author of all good, is author of our love in this way too, in that, creator of our nature as he is, he makes himself to its keeper also; for our nature is so constituted that it needs to be sustained, and he who made us is the one who meets that need. We depend on him for our subsistence, then, no less than for the fact that we exist. That we may grasp this fact and not (which God forbid!) take credit to ourselves for God's good gifts, his fathomless and loving wisdom has ordained we should be subjected to tribulations. We fail in these; and God comes to our aid. He sets us free; and we, as is most meet, give glory to his name. "Call upon me in the time of trouble; so will I hear thee and thou shalt praise me"[5] — that is what he says. In this way man, by nature animal and carnal,

---

4. Matt. 6:33; Luke 12:31.
5. Ps. 49 (50):15.

loving himself alone, begins to learn it is to his own profit to love God, because in him alone (as he has often proved) can he do all things which it profits him to do; he is quite powerless apart from him.

Chapter Nine

The Second Degree of Love, Which Is the Love of God for What He Gives. The Third, Which Is the Love of God for What He Is

Man begins by loving God, not for God's sake but for his own. It is, however, something that he should know his limitations and that he cannot do without God's help. And it is something too, if he knows what he can do by himself and what with God's help only, and if he can keep himself from giving God offense, who keeps him from all harm. But and if troubles come one after another, and he betake himself to God and find deliverance every time, though his heart be of stone within a breast of iron, he surely must melt down in gratitude at last. The love of God *for what God gives* will thus begin to dawn.

Recurrent troubles throw us back on God, and each occasion proves how kind he is. And this experience of his sweetness provides an urge to the pure love of God, more powerful than the impetus our trouble gave before. We say with the Samaritans, told by the woman that the Lord was there, "Now we believe, not because of thy saying, for we have heard him for ourselves and know that this is indeed the Saviour of the world."[6] We say this to our natural self, our carnal appetites. "It is not because of your demands," we tell them, "that we now love God, but because we have tasted for ourselves and know how gracious the Lord is." In this way our needs of the flesh become a kind of language, proclaiming joyfully the benefits of which they have taught us the value; and, once this has been learned, we find no difficulty in obeying the command to love our neighbor. The man who loves like this loves truly; and in so doing he loves the things of God. He loves purely and without self-interest, and so will readily obey God's pure command, purifying his heart in love's obedience, as Peter says. He loves justly, and takes this just commandment to his heart. This love — true, pure, and just — he does not offer upon terms, and so it is acceptable with God. It is pure love, for it is shown in deed and truth, not merely in vain words. It is just love, because he freely gives who

---

6. John 4:42.

freely has received. Love of the quality of God's own love is this, seeking no more its own but those things which are Christ's, even as he sought ours — or rather *us,* and never sought his own. "O give thanks unto the Lord, for he is gracious" — that is what this love says, gracious and good, not only to his lovers but in his very self. It is the love of God *for* God, not merely for oneself. But he of whom the psalmist says, "He will give thanks to Thee when Thou hast done him kindness,"[7] loves God as yet but in the second degree. The third degree is that in which the love of God is purely for Himself.

Chapter Ten

The Fourth Degree of Love, Which Is the Love Even of Self Only for God's Sake[8]

Happy is he who can attain the fourth degree of love, and love *himself* only for God's sake! "Thy righteousness, O God, is as the mountains of God." A mountain is this fourth degree of love, God's own "high hill," a mountain strong, fertile, and rich. Who shall go up into this mountain of the Lord? "O that I had wings as a dove, that I might flee away and be at rest," in that dear place of peace! Woe is me that my sojourn here must be so long! When will this flesh and blood, this mortal clay, this earthly frame, arrive up there? When shall I know this kind of love, when will my soul, inebriated by his love, forget herself, yea, know herself but as a broken vessel, and go clean out to God and cleave to him, her spirit one with his?[9] When shall I make the psalmist's words my own, "My flesh and my heart faileth, but God is the strength of my life and my portion forever"?[10] Happy is he, and holy too, to whom it has been given, here in this mortal life rarely or even once, for one brief moment only, to taste this kind of love! It is no merely human joy to lose oneself like this, so to be emptied of oneself as though one almost ceased to be at all; it is the bliss of heaven. And yet, if some poor mortal do attain to swift and sudden rapture such as this, forthwith this present evil world must drag him back, the daily ills of life must harass him, the body of this death will weigh him down, his fleshly needs cry out for satisfaction, the weakness of his fallen

---

7. Ps. 48:19 (49:18).
8. On Williams' summation of the four grades see *De diligendo Deo.*
9. Cf. Augustine, *De quantitate animae.*
10. Ps. 72 (73):26.

nature fails. Most violent of all, his brother's need calls on him to return. Alas, he has no choice but to come back, back to himself and to his own affairs; and in his grief he cries, "O Lord, I am oppressed, undertake for me," or yet again, "O wretched man that I am, who shall deliver me from the body of this death?"[11]

We read in Scripture that God has made all things for himself. His creatures must aim, therefore, at conforming themselves perfectly to their creator and living according to his will. So we must fix our love on him, bit by bit aligning our own will with his, who made all for himself, not wanting either ourselves or anything else to be or to have been, save as it pleases him, making his will alone, and not our pleasure, our object of desire. The sating of our own requirements, the happiness that *we* choose for ourselves, will never bring us to the joy that comes from finding his will done in and concerning us, even as every day we ask in prayer, "Thy will be done, in earth as it is in heaven."[12] O chaste and holy love, affection sweet and lovely! O pure and clean intention of the will, the purer in that now at last it is divested of self-will, the lovelier and the sweeter since its perceptions at last are all divine! To become thus is to be deified.[13] As a small drop of water, mingled in much wine, takes on its taste and color so completely that it appears no longer to exist apart from it; as molten, white-hot iron is so like the fire, it seems to have renounced its natural form; as air when flooded with the sun's pure light is so transformed as to appear not lit so much as very light itself; so, with the saints, their human love will then ineffably be melted out of them and all poured over, so to speak, into the will of God. It must be so. How otherwise could God be "all in all," if anything of man remained in man? And yet our human substance will remain: we shall still be ourselves, but in another form, another glory and another power. When will that be? Who will be there to see? Who will possess it? "When shall I come to appear before the presence of God?" O Lord my God, "my heart hath talked of thee, my face hath sought thee: thy face, Lord, will I seek." Shall *I* see, thinkest thou, thy holy house?[14]

---

11. Cf. Isa. 38:14 and Rom. 7:24.
12. Matt. 6:10.
13. *Sic affici, deificari est.*
14. Ps. 41:3 (42:2); 26 (27):8; 26 (27):4; etc.

63. Exposition of the Lord's Prayer and Pray and Work

From *Exposition of the Lord's Prayer* and the *Rule of St. Francis* (1209–23)

FRANCIS OF ASSISI

By the turn of the thirteenth century, the staggering wealth of the church and an emerging money economy prompted a new kind of piety based on the renunciation of all forms of property. The followers of Peter Valdes (previously known incorrectly as Waldo) (d. 1215), a former merchant of Lyon, tried to live like the first Christians in apostolic poverty. Although the Waldensians respected the traditional priestly office, they felt that lay men and women had a divine calling to preach the gospel to the poor. They tried to keep themselves pure by refusing to receive the sacraments from unworthy priests, which led to their excommunication and severe persecution (a position similar to that of the earlier Donatists, see vol. 1:201–9). A small remnant of the Waldensians survived in the Italian Alps, and their descendants later became part of the Protestant Reformation.

It was actually the Dominicans and Franciscans, the great mendicant (itinerant begging, rather than cloistered) orders, that developed more acceptable popular ideals of evangelical poverty. Giovanni Bernadone, known as Francis of Assisi (1182–1226), was the son of a wealthy Italian merchant and his French wife. Giovanni spent his early adult years trying to find himself and spending his family's money. About 1207, after a series of profound spiritual experiences, he resolved to follow Jesus' counsel to the rich young ruler (Matt. 19:21) and to give all that he had to the poor. He renounced his inheritance and "married Lady Poverty."

Almost immediately, Francis of Assisi attracted large numbers of like-minded disciples. In 1209 he wrote up a "Rule" to guide their life, and a year later he applied to Rome for official recognition of his order. A friend and disciple, Clare of Assisi (1194–1253), established a women's branch in 1212 with identical principles (the Poor Clares, later known as the Second Order of St. Francis).

Francis of Assisi and his followers, the "Minor (more humble) Brothers" and the "Poor Clares," took vows of poverty. They took the vows, not as a discipline but as a mark of liberation and solidarity with the poor. They did not withdraw from the world but went out to practice the love of Christ, to care for the sick and needy, to proclaim the goodness of God's creation, and to sing the joy of salvation as Christian troubadours.

A story tells of a young Franciscan brother who asked Francis if it were all right to have a Psalter. Francis replied, "When you have a Psalter, you'll want a breviary, and when you have a breviary, you'll want to climb the pulpit like a prelate."

The writings of Francis of Assisi are devotional rather than theological; they are from the heart rather than the intellect. His words about prayer and work from his "Rule" and his brief exposition of the Lord's Prayer are important expressions of faith's struggle in difficult times.

Exposition of the Lord's Prayer

Our Father, our most blessed, most holy Creator, our Saviour and our Comforter; who art in heaven, in the angels, in the saints, enlightening them to know thee; because thou, O Lord, art the light that inflames them by thy divine love; because thou, O Lord, art the love which is in them

---

SOURCE: Ray C. Petry, ed., *Late Medieval Mysticism*, vol. 13 of *Library of Christian Classics* (Philadelphia: Westminster Press, 1957). Used by permission of Westminster John Knox Press.

and fills them to render them blessed; because thou, O Lord, art the highest good, and the eternal good, from which all good things come, and without which there is no good anywhere.

Hallowed be thy name: let the knowledge of thee become apparent to us, so that we may know how plentiful are thy blessings, how long thy promises, how lofty thy majesty, how profound thy judgments.

Thy Kingdom come; that thou shouldst reign within us with thy grace and let us come to thy Kingdom, where we will see thee face to face, and have perfect love, blessed company, and sempiternal joy.

Thy will be done on earth as it is in heaven; so that we may love thee with all our heart, thinking ever of thee; with all our soul, ever desiring thee; with all our mind, directing all our intentions to thee, and seeking thy honor in all things; and with all our strength, employing all the power of our spirit and all the senses of our body in the service of thy love, and in naught else: and that we may also love our neighbors as ourselves, drawing all men, as far as it is in our power, toward thy love, rejoicing in the good things of others and grieving at their ills as at our own, and never giving offense to anyone.

Give us this day our daily bread, that is thy beloved Son, our Lord Jesus Christ, in memory of the love he bore us, and of what he said, did and suffered for us.

And forgive us our trespasses as we forgive those who trespass against us; and what we do not forgive entirely, make thou, O Lord, that we should forgive, so that for thy sake we should sincerely love our enemies, and intercede devoutly for them with thee, and never render evil for evil, and strive with thy help to be of assistance to all men.

And lead us not into temptation, hidden or manifest, sudden or protracted.

And deliver us from evil, past, present, and future.

So be it, with good will and without hope of reward.

Pray and Work

FROM THE *Rule of St. Francis*

3. The clerical brothers shall perform the divine service according to the order of the holy Roman Church; excepting the psalter, of which they

SOURCE: Henry Bettenson, *Documents of the Christian Church* (New York: Oxford University Press, 1963). Used by permission of Oxford University Press.

may have extracts. But the lay brothers shall say twenty-four Paternosters at matins, five at lauds, seven each at Prime, Terce, Sext and None, twelve at Vespers, seven at the Completorium; and they shall pray for the dead. And they shall fast from the feast of All Saints to the Nativity of the Lord; but as to the holy season of Lent, which begins after the Epiphany of the Lord and continues forty days, a season the Lord consecrated by his holy fast—those who fast during this time shall be blessed of the Lord, and those who do not wish to fast shall not be bound to do so; but otherwise they shall fast until the Resurrection of the Lord. At other times the brothers shall not be bound to fast save on the sixth day (Friday); but when there is a compelling reason the brothers shall not be bound to observe a physical fast. But I advise, warn and exhort my brothers in the Lord Jesus Christ, that, when they go into the world, they shall not quarrel, nor contend with words, nor judge others. But let them be gentle, peaceable, modest, merciful and humble, with honourable conversation towards all, as is fitting. They ought not to ride, save when necessity or infirmity clearly compels them so to do. Into whatsoever house they enter let them first say, "Peace be to this house." And according to the holy Gospel it is lawful for them to partake of all dishes placed before them.

4. I strictly command all the brothers never to receive coin or money either directly or through an intermediary. The ministers and guardians alone shall make provision, through spiritual friends, for the needs of the infirm and for other brothers who need clothing, according to the locality, season or cold climate, at their discretion. . . .

5. Those brothers, to whom God has given the ability to work, shall work faithfully and devotedly and in such a way that, avoiding idleness, the enemy of the soul, they do not quench the spirit of holy prayer and devotion, to which other and temporal activities should be subordinate. As the wages of their labour they may receive corporal necessities for themselves and their brothers but not coin nor money, and this with humility, as is fitting for servants of God, and followers of holy poverty.

6. The brothers shall possess nothing, neither a house, nor a place, nor anything. But, as pilgrims and strangers in this world, serving God in poverty and humility, they shall confidently seek alms, and not be ashamed, for the Lord made Himself poor in this world for us. This is the highest degree of that sublime poverty, which has made you, my dearly beloved brethren, heirs and kings of the Kingdom of Heaven; which has made you poor in goods but exalted in virtues. Let this be "your portion," which leads you to "the land of the living" [Ps. cxlii. 5]. If you cleave wholly to this, beloved, you will wish to have for ever in Heaven nothing

save the name of Our Lord Jesus Christ. Wherever the brethren are, and shall meet together, they shall shew themselves as members of one family; each shall with confidence unfold his needs to his brother. A mother loves and cherishes her son in the flesh; how much more eagerly should a man love and cherish his brother in the Spirit? And if any of them fall sick the other brothers are bound to minister to him as they themselves would wish to be ministered to.

7. But if any of the brethren shall commit mortal sin at the prompting of the adversary: in the case of those sins concerning which it has been laid down that recourse must be had to the provincial ministers, the aforesaid brethren must have recourse to them without delay. Those ministers, if they are priests, shall with mercy enjoin penance: if they are not priests they shall cause it to be enjoined through others, who are priests of the order, as it seems to them most expedient in the sight of God. They must beware lest they become angry and disturbed on account of the sin of any brother; for anger and indignation hinder love in ourselves and others.

64. On Spiritual and Mystical Ecstasy
From *The Soul's Journey into God*
(c. 1259)

BONAVENTURE

In 1243, Giovanni di Fidanza, a native of Tuscany and a student in Paris, joined the Franciscan order and took the new name of Bonaventure. He became a devoted disciple of the renowned Franciscan theologian, Alexander of Hales (d. 1245), at the University of Paris. Alexander was lavish in praising his student's character and intellect. It seemed, he said, that "Adam had never sinned in him [Bonaventure]." From an Augustinian theological standpoint, this concession was amazing. Bonaventure eventually succeeded and surpassed his mentor as an important Franciscan theologian in Paris. In 1257 Bonaventure was chosen Minister General of the Franciscan Order, an office he held until his death seventeen years later.

From the very beginning, the Franciscans were almost too successful. In 1221, five years before Francis of Assisi died, their general chapter (assembly) drew between 3000 and 5000 friars from all over Latin Europe and North Africa. Factions developed within the order, causing a

---

SOURCE: Bonaventure, *Bonaventure: The Soul's Journey into God*, trans. and introduced by Ewert Cousins, Classics of Western Spirituality Series (New York: Paulist Press, 1978). © 1978 by the Missionary Society of St. Paul the Apostle in the State of New York. Used by permission of Paulist Press.

rift between the "spirituals" and the "conventuals." The "spirituals" clung to the simple ways of Francis of Assisi, waiting for a new "age of the Spirit," which they expected to come in their lifetime. The "conventuals," saw the need for "stability." In order to manage the expansion of the order they were willing to relax the ideal of poverty.

Bonaventure was an extraordinary leader, later known as the second founder of the Franciscan order. His personal piety was beyond reproach, but he did not agree with Francis of Assisi who told the early friars to stay away from theology. Bonaventure was a speculative theologian in the Augustinian tradition with intellectual strength equal to his Dominican counterpart, Thomas Aquinas. In his writings he developed a solid Franciscan theological tradition, while preserving the ideal of spontaneous spirituality and selfless service.

Bonaventure wrote extensively, including a definitive biography of Francis of Assisi. His The Soul's Journey into God *has been called the classical text of medieval spirituality. It describes the soul's spiritual progress toward God, culminating in the vision of the Trinity.*

---

1. We have, therefore, passed through
these six considerations.
They are like
the six steps of the true Solomon's throne,
by which we arrive
at peace,
where the true man of peace
rests in a peaceful mind
as in the interior Jerusalem.

They are also like
the six wings of the Seraph[1]
by which the mind of the true contemplative
can be borne aloft,
filled with the illumination of heavenly wisdom.

---

1. Although the critical text has "Cherub," we have read "Seraph," since Bonaventure is clearly referring to the six-winged Seraph of Francis's vision (cf. prologue, 2–3), which serves as the symbolic matrix of the entire treatise.

They are also like the first six days,
in which the mind has been trained so that it may reach
the sabbath of rest.

After our mind has beheld God
outside itself
through his vestiges and in his vestiges,
within itself
through his image and in his image,
and above itself
through the similitude of the divine Light shining above us
and in the Light itself,
insofar as this is possible in our state as wayfarers
and through the exercise of our mind,
when finally in the sixth stage
our mind reaches that point
where it contemplates
in the First and Supreme Principle
and in the *mediator of God and men*,[2]
Jesus Christ,
those things whose likenesses can in no way be found
in creatures
and which surpass all penetration
by the human intellect,
it now remains for our mind,
by contemplating these things,
to transcend and pass over not only this sense world
but even itself.
In this passing over,
Christ is the *way and the door*;[3]
Christ is the ladder and the vehicle,
like the Mercy Seat placed above the ark of God[4]
and the *mystery hidden from eternity.*[5]

2. Whoever turns his face fully to the Mercy Seat
and with faith, hope and love,

---

2. 1 Tim. 2:5.
3. Cf. John 14:6, 10:7.
4. Cf. Exod. 25:21.
5. Eph. 3:9.

devotion, admiration, exultation,
appreciation, praise and joy
beholds him hanging upon the cross,
such a one makes the Pasch, that is, the passover,
with Christ.
By the staff of the cross
he passes over the Red Sea,[6]
going from Egypt into the desert,
where he will taste the *hidden manna*;[7]
and with Christ
he rests in the tomb,
as if dead to the outer world,
but experiencing,
as far as is possible in this wayfarer's state,
what was said on the cross
to the thief who adhered to Christ;
Today you shall be with me in paradise.[8]

3. This was shown also
to blessed Francis,
when in ecstatic contemplation
on the height of the mountain —
where I thought out these things I have written —
there appeared to him
a six-winged Seraph fastened to a cross,
as I and several others heard
in that very place
from his companion who was with him then.[9]
There he passed over into God in ecstatic contemplation
and became an example of perfect contemplation
as he had previously been of action,
like another Jacob and Israel,[10]
so that through him,
more by example than by word,
God might invite all truly spiritual men

---

6. Cf. Exod. 12:11.
7. Apoc. 2:17.
8. Luke 23:43.
9. Cf. Bonaventure's *Life of St. Francis,* XIII, 3.
10. Cf. Gen. 35:10.

to this kind of passing over
and spiritual ecstasy.

4. In this passing over,
if it is to be perfect,
all intellectual activities must be left behind
and the height of our affection
must be totally transferred and transformed
into God.
This, however, is mystical and most secret,
which *no one knows
except him who receives it*,[11]
no one receives
except him who desires it,
and no one desires except him
who is inflamed in his very marrow by the fire of the Holy Spirit
whom Christ sent into the world.[12]
And therefore the Apostle says that
this mystical wisdom is revealed
by the Holy Spirit.[13]

5. Since, therefore, in this regard
nature can do nothing
and effort can do but little,
little importance should be given to inquiry,
but much to unction;
little importance should be given to the tongue,
but much to inner joy;
little importance should be given to words and to writing,
but all to the gift of God,
that is, the Holy Spirit;
little or no importance should be given to creation,
but all to the creative essence,
the Father, Son and Holy Spirit,
saying with Dionysius
to God the Trinity:

---

11. Apoc. 2:17.
12. Cf. Luke 12:49.
13. Cf. 1 Cor. 2:10 ff.

"Trinity,
superessential, superdivine and supereminent
overseer of the divine wisdom of Christians,
direct us into
the super-unknown, superluminous and most sublime summit
of mystical communication.
There
new, absolute and unchangeable mysteries of theology
are hidden
in the superluminous darkness
of a silence
teaching secretly in the utmost obscurity
which is supermanifest —
a darkness which is super-resplendent
and in which everything shines forth
and which fills to overflowing
invisible intellects
with the splendors of invisible goods
that surpass all good."[14]
This is said to God.
But to the friend to whom these words were written,
let us say with Dionysius:
"But you, my friend,
concerning mystical visions,
with your journey more firmly determined,
leave behind
your senses and intellectual activities,
sensible and invisible things,
all nonbeing and being;
and in this state of unknowing
be restored,
insofar as is possible,
to unity with him
who is above all essence and knowledge.
For transcending yourself and all things,
by the immeasurable and absolute ecstasy of a pure mind,
leaving behind all things

---

14. Dionysius, *De mystica theologia,* I, 1.

and freed from all things,
you will ascend
to the superessential ray
of the divine darkness."[15]

6. But if you wish to know how these things come about,
ask grace not instruction,
desire not understanding,
the groaning of prayer not diligent reading,
the Spouse not the teacher,
God not man,
darkness not clarity,
not light but the fire
that totally inflames and carries us into God
by ecstatic unctions and burning affections.
This fire is God,
and *his furnace is in Jerusalem*;[16]
and Christ enkindles it
in the heat of his burning passion,
which only he truly perceives who says:
My soul chooses hanging and my bones death.[17]

Whoever loves this death
can see God
because it is true beyond doubt that
man will not see me and live.[18]
Let us, then, die
and enter into the darkness;
let us impose silence
upon our cares, our desires and our imaginings.
With Christ crucified
let us pass *out of this world to the Father*[19]
so that when the Father is shown to us,
we may say with Philip:

---

15. Ibid.
16. Isa. 31:9.
17. Job 7:15.
18. Exod. 33:20.
19. John 13:1.

It is enough for us.[20]
Let us hear with Paul:
My grace is sufficient for you.[21]
Let us rejoice with David saying:
My flesh and my heart have grown faint;
You are the God of my heart,
and the God that is my portion forever.
Blessed be the Lord forever
and all the people will say:
Let it be; let it be.
Amen.[22]

HERE ENDS THE SOUL'S JOURNEY INTO GOD.

---

20. John 14:8.
21. 2 Cor. 12:9.
22. Ps. 72:26, 105:48.

65. The Divine Spark in the Soul and Blessed Are the Poor!

From *Sermon 48* and *Sermon 28*
(early 14th century)

MEISTER ECKHART

April 15, 1329, the Franciscan archbishop of Cologne received a papal bull that condemned twenty-eight propositions of "one Eckhart by name of the Order of Preaching Brothers [the Dominicans] and, so it is said, doctor and professor of the Holy Scriptures, who endeavored to know more than is needful." The bull judged seventeen of Eckhart's statements to be heretical, the others questionable.

The accused, Meister Eckhart (1260–1328), had died the year before. Prior to his death, Eckhart had denounced the charges as a Franciscan plot. "I am able to err," he wrote, "but I cannot be a heretic, since the one has to do with the intellect, the other with the will."

When Eckhart came to Cologne in 1322, he was the most famous

SOURCE: Meister Eckhart, *Meister Eckhart: The Essential Sermons, Commentaries, Treatises and Defense*, ed. Edmund Colledge and Bernard McGinn (New York: Paulist Press, 1981). © 1981 by the Missionary Society of St. Paul the Apostle in the State of New York. Used by permission of Paulist Press.

preacher in Germany. As a professor in Paris and Strassburg, he had been a leading exponent of a mystical spirituality that was sweeping Europe. His initial success was due to the dismal state of the official church. Four years later, the archbishop accused him of being a heretic.

Meister Eckhart was a mystic. But unlike the more conventional spirituality of Assisi and Bonaventure, Meister Eckhart's mysticism was intellectual. He cared about the metaphysical problem of how the One (God) relates to many (human souls). He cared about the unity of the soul with God. The divine (Gottheit), according to Eckhart, is beyond being; it is the ground where knowing and being are at rest (quies). At the same time, God "is" by way of the Trinity, where essence flows into essence — or where the divine ground flows into "being" the one-in-three. Furthermore, Eckhart sees this divine "being," flowing into every aspect of creation. Thus, in a neo-Platonic fashion, all being flows from the Godhead. Without the light or spark from the divine, nothing is that is. In fact the very argument "soars above grace"!

Eckhart preaches about the divine "spark in the soul, which has never touched time or place . . . which comprehends God without a medium." Turning away from all created things, contemplating the "naked God in the soul," he asserts that we are led beyond the Trinity to the "birth of God in the soul" or back to the ground where nothing dwells. Eckhart's version of the mystical union, like other versions of mystical ecstasy, is difficult to reconcile with the life and work of Jesus of Nazareth. If the mystical vision is a common bond of religion in general, then everything or everyone is God, and it is difficult to explain how God is in Christ reconciling the world.

Two sermons, "The divine spark in the soul" and a more biblical exposition entitled "Blessed are the poor," reflect the essence of Eckhart's mystical theology.

The Divine Spark in the Soul

Sermon 48: Ein meister sprichet: alliu glîcbiu dinc minnent sich under einander.

An authority says: "All things that are alike love one another and unite with one another, and all things that are unlike flee from one another and hate one another."[1] And one authority says that nothing is so unlike as are heaven and earth.[2] The kingdom of earth was endowed by nature with being far off from heaven and unlike it. This is why earth fled to the lowest place and is immovable so that it may not approach heaven. Heaven by nature apprehended that the earth fled from it and occupied the lowest place. Therefore heaven always pours itself out fruitfully upon the kingdom of earth; and the authorities maintain that the broad and wide heaven does not retain for itself so much as the width of a needle's point, but rather bestows it upon the earth.[3] That is why earth is called the most fruitful of all created things that exist in time.

I say the same about the man who has annihilated himself in himself and in God and in all created things; this man has taken possession of the lowest place, and God must pour the whole of himself into this man, or else he is not God. I say in the truth, which is good and eternal and enduring, that God must pour out the whole of himself with all his might so totally into every man who has utterly abandoned himself that God withholds nothing of his being or his nature or his entire divinity, but he must pour all of it fruitfully into the man who has abandoned himself for God and has occupied the lowest place.

As I was coming here today I was wondering how I should preach to you so that it would make sense and you would understand it. Then I thought of a comparison: If you could understand that, you would understand my meaning and the basis of all my thinking in everything I have ever preached. The comparison concerns my eyes and a piece of wood. If my eye is open, it is an eye; if it is closed, it is the same eye. It is not the wood that comes and goes, but it is my vision of it. Now pay good heed to me! If it happens that my eye is in itself one and simple (Matt. 6:22), and it is opened and casts its glance upon the piece of wood, the eye and the wood remain what they are, and yet in the act of vision they become as one, so that we can truly say that my eye is the wood and the wood is my eye. But if the wood were immaterial, purely spiritual as is the sight of my eye, then one could truly say that in the act of vision the wood and my eye

---

1. Of the possible sources indicated by Quint, the closest is Thomas Aquinas, *STb* Iallae.29.1.

2. The "authority" seems to be Aristotle, *On Heaven and Earth, passim*, as used by Maimonides and others.

3. The parallel passages, e.g., *Sermon* XXXVIII, seem to indicate that Eckhart is citing himself again as "the authorities."

subsisted in one being.⁴ If this is true of physical objects, it is far truer of spiritual objects. You should know that my eye has far more in common with the eye of a sheep which is on the other side of the sea and which I never saw, than it has in common with my ears, with which, however, it shares its being; and that is because the action of the sheep's eye is also that of my eye. And so I attribute to both more in common in their action than I do to my eyes and my ears, because their actions are different.

Sometimes I have spoken of a light that is uncreated and not capable of creation and that is in the soul.⁵ I always mention this light in my sermons; and this same light comprehends God without a medium, uncovered, naked, as he is in himself; and this comprehension is to be understood as happening when the birth takes place.⁶ Here I may truly say that this light may have more unity with God than it has with any power of the soul,⁷ with which, however, it is one in being. For you should know that this light is not nobler in my soul's being than is the feeblest or crudest power, such as hearing or sight or anything else which can be affected by hunger or thirst, frost or heat; and the simplicity of my being is the cause of that. Because of this, if we take the powers as they are in our being, they are all equally noble; but if we take them as they work, one is much nobler and higher than another.

That is why I say that if a man will turn away from himself and from all created things, by so much will you be made one and blessed in the spark in the soul, which has never touched either time or place. This spark rejects all created things, and wants nothing but its naked God, as he is in himself. It is not content with the Father or the Son or the Holy Spirit, or with the three Persons so far as each of them persists in his properties. I say truly that this light is not content with the divine nature's generative or fruitful qualities. I will say more, surprising though this is. I speak in all truth, truth that is eternal and enduring, that this same light is not content with the simple divine essence in its repose,⁸ as it neither gives nor receives; but it wants to know the source of this essence, it wants to go

---

4. Aristotle, *Soul* 2.7.
5. The Bull "In agro dominico" condemned as heretical the proposition that there is something in the soul that is uncreated and not capable of creation, although Eckhart denied making such statements. It seems clear from this passage and others, however, that he did.
6. A conjectural rendering of a difficult and unclear phrase.
7. "Of the soul" is Quint's gloss, plainly justified.
8. "Divine essence" = MHG; *götlich wesen*.

into the simple ground, into the quiet desert, into which distinction never gazed, not the Father, nor the Son, nor the Holy Spirit. In the innermost part, where no one dwells, there is contentment for that light, and there it is more inward than it can be to itself, for this ground is a simple silence, in itself immovable, and by this immovability all things are moved, all life is received by those who in themselves have rational being.

May that enduring truth of which I have spoken help us that we may so have rational life. Amen.

Blessed Are the Poor!

BEATI PAUPERES SPIRITU, QUIA IPSORUM EST REGNUM COELORUM.
(Matthew 5:3)

Blessedness opened the mouth that spake wisdom and said: "Blessed are the poor in spirit, for theirs is the kingdom of heaven." All the angels and all the saints and all that were ever born must keep silence when the eternal wisdom of the Father speaks; for all the wisdom of angels and creatures is pure nothing, before the bottomless wisdom of God. And this wisdom has spoken and said that the poor are blessed.[1]

Now, there are two kinds of poverty. One is external poverty and it is good, and much to be praised in people who take it upon themselves willingly, for the love of our Lord Jesus Christ, for he himself practiced it in the earthly realm. Of this poverty I shall say nothing more, for there is still another kind of poverty, an inward poverty, with reference to which, this saying of our Lord is to be understood: "Blessed are the poor in spirit, or of spirit."

Now, I pray you that you may be like this, so that you may understand this address; for, by the eternal truth, I tell you that if you haven't this truth of which we are speaking in yourselves, you cannot understand me.

Certain people have asked me what this poverty is. Let us answer that.

SOURCE: Meister Eckhart, *Meister Eckhart: A Modern Translation*, trans. Raymond Bernard Blakney (New York: Harper & Brothers, 1941), 227–32. Copyright 1941 by Harper & Brothers; copyright renewed. Used by permission of HarperCollins Publishers, Inc.

1. This sermon bears such unmistakable earmarks of Eckhart's touch that external evidence is hardly required. As Quint shows, it occurs in all the earliest and best manuscripts. It harks back to *Sermons* 1–4 but is obviously the work of an older man under great stress. It is the logical outcome of Eckhart's central idea, of the unity of God and man: "God and I are one." John 10:30. It is a complete expression of this great idea.

Bishop Albert says: "To be poor is to take no pleasure in anything God ever created," and that is well said. But we shall say it better and take "poverty" in a higher sense. He is a poor man who wants nothing, knows nothing, and has nothing. I shall speak of these three points.

In the first place, let us say that he is a poor man who wants nothing. Some people do not understand very well what this means. They are people who continue very properly in their penances and external practices of piety (popularly considered of great importance — may God pardon it!) and still they know very little of the divine truth. To all outward appearances, these people are to be called holy, but inwardly they are asses, for they understand not at all the true meaning of the divine reality. They say well that to be poor is to want nothing, but they mean by that, living so that one never gets his own way in anything, but rather so disposes himself as to follow the all-loving will of God. These persons do no evil in this, for they mean well, and we should praise them for that — may God keep them in his mercy!

I tell you the real truth, that these people are not poor, nor are they even like poor people. They pass for great in the eyes of people who know no better. Yet I say that they are asses, who understand the truth of the divine not at all. For their good intentions they may possibly receive the Kingdom of Heaven, but of this poverty, of which I shall now speak, they have no idea.

If I were asked, then, what it is to be a poor man who wants nothing, I should answer and say: As long as a person keeps his own will, and thinks it his will to fulfill the all-loving will of God, he has not that poverty of which we are talking, for this person has a will with which he wants to satisfy the will of God, and that is not right. For if one wants to be truly poor, he must be as free from his creature will as when he had not yet been born. For, by the everlasting truth, as long as you will do God's will, and yearn for eternity and God, you are not really poor; for he is poor who wills nothing, knows nothing, and wants nothing.

Back in the Womb[2] from which I came, I had no god[3] and merely was,

---

2. Lit. "in miner ersten ursache," "in my prime origin."

3. The reader of this sermon will be bothered by the not unusual distinction between God and god. I (i.e. the translator) judge that this reflects the reading of Plato's *Timaeus*, where the divine name is spelled both ways, with the upper and lower case G. The *Timaeus* tells about the "created gods," who were responsible for the soul. There is, however, the other distinction in Eckhart, perhaps more important: God is beyond my thinking; god is what I think god is.

myself. I did not will or desire anything, for I was pure being, a knower of myself by divine truth. Then I wanted myself and nothing else. And what I wanted, I was and what I was, I wanted, and thus, I existed untrammeled by god or anything else. But when I parted from my free will and received my created being, then I had a god. For before there were creatures, God was not god, but, rather, he was what he was. When creatures came to be and took on creaturely being, then God was no longer God as he is in himself, but god as he is with creatures.

Now we say that God, in so far as he is only god, is not the highest goal of creation, nor is his fullness of being as great as that of the least of creatures, themselves in God. And if a flea could have the intelligence by which to search the eternal abyss of divine being, out of which it came, we should say that god, together with all that god is, could not give fulfillment or satisfaction to the flea! Therefore, we pray that we may be rid of god, and taking the truth, break into eternity, where the highest angels and souls too, are like what I was in my primal existence, when I wanted what I was, and was what I wanted. Accordingly, a person ought to be poor in will, willing as little and wanting as little as when he did not exist. This is how a person is poor, who wills nothing.

Again, he is poor who knows nothing. We have sometimes said that man ought to live as if he did not live, neither for self, nor for the truth, nor for God. But to that point, we shall say something else and go further. The man who is to achieve this poverty shall live as having what was his when he did not live at all, neither his own, nor the truth, nor god. More: he shall be quit and empty of all knowledge, so that no knowledge of god exists in him; for when a man's existence is of God's eternal species, there is no other life in him: his life is himself. Therefore we say that a man ought to be empty of his own knowledge, as he was when he did not exist, and let God achieve what he will and be as untrammeled by humanness as he was when he came from God.

Now the question is raised: In what does happiness consist most of all? Certain authorities have said that it consists in loving. Others say that it consists in knowing and loving, and this is a better statement. But we say that it consists neither in knowledge nor in love, but in that there is something in the soul, from which both knowledge and love flow[4] and which, like the agents of the soul, neither knows nor loves. To know this is to know what blessedness depends on. This something has no "before" or "after" and it waits for nothing that is yet to come, for it has nothing to

---

4. Sermon 14, note 7. *Defense* IX, 3, 12.

gain or lose. Thus, when God acts in it, it is deprived of knowing that he has done so. What is more, it is the same kind of thing that, like God, can enjoy itself. Thus I say that man should be so disinterested and untrammeled that he does not know what God is doing in him. Thus only can a person possess that poverty.

The authorities say that God is a being, an intelligent being who knows everything. But I say that God is neither a being nor intelligent and he does not "know" either this or that. God is free of everything and therefore he is everything. He, then, who is to be poor in spirit must be poor of all his own knowledge, so that he knows nothing of God, or creatures, or of himself. This is not to say that one may not desire to know and to see the way of God, but it *is* to say that he may thus be poor in his own knowledge.[5]

In the third place, he is poor who has nothing. Many people have said that this is the consummation, that one should possess none of the corporeal goods of this world, and this may well be true in case one thus becomes poor voluntarily. But this is not what I mean.

Thus far I have said that he is poor who does not want to fulfill the will of god but who so lives that he is empty of his own will and the will of god, as much so as when he did not yet exist. We have said of this poverty that it is the highest poverty. Next, we said that he is poor who knows nothing of the action of god in himself. When a person is as empty of "knowledge" and "awareness" as God is innocent of all things, this is the purest poverty. But the third poverty is most inward and real and I shall now speak of it. It consists in that a man *has* nothing.

Now pay earnest attention to this! I have often said, and great authorities agree, that to be a proper abode for God and fit for God to act in, a man should also be free from all [his own] things and [his own] actions, both inwardly and outwardly. Now we shall say something else. If it is the case that a man is emptied of things, creatures, himself and god, and if still god could find a place in him to act, then we say: as long as that [place] exists, this man is not poor with the most intimate poverty. For God does not intend that man shall have a place reserved for *him* to work in, since true poverty of spirit requires that man shall be emptied of god and all his works, so that if God wants to act in the soul, he himself must be the place in which he acts — and that he would like to do. For if God once found a person as poor as this, he would take the responsibility of his

---

5. The meaning of this sentence is that we should be very humble indeed about what we think we know about God.

own action and would himself be the *scene* of action, for God is one who acts within himself. It is here, in this poverty, that man regains the eternal being that once he was, now is, and evermore shall be.

There is the question of the words of St. Paul:[6] "All that I am, I am by the grace of God," but our argument soars above grace, above intelligence, and above all desire. (How is it to be connected with what St. Paul says?) It is to be replied that what St. Paul says is true, not that this grace was in him, but the grace of God had produced in him a simple perfection of being and then the work of grace was done. When, then, grace had finished its work, Paul remained as he was.

Thus we say that a man should be so poor that he is not and has not a place for God to act in. To reserve a place would be to maintain distinctions. *Therefore I pray God that he may quit me of god*, for [his] unconditioned being is above god and all distinctions. It was here [in unconditioned being] that I was myself, wanted myself, and knew myself to be this person [here before you], and therefore, I am my own first cause, both of my eternal being and of my temporal being. To this end I was born, and by virtue of my birth being eternal, I shall never die. It is of the nature of this eternal birth that I *have been* eternally, that I *am* now, and *shall be* forever. What I am as a temporal creature is to die and come to nothingness, for it came with time and so with time it will pass away. In my eternal birth, however, everything was begotten. I was my own first cause as well as the first cause of everything else. If I had willed it, neither I nor the world would have come to be! If I had not been, there would have been no god. There is, however, no need to understand this.

A great authority[7] says: "His bursting forth is nobler than his efflux." When I flowed forth from God, creatures said: "He is a god!" This, however, did not make me blessed, for it indicates that I, too, am a creature. In bursting forth, however, when I shall be free within God's will and free, therefore of the will of god, and all his works, and even of god himself, then I shall rise above all creature kind, and I shall be neither god nor creature, but I shall be what I was once, now, and forevermore. I shall thus receive an impulse which shall raise me above the angels. With

---

6. 1 Corinthians 15:10.

7. Probably Plato, again, in the *Timaeus* 40–41. The phrase "bursting forth" refers to the "eternal birth" in which one gets out of self, space, and time into eternity, the habitation of God; "efflux" means the birth of the individual out of undifferentiated eternity. Thus Eckhart means to say: I was not blessed by being born in the first place, but I am blessed by a second and more glorious birth. Which is good Johannine doctrine: John 3:3.

this impulse, I receive wealth so great that I could never again be satisfied with a god, or anything that is a god's, nor with any divine activities, for in bursting forth I discover that God and I are One. Now I am what I was and I neither add to nor subtract from anything, for I am the unmoved Mover, that moves all things. Here, then, a god may find no "place" in man, for by his poverty the man achieves the being that was always his and shall remain his eternally. Here, too, God is identical with the spirit and that is the most intimate poverty discoverable.

If anyone does not understand this discourse, let him not worry about that, for if he does not find this truth in himself he cannot understand what I have said — for it is a discovered truth[8] which comes immediately from the heart of God. That we all may so live as to experience it eternally, may God help us! Amen.

---

8. "Discovered" or "uncovered" truth — that is to say, a truth Eckhart found himself uttering without premeditation in the course of a sermon as he delivered it. It was this kind of "truth" that really got him into trouble with the Inquisition — the utterances in which he "went too far" and said things "which might easily lead his listeners into error." But Eckhart obviously had great respect for the "discovered" truth. It came immediately from the heart of God!

66. *The Flowing Light of the Godhead*
(1250–65)

MECHTHILD OF MAGDEBURG

Medieval mysticism shows an extraordinary breadth of vision — from the rigorous intellectualism of Meister Eckhart to the lyrical, spiritual ecstasy of the late medieval "women's movement." A case in point is the so-called brautmystik *(bridal mysticism) represented by Mechthild of Magdeburg (1210–c. 1280).*

*The visions of Mechthild and other mystical women, take the form of an intimate talk between two lovers. In sensual and poetic language, God (the bridegroom) and the human soul (the bride) explore their relationship in the language and imagery of the songs of courtly love (*minnesang*).*

How the Bride Who Is United with God Refuses All Creaturely Comfort and Accepts It of God Alone; How She Sinks under Suffering.

Thus speaks the Bride of God who has dwelt in the enclosed sanctuary of the Holy Trinity — "Away from me all ye creatures! Ye pain me and cannot comfort me!" And the creatures ask, "Why?" The Bride says,

---

SOURCE: Walter H. Capps and Wendy M. Wright, eds., *Silent Fire: An Invitation to Western Mysticism* (San Francisco: Harper & Row, 1978). Used by permission of the author.

"My Love has left me while I rested beside him and slept." But the creatures ask, "Can this beautiful world and all your blessings not comfort you?" "Nay," says the Bride, "I see the serpent of falsehood and false wisdom creeping in to all the joy of this world. I see also the hook of covetousness in the bait of ignoble sweetness by which it ensnares many."

"Can even the Kingdom of Heaven not comfort you?" ask the creatures. "Nay! it were dead in itself were the living God not there!" "Now, O Bride, can the saints not comfort thee?"

"Nay! for were they separated from the living Godhead which flows through them, they would weep more bitterly than I for they have risen higher than I and live more deeply in God."

> "Can the Son of God not comfort thee?"
> Yes! I ask Him when we shall go
> Into the flowery meadows of heavenly knowledge.
> And pray Him fervently,
> That He unlock for me
> The swirling flood which plays about the Holy Trinity,
> For the soul lives on that alone.
>   If I am to be comforted.
> According to the merit to which God has raised me,
> Then His breath must draw me effortlessly into Himself.
> For the sun which plays upon the living Godhead
> Irradiates the clear waters of a joyful humanity;
> and the sweet desire of the Holy Spirit
> Comes to us from both. . . .
> Nothing can satisfy me save God alone,
> Without Him I am as dead.
> Yet would I gladly sacrifice the Joy of His presence
> Could He be greatly honoured thereby.
> For if I, unworthy, cannot praise God with all my might,
> Then I send all creatures to the Court of Heaven
> And bid them praise God for me,
> With all their wisdom, their love,
> Their beauty; all their desires,
> As they were created, sinless by God,
> To sing with all the sweetness of their voices
> As they now sing.
> Could I but witness this praise
> I would sorrow no more.

Neither can I bear that a single consolation be given me save by Love alone. I love my earthly friends in a heavenly fellowship and I love my enemies with a holy longing for their salvation. God has enough of all good things save of intercourse with the soul; of that He can never have enough.

When this wonder and this consolation had continued for eight years God wished to comfort me more mightily, far above my deserts. "Nay, dear Lord! do not raise me up too high!" cried this unworthy soul. "It is even now too much for me here in the lowest place. Gladly will I stay here to Thy honour." Then the soul fell down below the ill-fated souls who had forfeited their reward, and it seemed good to her so. There our Lord followed her as some others also did, who, so far as they could bear it, had gone to the state of least joy. For God appeared to them all beautiful and glorious, according as they had here been sanctified in love and ennobled in virtue. St. John says, "We shall see God as He is" (1 John 3:2). That is true, but the sun shines after the storm and there are many kinds of storms in this world, just as there are many mansions in Heaven. According as I can bear it and see it, so is it with me.

Then our Lord said: "How long wouldst thou stay here?" The Bride answered: "Ah! leave me dear Lord and let me sink further down, to Thy Glory!" Then soul and body came into such gross darkness that I lost light and consciousness and knew no more of God's intimacy; ever-blessed Love also went its way. Then the soul spoke: "Constancy! where art thou? I entrust to thee the mission of love; thou shalt uphold the glory of God in me!" Then this servitor Constancy strengthened her mistress with such holy patience and joyful forbearance that she lived without care. But Unbelief came and surrounded me with such darkness and roared at me in such fury that his voice frightened me and I said to myself, "If thy former grace had been from God He would not so utterly have forsaken thee!"

Then my soul cried: "Where art thou now, O Constancy? Bid true Faith to come to me!" And the heavenly Father spoke to the soul: "Remember what thou didst see and experience when there was nothing between Me and thee!" Then spoke the Son: "Remember what thy body has suffered for My pain." And the Holy Spirit said: "Remember what thou hast written!" Then both soul and body answered with the true faith of Constancy: "As I have praised and loved, enjoyed and known, thus will I go unchanged from here!"

After this came the state of Forsaken-ness of God and so surrounded the soul that it cried: "Welcome blessed Forsaken-ness! Well for me that

I was born and that thou, Constancy, shalt now be my waiting-maid, for thou bringest me unaccustomed joy and inconceivable wonders and sweetness beyond what I can bear. But, Lord, Thou must take this sweetness from me and leave me only Forsaken-ness. Well for me, O faithful Lord, that after the transformation of love I can yet bear it in the palate of my soul."

And here I asked all creatures to praise our Lord in the *Te Deum Laudamus*. But they would not and turned their backs on me. Then my soul was glad and said: "Well for me that ye despise me and turn your backs on me, for that praises our Lord immeasurably!"

Now is God marvellous to me and his Forsaken-ness better even than Himself. That the soul knew full well. For as God was about to comfort her she said: "Remember, O Lord, how lowly I am and withhold Thyself from me!" Then our Lord spoke to me: "Grant me that I may cool the glow of My Godhead, the desire of My humanity and the delight of My Holy Spirit in thee." The soul answered: "Yes, Lord, but only if that is well for Thee alone—and not for me!"

After that the Bride came into such great darkness that sweat and cramp racked her body. She was asked by some if she would be a messenger from them to God. She said: "Pain! I command thee that thou now release me, seeing that thou hast reached thy highest power in me." Then Pain rose from soul and body like a dark cloud and went to God and cried with a loud voice: "Lord! Thou knowest well what I desire!" Our Lord met Pain before the gate of the Kingdom and said: "Welcome, Pain! Thou art the garment I wore on my body upon earth: the contempt of the whole world was My most glorious cloak. But however much I prized thee there, thou canst not enter here. But to the maid who will do two things I will give two things. She must be modest and wise and it would help her if thou wouldst be her messenger; then will I embrace her and take her to my heart in union." Pain spoke thus: "Lord! I make many holy, though I myself am not holy and I nourish many holy bodies though I myself am evil, and I bring many to Heaven, though I may never enter in myself." To this our Lord answered: "Pain! thou wast not born in Heaven, therefore canst thou not enter therein. Moreover, thou wast born out of Lucifer's heart, there thou must return and live for evermore."

Ah! blessed Forsaken-ness of God, how lovingly I am bound to thee! Thou strengthenest my will in suffering and makest dear to me the long difficult waiting in this poor body. The nearer I come to thee, the greater and more wonderful God appears to me. Ah! Lord! even in the depths of unmixed humility. I cannot sink utterly away from Thee—

In pride I so easily lost Thee —
But now the more deeply I sink
The more sweetly I drink
Of Thee!

• • •

Of Ten Characteristics of the Divine Fire and of the Nobility of God.

An unworthy creature thought simply about the nobility of God. Then God showed him in his senses and the eyes of his soul, a Fire which burned ceaselessly in the heights above all things. It had burned without beginning and would burn without end. This Fire is the everlasting God Who has retained in Himself Eternal Life from which all things proceed. The sparks which have blown away from the Fire are the holy angels. The beams of the Fire are the saints of God for their lives cast many lovely lights on Christianity. The coals of the Fire still glow; they are the just who here burn in heavenly love and enlighten by their good example: as they were chilled by sin they now warm themselves at the glowing coals. The crackling sparks which are reduced to ashes and come to nothing are the bodies of the blessed, who in the grave will await their heavenly reward. The Lord of the Fire is still to come, Jesus Christ to whom the Father entrusted the first Redemption and the last Judgment. On the Last Day He shall make a glorious chalice for the heavenly Father out of the sparks of the Fire; from this chalice the Father will on the day of His Eternal Marriage drink all the holiness which, with His Beloved Son, He has poured into our souls and our human senses.

Yea! I shall drink from thee
And Thou shalt drink from me
All the good God has preserved in us.
Blessed is he who is so firmly established here
That he may never spill out
What God has poured into him.

• • •

67. God in Christ, Our True Mother
From *Showings*
(c. 1388)

JULIAN OF NORWICH

A women's movement (Frauenbewegung) *supported, and often sustained, medieval mysticism. Beginning in the late twelfth century, a growing number of women sought refuge in the spiritual life. Their leaders and teachers were remarkable women: the Benedictine abbesses Hildegard of Bingen (d. 1179) and Elizabeth of Schoenau (d. 1165); the Cistercian nuns Mechthild of Magdeburg (d.c. 1280) and Gertrude the Great (d. 1282); women from the third-order mendicants, such as Franciscan Birgitta of Sweden (d. 1344) and Dominican Catherine of Siena (d. 1380). These and many other women were instrumental in shaping late medieval spirituality.*

One of the most remarkable women mystics was the English anchoress Julian of Norwich (1342–c. 1416). During a severe illness, as she lay close to death, a priest asked her to look at a crucifix and to meditate on Christ's suffering for her. She followed the priest's advice and

---

SOURCE: Julian of Norwich, *Showings*, ed. Edmund Colledge and James Walsh, Classics of Western Spirituality Series (New York: Paulist Press, 1978). © 1978 by the Missionary of St. Paul the Apostle in the State of New York. Used by permission of Paulist Press.

received a vision of fifteen "showings," or revelations, of Christ's passion and love.

After her recovery, she became an anchorite, a person who retires into solitude for religious reasons. She spent the rest of her life in a small room attached to St. Julian's of Norwich, the church from which she took her name. Her small cell had only two small windows: one to the outside, so she could talk to visitors seeking her counsel; another facing the sanctuary, so she could join in worship. Confined voluntarily to this small space, Julian wrote two accounts of her visions or "showings." She wrote a "short text" soon after coming to Norwich. A "long text" grew out of twenty years of reflection on her experience.

Recent scholarship on Julian of Norwich notes that despite her humble disclaimers, she is a gifted writer, the first known woman of letters in English literature. Her style is direct and free of the theological jargon of her time. At the same time, her mysticism is thoroughly Christ-centered.

The first nine of Julian's fifteen visions focus on the crown of thorns. The remainder testify to Christ's suffering as the disclosure of God's love and power over sin. Such suffering convinces Julian that Christ cannot allow the loss of a single soul. In Christ, the second human, "all will be well." In fact, these thoughts of God's loving compassion lead her to speak of God or Christ as a loving mother. Her maternal images of God, Christ, and even of the Trinity, reflect ongoing theological concerns about God and gender.

The Fifty-Second Chapter

And so I saw that God rejoices that he is our Father, and God rejoices that he is our Mother, and God rejoices that he is our true spouse, and that our soul is his beloved wife. And Christ rejoices that he is our brother, and Jesus rejoices that he is our saviour. These are five great joys, as I understand, in which he wants us to rejoice, praising him, thanking him, loving him, endlessly blessing him, all who will be saved.

During our lifetime here we have in us a marvellous mixture of both well-being and woe. We have in us our risen Lord Jesus Christ, and we have in us the wretchedness and the harm of Adam's falling. Dying, we are constantly protected by Christ, and by the touching of his grace we are raised to true trust in salvation. And we are so afflicted in our feelings by Adam's falling in various ways, by sin and by different pains, and in this we are made dark and so blind that we can scarcely accept any comfort.

But in our intention we wait for God, and trust faithfully to have mercy and grace; and this is his own working in us, and in his goodness he opens the eye of our understanding, by which we have sight, sometimes more and sometimes less, according to the ability God gives us to receive. And now we are raised to the one, and now we are permitted to fall to the other. And so that mixture is so marvellous in us that we scarcely know, about ourselves or about our fellow Christians, what condition we are in, these conflicting feelings are so extraordinary, except for each holy act of assent to God which we make when we feel him, truly willing with all our heart to be with him, and with all our soul and with all our might. And then we hate and despise our evil inclinations, and everything which could be an occasion of spiritual and bodily sin. And even so, when this sweetness is hidden, we fall again into blindness, and so in various ways into woe and tribulation. But then this is our comfort, that we know in our faith that by the power of Christ who is our protector we never assent to that, but we complain about it, and endure in pain and in woe, praying until the time that he shows[1] himself again to us. And so we remain in this mixture all the days of our life; but he wants us to trust that he is constantly with us, and that in three ways.

He is with us in heaven, true man in his own person, drawing us up; and that was revealed in the spiritual thirst. And he is with us on earth, leading us; and that was revealed in the third revelation, where I saw God in a moment of time. And he is with us in our soul, endlessly dwelling, ruling and guarding;[2] and that was revealed in the sixteenth revelation, as I shall say.

And so in the servant there was shown the blindness and the hurt of Adam's falling; and in the servant there was shown the wisdom and the goodness of God's Son. And in the lord there was shown the compassion and the pity for Adam's woe; and in the lord there was shown the great nobility and the endless honour that man has come to, by the power of the Passion and the death of God's beloved Son. And therefore he greatly rejoices in his falling, for the raising on high and the fulness of bliss which mankind has come to, exceeding what we should have if he had not fallen. And so, to see the surpassing nobility, my understanding was led into God at the same time as I saw the servant fall.

And so we have matter for mourning, because our sin is the cause of

---

1. "Showed."
2. "Guiding."

Christ's pains, and we have constantly matter for joy, because endless love made him suffer. And therefore the creature which sees and feels the operation of love by grace hates nothing but sin, for of all things, as I see it, love and hate are the hardest and most immeasurable contraries. And all this notwithstanding, in our Lord's intention I saw and understood that we cannot in this life keep ourselves completely[3] from sin, in the perfect purity that we shall have in heaven. But we can well by grace keep ourselves from the sins which would lead us to endless torment, as Holy Church teaches us, and eschew venial sin, reasonably, to the extent of our power. And if we through our blindness and our wretchedness at any time fall, then let us quickly rise, knowing the sweet touching of grace, and willingly amend ourselves according to the teaching of Holy Church, as may fit the grievousness of the sin, and go on our way with God in love, and neither on the one side fall too low, inclining to despair, nor on the other side be too reckless, as though we did not care; but let us meekly recognize our weakness, knowing that we cannot stand for the twinkling of an eye except with the protection of grace, and let us reverently cling to God, trusting only in him.

For God sees one way and man sees another way. For it is for man meekly to accuse himself, and it is for our Lord God's own goodness courteously to excuse man. And these are two parts which were shown in the double demeanour with which the lord saw his beloved servant falling.

The one was shown outwardly, very meekly and mildly, with great compassion and pity; and the other was of inward endless love and justice. So[4] does our good Lord want us willingly to accuse ourselves, and to see truly and know our falling, and all the harms which come from it, seeing and knowing that we can never repair it; and also we willingly and truly see and know[5] the everlasting love which he has for us, and his plentiful mercy. And so by grace to see and know both together is the meek self-accusation which our good Lord asks from us. And he himself works where it is, and this is the lower part of man's life; and it was shown in the outward demeanour, and in this showing I saw two parts. One is man's pitiful falling; the other is the glorious atonement which our Lord has made for man. The other demeanour was inwardly shown, and that was more exaltedly shown, and it was all one; for the life and the power

---

3. Or, less probably, "all holy."
4. Or, less probably, "endless love. And just so. . ."
5. "Our falling, and all . . . see and know."

that we have in the lower part is from the higher, and it comes down to us from the substantial love of the self, by grace. In between the one and the other is nothing at all, for it is all one love, which one blessed love now has a double operation in us; for in the lower part there are pains and sufferings, compassions and pities, mercies and forgiveness and other such, which are profitable. But in the higher part there are none of these, but all is one great love and marvellous joy, in which marvellous joy all pains are wholly destroyed. And in this our good Lord showed not only that we are excused, but also the honourable nobility to which he will bring us, turning all our blame into endless honour.

• • •

The Fifty-Fourth Chapter

And for the great endless love that God has for all mankind, he makes no distinction in love between the blessed soul of Christ and the least soul that will be saved. For it is very easy to believe and trust that the dwelling of the blessed soul of Christ is very high in the glorious divinity; and truly, as I understand our Lord to mean, where the blessed soul of Christ is, there is the substance of all the souls which will be saved by Christ.

Greatly ought we to rejoice that God dwells in our soul; and more greatly ought we to rejoice that our soul dwells in God. Our soul is created to be God's dwelling place, and the dwelling of our soul is God, who is uncreated. It is a great understanding to see and know inwardly that God, who is our Creator, dwells in our soul, and it is a far greater understanding to see and know inwardly that our soul, which is created, dwells in God in substance, of which substance, through God, we are what we are.

And I saw no difference between God and our substance, but, as it were, all God; and still my understanding accepted that our substance is in God, that is to say that God is God, and our substance is a creature in God. For the almighty truth of the Trinity is our Father, for he made us and keeps us in him. And the deep wisdom of the Trinity is our Mother, in whom we are enclosed. And the high goodness of the Trinity is our Lord, and in him we are enclosed and he in us. We are enclosed in the Father, and we are enclosed in the Son, and we are enclosed in the Holy Spirit. And the Father is enclosed in us, the Son is enclosed in us, and the Holy Spirit is enclosed in us, almighty, all wisdom and all goodness, one God, one Lord. And our faith is a power which comes from our natural substance into our sensual soul by the Holy Spirit, in which power all our powers come to us, for without that no one can receive power, for it is nothing else than right understanding with true belief and certain trust in our being, that we are in God and he in us, which we do not see.

And this power with all the others which God has ordained for us, entering there, works great things in us; for Christ is mercifully working in us, and we are by grace according with him, through the gift and the power of the Holy Spirit. This working makes it so that we are Christ's children and live Christian lives.

• • •

The Fifty-Sixth Chapter

And so I saw most surely that it is quicker for us and easier to come to the knowledge of God than it is to know our own soul. For our soul is so deeply grounded in God and so endlessly treasured that we cannot come to knowledge of it until we first have knowledge of God, who is the Creator to whom it is united. But nevertheless I saw that we have, naturally from our fulness, to desire wisely and truly to know our own soul, through which we are taught to seek it where it is, and that is in God. And so by the leading through grace of the Holy Spirit we shall know them[6] both in one; whether we are moved to know God or our soul, either motion is good and true. God is closer to us than our own soul, for he is the foundation on which our soul stands, and he is the mean which keeps the substance and the sensuality together, so that they will never separate. For our soul sits in God in true rest, and our soul stands in God in sure strength, and our soul is naturally rooted in God in endless love. And therefore if we want to have knowledge of our soul, and communion and discourse with it, we must seek in our Lord God in whom it is enclosed.

And of this enclosing I saw and understood more in the sixteenth revelation, as I shall say, and as regards our substance, it can rightly be called our soul, and as regards our sensuality, it can rightly be called our soul, and that is by the union which it has in God.

That honourable city in which our Lord Jesus sits is our sensuality, in which he is enclosed; and our natural substance is enclosed in Jesus, with the blessed soul of Christ sitting in rest in the divinity. And I saw very certainly that we must necessarily be in longing and in penance until the

---

6. "Hem" (i.e., "them"); "him" is defensible but less probable.

time when we are led so deeply into God that we verily and truly know our own soul; and I saw certainly that our good Lord himself leads us into this high depth, in the same love with which he created us and in the same love with which he redeemed us, by mercy and grace, through the power of his blessed Passion.

And all this notwithstanding, we can never come to the full knowledge of God until we first clearly know our own soul. For until the time that it is in its full powers, we cannot be all holy; and that is when our sensuality by the power of Christ's Passion can be brought up into the substance, with all the profits of our tribulation which our Lord will make us obtain through mercy and grace.

I had a partial touching,[7] and it is founded in nature, that is to say: Our reason is founded in God, who is nature's substance. From this substantial nature spring mercy and grace, and penetrate[8] us, accomplishing everything for the fulfillment of our joy. These are our foundations, in which we have our being, our increase and our fulfillment. For in nature we have our life and our being, and in mercy and grace we have our increase and our fulfillment. This is three properties in one goodness, and where one operates all operate in the things which now pertain to us.

God wants us to understand, desiring with all our heart and all our strength to have knowledge of them, always more and more until the time that we are fulfilled; for to know them fully and to see them clearly is nothing else than endless joy and bliss, which we shall have in heaven, which God wants us to begin here in knowledge of his love. For we cannot profit by our reason alone, unless we have equally memory and love; nor can we be saved merely because we have in God our natural foundation, unless we have, coming from[9] the same foundation, mercy and grace. For from these three operating[10] all together we receive all our good, the first of which is the good of nature. For in our first making God gave us as much good and as great good as we could receive in our spirit alone; but his prescient purpose in his endless wisdom willed that we should be double.

---

7. On Julian's use of this technical term "to convey that she is being directly affected and moved by the Holy Spirit to experience the reality of God, in a way which is above intellectual comprehension, but which accompanies and supports some form of inner seeing," see *Showings*, II.

8. Literally, "spread into us," see *Showings*, II.

9. "Connyng" ("knowledge") of.

10. "Operations."

The Fifty-Seventh Chapter

And as regards our substance, he made us so noble and so rich that always we achieve his will and his glory. When I say "we," that means men who will be saved. For truly I saw that we are that which he loves, and that we do what is pleasing to him, constantly, without any stinting. And from this great richness and this high nobility, commensurate powers come into our soul, whilst it is joined to our body, in which joining we are made sensual. And so in our substance we are full and in our sensuality we are lacking, and this lack God will restore and fill by the operation of mercy and grace, plentifully flowing into us from his own natural goodness. And so this natural goodness makes mercy and grace to work in us, and the natural goodness that we have from him enables us to receive the operation of mercy and grace.

I saw that our nature is wholly in God, in which he makes diversities flowing out of him to perform his will, which[11] nature preserves and mercy and grace restore and fulfil. And of these none will be destroyed, for our nature, which is the higher part, is joined to God in its creation, and God is joined to our nature, which is the lower part in taking flesh. And so in Christ our two natures are united, for the Trinity is comprehended in Christ, in whom our higher part is founded and rooted; and our lower part the second person has taken, which nature was first prepared for him.

For I saw most truly that all the works which God has done or will ever do were fully known to him and foreseen from without beginning. And for love he made mankind, and for the same love he himself wanted to become man. The next good which we receive is our faith, in which we begin to profit; and it comes from the great riches of our natural substance into our soul, which is sensual; and it is founded in us and we in it through the natural goodness of God by the operation of mercy and grace. And from that comes all our good, by which we are led and saved. For in that come the commandments of God, of which we ought to have two kinds of understanding. One is that we ought to understand and know what things he commands, to love them and to keep them. The other is that we ought to know what things he forbids, to hate them and refuse them. For in these two is all our activity comprehended. Also in our faith come the seven sacraments, one following another in the order God has ordained them in

---

11. "Whose"; "whom."

for us, and every kind of virtue. For the same virtues which we have received from our substance, given to us in nature by the goodness of God, the same virtues by the operation of mercy are given to us in grace, renewed through the Holy Spirit; and these virtues and gifts are treasured for us in Jesus Christ. For in the same time that God joined himself to our body in the maiden's womb, he took our soul, which is sensual, and in taking it, having enclosed us all in himself, he united it to our substance. In this union he was perfect man, for Christ, having joined in himself every man who will be saved, is perfect man.

So our Lady is our mother, in whom we are all enclosed and born of her in Christ, for she who is mother of our saviour is mother of all who are saved in our saviour; and our saviour is our true Mother, in whom we are endlessly born and out of whom we shall never come.

Plenteously, fully and sweetly was this shown; and it is spoken of in the first revelation, where it says that we are all enclosed in him, and he is enclosed in us. And it is spoken of in the sixteenth revelation, where he says that he sits in our soul, for it is his delight to reign blessedly in our understanding, and sit restfully in our soul, and to dwell endlessly in our soul, working us all into him. In this working he wants us to be his helpers, giving all our intention to him, learning his laws, observing his teaching, desiring everything to be done which he does, truly trusting in him, for I saw truly that our substance is in him.

The Fifty-Eighth Chapter

God the blessed Trinity, who is everlasting being, just as he is eternal from without beginning, just so was it in his eternal purpose to create human nature, which fair nature was first prepared for his own Son, the second person; and when he wished, by full agreement of the whole Trinity he created us all once. And in our creating he joined and united us to himself, and through this union we are kept as pure and as noble as we were created. By the power of that same precious union we love our Creator and delight in him, praise him and thank him and endlessly rejoice in him. And this is the work which is constantly performed in every soul which will be saved, and this is the godly will mentioned before.

And so in our making, God almighty is our loving Father, and God all wisdom is our loving Mother, with the love and the goodness of the Holy Spirit, which is all one God, one Lord. And in the joining and the union he is our very true spouse and we his beloved wife and his fair maiden, with which wife he was never displeased; for he says: I love you and you love me, and our love will never divide in two.

I contemplated the work of all the blessed Trinity, in which contemplation I saw and understood these three properties: the property of the fatherhood, and the property of the motherhood, and the property of the lordship in one God. In our almighty Father we have our protection and our bliss, as regards our natural substance, which is ours by our creation from without beginning; and in the second person, in knowledge and wisdom we have our perfection, as regards our sensuality, our restoration and our salvation, for he is our Mother, brother and saviour; and in our good Lord the Holy Spirit we have our reward and our gift for our living and our labour, endlessly surpassing all that we desire in his marvellous courtesy, out of his great plentiful grace. For all our life consists of three: In the first we have our being, and in the second we have our increasing, and in the third we have our fulfillment. The first is nature, the second is mercy, the third is grace.

As to the first, I saw and understood that the high might of the Trinity is our Father, and the deep wisdom of the Trinity is our Mother, and the great love of the Trinity is our Lord; and all these we have in nature and in our substantial creation. And furthermore I saw that the second person, who is our Mother, substantially the same beloved person, has now become our mother sensually, because we are double by God's creating, that is to say substantial and sensual. Our substance is the higher part, which we have in our Father, God almighty; and the second person of the Trinity is our Mother in nature in our substantial creation, in whom we are founded and rooted, and he is our Mother of mercy in taking our sensuality. And so our Mother is working on us in various ways, in whom our parts are kept undivided; for in our Mother Christ we profit and increase, and in mercy he reforms and restores us, and by the power of his Passion, his death and his Resurrection he unites[12] us to our substance. So our Mother works in mercy on all his beloved children who are docile and obedient to him, and grace works with mercy, and especially in two properties, as it was shown, which working belongs to the third person, the Holy Spirit. He works, rewarding and giving. Rewarding is a gift for our confidence which the Lord makes to those who have laboured; and giving is a courteous act which he does freely, by grace, fulfilling and surpassing all that creatures deserve.

---

12. "United."

Thus in our Father, God almighty, we have our being, and in our Mother of mercy we have our reforming and our restoring, in whom our parts are united and all made perfect man, and through the rewards and the gifts of grace of the Holy Spirit we are fulfilled. And our substance is in our Father, God almighty, and our substance is in our Mother, God all wisdom, and our substance is in our Lord God, the Holy Spirit, all goodness, for our substance is whole in each person of the Trinity, who is one God. And our sensuality is only in the second person, Christ Jesus, in whom is the Father and the Holy Spirit; and in him and by him we are powerfully taken out of hell and out of the wretchedness on earth, and gloriously brought up into heaven, and blessedly united to our substance, increased in riches and nobility by all the power of Christ and by the grace and operation of the Holy Spirit.

The Fifty-Ninth Chapter

And we have all this bliss by mercy and grace, and this kind of bliss we never could have had and known, unless that property of goodness which is in God had been opposed, through which we have this bliss. For wickedness has been suffered to rise in opposition to that goodness; and the goodness of mercy and grace opposed that wickedness, and turned everything to goodness and honour for all who will be saved. For this is that property in God which opposes good to evil. So Jesus Christ, who opposes good to evil, is our true Mother. We have our being from him, where the foundation of motherhood begins, with all the sweet protection of love which endlessly follows.

As truly as God is our Father, so truly is God our Mother, and he revealed that in everything, and especially in these sweet words where he says: I am he; that is to say: I am he, the power and goodness of fatherhood; I am he, the wisdom and the lovingness of motherhood; I am he, the light and the grace which is all blessed love; I am he, the Trinity; I am he, the unity; I am he, the great supreme goodness of every kind of thing; I am he who makes you to love; I am he who makes you to[13] long; I am he, the endless fulfilling of all true desires. For where the soul is highest, noblest, most honourable, still it is lowest, meekest and mildest.

And from this foundation in substance we have all the powers of our sensuality by the gift of nature, and by the help and the furthering of mercy and grace, without which we cannot profit. Our great Father, al-

---

13. "Love, I am he who makes you to."

mighty God, who is being, knows us and loved us before time began. Out of this knowledge, in his most wonderful deep love, by the prescient eternal counsel of all the blessed Trinity, he wanted the second person to become our Mother, our brother and our saviour. From this it follows that as truly as God is our Father, so truly is God our Mother. Our Father wills, our Mother works, our good Lord the Holy Spirit confirms. And therefore it is our part to love our God in whom we have our being, reverently thanking and praising him for our creation, mightily praying to our Mother for mercy and pity, and to our Lord the Holy Spirit for help and grace. For in these three is all our life: nature, mercy and grace, of which we have mildness, patience and pity, and hatred of sin and wickedness; for the virtues must of themselves hate sin and wickedness.

And so Jesus is our true Mother in nature by our first creation, and he is our true Mother in grace by his taking our created nature. All the lovely works and all the sweet loving offices of beloved motherhood are appropriated to the second person, for in him we have this godly[14] will, whole and safe forever, both in nature and in grace, from his own goodness proper to him.

I understand three ways of contemplating motherhood in God. The first is the foundation of our nature's creation; the second is his taking of our nature, where the motherhood of grace begins; the third is the motherhood at work. And in that, by the same grace, everything is penetrated, in length and in breadth, in height and in depth without end; and it is all one love.

The Sixtieth Chapter

But now I should say a little more about this penetration, as I understood our Lord to mean: How we are brought back by the motherhood of mercy and grace into our natural place, in which we were created by the motherhood of love, a mother's love which never leaves us.

Our Mother in nature, our Mother in grace, because he wanted altogether to become our Mother in all things, made the foundation of his work most humbly and most mildly in the maiden's womb. And he revealed that in the first revelation, when he brought that meek maiden before the eye of my understanding in the simple stature which she had when she conceived; that is to say that our great God, the supreme wis-

---

14. "Goodly"; but Julian may be referring to the doctrine of the godly will which never assents to sin.

dom of all things, arrayed and prepared himself in this humble place, all ready in our poor flesh, himself to do the service and the office of motherhood in everything. The mother's service is nearest, readiest and surest: nearest because it is most natural, readiest because it is most loving, and surest because it is truest. No one ever might or could perform this office fully, except only him. We know that all our mothers bear us for pain and for death. O,[15] what is that? But our true Mother Jesus, he alone bears us for joy and for endless life, blessed may he be. So he carries us within him in love and travail, until the full time when he wanted to suffer the sharpest thorns and cruel pains that ever were or will be, and at the last he died. And when he had finished, and had borne us so for bliss, still all this could not satisfy his wonderful love. And he revealed this in these great surpassing words of love: If I could suffer more, I would suffer more. He could not die any more, but he did not want to cease working; therefore he must needs nourish us, for the precious love of motherhood has made him our debtor.

The mother can give her child to suck of her milk, but our precious Mother Jesus can feed us with himself, and does, most courteously and most tenderly, with the blessed sacrament, which is the precious food of true life; and with all the sweet sacraments he sustains us most mercifully and graciously, and so he meant in these blessed words, where he said: I am he whom Holy Church preaches and teaches to you. That is to say: All the health and the life of the sacraments, all the power and the grace of my word, all the goodness which is ordained in Holy Church for you, I am he.

The mother can lay her child tenderly to her breast, but our tender Mother Jesus can lead us easily into his blessed breast through his sweet open side, and show us there a part of the godhead and of the joys of heaven, with inner certainty of endless bliss. And that he revealed in the tenth revelation, giving us the same understanding in these sweet words which he says: See, how I love you, looking into his blessed side, rejoicing.

This fair lovely word "mother" is so sweet and so kind in itself that it cannot truly be said of anyone or to anyone except of him and to him who is the true Mother of life and of all things. To the property of motherhood belong nature, love, wisdom and knowledge, and this is God. For though it may be so that our bodily bringing to birth is only little, humble and simple in comparison with our spiritual bringing to birth, still it is he who does it in the creatures by whom it is done. The kind, loving mother who

---

15. "And."

knows and sees the need of her child guards it very tenderly, as the nature and condition of motherhood will have. And always as the child grows in age and in stature, she acts differently, but she does not change her love. And when it is even older, she allows it to be chastised to destroy its faults, so as to make the child receive virtues and grace. This work, with everything which is lovely and good, our Lord performs in those by whom it is done. So he is our Mother in nature by the operation of grace in the lower part, for love of the higher part. And he wants us to know it, for he wants to have all our love attached to him; and in this I saw that every debt which we owe by God's command to fatherhood and motherhood is fulfilled in truly loving God, which blessed love Christ works in us. And this was revealed in everything, and especially in the great bounteous words when he says: I am he whom you love.

The Sixty-First Chapter

And in our spiritual bringing to birth he uses more tenderness, without any comparison, in protecting us. By so much as our soul is more precious in his sight, he kindles our understanding, he prepares our ways, he eases our conscience, he comforts our soul, he illumines[16] our heart and gives us partial knowledge and love of his blessed divinity, with gracious memory of his sweet humanity and his blessed Passion, with courteous wonder over his great surpassing goodness, and makes us to love everything which he loves for love of him, and to be well satisfied with him and with all his works. And when we fall, quickly he raises us up with his loving embrace and his gracious touch. And when we are strengthened by his sweet working, then we willingly choose him by his grace, that we shall be his servants and his lovers, constantly and forever.

And yet after this he allows some of us to fall more heavily and more grievously than ever we did before, as it seems to us. And then we who are not all wise think that everything which we have undertaken was all nothing. But it is not so, for we need to fall, and we need to see it; for if we did not fall, we should not know how feeble and how wretched we are in ourselves, nor, too, should we know so completely the wonderful love of our Creator.

For we shall truly see in heaven without end that we have sinned grievously in this life; and notwithstanding this, we shall truly see that we were never hurt in his love, nor were we ever of less value in his sight.

---

16. Or, less probably in the context, "lightens."

And by the experience of this falling we shall have a great and marvellous knowledge of love in God without end; for enduring and marvellous is that love which cannot and will not be broken because of offences.

And this was one profitable understanding; another is the humility and meekness which we shall obtain by the sight of our fall, for by that we shall be raised high in heaven, to which raising we might never have come without that meekness. And therefore we need to see it; and if we do not see it, though we fell, that would not profit us. And commonly we first fall and then see it; and both are from the mercy of God.

The mother may sometimes suffer the child to fall and to be distressed in various ways, for its own[17] benefit, but she can never suffer any kind of peril to come to her child, because of her love. And though our earthly mother may suffer her child to perish, our heavenly Mother Jesus may never suffer us who are his children to perish, for he is almighty, all wisdom and all love, and so is none but he, blessed may he be.

But often when our falling and our wretchedness are shown to us, we are so much afraid and so greatly ashamed of ourselves that we scarcely know where we can put ourselves. But then our courteous Mother does not wish us to flee away, for nothing would be less pleasing to him; but he then wants us to behave like a child. For when it is distressed and frightened, it runs quickly to its mother; and if it can do no more, it calls to the mother for help with all its might. So he wants us to act as a meek child, saying: My kind Mother, my gracious Mother, my beloved Mother, have mercy on me. I have made myself filthy and unlike you, and I may not and cannot make it right except with your help and grace.

And if we do not then feel ourselves eased, let us at once be sure that he is behaving as a wise Mother. For if he sees that it is profitable to us to mourn and to weep, with compassion and pity he suffers that until the right time has come, out of his love. And then he wants us to show a child's characteristics, which always naturally trusts in its mother's love in well-being and in woe. And he wants us to commit ourselves fervently to the faith of the Holy Church, and find there our beloved Mother in consolation and true understanding, with all the company of the blessed. For one single person may often be broken, as it seems to him, but the entire body of Holy Church was never broken, nor ever will be without end. And therefore it is a certain thing, and good and gracious to will, meekly and fervently, to be fastened and united to our mother Holy Church, who is Christ Jesus. For the flood of mercy which is his dear

---

17. "The one."

blood and precious water is plentiful to make us fair and clean. The blessed wounds of our saviour are open and rejoice to heal us. The sweet gracious hands of our Mother are ready and diligent about us; for he in all this work exercises the true office of a kind nurse, who has nothing else to do but attend to the safety of her child.

It is his office to save us, it is his glory to do it, and it is his will that we know it; for he wants us to love him sweetly and trust in him meekly and greatly. And he revealed this in these gracious words: I protect you very safely.

• • •

The Sixty-Third Chapter

Here we may see that truly it belongs to our nature to hate sin, and truly it belongs to us by grace to hate sin, for nature is all good and fair in itself, and grace was sent out to save nature and destroy sin, and bring fair nature back again to the blessed place from which it came, which is God, with more nobility and honour by the powerful operation of grace. For it will be seen before God by all his saints in joy without end that nature has been tried in the fire of tribulation, and that no lack or defect is found in it.

So are nature and grace of one accord; for grace is God, as uncreated nature is God. He is two in his manner of operation, and one in love, and neither of these works without the other, and they are not separated. And when we by the mercy of God and with his help reconcile ourselves to nature and to grace, we shall see truly that sin is incomparably worse, more vile and painful than hell. For it is in opposition to our fair nature; for as truly as sin is unclean, so truly is sin unnatural. All this is a horrible thing to see for the loving soul which would wish to be all fair and shining in the sight of God, as nature and grace teach. But do not let us be afraid of this, except insofar as fear may be profitable; but let us meekly lament to our beloved Mother, and he will sprinkle us all with his precious blood, and make our soul most pliable and most mild, and heal us most gently in the course of time, just as it is most glory to him and joy to us without end. And from this sweet and gentle operation he will never cease or desist, until all his beloved children are born and brought to birth; and he revealed that when he gave understanding of the spiritual thirst which is the longing in love which will last till the day of judgment.

So in our true Mother Jesus our life is founded in his own prescient wisdom from without beginning, with the great power of the Father and the supreme goodness of the Holy Spirit. And in accepting our nature he gave us life, and in his blessed dying on the Cross he bore us to endless life. And since that time, now and ever until the day of judgment, he feeds us and fosters us, just as the great supreme lovingness of motherhood wishes, and as the natural need of childhood asks. Fair and sweet is our heavenly Mother in the sight of our soul, precious and lovely are the children of grace in the sight of our heavenly Mother, with gentleness and meekness and all the lovely virtues which belong to children by nature. For the child does not naturally despair of the mother's love, the child does not naturally rely upon itself, naturally the child loves the mother and either of them the other.

These, and all others that resemble them, are such fair virtues, with which our heavenly Mother is served and pleased. And I understood no greater stature in this life than childhood, with its feebleness and lack of power and intelligence, until the time that our gracious Mother has brought us up into our Father's bliss. And there it will truly be made known to us what he means in the sweet words when he says: All will be well, and you will see it yourself, that every kind of thing will be well. And then will the bliss of our motherhood in Christ be to begin anew in the joys of our Father, God, which new beginning will last, newly beginning without end.

68. German Theology
(late 14th century)

The resurgence of mysticism in the late Middle Ages was a broadly based, popular movement, centered in the lower Rhine region of Germany and Holland. The best-known German mystics of the fourteenth century were Dominicans: Meister Eckhart (see vol. 1:442–51), Heinrich Suso (d. 1360), and Johannes Tauler (d.c. 1361). All of them taught and preached in the vernacular (the language of the common people) in order to meet the needs of the growing number of lay members in their order. Tauler and Suso especially articulated a popular German spirituality that tried to combine a practical emphasis on "outer works" with the ecstatic experience of the presence of God.

During the same period, informal associations of women, known as Beguines, arose. These women did not enter cloisters but followed the mendicant (itinerant) ideal of service and contemplation. Their male counterparts were the Beghards. Also in the Rhineland and reaching south into Switzerland, were the "friends of God" (Gottesfreunde), another of the many "mystical societies," who were the source of a popular fourteenth-century treatise known as the "German Theology."

SOURCE: Ray C. Petry, ed., *Late Medieval Mysticism*, vol. 13 of *Library of Christian Classics* (Philadelphia: Westminster Press, 1957). Used by permission of Westminster John Knox Press.

The anonymous author of the "German Theology" attempts to strike a balance between practical obedience to the law of God and the "deification" of humans by ecstatic union with Christ. "Outer works" are not enough; yet without obedience to Christ by "way of suffering" and "actively serving," one cannot perfectly imitate Christ (i.e., deification), which is the object of the ecstatic union. The writings of the German mystics, especially the "German Theology," greatly influenced Luther and some of the radical reformers of the sixteenth century. Chapter 53 of the "German Theology" describes the attainment of perfection in mystical union with Christ.

Christ says further: "No man cometh unto me, except the Father draw him."[1] Now mark: By the Father, I understand the perfect, simple Good, which is All and above All, and without which and besides which there is no true Essence nor true Good, and without which no good work ever was or will be done. And in that it is All, it must be in All and above All. And it cannot be any one of those things which the creature, as creature, can comprehend and understand. For whatever the creature, as creature, can comprehend and understand, conforms with its creature nature; it is something, this or that, and therefore is likewise all creature. Now if the simple perfect Good were a something, this or that, which the creature understands, it would not be All, and in All, and therefore also not perfect. Therefore we name it also "Nothing"; meaning thereby that it is none of all the things which the creature can comprehend, know, conceive, or name, in virtue of its creature nature. Now behold, when this Perfect and Unnamable flows into a person able to bring forth, and brings forth the only-begotten Son in that person, and itself in him, we call it the Father.

Now hear how the Father draws men to Christ. When somewhat of this perfect Good is discovered and revealed to the soul of man, as it were in a vision or an ecstasy, there is born in the man a longing to draw near to the perfect Goodness, and unite himself with the Father. And the stronger this longing grows, the more is revealed to the man; and the more is revealed to him, the more he longs and is drawn. In such wise is a man drawn and called to a union with the eternal Goodness. And this is the drawing of the Father, and thus the man is taught of Him who draws him, that he cannot come to that union except he come by the Christ life. Behold! now he puts on that life, of which I have spoken before.

---

1. John 6:44.

Now consider again those two sayings of Christ's. The one: "No man cometh unto the Father, but by me"; that is, through my life, as set forth above. The other saying: "No man cometh unto me," that is, he does not take my life upon him and follow me, "except he be moved and drawn of my Father"; that is, of the simple and perfect Good, of which Saint Paul says: "When that which is perfect is come, then, that which is in part shall be done away." That is to say: In whatever man this Perfect is known, felt, and tasted, so far as may be in this temporal world, to that man all created things seem as nought compared with the Perfect, as in truth they are. For beside or without the Perfect is neither true Good nor true Essence. Whosoever, then, has, recognizes, and loves the Perfect, has and recognizes all that is good. What more or else, then, should he want, or what is all that "is in part" to him, seeing that all the parts are united in the Perfect, in the one Essence.

What has here been said wholly concerns the outward life; it is the way or access to the true inward life. But the inward life begins in this wise: Once a man has tasted the Perfect as far as is possible in this temporal world, all created things, and even himself, become as nought to him. And when he recognizes in truth that the Perfect alone is All and above All, it needs must follow that he ascribes all that is good, such as essence, life, cognition, knowledge, power, and the like, to the Perfect alone, and to no creature. Hence it follows that the man arrogates nothing to himself, neither Essence nor Like, Knowledge nor Power, Doing nor Refraining, nor anything that we can call good. And thus the man comes wholly to poorness, and indeed he becomes nought to himself, and in him becomes nought all that is somewhat, that is, all created things. Such is the first beginning of his true inward life; and, thereafter, God himself becomes the man, so that nothing is left that is not God or of God, and nothing is left that arrogates anything to itself. And thus God himself, that is, the one eternal Perfect alone, is, lives, knows, works, loves, wills, does, and refrains in the man. And thus should it be in truth, and where it is otherwise, let it be improved and rectified.

And the good way or access is to look to it that the best be always the most loved, and to choose the best, and cleave to it, and unite oneself to it. First: In the creatures. But what is best in the creatures? Be assured: That, in which the eternal perfect Goodness and what is thereof, that is, all which belongs thereto, is most manifested and works, and is best recognized and loved. But what is that which is of God, and belongs to him? I answer: Whatever with justice and truth we may call good. When therefore among the creatures a man cleaves to that which is the best that he can recognize, and keeps steadfastly to that, and does not backslide, he comes time after time to a better, until at last he recognizes and tastes that the eternal Good is a perfect Good, immeasurably and numberlessly above all created good.

Now, if what is best is to be most loved by us, and we are to follow after it, the one eternal Good must be loved above all and alone, and we must cleave to it alone, and unite ourselves with it as much as we may. And, now, if we must ascribe all good things to the one eternal Good, as of right and truth we ought, so must we also of right and truth ascribe to it our beginning, progress, and perfection, so that nothing remain to man or the creature. So it should be in truth, let men write and rhyme what they will. On this wise we should attain to a true inward life. And what then further befalls, what is revealed to us, and what our life is thenceforward, none can rhyme or write. It has never been uttered by man's lips, nor has it entered into the heart of man to conceive, the manner thereof in truth.

This our long discourse, briefly recapitulated, declares: In right and truth there should be in a man nought which would arrogate aught to itself, or desire, will, love, or strive after aught in all things, save only God and what is divine, that is: the one, eternal, perfect Goodness.

But if there be aught else in a man, so that he arrogates somewhat to himself, or wills, strives after, and desires this or that, whatever it may be, beside or more than the eternal and perfect Good, which is God himself, this is all too much and a great fault, and hinders the man from a perfect life; wherefore he can never reach the perfect Good, unless he first forsake all things and himself first of all. For no man can serve two masters who are contrary the one to the other. He who will have the one must let the other go. Therefore, if the Creator shall enter in, all creature must depart. Of this be assured.

Reformation Beginnings

69. Tractate on the Unity of the Church
(1409)

JOHN GERSON

After the death of Boniface VIII (d. 1303), the papacy moved to Avignon in southern France in an unholy alliance with the French crown. Although the "Babylonian captivity" of the papacy in France — a misleading label since all the Avignon popes were French — lasted for only seventy years (1309–1377), the damage done to the religious leadership of the church had long-lasting effects. The heavy-handed policies of the Avignon popes created a major rift between the curia *(papal court) and the rank and file.*

In 1377 Gregory XI (d. 1378) agreed to return to Rome, supposedly at the urging of the Italian mystic Catherine of Siena (1347–1380). But the situation went from bad to worse. When Gregory died, the council of cardinals, under pressure from the Roman populace, elected an Italian

SOURCE: Matthew Spinka, ed., *Advocates of Reform: From Wyclif to Erasmus*, vol. 14 of *Library of Christian Classics* (Philadelphia: Westminster Press, 1953). Used by permission of Westminster John Knox Press.

pope, Urban VI (reigned 1378–1389). Later in the same year, the council of cardinals, yielding to French influence, declared itself in error and replaced the Italian pope (i.e., Urban VI) with a cardinal from Geneva, Clement VII (reigned 1378–1394). Urban refused to yield and continued his papacy in Rome.

Clement, of course, returned the seat of his papacy to Avignon. Thus began the Great Schism, with popes at both Rome and Avignon. For the next forty years, two popes (and after 1409, three popes) were busily excommunicating each other, raising revenues from the faithful, and competing for the support of bishops and princes.

This impasse turned many minds to a consideration of the status of the papacy and the nature of church unity. In the tradition of the ancient church, some leaders argued that a general council of bishops ought to resolve the schism and reassert the authority of bishops in the church. "Conciliarism," as this reform movement was called, included many professors at the University of Paris: Marsiglio of Padua, William of Ockham, Pierre d'Ailly, and John (also known as Jean) Gerson (1363–1429). Gerson's tract "On the Unity of the Church" states the conciliar position. He wrote it in 1409, the year a Council held at Pisa tried but failed to end the schism. It did, however, establish precedents for the final resolution of the schism at the Council of Constance in 1417.

To those who treat of the unity of the Church, one of the zealots of this very cause gladly presents for their consideration a way of peace. Although his body is bound by the chains of affairs, thus preventing him from going in person to the sacred council which is, God favoring us, to be held at Pisa, nevertheless "the word of God," as the apostle says, "is not bound."[1] Therefore, [his] spirit, inclined to and most anxious for peace, has decided to spread abroad in every direction, where the infirm flesh is unable to go, some word of God; not, of course, to determine anything — away with such boldness — but to state and examine in "the tabernacle of God with men"[2] whatever has been entrusted to him out of the fund of knowledge.

The unity of the Church in one undoubted vicar of Christ must not, in the present situation, which now confronts the Church on January 29, 1408,[3] be retarded on account of certain allegations derived from positive

---

1. 2 Tim. 2:9.
2. Rev. 21:3.
3. New Series, 1409.

law against the holding of a general council or the way of abdication. [Such allegations are:] that a council cannot be held without the authority of the pope; that anyone who has been deprived must before all else be reinstated; and that those who have withdrawn from obedience are to be dealt with as enemies. Righteous fear may also allege that no one is able to say to the pope, "Why do you act in this way?," especially if he is not expressly erring against the articles of faith, since he cannot be judged by anyone, subjected to anyone, or dealt with as a schismatic. [It may be also alleged] that it is dangerous for a shepherd to abandon his flock by abdicating; that each has done what has been required of him for the union of the Church, and is not in sin; and, finally, that an inquiry must be made into the justice of the true party, for without this knowledge those who have erred cannot do penance, etc. Therefore, against these allegations, twelve general considerations are set forth, a particular application of which is sufficient for the informed to refute them.

The First Consideration

The general unity of the Church has been hampered by divisions among her sons, as putrefying members and sinners against God. "Our sins," according to the words of the prophet, "have separated us from God."[4] Thus through the opposite process, that is, the reconciliation of each to God by the correction of evil practices, by self-humiliation, and by prayer, this unity must once again be secured. If this does not take place, and if the cause of the schism remains, what hope can we have that the schism will end, unless, however, in the pure grace of our Lord Jesus Christ, who is wont to bestow great benefits on the undeserving and the ungrateful? Nevertheless, it behooves us to be his fellow workers, especially now when, as the return of peace seems nearer, the enemy of peace is raging more savagely; and whenever he will introduce, if he is able, in order to continue the schism, the most powerful impediment, namely, division among those who are about to effect a union, by means of pride, lust, or envy.

The Second Consideration

The essential unity of the Church always remains in Christ, her spouse, for "Christ is the head of the Church,"[5] "in whom all are one,"[6] according

---

4. Isa. 59:2.
5. Eph. 5:23.
6. Gal. 3:28.

to the apostle. If she does not have a vicar, as when he is dead, corporally or civilly, or because it is not credibly to be expected that obedience will be conferred any longer on him or his successors by Christians, then the Church, by divine as well as by natural law (which no positive law properly understood hinders), is able to assemble in a general council representing her in order to procure for herself one undoubted vicar. This action can be taken not only on the authority of the cardinals, but even with the help and co-operation of any prince or other Christian. For the mystical body of the Church, perfectly established by Christ, has, no less than any civil, mystical, or truly natural body, the right and the power to procure its own union. It is not in accordance with the absolute and immutable law, divine or natural, that the Church should be unable to assemble or unite without the pope, or anyone of a particular rank or association, when death or error may occur at any time.

The Third Consideration

The unity of the Church in one undoubted vicar of Christ, who is, to a certain extent [*quodammodo*] unessential [*accidentalis*] and mutable [*mutabilis*], must in no way be hindered or deferred on account of the contention of two men over the papacy, or of their supporters, if these seek to maintain their position on the strength of allegations drawn from positive law, and on various pleas and complaints, such as: that they have suffered deprivation, and must, therefore, before all else be reinstated. On account of the council it is expedient that they should, as the apostle says, forget what is behind and strain forward to what lies ahead.[7] For according to Augustine, greater attention should be given to finding out how the Church is to be delivered from this exceedingly deep pit of schism than how and through whom it fell into it.

The Fourth Consideration

The unity of the Church in one undoubted vicar of Christ must be so greatly beloved that, for the sake of its attainment, the majority of the evils that have been committed by the individuals themselves should, according to reason, be dismissed now, or at some later date, without punishment. Certain rights [*iura*], true or pretended, can be put aside, that a voluntary abdication may be made by them or even forced upon them by the authority of the Council. The law of nature undoubtedly prescribes

---

7. Phil. 3:13.

that every part should surrender itself for the sake of the well-being of the whole. Why, if any of the contestants strives to justify himself or complain that he has been treated unjustly, let this be said to him: "You owe yourself and all that you have to the Church; you, who call yourself a shepherd, however innocent you may be, must be prepared to offer your own life for her, that she be saved, united, or not seriously scandalized. How much more, then, [must you be prepared to surrender] your present dignity, in seeking those things that are Jesus Christ's? This must not be done in accordance with the dictates of personal or carnal interest, but of public and incorrupt spiritual interest, according as the council, which is indeed wise, shall judge. In doing this you will by no means be abandoning the flock, but feeding and uniting it; and you will be called to remain."

The Fifth Consideration

The unity of the Church in one vicar of Christ does not for its attainment at the present time require a literal observance of the outward terms of positive law, or of ordinary processes in summonses, accusations, denunciations, or similar matters. This General Council may proceed summarily, and with the good and important [principle] of equity. It shall have sufficient judicial authority to use ἐπιείκεια, i.e., the power to interpret all positive law, to adapt it for the sake of accomplishing the union more speedily and more advantageously, and, if need be, to abandon it because it was instituted for the peace and well-being of the Church. If it has been instituted properly and not by any tyrannical malignity, it should not militate against the Church, lest the power that has been conferred on human institutions bring about the destruction rather than the edification of the Church. In fact the power of using ἐπιείκεια with regard to a matter of doctrine [*doctrinaliter*] belongs principally to those learned in theology, which in relation to other [sciences] is fundamental [*architectoria*], and thereafter with those skilled in the science of canon and civil law, as they have to take their basic ideas from the principles of divine and natural law.

The Sixth Consideration

The unity of the Church in one undoubted vicar of Christ should, it seems, be obtained by the council now to be held, in the following manner. First, security should be granted by the princes and others that the two contestants, if they wish to appear, may proceed to fulfill their oaths and vows. If they refuse to comply, abdication through legitimate proctors should be obtained from them. If they absolutely refuse to do either of these, both contestants should be condemned, then procedure set in motion for the election of one [vicar] with the common consent of the entire council, which would corroborate and approve what two thirds of the college of cardinals, or the greater and wiser part of them, agreed upon or accomplished. If some wish to adhere pertinaciously to one or other of the two contestants, and not follow the decision of the council (this is not to be entered upon lightly), let them look to their own salvation, because this council and its followers shall have in the sight of God and man delivered itself from the accusation of schism.

The Seventh Consideration

The unity of the Church in one undoubted vicar of Christ is so privileged and holy that those who sincerely seek it must by no means be regarded by the contestants as their adversaries, but as their best friends in Christ. For they ask for their voluntary abdication, or, if they refuse, seek to overthrow them, that their souls may thereby be saved and the Church no longer disturbed. Actually in so acting toward these contestants, they are doing what every Christian must do. Indeed, in this desperate and inveterate disease of our common Mother, they have a command from God. This is the inviolable basis, strengthened by necessity and piety, on which the Most Christian King of the Franks, who is most upright, neither seeking his own interest nor harboring hatred against any, has supported every kind of praiseworthy activity for the restoration of peace, as his open letter *Pax ecclesiastica* demonstrates.[8] Cicero, when he had been accused of having wavered and of having been fickle in his friendship toward Caesar, brought forward in the *Philippics* a famous plea, of which this is only the sense, as I do not have the exact words. "I never loved Caesar," he said, "except in so far as he was seen to love the State. Therefore, when he, by becoming a tyrant, had altered his love toward the State, I completely turned away my friendship from him."[9]

---

8. Bourgeois du Chastenet, *Nouvelle histoire du Concile de Constance* (Paris, 1718). In this letter, dated January 12, 1408, Charles VI threatened to withdraw obedience once again from Benedict XIII.

9. For the *sententia*, cf. *Philippics*, II, 45, 116–118; for Cicero's attitude to Caesar, cf. R. Y. Tyrrell, *Cicero in His Letters* (London, 1901), xxxi. For this note I am indebted to Professor G. Johnston, Toronto.

The Eighth Consideration

The unity of the Church in one undoubted vicar of Christ must not be hindered on the ground that a restoration of obedience must first be made to both contestants, because they have suffered deprivation. [For the argument that] an unjust detainer, or a robber who has been deprived, must be reinstated is derived rather from positive regulation than from the purely natural and divine law. Therefore [positive regulation] holds in stated cases only, and is in no way to be observed to the disadvantage of the natural and divine law and the common good. Thus, for example, no restitution ought to be made to heretics; to those who are obviously schismatics; to the mad and the drunk to their own harm; to those who have been intruded into the papacy; to those who seek to take as a wife one who is not marriageable or a relative within the decrees prohibited by the divine law; to him who seeks to obtain possession of a benefice which he cannot hold, as the legal possessor is still alive; or, finally, to those who seek to use their possessions to the contempt of the Creator, or the enslavement of free men, or against the chastity and life of anyone, etc. Against each contestant it is easy to bring forward many exceptions of this kind.

The Ninth Consideration

The unity of the Church in one undoubted vicar of Christ might be more easily accomplished if neither before, during, nor after the council they seek to have put into effect the just or unjust decisions which they have heretofore published. These concern the intrusion of one or other into the papacy; the processes fulminated against each other from the beginning; the violation of oaths and vows; the withdrawal of obedience or neutrality; the restoration of the freedom of particular churches; the accusations of schism or heresy; the approval or condemnation of the allegiance of one or other part of the obedience; and the sentences of excommunication or other forms of punishment. Such activity should in fact cease and procedure be set in motion to bring about the way of abdication in accordance with the conditions [*rationes*] and the practice demonstrated many times elsewhere, namely, by removing the processes that have been executed; by the justification, ratification, or even toleration of what took place in the past, as the nature of things will allow; or by the replacement without further discussion of most things to the condition in which they were before the outbreak of the present schism; and, finally, by providing both contestants with sufficient security and rank after abdication, if they at this late date wish to do this either in person or through legitimate proctors. Such an abdication carried out by them through the council would be considered as of sufficient worth to free them of all former impositions.

The Tenth Consideration

The unity of the Church in one undoubted vicar of Christ has to be sought after with such great earnestness that it can scarcely be the sober and responsible judgment of any Christian that he has sufficiently fulfilled his duty in this. Far less ought anyone to dare to affirm this on oath, especially when most men are of the contrary opinion. What else would this be for such a person but to remain pertinaciously and incorrigibly in his errors? Again, many cases may arise in which, as it would be permissible to resist force by force to obtain public peace or just protection, so it would be permissible to withdraw obedience from one duly elected to be pope; to remain in neutrality; to cast him into prison; to forbid him all public assistance; or to oppose him by appeal or similar remedy, and in this way true obedience rather than opposition and resistance would be offered. [There are many cases] when it is permissible not to fear any of his pretended sentences, or assert that they are to be feared, but to tear them to pieces and turn them against his own head. Again, it would be permissible to accuse him of schism or heresy by instruction [*doctrinaliter*] both in public assemblies by theologians and men of learning as well as privately in brotherly correction, to which he as a sinner is subject in the forum of penance, and lawfully before the whole Church, to which he is subject in the same manner as one who is capable of erring to what can never err [*deviabilis indeviabili*]: It would be permissible to hold a general council against his will; and, finally, to force him to abdicate, or, if he resisted, to deprive him of all honor and rank, and even his life. In a word, all these and similar actions are permissible according to the immutable divine and natural law, because against this truth no law or constitution of a mere man ought to be made without fresh authorization from God, except to be condemned as intolerable error. Whether the abovementioned instances have arisen in the present schism we have by no means assumed in our discussion, since we are of the opinion that the distinguishing of particular instances ought rather to be omitted.

The Eleventh Consideration

The unity of the Church in one undoubted vicar of Christ does not necessitate that those who are wandering in error, especially those in reasonable doubt about the obedience of the true pope, are not able to do penance, and are not in a state of salvation, unless they absolutely and expressly confess their error, since often in such instances a conditional penance or absolution is sufficient. It is not proper to accuse of schism all who, in this great uncertainty about the papal right which has arisen from various doubtful actions, do not remain in sure and steadfast obedience to the true pope. Indeed, just as a true pope could fall into the sin of schism by remaining pertinacious in rejecting what would be able to bring about a restoration of universal peace, such as a general council, or promptitude of mind for the way of cession to which he had sworn and the fulfillment of his vow, so also the many who have opposed him could be excused, if this were done out of zeal to achieve union, or from some reasonable doubt and ignorance, since they have shown themselves at all times prepared to obey the Church, and the truth that was known to them.

The Twelfth Consideration

The unity of the Church in one undoubted vicar of Christ must be earnestly sought after by means of devout prayer and the correction of morals. And in the reformation of the Church from top to bottom vehement and continued enthusiasm must be restrained by the complete uniting (when this has been accomplished) of its members, important and unimportant alike. This must be done lest anything worse in the just judgment of God befall us; lest, after a wholesome union has, through the mercy of God, been granted, the former situation return. The book of experience, as well as the numerous documents that have been issued on the subject, and the trustworthy reports of the ecclesiastics to the council, can inform us of where reformation is necessary in the government of the Church. Finally, it may happen that the general council will be delayed on account of the divisions among the princes and others in the various countries, or for some other reason, so that many important persons will either be unable or refuse to appear, or to send representatives, preferring to abstain. Further, the cardinals from both sides may discover from trustworthy conjecture that so many of the important members of each side would not adhere to their election. Then it would seem expedient in these instances that the cardinals themselves, being present at the council, at least put forward a method for ending the schism by providing (unless peace has been secured sooner, and because it would be better late than never) that after the death of both contestants peace be secured in accordance with the method agreed upon in the Council of France,[10] namely, that they should seek and obtain through their ambassadors from both contestants and their colleges [an agreement] that there be no election in the event of the death of the one or the other, with other clauses pertaining to this end.

---

10. Gerson is probably referring to the fifth French National Council (August to November, 1408), although no other account of this decision is apparently extant; cf. N. Valois, *La France et le grand schisme* (Paris, 1902), IV, 21 ff.).

70. On the Eucharist (1:1–15, 17)
(1380)

JOHN WYCLIFFE

Historians record that during the "captivity" of the popes in southern France in the fourteenth century, the church collected more revenue from the population than the French kings. The gulf between the monastic ideal of apostolic poverty and the real world of "prince bishops" was a scandal of major proportion, which undermined the foundations of church and society. Everyone agreed that the church needed reform "in head and members," but there was no consensus on how to accomplish it.

John Wycliffe (also known as Wyclif) (c. 1325–84), a popular master of theology at Oxford, argued early in the 1370s that any office in the church is a "loan" from God and not the property of the office holder. He insisted that the authority of bishops and popes is spiritual, not temporal. The use of "dominion" over the faithful for personal ends constitutes usurpation. Such usurpation can be justly punished by secular leaders, if need be with the loss of office and all unlawful gain.

King Edward III, king of England, chafing under the burden of papal taxation, considered Wycliffe's argument eminently reasonable. He

---

SOURCE: Matthew Spinka, ed., *Advocates of Reform: From Wyclif to Erasmus*, vol. 14 of *Library of Christian Classics* (Philadelphia: Westminster Press, 1953). Used by permission of Westminster John Knox Press.

made Wycliffe a theological consultant to the crown and appointed him rector of Lutterworth parish. Unfortunately, when Wycliffe applied the same logic to the conduct of royal or temporal authority, official support began to evaporate. Wycliffe was returned to Oxford but kept his parish at Lutterworth, where he retired in 1381 and died of a stroke three years later.

Wycliffe's ideas during the last few years of his life were very popular. After the Great Schism of 1377, he wrote a treatise, "On the Truth of the Holy Scriptures" (1378), stating that even though the church holds the key to scripture, scripture belongs to all Christians and should be accessible to all. His writings inspired two of his followers to translate the Vulgate (the Latin translation of the Bible) into English.

Wycliffe also turned his attention to the doctrine of the church. Writing on the church (1378) and the papacy (1379), he argued that the true church is the church of the elect who are known ultimately only to God; whereas the pope is the head of the visible church, which is a human institution. The church always consists of both saints and sinners who are known "by their fruits" (Matt. 7:16). Unworthy members of the visible church, including popes and prelates, place themselves outside the true church. Following this logic, Wycliffe argued that unworthy priests cannot rightly administer the sacraments. He also launched an attack on the doctrine of transubstantiation (the medieval church belief that the bread and wine of the Eucharist become the actual body and blood of Jesus Christ).

In his treatise, "On the Eucharist" (1380), Wycliffe insists that universals (i.e., the substance of bread) cannot disappear, and accidents (the appearance of bread) cannot exist without their matching universal. Therefore, the substances of bread and wine are not "annihilated" but remain. Along with the bread and wine, Christ is sacramentally and "efficaciously" present in the Eucharist. Wycliffe's views on the sacrament became a major factor in his posthumous conviction of heresy.

---

(1) In dealing with the Eucharist[1] it is necessary to set forth the more commonly known facts, and first to consider whether the sacrament of the

---

1. The text used is that edited by J. Loserth for the Wyclif Society (London, 1892), from which edition most of the footnotes to the present translation have been derived. Citations of this work by the original Latin title refer to sections not included in the present translation; citations of Wyclif, *On the Eucharist,* are from the translation as printed. Paragraph numbers have been assigned by the translator to the Latin text as printed.

altar is the real body of Christ. On this topic I have often said in public[2] that there are three aspects of the sacrament of the altar to be considered, namely, the bare sacrament, apart from the matter of the sacrament,[3] as the consecrated host; second, the sacrament and the matter of the sacrament as the true body and blood of Christ; and third, the matter of the sacrament, apart from the sacrament itself, as the union of Christ with his mystical body the Church. This is nowhere comprehensible by the senses, and consequently is not anywhere a sacrament. From this belief arise the objections of the pagans. For they argue that a hog, a dog, or a mouse can eat our Lord, because they can eat the body of Christ, that is, God.

(2) But we reply to them in accordance with this belief. Their assumption is false; beasts can eat the consecrated host, but it is the bare sacrament and not the body or blood of Christ. When a lion devours a man, it does not also devour his soul; yet his soul is present in every part of his body. Thus should one believe concerning the body of Christ in the sacrament of the altar. For this is whole, sacramentally, spiritually, or virtually in every part of the consecrated host, even as the soul is in the body.

(3) Secondly, they object on this account, that we priests break the body of Christ, and thus the head, neck, arms, and other members; this would be an utterly horrible thing to do to our God.

(4) But we reply according to the prior belief that they falsely assume this. We break the sacrament or consecrated host, but not the body of Christ, which is something different, just as we do not break a ray of the sun, even though we break a glass or a crystal stone. And this view is upheld by a hymn of the Church which sings,

> "When they this sacrament dismember,
> Without the slightest doubt, remember
> He lieth hid in every member
>   As in the very whole."[4]

(5) Since, therefore, we cannot deny that the sacrament is broken, as the custom of the Church teaches (the senses will otherwise be led astray, through false reasonings based upon the truth), and the body of Christ is not broken, it is clear that the sacrament which is broken is not the body of Christ, because otherwise to the inquirer what is broken would be less

---

2. Cf. Wyclif, *Trialogus,* ed. Lechler (1849), 248.

3. *Res sacramenti:* "matter of the sacrament."

4. From the Sequence attributed to Thomas Aquinas, *Lauda Sion salvatorem,* lines 55–58. See Daniel, *Thesaurus hymnologicus* (Leipzig, 1841–1856), II, 98. My translation.

truly spoken of as the body of Christ: what indeed he seeks is the substance of the thing.

(6) The third objection they make is this, that unless the consecrated host is the body of Christ, we would not see nor eat the body of Christ, that is, we do not bite it with the teeth, and thus we would not receive it. Such a conclusion would be embarrassing for Christians.

(7) But here we reply by distinguishing two kinds of seeing, of eating, and of digesting: namely, corporeal and spiritual.[5] Thus we agree that we do not see the body of Christ in that sacrament with the bodily eye, but rather with the eye of the mind, that is, in faith through a mirror darkly. And just as the image is perfect in every part of the mirror, so that it can be seen either in part or completely by any bodily eye placed anywhere, so also should one believe in part concerning the body of Christ in the consecrated host as in a mirror. And in the same manner it is said that we do not physically touch or seize the body of Christ, just as we do not eat it corporeally. And this is the meaning of the hymn of the Church which sings,

> "What thou canst not take nor see,
> Faith yet affirms courageously,
> Beyond the things of sense."[6]

(8) Nor do we crush the body of Christ with the teeth, but rather we receive it in a spiritual manner, perfect and undivided. And so we understand the same hymn in which we sing,

> "The thing within sustains no tear;
> The sign alone is broken there;
> No loss the state or size doth bear
> Of this, the Signified."[7]

(9) But at this point certain folk object concerning our views that these ideas should not be mentioned to laymen who cannot understand or observe them, since from such ideas they might lose their former faith. But nothing is more absurd than such an objection; for entirely too many laymen as well as clergy are so unfaithful in this matter that they believe,

---

5. Cf. John Hus, *De corpore Christi*, in *Joannis Hus . . . historia et monumenta* (Nüremberg, 1558), I, fol. 174a, 15.

6. Daniel, op. cit., II, 97, lines 34–36. My translation, with assistance of Professor J. T. McNeill.

7. Ibid., II, 98, lines 59–62. My translation.

worse than pagans, that the consecrated host is their God. Then, of course, they arrive at the aforesaid pagan arguments. Therefore, he who does not understand these matters ill understands the belief in the Trinity or the incarnation. Nor is the above-mentioned lay belief a belief that is pleasing to the Lord of Truth, but the vilest disbelief because it is a form of idolatry whereby a creature, cast down rather than lifted up, is worshiped as God. So according to this stupidity any error in faith would never be taught or argued, but lest worse things come to pass, the Christian, teachable though he might be, would wallow in unbelief, as if he were to be told that he ought not to take a thorn out of his foot, a spear out of his flesh, or to remove some deadly poison, the cause of illness in his body, lest perchance things might grow worse. Therefore it is the duty of bishops to destroy these heresies; otherwise they would become heretics themselves by condoning such views.

(10) Their second objection is that if this idea were spread among the laity the honor and devotion of the people to this venerable sacrament would thereby be destroyed or at least lessened.

(11) But this fiction involves the same falsity. For just as the apostle says..., "Why not do evil that good may come?",[8] one might much more faithfully say, "Why not commit idolatry that the people might be the more completely seduced out of false and faithless devotion?" For certainly it might lie a little less open to popular belief that the cup in which is the blood of Christ and the wood through which, crucified, he is worshiped are really our God. Just as when the cup is seen we break forth into profound worship, so also when the consecrated host is seen we do the same, not on account of the fact that that very cup has been consecrated by the priest, but because of the excellent sacrament hidden in the vessel. Thus when we see the host we ought to believe not that it is itself the body of Christ, but that the body of Christ is sacramentally concealed in it.[9] And this is the meaning of the Church when it sings,

> "Beneath these many forms we see
> Signs only, not reality;
> The wonder lies concealed."[10]

(12) And it is clear that when this error of idolatry has been destroyed, we can worship God more purely than we now worship him, because we

---

8. Rom. 3:8, slightly altered.
9. On the belief that Christ lies hidden in the elements, see also Wyclif, *De Eucharistia,* 29. Cf. Wyclif, *Sermons,* IV, 344, where the Eucharist is called the "tomb of Christ."
10. Daniel, op. cit., II, 97, lines 37–39. My translation.

ought to believe that Christ, present, is hidden in these sacraments. Why therefore should we not worship Christ when the host is seen just as we do when the cup is seen, and just as the faithful more devotedly worship the divine Majesty when any creature whatsoever is seen by them? Therefore, when this meaning is understood, the true worship which is due to God will be pleasing to him, just as now the worship of falsehood is indeed abominable to God. And this is the true meaning even though it may be displeasing to the priests of idols.

(13) Their third objection is this: that priestly authority would be damaged if the privilege of making the blood and body of Christ were not admitted to exist. . . . But who then would hear the Mass? Who would devotedly hire Masses to be said? Or who would receive the sacrament according to the custom of the Church?

(14) Here it is said that the first does not follow, but when the error of blasphemy has been destroyed, the priestly authority would be kept and comprehended within its proper limits. Nothing can be more awful than that any priest can daily make or consecrate the body of the Lord by saying Mass. For our God is not a God newly made; nor is his body, since it is supremely holy and everlasting, thus sacramental or freshly to be created. But we priests make and bless the consecrated host, which is not the Lord's body, but an efficacious sign thereof. . . . Hence, because the priest does not have the power of making this sacrament except when God is the principal minister thereof, so the priest is said to complete, not the body of Christ, but the bare sacrament. And so because of sanctity of life, and not for that reason, ought he to be praised. So the Mass of the holy priest ought the more devotedly to be heard, and the Mass of the notorious sinner ought to be shunned. We do not buy the approbation of priests as if it were money; but without civil agreement we render to them the necessaries of life just as the apostle teaches us to do with respect to preachers.[11] . . . Yet note that just as we bless God and our Lord because they are worthy of praise, not because of what they do, so also do we bless the body and blood of Christ, not by making it blessed or holy, but by praising and spreading abroad its holiness and blessedness which God has instituted in his body, and thus we sacrifice Christ and offer him to God the Father.

(15) Note also further with respect to the spiritual receiving of the body of Christ that it does not consist in bodily receiving, chewing, or touching of the consecrated host, but in the feeding of the soul out of the fruitful

---

11. 1 Cor. 9:14 ff.

faith according to which our spirit is nourished in the Lord. And on account of ignorance of the eating of the body of Christ and drinking of his blood, many disciples have turned aside . . . : "Hard, they say, is this word, and who can hear it?"[12] For nothing is more horrible than the necessity of eating the flesh carnally and of drinking the blood carnally of a man loved so dearly. Therefore Christ speaks to the apostles, who, over and above the unworthy disciples who turned back, were worthy to be instructed in the life-giving sense because the carnal meaning of this will not benefit. But it is the spirit, that is, the spiritual meaning, which gives life,[13] while the other sense brings scandal when it is taken in evil part. Therefore, the faithful person must believe that that upon which his soul feeds in an objective sense is the spiritual food of the soul, and thus ought the flesh of Christ and his blood for sinners in dire straits to kindle in our spirits that love which is the food of the soul in order that we may in some measure willingly make recompense. . . . Augustine says . . . : "This it is therefore for a man to eat that meat and to drink that drink, to dwell in Christ, and to have Christ dwelling in him. Consequently he that dwells not in Christ, and in whom Christ dwells not, without any doubt neither eats His flesh spiritually nor drinks His blood, although he may press the sacrament of the body and blood of Christ carnally and visibly with his teeth. But rather does he eat and drink the sacrament of so great a thing to his own judgment."[14] And thus in the words of Christ and of his disciple Augustine three notable things ought to be pointed out: First, it is customarily supposed that the body and blood of Christ are eaten only in a spiritual sense, for God has ordained eternally that "his Holy One shall not see corruption"[15] in any of his members. Secondly, it is clear that neither a beast nor a man eternally foreknown to be reprobate eats Christ's body with his teeth, although he corporeally chews the sacrament. And thirdly, the wonderful subtlety of the words of the doctor is clear in which he says not that an unworthy person visibly presses the body of Christ with his teeth, but that he visibly presses the sacrament of the body and blood of Christ with his teeth. For that sacrament ought especially to be distinguished from the body of Christ which is the matter of the sacrament thereof.

---

12. John 6:61.
13. John 6:64, Vg.; 6:63, E. V.
14. Augustine, *In Joannem,* XXVI, 18, in Migne, *Patrologia Latina* (hereafter *PL*), 35:1614.
15. Ps. 15:10, Vg.; 16:10, E. V.

(17) We ought to mark well the difference which Augustine posits between carnal and spiritual eating;[16] for in carnal eating that which is eaten changes into nourishment for the eater when it is taken in by his members. But in spiritual eating it is otherwise. When one eats the body of Christ spiritually, one is thereby incorporated into the members of the Church, and thus into Christ. The act of spiritual eating then exceeds mere carnal eating. . . .

---

16. Augustine, op. cit., *PL*, 35:1614.

71. Treatise of Divine Providence
(1378)

CATHERINE OF SIENA

Unlike her contemporary, Julian of Norwich, Catherine of Siena (1347–1380), an Italian, was no anchorite. As a member of a Dominican third order (an uncloistered religious order whose members lived in their own homes), Catherine of Siena combined mystical devotion with practical service to the sick and the poor. She became an activist for peace among warring factions in Italy and a leader of moral reform in the church.

Catherine attracted a large following, including some of the leading clergy of her time. Lamenting the so-called "Babylonian captivity" of the papacy in Avignon, France, in 1377 she played a key role in persuading Pope Gregory XI to return to Rome. Unfortunately, instead of restoring the papacy, rival papal claims led to the Great Schism, with several persons declared pope at the same time. However, her mystical writings continued to inspire the Christian rank and file.

Filled with prophetic zeal for Christian conduct in church and society, Catherine cultivated a Christian spirituality typical of many women in the late Middle Ages. In her "Treatise of Divine Providence," a dialogue

---

SOURCE: Ray C. Petry, ed., *Late Medieval Mysticism*, vol. 13 of *Library of Christian Classics* (Philadelphia: Westminster Press, 1957). Used by permission of Westminster John Knox Press.

between God and the soul, she suggests that the experience of God's love leads the soul back to loving the neighbor.

"I have told thee how all sins are accomplished by means of thy neighbor, through the principles which I exposed to thee, that is, because men are deprived of the affection of love, which gives light to every virtue. In the same way self-love, which destroys charity and affection toward the neighbor, is the principle and foundation of every evil. All scandals, hatred, cruelty, and every sort of trouble proceed from this perverse root[1] of self-love, which has poisoned the entire world, and weakened the mystical body of the holy church, and the universal body of the believers in the Christian religion; and, therefore, I said to thee, that it was in the neighbor, that is to say, in the love of him, that all virtues were founded; and, truly, indeed did I say to thee, that charity gives life to all the virtues, because no virtue can be obtained without charity, which is the pure love of me.

"Wherefore, when the soul knows herself, as we have said above, she finds humility and hatred of her own sensual passion, for she learns the perverse law, which is bound up in her members, and which ever fights against the spirit. And, therefore, arising with hatred of her own sensuality, crushing it under the heel of reason, with great earnestness, she discovers in herself the bounty of my goodness, through the many benefits which she has received from me, all of which she considers again in herself. She attributes to me, through humility, the knowledge which she has obtained of herself, knowing that, by my grace, I have drawn her out of darkness and lifted her up into the light of true knowledge. When she has recognized my goodness, she loves it without any medium, and yet at the same time with a medium, that is to say, without the medium of herself or of any advantage accruing to herself, and with the medium of virtue, which she has conceived through love of me, because she sees that in no other way can she become grateful and acceptable to me but by conceiving hatred of sin and love of virtue; and, when she has thus conceived by the affection of love, she immediately is delivered of fruit for her neighbor, because in no other way can she act out the truth she has conceived in herself, but, loving me in truth, in the same truth she serves her neighbor.

"And it cannot be otherwise, because love of me and of her neighbor are one and the same thing,[2] and so far as the soul loves me she loves her

---

1. *Perversa radice.*
2. *È una medesima cosa.*

neighbor, because love toward him issues from me. This is the means which I have given you, that you may exercise and prove your virtue therewith; because, inasmuch as you can do me no profit, you should do it to your neighbor. This proves that you possess me by grace in your soul, producing much fruit for your neighbor and making prayers to me, seeking with sweet and amorous desire my honor and the salvation of souls. The soul, enamored of my truth, never ceases to serve the whole world in general, and more or less in a particular case according to the disposition of the recipient and the ardent desire of the donor, as I have shown above, when I declared to thee that the endurance of suffering alone, without desire, was not sufficient to punish a fault.

"When she has discovered the advantage of this unitive love in me, by means of which she truly loves herself, extending her desire for the salvation of the whole world, thus coming to the aid of its neediness, she strives, inasmuch as she has done good to herself by the conception of virtue, from which she has drawn the life of grace, to fix her eye on the needs of her neighbor in particular. Wherefore, when she has discovered, through the affection of love, the state of all rational creatures in general, she helps those who are at hand, according to the various graces which I have entrusted to her to administer; one she helps with doctrine, that is, with words, giving sincere counsel without any respect of persons; another with the example of a good life, and this indeed all give to their neighbor, the edification of a holy and honorable life. These are the virtues, and many others, too many to enumerate, which are brought forth in the love of the neighbor; but, although I have given them in such a different way — that is to say, not all to one, but to one one virtue, and to another another — it so happens that it is impossible to have one, without having them all, because all the virtues are bound together. Wherefore, learn that in many cases I give one virtue, to be as it were the chief of the others; that is to say, to one I will give principally love, to another justice, to another humility, to one a lively faith, to another prudence or temperance or patience, to another fortitude. These, and many other virtues, I place, indifferently, in the souls of many creatures; it happens, therefore, that the particular one so placed in the soul becomes the principal object of its virtue; the soul disposing herself, for her chief conversation, to this rather than to other virtues, and, by the effect of this virtue, the soul draws to herself all the other virtues, which, as has been said, are all bound together in the affection of love; and so with many gifts and graces of virtue, and not only in the case of spiritual things but also of temporal. I use the word "temporal" for the things necessary to the physical life of man; all these I have given indifferently, and I have not placed them all in one soul, in order that man should, perforce, have material for love of his fellow. I could easily have created men possessed of all that they should need both for body and soul, but I wish that one should have need of the other, and that they should be my ministers to administer the graces and the gifts that they have received from me. Whether man will or no, he cannot help making an act of love.[3] It is true, however, that that act, unless made through love of me, profits him nothing so far as grace is concerned. See, then, that I have made men my ministers, and placed them in diverse stations and various ranks, in order that they may make use of the virtue of love.

"Wherefore, I show you that in my house are many mansions, and that I wish for no other thing than love, for in the love of me is fulfilled and completed the love of the neighbor, and the law observed. For he only can be of use in his state of life who is bound to me with this love."

---

3. *Che voglia l'Uomo, o nò, non può fare, che per forza non usi l'atto della Carità.*

72. The Congregation of the Elect
From *De Ecclesia* (On the Church)
(1413)

JOHN HUSS

In 1382, Richard II of England married Anne of Bohemia, a daughter of Emperor Charles IV. The marriage of a Czech princess to an English king led to close ties between the followers of Wycliffe at Oxford University and a group of like-minded reformers at Prague. Although the Czech reformation of the late fourteenth and early fifteenth centuries had its roots in indigenous anticlerical and nationalist sentiments, the Czech students and scholars who visited Oxford eagerly accepted Wycliffe's ideas and writings. Prague became a center of Wycliffite teaching on the continent.

John Huss (c. 1372–1415) was a university teacher at Prague and a preacher at the renowned Bethlehem Chapel. He shared Wycliffe's Augustinian "realism" and agreed with much of the English reformer's doctrine of the church. Like Wycliffe, Huss believed that the church was the "congregation of the elect," where the righteous can be known by their "fruits." He asserted that popes and prelates often are found on the

---

SOURCE: John Huss, *The Church*, trans. and introduced by David Schaff (New York: Charles Scribner's Sons, 1915). Reprinted with the permission of Scribner, an imprint of Simon & Schuster, Inc. Copyright 1915 Charles Scribner's Sons; copyright renewed.

side of the devil, and that scripture and tradition — not hierarchy or canon law — should guide the people of God.

Since Christ asked all of his disciples to share the cup, Huss and his followers insisted on frequent communion "in both kinds." Huss, however, was less radical than Wycliffe. He did not question the doctrine of transubstantiation; his treatise, On the Church, *stops just short of arguing that unworthy priests lose the powers of their office (the Donatist heresy — see vol. 1: 201–2 and 429–30). More than Wycliffe, Huss was a moral reformer who considered himself as orthodox as his detractors. His self-confidence, however, was his undoing.*

In 1412 the notorious Pope John XXIII of the Pisa line, issued an indulgence (a promise from the church to lift the punishment for a sin in return for a monetary payment) to raise funds for a crusade against the Christian king of Naples, with whom he had a dispute over territory. Huss strongly opposed this abuse of the pope's spiritual authority for personal political ends. Although he did not attack the indulgence system as such, Huss spoke out against the pope. He gained the tumultuous admiration of the Bohemian people but lost the support of his king and many of his colleagues who supported the Pisa papacy.

Huss was excommunicated (denied personal access to the sacraments), and the city of Prague was placed under an interdict (which barred sacramental benefits to all of its inhabitants). Huss left the city and spent the next few years in voluntary exile, writing his treatise On the Church. *In 1415 he made an ill-fated journey to the Council of Constance to plead his orthodoxy. However, his guaranteed safe passage was not honored, and he was burned at the stake in 1415. Later Protestant reformers remember John Huss's death with passion.*

As every earthly pilgrim[1] ought faithfully to believe the holy catholic church just as he ought to love Jesus Christ, the Lord, the bridegroom of that church, and also the church herself, his bride; but as he does not love this, his spiritual mother, except he also know her by faith — therefore ought he to learn to know her by faith, and thus to honor her as his chief mother.[2]

---

1. *Viator,* a current word. See Wyclif, *de Eccles.,* 4, 42, 350. Gerson, Du Pin's ed., 2:22.

2. The designation mother is nowhere given to the church in the N. T. It is derived from the relation the church bears to Christ as his bride. Later on Augustine represents her as

Therefore, in order to reach a proper knowledge of her, it is to be noted, (1) That the church signifies the house of God, constituted for the very purpose that in it the people may worship its God, as it is written, 1 Cor. 2:22: "Have ye not houses to eat and to drink in?" Or, to speak with Augustine: "Do you despise the church of God, the house of prayer?" (2) The church signifies the ministers belonging to the house of God. Thus the clerics belonging to one material church call themselves the church. But according to the Greeks, a church—*ecclesia*—is a congregation—*congregatio*—held together under one rule, as Aristotle teaches, *Polit.* 2:7,[3] when he says: "All have part in the church." In view of this meaning, therefore, the congregation of all men is called the church—*ecclesia*. This appears in Matt. 25:31–33, which says: "When the Son of Man shall come in his glory and all his angels with him, then shall he sit upon the throne of his glory and before him shall be congregated all nations." What a great congregation of all men under the rule of Christ the king that will be! Because, however, the whole of that congregation is not the holy church it is added, "and he will separate them, the one from the other, as a shepherd separates the sheep from the goats."

From this it is evident that there is one church—*ecclesia*—of the sheep and another of the goats, one church of the righteous and another of the reprobate—*præsciti*.[4] Likewise the church of the righteous is on the one hand catholic, that is, universal, which is not a part of anything else. Of this I am now treating. On the other hand, it is particular, a part with other parts, as the Saviour said, Matt. 18:20: "Where two or three are congregated together in my name, there am I in the midst of them." From this it follows that two righteous persons congregated together in Christ's

---

giving birth to children. So Wyclif, *de Eccles.*, 117: "The church is a virgin since she is the bride of the virgin Jesus Christ, by whom as a mother we are born after a spiritual manner." It followed that Christ was the spiritual father or "father by faith," Wyclif, p. 1, and Grosseteste in this treatise, chap. IV. In his *Com. on the Lombard*, p. 469, Huss speaks of the church as "our most dear mother, the most worthy mother of the predestinate."

3. Aristotle, the authority of the Schoolmen in philosophy, and called, in the Middle Ages, The Philosopher. So Huss in this treatise, chap. IV, and often in his *Com. on the Lombard*.

4. The foreknown, that is, those of whom God knows beforehand that they are not in a state of permanent grace. Their condition is not the result of an active decree, though it is a subject of God's previous knowledge. The foreknown are in grace according to present righteousness and desire through merit at once eternal bliss and at the same time their damnation. This apparent contradiction Huss explains to lie in this, that they are not willing to use the means to the attainment of eternal bliss, just as a person may wish a coat and yet not possess it. *Super IV. Sent.*, 188.

name constitute, with Christ as the head, a particular holy church, and likewise three or four and so on to the whole number of the predestinate without admixture. In this sense the term church is often used in Scripture, as when the apostle says, 1 Cor. 1:1: "To the church which is in Corinth, to the sanctified in Jesus Christ." Likewise Acts 20:28: "Take heed to yourselves and to the whole flock in which the Holy Spirit hath made you bishops, to feed the church which he hath purchased with his own blood." And in this sense, all the righteous now living under Christ's rule in the city of Prague, and more particularly the predestinate, are the holy church of Prague, and the same is true of other particular churches of saints of which Ecclesiasticus 24:2, speaks: "In the congregations — *ecclesiis* — of the Most High shall she [wisdom] open her mouth," and also 31:11: "All the congregation of the saints shall declare his alms."[5]

But the holy catholic — that is, universal — church is the totality of the predestinate — *omnium predestinatorum universitas* — or all the predestinate,[6] present, past, and future. This definition follows St. Augustine on John, *C. Recur.* 32:4 [Friedberg, 1:1126], who shows how it is that one and the same church of the predestinate, starting at the beginning of the world, runs on to the apostles, and thence to the day of judgment. For Augustine says: "The church which brought forth Abel, Enoch, Noah and Abraham, also brought forth Moses, and at a later time the prophets before the Lord's advent and she, which brought forth these, also brought forth the apostles and our martyrs and all good Christians. For she has brought forth all who have been born and lived at different periods, but they have all been comprised in a company of one people. And the citizens of this city have experienced the toils of this pilgrimage. Some are experiencing them now, and some will be experiencing them, even to the end of the world." How clearly that holy man shows what the holy catholic church is! And, in the same place and in a similar way, he speaks of the church of the wicked. This, he says, "brought forth Cain, Ham, Ishmael, and Esau, and also Dathan and other like persons of that people. And she, which brought forth these, also brought forth Judas, the

---

5. See Bissell, *Com. on Apocrypha,* Lange Series, 343, 359. Also *Apocrypha* trsl. out of the Greek and Latin, Cambr., 1895.

6. Huss takes up the decree of predestination in his *Super IV. Sent.,* 153–188. He makes a slight distinction between elect and predestinate, although he says the Masters use the terms interchangeably. Election may only be for the present life, as in the case of Judas, of whom Christ said: "Did not I elect you twelve, yet one of you is a devil?" John 6:70. The predestinate cannot fall, and yet no necessity is placed upon their free will.

false apostles, Simon Magus, and other pseudo-Christians, down to these days — all obstinately hardened in fleshly lusts, whether they are mixed together[7] in a union or are clearly distinguished the one from the other." So much, Augustine.

From this statement it appears that the holy universal church is one, the church which is the totality of the predestinate, including all, from the first righteous man to the last one to be saved in the future. And it includes all who are to be saved who make up the number, in respect to the filling up of which number all the saints slain under the altar had the divine assurance that they should wait for a time until the number should be filled up of their fellow servants and brethren, Rev. 6:9–11. For the omniscient God, who has given to all things their weight, measure and number, has foredetermined how many shall ultimately be saved. Therefore, the universal church is also Christ's bride about whom the Canticles speak, and about whom Isaiah, 61:10, "as a bridegroom decked with a crown, and as a bride adorned with jewels." She is the one dove of which Christ said: "My dove is one, my excellent one," Canticles 6:9.[8] She is also the strong woman whose maidens are clothed with double garments, Prov. 21:2. She is the queen, of whom the Psalmist says: "The queen stands at thy right hand in vestments of gold" [Psalms 45:9]. This is Jerusalem, our mother, the temple of the Lord, the kingdom of heaven and the city of the Great King; and this whole church, as Augustine, *Enchiridion,* 41 [*Nic. Fathers*, 3:255, 256], says, "is to be understood not only of that part which sojourns here, praising God from the rising to the setting of the sun, and which, after its old captivity, is singing the new

---

7. *Permixli,* which the Decretum has instead of *proximi,* Huss's text.

8. This text *una est columba, una perfecta mea,* was a chief biblical proof used by the Schoolmen for the unity of the church. The Song of Solomon had a great fascination for the Schoolmen — the book upon which, one after another, they exercised their allegorical skill. It was regarded as an inspired anthology of the bodily and spiritual excellences of the Virgin Mary, and the perfections of the church. They found in it a storehouse of devotional meditation, as did Bernard, whose sermons on the Canticles are full of tropical effusions to Christ and to Mary, and the chief source of his mystical theology. Paschasius Radbertus, *de corpore et sanguine,* Migne 120:1295, says, "The Canticles treat of the holy church of God, which is called in the Canticles the paradise of delights." Damiani represented God as inflamed with love for Mary, singing the Canticles to her praise. Albertus Magnus, in his elaborate panegyric of Mary, dwells again and again upon its passages, devoting no less than two hundred and forty pages to the words, "a garden shut up is my sister, my bride," Cant. 4:12. Alanus ab Insulis speaks of the Canticles as referring to the church, but in the highest spiritual sense to Mary, and another of the saner Schoolmen, Rupert of Deutz, fills his commentary on the Canticles with the most tropical language.

song, but also of that part in heaven which, continuing true to the purpose for which it was constituted, has always been loyal to God, and has never felt misery from any fall. This part among the holy angels remains blessed and, as it behooves it to do, helps the part sojourning upon the earth, because she who is to be one by the companionship of eternity is now also one by the bond of love. And this whole church was constituted to worship God. Therefore, neither the whole nor any part of it wishes to be worshipped as God." So far, Augustine.

This is the holy catholic church which Christians profess immediately after professing their faith in the Holy Spirit.[9] First, because, as Augustine says,[10] she is the highest creature, therefore she is placed immediately after the Trinity, which is uncreate, and second, because she is bound to Christ in a never-ending matrimony, and by the love of the Holy Spirit. And third, because, the Trinity being once acknowledged, it is proper that it should have her as a temple in which to dwell.[11] Therefore Augustine, as above [*Enchiridion,* 41] concludes: "That God dwells in his temple — not only the Holy Spirit, but the Father likewise, and also the Son. And of his body — by virtue of which he is made head of the church of God which is among men, in order that in all things he might have the pre-

---

9. The reference is to the Apostles' Creed, "I believe in the holy catholic church," which is preceded by the confession of God the Father, Son and Holy Ghost. Also the Nicene creed. See Schaff, *Creeds,* 2:57 *sq.* With regard to the intercession of the saints in heaven and on earth, the council of Trent, XXV, says: "That the saints who reign together with Christ offer up their own prayers to God for men, and it is good and useful suppliantly to invoke them, and to have recourse to their prayers and help for obtaining benefits from God through his Son, Jesus Christ, our Lord, who is our only Redeemer and Saviour."

10. In the *Enchiridion,* as quoted above. Augustine makes a similar statement in his sermon to catechumens, *Nic. Fathers,* 3:375.

11. The writers of the M. A. also made Mary the dwelling-place of the Trinity, especially the hymn-writers. So the great hymnist, Adam of St. Victor, in the lines

Salve mater pietatis
Et totius trinitatis
  Nobile triclinium.

Hail, mother of piety;
And of the whole Trinity
  Excellent refectory (monastic hall).

As the church is the bride of Christ, so Mary was also represented as the spouse of the Holy Spirit. Alfonso da Liguori delights so to represent her, as for example, in the prayer: "I thank thee, O eternal Spirit, for the love given to Mary, thy spouse." In his encyclical to the French bishops, Jan. 15, 1907, Pius X spoke "of his full confidence in the Virgin Immaculate, daughter of our Father, mother of the Word and spouse of the Holy Ghost," etc.

eminence — the Son said: 'Destroy this temple and in three days I will build it up again'" [John 2:21]. From these words of Augustine we deduce (1) that the universal church is one, praising God from the beginning of the world to the end; (2) that the holy angels are a part of the holy catholic church; (3) that the part of the church called pilgrim or militant is helped by the church triumphant; (4) that the church triumphant and the church militant are bound together by the bond of love; (4) that the whole church and every part of it are to worship God, and that neither she nor any part of it wishes to be worshipped as God.

From all this the conclusion follows, that the faithful ought not to believe *in* the church, for she is not God, but the house of God, as Augustine in his *Exposition of the Creed* says,[12] but they should believe that the catholic church is the bride of the Lord Jesus Christ — bride, I say, chaste, incorrupt, and never capable of being corrupted. For St. Cyprian, the bishop and glorious martyr, 24:1, *C. Loquitur* [Friedberg, 1:971, *de Unitate Eccles.*, 5; *Ante-Nic. Fathers*, 5:423], says: "The church is one, which is spread abroad far and wide by the increase of her fruitfulness." And he adds: "nevertheless the head is one, the origin is one, and one is the copious mother of fruitfulness. The bride of Christ cannot be defiled. She is incorrupt and chaste. She knows one house and guards with chaste modesty the sanctity of one couch."[13] The holy church is also the husbandman's vineyard, of which Gregory in his Homilies [Migne, 76:1154] says: "Our Maker has a vineyard, namely the universal church, which starts from righteous Abel and goes down to the last elect person who shall be born in the end of the world, which bears as many saints as the vineyard sends forth branches." Of the church St. Remigius[14] also says in his Homily Quadragesima on the text: "'The men of Nineveh shall rise up in judgment with this generation and condemn it.' The holy church is made up of two parts, those who have not sinned and those who have ceased to sin." St. Isidore also, in speaking of the church, *de Summo Bono*, 14 [Migne, 83:572][15] says: "The holy church is called catholic for

---

12. *Sermo de symbolo*, falsely ascribed to Augustine and given in the Appendix to his Works (Migne, 40:1196). Three of Augustine's genuine treatises on the creed are given in translation, *Nic. Fathers*, vol. III, 282–314; 321–333; 369–375.

13. *Cubilis*. The Decretum has *cubiculi*, bedchamber.

14. Remigius, d. about 908, a Benedictine monk of Auxerre, who also taught at Paris. He wrote commentaries on the Psalms, Genesis, etc., and 12 Homilies on Matthew, all found in Migne, 131. He supported Paschasius's view of the change of the eucharistic elements.

15. Usually known as the *de sententiis*, the first Latin compend of theology, and a forerunner of the *Sentences of Peter the Lombard* and the systems of the summists of the

the reason that it is universally distributed over all the world." Augustine and Ambrose likewise in their canticle, *Praising God,* say: "The holy church throughout all the world doth acknowledge Thee."[16] And Ambrose, 24:1 [Friedberg, 1:976] speaks thus of her: "What house is more worthy of the entrance of apostolic preaching than is the holy church? Or who else is to be preferred above all others than Christ, who was accustomed to wash the feet of his guests and did not suffer any whom he received into his house to dwell there with soiled steps, that is, works?" And, speaking of this church, Pope Pelagius, 24:1, *C. Schisma* [Friedberg 1:980],[17] cites Augustine as saying, "There cannot be two churches," and then adds: "Truly, as it has often been said, there can be only one church, the church which is Christ's body, which cannot be divided into two or more bodies." Jerome also says of the church, *de Pœn., Dist.* 1: *C. Eccl.* [Friedberg 1:1179]: "The church of Christ has no spot or wrinkle or anything of that sort, but he who is a sinner or is soiled with any filth cannot be said to be of Christ's church." This holy universal church is Christ's mystical body, as the apostle says, Eph. 1:22: "He gave himself to be the head over all the church, which is his body." Again he said, Col.

Middle Ages. Isidore, archbishop of Seville (d. 636), exercised a large influence over the scholastic studies of the Middle Ages, especially by his encyclopedic works, the *Etymologiæ* and the *de natura rerum.* The former is a general encyclopedia giving curious information derived from ancient authors, classic and ecclesiastical, on a large variety of subjects: medicine, law, the Bible, grammar, warfare, etc. See Bréhaut, *An Encyclopedist of the Dark Ages,* New York, 1912. Isidore was one of the very first to write a treatise designed to convince the Jews, *de fide catholica c. Judæos.* The high church fraud, the pseudo-Isidorian Decretals, which appeared about 853, was for centuries ascribed to Isidore. In the chapter quoted by Huss Isidore says, "The holy catholic church tolerates with patience in herself those who live ill, but casts out from herself those who believe ill," and again, "They are heretics who, leaving the church of God, have chosen private societies, that is, they have hewn out broken cisterns for themselves."

16. The *Te Deum,* or canticle to the Trinity, beginning, "We praise Thee, O God." According to the legend, first noted by Hincmar in the ninth century, Augustine and Ambrose at Augustine's baptism, 387, under supernatural inspiration, improvised the hymn. In the West it became a part of the church service as early as the sixth century, if not earlier. See Julian, *Hymnology,* p. 1119 *sqq.;* Augustine, *Conff.,* 9:7, refers to the moving impression made upon him by the "hymns and canticles" sung in the church of Milan. For these reasons, Raphael gave Augustine a place in his painting of St. Cecilia, in Bologna.

17. Pelagius I, pope, 555–561, witnessed the ravages of the Goth, Totila, in Rome, and helped to repair them during his pontificate. He was Justinian's choice for the papal office. The quotation is from Pelagius's letter to a certain patrician, John, condemning the ordination of Paulinus of Aquileja by the schismatic bishop of Milan as something to be execrated rather than to be regarded as sacred. See Jaffa, *Regesta pontificum,* p. 88. In this letter, Pelagius also quotes for the unity of the church Cant. 6:9: "My dove is one."

1:18, "He is the head of the body, which is the church," and again, Col. 1:24, "For his body's sake, which is the church," and Eph. 5:23, "Christ is the head of the church and himself is the Saviour of his body," and further on: "Christ loved the church and gave himself for it that he might sanctify it, washing it with the washing of water in the word of life that he might present it to himself a glorious church, not having spot or wrinkle or anything of that kind, but that it should be holy and without spot."

Upon this text the holy doctors lean, as when Augustine says, *de doctrina Christi* [3:37, *Nic. Fathers,* 2:573]: "Christ is the head of the church, which is his body destined in the future to be with him in his kingdom and unending glory." Gregory, *Moralia,* 35:9 [Migne, 76:762] says: "Because Christ and the church are one, the head and the body are one person." And on Ezekiel, homily 15, he says: "The church is one substance with Christ, its head." And Bernard on the Canticles, homily 12 [Migne, 183:831]: "The church is Christ's body, more dear than the body he gave over to death."[18] And Paschasius, *de sacra. corporis Christi* [Migne, 120:1284][19] says: "Even as it is found in the Scriptures — the church of Christ, or the bride of God, is truly called Christ's body, truly because the general church of Christ is his body and Christ is called the head and all the elect are called members. From these members the one body of the church is brought unto a perfect man and the measure of the fulness of Christ. But the body of Christ, that is, the bride of God, is called in law the church. This is according to the apostle's words: 'And they twain shall be one flesh.' This, he says, is a great sacrament in Christ and the church.[20] For, if Christ and the church are one flesh, then certainly

---

18. The passage runs: "The catholic lives and eats of the living bread which came down from heaven. She is the more precious body of Christ, and lest she should taste of death the other was given over to death."

19. This treatise of Paschasius, d. 865, usually quoted as *de corpore et sanguine Christi,* is one of the most important treatises bearing on the development of the doctrine of transubstantiation. Without using the word, Paschasius set forth the view in the Lord's Supper the very body "which was born of the Virgin Mary, suffered on the cross and rose again," is distributed by the priest. He supports this view by the literal interpretation of John 6:54: "Whoso eateth my flesh and drinketh my blood." Paschasius was a monk and then, 844–851, abbot of the convent of Corbie, nearer Amiens. His tract was written 831 and sent to Charles the Bald 844. His doctrine was opposed by the monk Ratramnus, and others. The next controversy over the Lord's Supper was led by Berengar, d. 1088. Transubstantiation was made a dogma of the church at the fourth Lateran council, 1215. Wyclif denied it, declaring that transubstantiation would involve transaccidentation. Huss was also charged with denying the doctrine, but emphatically repudiated the charge. Ratramnus's work was put on the Index by the council of Trent.

20. Eph. 5:32. The false translation of Jerome, rendering the Greek word mystery by

there is one body, one head, one bridegroom, but different elect persons, members the one of the other." So far, Paschasius.

These quotations from the saints show that the holy catholic church is the number of all the predestinate[21] and Christ's mystical body — Christ being himself the head — and the bride of Christ, whom he of his great love redeemed with his blood that he might at last possess her as glorious, not having wrinkle of mortal sin or spot of venial sin, or anything else defiling her, but that she might be holy and without spot, perpetually embracing Christ, the bridegroom.

---

sacrament, a rendering used to justify the inclusion of marriage among the sacraments and repeated in the Rheims version.

21. Wyclif, *Congregatio omnium predestinatorum, solum numerus predestinatorum, de Eccles.*, 2, 5, etc. In his *Com. on the Lombard*, p. 36, Huss defines the church as "the congregation of all the faithful about to be saved. It is the mystical body of Christ, that is now hidden to us, of which body the damned do not really have part, but they are like dung which in the day of judgment are to be separated from the body of Christ."

73. Reformers Against the Reformers
1414–18

THE COUNCIL OF CONSTANCE

The first reform Council at Pisa (1409) not only failed to end the Great Schism (two rival popes: one in Avignon and one in Rome), it resulted in three competing popes (see vol. 1:414). In 1414, the conciliar reformers vowed to try again. This time, Emperor Sigismund and Pope John XXIII (the pope in the Pisan line who hoped that the new council would confirm him in office) issued a joint call to a general council in the city of Constance.

John tried to improve his chances by appointing a new group of cardinals, but the conciliar party blocked this effort with a procedural change. Rather than be deposed, John fled the city. Prompted by John Gerson, the Council of Constance passed its most famous decree. The decree, entitled "Sacrosancta," declared that a general council receives its authority directly from Christ. Therefore, all Christians, including popes and prelates, are bound to obey its decisions. "Sacrosancta" marked the high point of representative governance in the Roman church.

The "way of the council" (via concilii) ended the Great Schism. It deposed two of the rival popes and forced the third to resign. In 1417, the cardinals at the Council of Constance elected Martin V (d. 1431), a strong leader who restored unity to the church by reasserting papal control. The Council of Constance also passed numerous minor reforms.

The conciliar reformers at Constance were tired of schism and concerned about heresy. They pressed toward unity at almost any cost, unwilling to tolerate dissent. The council condemned the teachings of John Wycliffe and ordered that his remains be exhumed from dedicated ground at Lutterworth and burned. His ashes were scattered in the River Swift.

Furthermore, when John Huss arrived from Bohemia, the conciliar party allowed him to be arrested by Pope John XXIII, a man they themselves uniformly despised. Pierre d'Ailly induced the reluctant Emperor Sigismund to accept the argument that promises to heretics need not be kept. Therefore, Huss's safe conduct was revoked; he was tried and burned as a heretic. When Jerome of Prague came to Constance to join his friend, he too was arrested. Although Jerome recanted at first, in the end he revoked his confession and followed Huss to the stake. Christian history records the Council of Constance as one of its bleakest moments—a place and time where reformers burned reformers.

Excerpts from Fillastre's Diary *give a careful account of the proceedings against John Huss in 1415 and against Jerome of Prague a year later. Another eyewitness report of the executions of Huss and Jerome, written by local resident Richental, describes the courage of the Bohemian reformers. Notice his last paragraph, describing the diversions available to visiting clergy who happened to be in town for the occasion.*

As in the ancient church, the blood of the martyrs was the seed for church renewal. In spite of severe persecution, remnants of Wycliffe's movement (the Lollards, "mumblers") survived in England until the sixteenth century. The death of Huss and Jerome touched off a Bohemian revolt against the church and the empire. The Hussites demanded freedom of the pulpit, apostolic poverty for the clergy, punishment for simony (the buying or selling of ecclesiastical offices or pardons), and the right to celebrate the Eucharist in both kinds. Their zeal to celebrate the Eucharist in both kinds became the nonnegotiable symbol of the Hussite movement.

In the ensuing conflict, Czech armies defeated three imperial "crusades" against them between 1421 and 1431, using peasant carts spiked with scythes. At the Council of Basel in 1436, a conservative wing of the Hussite movement (Utraquists) gained limited recognition from the pope and the emperor, including permission to celebrate communion in both (utra) *kinds. Called the "First Reformation" by the descendents of this movement, the Hussite movement survived as the* Unitas Fratrum *(literally the "unity of brethren"). Today the Moravians carry on this legacy.*

"Sacrosancta"
(1415)

This holy Council of Constance . . . declares, first that it is lawfully assembled in the Holy Spirit, that it constitutes a General Council, representing the Catholic Church, and that therefore it has its authority immediately from Christ; and that all men, of every rank and condition, including the Pope himself, is bound to obey it in matters concerning the Faith, the abolition of the schism, and the reformation of the Church of God in its head and its members. Secondly it declares that any one, of any rank and condition, who shall contumaciously refuse to obey the orders, decrees, statutes or instructions, made or to be made by this holy Council, or by any other lawfully assembled general council . . . shall, unless he comes to a right frame of mind, be subjected to fitting penance and punished appropriately: and, if need be, recourse shall be had to the other sanctions of the law. . . .

Propositions of Wyclif Condemned at London, 1382, and at the Council of Constance, 1415.

1.[1] That the material substance of bread and the material substance of wine remain in the Sacrament of the altar.

2. That the accidents of bread do not remain without a subject (substance) in the said Sacrament.

3. That Christ is not in the Sacrament essentially and really, in his own corporeal presence.

4. That if a bishop or a priest be in mortal sin he does not ordain, consecrate or baptize.

SOURCE: Henry Bettenson, *Documents of the Christian Church* (New York: Oxford University Press, 1963). Used by permission of Oxford University Press.

1. The propositions are numbered as at Constance.

5. That it is not laid down in the Gospel that Christ ordained the Mass.

6. That God ought to obey the devil.[2]

7. That if a man be duly penitent any outward confession is superfluous and useless.

10. That it is contrary to Holy Scripture that ecclesiastics should have possessions.

14. That any deacon or priest may preach the word of God apart from the authority of the Apostolic See or a Catholic bishop.

15. That no one is civil lord, or prelate, or bishop, while he is in mortal sin.

16. That temporal lords can at their will take away temporal goods from the church, when those who hold them are sinful (habitually sinful, not sinning in one act only).

17. That the people can at their own will correct sinful lords.

18. That tithes are mere alms, and that parishioners can withdraw them at their will because of the misdeeds of their curates.

20. That he who gives alms to friars is by that fact excommunicate.

21. That any one who enters a private religion [i.e. religious house], either of those having property or of mendicants, is rendered more inapt and unfit for the performance of the commands of God.

22. That holy men have sinned in founding private religions.

23. That the religious who live in private religions are not of the Christian religion.

24. That friars are bound to gain their livelihood by the labour of their hands, and not by begging.

[The above are common to the proceedings at London and at Constance. Many other propositions, of which a few are given below, were condemned at Constance. They are more extreme in tone and are probably to be attributed more to the Lollards than to Wycliffe himself.]

28. That the confirmation of young men, the ordination of clerics, the consecration of places are reserved for the Pope and bishops on account of the desire for temporal gain and honour.

30. That the excommunication of the Pope or of any prelate is not to be feared, because it is the censure of antichrist.

34. That all of the order of mendicants are heretics.

35. That the Roman Church is the synagogue of Satan, and the Pope is not the next and immediate vicar of Christ and the Apostles.

---

2. I.e., "Dominion by grace" cannot be put into operation in the world as it is.

42. That it is fatuous to believe in the indulgences of the Pope and the bishops.

43. That all oaths made to corroborate human contracts and civil business are unlawful.

The Trial of the Bohemian Reformers

FROM *Fillastre's Diary*

[*Session XII.*] Accordingly, on Wednesday, May 29, anno Domini 1415, the vigil of the feast of the Holy Eucharist,[1] the Council held a session, with the King present and the Cardinal of Ostia presiding, and pronounced the sentence of deposition of the Pope. It was read by the Bishop of Arras, who has a loud, deep voice.[2] The tenor of it was as follows:

"The sacrosanct general synod of Constance, representing the Catholic Church . . . decrees, enacts, and ordains that if the Apostolic See should for any reason become vacant, no steps whatever shall be taken at the beginning of the vacancy to elect a future supreme pontiff without the decision and consent of this sacred general Council. If any such steps are taken, they shall be *ipso facto,* by authority of the said sacred Council, null and void. . . .

"Further, the said holy synod decrees, enacts, and ordains, for the good of the union of the Church of God, that lord Baldassarre Cossa, Pedro de Luna, and Angelo Corario, known of late by their obediences as John XXIII, Benedict XIII, and Gregory XII, shall never be reelected to the papacy."[3]

SOURCE: John Hine Mundy and Kennerly M. Woody, eds., *The Council of Constance: The Unification of the Church*, trans. Louise Ropes Loomis (New York: Columbia University Press, 1961). Copyright © 1961 by Columbia University Press. Used by permission of the publisher.

1. Now better known as Corpus Christi.
2. Martin Poree, ambassador of Duke of Burgundy.
3. Hardt, Heinrich von der, *Magnum oeccuminicum Constantiense concilium*, 6 vols.,

"In the name of the Holy and Indivisible Trinity, Father, Son, and Holy Spirit. Amen. The sacrosanct general synod of Constance, lawfully assembled in the Holy Spirit, invoking the name of Christ and keeping God only before its eyes, has noted the articles formulated and presented in the case against the lord Pope John XXIII, the proofs of the same and his own voluntary submission, as also the entire procedure in the case, and after mature deliberation pronounces, decrees, and declares this definitive sentence, which it now issues in writing.

"The clandestine departure of the said lord Pope John XXIII from this city of Constance and the sacred general Council, at a suspicious hour of night, in unsuitable disguise, was and is unwarrantable, a notorious scandal to the Church of God and the Council, a disturbing obstacle to the peace and union of the Church, an aid to prolonging the schism and a violation of the vow, promise, and oath sworn by the same lord Pope John to God and the Church and this sacred Council. The same lord Pope John was and is a notorious simoniac, a notorious waster of the property and rights of the Roman and other churches and of many other pious institutions, and an evil administrator and dispenser of the spiritual and temporal treasures of the Church. By his detestable and dishonorable life and character he has notoriously scandalized the Church of God and Christian people, both before his elevation to the papacy and since, down to the present. On all these counts he has been and is in himself a notorious scandal to the Church of God and Christian people. In spite of due and charitable warnings, repeated on many occasions, he has persisted obstinately in his wicked course and proved himself notoriously incorrigible.

"Therefore, for these and other crimes, set forth and related in the proceedings of the case against him, he deserves to be unseated, removed, and deposed from the papacy and all administration, spiritual and temporal, as unworthy, unprofitable, and dangerous. And the said holy synod hereby unseats, removes, and deposes him, declaring all and every Christian of whatever rank, dignity, or condition released from obedience, fealty, and obligation to him, and forbidding all the faithful of Christ, now that he is herewith deposed from the papacy, from receiving him henceforth as pope or calling him pope or adhering to him as pope or paying him any obedience.... Other penalties that by canonical rules should be inflicted for his crimes and excesses the Council reserves to be pro-

---

Frankfurt and Leipzig. Gensius, 1692–1700. Completed by a seventh volume of indices by C. Ch. Bohnstedt. Berlin, Henningius, 1742; IV, 280–284.

nounced and inflicted at its discretion, as strict justice or considerations of mercy may dictate."

After passing the sentence, the Council sent it to the Pope, who was still confined at Radolfzell, and the Pope accepted it and performed an unconditional abdication according to the formula then prepared.

Then action was taken against John Hus, that is, the heretic already mentioned. He was convicted of many heresies and errors, both by witnesses and by a book of his own composition, which he called, *De Ecclesia*. The book was written by his own hand and acknowledged by him. He agreed to abide by the decision of the Council, but, when ordered to abjure certain statements, he raised difficulties and said he had never made them. However, proof was brought to the contrary. Action was also taken on the further errors of Wyclif, the 266 articles mentioned above.

• • •

[*Session XV.*] On the following Saturday, which was the 6th of July, the Council held a session to deal with the errors of Master John Wyclif of England, deceased, condemn his memory, and pass sentence on Master John of Bohemia. The following sentences were passed. First, as regards Wyclif, the Council condemned the forty-five articles, enumerated below, on the one hand, and the 260 articles on the other hand, and approved the sentence of the last Roman council, which had condemned his books and his memory. The same day it passed sentence on Master John Hus, who was present, condemned and degraded him for heresy, and delivered him to the secular court. For he persisted in his errors and when urged in the Council to repent, recant, and abjure, stood up and declared in a loud voice that he would not recant, because he believed that by so doing he would displease God and the saints; nor would he be a scandal to the multitude to whom he had preached his doctrines in Bohemia. So that very day he was conducted by the secular court outside the city and burned, impenitent....

• • •

From Richental's *Chronicle*

On Wednesday, May 27, 1416, the second year of the Council, the vigil of the Lord's Ascension, the Council held a session, without solemnities, and gave public audience to Jerome of Prague, at his own request.[4] For the new commissioners had begun new proceedings against him, an examination on the charge of heresy. He made a great speech to prove that hatred, false witnesses, and lies were being employed to convict him. In the course of it, he cited many examples from the Old and New Testaments of holy men who had suffered for the truth from false testimony and hate and showed that no one had ever been overcome by so many false means as he. At the end, he revoked forever, as he said, the abjuration, confession, and declaration which he had made in the session of the Council on Monday, September 23 [1415], in which he had approved and assented to the sentence of condemnation passed on Wyclif and John Hus, condemned for heresy of teaching and writing. This John Hus had been condemned for heresy in July and burned by the secular court, and the memory of Wyclif, long dead, had been condemned.

Jerome now said that he had made that confession and abjuration and had assented to and approved those verdicts wickedly and falsely, in foolish terror of an imaginary fire. He was not afraid to confess his falsehood and spoke of Hus always as a good man. But with regard to the article on the sacrament of the altar and the transsubstantiation of the bread into the body of Christ, he said he held and believed what the Church believed and on this point he preferred to believe Augustine and the other doctors rather than Wyclif or Hus.

[*Session XXI.*] On the Saturday after the Lord's Ascension, May 30, the Council held a session with solemnities, in miters and copes, and Mass was performed. The lord Cardinal Bishop of Ostia presided at the condemnation of Jerome. After Mass and the customary prayers, the oft-mentioned Bishop of Lodi preached a fine sermon, taking his text from the Gospel for the Lord's Ascension: "He upbraided them for their unbelief and hardness of heart."[5] He spoke with great eloquence, urging Jerome, who was present, to repent and save his soul. After the sermon, the Patriarch of Constantinople read the declaration which Jerome had made on the 23rd of the previous September, before the Council, as stated above, and said that Jerome had revoked it some days since and therefore had relapsed into heresy. In a loud voice Jerome confessed that he had revoked it, as he did on the Wednesday preceding, and went on to make many allegations, asserting, as he did before, that he was overcome by

---

4. Hardt, IV, 37 records this examinatory session as running from May 18 to May 21.
5. Matt. 16:14.

false witnesses, hatred, and lies and citing the examples of Paul and Christ, who were overcome by the Jews.

Finally, he professed the Catholic faith in general and refused to recant in any particular. He said also that Hus had been called a heretic because he preached against the arrogance of the clergy. To which the Cardinal of St. Mark replied that he ought not to invent such grounds for Hus's condemnation. The sacred Council knew and deplored the fact that many ecclesiastics did assume excessive arrogance and pomp, and had assembled in order to reform that and other bad customs and expected to do so. But it was characteristic of heretics to mix some truth in with their false doctrines, so that simple people who heard the truth would believe the false remainder was true also.

The Patriarch of Constantinople then read the sentence against Jerome. . . .[6] After the reading of the sentence a paper cap, painted over with devils, was given to Jerome, who took it boldly and set it on his head, saying: "Christ wore a crown of thorns." And he was received by the secular court, led to the fire, and burned.

• • •

Now turn I again to the Council to tell how it dealt with those two and what took place and how our lord King departed to go to other kings and lords and how he came back again. On the Saturday after St. Ulrich's Day, July 8, 1415, there was a session. Our lord King was present and Duke Louis of Bavaria-Heidelberg and many other temporal princes and lords, and the session was held the sixth hour after midnight. Master John Hus of Bohemia, the heretic, was brought in, and the reverend, devout Master John Dachery, rector in divinity at the High School of Paris, preached to him of his wicked heresy.[7] And Hus was confuted by holy, divine teaching from Holy Writ, proving that the articles which he had preached and taught were truly false heresy and that the sentence passed on him was just.

Since he was a consecrated priest, he was first degraded and his consecration stripped from him. Lord Nicholas, grandmaster and the lord

---

6. Hardt, IV, 769–71.

7. Richental's *Chronicle* is the only source to say that Dachery preached against Hus at this time. The preacher for the session was Bishop Jacob of Lodi, Master (of theology) of the Sacred Palace. The date was Saturday, July 6.

Archbishop of Milan,[8] two cardinals, two bishops, and two bishops-elect stood up and dressed him in a priest's habit and took it off again with prayers and divested him of his office. But he made only a mock of that. When it was done, they pronounced sentence upon him, that he was a heretic and must be punished for his iniquity. Then they delivered him over to the civil justice, requesting our lord King and the civil court not to put him to death but to keep him imprisoned.[9]

The King then said to Duke Louis: "Since I am one who wields the temporal sword, take him, dear uncle, Duke Louis, our Elector of the Holy Roman Empire and Lord High Steward, and deal with him as a heretic, in our stead." Then Duke Louis called to Hans Hagen, the advocate of Constance, who was advocate on behalf of the Empire and there present, and said to him: "Advocate, take him, under the joint sentence of us both and burn him as a heretic." The advocate then summoned the soldiers of the town council and the executioner to take him away to be burned but forbade them to remove his gown, girdle, purse, knife, money, stockings, or shoes. So it was done. He wore two good black coats of good cloth and a girdle with small ornaments on it and two knives in one sheath and a leather purse which might have contained something. He had a white miter on his head, on which two devils were painted, and between them was the word "Heresiarch," which means Archbishop of all Heretics.

They led him out of Constance with more than a thousand armed men, and the princes and lords went also armed. Two servants of Duke Louis guarded him, one on his right hand and one on his left. He was not in fetters, for they walked close beside him, and they called me, Richental, to go with them. Before and behind him were the soldiers of the town council and they took him out through the Gelting Gate. Because of the dense crowds that thronged about them, they were forced to take a way around the meadow, by Richman's dower house. The men in armor grew still more numerous, about three thousand, in addition to the unarmed men and the women. At the bridge by the Gelting Gate they had to keep back the mob and compel them to pass in file for fear the bridge would break. They led him into the middle of the small outer field. On the way

---

8. Nicholas has been described before as Chief Prior of the Order of the Holy Sepulcher. The Archbishop of Milan was Bartholomew Francisci della Capra. He was president of the Italian nation (at the Council).

9. A pure formality. Relaxation to the secular arm implied death in such a case.

out, he uttered only the prayer: "*Jesu Christe, fili Dei Vivi, miserere mei*" [Jesus Christ, Son of the Living God, have mercy upon me!]. When he came to the outer field and saw the pyre, the wood and straw, he fell three times on his knees and cried aloud: "*Jesu Christe, fili Dei Vivi, qui passus es pro nobis, miserere mei!*" [Jesus Christ, Son of the Living God, who suffered for us, have mercy upon me!]

They asked him if he wished to confess and he answered: "I would gladly, but there is no space here." For now he was ringed about with people. They made the ring wider, and then I asked him if he wished to confess. There was a priest there, called Lord Ulrich Schorand, who had authority from the Council and the bishop. I called this Lord Ulrich, and he came to Hus and said to him: "Dear lord and master, if you will renounce the unbelief and heresy for which you must suffer, I will gladly hear your confession. But if you will not, you yourself know well that the spiritual law forbids us to perform any divine service for a heretic." And Hus replied: "I do not need it. I am no mortal sinner." Then He started to preach in German, but Duke Louis would not permit that and ordered them to burn him. The executioner then took and bound him hurriedly in his gown to an upright stake, set a stool under his feet, piled wood and straw around him, scattering a little pitch over it, and lighted the fire. He began to cry out terribly but soon was burned.

When he himself had been entirely burned, the miter on his head was still whole. The executioner knocked it down, and it burned also. Then the worst stench arose that one could smell, for Cardinal Pancratius[10] had had a mule that died of old age and was buried there, and when the heat went into the earth, the stench arose. All the ashes that were left they threw into the Rhine. . . .

• • •

On Sunday [September 8] before Holy Cross Day, 1416, in the autumn, a great session was held with all the spiritual folk and learned lords and the entire Council. Duke Louis of Bavaria-Heidelberg took part in it, and our lord King had committed to him the care of the Council. The bells were rung, first after Matins, again early, before morning Mass, and then all together after morning Mass. They sang the Solemn Mass of the Holy

---

10. This refers to Rainald Brancacci who was created cardinal deacon of SS. Vito and Modesto by Urban VI in 1385, and who died in 1427. Rainald (was customarily) called the cardinal of Brancaccio.

Trinity. After Mass, Jerome, the heretic, was brought in and a master of theology from England preached. After the sermon, the masters of theology proved that Jerome had preached and taught falsehoods and would not renounce them or write the letter to Bohemia.[11] So he was condemned as a heretic and delivered to Duke Louis of Bavaria, who ordered him to be led out and burned. Then they took him out, as they did Hus, although not so many armed men went with them, for the majority of the Bohemians and the laity who had been at Constance had left with our lord King, and others had gone to their homes.

As they led him out of the city, he repeated the creed, and, when he was outside, he sang the litany and then once more the creed. He was burned on the spot where Hus was burned, and, as with Hus, no one heard his confession. He lived much longer in the fire than Hus and shrieked terribly, for he was a stouter, stronger man, with a broad, thick, black beard. After he was burned, they threw all the ashes and everything else into the Rhine. Many learned men were grieved that he had to die, for he was a far greater scholar than Hus. He was a Master of Arts at Prague, in the city of London in England, at Cologne, and at Erfurt.

Thereafter the Council continued in good peace, and there was no dispute between anyone. Strangers were so secure and peaceful that they would ride out or stroll a mile beyond Constance, through the cities and forests, wherever they liked. Especially into the Aichorn they went every day. In that wood, there were taverns that sold all manner of wines, whatever were wanted. And roast fowls, sausage, meat, and broiled fish were to be found there and whatever else was wanted, and gay women who belonged to the establishments. The spiritual lords wandered in any gardens they chose, and no one opposed them, and they did no harm. So the lords passed their time.

---

11. Richental has Jerome's dates wrong. He first recanted on September 11 and then again on September 23, 1415. He revoked his recantations on May 26, 1416, and was burned on May 30.

Praise and Prayer

74. Two Twelfth-Century Hymns

PETER ABELARD AND BERNARD OF CLAIRVAUX

Peter Abelard (c. 1079–1142) is better known for his critical scholarship and for a calamitous relationship with a lover named Heloise, than for his poetry. Yet this great teacher and "rationalist" of the twelfth century, known as a forerunner of the enlightenment, was also a person of deep faith. Abelard's "Hymn for Saturday vespers" is a beautiful liturgical poem originally written in Latin.

Bernard of Clairvaux (1090–1153), the famous and revered Cistercian monk who supported the church during one of its bleakest periods (see vol. 1:423–38), is considered the author of the well-known Latin hymn "Jesus the very thought of thee." Bernard believed that the highest attainment of the soul was the mystical experience of the love of Christ. This nineteenth-century version by Edward Caswall is found in the Hymnal of the United Church of Christ *(1974).*

Hymn for Saturday Vespers

O what their joy and their glory must be,
Those endless Sabbaths[1] the blessed ones see!
Crown for the valiant; to weary ones rest;
God shall be all, and in all ever blest.[2]

What are the Monarch, his court, and his throne?[3]
What are the peace and the joy that they own?
Tell us, ye blest ones, that in it have share,
If what ye feel ye can fully declare.

Truly "Jerusalem" name we that shore,[4]
"Vision of peace," that brings joy evermore!
Wish and fulfillment can severed be ne'er,
Nor the thing prayed for come short of the prayer.

We, where no trouble distraction can bring,
Safely the anthems of Sion shall sing;[5]
While for thy grace, Lord, their voices of praise
Thy blessed people shall evermore raise.[6]

There dawns no Sabbath, no Sabbath is o'er,
Those Sabbathkeepers have one and no more;[7]
One and unending is that triumph song
Which to the angels and us shall belong.

Now in the meanwhile, with hearts raised on high,
We for that country must yearn and must sigh,

SOURCE: Eugene R. Fairweather, ed., *A Scholastic Miscellany: Anselm to Ockham*, vol. 10 of *Library of Christian Classics* (Philadelphia: Westminster Press, 1956). Used by permission of Westminster John Knox Press.

1. In the Latin liturgical books, *sabbatum* means Saturday, not Sunday!
2. Cf. 1 Cor. 15:28.
3. Note the characteristically medieval court symbolism: *rex, curia, palatium*.
4. Cf. Gal. 4:26, and the noble old hymn "Urbs beata Hierusalem" (*Oxford Book of Medieval Latin Verse*, 36).
5. Cf. Ps. 136:3 f.
6. In the original, there is a play on *gratia* (grace) and *gratias* (thanks).
7. Cf. Heb. 4:9.

Seeking Jerusalem, dear native land,
Through our long exile on Babylon's strand.[8]

Low before Him with our praises we fall,
Of whom, and in whom, and through whom are all;
Of whom, the Father; and through whom, the Son;
In whom, the Spirit, with these ever One.[9]

Jesus, the Very Thought of Thee

1. Jesus, the very thought of thee, With sweetness fills my breast;
But sweeter far thy face to see, And in thy presence rest.

2. No voice can sing, no heart can frame, Nor can the memory find
A sweeter sound than thy blest name, O Savior of mankind.

3. O hope of every contrite heart, O joy of all the meek,
To those who fall, how kind thou art! How good to those who seek!

4. But what to those who find? Ah, this Nor tongue nor pen can show;
The love of Jesus, what it is None but his loved ones know.

5. Jesus, our only joy be thou, As thou our prize wilt be;
Jesus, be thou our glory now, And through eternity.

---

8. Note the echoes of Augustine, *De civ. dei.*
9. Common doxology for Abailard's hymns in this meter.

SOURCE: *Hymnal of the United Church of Christ* (Philadelphia: United Church Press, 1974).

75. *The Song of the Virtues* (Ordo Virtutum)
From the *Scivias*
(1141–51)
HILDEGARD OF BINGEN

Hildegard of Bingen (1098–1179) called herself a homo simplex *(a simple woman), a mere channel of the Word of God. In truth, the only simple thing about her was her devotion to the vision of what she called the "living light." God's light had illuminated her since early childhood "with a complete understanding of the scriptures." It also enabled her to behold "wide awake and clearly, with the mind, eyes, and ears of her inner being" the Trinity as a "most loving and gentle fire . . . manifesting one light, one virtue and one power." Like Bernard of Clairvaux (see vol. 1:423–28), who supported her request for official recognition before a papal commission, Hildegard was a practical visionary involved in the ordinary life of her order and of the larger church.*

As the founder and abbess of a Benedictine convent near Bingen on the river Rhine, Hildegard traveled extensively in Germany and France, preaching against the moral laxity of the clergy and advocating social and clerical reform. Her convent was known as a place of healing; two of her many writings are medical treatises.

SOURCE: Hildegard of Bingen, *Scivias*, trans. Bruce Hozeski (Santa Fe: Bear & Company, 1986). Copyright 1986, Bear & Co., Inc., P.O. Box 2860, Santa Fe NM 87504. Used by permission.

Hildegard of Bingen was a prolific author, writing poetry, music, the "lives of the saints," and spiritual treatises in a strange secret language code. She preserved her mystical visions in three books: Know the Way of the Lord *(the* Scivias *or* Scitas, *written around 1141–1151); the* Book of the Divine Works of a Simple Woman *(*Homo Simplex . . . , *written around 1163–1173); and the* Book of the Life of Good Works, *written around 1158–1163. Her best-known work is the* Scivias, *a graphic account of thirteen of her visions. Scholars regard her thirteenth vision, called the "Order of Virtues" (*Ordo Virtutum*), as the earliest known liturgical morality play.*

Thereupon, the sky got very bright, and I heard all the previously mentioned virtues sing in a wondrous manner to the various types of music. They persisted strongly in the way of truth as they sang the praises of the city of celestial joy. They persisted strongly as they called those with complaints back to praising with joy. And they persisted in exhorting and encouraging themselves so that they might fight back the snares of the devil and help people gain salvation. But these virtues do overcome the snares of the devil, so that the faithful may pass over at last from sin to celestial reward through repentance.

And the sound was that of the voice of a multitude singing a musical performance with harmony in praise of the celestial orders. They sang the following.

Vision Thirteen: 1

They sang this song about holy Mary:

> O most brilliant gem and serene glory of the sun,
> you who the leaping fountain has been poured into
>   from the heart of God,
> the fountain is God's only Word
> through which God created the first material of the
>   world
> which Eve threw into confusion;
> God formed the Word — a person — from you,

and because of this you are that bright material
through which this very Word breathed out all the
   virtues,
just as God brought forth all the creatures from
   the first material.

O you, the sweetest virgin sprouting from the root
   of Jesse,
O how great is the virtue
which the divinity beheld in this most beautiful
   daughter,
as a water drop put into the divine eye — the sun,
when God directed the divine attention to the
   brightness of the Virgin
where God wishes the Word to be made flesh in her.

For by the mystical mystery of God, the bright
   flower went forth from this very Virgin, with
   the mind of the Virgin made wondrously light.

Vision Thirteen: 2

They sang this song about the Nine Orders of the Heavenly Spirits:

O most glorious light — a living angel, you who
   below the divinity —
behold with burning desires
the divine eyes with the mystical obscurity of
   every creature,
whence you will never be satisfied with power:
o how the glorious joy — your garment — has a form
which is untouched in you by every depraved work,
the depraved work which first sprang up in your
   companion, the destroyed angel,
who wanted to fly upward inside the concealed
   pinnacle of God,
whereby this angel, a tortuous one, was plunged
   down into ruin;
but by means of this fall
the devil was able to take counsel of the thing
   which the finger of God was about to do.

For o you angel
who protects the people,
whose form shines in your face,
and o you archangel
who receives the souls of the just ones,
and you virtues, powers, principalities,
    dominations, and thrones,
who are counted in the fifth hidden number,
and o you cherubin and seraphin of the hidden
    images of God,
praise be to you,
who behold the little place of the ancient heart in
    the fountain.
For you see the inner strength of God
which breathes out from the heart of God as if it
    were a face.

Vision Thirteen: 3

They sang this song about the Patriarchs and Prophets:

O remarkable teachers
who pass through the eyes of the spirit, with you
    beholding the hidden things
and announcing in the bright shade the sharp and
    living light
sprouting forth in the green twig,
which alone flowered from the beginning of the
    rooting light;

You holy ancient ones
prophesied the salvation of banished souls,
which had been immersed in death,
you who turn around as wheels, speaking wondrously
    the mystical things of the mountain,
which touches heaven
with heaven passing through many waters with
    anointing,
when also among you there rose up a bright light
which — running before — shows this mountain.

O you happy roots,
with whom the work of miracles,
and not the work of crimes,
has been planted through the parched way of bright
   shade,
and o you ruminating fiery voice,
running before the polishing stone destroying the
   abyss,
rejoice in your head!
Rejoice in that one
whom many did not see in earthly things
many who called that one lovingly.

Vision Thirteen: 4

They sang this song about the Apostles:

O cohort of the military,
of the flower of a green twig not thorned,
you, the sound of the circle of the land,
you, going around the regions of the insane senses
   feasting with the pigs
which you cast out through a poured-in helper,
you are the flower putting roots in the tabernacle
   of the full work of the Word of God:
you also are noble, a type of savior,
entering the way of the regeneration of the water
   through the lamb
who sends you with a sword among most furious dogs,
who destroyed their own glory with the works of
   their own fingers,
the dogs setting up one not having been handmade
in the subjection of their own hands,
with which subjection they did not invent this one.

For, o very bright whirling round of the apostles,
the whirling round rising up in recognition
and opening the door of the magistracy of the
   devil,
by washing the devil's captives in the fountain of
   living water,

you are the brightest light in the blackest
    darkness,
and the strongest type of columns
with you sustaining *the bride of the lamb*
    (*Revelation 21:9*) with all her embellishments,
through the bride's joy, the very Mother and Virgin
is a banner.
For the unspotted lamb
is the bridegroom of this unspotted bride.

Vision Thirteen: 5

They sang this song about the Martyrs:

O most victorious triumphant ones,
who — in the pouring out of your blood,
saving the building of the church —
are among the blood of the lamb, with your
    feasting with a slain calf:
o how great the wages you have,
because you despise your living body,
by imitating the lamb of God,
by embellishing the lamb's punishment
by which the lamb led you into the restoration of
    your heredity.

You flowers of roses
who in the pouring out of your blood are blessed
    with the greatest joys,
which emit an aroma and drip with moisture in a
    purchase
which flowed from the inner mind of the
    deliberation
remaining before the lifetime of that one
in whom the disposition was not from the Word's
    head.

May honor be in your company,
you who are the instruments of the church
and you who rise in waves in the wounds of your
    blood.

Vision Thirteen: 6

They sang this song about the Confessors:

> O successors of the strongest lion
> being lords within the temple and on the altar in
>   the lion's service,
> as angels sound with praises
> and as angels are present to people with help,
> you are among those who do these things,
> always having a cure in the office of the lamb.
>
> O you imitators of a lofty person
> with a most precious and most glorious
>   significance,
> o how great is your embellishment,
> where a person proceeds, loosening and binding in
>   God
> the lazy ones and the foreigners,
> with the person also embellishing the white ones
>   and sending back the black ones and the great
>   burdens.
>
> For you also hold the offices of the angelic order
> and you foreknow the strongest foundation,
> wherever it ought to be established,
> when your honor is great.

Vision Thirteen: 7

They sang this song about the Virgins:

> O beautiful faces beholding God
> and building in the dawn,
> o blessed virgins, how noble you are,
> in whom the king settled himself,
> when he showed beforehand all the heavenly
>   embellishments in you
> where you also are the sweetest garden
> where you emit an odor in all your embellishments.

O most noble greenness which roots in the sun
and which gives light in white serenity in a wheel,
a wheel which no earthly excellence understands,
you are surrounded with the embraces of the divine
    mysteries.

You are red as the dawn,
and you burn as the flame of the sun.

And again the sound was that of a multitude singing in harmony the complaints of those who had been called back to the same order.

Vision Thirteen: 8

They sang this song about Those Having Been Called Back to the Same Orders:

O bewailing voice, this is
of the greatest sorrow.
Ach, ach!
a certain wondrous victory rose up in the
    wondrous desire of God,
        the victory in which the pleasure of the flesh
        concealed itself hiddenly;
alas, alas!
where the will did not know of any crimes,
and where the desire of humans fled wantonness.
Mourn, mourn therefore the innocence in these,
you are the voice which did not send away the
    integrity within good modesty,
and the voice which did not swallow there
the avarice of the throat of the ancient serpent.

O living fountain, how great is your sweetness,
who did not send away the face of these in
    yourself,
but you saw how keenly beforehand, dragging them
    away from the angelic fall,
who were valuing themselves to have that
which is not allowed thus to stand.

Whence rejoice, daughter Zion,
because God gave many back to you
whom the serpent wished to hide from you;
who now shine in a light greater
than the motive of those had been previously.

For the living light says concerning these:
I scandalized the tortuous serpent at the serpent's
 own suggestion,
which had not been so full as that one was
 thinking.

Whence I took an oath through myself
that I did more and more in these motives
that, o serpent, your joy might advance in them:
because I cut off at your suggestion
what never was invented
in your rage
o most foul deceiver.

Vision Thirteen: 9

And then that sound of the voice of the multitude sang aloud harmoniously an exhortation of the virtues — the helpers of people — and a contradiction of the opposing skills of the devil, with the virtues overcoming faults and with people at length coming back by divine inspiration to repentance:

We virtues are in God
and we remain in God;
we are soldiers for the king of kings
and we overcome evil by good.
For we began visible in the first action
where we existed as victorious,
while that one fell to the ground who wished to fly
 above God.
Therefore let us even now be soldiers,
coming up to aid those who call upon us,
and trampling on the skills of the devil,
and leading through to blessed mansions
those who will have wished to imitate us.

The Complaint of the Souls Placed in a Body

Alas, we are strangers.
What have we done, straying into sins?
We ought to be daughters of the king,
but into the shadow of sins we fell.
O living sun,
carry us on your shoulders
into the most righteous inheritance,
which we lost through Adam!
O king of kings,
we are fighting in your battle.

The Invocation of the Faithful Soul

O sweet divinity
and o pleasant life,
in which I will wear a bright garment,
accepting the one which I lost in my first
   appearance,
to you I sigh and I invoke all the virtues.

The Answer of the Virtues

O happy soul,
and o sweet creature of God,
you who have been built on the profound height of
   the wisdom of God,
you love much.

The Faithful Soul

O freely I will come to you,
in order that you may offer me the kiss of your
   heart.

Virtues

We ought to serve as soldiers with you,
o daughter of the king.

But the Burdened Soul Complained

O the heavy labor and the harsh weight
which I have in the garment of this life,
because it is very hard for me to fight against the
  body.

Virtues

O soul, created by the will of God,
and o happy instrument,
why are you so weak against this body
which God created with a virgin nature?
You ought to overcome the devil with us.

The Soul

Hasten to help me,
so that I might be able to stand.

76. The Canticle of the Sun
(1225)

FRANCIS OF ASSISI

Francis of Assisi (c. 1181–1226) was one of those rare Christians of any age, who for the "love and compassion of Christ," was truly able to become poor in things and rich in soul. Church historian Roland Bainton cites the Mirror of Perfection, *a legendary account of the saint's life: "Inebriated with the love and compassion of Christ, the blessed Francis would betimes voice in the French tongue the most sweet melodies that welled up within him."*

"The Canticle of the Sun," is the most famous hymn of Francis in which he celebrates the love and grace of God in solidarity with all of God's creation. Two versions of the famous canticle are a translation of the original text by N. Wydenbruck and a metric paraphrase, "All creatures of our God and king," written in 1926 by William H. Draper and found in the Hymnal of the United Church of Christ *(1974).*

SOURCE: Ray C. Petry, ed., *Late Medieval Mysticism*, vol. 13 of *Library of Christian Classics* (Philadelphia: Westminster Press, 1957). Used by permission of Westminster John Knox Press.

Most high, omnipotent, merciful Lord,[1]
Thine is all praise, the honor and the glory and every benediction
To thee alone are they confined,
And no man is worthy to speak thy name.

Praised be thou, my Lord, with all thy creatures,
Especially for Sir Brother Sun.
Through him thou givest us the light of day,
And he is fair and radiant with great splendor,
Of thee, Most High, giving signification.[2]

Praised be thou, my Lord, for Sister Moon and the stars
Formed in the sky, clear, beautiful, and fair.
Praised be thou, my Lord, for Brother Wind,
For air, for weather cloudy and serene and every weather
By which thou to thy creatures givest sustenance.

Praised be thou, my Lord, for Sister Water,
Who is very useful and humble, precious and chaste.

Praised be thou, my Lord, for Brother Fire,
By whom thou dost illuminate the night;
Beauteous is he and jocund, robustious, and strong.[3]

Praised be thou, my Lord, for our Mother Earth,
Who sustains and rules us
And brings forth divers fruits and colored flowers and herbs.
Praised be thou, my Lord, for those who grant forgiveness
    through thy love
And suffer infirmities and tribulation.
Blessed are they who bear them with resignation,
Because by thee, Most High, they will be crowned.

Karrer reminds us that this is the only text certainly known to have been conceived in the " 'sweet' tongue of St. Francis's Umbria." *Legends,* p. 258. Cf. the account in the *Speculum perfectionis* for the addition of the verses on death.

1. *Altissimu omnipotente bon Signore.*
2. *Porta significatione.*
3. *Et ello è bello e jocondo e robustoso e forte.*

Praised be thou, my Lord, for our [sister][4] bodily Death,
From whom no living man can ever 'scape.
Woe unto those who die in mortal sin.
Blessed those who are found in thy most holy will;
To them the second death will bring no ill.
Praise and bless my Lord, render thanks to him
And serve him with great humility.

All Creatures of Our God and King

1. All creatures of our God and King, Lift up your voice and with us sing
Alleluia, Alleluia! Thou burning sun with golden beam,
Thou silver moon with softer gleam, O praise him,
O praise him, Alleluia, Alleluia, Alleluia!

2. Thou rushing wind that art so strong, Ye clouds that sail in heav'n along,
O praise him, Alleluia! Thou rising morn, in praise rejoice,
Ye lights of evening, find a voice, O praise him,
O praise him, Alleluia, Alleluia, Alleluia!

3. Thou flowing water, pure and clear, Make music for thy Lord to hear,
Alleluia, Alleluia! Thou fire so masterful and bright,
That givest man both warmth and light, O praise him,
O praise him, Alleluia, Alleluia, Alleluia!

4. And all ye men of tender heart, Forgiving others, take your part,
O sing ye, Alleluia! Ye who long pain and sorrow bear,
Praise God and on him cast your care. O praise him,
O praise him, Alleluia, Alleluia, Alleluia!

5. Let all things their creator bless, And worship him in humbleness,
O praise him, Alleluia! Praise, praise the Father, praise the Son,
And praise the Spirit, Three in One. O praise him,
O praise him, Alleluia, Alleluia, Alleluia!

---

4. The original Italian reads: *per sora nostra morte corporale* — "for our sister bodily Death." Karrer, *Franz,* p. 522; *Speculum perfectionis,* cap. 120.

SOURCE: *Hymnal of the United Church of Christ* (Philadelphia: United Church Press, 1974). Copyright © 1923 (Renewed) by J. Curwen & Sons, Ltd. All rights for the U.S. and Canada controlled by G. Schirmer, Inc. (text by St. Francis of Assisi, English translation and musical arrangements by William Draper). International Copyright Secured. All Rights Reserved. Used by permission.

77. Canon of the Mass or The Great Eucharistic Prayer

The core of Christian worship is the sharing of bread and wine. Protestant worship has its roots in the Latin Mass, parts of which we can trace back to the sixth century. The most solemn moment of the Mass, "The Great Prayer or Canon of the Mass," took on a fixed form very early.

The Mass begins with a dialogue between the celebrant and the worshipers, known as the Sursum Corda *("Lift up your hearts . . ."), affirming that the Eucharist is a celebration of the entire congregation. The actual thanksgiving prayer begins with a brief invocation that introduces the commemorative narrative of Christ's passion. The dedication of the elements follows. The prayer keeps the dialogue going, with the people's saying/singing the* Sanctus *("Holy, holy, holy . . .") in response. After offering intercessions for the dead, the prayer concludes with a benediction,* Per ipsum, et cum ipso, et in ipso . . . *("Through him, and with him and in him . . ."). The congregation responds with the final "Amen."*

SOURCE: Bard Thompson, ed., *Liturgies of the Western Church* (Philadelphia: Fortress Press, 1980). Used by permission of the Estate of Bard Thompson.

*The Canon of the Mass is more than a liturgical relic of the past. Its earliest form demonstrates the truth of the ancient principle that the rule of prayer is the rule of faith (*lex orandi, lex credendi*). The prayers of the people express the true faith of the community more clearly than any official statements.*

The Eucharistic Prayer is an act of grateful remembrance, an ecumenical event, global in time and place. It gathers together all who bear Christ's name around the Word and around Christ's table. To paraphrase Luther's words about scripture, the Eucharist is its own interpreter. For this reason many Christians believe that the "Great Prayer" at the Eucharist or Holy Communion is the essence of Christian worship.

In the history of the United Church of Christ, a nineteenth century liturgical and theological renewal at the Mercersburg Seminary of the German Reformed Church generated a deep appreciation for the importance of the Eucharist. We find the "long" Order of Holy Communion in the Hymnal *(1941) of the Evangelical and Reformed Church. It incorporates many of the traditional elements of the Latin Mass. The more contemporary version of the eucharistic prayer includes everything except the prayers for the dead.*

Selections from the Canon of the Latin Mass

The Preface to the Canon

The celebrant, with hands laid upon the altar, says or chants:
C. The Lord be with you.
R. And with you.
C. Let us lift up our hearts.
R. We lift them up to the Lord.
C. Let us give thanks to the Lord our God.
R. That is just and fitting.

The Common Preface

Just it is indeed and fitting, right, and for our lasting good, that we should always and everywhere give thanks to thee, Lord, holy Father, almighty and eternal God, through Christ our Lord. It is through him that thy majesty is praised by Angels, adored by Dominations, feared by Powers; through him that the heavens and the celestial Virtues join with the blessed Seraphim in one glad hymn of praise. We pray thee let our voices blend with theirs as we humbly praise thee, singing:

• • •

Here the bell is rung thrice.
Holy, holy, holy art thou, Lord God of hosts. Thy glory fills all heaven and earth. Hosanna in high heaven! Blessed be he who is coming in the name of the Lord. Hosanna in high heaven!

• • •

The celebrant, bowing low over the altar, says silently:
And so, through Jesus Christ, thy Son, our Lord, we humbly pray and beseech thee, most gracious Father, to accept and bless these offerings, these oblations, these holy, unblemished sacrificial gifts. We offer them to thee in the first place for thy holy Catholic Church, praying that thou wilt be pleased to keep and guide her in peace and unity throughout the world; together with thy servant our Pope *N.*, and *N.* our Bishop, and all who believe and foster the true Catholic and Apostolic faith.

Remember, Lord, thy servants *N.* and *N.* (*here the celebrant makes silent mention of those for whom he wishes to pray*), and all here present.

• • •

The bell is rung once as the celebrant spreads his hands over the bread and wine. He continues:

And so, Lord, we thy servants, and with us thy whole household, make this peace-offering which we entreat thee to accept. Order our days in thy peace, and command that we be rescued from eternal damnation and numbered with the flock of thy elect: through Christ our Lord. Amen.

We pray thee, God, be pleased to make this offering wholly blessed, a thing consecrated and approved, worthy of the human spirit and of thy acceptance, so that it may become for us the Body and Blood of thy dearly beloved Son, our Lord Jesus Christ.

He takes the host in his hands and consecrates it, saying:

He, on the day before he suffered death, took bread into his holy and worshipful hands, and lifting up his eyes to thee, God, his almighty Father in heaven, and giving thanks to thee, he blessed it, broke it, and gave it to his disciples, saying: Take, all of you, and eat of this,

>For This Is My Body.

The bell is rung thrice as he genuflects, shows the Sacred Host to the people, and genuflects again.

He now consecrates the wine, saying:
In like manner, when he had supped, taking also this goodly cup into his holy and worshipful hands, and again giving thanks to thee, he blessed it, and gave it to his disciples, saying: Take, all of you, and drink of this,

>For This is the Chalice of My Blood, of the New and Everlasting Covenant, a Mystery of Faith. It Shall be Shed for You and Many Others, so That Sins May be Forgiven.

He genuflects, saying:
Whenever you shall do these things, you shall do them in memory of me.

He then shows the chalice to the people, genuflecting after doing so. The bell is again rung thrice. He continues:
Calling therefore to mind the blessed Passion of this same Christ, thy Son, our Lord, and also his resurrection from the grave, and glorious ascension into heaven, we thy servants, Lord, and with us all thy holy people, offer to thy sovereign majesty, out of the gifts thou hast bestowed upon us, a sacrifice that is pure, holy, and unblemished, the sacred Bread of everlasting life, and the Cup of eternal salvation.

Deign to regard them with a favourable and gracious countenance, and to accept them as it pleased thee to accept the offerings of thy servant Abel the Just, and the sacrifice of our father Abraham, and that which thy great priest Melchisedech sacrificed to thee, a holy offering, a victim without blemish.

Bowing low over the altar, he says:
Humbly we ask it of thee, God almighty: bid these things be carried by the hands of thy holy angel up to thy altar on high, into the presence of thy divine majesty. And may those of us who by taking part in the sacrifice of this altar shall have received the sacred Body and Blood of thy Son, be

filled with every grace and heavenly blessing: through the same Christ our Lord. Amen.

• • •

The celebrant makes the sign of the cross thrice over the chalice with the Sacred Host, and twice between the chalice and himself, then raises the Host and chalice slightly, saying meanwhile:

Through him, and with him, and in him, thou, God, almighty Father, in the unity of the Holy Spirit, hast all honour and glory,

Replacing the Host and chalice upon the altar, he then chants or says aloud:

    C. World without end.
    R. Amen.

Let us pray. Urged by our Saviour's bidding, and schooled by his divine ordinance, we make bold to say:
Pater noster, qui es in caelis, sanctificetur nomen tuum. Adveniat regnum tuum. Fiat voluntas tua, sicut in caelo, et in terra. Panem nostrum quotidianum da nobis hodie. Et dimitte nobis debita nostra, sicut et nos dimittimus debitoribus nostris. Et ne nos inducas in tentationem:

    R. Sed libera nos a malo.
    C. *silently:* Amen.

Taking the paten in his right hand, he continues silently:
Libera nos, quaesumus, Domine, ab omnibus malis, praeteritis, praesentibus, et futuris: et intercedente beata et gloriosa semper Virgine Dei Genitrice Maria, cum beatis Apostolis tuis Petro et Paulo, atque Andrea, et omnibus Sanctis (*he crosses himself with the paten and kisses it*), da propitius pacem in diebus nostris: ut ope misericordiae tuae adjuti, et a peccato simus semper liberi, et ab omni perturbatione securi.

He then breaks the Sacred Host over the chalice, saying:
Per eundem Dominum nostrum Jesum Christum, Filium tuum, qui tecum vivit et regnat in unitate Spiritus Sancti Deus.

He concludes the prayer aloud:
    C. Per omnia saecula saeculorum.
    R. Amen.

He makes the sign of the Cross thrice with a particle of the Sacred Host over the chalice, chanting or saying aloud:

C. Pax Domini sit semper vobiscum.
R. Et cum spiritu tuo.

Then he drops the particle into the chalice and continues silently:

Haec commixtio, et consecratio Corporis et Sanguinis Domini nostri Jesu Christi, fiat accipientibus nobis in vitam aeternam. Amen.

He strikes his breast three times as he says aloud:
Agnus Dei, qui tollis peccata mundi: miserere nobis.
Our Father, who art in heaven, hallowed be thy name. Thy kingdom come. Thy will be done, on earth as it is in heaven. Give us this day our daily bread. And forgive us our trespasses, as we forgive those who trespass against us. And lead us not into temptation:

R. But deliver us from evil.
C. *silently:* Amen.

Taking the paten in his right hand, he continues silently:
Deliver us, we pray thee, Lord, from every evil, past, present, and to come, and at the intercession of the blessed and glorious ever-virgin Mary, Mother of God, of thy blessed apostles Peter and Paul, of Andrew, and of all the saints (*he crosses himself with the paten and kisses it*), be pleased to grant peace in our time, so that with the help of thy compassion we may be ever free from sin and safe from all disquiet.

He then breaks the Sacred Host over the chalice, saying:
Through the same Jesus Christ, thy Son, our Lord, who is God, living and reigning with thee in the unity of the Holy Spirit:

He concludes the prayer aloud:
C. World without end.
R. Amen.

The Eucharistic Prayer

THE VESSELS CONTAINING BREAD AND WINE
HAVING BEEN MADE READY, AND THE CONGREGATION STANDING,
THE SERVICE SHALL THEN PROCEED AS FOLLOWS:

SOURCE: General Synod of the Evangelical and Reformed Church, *The Hymnal* (St. Louis: Eden Publishing House, 1941).

CANON OF THE MASS OR THE GREAT EUCHARISTIC PRAYER • 545

Minister. The Lord be with you.
Congregation. And with thy spirit.
Minister. Lift up your hearts.
Congregation. We lift them up unto the Lord.
Minister. Let us give thanks unto the Lord our God.
Congregation. It is meet and right so to do.

THE MINISTER, PROCEEDING, SHALL SAY,

It is very meet, right, and our bounden duty, that we should at all times and in all places give thanks unto thee, O Holy Lord, Father Almighty, Everlasting God, who didst create the heavens and the earth and all that in them is, who didst make man in thine own image, and whose tender mercies are over all thy works.

For all thy mercies and favors, known to us and unknown, we give thee thanks. But most of all we praise thee, the Father everlasting, for the gift of thine adorable, true, and only Son, our Saviour Jesus Christ, who by his appearing hath abolished death and brought life and immortality to light through the Gospel. We bless thee for his holy incarnation, for his life on earth, for his precious sufferings and death upon the cross, for his resurrection from the dead, and for his glorious ascension to thy right hand. We bless thee for the giving of the Holy Spirit, for the institution of the Church, for the means of grace, for the hope of everlasting life, and for the glory which shall be brought unto us at the coming, and in the kingdom, of thy dear Son.

Thee, mighty God, heavenly King, we magnify and praise. With patriarchs and prophets, apostles and martyrs, with the holy Church throughout all the world; with the heavenly Jerusalem, the joyful assembly and congregation of the firstborn on high; with the innumerable company of angels round about thy throne, the heaven of heavens, and all the powers therein, we worship and adore thy glorious Name, joining in the song of the Cherubim and Seraphim:

HERE THE MINISTER AND CONGREGATION SHALL SAY OR SING THE SERAPHIC HYMN OR THE SANCTUS.

Seraphic Hymn (No. 522)
Holy, Holy, Holy, Lord God of Sabaoth;
Heaven and earth are full of the majesty of thy glory;
Hosanna in the highest!

Blessed is he that cometh in the Name of the Lord;
Hosanna in the highest!

Sanctus (No. 521)
Holy, Holy, Holy, Lord God of hosts,
Heaven and earth are full of thy glory;
Glory be to thee, O Lord Most High.

THE MINISTER SHALL CONTINUE,

The Lord Jesus, the same night in which he was betrayed, took bread, (*Here the Minister shall take the bread into his hands*) and when he had given thanks, he brake it, (*Here the Minister shall break the bread*) and said: Take, eat; this is my Body which is broken for you; this do in remembrance of me. After the same manner also, he took the cup, (*Here the Minister shall take the cup into his hands*) when he had supped, saying: This cup is the New Testament in my Blood; this do ye, as oft as ye drink it, in remembrance of me.

Wherefore, we beseech thee, O merciful Father, to send thy Holy Spirit upon us, and upon these elements of bread and wine, that the bread which we break may be to us the Communion of the Body of Christ, and the cup of blessing which we bless, the Communion of the Blood of Christ. And be pleased now, O most merciful Father, graciously to receive this memorial of the blessed sacrifice of thy Son which we here offer unto thee, in union with the sacrifice of our thanksgiving and praise, consecrating ourselves in soul and body, property and life, to thy most blessed service and praise. Look upon us through the mediation of our great High Priest. Make us accepted in the Beloved, and let his Name be as a pure and holy incense, through which all our worship may come up before thee, a sacrifice acceptable and well pleasing in thy sight; through Jesus Christ our Lord, to whom, with thee, and the Holy Spirit, be all honor and glory, world without end. *Amen.*

THEN MAY BE SAID ANY OR ALL OF THE FOLLOWING PRAYERS:
Here intercessions may be made.

O God, the Father and our Lord Jesus Christ, of whom the whole family in heaven and earth is named, we rejoice before thee in the blessed communion of all thy saints, wherein thou givest us also to have part. We praise thee for the holy fellowship of patriarchs and prophets, apostles and martyrs, and the whole glorious company of the redeemed of all ages, who have died in the Lord, and now live with him forevermore. We give thanks unto thee for thy great grace and many gifts bestowed on those who have thus gone before us in the way of salvation, and by whom we are now compassed about in our Christian course, as a cloud of witnesses looking down upon us from the heavenly world. Enable us to follow their faith, that we may enter at death into their joy, and so abide with them in rest and peace, till both they and we shall reach our common consummation of redemption and bliss in the glorious resurrection of the last day. *Amen.*

MINISTER AND CONGREGATION.

Our Father, who art in heaven, Hallowed be thy Name. Thy kingdom come. Thy will be done, on earth as it is in heaven. Give us this day our daily bread. And forgive us our debts, as we forgive our debtors. And lead us not into temptation, but deliver us from evil. For thine is the kingdom, and the power, and the glory, for ever. Amen.

THE AGNUS DEI MAY BE SUNG OR SAID. (NO. 525)

Minister. O Christ, thou Lamb of God, that takest away the sin of the world,
Congregation. Have mercy upon us.
Minister. O Christ, thou Lamb of God, that takest away the sin of the world,
Congregation. Have mercy upon us.
Minister. O Christ, thou Lamb of God, that takest away the sin of the world,
Congregation. Grant us thy peace. Amen.

THEN THE MINISTER MAY SAY,

The peace of our Lord Jesus Christ be with you all. *Amen.*

Sources

Aquinas, Saint Thomas. *The Basic Writings of St. Thomas Aquinas.* 2 vols. Edited by Anton C. Pegis. New York: Random House, 1945.
Augustine, Saint. *Augustine: Earlier Writings.* Edited by J. H. S. Burleigh. Vol. 6 of *Library of Christian Classics.* Philadelphia: Westminster Press, 1957.
———. *Augustine: Later Works.* Edited by John Burnaby. Vol. 8 of *Library of Christian Classics.* Philadelphia: Westminster Press.
———. *The Basic Writings of Saint Augustine.* Vol. 1. Edited by Whitney Oates. New York: Random House, 1948.
Bettenson, Henry. *Documents of the Christian Church.* New York: Oxford University Press, 1963.
Bonaventure. *Bonaventure: The Soul's Journey into God.* Translated and introduced by Ewert Cousins. Classics of Western Spirituality Series. New York: Paulist Press, 1978.
Boniface, Saint. *The English Correspondence of St. Boniface.* Edited by Edward Kylie. New York: Cooper Square Publishers, 1966.
———. *The Letters of Saint Boniface.* Translated and introduced by Ephraim Emerton. Records of Civilization Series. New York: Columbia University, 1940.
Capps, Walter H., and Wendy M. Wright, eds. *Silent Fire: An Invitation to Western Mysticism.* San Francisco: Harper & Row, 1978.
Chadwick, Henry, and J. E. L. Oulton, eds. *Alexandrian Christianity.* Vol. 2 of *Library of Christian Classics.* Philadelphia: Westminster Press, 1954.

Chadwick, Owen, ed. *Western Asceticism*. Vol. 12 of *Library of Christian Classics*. Philadelphia: Westminster Press, 1958.
Eckhart, Meister. *Meister Eckhart: The Essential Sermons, Commentaries, Treatises and Defense*. Edited by Edmund Colledge and Bernard McGinn. New York: Paulist Press, 1981.
———. *Meister Eckhart: A Modern Translation*. Translated by Raymond Bernard Blakney. New York: Harper & Brothers, 1941.
English Language Liturgical Consultation. *Praying Together*. Nashville: Abingdon Press, 1988.
Eusebius. *The History of the Church from Christ to Constantine*. Translated and introduced by G. A. Williamson. New York: Dorset Press, 1965.
Fairweather, Eugene R., ed. *A Scholastic Miscellany: Anselm to Ockham*. Vol. 10 of *Library of Christian Classics*. Philadelphia: Westminster Press, 1956.
Fremantle, Anne, ed. *A Treasury of Early Christianity*. New York: Mentor Books, 1960.
General Synod of the Evangelical and Reformed Church. *The Hymnal*. St. Louis: Eden Publishing House, 1941.
Greenslade, S. L., ed. *Early Latin Theology*. Vol. 5 of *Library of Christian Classics*. Philadelphia: Westminster Press, 1956.
Gregory VII. *The Correspondence of Pope Gregory VII: Selected Letters from the Registrum*. Translated and introduced by Ephraim Emerton. Records of Civilization Series. New York: W. W. Norton, 1969.
Hardy, Edward Rochie, ed. *Christology of the Later Fathers*. Vol. 3 of *Library of Christian Classics*. Philadelphia: Westminster Press, 1954.
Hildegard of Bingen. *Scivias*. Translated by Bruce Hozeski. Santa Fe: Bear & Company, 1986.
Huss, John. *The Church*. Translated and introduced by David Schaff. New York: Charles Scribner's Sons, 1915.
Hymnal of the United Church of Christ. Philadelphia: United Church Press, 1974.
John of Damascus. *Writings*. Vol. 37 of *The Fathers of the Church: A New Translation*. New York: Fathers of the Church, Inc., 1958.
Julian of Norwich. *Showings*. Edited by Edmund Colledge and James Walsh. Classics of Western Spirituality Series. New York: Paulist Press, 1978.
Leith, John H., ed. *Creeds of the Churches: A Reader in Christian Doctrine from the Bible to the Present*. Atlanta: John Knox Press, 1978.
McCracken, George E., ed. *Early Medieval Theology*. Vol. 9 of *Library of Christian Classics*. Philadelphia: Westminster Press, 1957.
McDonald, Lee Martin. *The Formation of the Christian Biblical Canon*. Nashville: Abingdon Press, 1988.

Meecham, Henry G. *The Epistle to Diognetus.* Manchester: Manchester University Press, 1949.

Mundy, John Hine, and Kennerly M. Woody, eds. *The Council of Constance: The Unification of the Church.* Translated by Louise Ropes Loomis. New York: Columbia University Press, 1961.

Petry, Ray C., ed. *Late Medieval Mysticism.* Vol. 13 of *Library of Christian Classics.* Philadelphia: Westminster Press, 1957.

Pilgrim Hymnal. Boston: Pilgrim Press, 1958.

Richardson, Cyril C. ed., *Early Christian Fathers.* Vol. 1 of *Library of Christian Classics.* Philadelphia: Westminster Press, 1953.

Schaff, Philip. *Creeds of Christendom.* 3 vols. 1877; reprint New York: Baker Book House, 1977.

Spinka, Matthew, ed. *Advocates of Reform: From Wyclif to Erasmus.* Vol. 14 of *Library of Christian Classics.* Philadelphia: Westminster Press, 1953.

Thompson, Bard, ed. *Liturgies of the Western Church.* Philadelphia: Fortress Press, 1980.

United Church of Christ Office for Church Life and Leadership, *Book of Worship, United Church of Christ.* New York: United Church of Christ Office for Church Life and Leadership, 1986.

Wiles, Maurice, and Mark Santer, eds. *Documents in Early Christian Thought.* Cambridge: Cambridge University Press, 1979.

Index

Aaron, 29
Abel, 221
Abelard, Peter, 416, 522, 523–24
Abgar, 291–92
abortion, 121
Abraham, 51, 127, 291
"accidents," 405–6, 489
Acts of the Apostles, 11, 56, 133, 193, 356
Adam, 148–49, 162–63, 169, 275, 288, 310–12
Adam of St. Victor, 505n. 11
Adam's Fall, 8–10, 69–80, 213–14, 217–21, 458–59
adultery, 17, 28, 99–100, 119–20, 174, 350–51
Advocates of Reform: From Wyclif to Erasmus, 478n, 488n
Aebbe, 366
Aeschylus, 319n. 14
"Against Celsus" (Origen), 13, 279
Against Heresies (Irenaeus), 32–40
"Against Praxeas" (Tertullian), 151, 228
Albertus Magnus, 380, 504n. 8
Albigensian sect, 334
Alexander, 37, 66–67
Alexander of Hales, 391n. 7, 434
Alexandrian Christianity, 146–47, 153, 157–83, 241, 274, 279
Alexandrian Christianity, 166n, 274n
Alfonso da Liguori, 505n. 11
"All creatures of our God and King," 416, 538

allegorical method, 10, 13, 146; Gregory on, 315–23; Origen on, 10, 49–54, 146, 158; Tertullian on, 41–47; Theodore on, 158, 162–65
Ambrose, 147–48, 256, 258–59, 368, 392, 397n. 5, 507n. 16
Amphilochus, 103
Ananias, 30
anchorites, 458
Anencletus, 36
angels, 98, 117
Anicetus, 37
Anne of Bohemia, 500
Anselm of Canterbury, 301–2, 376–79, 381
Antiochene Christianity, 137n. 1, 146–47, 153, 157–83, 241, 282, 309–13
Antoninus Pius, 95n. 1
Apelles, 43, 47
apocryphal writings, 10–11, 57
Apollinarians, 240
Apollinarius, 191n. 1
Apollos, 31
Apologetics, 12–14, 84–122, 145–46; "First Apology," 13, 94–108; "Letter to Diognetus," 13, 84–93; plea for fair hearing, 95–103; "Plea Regarding the Christians," 13, 109–22
Apology (Plato), 97n. 7
Apology (Tertullian), 41
apostles, 529–30; church governance and, 25–31

553

Apostles' Creed, 147, 149, 151, 153–54, 246–48, 505n. 9; Augustine of Hippo on, 184–200
Apostolic See, 323, 345, 355, 513, 514
apostolic succession, 37. *See also* apostolic tradition
apostolic tradition, 9–12, 14–24, 34–39, 55, 150–54, 246
"Apostolic Tradition of Hippolytus," 250–54
Aquinas, Thomas, 405–9, 435, 444n. 1, 490n. 4; on Aristotle, 302–3, 380–81, 391, 393, 395, 405–6; on Eucharist, 405–9; "Five Ways to Prove the Existence of God," 302, 380–89; "Natural and Theological Virtues," 395–404; "Whether the Trinity of the Divine Persons Can By Known by Natural Reason?," 390–94
Archbishop of Canterbury. *See* Augustine; Cuthbert; Theodore
Ariadne, 103
Arianism, 152–53, 175, 189, 231, 235–36
Aristotle, 384n. 15, 396n. 1, 398n. 1, 444n. 2, 445n. 4, 502; Aquinas on, 302–3, 380–81, 391, 393, 395, 405–6
Arius, 152, 394
Arnou, R., 391n. 1
Artaxius, 75
Asceticism, 147, 214, 268, 275, 412, 417–18
Asclepius, 103, 104
Aspasius, 76
Athanasian Creed, 153–54, 242–45
Athanasius, 11, 55–56, 152–53, 175, 232n. 6, 235, 355
atheism, 13–14, 94, 109, 111–18
Athenagoras, 13, 109–22, 114n. 12
Athens, 146, 148, 150

Atlas, 319n. 14
atonement, 301, 377
Atreus, 111n. 2
Attalus, 61, 64, 65, 66
Attila the Hun, 298, 308, 324
Auctoritas, 45n. 8
Augustine (archbishop of Canterbury), 298, 300, 315, 324, 340–44, 397n. 5, 400, 403
Augustine: Earlier Writings (Burleigh), 184n
Augustine: Later Works (Burnaby), 201n
Augustine of Hippo, 14, 147–50, 302, 367–68, 378n. 1, 384n. 15, 427n. 9, 494n. 14, 495n. 16, 507n. 16, 524n. 8; on Apostles' Creed, 184–200; "The Church as the Company of the Elect," 140–44; on Epistle of John, 201–9, 502–8; on evil, 388; on Holy Communion, 210–11, 300–301, 370–74; on natural reason, 381, 391–93; on nature and grace, 213–25; on the Trinity, 149–50, 153–55, 185–86, 193–95, 197–98, 240
Augustine the Bishop (van der Meer), 211n. 1
Augustus, 95, 103n. 38, 331
Augustus (Suetonius), 103n. 38
Aurelius. *See* Prudentius, Aurelius Clemens
Azarias, 30

"Babylonian captivity" of papacy, 414, 478, 488, 496
Bacchius, 95
Bainton, Roland, 536
Baker, Henry W., 256
baptism, 140–44, 150–51, 210–12, 246–47, 335–36; apostasy after, 81; in apostolic tradition, 15–24;

Augustine on, 140–41; confession and, 170n. 12; rebaptism, 129–34
barbarians, 297–300; mission to, 340–66
Barth, Karl, 154
Bartholomew Francisci della Capra, 519n. 8
Basic Writings of Saint Augustine, 213n
Basic Writings of St. Thomas Aquinas, The, 380n, 390n, 395n
Basil, 290
Basil, "the Great," 175
Basilides, 34
Battles, F. L., 256
Bauer, Bruno, 9
Baxter, Richard, 243
begging orders, 334, 413, 429–30, 474
Beghards, 474
begotten, 152, 188–90, 195–96, 233–34
Beguines, 474
Bellerophon, 103
Benedictine Rule, 350, 412, 417–22, 424
Benedict XIII, 483n. 8, 514
Benedict of Nursia, 350, 412, 417–22
Benefit of Patience, The (Cyprian), 134
Benson, Louis F., 256
Berengar, 508n. 19
Bernard of Clairvaux, 412, 416, 423–28, 504n. 8, 508, 522–25
Bettenson, Henry, 331n, 337n, 342n, 405n, 431n, 512n
Bible. *See* scripture
biblical literalism, 9
biblical reformers, 415
biblical theology, 145–46
Biblis, 62–63
Bindley, T. H., 379n. 5

Birgitta of Sweden, 457
birthright, 133
bishops, 82–83; appointment of, 28–30; authority of, 12, 33, 124–27, 308–13, 349, 479, 488; decrees of Council of Hertford, 345–46; election of, 16, 23, 327–32; succession of, 35
Bisi, 345
Blakney, Raymond B., 446n
Blandina, 59, 61–62, 64–65, 67
blasphemy, 9, 17–18, 31, 35, 272
"Blessed Are the Poor" (Meister Eckhart), 442–43, 446–51
Blessing of Cheese and Olives, 252–53
Blessing of Oil, 252
blood of Christ, 20n. 32, 210–12, 283–84, 369–75, 405–9
body, 121–22, 136–38, 198–99
body of Christ, 14, 20n. 32, 33, 82, 136–38, 210–12, 367–75, 405–9; church as, 135–39
Boethius, 383
Bollard, J., 316n. 1
Bonaventure, 391n. 7, 413, 434–41
Boniface, 347–49, 352–66, 371
Boniface VIII, 298, 299–300, 337–39, 478
Book of the Divine Works of a Simple Woman (Hildegard of Bingen), 526
Book of the Life of Good Works (Hildegard of Bingen), 526
Book of Worship, 154, 237–39, 247, 248
Bourgeois du Chastenet, 483n. 8
Brancacci, Rainald, 520n. 10
brautmystik, 452
bread and wine, 16, 106–8, 210–12, 289, 301, 303, 333–36, 367–75, 405–9, 539
breaking bread, 20n. 34, 23
bridal mysticism, 452

brotherly love, 202–9
Browning, Elizabeth Barrett, 255
Brunichild, 340–41, 342
Bruno of Cologne, 412
Burchard, 348
Burleigh, J. H. S., 184n
Burnaby, John, 201n, 214n. 1
Burrhus, 128

Cabiri, 112
Caelestius, 213
Caesarean Creed, 230–34
Caliph Al-Walid, 286
Calixtus II, 328, 331–32
Callistus, 250
Calvin, 246
Candidus, 341
cannibalism, 13, 118, 121. *See also* Thyestean feasts
canon, 55–57, 251–52, 333–36
Canon Law, 414
Canon of the Mass, 416, 539–47
Canossa, 329–31
"Canticle of the Sun" (Francis of Assisi), 416, 536–38
Cappadocians, 175, 185, 235
Capps, Walter H., 452n
captatio benevolentiae, 95n. 2
Carloman, 348
Carthusian order, 412
Cassian, 275
Caswall, Edward, 522
Catechetical Orations (Gregory), 146, 175
catechumens, 69, 70, 79, 131–32, 210
Cathars, 413
cathedrals, 416
Catherine of Siena, 413–14, 457, 478, 496–99
"Catholic" letters, 56
Celestine (pope), 256

celibacy, 276–77
Celsus, 146, 280, 281
Cephas, 31
Cerinthus, 34, 37, 39
Chadwick, Henry, 166n, 274n
Chadwick, Owen, 417n
chain of being, 167, 175
Chalcedon, definition of, 153–54
Chalcedonian Creed, 240–41
Chandler, John, 256
charity, 15, 202–9
Charlemagne, 299
Charles IV, 500
Charles VI, 483n. 8
Charles "the Bald," 242, 369, 508n. 19
chastity, 269–73
Childebert II, 299, 324–26
Christ: biblical theology and, 145–46; blood of, 20n. 32, 210–12, 283–84, 369–75, 405–9; body of, 14, 20n. 32, 33, 82, 210–12, 367–75, 405–9; dual natures of, 146–47, 151–54, 157–62, 166–74, 240, 308–13; marriage of, with church, 22n. 51; as mother, 458, 501n. 2; as second Adam, 9–10, 33; as Son of God, 104; speculative theology and, 145–46; suffering of, 458
Christian conduct, 84–93, 99–101, 154, 496–97
Christianity: Alexandrian, 146–47, 153, 157–83, 241, 274, 279; Antiochene, 137n. 1, 146–47, 153, 157–83, 241, 282, 309–13; moral teaching, 114–16; superiority over paganism, 103–5; view on demons, 117; way of life, 15
Christian Queen of Kent, 300
Christians, lapsed, 8, 81–83, 129, 140
"Christmas Sermon on the Two Na-

tures of Christ" (Pope Leo I), 308–13
Christology, 145–46, 151–56, 250, 298, 309, 377
Christology of the Later Fathers, 230n
"Christ's Body and Blood" (Ratramnus), 369–75
"Christ's Poor," 412
Chrysostom, John, 135, 155, 172n. 25, 264–65, 282–83, 319n. 12
Church as the Body of Christ, The (Cyril), 135–39
Church as the Company of the Elect (Augustine), 140–44
church governance, 16, 25–31, 510
"Church of Christ Is One, The," 255–56, 258
Cicero, 396, 483
Circumcellions, 140–41
circumcision, 87, 126
Cistercians, 412–13, 423–24
Clare of Assisi, 413, 430
clausulae, 322n. 29
Clement, 37, 48, 50, 255, 257, 274, 355; First Letter of, 25–31; on persecution, 30
Clement VII, 479
Clement's First Letter, 11, 25–31, 37n. 9
clergy: discipline of, 347–61; duties of, 299; instruction of, 348–51
Cluniac reformers, 412
Colledge, Edmund, 457n
Colossians, 56
commandments, 18, 101, 198, 224–25
"Commentary on Galatians 4:24" (Theodore of Mopsuestia), 158, 162–65
Commentary on Job (Pope Gregory I), 314–23

Commentary on the Sentences (Bonaventure), 435
communion, 15–16, 149–50, 155, 253, 288–90, 501, 512; Augustine of Hippo on, 210–11, 300–301, 370–74; "Communion as Participation," 282–85; as sacrifice, 368; "Sermon on Holy Communion," 210–12. *See also* Eucharist
"Communion as Participation," 282–85
Communion of the Saints, 14
concelebration, 251n. 1
conciliarism, 414–15, 479, 510–11
Concilium Germanicum, 300, 347–51
Concordat of Worms, 299, 328, 331–32
concupiscence, 148, 215
Conference of Carthage, 213
confession: baptism and, 170n. 12; ecumenical, 237–38
Confessions (Augustine), 148
"Confessions of the Presbyters at Smyrna," 226–27
congregationalism, 11–12, 16
"Congregation of the Elect, The" (Huss), 500–509
Constantine, 152, 230, 297–98, 304–5
Constantine V, 155–56, 293
Constantinople Council, 153
Constantinus Augustus. *See* Constantine
Constantius, 235
consubstantial, 152–53, 185–86, 230–34, 240–41, 309–13
conventicles, 418
conversion, 347–48
Corinthians, 56; Clement's letter to, 25–31
Cornelius (pope), 129, 355
cosmetics, 270–73

Council at Pisa, 510
Council of Basel, 511–12
Council of Chalcedon, 152–53, 236, 240–41, 309
Council of Constance, 415, 479, 501, 510–21
Council of Constance, The, 510n, 514n
Council of Constantinople (381), 235–36
Council of Constantinople (743), 287
Council of Ephesus, 135
Council of Hertford, 344–46
Council of Jerusalem, 9
Council of Nicaea (325), 151–53, 230–36
Council of Nicaea (787), 287, 295
Council of Pisa, 415, 479
Council of the Germans, 300, 347–51
Council of Toledo, 155, 315n. 1
Council of Trent, 505n. 9
courage, 303, 395–404
creation, 32–33, 40, 116, 146–47, 176–83, 186–87
creation *ex nihilo*, 13
"creation line," 157
Creed of the 150 Fathers, 153, 235–36
creeds, 147, 150–54; Caesarean Creed, 230–34; Chalcedonian Creed, 240–41; Creed of the 150 Fathers, 153, 235–36; Interrogatory Creed of Hippolytus, 151, 154, 246; Nicene-Constantinopolitan Creed, 235–36. *See* Apostles' Creed
Creeds of Christendom (Schaff), 154, 247
Creeds of the Churches, 226n, 235n, 293n, 333n
Crehan, J., 172n. 25
Crito (Plato), 108n. 55

cross, theology of, 148–49, 155, 214, 218–21
crown of thorns, 458
cuius regio, eius religio principle, 348
cup, 20n. 32
"Curb for Wild Horses" (Clement), 255, 257
Cur Deus Homo?, 376
Cuthbert (archbishop of Canterbury), 352–61
Cyneberht, 353
Cyprian, 14, 141–43, 355, 368, 506; hymns, 255–58; "Outside the Church, There Is No Salvation," 129–34; "The Problem of the Lapsed," 81–83
Cyril, 14, 135–36, 309n. 1
Czech reformation, 500

Dachery, John, 518
Dadanus, 348
d'Ailly, Pierre, 414, 479, 511
Damascene, 382
Damiani, 504n. 8
Daniel, 30
David, 159, 310–11
deacons, 12, 16, 28, 124–27; election of, 23
death, 115, 176; dangers of, 397
debates, 184
Decius, 8, 48, 81
"Decree Sacrosancta," 415, 510, 512
"Decrees of the Frankish Synods," 347–51
Decretals, 507n. 15
De Ecclesia (Huss), 500–509, 516
De Eucharistia (Wycliffe), 492n. 9
Definition of Chalcedon, 153–54
Definition of the Council of Chalcedon, 240–41
"De haeretico comburendo," 415
deification, 475

deity, 170–71, 196–97
Demetrius, 48
Demiurge, 35, 37, 40, 55
Democritus, 118
demons, Christian views of, 117
"Demonstration of the Apostolic Faith" (Irenaeus), 32
Descartes, 302
de sententiis, 506n. 15
Deuteronomy, 224
Diagoras, 112
dialectical method, 302, 376–77
"Dialogue of Origen with Heraclides and the Bishops with Him Concerning the Father and the Son and the Soul" (Origen), 166–74
"Dialogue with Heraclides" (Origen), 146
Diaspora, 7
Didache, 11–12, 15–24
Dinocrates, 73–74
Diocletian, 201, 297
Diognetus, 13, 84–93
Dionysius, 393, 439n. 14, 440n. 15
Dionysus, 103
Dioscuri, 103
discipline, 347–61
"Divine Spark in the Soul, The" (Meister Eckhart), 442–46
Dix, Gregory, 251n. 1
Docetism, 12, 124, 146–47, 275
Doctrine of Addai, 292n. 18
Documents in Early Christian Thought, 48n, 135n, 140n, 157n, 175n, 210n, 264n, 279n, 282n, 308n
Documents of the Christian Church (Bettenson), 331n, 337n, 342n, 405n, 431n, 512n
Dodona, 103
Dolger, F. J., 373n. 10
Dominicans, 334, 380, 413, 429–30, 474

Dominican third order, 496
Domitian, 26n. 2
Donatism, 140–41, 148–49, 185, 201–2, 213, 429, 501
Donatus, 140–41, 322
Draper, William H., 536
dress, 154, 353, 354, 360; for men, 271–72; for priests, 350; for women, 268–73
drunkenness, 360
dual natures of Christ, 137, 146–47, 151–54, 157–62, 166–74, 240, 308–13
Duke Louis, 518–21
Dynne, 365

Eadburga, 362–63, 366
Early Christian Fathers, 15n, 25n, 94n, 109n, 123n
Early Latin Theology, 41n, 81n, 129n
Early Medieval Theology, 314n, 367n, 369n
earrings, 272
Easter date, 344–45
Easter Letter (Athanasius), 11
Eastern Orthodoxy, 155–56, 282–95
Ebion, 43
ecclesiastical authority, 337–39
ecclesiastical reformers, 415
eclectic syncretism, 9
ecumenical confession, 237–38
ecumenical councils, 151–52
ecumenical theology, 9–12
Eddanus, 349
Edict of Galerius, 306n. 1
Edict of Henry V, 331–32
Edict of Milan, 297, 304–7
Edward III, 488–89
efficacy of the sacraments, 141, 489–95
Egyptian monasticism, 418
Eighth Homily (Augustine of Hippo), 201

Elect, the, 30, 87, 140–44, 489, 500–509
election: of bishops, 16, 23, 327–32; of deacons, 23
Eleusis, 112
Eleutherus, 37
Elijah, 133
Elizabeth of Schoenau, 457
Emerton, Ephraim, 329n, 347n
Empedocles, 103, 117
English Correspondence of St. Boniface, The, 352n
Eoba, 363
Ephesians, 56, 264
episcopacy, 29n. 16, 36
Epistle of John, 149, 201–9, 502–8
Epistle of Saint Peter, 363
Esau, 133
essence of God, 162–65
Esther, 57
Ethelbert, 300, 341
Etymologies, 372
Eucharist, 20–21, 98n. 10, 301, 333–36, 511; Aquinas on, 405–9; in First Apology, 107; Judaizers and, 125; prayer of, 416; Radbertus and Ratramnus on, 367–68; Wycliffe on, 415, 488–95
Eucharistic Prayer, 539–47
Eudoxia, 264
Eugenius III, 423
Eusebius, 36n. 8, 45n. 7, 152, 279, 291n. 18; Edict of Milan, 297, 304–7; letter describing Council of Nicaea, 230–34; letter from the churches of Lyon and Vienne, 58–68
Eutyches, 298, 309, 312
Evangelical and Reformed Church, 256
evangelists. *See* prophets
Evans, E., 44n. 4
Evarestus, 37

Eve, 148–49, 163, 169, 275
evil, 148–49, 176, 178–83, 388
excommunication, 328–29, 501
executions, 510–21
exegesis, 158, 162–65
exegetical theology, 145–46
Exodus, 51
Exposition of the Creed (Augustine), 506
"Exposition of the Lord's Prayer" (Francis of Assisi), 413, 429–33
Ezekiel, 356, 508

Fairweather, Eugene R., 376n, 522n, 523n
faith, 145–56, 210–12, 265–67, 303, 395–404; justification by, 214, 216–23; prayer and, 540; rule of, 11, 41–47, 55, 150–54, 246; in tradition, 32–40; understanding and, 367–68, 376–79
"Faith and the Creed" (Augustine of Hippo), 184–200
"Faith in Scripture and Tradition, The" (Irenaeus), 32–40
Fall, the, 8–10, 147, 149, 213–14, 217–21, 458–59
false prophets, 11, 16, 21–23
fasting, 16, 19, 87, 105
Felicitas, 8, 69–80
Ferguson, John, 258n
feudal system, 414
filioque, 155, 238, 242
Fillastre's Diary, 511, 514–21
"First Apology" (Justin Martyr), 13, 94–108
First Corinthians, 282
First Ecumenical Council, 152
First Epistle of John, 149, 201–9
First Reformation, 511
fish, sign of, 151
"Five Ways to Prove the Existence of God" (Aquinas), 302, 380–89

Flavian, 298, 309
flesh, mortification of, 418
Florentina, 315n. 1
"Flowing Light of the Godhead, The" (Mechthild of Magdeburg), 452–56
foreknown, the, 502n. 4
forgiveness, 198
Formation of the Christian Biblical Canon, The (McDonald), 55n
fornication, 277
fortitude, 303, 395–404
Fortunatus, 184
"Four Degrees of Love, The" (Bernard of Clairvaux), 423–28
Fourth Lateran Council, 299, 301, 369, 508n. 19; Canon I, 333–36
Franciscans, 334, 413, 429–30, 434–35, 442
Francis of Assisi, 411, 413, 416, 429–35, 536–38
Frankish synods, 347–51
Frauenbewegung. See women, in reform movement
Frederick II, 334
free choice, 149, 179
free prayer, 416
free will, 178–83, 213–14, 217, 222, 310–11
Fremantle, Anne, 69n, 228n, 257n, 263n, 268n, 324n, 341n, 342n
French National Council, 498n. 10
Frend, W. H. C., 7n. 1, 59, 69n. 1
Friends of God, 414, 474
Fulgentius, 315n. 1

Galatians, 56, 158, 162–65
Galerius, 306n. 1
Galtier, P., 36n. 8
Ganymede, 104
gender, 59, 69, 269, 411–12, 458
Geneseric, 308

"German Theology," 414, 474–77
Germanus, 293
Gerson, John, 414, 478–87, 510
Gertrude the Great, 457
Giovanni Bernadone. *See* Francis of Assisi
Giovanni di Fidanza. *See* Bonaventure
Gnosticism, 41, 146–47, 275; founder of, 43n. 2; refutation of, 12, 39–40; rejection of natural world, 9–10, 32–33, 48
God: becoming human, 376–79; as bridegroom, 452; essence of, 162–65; gender and, 458; image of, 193; imitation of, 91–92; indwelling of, 157–62; knowledge of, 390–94; love of, 185–86, 196–97, 423–27; as mother, 458, 501n. 2; nature of, 89–90; proving existence of, 302, 380–89
"God in Christ, Our True Mother" (Julian of Norwich), 457–73
God-Man, 377–79
God's "effects," 302
God's elect, 30
God's honor, 377
Golden Mean, 395
Gospel, 10–11, 23, 56; traditions of, 33–34
Gospel of John, 11
governance: church, 16, 25–31, 510; Monasticism and, 353–61
grace, 18, 20n. 31, 20n. 34, 20–21, 148–49, 164–65; justice and, 303; means of, 149–50; nature and, 213–25; salvation by, 9–10, 146–47, 149–50, 216–18, 223
grace, theology of, 184–225
Grapte, 50
Great Eucharistic Prayer, 539–47
Great Schism, 414, 479, 489, 496, 510–11

Greek and Latin Creeds, The, 240n, 242n, 246n
Green, F. W., 379n. 5
Greenslade, S. L., 41n, 81n, 129n
Gregory, 396, 397n. 5
Gregory I, 298–300, 314–26, 340–43, 353, 359
Gregory III, 347
Gregory VI, 327
Gregory VII, 299, 327–31, 412
Gregory XI, 478–79, 496
Gregory XII, 514
Gregory of Nazianzus, 175, 287n. 1
Gregory of Nyssa, 146, 174–75, 289n. 8
Gregory of Tours, 322n. 30
Gummere, R. M., 397n. 6

Hadrian, 95n. 1
Hagar, 162, 164
Hagen, Hans, 519
hair coloring, 270–71
Hardt, Heinrich von der, 514n. 3
Hardy, Edward Rochie, 230n
Hebrews (book of), 10, 56
Hellenistic culture, 7–9, 145
Henry IV, 299, 327–29
Henry V, 328, 331–32
Heracles, 103
Heraclides, 146, 166–74
Heraclitus, 118
heresy, 38–40, 44, 46–47, 130–34, 198; Council of Constance on, 511–21; of John Huss, 415; mysticism and, 413; New Testament canon and, 55–57; of Origen, 10; Praxeas and, 250
Hermas, 49–50
Hermes, 103, 104
Hesiod, 319n. 14
high priesthood, 23n. 53
Hilarian, 69, 73, 78
Hilary, 392

Hildebrand. *See* Gregory VII
Hildegard of Bingen, 416, 457, 525–35
Hincmar, 507n. 16
Hippolytus, 147, 172n. 25, 250–54
History of the Church from Christ to Constantine, The (Eusebius), 58, 304
History of the Primitive Church, The (Lebreton), 36n. 7
holiness, 9, 225
Holy Communion. *See* communion
Holy Spirit, 113–14, 155, 185, 193–98
Homer, 103
Homilies on Ephesians 1:1–2, 264
Homilies on 1 Corinthians 24:1–2, 282
homo-ousios. *See* consubstantial
homosexuality, 120, 174
honey and milk, 253
hope, 303, 395–404
hospitality, 26
human reason, 302–3
human soul, 13, 88, 102–3, 146–47, 198–99; as bride, 452; unity with God, 443
humility, 396, 417–22
hunting of animals, 349, 354
Huss, John, 415, 491n. 5, 500–521
Hussite movement, 512
Hyginus, 37
Hymnal, The (Evangelical and Reformed Church), 259n, 260n
Hymnal of the United Church of Christ, 258n, 522, 524n, 536, 538n
"Hymn for Saturday Vespers" (Abelard), 416, 522, 523–24
hymns, 154, 249, 255–63, 416, 422–24
hypostases, 153, 154, 236

iconoclasts, 286–87, 293–95

icons, 155–56, 293–95
Ignatius, 12, 14, 123–28, 226
Iliad, 115n. 15, 116n. 17
illumination, 106
image controversy, 155–56, 293–95
image of God, 193
images, 85–87, 286–92, 301
incarnation, 146, 155, 158–62, 190–92, 195, 228
incest, 13, 61, 111–12, 118–21, 346, 351
indulgence, 501
indwelling of God, 157–62
Innocent II, 423
Innocent III, 299, 333–36, 411
intellectual virtues, 303, 395–97
interdict, 333, 414, 501
International Consultation on English Texts (ICET), 237
Interrogatory Creed of Hippolytus, 151, 154, 246
investiture, 299, 327–32
Irenaeus, 9–12, 14, 36n. 8, 37n. 9, 42, 44n. 4, 55, 279; escape from persecution, 32; "The Faith in Scripture and Tradition," 32–40; on Word, 33, 39
Isaac, 127, 164
Isaiah, 105, 113, 360
Isidore, 315n. 1, 372, 391n. 4, 506, 507n. 15

Jacob, 127
Jacob of Lodi, 518n. 7
Jacobus, 215
Jalland, T. G., 45n. 8
James, 45n. 7, 56
Jenkins, J. T. S., 174n. 33
Jeremiah, 113, 339
Jerome, 298, 315, 322n. 30, 394n. 25, 508n. 20
Jerome of Prague, 416, 510–21
Jerusalem, 146, 148, 150

Jesus. *See* Christ
Jesus kyrios, 8
"Jesus the very thought of Thee" (Bernard of Clairvaux), 416, 522–23, 524
jewelry, 272–73
Job, 314–23
John, 34, 37, 39–40, 45–46, 134, 197, 202–9, 454; Epistle of, 149, 201–9, 502–8; Gospel of, 11
John XXIII, 501, 510–11, 514
John of Bohemia, 516
John of Damascus, 155–56, 286–87, 293–94
Johnston, G., 483n. 9
John the Deacon, 316n. 2
Jubaianus, 130
Jucundus, 75
Judaism, 8, 126
Judaizers, 7–9, 12, 125, 125n. 7, 125n. 11
Judas, 220
Jude, 11, 56
judgment, 193
Judith, 57
Jugurtha, 215n. 1
Julian of Norwich, 413, 457–73
Julianus Pomerius, 355n. 1
Julius Caesar, 103n. 38
justice, 303, 395–404; grace of God and, 303
justification by faith, 214, 216–23
Justin Martyr, 35, 94–108
just war, 149

Karlmann, 348
Keil, H., 322n. 30
Kelly, J. N. D., 44n. 4
keys, power of, 82, 299, 338–39
knowledge, 92–93; of God, 390–94; of Trinity, by natural reason, 390–94

"Know the Way of the Lord" (Hildegard of Bingen), 416, 526
Knox, W. L., 36n. 8
Kore, 119
Kylie, Edward, 352n

Lactentius, 304–5
laity: duties of, 299; instruction of, 348–51
Lampe, G. W. H., 46n. 12
Lanfranc, 376
lapsed Christians, 8, 81–83, 129, 140
lapsi, 81
Late Medieval Mysticism, 423n, 429n, 430n, 474n, 496n, 536n
Latin Mass, 539
Latin theology, 148, 153, 297–303
laughing, 421
law, 35, 52–54
lay investiture, 299, 327–32
Lazarus, 220
Leander, 315, 321n. 25
Leda, 103
Leith, John H., 226n, 235n, 293n, 333n
Leo, 314, 378n. 4
Leo I, 298, 308–13
Leo III, 293, 299
Leo IX, 412
Leo XIII, 381
Leonidas, 279
Letter 33 (Cyprian), 81, 82
Letter 73 (Cyprian), 129–30
"Letter from the Churches of Lyon and Vienne," 58–68
"Letter of Eusebius of Caesarea Describing the Council of Nicaea," 230–34
Letters of Saint Boniface, 347n
"Letter to Childebert, King of the Franks" (Pope Gregory I), 324–26
"Letter to Cuthbert, Archbishop of Canterbury on the German Synods and Other Matters of Church Discipline," 352–61
"Letter to Diognetus," 13, 84–93
"Letter to the Philadelphians," 123–28
Leutherius, 345
libelli, 81
libelli pacis, 82
Licinius, 152, 297, 305
Life of St. Francis (Bonaventure), 437n. 9
Linus, 36
Lioba, 362, 365–66
Liturgies of the Western Church, 250n, 529n
liturgy, 151, 246–47, 250–54, 341, 343, 416, 539–47
Liturgy of St. James, 289n. 7
Logos, 107n. 50, 151, 176n. 1, 185, 235–36, 240, 250; John Chrysostom on, 282; Cyril on, 135–36; Irenaeus on, 33, 39; Justin Martyr on, 94; Tertullian on, 228; Theodore on, 157–62. *See also* Word
Lollards, 415, 511
Lombard, Peter, 393n. 17
"Lord's Body and Blood, The" (Radbertus), 367–68
Lord's Day, 23
Lord's Prayer, 413, 430–31
Lord's Supper, 20n. 31, 20n. 34, 508n. 19
"Lorica of St. Patrick," 256, 261–63
Loserth, J., 489n. 1
love, 202–9, 303, 395–404; brotherly, 202–9; commandment of, 198; four degrees of, 423–28; of God, 185–86, 196–97, 423–27; ordinate, 149; of self, for God's sake, 427–28; of self for self, 424–26
Lucius, 95

Lucius Aurelius Commodus, 109
Luke, 34, 56
Lul, 362–65
lust, 119, 278, 419
Luther, Martin, 210–12, 242–43, 414, 475, 540

Mabillon, J., 316n. 1
Macrobius, 393n. 21, 394
magnanimity, 396
Maimonides, 384n. 15, 444n. 2
Manicheanism, 147, 148, 181, 184, 192
Marcellinus, 213
Marcion, 9, 10, 34, 37, 40, 43, 47, 55, 275
Marcionism, 32–33, 172n. 27
Marcus Aurelius, 32, 58n
Marcus Aurelius Antoninus, 109
Mark, 34, 56
marriage, 99, 120, 274–78, 336, 346, 509n. 20; of church and Christ, 22n. 51
Marsiglio of Padua, 414, 479
Martel, Charles, 348, 351
Martin V, 415, 510
Martin Poree, 514n. 2
martyrdom, 8, 279, 417–18, 530; of Felicitas, 69–80; of Jerome of Prague, 510–21; of John Huss, 510–21; of Perpetua, 69–80; of Polycarp, 37. *See also* persecution
Mary, 40, 191, 228, 310–12, 504n. 8; as dwelling for Trinity, 505n. 11; song for, 526–27; *theotokos*, 135
matter and spirit, dualism of, 10
Matthew, 34, 56
Maturus, 61, 64
Maxentius, 304
Maximilla, 411
Maximinus, 305
Maximus, 171

McCracken, George E., 314n, 367n, 369n
McDonald, Lee Martin, 55n
McNeill, J. T., 491n. 6
means of grace, 149–50
Mechthild of Magdeburg, 413, 452–56, 457
Meecham, Henry G., 84n
Meister Eckhart, 413, 442–51, 474
mendicant orders, 334, 413, 429–30, 474
Mercersburg Seminary, 540
Messianic community, 20n. 33
Messianic promise, 20n. 33
metacism, 322
Migne, 504n. 8, 506n. 12
military service, 13, 154, 279–81, 349, 354
milk and honey, 253
mind, 394
ministry, 23, 36, 301, 413
Minor Brothers, 430
Minos, 115
Minucius Timinianus, 73
Mirror of Perfection (a "life" of St. Francis cited by Bainton), 536
Miscellanies, Book III (Clement), 274
Mishael, 30
missions, 12, 315; to barbarians, 340–66; in England, 300, 324–26, 340–46; to Germans, 347–51; Monasticism and, 411–16; support of women, 362–66
Mithra, 107
Monarchianism, 41, 151, 228, 250
monarchical episcopate, birth of, 22n. 53
Monasticism, 175, 411–22; Egyptian, 418; enslavement of monks, 361; governance in, 353–61; missions and, 411–16; monastic communities, 417–18; reform of, 412–16; tonsure of monks, 344–46

Monophysites, 294
monotheism, 185
Montanism, 41, 228–29, 250, 268, 411–12
Montanus, 411
morality play, 416, 526
Moravians, 512
mortification of flesh, 418
Moses, 9, 28–29, 52, 113, 163, 178, 290
mother, Christ/God as, 458, 501n. 2
Mundy, John Hine, 510n, 514n
music, 416. *See also* hymns
mysteries, 22, 35, 369–75
mystical ecstasy, 434–41, 443
mystical union, 155, 443
mysticism, 413, 442–51; bridal, 452; Germans and, 474–77; heresy and, 413; resurgence of, 474–77; women's movement in, 413–14, 452, 457–58, 474

Nahum, 355
"Natural and Theological Virtues" (Aquinas), 395–404
natural reason, 390–94
natural theology, 302
natural virtues, 303, 395–97
natural world, rejection of, 9–10, 32–33, 48
nature, grace and, 213–25
Nautin, P., 172n. 25
Neale, John M., 256
Nelson, William, 258n
Neoplatonism, 48, 167, 275, 443
nepotism, 414
Nero, 46n. 9
Nestorians, 240, 294
Nestorius, 135, 309, 312
new Nicene party, 175
New Testament, 33; authority of, 10–11; canon, 55–57

Nicene-Constantinopolitan Creed, 235–36
Nicene Creed, 152–55, 175, 185, 230–40, 247, 505n. 9
Niceta, 256
Nicholas, 518
Niedfeor, 350
Noah, 143, 338
Noetus, 151, 227, 228
Numbers, 51

Oates, Whitney, 213n
"O come, O come, Emmanuel," 416
Odin (Norse god), 348
Odysseus, 103
Odyssey, 103n. 35
Oedipean intercourse. *See* incest
Oedipus Rex, 111n. 3
"Of the Father's Love Begotten," 256, 260
"O Gladsome Light," 249, 255
Old Testament, 33, 127n. 19
On Baptism (Augustine), 140–41
On Christian Doctrine (Augustine), 370
"On Female Dress" (Tertullian), 268–73
On First Principles IV (Origen), 48
"On Human Sexuality and Christian Marriage" (Clement), 274–78
On Loving God (Bernard of Clairvaux), 424
"On Nature and Grace" (Augustine of Hippo), 150, 213–25
"On Public and Military Service" (Origen), 279–81
"On Sin and Salvation" (Gregory of Nyssa), 175–83
"On Spiritual and Mystical Ecstasy" (Bonaventure), 434–41
On the Christian Life, 214n. 2
On the Church (Huss), 500–509

INDEX • 567

"On the Eucharist" (Wycliffe), 415, 488–95
"On the Incarnation" (Theodore of Mopsuestia), 146, 158–62
"On the Lord's body and blood," 301
On the Love of God (Bernard of Clairvaux), 423–28
On the Rewards and Remissions of Sins (Augustine of Hippo), 213, 214n. 1
"On the Trinity" (Augustine of Hippo), 149, 185
"On the Truth of the Holy Scriptures" (Wycliffe), 489
On the Unity of the Catholic Church (Cyprian), 82
"On the Unity of the Church" (Gerson), 415, 478–87
On the Virgin's Veil (Tertullian), 228
ontological proof, 302
Optatus, 76, 140
"Order of Virtues" (Hildegard of Bingen), 526
ordinate love, 149
Ordo virtutum, 416, 525–35
Origen, 46n. 9, 231, 235, 274, 394; "Against Celsus," 13, 279; on allegorical method, 10, 49–54, 146, 158; on creation, 176; dialogue with Heraclides concerning the Father and the Son and the Soul, 166–74; on public and military service, 279–80; "On the Right Way of Reading the Scriptures," 48–54
original sin, 213–21
Orpheus, 119
Orthodoxy, 155–57, 282–95
"O Splendor of God's Glory Bright," 256, 258–59
Otto IV, 334
Oulton, J. E. L., 166n, 274n

"Outside the Church, There Is No Salvation" (Cyprian), 129–34

paganism, 348, 349–50, 354; sacrifices, problem of, 116; superiority of Christianity, 103–5
paideia, 255
Palestine, 7–8
Pancratius, 520
pantheism, 158
papacy: authority of, 297–303, 337–39, 414, 488; "Babylonian captivity" of, 414, 478, 488, 496; rise of, 304–39; schism, 414–15; supremacy of, 333–36; taxation, 102, 337–39, 488–89
Paraclete, 60n. 7, 229, 250
parousia, 11, 12
Paschal, 172n. 25
Paschal Mass, 253–54
Paschasius Radbertus. *See* Radbertus
pastoral care, 315–16
Pastoral Care (Saint Gregory), 359
Pastoral Rule (Pope Gregory I), 315, 325
paternal intellect, 394
patience, 396
patrimony, 341
Paul, 9, 31, 34–38, 45, 50–52, 214, 292, 360, 424, 450; baptism by, 133; on blood of Christ, 283–84, 375; on body of Christ, 136–38, 375; on charity, 204–5, 208; death of, 46n. 9; on faith, 265–67; on priesthood, 356–57; on resurrection of the flesh, 199; writings of, 11, 56
Paulinus of Aquileja, 507n. 17
Pax ecclesiastica, 483
Pax Romana, 7
Pegis, Anton C., 380n, 390n, 395n
Pelagianism, 367–68
Pelagius, 148, 150, 213–14, 218–20, 222–23, 507n. 17

Pepin, 348
perfect number, 50
Perpetua, 8, 69–80
persecution, 12, 26n. 2, 297, 415, 429, 510–21; Clement on, 30; escape of Irenaeus, 32; lapsed Christians and, 8, 81–83; letter from the churches of Lyon and Vienne, 58–68; Origen on, 279; plea of Athenagoras, 109–22; pressures of, 58–83; relief from, 304–7; unity and, 14. *See also* martyrdom
Perseus, 103, 104
person, 268
Peter, 9, 34–35, 45–46, 82, 338–39, 354, 357; on baptism, 143; on lust, 278; writings of, 11, 56, 363
Petry, Ray C., 423n, 429n, 430n, 474n, 496n, 536n
Philadelphians, 123–28
Philemon, 56
Philip IV, 299, 337–38
Philippians, 56
Philippics, 483
Philo, 50n. 3, 127–28
philosophical theology. *See* Apologetics
Physics (Aristotle), 398
Pilgrim Hymnal, 249
Pius, 37
Pius X, 505n. 11
Plato, 96n. 5, 97n. 7, 103, 108n. 55, 115, 122, 177n. 2, 377, 447n. 3, 450n. 7
Platonism, 94, 148, 175, 274, 381, 393–94
"Plea Regarding the Christians, A" (Athenagoras), 13, 109–22
pleasures of touch, 397
Pleroma, 39–40
pluralism, 7
poetry, 363–65
Polycarp, 32, 37, 38, 123

polytheism, 13
Pomponius, 71, 73, 74
Ponticus, 67
Pontius Pilate, 38, 98, 192
Poor Clares, 413
Porphyry, 13
Pothinus, 32, 63
poverty, 429–33, 435, 488, 511
power of the keys, 82, 299, 338–39
Praxeas, 228–29, 250
"Pray and Work" (Francis of Assisi), 429–33
prayer, 18–20, 105–8, 154, 431–33; Eucharistic Prayer, 539–47; faith and, 540; free, 416
prayer of the Eucharist, 416
Praying Together, 260n
predestinarianism, 213–14, 503–4
presbyters, 12, 29n. 16, 30–31, 124–27, 226–27
Prescription Against Heretics (Tertullian), 41–47, 228
pride, 202, 204
priesthood, 28–29, 127, 334–36, 356–57; carnal sins and, 350; dress for, 350; high, 23n. 53
Priscilla, 411
Priscus, 95
"Problem of the Lapsed, The" (Cyprian), 81–83
problem-solving approach, 376
prophets, 528–29; ecstatic utterances of, 22; false, 11, 16, 21–23; signs of, 22n. 48; tradition of, 9–12, 15–24
Proslogion (Anselm), 302
Protestantism, 147, 150, 154
Proverbs, 173
prudence, 303, 395–404
Prudentius, Aurelius Clemens, 184–85, 256, 260
public service, 279–81

Pudens, 74, 79
Putta, 345
Pythagoras, 103, 118, 122
Pytho, 103

Quintus, 75, 130

Rabanus Maurus, 369
Radbertus, 301, 367–68, 369, 504n. 8, 506n. 14, 508–9
Rahab, 82
Raphael, 507n. 16
Ratramnus, 301, 369–75, 508n. 19
reading verses, 21n. 45
realism, 368
reason, 302–3; natural, 390–94
rebaptism, 129–34
Recared, 324
reform, 478–521; biblical, 415; burning of reformers, 510–21; of church, 411–16; Cluniac reformers, 412; Czech reformation, 500; ecclesiastical reformers, 415; of Monasticism, 412–16; reformers against reformers, 510–21; women and, 413–14
"Refutation against the so-called Gnosis" (Irenaeus). *See Against Heresies*
Reginfried, 348
regional councils, 300
Regula Fidei, 44n. 4
Remigius, 506n. 14
Remissions of Sins (Augustine), 213
Republic (Plato), 96n. 5
resurrection, 121–22, 146, 163–64, 199
Revelation, 10–11, 56
Revocatus, 70, 78
Rhadamanthus, 115
Rhea, 119
Rheus Agathopus, 127–28
Richard II, 500

Richard of St. Victor, 391, 392n. 8
Richardson, Cyril C., 15n, 25n, 94n, 109n, 123n
Richental, 511, 516–21
Rise of Christianity, The (Frend), 7n. 1, 59, 69n. 1
Robert of Arbrissel, 412
Romans, Clement's letter to, 25–31
Roman symbol, 247
Roman theology, 297–303
Rome, fall of, 304–39
Rule of Faith, 11, 41–47, 55, 150–54, 246. *See also* apostolic tradition
"Rule of Faith, The" (Tertullian), 228–29
Rule of St. Benedict, 350, 412, 417–22, 424
Rule of St. Francis, 413, 429–33
Rule of Truth. *See* Rule of Faith
Rupert of Deutz, 504n. 8
Rusticus, 79

Sabbath, 87, 108
Sabellians, 189
sacramental symbol, 301
sacraments, 15, 413; Aquinas on, 405–9; Augustine on, 141; canon of Fourth Lateran Council, 334–36; efficacy of, 141, 489–95; Ratramnus on, 369–75; sermon on Holy Communion, 210–12; validity of, 14, 141; Wycliffe on, 489. *See also* baptism; communion
sacred scripture, 55. *See also* New Testament
sacrifice, 23, 28, 30, 87; communion as, 368; paganism and, 116
St. Albert, 394n. 23
St. Ambrose. *See* Ambrose
St. Augustine. *See* Augustine
St. Augustine of Hippo. *See* Augustine of Hippo

St. Bonaventure. *See* Bonaventure
St. Francis of Assisi. *See* Francis of Assisi
St. Gregory. *See* Gregory
St. Isidore. *See* Isidore
St. Jerome. *See* Jerome
St. John. *See* John
St. Patrick, 256, 261–63
St. Paul. *See* Paul
St. Peter. *See* Peter
St. Thomas, gnostic gospel of, 11
Saints, Communion of, 14
Saladin, 334
salvation, 33–34, 82, 129–34, 155, 174–83, 301, 377; by grace, 9–10, 146–47, 149–50, 216–18, 223; by water, 105–6, 130–31, 143–44
Sanctus, 61, 62, 64–65
Santer, Mark, 48n, 135n, 140n, 157n, 175n, 210n, 264n, 279n, 282n, 308n
Sarah, 164
Saturninus, 70, 75, 78
Saturus, 72, 75–76, 77, 78–79
Saviour, 35, 38, 40
Schaff, David, 500n, 505n. 9
Schaff, Philip, 154, 240n, 242n, 246n, 247
schism, 198, 228, 250; Cyprian on, 129–34; Donatism and, 140–41, 185, 201–2; Great Schism, 414, 479, 489, 496, 510–11; Ignatius on, 123–28; of papacy, 414–15
scholasticism, 367–409; Anselm on, 376–79; Aquinas on, 380–409; defined, 376, 381; Radbertus on, 367–68; Ratramnus on, 369–75
Scholastic Miscellany, A, 376n, 522n, 523n
Schorand, Lord Ulrich, 520
Scivias, 416, 526
scripture, 55, 57, 113, 489, 501, 540; faith in, 32–40; Hebrew, 9–10, 14–15; reading verses, 21n. 45; right way of reading, 48–54; Tertullian on, 10, 145–46; uses of, 41–47. *See also* allegorical method
Second Order of St. Francis, 413
secret writings. *See* apocryphal writings
Secundulus, 70, 76
self, love of, 424–28
self-control, 303, 395–404
Seneca, 397n. 6
sensuality. *See* concupiscence
Sentences of Peter the Lombard, 506n. 15
Sentences of Sixtus, 421n. 14
Septimius Severus, 69, 268
Septuagint, 10, 11, 55, 127n. 19
Sermon 28 (Meister Eckhart), 442
Sermon 48 (Meister Eckhart), 442
Sermon 272 (Augustine of Hippo), 210
"Sermon on Faith and Works" (John Chrysostom), 264–67
"Sermon on 1 John 4:12–16" (Augustine of Hippo), 201–9
"Sermon on Holy Communion" (Augustine of Hippo), 210–12
Sermon on the Mount, 214
Sermons (Wycliffe), 492n. 9
sexuality, 154, 274–78
Shape of the Liturgy, The (Dix), 251n. 1
Shepherd, 57
Shepherd of Hermas, 49n. 1
Shewring, W. H., 322n. 29
Showings (Julian of Norwich), 413, 457–73
Sigismund, 510, 511
sign of the fish, 151
Silent Fire: An Invitation to Western Mysticism, 452n
Simon, 43
Simon Magus, 43n. 2, 504

simony, 327, 414, 511
sin, 148–49, 173–83, 198–99, 213–21. *See also* Adam's Fall
social classes, 59, 69
Socrates, 97, 103, 118, 234n. 8, 377
sola scriptura principle, 49
Solomon, 49, 57, 173, 353, 359
Son, 113–14
Song of Solomon, 141, 355, 424, 504n. 8
Song of Songs. *See* Song of Solomon
"Song of the Virtues" (Hildegard of Bingen), 416, 525–35
Soter, 37
soul. *See* human soul
"Soul's Journey into God, The" (Bonaventure), 413, 434–41
speculative theology, 145–46, 228–29, 435
Speratus, 8
Spinka, Matthew, 478n, 488n
spirit and matter, dualism of, 10
spiritual ecstasy, 434–41
Staab, K., 163n. 1
Stephen (pope), 129–30
Stoicism, 15, 94, 95n. 3, 275
substance, 268
Suetonius, 103n. 38
Summa Contra Gentiles (Aquinas), 381
Summa Theologica (Aquinas), 302, 380–409
Suso, Heinrich, 474
swearing, 101
symbolism, 247, 286–92, 301, 368
"Symbols and Images" (John of Damascus), 286–92
Synod of Constantinople, 294
synods, 294, 347–51

Tacitus, 46n. 9
Tauler, Johannes, 474
tautology, 381

taxes, 102, 337–39, 488–89
teachers. *See* apostles
teaching, 114–16, 226–27, 255
Teaching of the Apostles, 57
Te Deum, 507n. 16
Te Deum Laudamus, 256, 259–60, 455
Telesphorus, 37
temperance, 303, 395–404
Templars, 423
temporal dispensation, 190–200
Tertius, 71
Tertullian, 32, 70, 96n. 6, 108n. 53, 134n. 11, 274, 309n. 1, 411; on allegorical method, 41–47; on apostasy after baptism, 81; on female dress, 268–73; on Praxeas, 250; on Rule of Faith, 151, 228–29; on scripture, 10, 145–46; on Word, 228
testimony, 150–54
textus receptus, 147
Thanksgiving, the, 20n. 31
Theoderic, 314
Theodore (archbishop of Canterbury), 300, 344–45
Theodore of Mopsuestia, 146, 157–62
Theodoret, 232n. 6
Theodosius, 147, 256
theological virtues, 303, 397–404
theology: biblical, 145–46; of the cross, 148–49, 155, 214, 218–21; ecumenical, 9–12; exegetical, 145–46; "German," 414, 474–77; of grade, 184–225; Latin, 148, 153, 297–303; natural, 302; Roman theology, 297–303; speculative, 145–46, 228–29, 435. *See also* Apologetics
Theophilus, 135
theory of the atonement, 377
theotokos, 135

Thessalonians, 56
Thirlby, 106n. 45
39th Easter Letter (Athanasius), 55–56
Thompson, Bard, 250n, 539n
Thyestean feasts, 61, 111–12. *See also* cannibalism
Thyestes, 111n. 2, 119
Tiberius Caesar, 98
Timaeus (Plato), 177n. 2, 447n. 3, 450n. 7
Timasius, 215
Timothy, 29n. 16, 56, 357, 360
tithing, 23n. 53
Titus, 29n. 16, 56
Titus Aelius Hadrianus Antoninus Pius Augustus Caesar, 95
Tobias, 57
Tome, 308–13
tonsure of monks, 344–46
torture, 61–68, 78–79
touch, pleasures of, 397
tradition: apostolic, 9–12, 14–24, 34–39, 55, 150–54, 246; faith in, 32–40; of prophets, 9–12, 15–24
Trajan, 123
transaccidentation, 508n. 19
transubstantiation, 508n. 19, 517; Aquinas on, 303, 405–9; defined, 489; Fourth Lateran Council on, 299, 301, 333–36; Ratramnus on, 369–75; Wycliffe on, 489
Treasury of Early Christianity, A, 69n, 228n, 257n, 263n, 268n, 324n, 341n, 342n
"Treatise of Divine Providence" (Catherine of Siena), 496–99
"Treatise on the Church" (Huss), 415
Trialogus (Wycliffe), 490n. 2
Trinity, 238, 240–43, 457–73; Athenagoras on, 109, 113–14; Augustine of Hippo on, 149–50, 153–55, 185–86, 193–95, 197–98, 240; Cyril on, 136–39; knowledge of, by natural reason, 390–94; Mary as dwelling for, 505n. 11; Tertullian on, 228
Trismegistus, 391, 394
"True Discourses," 13
"Twelve Degrees of Humility, The" (Benedict), 417–22
two natures, 166–74
two swords theory, 338–39
"Two Ways," 15
Tyrrell, R. Y., 483n. 9

Unam Sanctam (Boniface VIII), 337–39
understanding, faith and, 367–68, 376–79
Unitas Fratrum, 511
United Church of Christ, 540
unity, 123–44, 185, 283, 300, 415–16, 510–21; Augustine of Hippo on, 140–44; Cyprian on, 129–34; Cyril on, 135–39; forces toward, 7–14; Gerson on, 414, 478–87; letter to the Philadelphians on, 123–28; persecution and, 14; visions of, 14
universals, 489
Urban VI, 479
usurpation, 488
Utraquists, 511

Valdes, Peter, 429
Valentine, 275
Valentinus, 34, 37, 40, 43, 47
Valerian, 8, 81
validity of the sacraments, 14, 141
Valla, Lorenzo, 246
Valois, N., 498n. 10
van den Eynde, D., 44n. 4
van der Meer, F., 211n. 1
Verissimus, 95
vernacular, 474

verses, reading, 21n. 45
Verus, L. Aelius, 95n. 1
Vettius Epagathus, 60
Vibia Perpetua. *See* Perpetua
Virgilius, 325
Virgin Birth, 310–12
Virgin Mary. *See* Mary
virtues: natural, 303, 395–97; theological, 303, 397–404
Vulgate, 298, 315, 323n. 31, 489

Waldensians, 413, 429
Waldo, Peter. *See* Valdes, Peter
Walsh, James, 457n
war, just, 149
washing, 106–7
water, 253; mixing with wine, 373n. 10; salvation by, 105–6, 130–31, 143–44
Western Asceticism, 417n
"Whether the Substance of Bread and Wine Remain in the Sacrament after Consecration?" (Aquinas), 405–9
"Whether the Trinity of the Divine Persons Can Be Known by Natural Reason?" (Aquinas), 390–94
"Why Did God Become Human?" (Anselm of Canterbury), 376–79
Wiles, Maurice, 48n, 135n, 140n, 157n, 175n, 210n, 264n, 279n, 282n, 308n
Wilfrid, 345
William of Auxerre, 399n. 5

William of Ockham, 414, 479
Williamson, G. A., 58n
Willibald, 348
Willibrord, 347
wine, 210–12; mixing with water, 373n. 10. *See also* bread and wine
Winfrid, 345
Wintan, 348
women: dress of, 268–73; mysticism and, 413–14, 452, 457–58, 474; pilgrimage to Rome of, 353, 359; in reform movement, 413–14; spirituality of, 496–97; support of, in mission work, 362–66
Woody, Kennerly M., 510n, 514n
Word, 39–40, 92–93, 103–4, 113–14, 176–77, 183, 187–92. *See also* Logos; scripture
works, 101–2, 154, 204–9, 266, 301, 377, 474–77
worship, 101, 105–8, 154, 294, 416, 522–47, 539
Wright, Wendy M., 452n
Wyclif. *See* Wycliffe, John
Wycliffe, John, 414–15, 488–95, 489, 500, 509n. 21, 511, 512–14, 516–17
Wydenbruck, N., 536
Wynfrith. *See* Boniface

Xystus, 37

Zacharias, 60
Zeus, 103–4, 115n. 13, 119

Scriptural Index

Old Testament

Genesis

1:26	290n. 10
1:27	178
2:7	180
2:9	276n. 8, 276n. 9
2:24	169n. 8
3:5	189
3:19	312
3:22	276n. 9
6:16	338n. 2
8:21	291n. 15
27	133n. 7
35:10	437n. 10

Exodus

3:14	190, 386
8	391
8:19	391n. 4
12:11	437n. 6
15:6	313
20:2, 3	113n. 5
20:13–17	17n. 11
25:21	436n. 4
25:40, 20	290n. 13
33:10	290n. 12
33:20	440n. 18

Leviticus

11:44	278n. 26
19:2	278n. 26
19:15	170n. 13
19:18	16n. 1
20:7	278n. 26
26:12	158

Numbers

12:7	28n. 15
18:27	27n. 11
22:21–30	318n. 11

Deuteronomy

1:16, 17	18n. 16
4:12	18n. 19
4:34	27n. 11
6:4	193
6:4–5	150
12:32	18n. 19
14:2	27n. 11, 265
16:21	322n. 27
18:3–5	23n. 54
30:2	224n. 36
30:14	224n. 34
32:8, 9	27n. 10
32:39	169n. 11

Joshua

6	82

SCRIPTURAL INDEX • 575

1 Kings

6	290n. 14
8:46	220n. 23

2 Chronicles

31:14	27n. 11

Nehemiah

1:9	20n. 38
8:5, 6	106n. 48

Job

3:2	320n. 16
3:5	320n. 17
3:7	320n. 18
6:7	320n. 20
7:15	319n. 15, 440n. 17
7:19	320n. 19
7:20	320n. 21
9:13	319n. 13
13:26	320n. 22
14:2	220n. 23
14:4	311
15:6	383
27:6	320n. 23
31:16–20	321n. 24

Psalms

2 (27):4	428n. 13
4:2	19n. 22
4:6	358n. 12
7:9	419n. 2
14:1	220n. 23, 419n. 3
14:3	420n. 5
15:10	494n. 15
16:2	209n. 10
16:10	172n. 26
17:4	225n. 41
18:23	419n. 2
18:24	266
18:26, 27	30n. 18
19:1–3	27n. 7
22:6	421n. 11
26 (27):8	428n. 13
27:14	420n. 7
32:5	421n. 9
34:18	159
37:5	421n. 8
37:11	17n. 13
38:9	419n. 3
40:5	142
41:3 (42:2)	428n. 13
42:3	68n. 42
45:9	504
45:12	142
45:13	64n. 25
48:19 (49:18)	427n. 7
49 (50):15	425n. 5
50:21	420n. 5
51:11	159
52:5	432
53:1	383
53:2–3	420n. 5
66:10–12	420n. 7
67:36	378n. 3
72:26	441n. 22
72 (73):26	427n. 10
73:21–2	421n. 10
76:10	419n. 2
80:8	20n. 33
82:1, 7	281
82:6	194
88:15	421n. 11
90:1	359n. 15
94:11	419n. 2
105:48	441n. 22
106:1	421n. 8
110:1	312
118:19, 20	31n. 22
118:26	22n. 52
119:28	142

119:71	421n. 11	5:22	361n. 21
119:107	422n. 15	7:9	186, 211
131:1–2	418n. 1	11:1	20n. 33
136:3	523n. 5	22:13	115n. 14
139:1	419n. 2	27:1	65n. 28
139:7, 8	27n. 8	31:9	440n. 16
140:11	421n. 12	38:14	428n. 11
147:10–11	159	40:6–8	275n. 3
		43:10	169n. 11
		43:10, 11	113n. 7
		44:6	113n. 6

Proverbs

2:20	225n. 40	53:2	276n. 5
3:5, 6	359n. 13	53:8	233n. 7
3:34	28n. 12	53:11	313
8:13	360n. 18	58:6	126n. 18
8:22	114n. 10, 189	59:2	480n. 4
10:19	421n. 12	60:17	28n. 14
13:12	276n. 6	61:10	504
15:3	420n. 5	66:1	113n. 8
16:25	419n. 3	66:2	17n. 14
18:10	359n. 14		
20:9	173n. 30		
21:2	504		

Jeremiah

21:6	17n. 12	1:10	339n. 8
22:20–21	49	5:8	275n. 2
31:9	18n. 16	19	22n. 50

Ecclesiastes

Ezekiel

8:21	220n. 23

3:17	357n. 5
3:18	357n. 6
34:2, 9, 10	358n. 11
34:2–5	358n. 10
38	66n. 32
48:12	27n. 11

Song of Solomon (also Song of Songs or Canticles)

1:5	355n. 2
2:2	142
2:14	142
4:12–13	141
6:9	504

Daniel

3:15	68n. 44

Habakkuk

Isaiah

1:16–20	105n. 43
1:23	19n. 23

3:17	356n. 3

Zechariah

14:5	24n. 66

Malachi

1:11, 14	23n. 56

New Testament

Matthew

4:10	101n. 29
5:3	446–51
5:5	17n. 13
5:6	205n. 4
5:8	198
5:22, 41, 16	101n. 27
5:26	17n. 9
5:28	99n. 12, 119n. 21
5:29	99n. 13
5:32	99n. 14
5:33	17n. 11
5:34, 37	101n. 28
5:39, 40	101n. 26
5:39, 48	16n. 5
5:40, 41	16n. 6
5:42	100n. 19
5:44, 45	114n. 11
5:44, 46, 47	16n. 3
5:45	100n. 22
5:46	100n. 18, 202n. 1
6:1	101n. 25
6:5	19n. 29
6:9–13	19n. 30
6:10	428n. 12
6:16	19n. 28
6:19, 20	100n. 20
6:21	101n. 24
6:22	444
6:25, 26, 33	100n. 23
6:33	425n. 4
7:6	20n. 36
7:12	16n. 2
7:15, 16, 19	102n. 32
7:16	489
7:21–23	102n. 31
8:12	278n. 23
9:12	206n. 5, 216n. 8
9:13	100n. 17, 216n. 9
10:10	22n. 53
10:22	24n. 61, 420n. 7
10:40, 41	21n. 47
11:30	224n. 32, 359n. 16
12:30	36n. 7
12:31	22n. 48, 22n. 49
12:33–37	22n. 48
12:38	22n. 48
12:48	191
13:42, 43	102n. 32
15:13	125n. 4
15:19	18n. 20
16:14	517n. 5
16:18–19	82n. 1
16:19	339n. 10
16:26	100n. 21
18:20	502
19:5	169n. 8
19:9	120n. 25
19:11, 12	99n. 15
19:18	17n. 11
19:21	430
19:28	68n. 43
21:9	22n. 52
21:9, 15	21n. 42
22:11	66n. 33
22:20, 21	102n. 33
22:30	192
22:32	83n. 2
22:37	101n. 29, 424n. 1
22:37–39	16n. 1
22:39	424n. 3
22:43–44	310
23:9	191
23:27	126n. 14
24:4	19n. 25
24:10	24n. 60

24:13	24n. 61	6:35	96n. 6
24:24	24n. 59	6:35, 36	100n. 22
24:30	24n. 63, 24n. 66	9:25	100n. 21
24:31	21n. 40, 24n. 65	10:16	33n. 1
24:42, 44	23n. 57	10:30	222n. 27
25:31–33	502	10:34	222n. 28
25:34	265	11:5	43n. 3
25:35	193	11:23	36n. 7
25:46	63n. 21	12:4, 5	95n. 3
26:24	31n. 19	12:22, 24, 31	100n. 23
26:27	372n. 7	12:31	425n. 4
27:59	171n. 16	12:34	101n. 24
28:19	19n. 26, 19n. 27, 151	12:35	23n. 57
		12:48	102n. 34
Mark		12:49	438n. 12
		12:50	132n. 4
2:17	100n. 17	14:11	418n. 1
7:21, 22	18n. 20	14:23	202
9:47	99n. 13	15:4	209n. 11
10:11	120n. 25	15:8	43n. 3
10:17, 18	101n. 30	16:10	281
12:14–17	102n. 33	16:18	99n. 14
12:30	101n. 29	17:1, 2	31n. 19
14:22, 23	107n. 49	17:10	83n. 3
14:22–24	107n. 51	18:3	43n. 3
14:23	372n. 7	18:13	422n. 15
15:4	147	18:18, 19	101n. 30
15:46	171n. 16	18:42	45n. 6
		19:17	281
Luke		20:22–25	102n. 33
		21:34	360n. 19
1:6	60n. 4	22	338
1:15, 17	133n. 6	22:17, 19	372n. 7
1:67	60n. 8	22:19	368n. 1
1:75	31n. 23	22:38	339n. 5
4:8	101n. 29	23:34	206n. 6
5:32	100n. 17	23:43	437n. 8
6:27, 28	100n. 18, 114n. 11	23:46	171n. 21
6:27, 28, 32, 33	16n. 3	23:53	171n. 16
6:29	16n. 5, 101n. 26		
6:30	16n. 7, 16n. 8	*John*	
6:32	100n. 18		
6:32, 34	116n. 16	1:1	195
6:34	100n. 19	1:1–3	152, 167n. 2

1:1–5	39n. 14	14:28	195
1:2	52	16:2	61n. 13
1:3	168n. 6, 189	16:13	196
1:9	190	17:12	66n. 35
1:11	40n. 15	17:20–21	135–36
1:14	137, 189	17:21	136
2:4	191	17:24	265
2:6	50	18:11	339n. 6
2:11	63n. 23	19:34	62n. 16
2:12	49n. 1	19:36	284
2:21	506	20:17	173n. 28, 195
3:3	450n. 7	21:17	338n. 3
3:3, 4	105n. 42	21:18	46n. 9
3:5	131n. 3		
3:6	197	*Acts of the Apostles*	
3:8	126n. 15	2:27	172n. 26
4:24	197	2:36	150
4:42	426n. 6	2:47	66n. 36
5:21	220n. 22	4:29	66n. 37
5:43	22n. 52	4:32	212, 285
6:38	420n. 6	5:14	66n. 36
6:44	475n. 1	10:36–38	150
6:48	288n. 4	15	9
6:54	508n. 19	15:29	63n. 22
6:54–58	289n. 9	18:25	60n. 6
6:61	494n. 12	19:1–7	133n. 5
6:63	375n. 12	19:9	66n. 34
6:64	494n. 13	20:26–28	356n. 4
6:66	371n. 3	20:35	26n. 4
6:70	503n. 6	20:38	503
7:38	62n. 16	21:11	22n. 50
10:7	124n. 3, 436n. 3		
10:7, 8	38n. 12	*Romans*	
10:7, 9	127n. 21	1	391
10:16	338n. 4	1:3	168n. 7
10:30	169n. 10, 195, 446n. 1	1:3–4	150
13:1	440n. 19	1:9	198
13:1–15	288n. 5	1:20	385
13:34	224n. 37	1:21	393
14:6	436n. 3	1:27	120n. 27
14:8	441n. 20	1:29–31	18n. 20
14:9	195	2:29	50, 142
14:16	60n. 7		

3:8	492n. 8	1:23	390
3:23	218n. 17	1:25	191, 402
3:23, 24	216n. 7	1:28	61n. 15
3:24	218n. 16	2:2	222n. 29
4:5	215n. 6	2:6	34n. 3, 393
5:5	196, 208n. 8, 225n. 43	2:6,7	393
5:11	266	2:6–7	49
5:12	221n. 24	2:7–8	51
6:9	171n. 18	2:9	402
7:11	60n. 6	2:10	52, 438n. 13
7:14	49	2:10, 11	126n. 16
7:24	428n. 11	2:11	172n. 24
7:25	198	2:14–15	181
8:15	196	2:15	339n. 9
8:16	172n. 23	2:22	502
8:17	288n. 3	3:21, 23	197
8:18	59n. 3	4:9	65n. 27
8:22	198	5:9	277n. 15
8:24	208n. 9	6:9, 10	125n. 6
8:28	142	6:9–10	174n. 33, 174n. 34
8:29, 30	218n. 19	6:9–11	278n. 20
8:36–37	420n. 7	6:13, 16	277n. 15
9:23	218n. 18	6:17	169n. 9
10	216n. 11	7:5, 3	277n. 16
10:1	339n. 7	7:7	204n. 2, 267, 276n. 14
10:2	60n. 5	7:10–12, 14	277n. 17
10:2, 3	215n. 2	7:36	22n. 51
10:4	215n. 3	9:9–10	51
10:8	224n. 34, 224n. 35	9:14	493n. 11
10:9	150	10:4	51
10:10	186	10:11	51, 52
10:17, 18	216n. 12	10:16–17	282
11:4–5	52	10:17	138, 212
11:36	194, 287n. 2	11:2	292n. 19
12:1	116n. 18	11:3	195, 197
12:9	19n. 21	11:16	134n. 10
13:8	224n. 38	11:23–25	107n. 51
13:10	224n. 39	11:24	288n. 6
		11:25–26	289n. 7
1 Corinthians		11:26	375n. 11
1:1	221n. 25, 503	12:3	150
1:17	219n. 20	12:27	138, 211
1:20–25	9	13	303, 395

13:3	205n. 3	2:3	199, 217n. 14
13:13	401, 403	2:4, 5	217n. 15
15:3–7	151	2:14–16	136
15:10	450n. 6	3:5–6	138
15:12	170n. 15	3:9	436n. 5
15:23	28n.13, 171n. 19	4:2–6	139
15:28	195, 523n. 2	4:5	338n. 1
15:40	200	4:14–16	138
15:44	171n. 17	5:3	173n. 32
15:46	424n. 2	5:14	255
15:50	276n. 11	5:18	360n. 20
15:51	192	5:23	276n. 4, 480n. 5, 508
15:52	199, 200	5:27	142
15:54	200	5:32	508n. 20
16:22	21n. 44	6:11	280

2 Corinthians

Philippians

2:15	64n. 26	2:5–11	255
5:17	217n. 13	2:6	167n. 3, 189, 195
6:16	158	2:8	192
8:23	62n. 18	3:13	481n. 7
11:3	163	3:19	278n. 21
12:9	441n. 21	3:20	26n. 1
		4:8	278n. 24
		4:15	31n. 20

Galatians

Colossians

2:9	59n. 2	1:15	152, 168n. 4
2:21	215n. 5, 221n. 26	1:18	312, 507–8
3:3	276n. 12	1:24	508
3:13	24n. 62	2:8–10	313
3:24	215n. 4		
3:27	65n. 29		
3:28	480n. 6		
4:24	146, 158, 162–65		
4:26	523n. 4		
5:12–21	18n. 20		
6:12	126n. 13		
6:16	46n. 13		

1 Thessalonians

2:8	60n. 9
3:13	24n. 66
5:23	171n. 22

Ephesians

2 Thessalonians

1:1–2	264	2:7–9	59n. 1
1:4–5	264	2:14	292n. 19
1:22	276n. 4, 507		

1 Timothy

1:5	225n. 42
1:8	224n. 31
2:1–2	280
2:2	122n. 30
2:5	223n. 30, 436n. 2
3:2–74	277n. 18
3:15	59n. 2, 61n. 14
3:16	216n. 10, 255
4:4	180
4:4, 5	107n. 49
5:14	267
6:13	63n. 24
6:17	360n. 17
6:20	173n. 31

2 Timothy

2:9	479n. 1
2:11–13	255
2:19	142
2:26	62n. 20
4:1, 2	357n. 8
4:3	357n. 9

Titus

1:15	191, 278n. 19
1:16	277n. 18
3:10, 11	38n. 11

Hebrews

3:5	28n. 15
4:9	523n. 7
6:18	27n. 5
8:5	51, 290n. 13
10:1	49, 51
11:1	384, 392
11:9	26n. 1
11:31	82
12:6	207n. 7, 321n. 26
12:16–17	133n. 7
13:7	18n. 15

James

1:4	396
2:24	173n. 29
3:15	219n. 21
4:6	28n. 12

1 Peter

1:14–16	278n. 26
1:21	278n. 25
2:11	16n. 4, 26n. 1
3:20–21	143
5:5	28n. 12
5:8	62n. 19
5:8, 9	357n. 7

2 Peter

1:4	398
1:8	65n. 30
2:2	66n. 34
3:9	66n. 32

1 John

1:20	202
3:2	454
3:16	60n. 9
4:12–16	201–9
4:18	62n. 17
5:3	224n. 33

Revelation

1:8	193
3:9	126n. 12
4:11	21n. 39
6:9–11	504
14:4	60n. 10

19:9	67n. 39	*Ecclesiasticus (also Sirach)*	
20:12, 15	278n. 22		
21:3	479n. 2	2:8	398
21:27	278n. 22	10:12	199
22:11	68n. 41	18:1	21n. 39
22:17	38n. 12	18:30	419n. 3, 419n. 4
		21:20	421n. 13
		24:2	503
		31:11	503

Apocryphal/Deuterocanonical Books

Apocrypha

Baruch

2:17	437n. 7, 438n. 11	3:38	291n. 16

Wisdom (of Solomon)

2 Maccabees

1:14	21n. 39	7:21–41	67n. 38
7:27	188		
8:1	188	*Barnabas*	
10:21	318n. 10		
11:17	187	4:9	23n. 58
12:6	19n. 24	7:9	24n. 62
12:12	27n. 6	12:2–4	24n. 64